This book is dedicated to my teacher,
Prof. Fritz Gessner,
who first introduced me to hydrobiology,

and

to my old friend Prof. H.-H. Reichenbach-Klinke
who has always placed his great scientific
knowledge freely at my disposal.

Photographs

Front of cover
Ceratoichthys pinnatiformis, Verona Museum.

Back of cover
Top Left: *Rhamphosus aculeatus*, Verona M.
Top Right: *Pygaeus gazolai*, Verona Museum.
Bottom Left: *Acanthura ovalis*, Verona Museum.

Title page (opposite)
Priscacara liops, Eocene, Wyoming, (50 million years), Baensch Collection.

All rights reserved. No part of this book may be reproduced or transmitted in any form or by any means, electronic or mechanical, including photocopying, recording, or by any other information storage and retrieval system, without written permission of the publisher, except where permitted by law.

Library of Congress Cataloging-in-Publication Data
Frickhinger, Karl Albert
  [Fossilien Atlas Fische, English]
  Fossil atlas, fishes / Karl Frickhinger; translated by R. P. S. Jefferies.
  1st English language ed.
  1088 p. 12 x 18 cm
  Includes bibliographical references (30 p.) and indexes.
  ISBN 1-56465-115-0
  1. Fishes, Fossil - Atlas. 1. Title
  QE851.F89213 1995
  567'.022'3--dc20   95-138
                                                                        CIP

1st. Edition, 1995
ISBN 1-56465-115-0 (U.S.A. only)
ISBN 3-88244-019-8 (for other countries)
WL Code 16822

© Copyright 1991, 1995 Mergus® Verlag GmbH, Hans A. Baensch, P. O. Box 86, 49302 Melle   Mergus ® is a registered trademark.

Layout:	Dr. Gero W. Fischer, Quito, Ecuador
Lithography:	bücher- repro, Bielefeld, Germany
Press:	Mergus Press, Singapore
Editor:	K. A. Frickhinger, München, Germany
Original Publisher:	Hans A. Baensch, Melle, Germany

1st English Language Ed., 1995
Published in the USA: Tetra Press, Blacksburg, VA

Distribution:
USA:	Tetra Sales (Warner-Lambert-Company) Blacksburg, VA 24060
Canada:	Rolf C. Hagen Inc., 3225 Sartelon Street, Montreal, Que. H4R 1E8
Great Britain:	Rolf C. Hagen (U.K.) Limited, California Drive, Whitwood Industrial Estate, Castleford WF 10 50H, West Yorkshire
Australia:	Pets International Pty. Ltd., 5 Orchard Ind. Est., Orchard Road, P. O. Box 21, Chester Hill, N.S.W.
	Pet Pacific Pty. Ltd., Unit C, 30 Skarratt Street, Auburn N.S.W 2144 P. O. Box 398, Rydalmere N.S.W. 2116

Printed in Singapore

Karl Albert Frickhinger

Fossil Atlas
Fishes

Translated by Dr. R. P. S. Jefferies, London

Publishers for Natural History and Pet Books
Hans A. Baensch • Melle • Germany

Preface

There is no lack of general literature on fossil invertebrates. Ammonites and trilobites, especially, have been very thoroughly treated in the last one hundred years and there are many texts available on faunas and particular systematic groups. Above all, there is the well known "Treatise on Invertebrate Paleontology"— an available work that leaves very little to be desired.

It is true that the last few years have given us "The Handbook of Palaeoichthyology" and "The Handbook of Palaeoherpetology". Unfortunately, however, neither work is complete and we may have to wait many years before all the volumes are available. Moreover, both are purely scientific works whose main objective is the diagnosis of genera. It is therefore understandable that they do not give as many figures as the editors and authors would no doubt have wished. Because of this, the readership is effectively restricted to scientific professionals and a few especially interested amateurs.

Apart from these two important works, little choice remains. The vertebrate literature must be gathered laboriously together and all-inclusive works hardly exist. As to fish, the last and only attempt to record all known fossil fishes, and illustrate them with masterly engravings, was made by Agassiz. He wrote 150 years ago, however. Only a few complete copies are left and they fetch an extremely high price—more a book lover's rarity than a practical work.

These considerations prompted me to produce the present work. It is a "picture book." I do not intend it to compete with more scientific works, since I knew from the start that it could be no more than a useful supplement to the specialised literature.

Nevertheless, it was no easy task. I have visited most of the important museums in the world and suffered a great deal of drudgery. I have searched through the collections for hours at a time, finally to photograph only those fishes still lacking. At first, everything went quickly, but once I had reached a certain level, it became more and more difficult to find anything new. Above all, I had set myself to photograph very well preserved specimens only. Thus I soon discovered that many of the 2500 genera so far described were based on incomplete specimens only, or even on single dorsal shields, teeth, spines or scales. No doubt there is

Preface

much good material to which I never had access or have overlooked. This, however, could only be true of a fraction of the genera shown in this book.

Another great difficulty was the nomenclature. In many collections I came across old specimens labelled with antique synonyms, or even undetermined material. I have made great efforts to bring everything into order; with the willing help of certain specialists, to whom I am very grateful. Nevertheless, I cannot guarantee absolute correctness in all cases. I sincerely ask that, if the reader finds a mistake, he tells me of it.

What readership is this book intended for? The scientific specialist may find in it a pictorial supplement to the technical literature. Besides that, he may be glad to know in what museum the fishes are kept which interest him. The museum curator will be able, using this book, to look over what is on offer and thus discover how his collections may sensibly be expanded. The student of palaeontology will be given a general view of most of the fossil fish fauna. The book will be of greatest interest to fossil collectors. Finally, I do not forget the amateur , whether angler or aquarist, who is interested in fishes. Up till now he has not had the chance to see what the ancestors of his fishes looked like, how they evolved nor how long they have already been on earth.

Autumn, 1994, Planegg.

Contents

Preface 4

Acknowledgements 7

Collecting Fossils 11

The Photography of Fossils 13

Evolution in Geological Time 16–17

The Origin of Life and the Evolution of Fishes 18

The External Features of Fishes 26–33

The Groups of Fishes 68–994

Agnatha (Jawless Fishes) 68
Placodermi (Placoderms) 116
Chondrichthyes (Cartilaginous fishes) 147
Acanthodii (Acanthodians) 236
Chondrostei (Chondrosteans) 252
"Holostei" (Holosteans) 371
Teleostei (True Bony Fishes) 449
Euteleostei (Higher Bony Fishes) 573
Crossopterygii (Lobe-finned Fishes) 939
Dipnoi (Lung Fishes) 975

Literature 996–1025

Index of Genera and Synonyms 1027

Index of Orders, Suborders, and Families 1043

Index of Genera, Arranged by Formation 1059

Index of Genera, Arranged by Locality 1070

Index of Recent Families and Genera 1080

The Author 1087

Picture Credits 1088

Acknowledgements

This book, which involved great personal and financial outlay, could never have been finished without the most generous help from all parts of the world. It is therefore a pleasant duty to thank all the museums and institutes who allowed me to photograph the finest specimens in their collections or made photographs available free of charge. I would also like to thank all those who so willingly answered my questions when anything was unclear to me. I am particularly grateful to Prof. Schultze, of Lawrence, Kansas, U.S.A. and Dr. Patterson of London whom I sometimes burdened beyond all reason and whose advice was especially helpful as concerns the new systematics. Dr. Wellnhofer, of Munich, likewise deserves my special thanks. I am also deeply indebted to the firm of Tetrawerke, Melle, and its Director Herr J Sander, who not only organised my Moscow journey but financed it.

The following list is arranged alphabetically by town or city.

Adelaide, Australia, Museum of Natural History, Dr. N. Pledge.

Amsterdam, Netherlands, Universiteit van Amsterdam, Geological Museum, Dr. J. H. Werner.

Bergamo, Italy, Museo Civico di Scienze Naturali, Dr. Paganoni.

Berlin, Museum für Naturkunde, Dr. Jäger, Dr. W.-D. Heinrich.

Bloemfontein, South Africa, National Museum, Dr. C. M. Engelbrecht, Dr. B. Rubidge.

Brisbane, Australia, Queensland Museum, Dr. R. E. Molnar.

Bristol, England, University of Bristol, Prof. D. L. Dineley.

Brussels, Belgium, Institut Royale des Sciences Naturelles de Belgique, Dr. P. Sartenaar

Calgary, Alberta, Canada, Geological Survey of Canada, Dr. R. Thorsteinsson.

Canberra, Australia, Australian National University, Prof. K. S. W. Campbell.

Canberra, Australia, Division of Continental Geology, Dr. G. Young.

Capetown, South Africa, South African Museum, Dr. M. A. Cluver, Dr. R. Smith.

Chicago, Illinois, U.S A., Field Museum of Natural History, Dr. L. Grande, Dr. C. Forster.

Cleveland, Ohio, U. S. A., Cleveland Museum of Natural History, Dr. M. E. Williams, Dr. G. L. Jackson.

Copenhagen, Denmark, Geological Museum, Dr. B. S. Bang, Dr. S. Bendix-Almgren.

Acknowledgements

Drumheller, Alberta, Canada, Tyrell Museum of Paleontology, Dr. D. Brinkmann, Dr. Neumann.
Edinburgh, Scotland, National Museum of Scotland, Dr. W. D. I. Rolfe, Dr. R. Patton.
Edmonton, Canada, University of Alberta, Prof. Dr. M. V. H. Wilson.
Eichstätt, Germany, Jura-Museum, Willibaldsburg, Dr.G. Viohl.
Eichstatt-Harthof, Germany, Museum Berger, Herr R. Berger.
Frankfurt-am-Main, Germany, Naturmuseum Senckenberg, Prof. W. Ziegler, Dr. G. Plodowski, J. Oelkers-Schäfer.
Garden City, New Jersey, U. S. A., Adelphi University, Prof. R. Lund.
Glasgow, Scotland, Hunterian Museum, Prof. F. Willet, Dr. J. K. Ingham.
Grahamstown, South Africa, Albany Museum, Dr. B. C. Wilmot, Mr. W. J. de Klerk.
Haarlem, Netherlands, Teyler Museum, Mr. E. Ebbinge, Mr. J. C. van Veen.
Holzmaden, Germany, Urwelt Museum Hauff, Dr. B. Hauff.
Johannesburg, South Africa, Witwatersrand University, Prof. Kitching.
Karlsruhe, Germany, Staatliches Museum für Naturkunde, Prof. S. Rietschel, Prof. L. Trunkò.
Kassel, Germany, Naturkunde Museum in Ottoneum, Dr. J. Fichter.
Lausanne, Switzerland, Musée Géologique Cantonal, Dr. M. H. Septfontaine.
Lawrence, Kansas, U. S. A., University of Kansas, Museum of Natural History, Prof. H.-P. Schultze, Prof. G. Arratia-Schultze.
Leyden, Netherlands, Rijksmuseum van Geologie en Mineralogie, Dr. G. E. de Groot.
London, England, The Natural History Museum, Dr. C. Patterson, Dr. P. Forey, Dr. R. P. S. Jefferies.
Lyon, France, Musée Guimet d'Histoire Naturelle, Dr. M. L. David.
Milan, Italy, Museo Civico di Storia Naturale, Prof. G. Pinna, Dr. G. Teruzzi.
Milan, Italy, Università degli Studi di Milano, Dr. A. Tintori.
Montreal, Quebec, Canada, MacGill University, Redpath Museum, Prof. R. L. Carroll.
Moscow, Russia, Paleontologicheskii Muzei Russkoi Akademii Nauk, Prof. L. Tatarinov, Dr. L. Novitskaya, Mr. A. F. Bannikov, Ms. O. Affanasiyeva.
München, Germany, Bayerische Staatsammlung für Paläontologie, Prof. D. Herm, Dr. P. Wellnhofer.

Acknowledgements

Münster, Germany, Geologisch-Paläontologisches Institut und Museum, Dr. K. Oekentorp.
New Haven, Connecticut, U. S. A., Yale University, Peabody Museum of Natural History, Prof. J. Ostrom.
New York, N. Y., U. S. A., American Museum of Natural History, Dr. J. G. Maisey.
Nouvelle, Quebec, Canada, Musée Parc de Miguasha, Dr. M. Arsenault.
Oslo, Norway, Universitetet i Oslo, Paleontologisk Museum, Dr. N. Heintz.
Ottawa, Ontario, Canada, National Museum of Natural Sciences, Dr. D. Russell, Dr. A. Day.
Padua, Italy, Università di Padova, Dipartimento di Paleontologia, Dr. L. Altichieri.
Paris, France, Muséum National d'Histoire Naturelle, Prof. P. Taquet, Dr. M. Veran, Dr. D. Goujet, M. D. Serette.
Pittsburg, Pennsylvania, U. S. A., Carnegie Museum of Natural History, Dr. D. S. Berman.
Pretoria, South Africa, Transvaal Museum, Prof. C. K. Brain, Dr. V. Watson.
Solnhofen, Germany, Bürgermeister Müller Museum, Bürgermeister Güllich.
Stockholm, Sweden, Naturhistoriska Riksmuseet, Dr. H. C. Bjerring, Dr. Borger.
Stuttgart, Germany, Staatliches Museum für Naturkunde, Prof. B. Ziegler, Dr. R. Böttcher, Dr. R. Wild.
Sydney, Australia, Australian Museum, Dr. A. Ritchie.
Toronto, Ontario, Canada, Royal Ontario Museum, Dr. G. Edmund, Dr. K. Seymour.
Tübingen, Germany, Museum für Geologie und Paläontologie, Prof. F. Westphal, Dr. A. Liebau.
Uppsala, Sweden, Palaontologiska Museet, Dr. S. Stuenes.
Verona, Italy, Museo Civico di Storia Naturale, Dr. L. Sorbini, Sign. G. Bonato.
Vienna, Austria, Naturhistorisches Museum, Dr. H. Kollmann, Dr. O. Schulz.
Washington, D. C., U. S. A., National Museum of Natural History, Smithsonian Institution, Dr. F. Collier.
Zürich, Switzerland, Paläontologisches Institut und Museum, Prof. H. Rieber, Dr. K. A. Hünermann, Dr. Burgin.

Acknowledgements

I also thank the owners of the following private collections, who likewise allowed me to photograph their finest specimens and thus contributed greatly to this book:

Beyrouthy Collection, Toulouse, France
Dr. de Buisonje Collection, Amsterdam, Netherlands
Bürger Collection, Bad Hersfeld, Germany
Henne Collection, Stuttgart, Germany
Herrmann Collection, Buchendorf, Germany
Kandler Collection, Augsburg, Germany
Krauss Collection, Weissenburg, Germany
Leonhardt Collection, Ober-Kainsbach, Germany
Monk Collection, Karlsruhe, Germany
Dr. Pabst Collection, Zürich, Switzerland
Perner Collection, Bad Homburg, Germany
Peukert Collection, Waldstetten, Germany
Schwegler Collection, Langenaltheim, Germany
Schweitzer Collection, Langenaltheim, Germany
Siber & Siber Collection, Aathal, Switzerland
Stöbener Collection, Staufenberg, Germany
Tischlinger Collection, Stammham, Germany
Weiss Collection, Vienna, Austria.

In addition I have to thank Prof. H.-H. Reichenbach-Klinke of Munich, Frau R. Ageland of Oberägeri, Switzerland, and Dr. R. Riehl of Düsseldorf for undertaking the laborious task of reading the proofs.

I owe a special word of thanks to my wife, Frau Gertrud Frickhinger, who helped me in innumerable ways.

Frau A. Gehlen and Frau I. Weindl relieved me of much time-consuming labour and deserve my heartfelt thanks as also does Herr Konrad Götz, of Munich, who advised me on photography. Last, but not least, I must thank my publisher, Herr Hans A. Baensch of Mergus Verlag, Melle, who met all my wishes as regards format and the provision of expensive illustrations. To him, also, I owe the suggestion of placing photographs or drawings of recent fishes alongside the fossils so as to make this book of greater interest for those who love fishes, whether angler or aquarist.

Collecting Fossils

Collecting can be seen as an instinctive drive of mankind, for otherwise we would not refer to a whole cultural stage as that of hunting and collecting. Something from that time must remain in many people, for very little is not collected, whether stamps, coins, beer mats or matchboxes, to name a few. Here the primitive hunting instinct is at work, since we rightly speak of hunting for the desired object before coming home with the loot.

Fossils have obviously always fascinated people although in early times nobody knew what they were. Thus in Stone Age deposits fossils have been found which had obviously been collected. Were they used as charms or ornaments? Was it only their strange shapes which attracted? Or did they have legends woven about them, as when the belemnites were called thunderbolts and seen as relics of the lightning thrown by Thor?

Later on, fossils were condemned by the Church as the work of the Devil or at best were supposed to be relics of Noah's Flood. This was why Scheuchzer saw the remains of a giant salamander found by him as those of a poor sinner drowned in the Flood. Nevertheless, he brought together an important collection, as was fashionable at the end of the 18th and, especially, in the early 19th century. At first it was noblemen and princely houses who were proud to maintain a cabinet of natural objects. However, there were always unpredictable incidents, like the famous example of Beringer, the Professor at Würzburg, who collected fossils with zeal but had forgeries passed off on him by his students. It was his bad luck that he did not recognize them in time. Indeed Beringer's "lying stones" have become world-famous.

In the end there were more and more people who concerned themselves with collecting these stony relics of a distant past. The present time has brought an awakening interest in Nature and there are many collectors who pursue this fascinating hobby with more or less devotion.

There are many ways of collecting. Some people, and they are probably the majority, collect only what they come across, whether accidentally or on purpose. They bring everything home that comes into their hands and, lacking standards of comparison, have no sense of quality. Over the years they pile up great heaps

Collecting Fossils

of stone, often not even properly arranged. Sooner or later they, or perhaps their heirs, wish to sell this "collection". Then they cannot understand why they are paid, at most, a few Marks only. Others, again, make a local collection and have the ambition to possess all the fossils known from one locality. In the course of their lives they often acquire deep knowledge and thus achieve a remarkable contribution to science. Such collections always come, sooner or later, into the hands of a museum and thus finally reach the right place.

Others, again, collect only particular sorts of object, such as ammonites, trilobites or fishes. Commonly they are experts in their field and lay special value on complete specimens. Experience shows that such a collection will commonly finish in a museum after the owner's death, whether as a donation or at a reasonable price, as is only fair given the labour of amassing it.

Lastly, there are the aesthetes. They collect only what attracts the eye. Specimens can never be beautiful enough for them and they are ready to invest much time and money. In the course of their lives they bring collections together of which any museum could be proud. Indeed, museums are proud of them when, perhaps after several generations, such a collection comes on offer and is acquired. While such collectors live they have joy in their treasures every day. The clever ones among them see this pleasure as the "interest" earned by their often considerable "unemployed capital". When the values, or lack of value, of different ways of collecting are compared together, it is obvious that this last approach comes near the ideal. Nothing is more worthwhile than something which every day brings joy and in addition there is the pride of possessing something unique.

Unfortunately there are some museums today, and some scientists, who dislike the fact that private individuals are allowed to collect fossils. They would gladly claim a legal right to all such finds and would prefer to forbid private collecting entirely. But why should private initiative be suppressed? It is like the free market, without which nothing can prosper. Experience shows that every good collection lands, sooner or later, in a museum. It is only necessary to wait.

The Photography of Fossils

Many collectors try to photograph their treasures. Unfortunately this is less easy than it seems, for several factors must be considered. Thus the flash, otherwise so handy, must be forgotten, since illumination from in front leaves most fossils looking pale and flat and produces undesirable reflections. A side flash, however, may be useful in an emergency.

Best results are normally got under artificial light since only this form of illumination can be adapted to the requirements of the specimen. Even so, very bright light must, as a general rule, be avoided, for only a soft side light gives the desired results. This is particularly true of fossils that are hard to see, such as some insects. In such cases it is often important whether the light comes from left, right or above.

Furthermore the nature of the rock must be taken into account, because some rocks reflect light while others absorb it strongly. In this connection, automatic exposure meters often give wrong answers.

The photographic method used by me has aroused interest even among specialists. I work with a very simple trick—I use polarized light. The light source must have a polarizing filter, as likewise the lens of the camera. By rotating these polarizers, all reflections can be cut out. At the same time, the specimen grows darker and thus more brightly coloured. By turning the polarizers back slightly, a minimum of reflections can be brought back, giving a more lively picture.

When using this method, all disturbing outside light should be excluded. Since this can hardly be done with incident daylight—except by photographing only at night—I use a blue filter over my light source. This allows me to employ daylight film with the benefit that the camera can quickly be used for other purposes. Film sensitivity should not be greater than 100-200 ASA (21-24 DIN). I use Ektachrome Professional film.

Unfortunately, even with a daylight filter, a slight trace of purple often intrudes which can be countered by using a weak green filter (Kodak Gelatine Filter G005). Using a light amber filter brings other advantages. Of course, by applying all these different filters I lose at least three stops. It is therefore necessary to use a stand. Exposure times of 1 second are attainable in almost all cases.

The Photography of Fossils

As to exposure time, I have already mentioned that the characteristics of the different rocks must be thought of. In this connection while black and red rocks need underexposure, grey rocks are, in general, neutral.

In the following table I give examples of how the exposure meter value should be modified in particular cases:

Bolca	normal
Brazil	1–2 stops more
Bundenbach	1 stop less
Holzmaden	1 stop less
Kupferschiefer	1–2 stops less
Lebanon	1–2 stops more
Messel	normal
Pfalz	normal
Red rocks	1–2 stops more
Scottish Old Red	normal
Solnhofen	1–2 stops more
Wyoming	1–2 stops more

These are only a few examples. Other rocks can be interpolated as appropriate.

And now for the camera itself. I recommend a small-frame camera with an interchangeable lens and a double draw tube. An extension ring allows me an image magnification of 1:1, which has turned out to be enough in all cases. If a higher image magnification were needed, a bellows could be inserted.

All this sounds rather complicated and is not cheap to buy. But the results are well worth the trouble and expense. There is a paradoxical rule of thumb—light-coloured rocks require overexposure.

Phylogeny

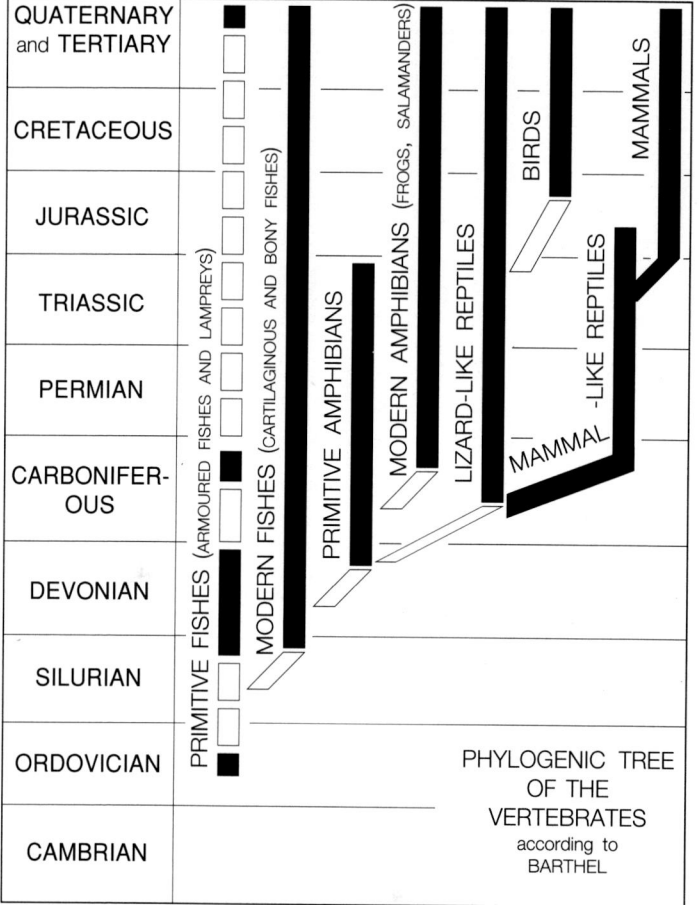

The Evolution of Life in Geological Time

Era	Period	Subdivisions (Epoch)	Years*	Animals and Plants
Cainozoic	Quaternary	Holocene (recent) — Pleistocene (Ice Age): Wurm Glacial, Riss Glacial, Mindel Glacial, Gunz Glacial, Pre-glacial	10,000; 50,000; 200,000; 500,000; 700,000; 2 million	Pre-historic, historical and cultural evolution of man. The extinction of animal and plant species by man's activity begins and increases. The first true men. Climatic fluctuations caused by the ice ages change the fauna and flora.
Cainozoic	Tertiary	Pliocene, Miocene, Oligocene, Eocene, Palaeocene	7 million; 26 million; 38 million; 54 million; 65 million	Highest development of the mammals and the flowering plants (angiosperms). Primates appear. Towards the end the first man-like organisms originate.
Mesozoic	Cretaceous	Upper Cretaceous, Lower Cretaceous	100 million; 136 million	Evolution of reptiles up to enormous sizes (dinosaurs). The first advanced birds appear. Ammonites develop strange forms. The first flowering plants (angiosperms) appear. At the end of the period most reptiles die out, including the pterodactyls and ichthyosaurs. Ammonites and belemnites likewise disappear.
Mesozoic	Jurassic	Upper Jurassic, Middle Jurassic, Lias	157 million; 172 million; 190 million	The acme of the reptiles, including especially the pterodactyls and the ichthyosaurs. Appearance of the primitive bird *Archaeopteryx*. Plants not much changed.
Mesozoic	Triassic	Keuper, Muschelkalk, Bunter	205 million; 215 million; 225 million	Origin of the first primitive reptiles. Further evolution of the reptiles and strong expansion of the gymnospermous plants.

The Evolution of Life in Geological Time

Paleozoic	Permian	Upper Permian	240 million	True bony fishes become numerous and mammal-like reptiles appear. Gymnosperms arise, including conifers, *Ginkgo* and others. Trilobites die out.
		Lower Permian	280 million	
	Carboniferous	Upper Carboniferous (Pennsylvanian)	325 million	Appearance of the first reptiles. The highest evolution of ferns, lycopods and horsetails to form luxuriant forests giving rise to coal. Graptolites and armoured fishes die out.
		Lower Carboniferous (Mississippian)	345 million	
	Devonian	Upper Devonian	360 million	Origin of amphibians and occurrence of the first insects. Land plants develop further as psilophytes.
		Middle Devonian	370 million	
		Lower Devonian	395 million	
	Silurian		430 million	Expansion of corals. Armoured fishes and giant scorpions occupy the sea. The first primitive land plants.
	Ordovician		500 million	Appearance of fishes as the first vertebrates. Considerable further evolution of the ancestors of the ammonites. Crinoids and sea urchins, corals and graptolites appear for the first time.
	Cambrian	Upper Cambrian	515 million	Sudden appearance of invertebrate marine animals, especially trilobites. Further evolution of primitive algae.
		Middle Cambrian	540 million	
		Lower Cambrian	570 million	
Precambrian			1.0 billion	The beginning of animal life. Gradual evolution of multicellular organisms.
			3.4 billion	Beginning of plant life. Gradual evolution of algae.

* The numbers refer to the start of the period in question.

Evolution

The Origin of Life and the Evolution of Fishes

Stromatolite from the Precambrian of Biwabik, U. S. A. Specimen and photograph: K. Götz, Munich.

The question as to when life began on this planet must be almost as old as paleontology itself. It is now supposed that plant life, in the form of bacteria and unicellular algae, started about 3.5 billion years ago, while animal life, in the form of unicellular flagellates, followed at about 1 billion years. This whole period, extending over billions of years, is called the Precambrian. Nobody should be surprised that fossil remains from this period are rare. Among the oldest are the stromatolites which are important both in the PRECAMBRIAN and in Lower Palaeozoic rocks. They are calcareous precipitates built mainly by green-blue algae. Stromatolites are among the most colourful fossils known and give a striking picture of the first organisms inhabiting this planet.

From the latest part of the PRECAMBRIAN a few finds of articulate animals (annelids, arthropods) are known and some jellyfish, but they are not very common.

Evolution

The CAMBRIAN Period, which began about 570 million years ago, brought an explosive evolution of invertebrate animals and lower algae. This is when the ancestors of fishes must have existed, which would likewise be ancestral to all vertebrates and to man himself. When the first proven jawless fishes appeared in the ORDOVICIAN, and thus about 450 million years ago, they were already fully developed and must have had a long period of evolution behind them.

It is no surprise that the question of the ancestors of our fishes has been, or still is, the subject of lively discussion. Among recent animals there is an extremely primitive organism known as the lancelet or amphioxus (*Branchiostoma*). This little creature belongs to the *Acraniata*. Throughout the length of the body it has a notochord which is comparable with the human vertebral column and can be seen as its predecessor. The general shape of amphioxus is also what might be expected for an ancestor of the fishes.

There has been a recent unique fossil find. *Palaeobranchiostoma hamatotergum* has been discovered in the Permian of South Africa, which leads as to believe that *Acraniata* and fishes share a common ancestor. Additional supporting evidence are other chordates with their "calcareous skeleta", especially the *Calciochordata*. JEFFERIES believes them to be direct ancestors of the vertebrates - a view which has every prospect of prevailing.

Branchiostoma, also known as the lancelet or amphioxus. It suggests what the ancestors of fishes were like. (Photograph: Prof. Ax, Göttingen.)

Evolution

Unnamed chordate from the Lower Carboniferous of Bear Gulch, Montana, U. S. A. Specimen: Adelphi University, Garden City, New Jersey, U. S. A.

But where do we go from there? It is a long way from such a calcareous chordate to lancelet or especially, to a true agnathan. We probably will never find all the links, though a beginning seems to have been made.

The fossil **Agnatha** differ considerably from the organisms that we now recognize as fishes. People still argue as to we should talk of them as fishes, or as fish-like. Their jawless mouth can probably be seen as their essential feature. At best they could suck or rasp, but never bite. Even their swimming ability may not have been very great, at least for most of them. Some of them reached lengths of 60-80 cm. Probably they lived mostly in fresh water. They reached their maximum in the Upper SILURIAN and finally disappeared in the Upper DEVONIAN.

A side branch of the agnathans, which differs in its anatomy in many ways from the classical representatives but shares the jawless mouth with them, still survives in the form of the hagfishes

Evolution

and the lampreys. Three such cyclostomes have been found in the Lower Carboniferous, at a time when no other agnathans still existed. An evolutionary connection is therefore very likely.

In the Lower DEVONIAN another group besides the agnathans was widespread. These were the **placoderms** (PLACODERMI). From the evolutionary point of view they were more advanced. They had mobile jaws which gave them the advantage of leading a predatory mode of life. Their body was protected at back and belly by powerful armour so that they would scarcely need to fear enemies. They were still far from our usual picture of a fish—at first sight they could even be taken for turtles—and their swimming ability may also have been limited. In the Upper DEVONIAN they reached fearful sizes, up to eight metres long. These big forms had the armour confined to the head region and so could have swum considerably quicker than other placoderms. They must have terrorized the seas of the time but, nevertheless, did not prevail. They disappeared without issue, at the same time as the fossil agathans, in the Upper DEVONIAN.

The puzzling **acanthodians** (ACANTHODII) had already appeared in the Upper SILURIAN. As the name indicates (*acanthos* = spine) all the fins except the caudal fin carried a powerful spine. In some species the spines continued in a paired series between the pectoral and the pelvic fins. In their external features, the acanthodians were the first organisms with an undeniable resemblance to what we call fishes. Nevertheless, this class is completely isolated. It can neither be derived from the placoderms nor be assigned to the sharks. Unlike the latter, the acanthodians had bony tissue both in the internal and the external skeleton. The body was covered with small, tessellate, non-overlapping scales some of which extended onto the fin membranes. These scales consist of a bony base covered with a layer of dentine. The acanthodians lasted into the Lower PERMIAN but then died without issue. It is still controversial whether the acanthodians should be classified in front of the sharks or after them. It has even been suggested that the first primitive bony fishes are descended from them.

Evolution

Perhaps it is not too daring to suppose that primitive, still unknown, ancestors of the acanthodians gave rise to all higher fishes.

The **cartilaginous fishes** (CHONDRICHTHYES) appeared considerably later, in the Upper DEVONIAN. As the name implies, they have no true bony tissue. The sharks belong to this group as do also the primitive but still surviving chimaeras. The sharks did not reach their maximum until the Upper Cretaceous, but there are still so many species today that the end of their evolution is by no means in sight. Ossification is often seen as an advanced feature and chondification as a primitive one. At least in this class, however, the opposite is true.

The first sharks lived in fresh water and were predators even then. Since the TRIASSIC, however, they have been able to live in the sea. The rays and skates, which are related to the sharks, are known first from the Upper Jurassic, but the beginning of their evolution may be considerably earlier.

Up till now, I have discussed three culs-de-sac of evolution and one successful branch road. Now, however, I come to the main route as followed by the **bony fishes** (OSTEICHTHYES). The most primitive representatives have been found in the Middle DEVONIAN, but their origins may lie considerably lower. At that time, the skeleton was not completely ossified, so at this evolutionary stage they are known as CHONDROSTEI. The scales were three-layered with the outer layer made of an enamel-like tissue **called ganoin**. The Lower CARBONIferous can be seen as the first maximum of the chondrosteans, but a second maximum followed in the Lower TRIASSIC. After that, they became very uncommon. In the recent fauna their only descendants are the sturgeons, the the lobe-finned pikes and the lobe-finned eel *Calamoichthys calabaricus* which arose from a side branch.

The next group, which is not truly self-contained, is the "**holosteans**" ("HOLOSTEI"). It separated off in the Upper PERMIAN. Their main common features are an increasing ossification of the internal skeleton and a reduction of the ganoin layer on the scales. This group reached a maximum in the Upper JURASSIC and were abundant even in the CRETACEOUS. Only in the TERTIARY did they lose importance. The only forms still existent are the garpike (*Lepisosteus*) and the bowfin (*Amia*).

Evolution

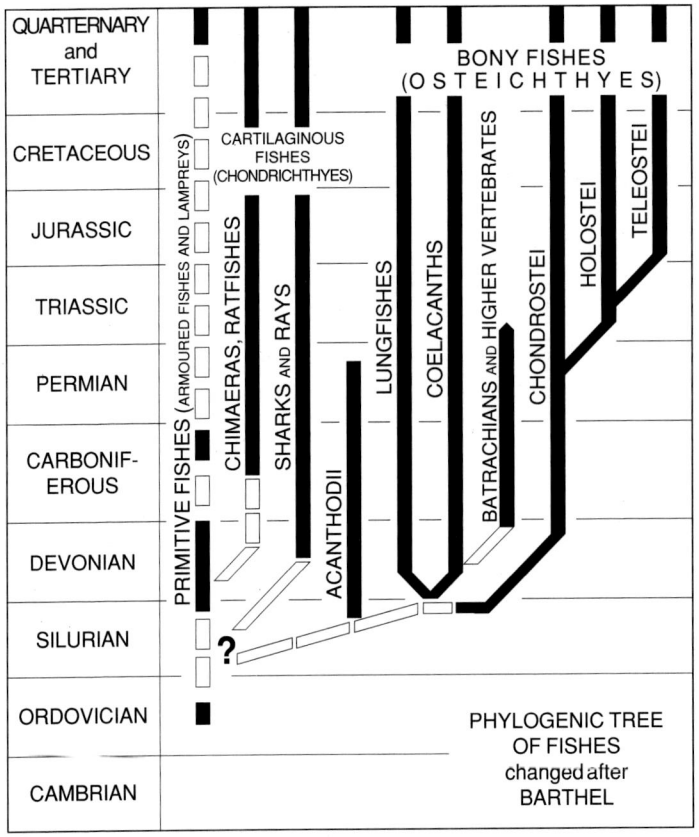

PHYLOGENIC TREE OF FISHES
changed after BARTHEL

Finally, in the Upper TRIASSIC, the ancestors should be sought of the true **bony fishes** (TELEOSTEI). This is a group of at least 25,000 species and forms the majority of all living fishes. Most of them were small herring-like fishes that still retained a thin layer

Evolution

of ganoin on the scales. In addition there were somewhat larger fishes, grouped into a total of four orders, which were the only true bony fishes during the whole of the JURASSIC and the greater part of the CRETACEOUS. Then eight new orders were added, while the Lower TERTIARY brought a further nine orders and the Middle TERTIARY another three. All the remaining, rather numerous, orders consist of recent fishes only. Thus about a third of all true bony fishes have only arisen recently. This suggests that the evolution of this, the most successful of all fish groups, is far from exhausted.

Which is descended from which can, in many cases, only be guessed. It is not even known with certainty whether we are dealing with a monophyletic or a polyphyletic group. Perhaps they can all be derived from the lineage of *Pholidophorus* and *Leptolepis*. Finally, however, the Pholidophoriformes may be split up into several branches and it may not be too outrageous to suppose that other ganoid fishes may also be involved.

All the **bony fishes** so far mentioned are placed in the subclass of the ACTINOPTERYGII. In these all the paired fins are carried by strong rays with a radial arrangement. There are, however, two further fish groups which are separated from them as "flesh-finned" (SARCOPTERYGII). These are the **lungfishes** (DIPNOI) and the **lobe-finned fishes** (CROSSOPTERYGII). Both of them are known since the Lower DEVONIAN.

There is evidence to suggest, however, that they separated off still earlier from the main branch which led to the bony fishes. Both possessed, at that time, the unusual ability to breathe air.

Lungfishes reached their maximum in the Upper DEVONIAN and still persist as a few genera today with an enormous geographical range including Africa, Australia and South America. They can survive droughts embedded in cocoons of mucus.

The maximum of the lobe-finned fishes was in the Middle DEVONIAN. No representative of this group of fishes has ever been found in the Tertiary and they were believed to have died out at the end of the Cretaceous. In 1938, however, the famous coelacanth *Latimeria chalumnae* was discovered. As a living fossil it showed that the lobe-finned fishes had survived to the present day.

Evolution

Photograph of a live *Latimeria* at the coastal region of the Comoros Islands. Photo: Prof. Fricke, Seewiesen.

The original habitat of all lobe-finned fishes was in fresh water. The representatives of the order *Coelacanthiformes*, however, may from early times have preferred life in the sea. *Latimeria* itself belongs to this order. Among the other orders, included in the higher group *Rhipidistia*, those fishes must be sought which already attempted, at the end of the DEVONIAN, to conquer the land and which thus became, by way of the amphibians and the reptiles, the ultimate ancestors of all land-dwelling vertebrates.

Today we know that the last representatives of the lobe-finned fishes prefer to live at great depth in the lava cliffs off the Comores islands. They are active at night. The females are up to two metres long and viviparous. The number of still living animals is estimated at 250. Thus this living fossil, so recently discovered, is threatened with extinction. The fishermen of the Comoros catch a few every year and recently there have even been expeditions to try to catch living specimens for exhibition. Only the strictest conservation measures may call a halt and maintain the last lobe-finned fishes for the future.

The External Features of Fishes

The Fins

Fins are very important for fishes since they are the propulsive organs. Because of their very diverse structure they are often used for identification.

Basically there are two types of fin—paired and unpaired. The unpaired fins include the **dorsal** fin along the mid line of the back, the **anal** fin situated in the ventral mid line behind the anus and the **caudal** fin (tail fin) which forms the posterior end of the fish.

The paired fins are the **pectoral** and **pelvic**. The pectoral fins are always lateral and just behind the mouth. The pelvic fins, though always located ventrally, vary greatly in position. In evolutionary terms the pectoral and pelvic fins correspond to the fore and hind limbs of land vertebrates.

It is thought that the first ancestors of fishes had no fins and could move only by undulating their bodies. The predecessors of fins may have been almost undifferentiated stabilization keels. These may have arisen from an uninterrupted fold of tissue as found today in the larval stages of almost all fishes. Perhaps at first ridges of cartilage developed in these folds which later divided into a basal portion, transverse to the body, and a radial portion extending perpendicularly into the tissue fold. In any case, this is the type of fin still found in living agnathans, both hagfishes and lampreys. Since these represent the most primitive living fishes, the median fins may have arisen in this manner. The origin of the paired fins cannot be imagined so easily. Perhaps a fold running on left and right from the gill openings to the anal region may have played a role corresponding to the median fin fold. As yet, however, such a paired fold has been found only in the fossil agnathan *Jamoytius*.

In the sharks the supporting rays are further subdivided, although this cannot be seen from outside since they are covered by skin and muscle. The still-living sturgeon also has fins of primitive type. In these fishes the dorsal and anal fins have a muscular lobe at the base which surrounds rod-like structures in the body and rays in the externally visible parts of the lobes. Such fins are similar to typical shark fins but, unlike them, the outer part of the fin is supported by bony rays—the so-called

The External Features of Fishes

Lepidotrichia. Higher fishes lack this lobe at the base of the fin and the lepidotrichia, attached to little nodes in the body, have become the only support for the external part of the fin.

The supporting skeleton of the caudal fin is different, for modifications of the posterior part of the vertebral column are involved. If the vertebral column remains straight and the fin runs around it as a sort of fringe, we speak of a **protocercal** caudal fin. If the column bends upward and extends into a longer upper lobe, while the lower lobe remains shorter, then we have a **heterocercal** caudal fin. This type is found among all sharks and chondrosteans. The opposite case, when the vertebral column bends downwards and runs into the lower lobe, is called a **hypocercal** caudal fin. This type occurs in the agnathans and also in the ichthyosaurs. (These are not fishes but I mention them for the sake of completeness.) If the caudal fin is divided symmetrically into equal-sized upper and lower lobes, or is undivided, then the fin is **homocercal**. Externally this type of fin looks absolutely symmetrical but anatomy shows that here also, in the more primitive forms, the vertebral column turns upward at the end. This strongly indicates that the homocercal fin arose in evolution from the heterocercal fin. The homocercal fin is typical for most bony fishes. Finally there is the **diphycercal** caudal fin in which the vertebral column remains straight and the caudal fin is divided into two equal lobes. Perhaps this is the most primitive type of caudal fin. It is found in some of the lobe-finned fishes.

In general the caudal fin, like the dorsal and anal fin, is made up of simple rays and jointed rays which serve to support a thin membrane. Spines are never present.

Finally, for completeness, I mention a type of fin which only occurs in the headfish *Mola*. This is the **gephyrocercal** caudal fin. It terminates the body by running as a fringe between the dorsal and anal fins.

The External Features of Fishes

Types of Caudal Fins

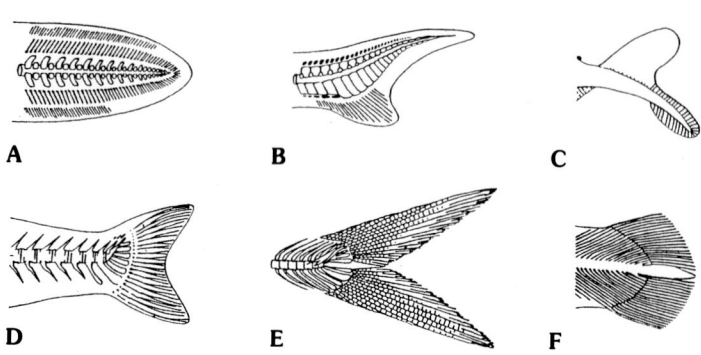

A = protocercal and diphycercal B = heterocercal C = hypocercal
D = homocercal E = homocercal F = triphycercal
  (primitive type) (more advanced type)

Shapes of Caudal Fins

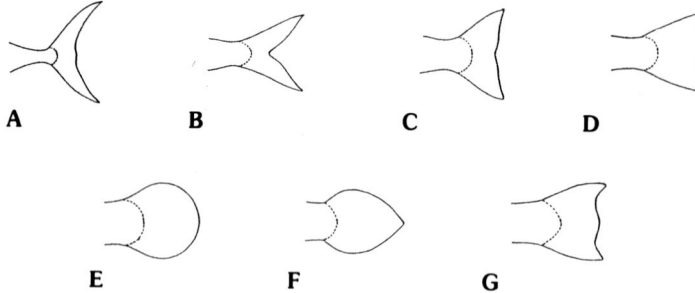

A = sickle-shaped B = forked C = slightly forked D = truncate
E = rounded F = pointed G = double-curved

The External Features of Fishes

Scales and Spines

The skin of fishes is fundamentally like that of other vertebrates. It consists of a very thin outer layer (epidermis) and a thicker layer beneath (dermis). The epidermis is made up of several layers of simple cells, the outermost layers being continually worn away by natural means and replaced. The dermis, on the other hand, is formed of a thick layer of connective tissue into which muscle fibres, nerves and blood vessels extend. The fine mucus which covers a fish and makes it slippery is secreted by special gland cells in the epidermis.

In addition to the skin, most fishes have another body covering i.e. the scales, which are sometimes referred to as an exoskeleton. In scaleless fishes the skin is always strengthened in some way. When it serves as a substrate for scales, however, it remains soft and also relatively thin.

Sharks and rays have dermal denticles which are also known as **placoid scales**. Each of these has a bone-like base embedded in the skin which at the surface bears a spine pointing backwards and covered with enamel. The rudiments of these denticles arise already in the skin of the embryo. Placoid scales, unlike the scales of bony fishes, do not enlarge as the fish grows. Rather do new placoid scales insert themselves between those already there, so that the growing body always remains covered. The shape of the dermal denticles varies with the genus and ranges from spine-like to wart-like. Some rays have even completely lost their denticles and retain only a smooth skin. Stingrays have a tail spine instead of the dorsal fin. This spine can be cast off if necessary and replaced by a new one. The chimaeras and their relatives (*Holocephali*) have largely a naked skin but there are places with little denticles almost like those of sharks.

In bony fishes the scales arise from the dermis. I start by describing **cosmoid scales** which are found in many lobe-finned fishes and fossil lungfishes. The individual scale is here made of four layers. The innermost layer consists of dense bone. Above this is a layer of porous bone, then a dentine-like cosmine layer and finally a thin superficial layer of enamel.

The chondrosteans have evolved another type of scale—the **ganoid scale**. In these the dentine layer is thinner and the bony layer correspondingly thicker. The most striking feature of this type of scale, however, is the thick layer of enamel which is referred to as

The External Features of Fishes

the ganoine layer. These layers are deposited concentrically around a tiny cosmoid scale. It is supposed that ganoid scales evolved earlier than cosmoid scales and that the latter originated by a reduction of the thick ganoin layer. Among still living fishes the primitive type of scale is found only in paddlefishes and in the African bichir and its relatives. In the "holosteans" a reduced type of ganoid scale occurs. It consists of only two layers and of these the enamel-like ganoine layer has become appreciably thinner. Such scales are found today only in the garpike *Lepisosteus* and are sometimes therefore referred to as the "lepisostoid" type of scale. Most ganoid scales are rhomboidal in outline.

All "ganoid" fishes were thus enclosed in a thick, rather inflexible armour which must have made them relatively immobile. On the other hand such scales offered a more or less effective defence against predators. Such fishes were therefore not adapted for rapid swimming and even the predators among them may have contented themselves with slow-moving or even sessile prey. Only with the gradual reduction and final loss of the enamel layer could modern types of fishes arise.

Among advanced recent fishes we have to distinguish between two basically different types of scale—**cycloid** and **ctenoid**. Cycloid scales are circular and overlap each other like tiles on a roof. They cover the whole body except for the fins and the head. The anterior end of each cycloid scale extends into a pocket in the dermis. Typical examples of cycloid scales are found in the carp.

With ctenoid scales, on the other hand, the hinder edge of the scale has small tooth-like spines. These spines can be long and pointed, or rather soft and hair-like, or anything between. A typical example of a ctenoid scale is found in the perch. With a few exceptions it can be said that cycloid scales are mostly larger than ctenoid scales and that fish with only soft fins in general have cycloid scales while those with hard fin rays have ctenoid scales. There are some fishes, however, in which both types of scale occur.

One particular exception must be mentioned. Among true bony fishes some retain a thin layer of enamel on the scales. These are the primitive true bony fishes e.g. *Pholidophorus*. Others evolved armour secondarily such as the snipefishes, sea-horses, sticklebacks, armoured catfishes and cofferfishes.

Some fishes have replaced their scales by spines. The best known example is the porcupinefish, in which the spines stick out at right

The External Features of Fishes

angles when the fish inflates itself. The same happens in some pufferfishes. The armour of many cofferfishes ends in sharp points and there are even some which have long spines extending from the head. The surgeonfishes have a lancet-shaped spine on either side of the tail base. These spines are normally enclosed in a fold of skin but in danger are protruded and can cause serious injury. The snipefishes have scales in the form of rhomb-shaped bony plates each of which extends posteriorly into a spine. Some armoured catfishes likewise show little spines on their bony plates which, like those of sharks, are formed of dentine and covered with enamel.

Among holosteans, as also among true bony fishes, there are some which have completely lost any scales and are content with a naked, though thickened, skin. In some superficially naked fishes, however, scales are present deeply embedded in the skin. This is a transitional condition to complete loss of scales. The best, and best known, example of a fish on the way to scalelessness is the European eel. Its tiny, almost buried scales are easily visible under the microscope.

Types of Scales

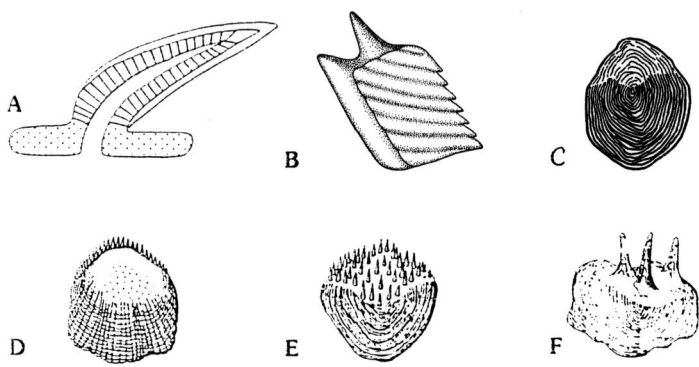

A = **placoid scale** (dermal denticle) of a shark
B = **ganoid scale** of a primitive bony fish
C = **cycloid scale** of a true bony fish
D–F = **ctenoid scales** of various types in true bony fishes.

The External Features of Fishes

Teeth

Teeth, and the type of dentition, give much information about the mode of feeding of different genera. There has been much modification in the course of evolution. Thus the oldest fishes had no true teeth. Lacking jaws, they would not have been able to grasp large prey with their teeth. In the mouth of the lamprey (*Petromyzon*) there are only conical structures and two horny plates with notched edges. The extendable tongue has other plates which serve to rasp away the surface of the prey fish. It is likely that fossil agnathans were similarly equipped.

Some placoderms had toothless cutting jaws while others had small or massive bony teeth. True teeth with dentine still did not exist. The sharks represent a great advance. Here teeth have arisen from placoid scales and are still, therefore, somewhat primitive. Each nevertheless consists of a bone-like substance called dentine covered by a layer of enamel. Enclosed by the dentine there is a pulp cavity which contains blood vessels and nerves. Such teeth are not fixed directly to the jaw but rest on a fibrous layer and are held in place additionally by the soft tissue of the gums. Sharks do not keep the same set of teeth throughout life. Whenever a tooth is lost, a replacement is ready to insert itself into the gap. Such continually self-renewing dentitions are called polyphyodont.

Sharks vary greatly in the size and shape of the teeth. They can be long and slender, or broadly triangular. There may be several types of tooth within a dentition. Even the forms of dentition are very variable. Sharks which swim freely in the water and live mainly on fishes have a typical predatory dentition which consists of two rows of sharp pointed teeth. Benthic sharks have a grasping dentition of small pointed teeth arranged in several rows one behind the other.

The chimaeras and many rays live on hard-shelled food and have crushing dentitions. These are pavement-like and consist of rounded or flat teeth or fused tooth-plates. The teeth of chondrichthyans are in general very characteristic and can therefore useful for identification.

The External Features of Fishes

Some acanthodians were toothless, some had teeth only in the lower jaw and a few had teeth in both jaws.
In the classes of fishes so far discussed, teeth are developed on the jaws only. In bony fishes, however, they can also be present on the tongue, on the palate and in the throat. Thus in many carp there are teeth in the throat but the jaws themselves are toothless. In general the teeth of bony fishes are more firmly fixed than in sharks. They vary greatly in shape, in correlation with the mode of feeding. Fish-eating fishes have especially strong sharp pointed teeth which are used for seizing prey but never for chewing it. Chewing occurs only in fishes with a pavement- or plate-like dentition. Some predatory fishes, such as the pike, have teeth also on the palate. These point backwards and can be pushed downwards in this direction to help prey to enter. They cannot be pushed forward, however, so that the prey, once in, cannot get out.
Other predatory fishes, such as the piranha, have very short upwardly directed jaws with razor-sharp teeth. This structure gives great strength to the bite so that pieces of flesh can be torn out of bigger animals. There are still other predatory fishes whose teeth are differentiated between long and short. They are especially long at the anterior end of the jaw where they are used as grasping teeth. Such teeth sink deep into the body of the prey and hold it in a powerful grip.
Fishes with a mixed diet, or which feed only on plants, mostly have blunt teeth, if any. Among other fishes, such as the puffers, the teeth fuse to form two sharp-edged plates in each jaw. Indeed, the porcupine fish has only one such plate in each jaw. Triggerfishes have chisel-like teeth with which they can make holes in hard-shelled bivalves. Finally, there are some rudderfishes (Stromateoidei), which only have tiny teeth but to compensate have a muscular, toothed feeding tube. The related form *Tetragonurus* has a similar feeding tube but lacks teeth.

Systematics

All forms of systematics seem dry-as-dust at first sight and they frighten the layman off. Here I shall therefore try to explain the absolute necessity and, above all, the usefulness, of systematics.

A classification has the important task of inserting every species into a system so as to display its relationships as clearly as possible. Obviously, this is not always easy. Moreover a classification must change to take account of the latest researches. The more research advances, the more complicated the classification becomes.

Thus early classifications were simple. They were easy to understand but did not say very much. In particular it used to be customary to consider fossils separately from existent organisms, which at first sight seemed convenient. This simple approach, however, gave almost no indication of how fossils were related to recent organisms and scarcely suggested the course of evolution.

As regards fishes, the Russian ichthyologist L. S. Berg in 1940 was the first to unite fossils and recent organisms in one classification. This was a path-making act which soon stimulated others to move in the same direction. Thus in 1958, BERG'S classification was extended by C. ARAMBOURG and L. BERTIN. Their interpretation, which naturally did not go uncontradicted, is still given in the text books. In contrast to this classification, in 1966 the ichthyologists GREENWOOD, ROSEN, WEITZMANN & MYERS set up a new system of subdivisions which was adopted in the latest edition of the standard work "Vertebrate Paleontology" by the brilliant paleontologist A. S. ROMER.

This classification, especially in mainland Europe, is still widely accepted.

In English-speaking countries, however, a new classification has been proposed which in part differs considerably from the one just mentioned. This is a cladistic interpretation, based on a theory of divergent evolution, but not yet generally accepted. It was proposed by LAUDER & LIEM in 1983 and radically revised by J. S. Nelson in 1984. The classification of fishes given by R. L. Carroll in his new successor-work to ROMER'S "Vertebrate Paleontology" is to a large extent based on this new system.

Systematics

NELSON'S book "Fishes of the World" unfortunately deals mainly with recent fishes and only mentions fossil genera by way of example. In writing the present work, therefore, I could follow NELSON and CARROLL only with regard to the bony fishes (Osteichthys). For groups more primitive than them, however, and for the lobe-finned fishes, I had to compile a classification myself. This was necessary to produce a result even halfway up-to-date. Of course, I had the help of acknowledged experts and so I hope to have done the best possible.

I am sure that I shall not escape criticism, especially concerning a few arbitrary decisions (in my view unimportant) which I thought were necessary for clarity. Thus, for example, I adopt uniform terminations for all orders, all suborders and all superfamilies. Also, I did not have the courage to eliminate the old grouping "Holostei" before a suitable replacement is proposed. In the meantime I shall use the word in the systematic part in quotation marks, followed by the new subdivisions. The already cited A. S. Romer even said: "The difficulties of classifying the actinopterygians, and bringing them into a reasonable system, can drive the fish systematist to desperation. The task of giving even a passably coherent survey of the phylogeny of this group would be the death of me." It is likely that, even today, the last word has not been spoken on this subject.

After these introductory words, I wish to discuss the importance of systematics, especially with regard to the fishes. The subphylum *Vertebrata* (backboned animals) includes, besides the fishes, the amphibians, reptiles, birds and mammals. Thus the fishes are placed in the superclass *Pisces*. This includes everything from the agnathans to the rhipidistians. It is divided into individual classes called Agnatha, Placodermi, Chondrichthyes, Acanthodii and Osteichthyes. The agnathans are divided into three subclasses with a total of eight orders. The placoderms are divided into eight orders and four suborders. The chondrichthyans are divided into two subclasses, three superorders, 28 orders and 20 suborders. Finally the osteichthyans, which are by far the most diverse class, are divided into two subclasses, four infraclasses, three divisions, five subdivisions, five superorders, 66 orders and 92 suborders. Then come the families, genera and species.

Systematics

All this only serves to show the interconnections and relationships clearly. If I try, not very successfully, to express the matter in human terms, then all members of the same class could be seen as more or less distant cousins. This relationship becomes closer, the farther we go downwards. Thus members of the same family could be seen as third cousins, and all members of a genus as second cousins. Accordingly the species must contain first cousins down to siblings with all possible combinations.

So how are a carp and a catfish related to each other? They both belong to the same suborder and are therefore fairly close "cousins". A carp and a pike form part only of the same subdivision. They are therefore rather distant "cousins". And how is it with a perch and a shark? They belong to different classes—the degree of relationship between them can be expressed only by saying that they are both "fishes".

The classification given below includes all fishes, fossil and recent, divided to the family level. A large number of fossil genera are included in the systematic part of this book and with each one it is stated whether connections exist with recent fishes. I have not attempted to list the relevant subfamilies and species.

Classification of Fishes

CLASSIFICATION OF FISHES

103 orders
720 families

Of these
263 are only known fossil (†)
224 are known both fossil and recent
233 are only known recent (•)

CLASS AGNATHA — Agnathans
  SUBCLASS MYXINI — Hagfishes or Myxinoids

Order MYXINIFORMES
  †Family: Myxinidae (hagfishes)

SUBCLASS PTERASPIDOMORPHI

Order ASTRASPIDIFORMES
  †Family: Arandaspididae
  †Family: Astraspididae
  †Family: Eriptychidae

Order PTERASPIDIFORMES
  †Family: Cyathaspididae
  †Family: Amphiaspididae
  †Family: Corvaspididae
  †Family: Traquairaspididae
  †Family: Protopteraspididae
  †Family: Pteraspididae
  †Family: Cardipeltidae
  †Family: Drepanaspididae

Classification of Fishes

Order THELODONTIFORMES
- †Family: Katoporidae
- †Family: Loganiidae
- †Family: Turiniidae
- †Family: Apalolepididae
- †Family: Nikoliviidae

SUBCLASS CEPHALASPIDOMORPHI

Order CEPHALASPIDIFORMES
- †Family: Tremataspididae
- †Family: Dartmuthiidae
- †Family: Ateleaspididae
- †Family: Sclerodontidae
- †Family: Cephalaspididae
- †Family: Kiaeraspididae

Order EUGALEASPIDIFORMES
- †Family: Hanyangaspididae
- †Family: Eugaleaspididae
- †Family: Nanpanaspididae
- †Family: Polybranchiaspididae
- †Family: Hunanaspididae
- †Family: Duyunolepididae
- †Family: Lungmenshanaspididae
- †Family: Tridensaspididae
- †Family: Dayongaspididae

Order ANASPIDIFORMES
- †Family: Jamoytiidae
- †Family: Birkeniidae
- †Family: Euphaneropsidae
- †Family: Endeiolepididae
- †Family: Lasaniidae

Order PETROMYZONTIFORMES — Lampreys
- •Family: Petromyzontidae (lampreys)
- †Family: Mayomyzontidae

Classification of Fishes

CLASS PLACODERMI	Placoderms

Order STENSIOELLIFORMES
　　†Family: Stensioellidae

Order PSEUDOPETALICHTHYIFORMES
　　†Family: Paraplesiobatidae

Order RHENANIFORMES
　　†Family: Asterosteidae

Order PTYCTODONTIFORMES
　　†Family: Ptyctodontidae

Order ACANTHOTHORACIFORMES
　　†Family: Palaeacanthaspididae
　　†Family: Weejeraspididae

Order PETALICHTHYIFORMES
　　†Family: Macropetalichthyidae

Order PHYLLOLEPIDIFORMES
　　†Family: Antarctaspididae
　　†Family: Phyllolepididae

Order ARTHRODIRIFORMES

　Suborder Actinolepidoidei
　　†Family: Actinolepididae

　Suborder Wuttagoonaspidoidei
　　†Family: Wuttagoonaspididae

　Suborder Phlyctaenioidei
　　†Family: Phlyctaeniidae
　　†Family: Holonematidae
　　†Family: Williamsaspididae

　Suborder Heterosteoidei
　　†Family: Heterosteidae

Classification of Fishes

Suborder Coccosteoidei
    Superfamily Buchanosteoidea
        †Family: Buchanosteidae
        †Family: Goodradigbeonidae
    Superfamily: Gemuendenaspoidea
        †Family: Gemuendenaspididae
    SuperFamily: Homosteoidea
        †Family: Homosteidae
    Superfamily: Brachydeiroidea
        †Family: Brachydeiridae
        †Family: Leptosteidae
    Superfamily: Coccosteoidea
        †Family: Coccosteidae
        †Family: Camuropiscidae
        †Family: Pholidosteidae
        †Family: Incisoscutidae
        †Family: Rachiosteidae
    Superfamily: Pachyostoidea
        †Family: Dinichthyidae
        †Family: Leiosteidae
        †Family: Trematosteidae
        †Family: Pachyosteidae
        †Family: Mylostomatidae
        †Family: Titanichthyidae
        †Family: Bungartiidae
Order ANTIARCHIFORMES
        †Family: Bothriolepididae
        †Family: Asterolepididae
        †Family: Sinolepididae

CLASS CHONDRICHTHYES   Cartilaginous Fishes
    SUBCLASS ELASMOBRANCHII   Elasmobranchs

SUPERORDER UNNAMED

Order XENACANTHIFORMES
        †Family: Diploselachidae
        †Family: Xenacanthidae

Classification of Fishes

Order CLADOSELACHIFORMES   Cladoselachian Sharks
    †Family: Cladoselachidae

Order CORONODONTIFORMES
    †Family: unnamed

Order SYMMORIIFORMES
    †Family: Symmoriidae
    †Family: Stethacanthidae

Order EUGENEODONTIFORMES
    Superfamily: Caseodontoidea
        †Family: Casiodontidae
        †Family: Eugeneodontidae
    Superfamily: Edestoidea
        †Family: Agassizodontidae
        †Family: Edestidae

Order ORODONTIFORMES
    †Family: Orodontidae

Order PETALODONTIFORMES
    †Family: Petalodontidae
    †Family: Pristodontidae
    †Family: Belantseidae

Order SQUATINACTIFORMES
    †Family: Squatinactidae

SUPERORDER EUSELACHII

Order CTENACANTHIFORMES
    Superfamily: Ctenacanthoidea
        †Family: Ctenacanthidae
        †Family: Bandringidae
        †Family: Phoebodontidae

Classification of Fishes

    Superfamily: Hybodontoidea
      †Family: Hybodontidae
    Superfamily: Protacrodontoidea
      †Family: Tamiobatidae

SUPERORDER NEOSELACHII

Order GALEIFORMES
    †Family: Palaeospinacidae

Suborder Heterodontoidei
    Family: Heterodontidae (horn sharks)

Suborder Orectoloboidei
    Family: Orectolobidae (nurse sharks)
    •Family: Rhincodontidae (whale sharks)
    Family: Hemiscylliidae
    †Family: Parascylliidae

Suborder Lamnoidei
    Family: Carchariidae (cub sharks)
    †Family: Cretoxyrhinidae
    †Family: Otodontidae
    Family: Lamnidae (mackerel sharks)
    Family: Mitsukurinidae
    Family: Cetorhinidae (basking sharks)
    Family: Alopiidae (thresher sharks)
    Family: Anacoracidae

Suborder Carcharhinoidei
    Family: Scyliorhinidae (cat sharks)
    Family: Pseudotriakidae
    Family: Triakidae (hound sharks)
    Family: Carcharhinidae (requin sharks)
    Family: Sphyrnidae (hammerhead sharks)

Suborder Hexanchoidei
    †Family: Orthacodontidae
    Family: Hexanchidae (cow sharks)

Suborder Chlamydoselachoidei
    Family: Chlamydoselachidae (frill sharks)

Classification of Fishes

Order SQUALIFORMES
Suborder Squaloidei (angel and dogfish sharks)
 Family: Squalidae (spiny dogfishes)
 Family: Dalatiidae (sleeper sharks)
 Family: Echinorhinidae (bramble sharks)

Suborder Pristiophoroidei
 Family: Pristiophoridae (saw sharks)

Suborder Squatinoidei
 Family: Squatinidae (angel sharks)

Order RAJIFORMES (Rays and Skates)
Suborder Rhinobatoidei
 Family: Rhynchobatidae
 Family: Rhinobatidae (guitarfishes)
 †Family: Platyrhinidae

Suborder Rajoidei
 Family: Rajidae (true rays and skates)
 †Family: Cyclobatidae
 •Family: Pseudorajidae
 •Family: Anacanthobatidae

Suborder Sclerorhynchoidei
 †Family: Sclerorhynchidae

Suborder Pristoidei (sawfishes)
 Family: Pristidae

Suborder Torpedinoidei
 Family: Torpedinidae (electric rays)
 Family: Narcinidae
 •Family: Temeridae

Suborder Myliobatoidei
 Family: Dasyatidae (stingrays)
 Family: Urolophidae (round rays)
 Family: Potamotrygonidae (river stingrays)
 Family: Gymnuridae (butterfly rays)
 Family: Myliobatidae (eagle rays)
 Family: Rhinopteridae (cow-nosed rays)
 †Family: Rhombodontidae
 Family: Mobulidae (devil rays)

Classification of Fishes

SUBCLASS SUBTERBRANCHIALIA

SUPERORDER INIOPTERYGII

Order CHONDRENCHELYIFORMES
　　†Family:　Chondrenchelyidae

Order INIOPTERYGIIFORMES
　　†Family:　Iniopterygiidae
　　†Family:　Sibyrhynchidae

SUPERORDER HOLOCEPHALI　　　　　　　　　Chimaeras

Order HELODONTIFORMES
　　†Family:　Helodontidae

Order COPODONTIFORMES
　　†Family:　Copodontidae

Order PSAMMODONTIFORMES
　　†Family:　Psammodontidae

Order unnamed
　Suborder Cochliodontoidei
　　　†Family:　Cochliodontidae
　Suborder Menaspoidei
　　　†Family:　Menaspidae
　Suborder Squalorajoidei
　　　†Family:　Squalorajidae
　Suborder Myriacanthoidei
　　　†Family:　Acanthorhinidae
　　　†Family:　Chimaeropsidae
　　　†Family:　Myriacanthidae

Classification of Fishes

Order CHIMAERIFORMES
  Suborder Echinochimaeroidei
    †Family: Echinochimaeridae
  Suborder Chimaeroidei
    Family: Chimaeridae (chimaeras)
    Family: Rhinochimaeridae (longnose chimaeras)
    Family: Callorhynchidae (ploughnose chimaeras)

CLASS ACANTHODII — Acanthodians

Order CLIMATIIFORMES
  †Family: Climatiidae
  †Family: Diplacanthidae
  †Family: Gyracanthidae

Order ISCHNACANTHIFORMES
  †Family: Ischnacanthidae

Order ACANTHODIFORMES
  †Family: Acanthodidae

CLASS OSTEICHTHYES — Bony Fishes
SUBCLASS ACTINOPTERYGII — Ray-Finned Fishes
INFRACLASS CHONDROSTEI — Chondrosteans

Order POLYPTERIFORMES
  Family: Polypteridae (bichirs)

Order PALAEONISCIFORMES
  Suborder Palaeoniscoidei (palaeoniscoids)
    †Family: Cheirolepididae
    †Family: Stegotrachelidae

Classification of Fishes

†Family: Tegeolepididae
†Family: Rhabdolepididae
†Family: Rhadinichthyidae
†Family: Carbovelidae
†Family: Canobiidae
†Family: Cornuboniscidae
†Family: Styracopteridae
†Family: Cryphiolepididae
†Family: Holuriidae
†Family: Cosmoptychiidae
†Family: Pygopteridae
†Family: Elonichthyidae
†Family: Acrolepididae
†Family: Coccocephalichthyidae
†Family: Amblypteridae
†Family: Aeduellidae
†Family: Platysellidae
†Family: Commentryidae
†Family: Palaeoniscidae
†Family: Dicellopygidae
†Family: Boreolepididae
†Family: Birgeriidae
†Family: Scanilepididae
†Family: Centrolepididae
†Family: Coccolepididae

Suborder Platysomoidei
†Family: Platysomidae
†Family: Chirodontidae
†Family: Bobasatraniidae

Order HAPLOLEPIFORMES
†Family: Haplolepididae

Order DORYPTERIFORMES
†Family: Dorypteridae

Order TARRASIIFORMES
†Family: Tarrasiidae

Classification of Fishes

Order PTYCHOLEPIFORMES
  †Family: Ptycholepididae

Order PHOLIDOPLEURIFORMES
  †Family: Pholidopleuridae

Order LUGANOIIFORMES
  †Family: Luganoiidae
  †Family: Habroichthyidae
  †Family: Thoracopteridae

Order REDFIELDIIFORMES
  †Family: Redfieldiidae

Order PERLEIDIFORMES
  †Family: Perleididae
  †Family: Cleithrolepididae
  †Family: Platysiagidae
  †Family: Cephaloxenidae
  †Family: Aetheodontidae

Order PELTOPLEURIFORMES
  †Family: Peltopleuridae
  †Family: Polzbergiidae

Order PHANERORHYNCHIFORMES
  †Family: Phanerorhynchidae

Order SAURICHTHYIFORMES
  †Family: Saurichthyidae

Order ACIPENSERIFORMES   Sturgeons and Paddlefishes

  Suborder Chondrosteoidei
    †Family: Errolichthyidae
    †Family: Chondrosteidae

  Suborder Acipenseroidei (sturgeons)
    Family: Acipenseridae (sturgeons)

Classification of Fishes

Suborder Polyodontoidei (paddlefishes)
    Family: Polyodontidae (paddlefishes)

SUBCLASS NEOPTERYGII — Neopterygians
DIVISION GINGLYMODI — Garpikes

Order LEPISOSTEIFORMES — Garpikes
    Family: Lepisosteidae (gars)

DIVISION HALECOSTOMI

Order SEMIONOTIFORMES
    †Family: Semionotidae

Order PYCNODONTIFORMES
    †Family: Brembodontidae
    †Family: Pycnodontidae

Order MACROSEMIIFORMES
    †Family: Macrosemiidae
    †Family: Uarbryichthyidae

SUBDIVISION HALECOMORPHI — Bowfins

Order AMIIFORMES — Bowfins
    †Family: Parasemionotidae
    †Family: Caturidae
    Family: Amiidae (bowfins)
    †Family: Tomognathidae

Order PACHYCORMIFORMES
    †Family: Pachycormidae

Order ASPIDORHYNCHIFORMES
    †Family: Aspidorhynchidae

Classification of Fishes

SUBDIVISION TELEOSTEI — True Bony Fishes

Order PHOLIDOPHORIFORMES
- †Family: Pholidophoridae
- †Family: Ichthyokentemidae
- †Family: Majokiidae
- †Family: Ligulellidae
- †Family: Pleuropholidae
- †Family: Archaeomaenidae
- †Family: Oligopleuridae

Order LEPTOLEPIFORMES
- †Family: Leptolepididae

Order unnamed
- †Family: Varasichthyidae

Order ICHTHYODECTIFORMES
- †Family: Allothrissopidae
- †Family: Ichthyodectidae
- †Family: Saurodontidae
- †Family: Thryptodontidae

Order unnamed
- †Family: Tselfatiidae

INFRADIVISION OSTEOGLOSSOMORPHA — Bonytongues

Order OSTEOGLOSSIFORMES — Bonytongues
Suborder Osteoglossoidei
- †Family: Singididae
- Family: Osteoglossidae (bonytongues)
- Family: Pantodontidae (butterflyfishes)

Suborder Notopteroidei (knifefishes and featherbacks)
- †Family: Lycopteridae

Classification of Fishes

    Family: Hiodontidae (moon eyes)
    Family: Notopteridae (knifefishes)

Suborder Mormyroidei (mormyrids)
    Family: Mormyridae (elephantfishes)
    •Family: Gymnarchidae

INFRADIVISION ELOPOMORPHA

Order ELOPIFORMES   Tarpons

Suborder unnamed
    †Family: Anaethalionidae

Suborder Elopoidei
    Family: Elopidae (tenpounders)
    Family: Megalopidae (tarpons)

Suborder Albuloidei
    †Family: Osmeroididae
    Family: Pterothrissidae
    Family: Albulidae (bonefishes)
    †Family: Phyllodontidae (?)

Suborder Pachyrhizodontoidei
    †Family: Crossognathidae
    †Family: Pachyrhizodontidae
    †Family: Notelopidae

Order NOTACANTHIFORMES   Spiny Eels and Halosaurid Eels
    Family: Halosauridae (halosaurs)
    Family: Notacanthidae (spiny eels)
    •Family: Lipogenyidae
    †Family: Protostomiatidae

Order ANGUILLIFORMES   Eels
    †Family: Anguillavidae
    Family: Anguillidae (true eels)
    †Family: Paranguillidae
    Family: Heterenchelyidae
    •Family: Moringuidae (worm eels)
    Family: Xenocongridae (false morays)

Classification of Fishes

    •Family: Myrocongridae
    Family: Muraenidae (moray eels)
    †Family: Proteomyridae
    †Family: Anguilloididae
    †Family: Milananguillidae
    Family: Nemichthyidae (snipe eels)
    •Family: Cyematidae
    •Family: Synaphobranchidae (cutthroat eels)
    •Family: Simenchelyidae (snubnose parasitic eels)
    •Family: Dissomidae (mustard eels)
    Family: Ophichthidae (snake eels)
    •Family: Neenchelyidae
    Family: Nettastomatidae (duckbilled eels)
    •Family: Macrocephenchelyidae
    Family: Congridae (congers)
    Family: Muraenesocidae (pike eels)
    •Family: Derichthyidae (longneck eels)
    •Family: Nessorhamphidae
    •Family: Serrivomeridae
    †Family: Patavichthyidae
    †Family: Urenchelyidae

Suborder Saccopharyngoidei (gulper eels)
    •Family: Saccopharyngidae (swallowers)
    •Family: Eupharyngidae (gulpers)
    •Family: Monognathidae

INFRADIVISION CLUPEOMORPHA Herringlike Fishes

Order ELLIMMICHTHYIFORMES
    †Family: Ellimmichthyidae

Order CLUPEIFORMES
    Suborder Denticipitoidei
        Family: Denticipitidae (denticle herrings)
    Suborder Clupeoidei
        Family: Clupeidae (herrings)
        Family: Engraulididae (anchovies)
        Family: Chirocentridae (wolf herrings)

Classification of Fishes

INFRADIVISION EUTELEOSTEI — Higher Teleosts

SUPERORDER OSTARIOPHYSI — Carps and Catfishes

Order GONORHYNCHIFORMES

Suborder Chanoidei
    Family: Chanidae (milkfishes)

Suborder Gonorynchoidei
    Family: Gonorhynchidae
    †Family: Judeichthyidae

Suborder Knerioidei
    •Family: Kneriidae
    •Family: Phractolaemidae

Order CYPRINIFORMES — Carps
    Family: Cyprinidae (carps, tenches, minnows etc.)
    •Family: Psilorhynchidae
    •Family: Homalopteridae (torrentfishes)
    Family: Cobitididae (loaches)
    •Family: Gyrinocheilidae (algae eaters)
    Family: Catostomidae (suckers)

Order CHARACIFORMES — Characins
    †Family: Clupavidae
    •Family: Citharinidae (citharins)
    Family: Hemiodontidae (hemiodids)
    Family: Curimatidae (curimatas)
    Family: Anastomidae (headstanders)
    Family: Erythrinidae (trahiras)
    •Family: Lebiasinidae (pencil fishes and pyrrhulinins)
    •Family: Gasteropelecidae (freshwater hatchetfishes)
    •Family: Ctenoluciidae (pike-characins)
    •Family: Hepsetidae (Kafue pike)
    Family: Characidae (true American characins)

Classification of Fishes

Order SILURIFORMES   Catfishes
- •Family: Diplomystidae (diplomystid catfishes)
- †Family: Hypsidoridae
- Family: Ictaluridae (North American catfishes)
- Family: Bagridae (bagrid catfishes)
- •Family: Cranoglanididae (armorhead catfishes)
- Family: Siluridae (Eurasian catfishes)
- •Family: Schilbeidae (schilbeid catfishes)
- Family: Pangasiidae (shark catfishes)
- •Family: Amblycipitidae (Asiatic torrent catfishes)
- •Family: Amphiliidae (African hillstream catfishes)
- •Family: Akysidae (stream catfishes)
- Family: Sisoridae (sisorid catfishes)
- Family: Clariidae (airbreathing catfishes)
- •Family: Heteropneustidae (airsac catfishes)
- •Family: Chacidae (squarehead catfishes)
- •Family: Olyridae (bannertail catfishes)
- •Family: Malapteruridae (electric catfishes)
- Family: Ariidae (sea catfishes)
- Family: Plotosidae (catfish eels)
- Family: Mochokidae (upside-down catfishes)
- •Family: Doradidae (thorny catfishes)
- •Family: Auchenipteridae (driftwood catfishes)
- Family: Pimelodidae (antenna catfishes)
- •Family: Ageneiosidae (barbel-less catfishes)
- •Family: Helogenidae (marbled catfishes)
- •Family: Cetopsidae (whale-like catfishes)
- •Family: Hypophthalmidae (low-eyed catfishes)
- •Family: Aspredinidae (banjo catfishes)
- •Family: Trichomycteridae (parasitic catfishes)
- Family: Callichthyidae (callichthyid armoured catf.)
- •Family: Loricariidae (armoured catfishes)
- •Family: Astroblepidae (S. American hillstream catf.)

Order GYMNOTIFORMES
   Suborder Sternopygoidei
- •Family: Sternopygidae
- •Family: Rhamphichthyidae (knifefishes)
- •Family: Hypopomidae
- •Family: Apteronotidae (speckeled knifefishes)

Classification of Fishes

    Suborder Gymnotoidei
        •Family: Gymnotidae (knife eels)
        •Family: Electrophoridae (electric eels)

SUPERORDER PROTACANTHOPTERYGII

Order SALMONIFORMES

    Suborder Esocoidei
        †Family: Palaeoesocidae e
    Suborder Osmeroidei
        Family: Osmeridae (smelts)
    Suborder Salmonoidei
        •Family: Salangidae (icefishes)
        •Family: Retropinnidae (New Zealand smelts)
        Family: Galaxiidae (galaxiids)
        Family: Salmonidae (salmonids)

SUPERORDER STENOPTERYGII

Order STOMIIFORMES

    Suborder Gonostomatoidei
        Family: Gonostomatidae (bristlemouths)
        Family: Sternoptychidae (marine hatchetfishes)
    Suborder Photichthyoidei
        Family: Photichthyidae
        •Family: Astronesthidae (snaggletooths)
        •Family: Melanostomiidae (scaleless black dragonfishes)
        •Family: Malacosteidae (loosejaws)
        •Family: Idiacanthidae (black dragonfishes)

Classification of Fishes

SUPERORDER SCOPELOMORPHA

Order AULOPIFORMES

Suborder Enchodontoidei
    †Family: Enchodontidae
    †Family: Eurypholidae

Suborder Halecoidei
    †Family: Halecidae

Suborder Aulopoidei
    •Family: Aulopodidae (aulopus)
    •Family: Chlorophthalmidae (greeneyes)
    •Family: Scopelarchidae (pearleyes)
    •Family: Notosudidae

Suborder Alepisauroidei
    Family: Synodontidae (lizardfishes)
    •Family: Giganturidae (giganturids)
    Family: Paralepididae (barracudinas)
    •Family: Anotopteridae (daggertooth)
    •Family: Evermannellidae (sabretooth fishes)
    •Family: Omosudidae
    •Family: Alepisauridae (lancetfishes)
    •Family: Pseudotrichonotidae

Suborder Ichthyotringoidei
    †Family: Ichthyotringidae
    †Family: Cheirothricidae
    †Family: Dercetidae
    †Family: Cimolichthyidae
    †Family: Prionolepididae

Order MYCTOPHIFORMES
    †Family: Sardinoididae
    •Family: Neoscopelidae
    Family: Myctophidae (lanternfishes)

Order PATTERSONICHTHYIFORMES
    †Family: Pattersonichthyidae

Classification of Fishes

Order CTENOTHRISSIFORMES
†Family: Ctenothrissidae
†Family: Aulolepidae

SUPERORDER PARACANTHOPTERYGII

†Family: Mcconichthyidae

Order PERCOPSIFORMES
Suborder Sphenocephaloidei
 †Family: Sphenocephalidae
Suborder Percopsoidei
 Family: Percopsidae
Suborder Aphredoderoidei
 Family: Aphredoderidae (pirate perch)
 Family: Amblyopsidae (cavefishes)

Order GADIFORMES   Cods
Suborder Muraenolepidoidei
 •Family: Muraenolepididae (eel cods)
Suborder Gadoidei
 Family: Moridae (morid cod)
 •Family: Melanonidae (melanonids)
 Family: Bregmacerotidae (codlets)
 Family: Gadidae (cods)
 Family: Merlucciidae (merluccid hakes)
Suborder Macrouroidei
 Family: Macrouridae (grenadier fishes)

Order OPHIDIIFORMES
Family: Ophidiidae (brotulas and cusk-eels)
Family: Carapidae (carapids)

Order BATRACHOIDIFORMES
Family: Batrachoididae (toadfishes)

Classification of Fishes

Order LOPHIIFORMES　　　　　　　　　　　　　　Anglerfishes
    Suborder Lophioidei
        Family: Lophiidae (goosefishes)
    Suborder Antennarioidei
        Family: Antennariidae (frogfishes)
        Family: Brachionichthyidae (warty anglers)
       •Family: Chaunacidae (sea toads)
       •Family: Ogcocephalidae (batfishes)
    Suborder Ceratioidei
       •Family: Caulophrynidae
       •Family: Ceratiidae (sea devils)
       •Family: Gigantactinidae
       •Family: Neoceratiidae
       •Family: Linophrynidae
       •Family: Oneirodidae
       •Family: Thaumatichthyidae
       •Family: Centrophrynidae (deep-sea anglerfish)
       •Family: Diceratiidae
       •Family: Himantolophidae (footballfishes)
       •Family: Melanocetidae

SUPERORDER ACANTHOPTERYGII
  SERIES ATHERINOMORPHA

Order CYPRINODONTIFORMES

    Suborder Exocoetoidei
        Family: Exocoetidae (flying fishes)
        Family: Hemirhamphidae (halfbeaks)
        Family: Belonidae (needlefishes)
        Family: Scomberosocidae (sauries)
       †Family: Forficidae

    Suborder Adrianichthyoidei
        Family: Adrianichthyidae (adrianichthyids)

    Suborder Cyprinodontoidei
       •Family: Aplocheilidae (rivulines)
        Family: Cyprinodontidae (killifishes)

Classification of Fishes

      Family: Goodeidae (goodeids)
    •Family: Anablepidae (four-eyed fishes)
    •Family: Poeciliidae (livebearers)

Order ATHERINIFORMES
      Family: Atherinidae (silversides)
    •Family: Isonidae (surf sardines)
    •Family: Melanotaeniidae (rainbowfishes)
    •Family: Phallostethidae

SERIES PERCOMORPHA   Perches

Order LAMPRIDIFORMES

Suborder Lampridoidei
      Family: Lampridae (opah)
    †Family: Turkmenidae

Suborder Veliferoidei
      Family: Veliferidae

Suborder Trachipteroidei
      Family: Lophotidae (crestfishes)
    •Family: Trachipteridae (ribbonfishes)
    •Family: Regalecidae (oarfishes)

Suborder Stylephoroidei
    •Family: Stylephoridae (tube-eye)

Suborder Ateleopodoidei
    •Family: Ateleopodidae

Suborder Mirapinnatoidei
    •Family: Mirapinnidae (hairyfish)
    •Family: Eutaeniophoridae (tapetails)

Suborder Megalomycteroidei
    •Family: Megalomycteridae (largenose fishes)

Order BERYCIFORMES

Suborder Berycoidei
      Family: Monocentrididae (pinecone fishes)
      Family: Trachichthyidae (slimeheads)

Classification of Fishes

      •Family: Anomalopidae (lanterneye fishes)
      •Family: Diretmidae (spinyfins)
      •Family: Anoplogastridae (fangtooth)
      Family: Berycidae (alfonsinos)
      Family: Holocentridae (squirrelfishes)
Suborder Dinopterygoidei
      †Family: Dinopterygidae
      †Family: Aipichthyidae
      †Family: Pycnosteroididae
      †Family: Stichocentridae
      †Family: Digoriidae

Suborder Polymixoidei
      Family: Polymixiidae (beardfishes)

Suborder Stephanoberycoidei
      •Family: Stephanoberycidae (pricklefishes)
      Family: Melamphaidae (bigscale fishes)
      •Family: Gibberichthyidae (gibberfish)

Suborder Araripichthoidei
      †Family: Araripichthyidae

Order ZEIFORMES
      •Family: Parazenidae (parazen)
      •Family: Macrurocyttidae
      Family: Zeidae (dories)
      •Family: Oreosomatidae (oreos)
      •Family: Grammicolepididae (grammicolepids)
      Family: Caproidae (boarfishes)

Order GASTEROSTEIFORMES
      •Family: Hypoptychidae   (sand eels)
      Family: Aulorhynchidae (tubesnouts)
      Family: Gasterosteidae (sticklebacks)

Order INDOSTOMIFORMES
      •Family: Indostomidae

Classification of Fishes

Order PEGASIFORMES
      Family: Pegasidae (seamoths)

Order SYNGNATHIFORMES

  Suborder Aulostomoidei
      Family: Aulostomidae (trumpetfishes)
      †Family: Urosphenidae
      Family: Fistulariidae (cornetfishes)
      †Family: Parasynarcualidae
      Family: Macrorhamphosidae (snipefishes)
      Family: Centriscidae (shrimpfishes)
      †Family: Paraeoliscidae

  Suborder Syngnathoidei
      Family: Solenostomidae (ghost pipefishes)
      Family: Syngnathidae (pipefishes and seahorses)

Order DACTYLOPTERIFORMES
      Family: Dactylopteridae (flying gurnards)

Order SYNBRANCHIFORMES
      •Family: Synbranchidae (swamp-eels)

Order SCORPAENIFORMES

  Suborder Scorpaenoidei
      Family: Scorpaenidae (scorpionfishes)
      •Family: Synanceiidae (synancejidae)
      †Family: Pterygocephalidae
      †Family: Rhamphosidae
      •Family: Caracanthidae (orbicular velvetfishes)
      •Family: Aploactinidae (velvetfishes)
      •Family: Pataecidae
      •Family: Congiopodidae (racehorses)
      Family: Triglidae (searobins)

  Suborder Platycephaloidei
      Family: Platycephalidae (flatheads)
      •Family: Hoplichthyidae (ghost flatheads)

  Suborder Anoplopomatoidei
      •Family: Anoplopomatidae (sablefishes)

Classification of Fishes

Suborder Hexagrammoidei
      Family: Hexagrammidae (greenlings)
    •Family: Zaniolepididae (combfishes)

Suborder Cottoidei
    •Family: Normanichthyidae
    •Family: Ereuniidae
     Family: Cottidae (sculpins)
    •Family: Cottocomephoridae
    •Family: Comephoridae (Baikal oilfishes)
    •Family: Psychrolutidae
    •Family: Agonidae (poachers)
     Family: Cyclopteridae (lumpfishes and snailfishes)

Order PERCIFORMES

Suborder Percoidei
      Family: Centropomidae (snooks)
      Family: Percichthyidae (temperate basses)
      Family: Serranidae (sea basses)
    •Family: Grammistidae (soapfishes)
    •Family: Pseudochromidae (dottybacks)
    •Family: Grammidae (basslets)
    •Family: Plesiopidae (roundheads)
    •Family: Anisochromidae
    •Family: Acanthoclinidae
    •Family: Glaucosomatidae
    •Family: Teraponidae (tigerperches)
    •Family: Banjosidae
    •Family: Kuhliidae (aholeholes)
     Family: Centrarchidae (sunfishes)
     Family: Percidae (perches)
     Family: Priacanthidae (bigeyes)
     Family: Apogonidae (cardinalfishes)
     Family: Acropomatidae
     Family: Sillaginidae (smelt-whitings)
     Family: Malacanthidae
    •Family: Labracoglossidae
     Family: Lactariidae (false trevallies)
     Family: Pomatomidae (bluefishes)
    •Family: Rachycentridae (cobia)

Classification of Fishes

   Family: Echeneididae (remoras)
   Family: Carangidae (jacks and pompanos)
•Family: Nematistiidae
•Family: Coryphaenidae (dolphins)
•Family: Apolectidae
   Family: Menidae (moonfish)
   Family: Leiognathidae (slimys, slipmouths or ponyfishes)
   Family: Bramidae (pomfrets)
   Family: Caristiidae (manefishes)
•Family: Arripidae (Australian salmon)
•Family: Emmelichthyidae (bonnetmouths)
   Family: Lutjanidae (snappers)
•Family: Caesionidae
   Family: Lobotidae (tripletails)
•Family: Gerreidae (mojarras)
   Family: Haemulidae (grunts)
•Family: Inermiidae
   Family: Sparidae (porgies)
•Family: Lethrinidae (scavengers or emperors)
•Family: Nemipteridae (threadfin breams)
   Family: Sciaenidae (drums)
   Family: Mullidae (goatfishes)
   Family: Monodactylidae (fingerfishes)
•Family: Pempherididae (sweepers)
•Family: Leptobramidae (beachsalmon)
•Family: Bathyclupeidae
   Family: Toxotidae (archerfishes)
•Family: Coracinidae (galjoen fishes)
•Family: Kyphosidae (sea chubs)
†Family: Amphistiidae
   Family: Ephippidae (spadefishes)
   Family: Platacidae
   Family: Scatophagidae (scats)
•Family: Rhinoprenidae (threadfin scat)
   Family: Chaetodontidae (butterflyfishes)
•Family: Pomacanthidae (angelfishes)
   Family: Enoplosidae
•Family: Pentacerotidae (armourheads)
•Family: Nandidae (leaffishes)

Classification of Fishes

    Family: Oplegnathidae (knifejaws)
    Family: Cichlidae (cichlids)
    Family: Embiotocidae (surfperches)
    Family: Pomacentridae (damselfishes)
   †Family: Priscacaridae
  •Family: Gadopsidae (blackfish)
  •Family: Cirrhitidae (hawkfishes)
  •Family: Chironemidae (kelpfishes)
  •Family: Aplodactylidae
  •Family: Cheilodactylidae (morwongs)
  •Family: Latrididae (trumpeters)
    Family: Owstoniidae
    Family: Cepolidae (bandfishes)
    Family: Dipterichthyidae (Twowingbasses)

†Family: Arambourgellidae

Suborder Mugiloidei
    Family: Mugilidae (mullets)

Suborder Sphyraenoidei
    Family: Sphyraenidae (barracudas)

Suborder Polynemoidei
    Family: Polynemidae (threadfins)

Suborder Labroidei
    Family: Labridae (wrasses)
  •Family: Odacidae
    Family: Scaridae (parrotfishes)

Suborder Zoarcoidei
  •Family: Bathymasteridae (ronquils)
  •Family: Zoarcidae (eelpouts)
    Family: Stichaeidae (pricklebacks)
  •Family: Cryptacanthodidae (wrymouths)
    Family: Pholididae (gunnels)
    Family: Anarhichadidae (wolffishes)
  •Family: Ptilichthyidae (quillfish)
    Family: Zaporidae (prowfish)
  •Family: Scytalinidae (graveldiver)

Classification of Fishes

Suborder Notothenoidei
- •Family: Bovichthyidae
- Family: Nototheniidae (cod icefishes)
- •Family: Harpagiferidae (plunderfish)
- •Family: Bathydraconidae (Antartic dragonfishes)
- •Family: Channichthyidae (crocodile icefishes)

Suborder Trachinoidei
- •Family: Opisthognathidae (jawfishes)
- •Family: Congrogadidae (eelblennies)
- Family: Chiasmodontidae
- •Family: Chamsodontidae
- •Family: Notograptidae
- •Family: Pholidichthyidae
- •Family: Trichodontidae (sandfishes)
- Family: Trachinidae (weeverfishes)
- •Family: Uranoscopidae (stargazers)
- •Family: Trichonotidae (sandfishes)
- •Family: Creediidae
- •Family: Leptoscopidae
- •Family: Percophidae
- Family: Mugiloididae (sandperches)
- •Family: Cheimarrhichthyidae

Suborder Blennioidei
- Family: Tripterygiidae (threefin blennies)
- •Family: Dactyloscopidae (sand stargazers)
- Family: Labrisomidae
- Family: Clinidae (clinids)
- •Family: Chaenopsidae
- Family: Blenniidae (combtooth blennies)

Suborder Icosteoidei
- •Family: Schindleriidae

Suborder Ammodytoidei
- Family: Ammodytidae (sand lances)

Suborder Callionymoidei
- Family: Callionymidae (dragonets)
- •Family: Draconettidae (dragonets)

Suborder Gobiesocoidei
- Family: Gobiesosocidae (clingfishes)

Classification of Fishes

Suborder Gobioidei
- •Family: Rhyacichthyidae (loach gobies)
- •Family: Eleotrididae (sleepers)
- Family: Gobiidae (gobies)
- •Family: Gobioididae (eellike gobies)
- •Family: Tripauchenidae (burrowing gobies)
- •Family: Kraemeriidae (sand gobies)
- •Family: Microdesmidae (wormfishes)

Suborder Kurtoidei
- •Family: Kurtidae (nurseryfishes)

Suborder Acanthuroidei
- Family: Acanthuridae* (surgeonfishes)
- †Family: Caprovesposidae
- Family: Siganidae (rabbitfishes)
- †Family: Kushlukiidae

Suborder Scombroidei
- •Family: Scombrolabracidae
- Family: Gempylidae (snake mackerels)
- Family: Trichiuridae (cutlassfishes)
- Family: Scombridae (mackerels and tunas)
- Family: Xiphiidae (swordfish)
- •Family: Luvariidae (louvar)
- Family: Istiophoridae (billfishes)
- †Family: Palaeorhynchidae

Suborder Stromateoidei
- •Family: Amarsipidae
- •Family: Centrolophidae (medusafishes)
- Family: Nomeidae (driftfishes)
- •Family: Ariommatidae (amiommids)
- Family: Tetragonuridae (squaretails)
- Family: Stromateidae (butterfishes)

Suborder Anabantoidei
- Family: Anabantidae (climbing gouramies)
- •Family: Belontiidae (gouramies)
- •Family: Helostomatidae (kissing gourami)
- Family: Osphronemidae (giant gourami)

---

* Nelson places Zanclus in this family.

Classification of Fishes

Suborder Luciocephaloidei
 •Family: Luciocephalidae (pikehead)

 Suborder Channoidei
 Family: Channidae (snakeheads)

 Suborder Mastacembeloidei
 •Family: Mastacembelidae (spiny eels)
 •Family: Chaudhuriidae

Order PLEURONECTIFORMES

 Suborder Psettodoidei
 Family: Psettodidae (psettotids)

 Suborder Pleuronectoidei
 Family: Citharidae (citharids)
 Family: Bothidae (lefteye flounders)
 Family: Pleuronectidae (righteye flounders)

 Suborder Soleoidei
 Family: Cynoglossidae (tonguefishes)
 Family: Soleidae (soles)

Order TETRAODONTIFORMES

 Suborder Balistoidei
 Family: Aracanidae
 Family: Triacanthodidae (spikefishes)
 Family: Triacanthidae (triplespines)
 Family: Balistidae (triggerfishes and filefishes)
 Family: Ostraciidae (boxfishes)

 Suborder Tetraodontoidei
 •Family: Triodontidae (three-toothed puffer)
 Family: Tetraodontidae (puffers)
 Family: Diodontidae (porcupinefishes)
 Family: Molidae (molas)

Classification of Fishes

SUBCLASS: SARCOPTERYGII — Sarcopterygians
INFRACLASS: CROSSOPTERYGII — Lobe-Finnned Fishes

Order COELACANTHIFORMES (Actinistia) — Coelacanths
- †Family: Diplocercidae
- †Family: Hadronectoridae
- †Family: Rhabdodermatidae
- †Family: Coelacanthidae
- †Family: Laugiidae
- •Family: Latimeriidae (gombessa)

Order ONYCHODONTIFORMES
- †Family: Onychodontidae

Order RHIPIDISTIIFORMES (Rhipidistians)
Superfamily: Holoptychoidea
- †Family: Powichthyidae
- †Family: Porolepididae
- †Family: Holoptychidae

Superfamily: Osteolepidoidea
- †Family: Osteolepididae
- †Family: Eusthenopteridae
- †Family: Panderichthyidae
- †Family: Rhizodontidae

INFRACLASS: DIPNOI — Lungfishes

- †Family: Uranolophidae
- †Family: Dipnorhynchidae
- †Family: Dipteridae
- †Family: Rhynchodipteridae
- †Family: Phaneropleuridae
- †Family: Ctenodontidae
- †Family: Sagenodontidae
- †Family: Uronemidae
- †Family: Conchopomidae
- Family: Ceratodontidae (Australian lungfishes)
- Family: Lepidosirenidae (South American lungfishes)
- Family: Protopteridae (African lungfishes)

AGNATHA — Jawless Fishes

The first fish-like organisms to appear on earth were not much like our present concept of a typical fish. Most of them had a dorso-ventrally flattened body indicating a bottom-dwelling mode of life. They were probably weak swimmers. Their main common feature, from the evolutionary point of view, was the jawless mouth. They could not bite and therefore would not have been able to hunt for large swimming prey. Their circular mouths would allow them only to suck, or perhaps to rasp, so they would have fed mainly on small organisms and detritus. Their heads, and also the anterior parts of their bodies, were covered with thick bony armour which would have made an effective defence against enemies. Their eyes and nasal opening often lay close together and were directed upwards. The total size was usually small, though there were exceptions which reached a length of 60 cm or more.

Paired fins were usually developed only as pectorals. There are forms with one, or even two, dorsal fins while others lacked dorsal fins completely. The anal fin was sometimes present whereas the existence of pelvic fins is doubtful. The caudal fin was mostly heterocercal or hypocercal. The notochord (the evolutionary forerunner of the vertebral column) persisted throughout life. The order Anaspidiformes included some genera which looked truly fish-like. Instead of armour, they often had thick scales. A few of them had lost the scaly cover except for a few remnants. To judge by their shape, most members of this order would have been rather skillful swimmers in the open water.

Finally I must mention the hagfishes and lampreys which, except for the circular jawless mouth, were unlike other agnathans. They are known from the Upper Carboniferous onwards and still survive. They have scaleless eel-like bodies. They may represent a side branch which has survived from early times.

The **AGNATHA** first appeared in the Lower Ordovician, had their greatest maximum in the Upper Silurian and died out in the Upper Devonian except for the hagfishes and lampreys. About 200 fossil genera have been described, though most of them on the basis of isolated head shields and dorsal shields only. Complete agnathans are extremely rare.

AGNATHA — Jawless Fishes

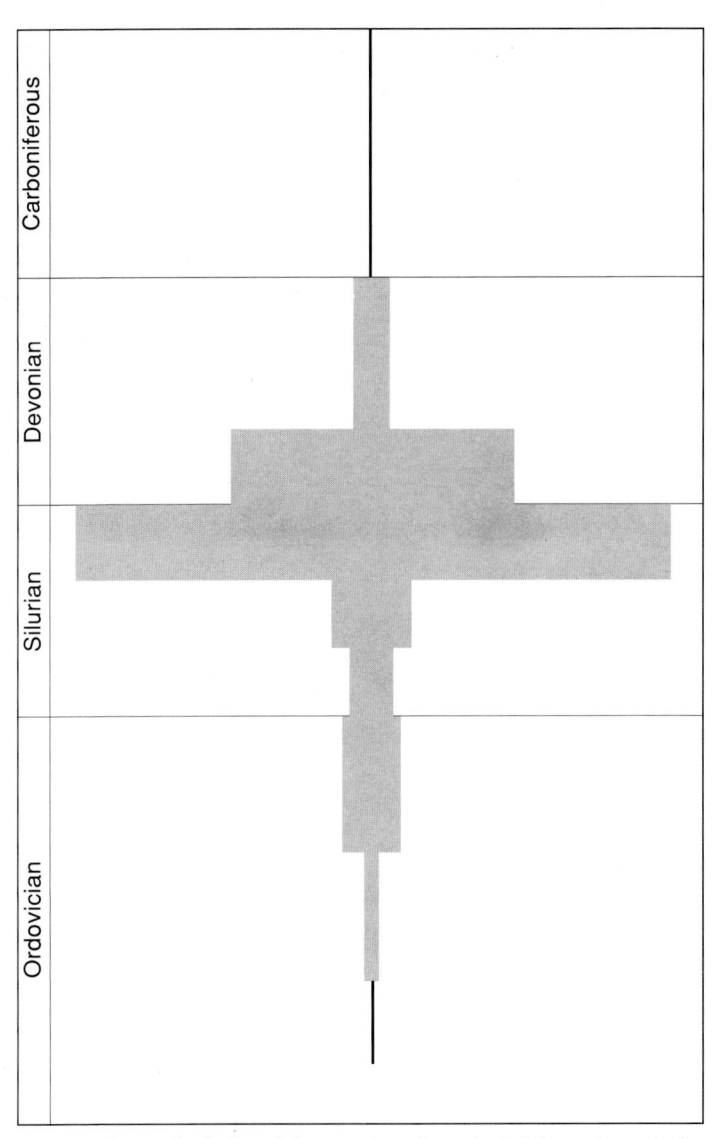

The approximate distribution of the agnathans in geological time, changed after MÜLLER

AGNATHA
Jawless Fishes
Order: Astraspidiformes
Family: Arandaspididae

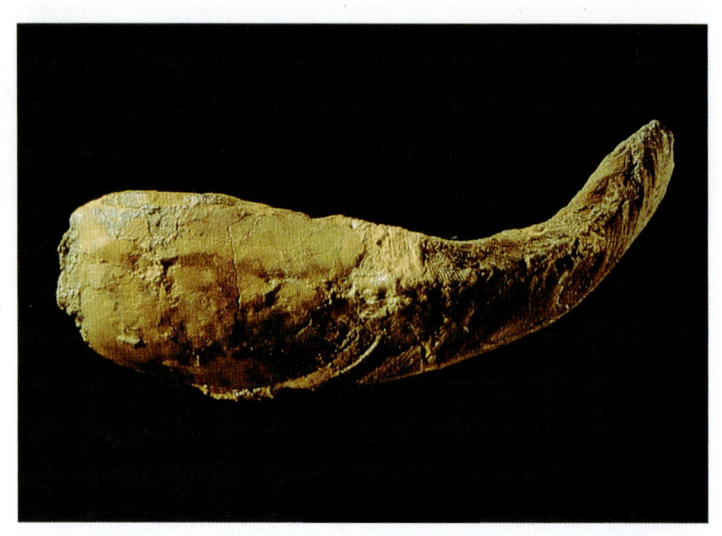

Sacabambaspis janvieri GAGNIER (length c. 35 cm), from the Upper Ordovician of Sacabamba, Bolivia. Original: Muséum National d'Histoire Naturelle, Paris, France. Photo: Serette, Paris.

Genus: *Sacabambaspis* GAGNIER, 1986.

Horizon: Upper Ordovician.

Geographical distribution: South America.

Features: Large agnathans, wide at the front and tapering rearwards. The head and part of the trunk were surrounded by thin relatively primitive armour. The body behind the armour covered with rod-like sculptured scales in a diagonal arrangement. Maximum length up to 35 cm.

Remarks: Probably bottom-dwelling.

Recent relatives: None. Died out in the Ordovician.

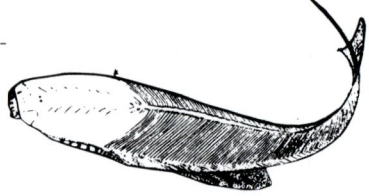

Sacabambaspis, reconstruction after GAGNIER.

AGNATHA
Order: Pteraspidiformes
Family: Cyathaspididae

Jawless Fishes

Anglaspis insignis KIAER & HEINTZ (length c. 5 cm) from the Lower Devonian of Spitzbergen. Original: Paleontologisk Museum, Oslo, Norway.

Genus: *Anglaspis* JAEKEL.

Synonym: *Fraenkelaspis*.

Horizon: Lower Devonian.

Geographical distribution: Europe, Spitzbergen.

Features: Small agnathans, approximately torpedo-shaped. Head and anterior part of back enclosed in armour. Dorsal armour extends forward into small pointed rostrum which overhangs the mouth. Eyes lateral. No dorsal spine but overlapping rearward-pointing elements in the dorsal and ventral mid-lines of trunk. Sides of body covered with long plates.

Remarks: Probably bottom-dwelling and very weak swimmers.

Recent relatives: None. Died out in the Silurian.

Anglaspis, reconstruction after HEINTZ.

AGNATHA
Order: Pteraspidiformes
Family: Cyathaspididae

Jawless Fishes

Irregulareaspis hoeli KIAER (length c. 6 cm) from the Lower Devonian of Spitzbergen. Original: Paleontologisk Museum, Oslo, Norway.

Genus: *Irregulareaspis* ZYCH, 1931.

Synonyms: *Dyctiaspidella*, *Dyctaspis*.

Horizon: Lower Devonian.

Geographical distribution: Europe, Spitzbergen.

Features: Middle-sized agnathans. Head and anterior part of the trunk enclosed in brief armour. Snout pointed. Mouth slightly ventral. Posterior part of trunk and rest of body heavily scaled. Scales large and elongate anteriorly but becoming smaller posteriorly. Caudal fin not subdivided. Eyes rather ventral. Maximum length c. 12 cm.

Remarks: Probably free-swimming.

Recent relatives: None. Died out in the Lower Devonian.

Irregulareaspis, reconstruction after BENDIX-ALMGREN.

AGNATHA
Jawless Fishes
Order: Pteraspidiformes
Family: Cyathaspididae

Pionaspis sp. (length c. 17 cm) from the Lower Devonian of Grizzly Bear Lake, Alberta, Canada. Original: University of Alberta, Edmonton, Alberta, Canada.

Genus: *Pionaspis* STADELMANN, 1897.

Horizon: Lower Devonian.

Geographical distribution: North America.

Features: Head and trunk enclosed above and beneath in armour. Plates elongate, oval and sculptured with little points. Eyes lateral. Mouth terminal or slightly ventral. Body behind armour covered with scales which are elongate anteriorly but become smaller posteriorly. Caudal fin hypocercal i.e. lower lobe larger than upper. Middle-sized agnathans. Maximum length c. 20 cm.

Remarks: Partly bottom-dwelling, partly free-swimming.

Recent relatives: None. Died out in the Lower Devonian.

AGNATHA
Order: Pteraspidiformes
Family: Cyathaspididae

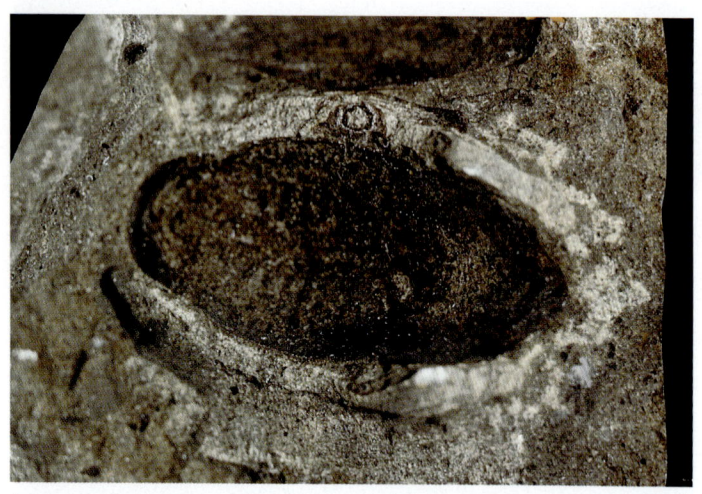

Jawless Fishes

Poraspis cylindrica KIAER & HEINTZ (length 4.5 cm) from the Lower Devonian of Bennevis, Spitzbergen. Original: Paleontologisk Museum, Oslo, Norway.

Genus: *Poraspis* KIAER, 1930.

Synonym: *Holaspis*.

Horizon: Lower Devonian.

Geographical distribution: Europe, Spitzbergen, northern North America.

Features: Head and part of trunk enclosed in rather brief armour. Plates of armour sculptured with regularly arranged lines directed outwards to right and left. Behind the armour, lateral scales of body long and large. Dorsal and ventral mid lines of body bearing much smaller keel scales. Eyes lateral. Mouth somewhat ventral. Dorsal armour of head shield undivided.

Remarks: Probably more free-swimming than bottom-dwelling.

Recent relatives: None. Died out in the Lower Devonian.

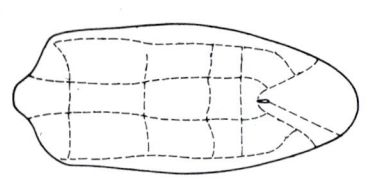

Poraspis, reconstruction after BLIECK

AGNATHA
Jawless Fishes
Order: Pteraspidiformes
Family: Cyathaspididae

Torpedaspis elongata BROAD & DINELEY (length c. 20 cm) from the Lower Devonian of Prince of Wales Island, Northwest Territories, Canada. Original: National Museum of Natural Sciences, Ottawa, Ontario, Canada.

Genus: *Torpedaspis* BROAD & DINELEY, 1973.

Horizon: Upper Silurian to Lower Devonian.

Geographical distribution: Northern North America.

Features: Head and trunk enclosed in unusually long narrow skeleton of armour. Scaly part of body considerably shorter than armoured part. Maximum length c. 25 cm.

Recent relatives: None. Died out in Lower Devonian.

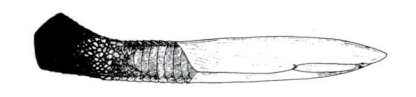

Torpedaspis, reconstruction after DINELEY.

AGNATHA
Jawless Fishes
Order: Pteraspidiformes
Family: Cyathaspididae

Athenaegis chattertoni SOEHN & WILSON (length c. 5 cm) from the Silurian of Avalanche Lake, Canada. Original: University of Alberta, Edmonton, Alberta, Canada.

Genus: *Atenaegis*   SOEHN & WILSON, 1990.

Horizon: Silurian.

Geographical distribution: North America.

Features: Little agnathans. Head and trunk rather wide with armour above and beneath. Plates sculptured with elongate ridges. Eyes somewhat dorsal. Mouth terminal to ventral. Scales decreasing in size rearwards. Caudal fin divided, hypocercal. Maximum c. 6 cm.

Remarks: Probably bottom-dwelling.

Recent relatives: None. Died out in Silurian.

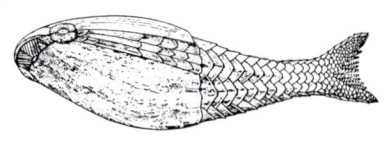

Athenaegis, reconstruction after SOEHN & WILSON.

AGNATHA
Jawless Fishes
Order: Pteraspidiformes
Family: Cyathaspididae

Vernonaspis sp. (length c. 10 cm) from the Upper Silurian of Cornwallis Island, Northwest Territories, Canada. Original: Thorsteinsson Collection, Calgary, Alberta, Canada.

Genus: *Vernonaspis* FLOWER & WAYLAND-SMITH, 1952.

Synonyms: *Anatiftopsis*, *Eoarchegonaspis*.

Horizon: Upper Silurian to Lower Devonian.

Geographical distribution: Northern North America.

Features: Little agnathans. Head and trunk armoured above and below. Armour finely sculptured with a pattern of lines. Body behind armour covered with scales which become appreciably smaller posteriorly. Eyes lateral. Mouth terminal to ventral. Maximum length scarcely more than 10 cm.

Remarks: Probably partly bottom-dwelling, partly free-swimming.

Recent relatives: None. Died out in Lower Devonian.

AGNATHA
Jawless Fishes
Order: Pteraspidiformes
Family: Amphiaspididae

Empedaspis inermis Novitskaya (length c. 7 cm) from the Lower Devonian of the Taimir Peninsula, Siberia, Russia. Original: Paleontologicheskii Muzei Russkoi Akademii Nauk, Moscow, Russia (Novitskaya Collection).

Genus: *Empedaspis* Novitskaya

Horizon: Lower Devonian.

Geographical distribution: Northern Asia.

Remarks: Middle-sized agnathans with greatly enlarged head. The shield enclosing the whole head and the anterior part of the back is oval in outline, flattened posteriorly and with a rounded keel in the posterior mid line. Anteriorly it tapers to an almost quadrangular "nose". Here, close together, are the small eyes and also the ventral mouth.

Remarks: Probably bottom-dwellers and almost unable to swim.

Recent relatives: None. Died out in the Lower Devonian.

Empedaspis, reconstruction after Novitskaya.

AGNATHA
Jawless Fishes
Order: Pteraspidiformes
Family: Protopteraspididae

Canadapteraspis sp. (length c. 6 cm) from the Lower Devonian of Prince of Wales Island, Northwest Territories, Canada. Original: Thorsteinsson Collection, Calgary, Alberta, Canada.

Genus: *Canadapteraspis* Dineley & Loeffler, 1976.

Horizon: Lower Devonian.

Geographical distribution: Northern North America.

Features: Middle-sized agnathans. Head and trunk armoured above and below. Snout region long and pointed. Dorsal armour with a strong, broad, posteriorly projecting spine in the dorsal mid line. Cornual plates paired, drawn into a point posteriorly. Eyes lateral. Mouth terminal to slightly ventral. Maximum size c. 12 cm.

Remarks: Partly bottom-dwelling, partly free-swimming.

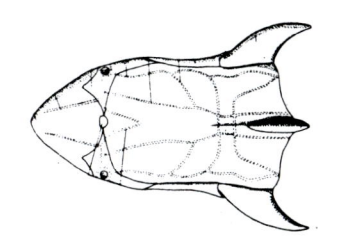

Recent relatives: None. Died out in the Lower Devonian.

Canadapteraspis, reconstruction after Dineley & Loeffler.

AGNATHA
Jawless Fishes
Order: **Pteraspidiformes**
Family: **Protopteraspididae**

Trygonaspis sp. (length c. 5 cm) from the Lower Devonian of Prince of Wales Island, Northwest Territories, Canada. Original: Thorsteinsson Collection, Calgary, Alberta, Canada.

Genus: *Trygonaspis* THORSTEINSSON

Horizon: Lower Devonian.

Geographical distribution: Northern North America.

Features: Middle-sized agnathans. Head and trunk armoured above and below, ventrally flattened. Armour ornamented with worm-like ridges with punctae between them. The dorsal armour with a rearward pointing spine in the mid line posteriorly. The paired cornual plates are expanded almost like fins and each ends in a point. Snout region pointed. Eyes lateral. Mouth ventral. maximum length c. 12 cm.

Remarks: Probably partly bottom-dwelling, partly free-swimming.

Recent relatives: None. Died out in the Lower Devonian.

AGNATHA Jawless Fishes
Order: Pteraspidiformes
Family: Pteraspididae

Doryaspis nathorsti (LANKESTER) (length c. 15 cm) from the Lower Devonian of Lytka, Spitzbergen. Original: Paleontologisk Museum, Oslo, Norway.

Genus: *Doryaspis* WHITE, 1935.
Synonyms: *Lyktaspis*, *Scaphaspis*.
Horizon: Lower Devonian.
Geographical distribution: Spitzbergen.
Features: Head and anterior part of trunk enclosed in thick armour. The dorsal and ventral plates are the largest elements of the upper and lower sides. Armour with dentine ridges. The paired cornual plates at the posterior end of the armour stick out sideways and extend as spines. The snout part of the armour projects as a long rostrum. Beneath and behind it is the wide mouth. Proximal to the rostrum are the paired nasal openings. Maximum length up to 20 cm.
Remarks: Probably bottom-dwellers but certainly also in part free-swimming. The significance of the extended rostrum is unclear.
Recent relatives: None. Died out in the Lower Devonian.

Doryaspis, reconstruction after MACMILLAN.

AGNATHA
Order: Pteraspidiformes
Family: Pteraspididae

Jawless Fishes

Larnovaspis goujeti BLIECK (length c. 10 cm) from the Lower Devonian of Spitzbergen. Original: Muséum National d'Histoire Naturelle, Paris, France. Photograph: Serette, Paris.

Genus: *Larnovaspis* BLIECK, 1984.

Horizon: Lower Devonian.

Geographical distribution: Europe, Spitzbergen.

Features: Middle-sized agnathans, probably with a spindle-shaped body. Head and anterior part of trunk enclosed above and below in thick armour. Eyes small. Snout broad at the base but extending into a pointed rostrum, beneath and behind which was the mouth. Total length perhaps 20 cm.

Remarks: Probably a bottom-dweller.

Recent relatives: None. Died out in Devonian.

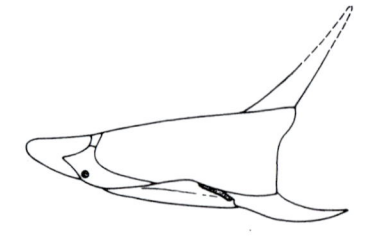

Larnovaspis, reconstruction after BLIECK.

82

AGNATHA
Jawless Fishes
Order: Pteraspidiformes
Family: Pteraspididae

Protaspis transversa DENISON (length c. 26 cm) from the Lower Devonian of Big Horn County, Wyoming, U.S.A. Original: Field Museum of Natural History, Chicago, Illinois, U.S.A.

Genus: *Protaspis* BRYANT, 1933.

Horizon: Upper Silurian to Lower Devonian.

Geographical Distribution: Northern North America, Europe, Spitzbergen.

Features: Elongate agnathans. Narrow flat armour above and below. The central plate, both dorsally and ventrally, is slender and surrounded by mosaic-like smaller plates. Snout region extends into a small rostrum. Relatively long scaly body behind the armour. Tail fin hypocercal. Maximum length about 30 cm.

Remarks: Probably partly bottom-dwelling and partly free-swimming.

Recent relatives: None. Died out in the Lower Devonian.

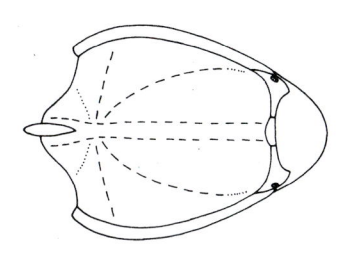

Protaspis, reconstruction after BLIECK.

AGNATHA
Order: Pteraspidiformes
Family: Pteraspididae

Jawless Fishes

Pteraspis rostrata WHITE (length c. 15 cm) from the Lower Devonian of Hereforeshire, England. Original: The Natural History Museum, London, U.K. (P16789).

Genus: *Pteraspis* KNER, 1847.

Synonyms: *Archaeoteuthis, Brachipteraspis, Lerichaspis, Palaeoteuthis, Parapteraspis, Plesiopteraspis, Pseudopteraspis, Simopteraspis.*

Horizon: Lower Devonian.

Geographical distribution: Western and eastern Europe, Spitzbergen, northern Asia, North America.

Features: Relatively slender, elongate agnathans. Head and trunk enclosed above and below in thick armour. The dorsal and ventral plates very large, forming almost all the dorsal and ventral armour respectively. Snout ends in a short rostrum directed slightly upwards and broad at the base. At posterior end of the armour is a characteristic dorsal spine. The scaly body behind the armour with a row of keeled scales in the dorsal and ventral mid line. Points of keeled scales directed rearward.

Remarks: Probably partly bottom-dwelling and partly free-swimming.

Recent relatives: None. Died out in the Lower Devonian.

Pteraspis, reconstruction after MACMILLAN.

AGNATHA
Jawless Fishes
Order: Pteraspidiformes
Family: Pteraspididae

Rhinopteraspis dunensis (ROEMER) (length c. 23 cm) from the Lower Devonian of Odenspiel, Rhineland, Germany. Original: Collection Brühn, Essen, Germany

Genus: *Rhinopteraspis* JAEKEL, 1919.

Synonym: *Belgicaspis*.

Horizon: Lower Devonian.

Geographical distribution: Western and Eastern Europe.

Features: Head and trunk enclosed above and below in thick armour. Snout extends into rostrum longer than the armour. Scaly body ends in a hypocercal caudal fin. Length, including rostrum, more than 30 cm.

Remarks: Probably bottom-dwelling and free-swimming. Significance of extended rostrum unclear.

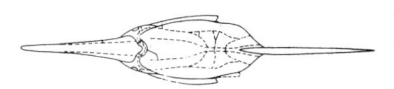

Recent relatives: None. Died out in the Lower Devonian.

Rhinopteraspis, reconstruction after GROSS.

AGNATHA
Jawless Fishes

Order: Pteraspidiformes
Family: Cardipeltidae

Cardipeltis bryanti DENISON (length c. 19 cm) from the Lower Devonian of Big Horn County, Wyoming, U.S.A. Original: Field Museum of Natural History, Chicago, Illinois, U.S.A.

Genus: *Cardipeltis* BRANSON & MEHL, 1931.

Horizon: Lower Devonian.

Geographical distribution: Spitzbergen, North America.

Features: Dorsal region oval but widening rearward and forming a heart-shaped embayment posteriorly. Further wide embayments at right and left received the external gill openings. Dorsal plates with a thin dentine layer but with worm-like ridges bearing flattened dentine pustules. Both the ridges and the pustules have smooth margins. Mouth somewhat ventral.

Remarks: Bottom-dwelling and probably not skillful swimmers.

Recent relatives: None. Died out in Lower Devonian.

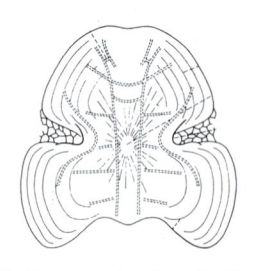

Cardipeltis, reconstruction after DENISON.

AGNATHA — Jawless Fishes
Order: Pteraspidiformes
Family: Drepanaspididae

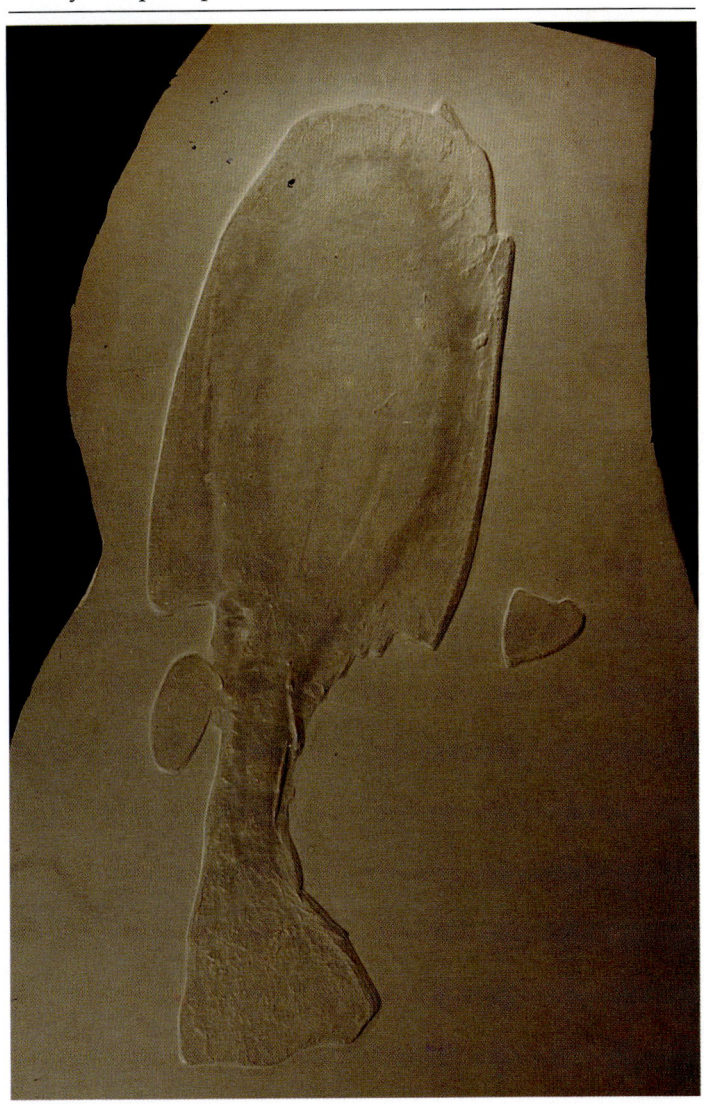

Drepanaspis gemuendensis SCHLÜTER (length c. 53 cm), from the Lower Devonian of Bundenbach, Rhineland, Germany. Original: Staatliches Museum für Naturkunde, Stuttgart, Germany.

AGNATHA
Order: Pteraspidiformes
Family: Drepanaspididae

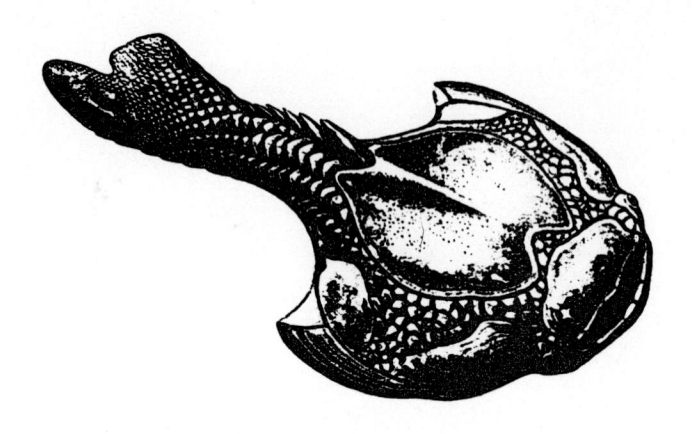

Jawless Fishes

Drepanaspis, reconstruction after MacMillan.

Genus: *Drepanaspis* Schlüter, 1887.

Horizon: Lower Devonian.

Geographical distribution: Europe.

Features: Large agnathans which could reach a length of almost 1 m. Head and trunk half-oval in dorsal aspect, ending behind at a straight transverse line. The large plates of the armour surrounded by mosaic-like fields of scales. The tail with a row of keeled scales in the dorsal and ventral mid lines. Caudal fin hypocercal. Mouth terminal.

Remarks: Probably bottom-dwellers, though the terminal mouth suggests that prey could be taken, at least in part, during swimming.

Recent relatives: None. Died out in Lower Devonian.

AGNATHA
Jawless Fishes
Order: Thelodontiformes
Family: Katoporidae

Lanarkia horrida Traquair (length c. 7 cm) from the Upper Silurian of Segholm, Ayrshire, Scotland, U.K. Original: National Museum of Scotland, Edinburgh, U.K.

Genus: *Lanarkia* Traquair, 1899.

Horizon: Upper Silurian

Geographical distribution: Europe.

Features: Body extremely depressed dorso-ventrally and covered with strong thorn-like denticles. Length rarely greater than 10 cm. Dorsal and anal fins present. Mouth probably slit-like and somewhat ventral. Beneath the 9 "lateral fins" there were eight pairs of gill slits. Caudal fin a-symmetrical (hypocercal). Dentine of dermal denticles like that of Pteraspidiformes and suggests a relationship with that order.

Remarks: The shape suggests relatively slow-moving bottom-dwellers.

Recent relatives: None. Died out in the Upper Silurian.

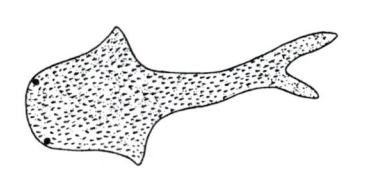

Lanarkia, reconstruction after Traquair.

AGNATHA
Order: **Thelodontiformes**
Family: **Katoporidae**

Jawless Fishes

Phlebolepis elegans PANDER (length c. 6 cm) from the Upper Silurian of Oesel, Estonia. Original: American Museum of Natural History, New York, N.Y., U.S.A.

Genus: *Phlebolepis* PANDER, 1856.

Horizon: Upper Silurian.

Geographical distribution: Western and eastern Europe, northern North America.

Features: Shape "fish-like" (unlike *Thelodus* and *Lanarkia*). Maximum length 7–9 cm. Body covered with thin, uniform, scale-like elements. Dorsal, anal and pectoral fins present. Caudal fin hypocercal. Mouth terminal.

Remarks: Probably rather skilful free-swimmers.

Recent relatives: None. Died out in Upper Silurian.

Phlebolepis, reconstruction after RITCHIE.

AGNATHA
Jawless Fishes
Order: Thelodontiformes
Family: Loganiidae

Logania scotica (Traquair) (length c. 14 cm) from the Upper Silurian of Lanarkshire, Scotland. Original: National Museum of Scotland, Edinburgh U.K.

Genus: *Logania* Distant, 1884.

Horizon: Upper Silurian to Lower Devonian.

Geographical distribution: Western and eastern Europe, North America, central Asia.

Features: Ventro-dorsally compressed body much like *Thelodus* but with considerably smaller dermal denticles, especially in head. Relatively large—individuals of length 15 cm and more not uncommon. Mouth probably slit-like and ventral. One dorsal and one anal fin. Caudal fin hypocercal. Gill slits beneath the "lateral fins".

Remarks: Bottom-dwellers like *Thelodus* and *Lanarkia*.

Recent relatives: None. Died out in Lower Devonian.

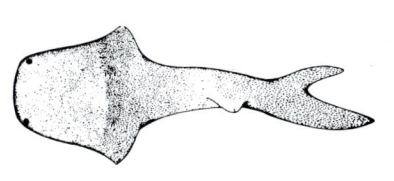

Logania, reconstruction after Traquair.

AGNATHA
Jawless Fishes
Order: Thelodontiformes
Family: Loganiidae

Thelodus scoticus TRAQUAIR (length c. 15 cm) from the Upper Silurian of Lanarkshire, Scotland. Original: National Museum of Scotland, Edinburgh, U.K.

Genus: *Thelodus* AGASSIZ, 1838.

Synonyms: *Thelolepis*, *Thelolepoides*, *Thelyodus*.

Horizon: Lower Silurian to Lower Devonian.

Geographical distribution: Western and eastern Europe, northern North America, Spitzbergen, central Asia.

Features: Body flattened. Head relatively large. Unlike *Lanarkia*, surface densely covered with fine dermal denticles. Dorsal and anal fin present. Mouth probably slit-shaped and slightly ventral. Eight gill slits beneath the "lateral fins". Relatively large. Individuals of length 15 cm and more are not unusual.

Remarks: The body shape suggests a bottom dweller.

Recent relatives: None. Died out in Lower Devonian.

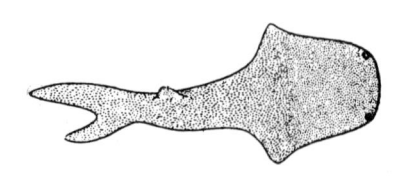

Thelodus, reconstruction after TRAQUAIR.

AGNATHA
Jawless Fishes
Order: Thelodontiformes
Family: Turiniidae

Turinia pagei (POWRIE), (length c. 32 cm) from the Lower Devonian of Angus, Scotland. Original: National Museum of Scotland, Edinburgh, U.K.

Genus: *Turinia* TRAQUAIR, 1896.

Horizon: Lower Devonian.

Geographical distribution: Western and eastern Europe, Spitzbergen, Australia, central Asia, northern Asia.

Features: All other thelodonts are at most 10-20 cm long but *Turinia* reaches a length of up to 40 cm. In outline it resembles *Thelodus* and *Lanarkia*, even in the presence of "lateral fins", but can always be distinguished by its greater size. The surface of the body is covered with very small synchronomorial scales. The mouth was probably slit-shaped. It was slightly ventral.

Remarks: The body shape suggests relatively slow-moving bottom-dwellers.

Recent relatives: None. Died out in the Lower Devonian.

AGNATHA
Jawless Fishes
Order: Thelodontiformes
Family: unnamed

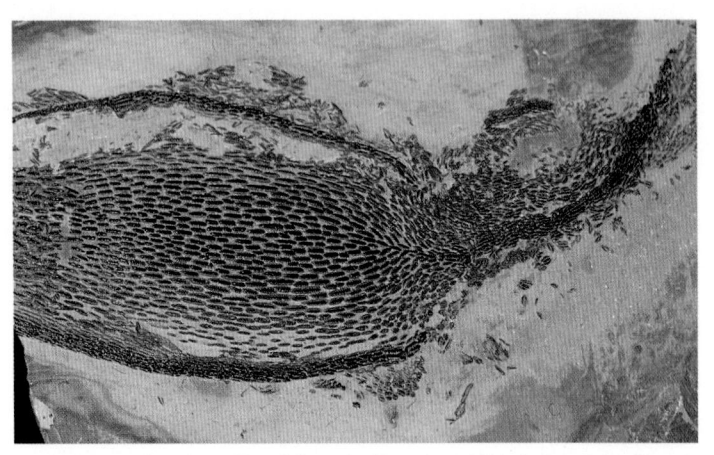

Lepidaspis sp. (length c. 23 cm) from the Devonian of Grizzly Bear Lake, Canada. Original: University of Alberta, Edmonton, Alberta, Canada.

Genus: *Lepidaspis* MacGillivray, 1921.

Horizon: Devonian.

Geographical distribution: North America.

Features: Middle-sized agnathans. Maximum length c. 25 cm. Body densely covered with short ridges. Tail strongly tapering. Caudal fin probably hypocercal. Dorsal fin present, and probably anal fin also. Mouth terminal to slightly ventral.

Remarks: Bottom-dwelling.

Recent relatives: None. Died out in Devonian.

AGNATHA
Jawless Fishes
Order: Cephalaspidiformes
Family: Dartmuthiidae

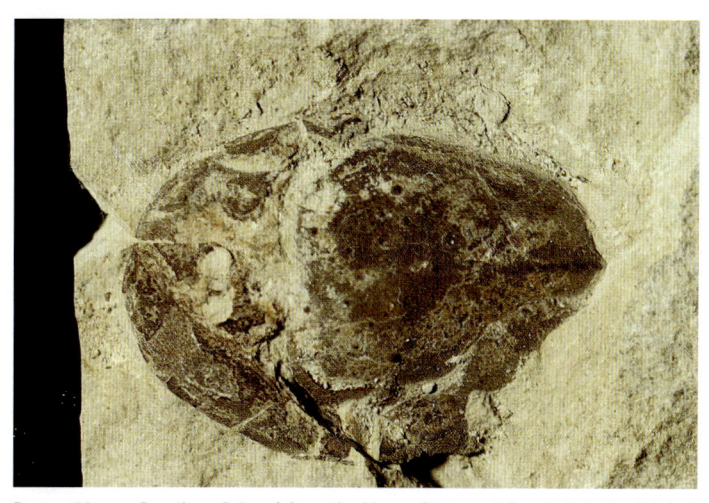

Dartmuthia sp. (length c. 3.5 cm) from the Upper Silurian of Oesel, Estonia. Original: American Museum of Natural History, New York, N.Y., U.S.A.

Genus: *Dartmuthia* PATTEN, 1931.

Synonyms: *Lophosteus*.

Horizon: Upper Silurian.

Geographical distribution: Europe.

Features: Small slender agnathans, supposedly with a strikingly large head. Head and anterior part of back enclosed in pustulate armour with undulating posterior margin but rounded anteriorly. Eyes relatively large, close together and directed upwards.

Remarks: Probably bottom-dwellers and scarcely able to swim.

Recent relatives: None. Died out in Silurian.

Dartmuthia, reconstruction after MACMILLAN.

AGNATHA
Jawless Fishes
Order: Cephalaspidiformes
Family: Dartmuthiidae

Tyriaspis whitei HEINTZ (length c. 9 cm) from the Upper Silurian of Ringerike, Norway. Original: Paleontologisk Museum, Oslo.

Genus: *Tyriaspis* HOPE, 1840.

Horizon: Upper Silurian.

Geographical distribution: Europe.

Features. The rounded head and the anterior part of the trunk are enclosed in bony pustulate armour. Eyes on upper surface. Plump, scaly body tapers strongly towards tail. Mouth terminal to ventral. Maximum length about 10 cm.

Remarks: Bottom-dwellers, probably sluggish swimmers.

Recent relatives: None. Died out in Upper Silurian.

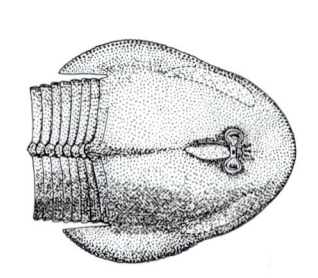

Tyriaspis, reconstruction after HEINTZ.

AGNATHA
Jawless Fishes
Order: Cephalaspidiformes
Family: Ateleaspididae

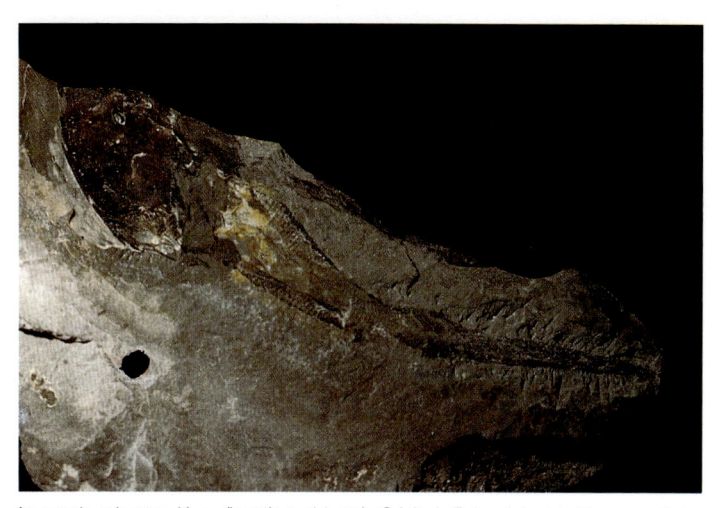

Aceraspis robustus KIAER (length c. 14 cm). Original: Paleontologisk Museum, Oslo, Norway.

Genus: *Aceraspis* KIAER, 1911.

Synonyms: *Hemiteleaspis*.

Horizon: Lower Devonian.

Geographical distribution: Europe.

Features: Shape elongate, flattened ventrally. The head and the anterior part of the body covered with bony armour. Eyes close together on the upper surface of the head armour. Nasal opening between the eyes. Gill slits circular. Body fish-like and covered with scales. Lobe-shaped, scaly pectoral fins. Two dorsal fins, the anterior halves of which are scaly. Caudal fin heterocercal, passing downwards into a marginal fin. Maximum length c. 15 cm.

Remarks: The flattened ventral surface and the position of the eyes suggest a bottom-dweller.

Recent relatives: None. Died out in Lower Devonian.

Aceraspis, reconstruction after STENSIÖ.

AGNATHA
Jawless Fishes
Order: Cephalaspidiformes
Family: Ateleaspididae

Hemicyclaspis murchisoni (EGERTON) (length c. 18 cm) from the Upper Silurian of Ledbury, Herefordshire, England, U.K. Original: The Natural History Museum, London, U.K. (P6023).

Genus: *Hemicyclaspis* LANKESTER, 1870.

Horizon: Upper Silurian to Lower Devonian.

Geographical distribution: Europe, northern North America.

Features: Head and anterior part of body covered in bony armour. Mouth ventral. Pectoral fins lobe-shaped and scaly. Anterior dorsal fin present only as a projecting ridge. Fish-like, scaly, ventrally flattened body ends in a heterocercal caudal fin. The lower margin of the caudal fin runs into a short broad marginal fin.

Remarks: The shape and the position of the mouth and eyes suggest a bottom dweller.

Recent relatives: None. Died out in Lower Devonian.

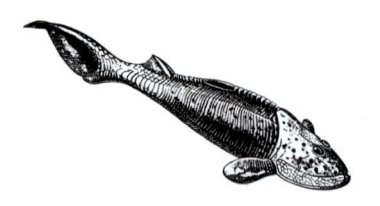

Hemicyclaspis, reconstruction after MACMILLAN.

AGNATHA
Jawless Fishes
Order: Cephalaspidiformes
Family: Ateleaspididae

Hirella gracilis (KIAER) (length c. 7 cm) from the Upper Silurian of Ringerike, Norway. Original: Paleontologisk Museum, Oslo.

Genus: *Hirella* COSSMANN, 1920.

Synonyms: *Micraspis*.

Horizon: Upper Silurian.

Geographical distribution: Europe.

Features: Little fishes, ventrally flattened. Head armour about as long as wide. No lateral horns to head armour. Mouth transversely elongate. Two dorsal fins. Pectoral fins present.

Remarks: Bottom dwellers.

Recent relatives: None. Died out in Upper Silurian.

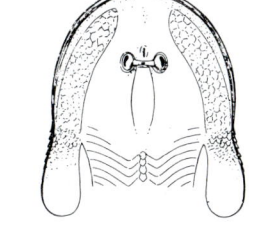

Hirella, reconstruction after KIAER.

AGNATHA
Jawless Fishes
Order: Cephalaspidiformes
Family: Cephalaspididae

Alaspis microtuberculata ORVIG (length c. 31 cm) from the Upper Devonian of Miguasha, Gaspé Peninsula, Quebec, Canada. Original: Musée d'Histoire Naturelle, Miguasha.

Genus: *Alaspis* ORVIG, 1957.
Horizon: Upper Devonian.
Geographical distribution: North America.

Features: Head and anterior part of the body enclosed in armour. Head rounded in anterior outline in dorsal aspect. Prominent lateral horns. Eyes very close together and approximately in the middle of the armour. Nasal opening between the eyes. Ventral surface flattened. Scaled body slender and ending in a heterocercal tail. Mouth ventral. Relatively large - maximum body length up to 35 cm.
Remarks: The flattened ventral surface and the position of the mouth suggest a bottom dweller.
Recent relatives: None. Died out in Upper Devonian.

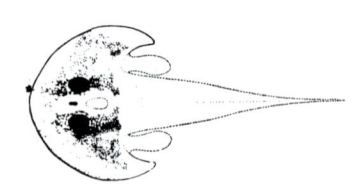

Alaspis, reconstruction after ORVIG.

AGNATHA
Jawless Fishes
Order: Cephalaspidiformes
Family: Cephalaspididae

Boreaspis puella Wängsjö (length c. 2 cm) from the Lower Devonian of Spitzbergen. Original: Naturhistoriska Riksmuséet, Stockholm, Sweden.

Genus: *Boreaspis* Stensiö.

Horizon: Lower Devonian.

Geographical distribution: Northern Europe.

Features: Little agnathans of slender shape. Head and anterior part of the body enclosed in armour. Dorsal surface of armour extends into long narrow pointed rostrum. Lateral spines broad at base and acute-triangular in shape. Eyes small, on the upper surface.

Remarks: Probably bottom-dwelling and scarcely free-swimming.

Recent relatives: None. Died out in Lower Devonian.

Boreaspis, reconstruction after Macmillan.

AGNATHA
Jawless Fishes
Order: Cephalaspidiformes
Family: Cephalaspididae

Cephalaspis powriei LANKESTER (length c. 12 cm) from the Lower Devonian of Angus, Scotland, U.K. Original: National Museum of Scotland, Edinburgh, U.K.

AGNATHA
Jawless Fishes
Order: Cephalaspidiformes
Family: Cephalaspididae

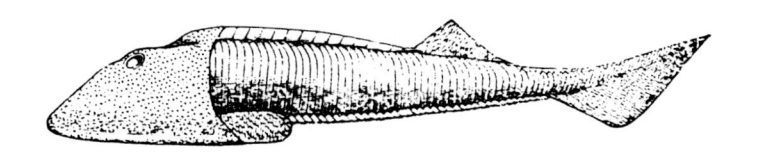

Cephalaspis, reconstruction after WOODWARD.

Genus: *Cephalaspis* AGASSIZ, 1835.

Synonyms: *Camptaspis, Escuminaspis, Eucephalaspis, Minestaspis, Pattenaspis, Scolenaspis, Zenaspis.*

Horizon: Upper Silurian to Upper Devonian.

Geographical distribution: Europe, Spitzbergen, East Asia, North America.

Features: The head and the anterior part of the body enclosed in armour. Long lateral horns. Eyes facing upward, approximately in the middle of the head armour, very close together. Nasal opening between the eyes. Pectoral fins lobe-shaped. Dorsal fin in the posterior third of the body. Caudal fin heterocercal. Lower lobe broad. Body scaly. Mouth circular, ventral in position. Ventral surface flattened. General shape elongate. Maximum length up to 20 cm.

Remarks: The flattened belly and ventral mouth suggest a bottom dweller.

Recent relatives: None. Died out in Upper Devonian.

AGNATHA
Jawless Fishes
Order: Cephalaspidiformes
Family: Cephalaspididae

Thyestes verrucosus Eichwald (length c. 2 cm) from the Upper Silurian of Saarema, Estonia. Original: Paleontologicheskii Muzei Russkoi Akademii Nauk, Moscow, Russia.

Genus: *Thyestes* Eichwald, 1854.

Synonyms: *Auchenaspis*.

Horizon: Upper Silurian to Lower Devonian.

Geographical distribution: Europe.

Features: Little agnathans with oval, tuberculate shield. This encloses the whole head and the anterior part of the trunk. The lateral horns run parallel to the head but separated by a small gap. Eyes relatively large, close together and facing upwards. Mouth ventral.

Remarks: Probably bottom-dwellers and weak swimmers.

Recent relatives: None. Died out in Lower Devonian.

Thyestes, reconstruction after Afanassieva.

AGNATHA
Jawless Fishes
Order: **Anaspidiformes**
Family: **Jamoytiidae**

Jamoytius kerwoodi WHITE (length c. 19 cm) from the Middle Silurian of Lanarkshire, Scotland, U.K. Original: The Natural History Museum, London U.K. (P47784).

Genus: *Jamoytius* WHITE, 1946.

Horizon: Middle Silurian.

Geographical distribution: Europe.

Features: Dorsal fin long and almost like a fin fold. Lateral fins likewise long and narrow, extending half length of body. Scales extremely weak and thin. Head naked. Eyes protected by sclerotic ring. Maximum length of long, spindle-shaped body perhaps 15 cm.

Remarks: Given the streamlined shape, possibly expert swimmers. Genus includes some of the oldest agnathans known.

Recent relatives: None. Died out in Middle Silurian.

Jamoytius, reconstruction after MACMILLAN.

AGNATHA
Order: Anaspidiformes
Family: Birkeniidae

Jawless Fishes

Birkenia elegans TRAQUAIR (length c. 4 cm) from the Upper Silurian of Muirkirk, Scotland. Original: Frickhinger Collection, Munich.

Genus: *Birkenia* TRAQUAIR.

Horizon: Middle Silurian to lower Devonian.

Geographical distribution: Europe.

Features: Anterior part of dorsal mid line consists of large low keeled scales whereas posterior part is of spine-like structures. The two parts separated but a much taller structure whose two spikes point forward and back. The spindle-shaped body covered with overlapping rows of scales. Eight pairs of external gill slits. Caudal fin hypocercal. Length c. 10 cm.

Remarks: Probably expert swimmers.

Recent relatives: None. Died out near the end of the Silurian.

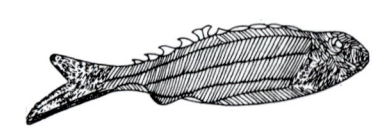

Birkenia, reconstruction after TRAQUAIR.

AGNATHA
Order: Anaspidiformes
Family: Birkeniidae

Jawless Fishes

Pharyngolepis oblongus KIAER (length c. 16 cm) from the Upper Silurian of Ringerike, Norway. Original: National Museum of Scotland, Edinburgh, U.K.

Genus: *Pharyngolepis* KIAER, 1911.

Horizon: Upper Silurian.

Geographical distribution: Europe.

Features: Streamlined shape. Greatest length up to 20 cm. Mouth terminal. Snout somewhat pointed. Eyes situated far forward on the head. The body passes into a hypocercal caudal fin. Along the dorsal mid line a row of small spines. 15 pairs of gill slits.

Remarks: Probably good swimmers.

Recent relatives: None. Died out in Upper Silurian.

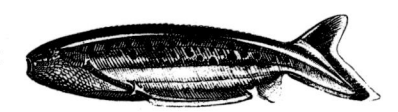

Pharyngolepis, reconstruction after MAC-MILLAN.

AGNATHA
Jawless Fishes
Order: Anaspidiformes
Family: Birkeniidae

Pterygolepis nitidus (KIAER) (length c. 7 cm) from the Upper Silurian of Ringerike, Norway. Original: Museum National d'Histoire Naturelle, Paris, France. Photograph: Serette, Paris.

Genus: *Pterygolepis* COSSMANN, 1920.

Synonyms: *Pterlepidops*, *Pterolepis*.

Horizon: Upper Silurian.

Geographical distribution: Europe.

Features: Mid-dorsal ridge of thorn-like scales, with points facing rearwards. Pectoral fins short. Body covered with five rows of overlapping scales. Ten pairs of gill slits. Caudal fin hypocercal. Maximum length 10 cm. Body spindle-shaped. Mouth slightly ventral.

Remarks: Probably expert swimmers.

Recent relatives: None. Died out in Upper Silurian.

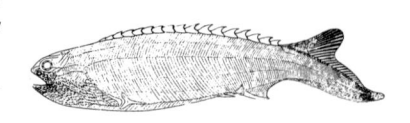

Pterygolepis, reconstruction after ORLOV.

108

AGNATHA
Jawless Fishes
Order: Anaspidiformes
Family: Birkeniidae

Rhyncholepis parvulus KIAER (length c. 6 cm) from the Lower Devonian of Ringerike, Norway. Original: Paleontologisk Museum, Oslo, Norway.

Genus: *Rhynocholepis* KIAER, 1911.

Horizon: Lower Devonian.

Geographical distribution: Europe.

Features: Mid-dorsal ridge of spine-like scales with points facing rearwards. Ventral fins short. Anal fin elongate with spine-like scales. Body covered in five rows of overlapping scales. Eight pairs of gill slits. Body broadly spindle-shaped. Length 6–7 cm.

Remarks: Somewhat plumper than other anaspids.

Recent relatives: None. Died out in Lower Devonian.

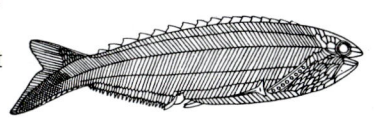

Rhyncholepis, reconstruction after KIAER.

AGNATHA　　　　　　　　　　　　　　Jawless Fishes
Order: Anaspidiformes
Family: Birkeniidae?

Unnamed anaspid (length c. 15 cm) from the Middle Silurian of Cornwallis Island, Northwest Territories, Canada. Original: Thorsteinsson Collection, Calgary, Alberta, Canada.

Genus: Unnamed.

Horizon: Middle Silurian.

Geographical distribution: Northern North America.

Features: Relatively large anaspids. Greatest length 15 cm or more. A row of thorn-like structures in the dorsal mid-line. General shape broadly elongate. Head slightly pointed. Mouth somewhat ventral. Eyes far forward on head.

Remarks: Free-swimming.

Recent relatives: None. Died out in Middle Silurian.

AGNATHA
Jawless Fishes
Order: Anaspidiformes
Family: Endeiolepididae?

Legendrelepis parenti ARSENAULT & JANVIER (length c. 8 cm) from the Upper Devonian of Miguasha, Gaspé Peninsula, Quebec, Canada. Original: Musée d'Histoire Naturelle, Miguasha, Quebec, Canada.

Genus: *Legendrelepis* ARSENAULT & JANVIER, 1991.

Horizon: Upper Devonian.

Geographical distribution: North America.

Features: Relatively small agathans. Greatest possible maximum length scarcely more than 10 cm. Streamlined shape. Mouth terminal. A row of thorns in the dorsal mid line with the points directed rearward. Caudal fin hypocercal with a strikingly long lower lobe. Body uniformly scaled.

Remarks: Probably clever swimmers.

Recent relatives: None. Died out in Upper Devonian.

AGNATHA
Jawless Fishes
Order: Anaspidiformes
Family: Lasaniidae

Lasanius problematicus Traquair (length c. 5 cm) from the Upper Silurian of Ayrshire, Scotland. Original: Royal Museum of Scotland, Edinburgh, Scotland.

Genus: *Lasanius* Traquair, 1899.

Horizon: Upper Silurian to Lower Devonian.

Geographical distribution: Europe.

Features: Scales of mid-dorsal ridge thorn-like with the points facing rearwards. Scales of flanks very weak and scarcely recognizable. Gill slits probably six to eight pairs. Maximum length c. 8 cm. General form spindle-shaped.

Remarks: Probably good swimmers.

Recent relatives: None. Died out in Lower Devonian.

Lasanius, reconstruction after Orlov.

AGNATHA
Jawless Fishes
Order: Petromyzontiformes
Family: Mayomyzontidae

Hardistiella montanensis JANVIER & LUND (length c. 5 cm) from the Lower Carboniferous of Bear Gulch, Montana. Original: Adelphi University, Garden City, N.J., U.S.A.

Genus: *Hardistiella* JANVIER & LUND, 1983.

Horizon: Lower Carboniferous.

Geographical distribution: North America.

Features: Elongate, eel-like shape. Skin without scales. Skeleton not calcified. No bony tissue. Dorsal and caudal fins probably separate from caudal fin. Eyes dorso-lateral. Mouth terminal.

Remarks: Probably bottom dwellers. It is uncertain whether they fed on detritus and small organisms or were parasitic. At present only known as larval stage.

Recent relatives: Genus and family extinct. However, a close relationship to the lampreys (family Petromyzontidae) is suspected.

Hardistiella, reconstruction after LUND.

AGNATHA
Jawless Fishes
Order: Petromyzontiformes
Family: Mayomyzontidae

Mayomyzon pieckoensis BARDACK & ZANGERL (length c. 6 cm) from the Middle Carboniferous of Francis Creek, Illinois, U.S.A. Original: Field Museum of Natural History, Chicago, Illinois, U.S.A.

Genus: *Mayomyzon* BARDACK & ZANGERL, 1968.

Horizon: Middle Carboniferous.

Geographical distribution: North America.

Features: Eel-shaped agnathans, when adult very elongate. Skin without scales. Skeleton uncalcified. No bony tissue. Dorsal fin separated from dorsal fin by a shallow constriction. Eyes dorsolateral. Mouth terminal. Internal organs commonly visible as dark patches. Length of adult probably between 15 and 20 cm.

Remarks: Probably bottom dwellers, though also readily able to swim. It is uncertain whether these animals fed on detritus and small organisms or were parasitic.

Recent relatives: Genus and family extinct. Close relationship to the lampreys (family Petromyzontidae) is suspected.

Lampetra planeri, the recent brook lamprey.

AGNATHA

Order: Unnamed
Family: Unnamed

Jawless Fishes

Gilpichthys greenei BARDACK (length c. 6 cm) from the Upper Carboniferous of Essex, Illinois, U.S.A. Original: Henne Collection, Stuttgart, Germany.

Genus: *Gilpichthys* BARDACK, 1979.

Horizon: Upper Carboniferous.

Geographical distribution: North America.

Features: Slender eel-like shape. Skin without scales. Mouth terminal. No bony tissue. End of body pointed.

Remarks: Probably bottom-dwelling. Uncertain whether they fed on detritus and small organisms or were parasitic.

Recent relatives: Genus extinct.
Relationships uncertain.

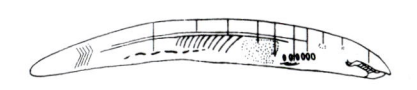

Gilpichthys, reconstruction after BARDACK & RICHARDSON.

PLACODERMI — Placoderms

The placoderms evolved an extremely important feature, for they are the first fish with movable jaws. Thus they were adapted to a predatory mode of life. Most of them, however, had a dorso-ventrally flattened body which suggests that they were bottom-dwellers. Most of them probably had only a limited swimming ability.

The head and the anterior part of the trunk were covered with a multiplated armour of dermal bones and individual regions of the armour were often articulated to each other. The body behind this armour was naked or covered with scales. It tapered posteriorly and ended in a diphycercal or heterocercal caudal fin. The mouth was usually terminal but sometimes ventral.

Paired extensions in the region of pectoral fins also had an armour of bony plates. The dorsal head armour, together with these extensions, looks in some ways more like a turtle than a fish. In some species, pelvic and anal fins have also been found. From the Middle Devonian on, some genera showed a tendency to a partial or complete loss of armour. The great majority of placoderms were small- to middle-sized animals. In the Upper Devonian, however, some were of very large size. In these same fishes, the armour was limited to the head region which gave them greater mobility. The largest forms, which were up to eight metres long, may, as dangerous predators, have played the role of Lords of the Sea. They certainly would have had no enemies.

Nevertheless, despite many advanced features, the placoderms were dominant only for a relatively short time. They appeared in the Lower Devonian and reached their maximum in the Upper Devonian. Whether they still existed in the Lower Carboniferous is doubtful. They had their widest distribution at the time when they died out. They had no descendants. Up to the present, some 200 genera have been described, mostly on the basis of isolated plates of the armour. Complete fishes are very rare.

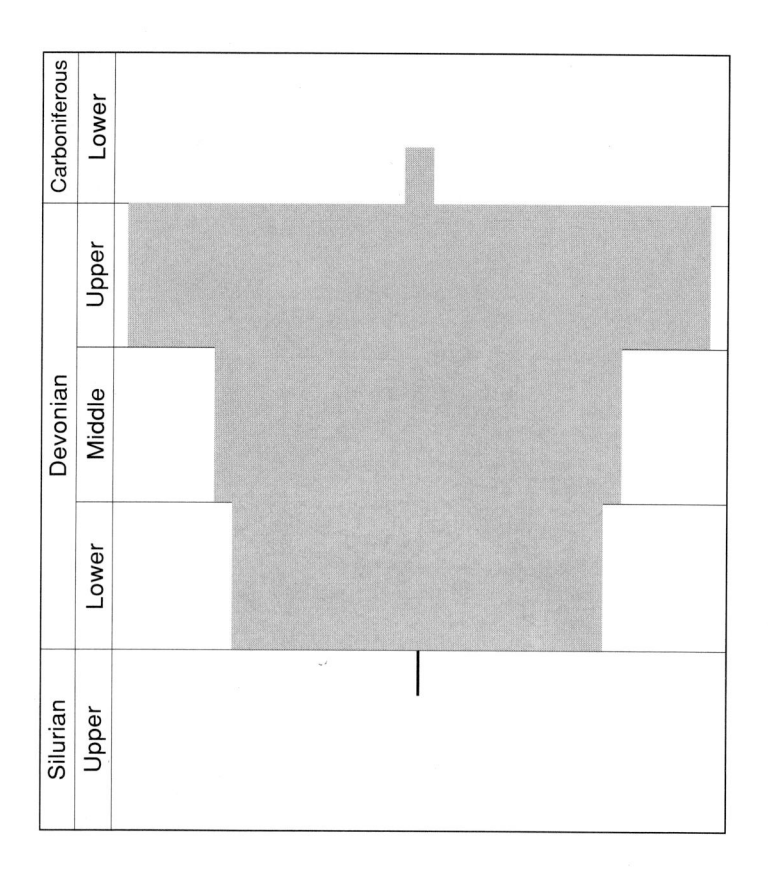

PLACODERMI — Placoderms

The approximate distribution of placoderms in geological time, changed after MÜLLER

117

PLACODERMI
Placoderms
Order: Stensioelliformes
Family: Stensioellidae

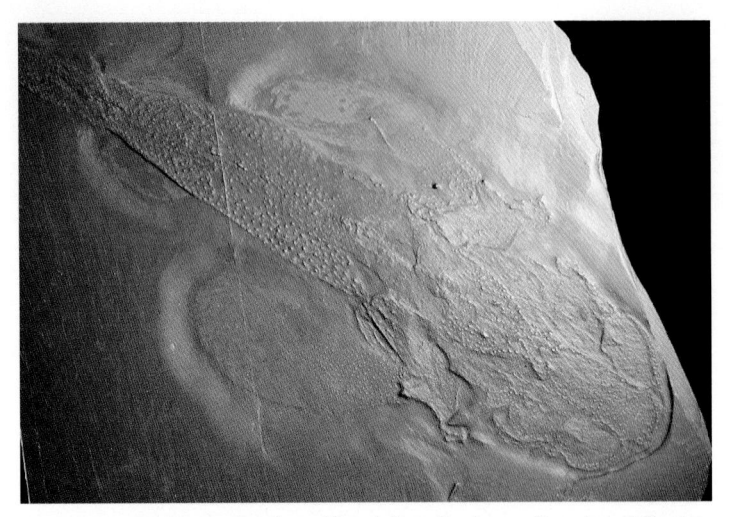

Stensioella heintzi BROILI (length c. 26 cm) from the Lower Devonian of Bundenbach, Rhineland, Germany. Original: Bayerische Staatssammlung für Paläontologie, Munich, Germany.

Genus: *Stensioella* BROILI, 1933.

Horizon: Lower Devonian.

Geographical distribution: Europe.

Features: Slender placoderms with extensive loss of exoskeleton. Head covered with bony plates and rigidly fused to the trunk. Pectoral fins large and without spines. Eyes small, widely separated from each other and protected by a sclerotic ring. Mouth ventral but far forward in the head. Lower jaw with tiny teeth. Paired fins well developed. Pelvic fins semi-circular. Dorsal fin small. A low ventral fin fold is present. Body covered with thin spiny scales.

Remarks: Bottom dwelling but also free-swimming.

Recent relatives: None. Died out in Lower Devonian.

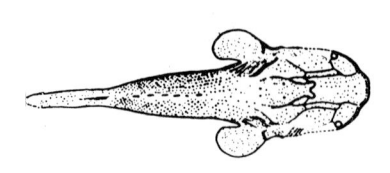

Stensioella, reconstruction after BROILI.

PLACODERMI
Order: Rhenaniformes
Family: Asterosteidae

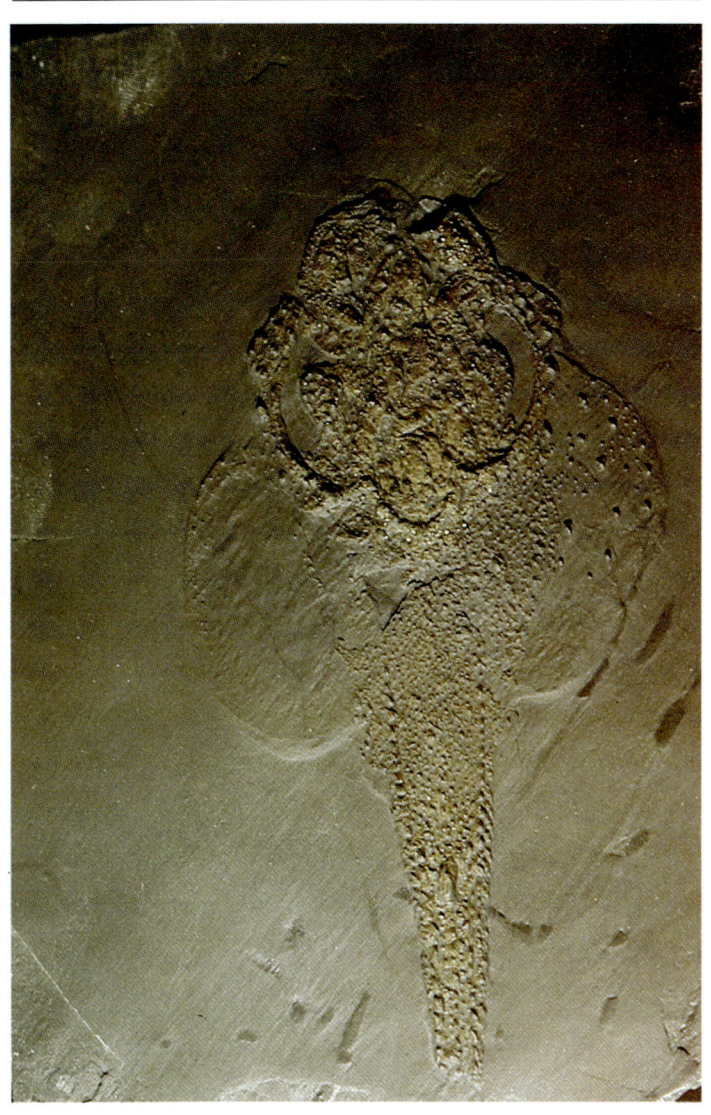

Placoderms

Gemuendina stuertzii Traquair (length c. 15 cm) from the Lower Devonian of Bundenbach, Rhineland, Germany. Original: Bayerische Staatssammlung für Paläontologie, Munich, Germany.

PLACODERMI
Order: Rhenaniformes
Family: Asterosteidae

Placoderms

Gemuendina, reconstruction after MacMillan.

Genus: *Gemuendina* Traquair, 1903.

Synonyms: *Broilina*.

Horizon: Lower Devonian.

Geographical distribution: Europe.

Features: Skate-like forms. Pectoral fins very large and semi-circular. Tail tapers to point posteriorly, with a little spine at anterior end. Head flat, with eyes and nasal opening directed upwards. Mouth opening dorsally. Exoskeleton extensively reduced. Body mostly covered with scales and polygonal platelets. Normal length up to 25 cm but specimens 1 m long have been found.

Remarks: Probably partly bottom-dwelling and partly free-swimming.

Recent relatives: None. Died out in Lower Devonian. It is widely suspected that this form, together with *Ctenurella*, was a blind-ending side branch of the group of fishes which gave rise to the ancestors of the sharks.

PLACODERMI
Placoderms
Order: Rhenaniformes
Family: Asterosteidae

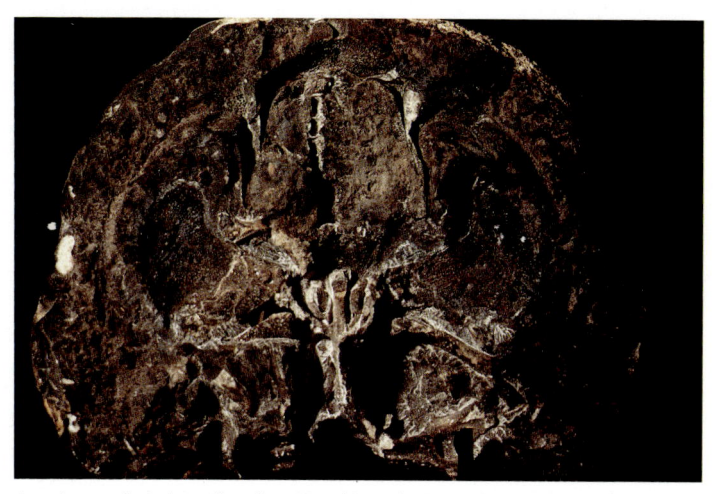

Jagorina pandora JAEKEL (length c. 19 cm) from the Upper Devonian of Bad Wildungen, Hesse, Germany. Original: Museum für Naturkunde, Berlin, Germany.

Genus: *Jagorina* JAEKEL, 1921.

Horizon: Upper Devonian.

Geographical distribution: Europe.

Features: Middle-sized fishes with a broad semicircular skull, somewhat like that of rays. Bony plates on dorsal surface tuberculate. Internal surface of brain cavity ossified with a thin layer of bone. Eyes large. Nasal opening between the eyes. Jaws with loosely attached shark-like teeth. Pectoral fins probably extended along the body.

Remarks: Probably bottom-dwelling predatory fishes.

Recent relatives: None. Died out in Upper Devonian.

PLACODERMI
Order: Ptyctodontiformes
Family: Ptyctodontidae

Placoderms

Ctenurella gladbachensis ORVIG (length c. 8 cm) from the Upper Devonian of Bombach, Bergisch Gladbach, Rhineland, Germany. Original: Naturmuseum Senckenberg, Frankfurt-am-Main, Germany.

Genus: *Ctenurella* ORVIG, 1960.

Horizon: Upper Devonian.

Geographical distribution: Europe, Australia.

Features: Small fishes with a weakly developed exoskeleton. Head short and deep. Eyes directed upwards. Mouth somewhat ventral. A pair of tooth plates in both the upper and lower jaw. Two dorsal fins, the anterior short and the posterior elongate. Caudal fin small, heterocercal. Pectoral fins relatively large. Pelvic fins show sexual dimorphism. Those of the male have hook-shaped claspers. Body largely naked. Maximum length about 18 cm.

Remarks: Bottom-dwellers.

Recent relatives: None. Died out in Devonian. Certain similarities suggest that this is a blind-ending side branch of the group of fishes from which the chimaeras are descended.

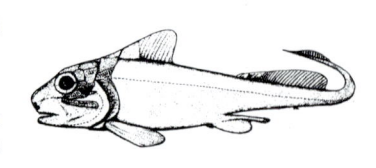

Ctenurella, reconstruction after MACMILLAN.

PLACODERMI — Placoderms
Order: Ptyctodontiformes
Family: Ptyctodontidae

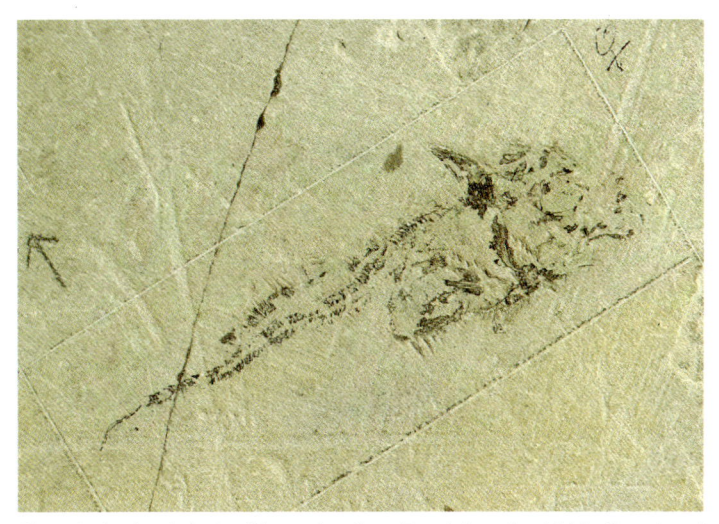

Rhamphodopsis trispinatus WATSON (length c. 7 cm) from the Middle Devonian of Caithness, Scotland. Original: Australian Museum, Sydney, Australia.

Genus: *Rhamphodopsis* WATSON, 1934.

Horizon: Middle Devonian.

Geographical distribution: Europe.

Features: Small fishes. Head relatively small. Eyes directed upwards. Mouth ventral. A pair of tooth plates on upper and lower jaw. The anterior part of the back has a posteriorly grooved spine. The posterior dorsal fin triangular and relatively large. Pelvic fins long, partly scaly in female and in the male with hook-shaped claspers. Maximum length c. 12 cm.

Remarks: Bottom-dwellers. Lived in fresh water.

Recent relatives: None. Died out in Middle Devonian.

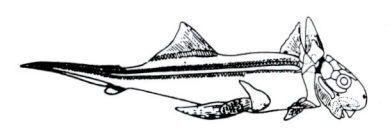

Rhamphodopsis, reconstruction after HOLMGREN.

PLACODERMI
Placoderms
Order: Petalichthyiformes
Family: Macropetalichthyidae

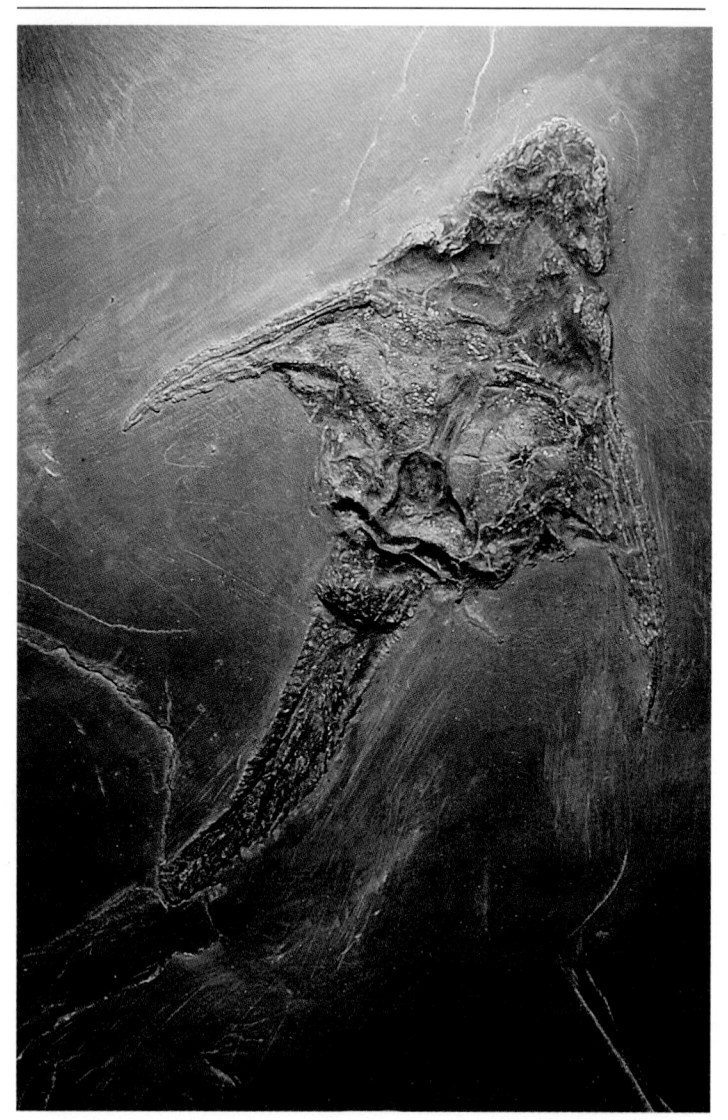

Lunaspis broilii Gross (length c. 19 cm) from the Lower Devonian of Bundenbach, Rhineland, Germany. Original: Bayerische Staatssammlung für Paläontologie, Munich, Germany.

PLACODERMI
Placoderms
Order: Petalichthyiformes
Family: Macropetalichthyidae

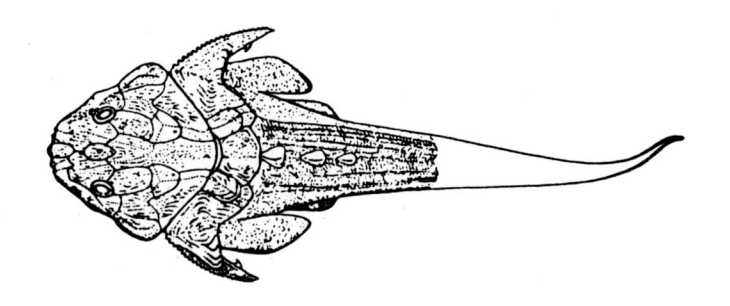

Lunaspis, reconstruction after STENSIÖ.

Genus: *Lunaspis* BROILI, 1929.

Horizon: Lower Devonian.

Geographical distribution: Europe.

Features: Middle-sized armoured fishes with a maximum length of c. 30 cm. Head armour and body armour not articulated to each other. Characteristic lateral spines with denticulate edges. Shape elongate. Tail tapering to point with diphycercal caudal fin. Other fins absent. Jaw never found. Body covered with thin scales. Three large keeled scales in the dorsal mid line.

Remarks: Bottom-dwelling.

Recent relatives: None. Died out in Lower Devonian.

PLACODERMI
Order: Petalichthyiformes
Family: Macropetalichthyidae

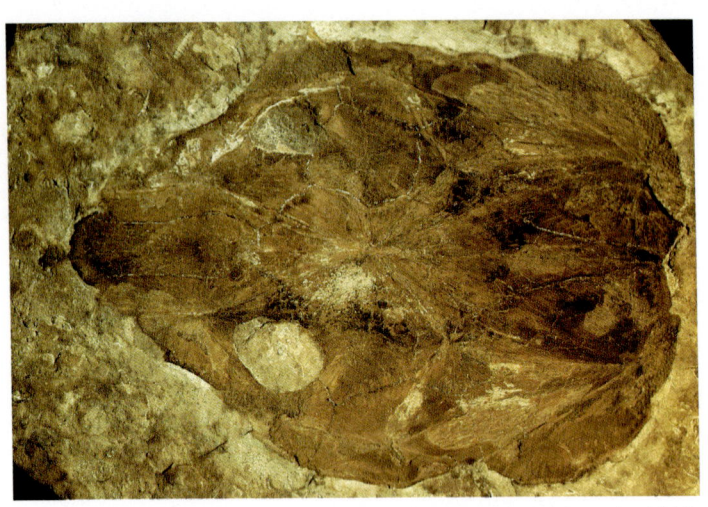

Placoderms

Macropetalichthys sullivani NORWOOD & OWEN (length c. 17 cm) from the Middle Devonian of Sanusky, Ohio, U.S.A. Original: Peabody Museum of Natural History, New Haven, Connecticutt, U.S.A.

Genus: *Macropetalichthys* NORWOOD & OWEN, 1846.

Synonyms: *Acanthaspis, Agassichthys, Heintzaspis, Ohiodurolites, Physichthys*.

Horizon: Middle Devonian.

Geographical distribution: Europe, North America.

Features: Relatively large fishes. Roof of skull may reach length of 25 cm. Eyes directed upwards but somewhat laterally placed. Mouth slightly ventral. Jaws not yet found. Trunk armour relatively brief.

Remarks: Probably largely bottom-dwellers.

Recent relatives: None. Died out in Middle Devonian.

Macropetalichthys, reconstruction after BROILI.

126

PLACODERMI

Order: Phyllolepidiformes
Family: Phyllolepididae

Placoderms

Phyllolepis sp. (length c. 12 cm) from the Upper Devonian of East Greenlan. Original: Geologisk Museum, Copenhagen, Denmark.

Genus: *Phyllolepis* AGASSIZ, 1844.

Synonyms: *Pentagonolepis*.

Horizon: Upper Devonian.

Geographical distribution: Western and Eastern Europe, Greenland, North America, Australia.

Features: Head shield broad and flat. Eyes small, antero-lateral in position. Dorsal and ventral shields likewise broad and flat. Lateral spines short. Pectoral fins narrow. Body behind armour slender and elongate, tapering to a point at end of tail. Maximum length, according to the species, 40 cm.

Remarks: Probably more bottom-dwelling than free-swimming.

Recent relatives: None. Died out in Upper Devonian.

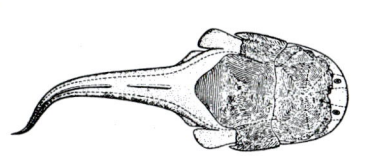

Phyllolepis, reconstruction after STENSIÖ.

PLACODERMI
Order: Arthrodiriformes
Family: Wuttagoonaspididae

Placoderms
Suborder: Coccosteoidei

Wuttagoonaspis fletsheri RITCHIE (length c. 7 cm) from the Middle Devonian of Wuttagoona, New South Wales, Australia. Original: Australian Museum, Sydney, Australia.

Genus: *Wuttagoonaspis* RITCHIE, 1973.

Horizon: Middle Devonian.

Geographical distribution: Australia.

Features: Middle-sized fishes with beautifully sculptured armour. Head shield convex. Eyes displaced sideways and rearwards. Snout rounded. No differentiated hinge between head shield and trunk armour. Shortly behind the eyes there are slender lateral spines. Head shield up to 18 cm in length.

Remarks: Inhabited fresh-water.

Recent relatives: None. Died out in Middle Devonian.

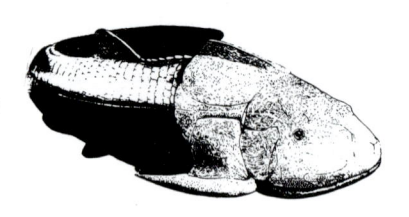

Wuttagoonaspis, reconstruction after RITCHIE.

128

PLACODERMI
Placoderms

Order: Arthrodiriformes
Suborder: Coccosteoidei
Family: Homosteidae

Homosteus milleri TRAQUAIR (length c. 42 cm) from the Middle Devonian of Caithness, Scotland, U.K. Original: National Museum of Scotland, Edinburgh, U.K.

Genus: *Homosteus* ASMUSS, 1856.

Synonyms: *Homostius*.

Horizon: Middle to Upper Devonian.

Geographical distribution: Western and Eastern Europe, Spitzbergen, Greenland, North America.

Features: Head and trunk arm form an ovoid. Eyes relatively large, anterior, close together and directed upwards. Trunk shield considerably smaller than head armour. Lateral spurs very small. Head and trunk armour together may reach a length of about 1 m in some species.

Remarks: The upward directed eyes suggest a bottom-dweller.

Recent relatives: None. Died out in Upper Devonian.

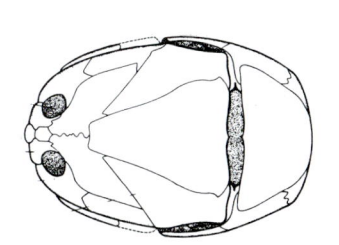

Homosteus, reconstruction after MILES.

PLACODERMI
Order: Arthrodiriformes
Family: Brachydeiridae

Placoderms
Suborder: Coccosteoidei

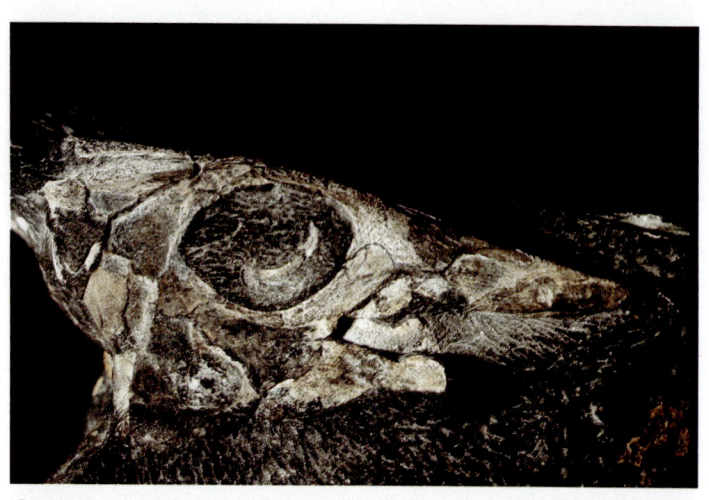

Oxyosteus sp. (length c. 9 cm) from the Upper Devonian of Bad Wildungen, Hesse, Germany. Original: Naturhistoriska Riksmuseet, Stockholm, Sweden.

Genus: *Oxyosteus* JAEKEL, 1911.

Synonym: *Platyosteus*.

Horizon: Upper Devonian.

Geographical distribution: Western and Eastern Europe.

Features: Head and body narrow and deep. Anterior part of the head elongated to form pointed snout. Eyes large and lateral. Jaws toothless. In some species skull up to 20 cm long.

Remarks: Probably good swimmers.

Recent relatives: None. Died out in Upper Devonian.

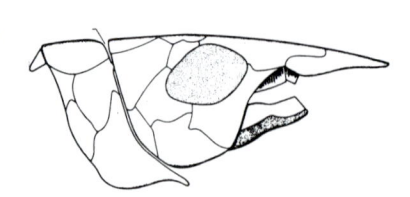

Oxyosteus, reconstruction after MILES.

PLACODERMI
Placoderms
Order: Arthrodiriformes
Suborder: Coccosteoidei
Family: Coccosteidae

Coccosteus cuspidatus MILLER (length c. 27 cm) from the Middle Devonian of Scotland. Original: Naturmuseum Senckenberg, Frankfurt-am-Main, Germany.

131

PLACODERMI
Order: Arthrodiriformes
Family: Coccosteidae

Placoderms
Suborder: Coccosteoidei

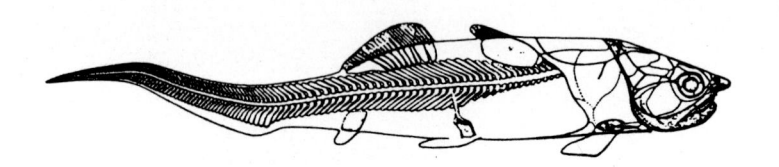

Coccosteus, reconstruction after STENSIÖ.

Genus: *Coccosteus* MILLER, 1841.

Horizon: Middle Devonian.

Geographical distribution: Western and Eastern Europe.

Features: Roof of skull relatively deep. Eyes of middle size and placed laterally. Pectoral fins roughly in the middle of the body. Dorsal fin present. Trunk armour broad. Body long and slender, ending in a pointed tail. Maximum length c. 40 cm.

Remarks: Probably good swimmers. The genus is known from both fresh-water and marine deposits.

Recent relatives: None. Died out in Middle Devonian.

PLACODERMI
Placoderms
Order: Arthrodiriformes
Suborder: Coccosteoidei
Family: Coccosteidae

Millerosteus minor (MILLER) (length c. 6 cm) from the Middle Devonian of Caithness, Scotland, U.K. Original: Field Museum of Natural History, Chicago, Illinois, U.S.A.

Genus: *Millerosteus* STENSIÖ, 1959.

Horizon: Middle Devonian.

Geographical distribution: Western and Eastern Europe.

Features: Small placoderms. Length about 10 cm. Head shield rather deep. Eyes relatively large. Median dorsal shield long and slender with a spine at the end. Lateral spines also long and slender. One of the smallest placoderms.

Remarks: Bottom dwellers with moderate ability for free-swimming.

Recent relatives: None. Died out in Middle Devonian.

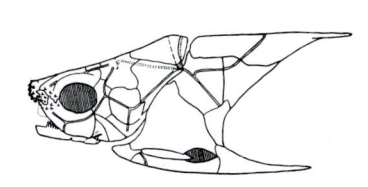

Millerosteus, reconstruction after DESMOND.

133

PLACODERMI
Order: Arthrodiriformes
Family: Coccosteidae

Placoderms
Suborder: Coccosteoidei

Watsonosteus fletti (WATSON) (length c. 58 cm) from the Middle Devonian of the Orkney Islands, Scotland, U.K. Copy: de Buisonje Collection, Amsterdam, Netherlands.

Genus: *Watsonosteus* MILES & WESTOLL, 1963.

Horizon: Middle Devonian.

Geographical distribution: Europe.

Features: Head shield moderately broad. Eyes middle-sized and lateral. Dorsal fin short and broad and located at anterior end of body behind armour. Tail long and ending in a point. Pectoral fins relatively large. Length about 60 cm.

Remarks: Probably good swimmers.

Recent relatives: None. Died out in Devonian.

PLACODERMI | Placoderms
Order: **Arthrodiriformes** | Suborder: **Coccosteoidei**
Family: **Pholidosteidae**

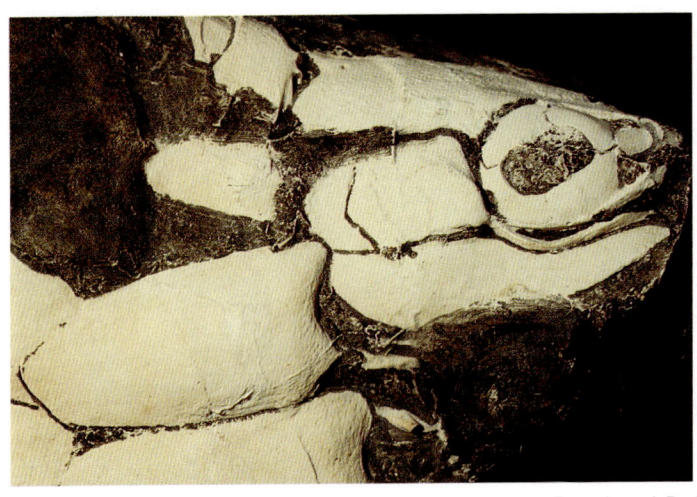

Pholidosteus friedelti JAEKEL (length c. 17 cm) from the Upper Devonian of Bad Wildungen, Rhineland, Germany. Cast: American Museum of Natural History, New York, N.Y., U.S.A.

Genus: *Pholidosteus* JAEKEL, 1907.

Horizon: Upper Devonian.

Geographical distribution: Europe.

Features: Middle-sized placoderms. Eyes extremely large, with sclerotic rings. Jaws toothed. Lateral spines short and narrow. Shape slender and elongate.

Remarks: Free-swimming.

Recent relatives: None. Died out in Upper Devonian.

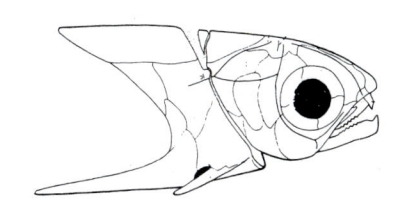

Pholidosteus, reconstruction after GROSS.

PLACODERMI
Order: Arthrodiriformes
Family: Dinichthyidae

Placoderms
Suborder: Coccosteoidei

Dunkleosteus terelli (NEWBERRY) (length c. 110 cm) from the Upper Devonian of Cleveland, Ohio, U.S.A. Original: Cleveland Museum of Natural History, Ohio, U.S.A.

Genus: *Dunkleosteus* LEHMAN, 1956.

Synonyms: *Dinichthys*.

Horizon: Upper Devonian.

Geographical distribution: Western and eastern Europe. North Africa, North America.

Features: Very large placoderms with massive skull. Maximum length about 6–8 m. Skull alone may be 65 cm long. Together with reduced body armour, may reach 110 cm. Enormous jaws toothless but strongly serrated. Eyes relatively small.

Remarks: Free-swimming, dangerous predators which need not even have feared sharks.

Recent relatives: None. Died out in Upper Devonian.

Dunkleosteus, reconstruction after MACMILLAN.

PLACODERMI
Order: Arthrodiriformes
Family: Dinichthyidae

Placoderms
Suborder: Coccosteoidei

Eastmanosteus calliaspis DENNIS-BRYAN (length c. 35 cm) from the Lower Devonian of Paddy's Springs, Western Australia. Original: Australian Museum, Sydney, Australia.

Genus: *Eastmanosteus* OBRUCHEV, 1964.

Horizon: Middle Devonian to Upper Devonian.

Geographical distribution: North Africa, North America, western and eastern Europe, southwest Asia.

Features: Large skull. Reduced dorsal and lateral armour. Relatively small eyes. Length probably 2–3 m. Powerful serrated toothless jaws. Much like *Dunkleosteus* but in some ways more primitive.

Remarks: Free-swimming predators.

Recent relatives: None. Died out in Lower Devonian.

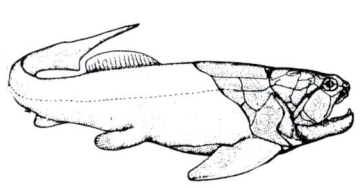

Eastmanosteus, reconstruction after West Australian Museum.

137

PLACODERMI
Order: Arthrodiriformes
Family: Trematosteidae

Placoderms
Suborder: Coccosteoidei

Brachyosteus dietrichi GROSS (length c. 5 cm) from the Upper Devonian of Bad Wildungen, Hesse, Germany. Original: Museum für Naturkunde, Berlin, Germany.

Genus: *Brachyosteus* JAEKEL, 1927.

Horizon: Upper Devonian.

Geographical distribution: Europe.

Features: Small to medium-sized fishes with rather deep head. Central dorsal plate short and with a weak keel.

Remarks: Predatory fishes.

Recent relatives: None. Died out in Upper Devonian.

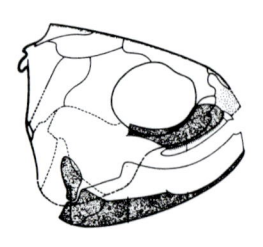

Brachyosteus, reconstruction after MILES.

PLACODERMI
Placoderms
Order: Antiarchiformes
Family: Bothriolepididae

Bothriolepis canadensis W<small>HITEAVES</small> (length c. 11 cm) from the Upper Devonian of Miguasha, Gaspé Peninsula, Quebec, Canada. Original: The Natural History Museum, London, U.K. (P56844).

PLACODERMI Placoderms
Order: **Antiarchiformes**
Family: **Bothriolepididae**

Bothriolepis, reconstruction after West Australian Museum.

Genus: *Bothriolepis* EICHWALD, 1840

Synonyms: *Bothryolepis*, *Glyptosteus*, *Homothorax*, *Macrobrachius*, *Parmphractus*, *Phoebammon*, *Placothorax*, *Shurcabroma*, *Stanacanthus*.

Horizon: Middle to Upper Devonian.

Geographical distribution: Western and eastern Europe, Antarctica, North America, Greenland, central Asia, northern Asia, southwest Asia, Australia.

Features: Head shield short and deep. Body armour almost egg-shaped. Body ends in pointed caudal fin with a narrow fin fold above and a broad lobe beneath. Eyes close together and facing forward. Mouth terminal and relatively small. Two dorsal fins. Maximum length 40–50 cm.

Remarks: Free swimming.

Recent relatives: None. Died out in Upper Devonian.

PLACODERMI — Placoderms
Order: Antiarchiformes
Family: Bothriolepididae

Asterolepis maxima (AGASSIZ) (length c. 28 cm) from the Upper Devonian of Scotland, U.K. Original: National Museum of Scotland, Edinburgh, U.K.

Genus: *Asterolepis* EICHWALD, 1840.

Horizon: Middle Devonian to Upper Devonian.

Geographical distribution: Western and Eastern Europe, North America, Greenland, Spitzbergen, eastern Asia, Australia.

Features: Head shield short and deep. Eyes close together. Body armour extending into a little point. Paired limbs reach back past the middle of the dorsal shield. A single dorsal fin. Body tapering in a point. Maximum length probably between 60 and 70 cm.

Remarks: Free-swimming.

Recent relatives: None. Died out in Upper Devonian.

Asterolepis, reconstruction after ORLOV.

PLACODERMI
Placoderms
Order: Antiarchiformes
Family: Asterolepididae

Microbrachius dicki TRAQUAIR (length c. 3 cm) from the Middle Devonian of the Orkney Islands, Scotland, U.K. Original: National Museum of Scotland, Edinburgh, U.K.

Genus: *Microbrachius* TRAQUAIR, 1888.

Synonyms: *Microbrachium*.

Horizon: Middle Devonian.

Geographical distribution: Europe.

Features: A dwarf among placoderms. Length scarcely more than 6 cm. Relatively large head shield and relatively short and broad dorsal armour. The paired limbs scarcely extend beyond the half length of the dorsal armour. Systematic position still uncertain.

Remarks: Free swimmers, lived in fresh water.

Recent relatives: None. Died out in Middle Devonian.

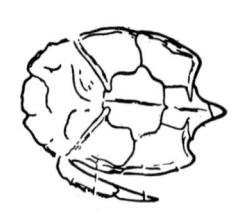

Microbrachius, reconstruction after TRAQUAIR.

PLACODERMI
Order: **Antiarchiformes**
Family: **Asterolepididae**

Placoderms

Pterichthyodes milleri AGASSIZ (length c. 15 cm) from the Middle Devonian of Caithness, Scotland. Original: Frickhinger Collection, Munich, Germany.

PLACODERMI
Placoderms
Order: Antiarchiformes
Family: Asterolepididae

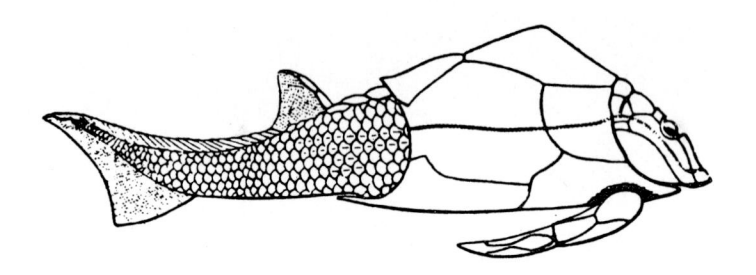

Pterichthyodes, reconstruction after TRAQUAIR.

Genus: *Pterichthyodes* BLEEKER, 1859.

Synonyms: *Pterichthys*.

Horizon: Lower to Middle Devonian.

Geographical distribution: Europe, Australia.

Features: Head shield short and deep. Eyes facing forward and close together. Together with the nasal opening between them form a common orbito-nasal opening. Lower surface of head shield not armoured, carrying very delicate jaws and the mouth. Armoured paired limbs which extend back to two-thirds the length of the trunk armour. These limbs correspond functionally to the pectoral fins of higher fishes. Length c. 30 cm.

Remarks: Fresh-water fishes. Partly bottom-dwellers, partly free-swimming.

Recent relatives: None. Died out in Middle Devonian.

PLACODERMI   Placoderms
Order: **Antiarchiformes**
Family: **Asterolepididae**

Remigolepis sp. (length c. 17 cm) from the Upper Devonian of Mount Smith Woodward, Greenland. Original: Geologisk Museum, Copenhagen, Denmark.

Genus: *Remigolepis* STENSIÖ, 1931.

Horizon: Upper Devonian.

Geographical distribution: Europe, Greenland, Australia.

Features: Head shield short and deep. Body armour long, narrow and low. Paired limbs of a single piece (with no included articulation), reaching back to the posterior two-thirds of the body armour. The body behind the armour covered with rounded-rectangular scales. Caudal fin consists of lower lobe only. Length c. 40 cm.

Remarks: Bottom dwelling but free-swimming.

Recent relatives: None. Died out in Upper Devonian.

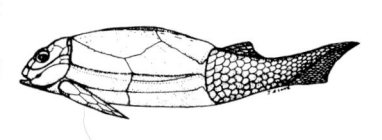

Remigolepis, reconstruction after West Australian Museum.

PLACODERMI
Order: Antiarchiformes

Placoderms

Diplognathus mirabilis NEWBERRY (length c. 18 cm) from the Upper Devonian of Cleveland, Ohio, U.S.A. Original: American Museum of Natural History, New York, N.Y., U.S.A.

Genus: *Diplognathus* NEWBERRY, 1878.

Horizon: Upper Devonian.

Geographical distribution: North America.

Features: Middle-sized placoderms with powerful jaws, which were probably up to 45 cm long and had a low sharp cutting edge and pointed teeth in the anterior part. In the posterior part the teeth are curved. Systematic position not yet resolved.

Remarks: Free-swimming predatory fishes.

Recent relatives: None. Died out in Upper Devonian.

CHONDRICHTHYES — Cartilaginous Fishes

As the name implies, the endoskeleton may be calcified in these fishes but never contains true bony tissue. In an evolutionary sense, ossification is usually seen as more advanced than cartilage but in these fishes cartilaginisation seems to have been a success.

Cartilaginous fishes include the sharks, angel sharks, rays and chimaeras. The surface of the body is mostly covered with placoid scales which consist of a basal plate and a tooth-like upper part of various shapes. From the evolutionary point of view, the teeth can be seen as placoid scales which have migrated into the mouth. When worn away or lost, they can be replaced. The following types of dentition are distinguished: 1) the catching dentition comprising two rows of sharp teeth—this is typical for free-swimming sharks; 2) the grasping dentition of bottom-dwelling sharks—this consists of several rows of small pointed teeth lying one behind the other; and, finally, 3) the crushing dentitions of rays and chimaeras where the teeth are rounded, or form pavements or are developed as tooth plates.

The paired pectoral fins are mostly lateral in position and situated near the most posterior gill slits. The ventral fins are simpler and often bear hook-like claspers which facilitate internal fertilization. One or two dorsal fins may exist and an anal fin is present. The caudal fin is usually heterocercal with the vertebral column bending upwards into the larger upper lobe. The fin rays consist of thin, flexible unjointed rods named actinotricha.

Sharks first appear in the Middle Devonian. They had a brief maximum in the Lower Carboniferous and then the number of species decreased continuously up to the Lower Triassic. After this a new progressive phase began which led to an absolute maximum in the Upper Cretaceous. Then there was a new decline followed by another period of prosperity in the Eocene which continues to the present day with 100 recent genera and 340 species. The first sharks lived in fresh water. Up to the present, about 370 fossil genera have been described, though many of them only on the basis of incomplete specimens or even just teeth, fin spines etc. Complete fossil specimens are very rare.

CHONDRICHTHYES — Cartilaginous Fishes

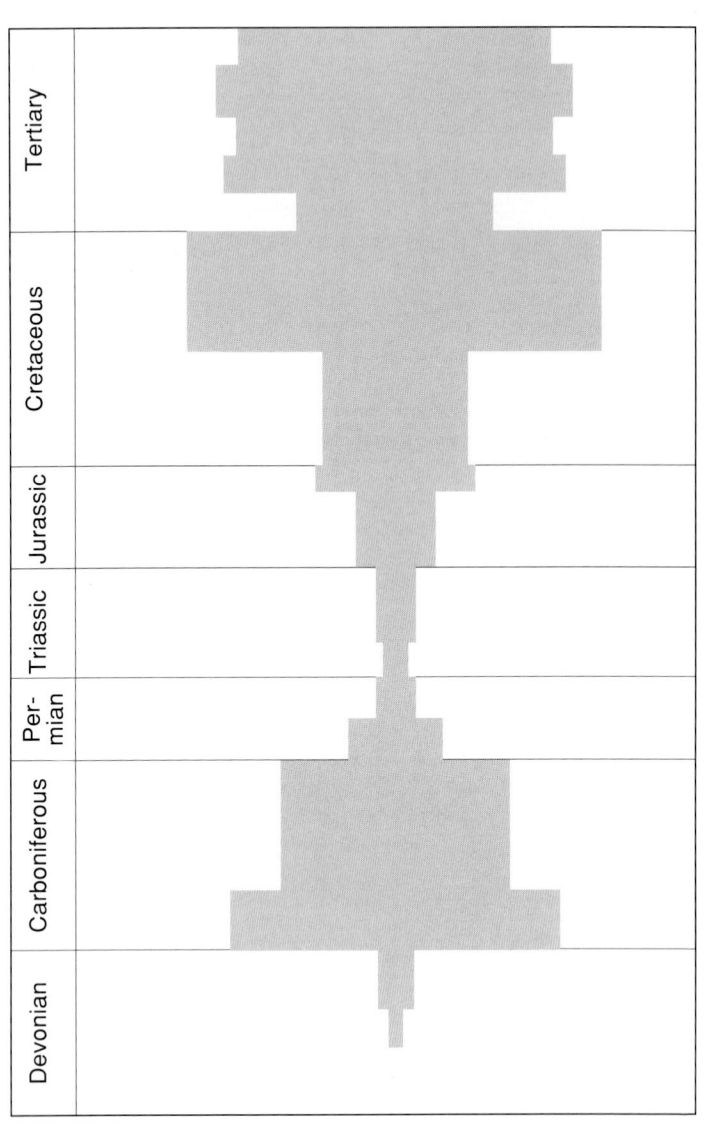

The approximate distribution of cartilaginous fishes in geological time, changed after MÜLLER

CHONDRICHTHYES — Cartilaginous Fishes
Order: Palaeospondyliformes
Family: Palaeospondylidae

Palaeospondylus gunni Traquair (length c. 4 cm) from the Middle Devonian of Scotland. Original: Henne Collection, Stuttgart.

Genus: *Palaeospondylus* Traquair, 1890.

Horizon: Middle Devonian.

Geographical distribution: Europe.

Features: Little fishes scarcely 4 cm long. All trace of exoskeleton absent. Vertebral column of calcified ring-shaped centra. Skull relatively large. Pectoral and pelvic fins supposedly present.

Remarks: Systematic position unclear. Possibly larvae of larger fishes or dwarfed forms.

Recent relatives: None.

Palaeospondylus, reconstruction after Macmillan.

CHONDRICHTHYES — Cartilaginous Fishes
Order: Xenacanthiformes
Family: Xenacanthidae

Expleuracanthus gaudryi Heyler (length c. 58 cm) from the Upper Carboniferous of Commentry, France. Original: Muséum National d'Histoire Naturelle, Paris, France. Photograph: Serette, Paris.

Genus: *Expleuracanthus* Brongniart, 1888.

Horizon: Upper Carboniferous.

Geographical distribution: Europe.

Features: Slender Middle-sized sharks. Head deep and elongate. Eyes large. Mouth deeply incised and ventral. A long spine in the middle of the head. Dorsal fin low and fin-fold like. Begins shortly behind the head and extends back to the caudal fin. The latter surrounds the posterior end of the body and runs forward along the belly. Pelvic fins relatively broad. Pectoral fins narrow. Teeth very weak.

Remarks: *Expleuracanthus* has recently been considered as a synonym of *Triodus*.

Recent relatives: None. Died out in Carboniferous.

CHONDRICHTHYES — Cartilaginous Fishes
Order: Xenacanthiformes
Family: Xenacanthidae

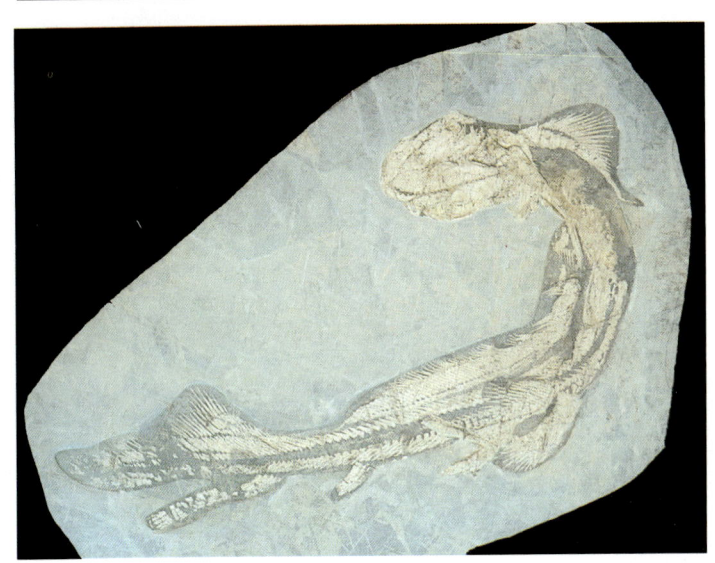

Orthacanthus senckenbergianus FRITSCH (length c. 220 cm) from the Lower Permian of Rockenhausen, Palatinate, Germany. Original: Naturmuseum Senckenberg, Frankfurt-am-Main, Germany.

Genus: *Orthacanthus* AGASSIZ, 1843.

Synonyms: *Aganodus*, *Compsacanthus*, *Diplodus*, *Dissodus*, *Eucompsacanthus*, *Ochlodus*, *Pternodus*.

Horizon: Upper Carboniferous to Lower Permian.

Geographical distribution: Europe, North America, East Asia.

Features: Large sharks with an occipital spine situated immediately behind the head and attached to the shoulder girdle. This spine is long, pointed and oval or circular in section. Its posterior side ornamented with two parallel rows of thorns. Teeth relatively large, with two longer lateral cusps and a smaller central cusp. Pectoral fins long and pointed. Snout rounded. Mouth large.

Remarks: Predatory fish which were able to overpower even large prey.

Recent relatives: None. Died out in Permian.

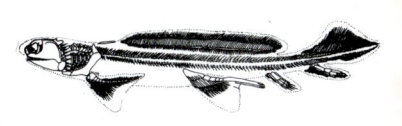

Orthacanthus, reconstruction after HEIDTKE.

CHONDRICHTHYES
Cartilaginous Fishes
Order: Xenacanthiformes
Family: Xenacanthidae

Triodus sesselis JORDAN (length c. 50 cm) from the Permian of Odernheim, Palatinate, Germany. Original: Interfoss, Munich, Germany.

Genus: *Triodus* JORDAN, 1849.

Synonyms: *Expleuracanthus*.

Horizon: Lower Permian.

Geographical distribution: Europe.

Features: Occipital spine like that of *Orthacanthus* but weaker. Teeth very small with two larger lateral cusps and a smaller middle cusp. Mouth large, slightly ventral. Fin extends from the neck region, over the pointed caudal end of the body forward to the posterior end of the belly. Pelvic and pectoral fins somewhat expanded.

Remarks: Predatory fishes.

Recent relatives: None. Died out in Lower Permian.

CHONDRICHTHYES — Cartilaginous Fishes
Order: Xenacanthiformes
Family: Xenacanthidae

Xenacanthus meisenheimensis HAMPE (length c. 75 cm) from the Lower Permian of Meisenheim, Palatinate, Germany. Original: Interfoss, Munich, Germany.

Genus: *Xenacanthus* BEYRICH, 1848.

Synonyms: *Hypospondylus*.

Horizon: Lower Permian.

Geographical distribution: Europe.

Features: Middle-sized sharks with a long, slender body. Occipital spine long, relatively thin, of oval section. This spine has lateral thorns near the base. Teeth small, with two strong lateral cusps and an appreciably smaller middle cusp. End of tail bent slightly upwards. Caudal fin extends far forwards as a fin fold and separated from equally fold-like dorsal fin by a constriction. Pectoral and pelvic fins broad.

Remarks: Predatory fishes.

Recent relatives: None. Died out in Lower Permian.

Xenacanthus, reconstruction after FRITSCH.

153

CHONDRICHTHYES — Cartilaginous Fishes
Order: Cladoselachiformes
Family: Cladoselachidae

Cladoselache clarki CLAYPOLE (length c. 60 cm) from the Devonian of Cleveland, Ohio, U.S.A. Original: Museum of Natural History, Cleveland, Ohio, U.S.A.

Genus: *Cladoselache* DEAN, 1894.

Synonyms: *Cladodus*.

Horizon: Upper Devonian.

Geographical distribution: North America.

Features: Sharks with slim spindle-shaped body. Head with blunt snout. Two dorsal fins. Heterocercal forked caudal fin which nevertheless externally looks almost homocercal. Skin largely naked. Teeth with a large middle cusps and smaller lateral cusps (cladodont). Very large pectoral fins. A strong spine in front of the first dorsal fin. Maximum length c. 1 m.

Remarks: Probably rapid swimmers and formidable predators.

Recent relatives: None. Died out in Upper Devonian.

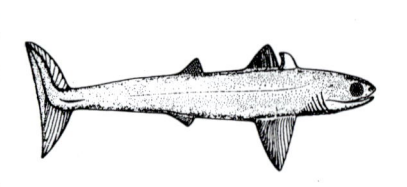

Cladoselache, reconstruction after HARRIS.

CHONDRICHTHYES — Cartilaginous Fishes
Order: Coronodontiformes
Family: Unnamed

Diademodus hydei Harris (length c. 39 cm) from the Upper Devonian of Cleveland, Ohio, U.S.A. Original: Museum of Natural History, Cleveland, Ohio, U.S.A.

Genus: *Diademodus* Harris, 1951.

Synonyms: *Tiaradontus*.

Horizon: Upper Devonian.

Geographical distribution: North America.

Features: Small primitive sharks. Body covered with blunt dermal denticles. Teeth small, symmetrical. Two higher cusps in middle and a smaller one at each end. Probably only one dorsal fin. Male with claspers.

Remarks: Small sharks but nevertheless, in view of the sharp teeth, formidable predators.

Recent relatives: None. Died out in Upper Devonian.

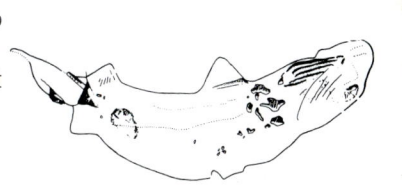

Diademodus, reconstruction after Harris.

CHONDRICHTHYES
Cartilaginous Fishes
Order: Symmoriiformes
Family: Symmoriidae

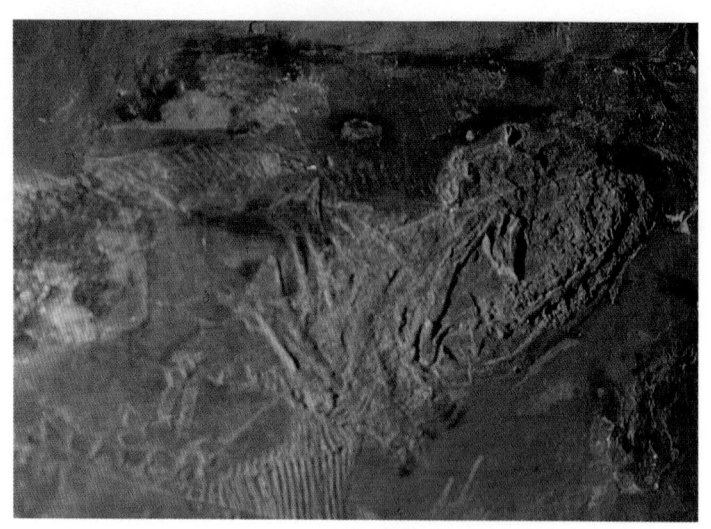

Symmorium reniforme COPE from the Upper Carboniferous of Indiana, U.S.A. Original: Field Museum of Natural History, Chicago, Illinois, U.S.A.

Genus: *Symmorium* COPE, 1839.

Synonyms: *Cladodus*.

Horizon: Lower Carboniferous to Upper Carboniferous.

Geographical distribution: Europe, North America.

Features: Maximum length 3 m. Head relatively small. Lower jaw somewhat longer than upper jaw. Only one dorsal fin which lies in the posterior third of the body. Caudal fin slightly forked. Teeth cladodont (see *Cladoselache*). Body without spines.

Remarks: Predators with sharp teeth.

Recent relatives: None. Died out in Upper Carboniferous.

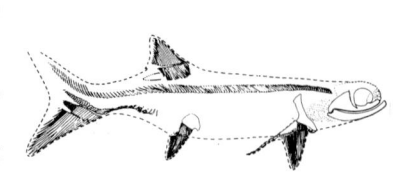

Symmorium, reconstruction after WILLIAMS.

CHONDRICHTHYES — Cartilaginous Fishes
Order: Symmoriformes
Family: Stethacantidae

Damocles serratus LUND (length c. 5 cm) from the Lower Carboniferous of Bear Gulch, Montana, U.S.A. Original: Adelphi University, Garden City, N.J., U.S.A.

Genus: *Damocles* LUND, 1986.

Horizon: Lower Carboniferous.

Geographical distribution: North America.

Features: Small slender sharks. Dorsal fin small and located in posterior third of body. Caudal fin forked. Upper part of head elongated to a point. Mouth displaced posteriorly. Characteristic recurved occipital spine stretched horizontally over head. Lower surface of this spine denticulate. Males with claspers in posterior third of ventral surface.

Remarks: Small predators.

Recent relatives: None. Died out in Lower Carboniferous.

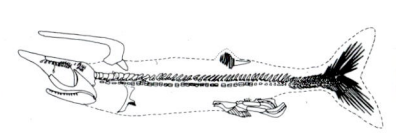

Damocles, reconstruction after LUND.

CHONDRICHTHYES — Cartilaginous Fishes
Order: Symmoriiformes
Family: Stethacantidae

Falcatus falcatus (ST. JOHN & WORTHEN) (length c. 15 cm) from the Lower Carboniferous of Bear Gulch, Montana, USA. Original: Staatliches Museum für Naturkunde, Karlsruhe, Germany.

Genus: *Falcatus* LUND, 1985.

Synonyms: *Physonemus.*

Horizon: Lower Carboniferous.

Geographical distribution: North America.

Features: Small slender fishes. Upper snout area very pointed. Mouth posterior. Eyes large. Caudal fin forked. Characteristic occipital spine pointed forward over head. It is relatively long and originates from a broad base.
The upper section is flattened.

Remarks: Small predators.

Recent relatives: None. Died out in Lower Carboniferous.

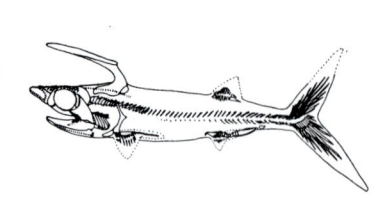

Falcatus, reconstruction after LUND

CHONDRICHTHYES — Cartilaginous Fishes
Order: Symmoriiformes
Family: Stethacantidae

Stethacanthus sp. (length c. 70 cm) from the Upper Carboniferous of Bearsden, Glasgow, Scotland, U.K. Original: Hunterian Museum, Glasgow, U.K. Photograph: Hunterian Museum.

Genus: *Stethacanthus* NEWBERRY, 1889.
Synonyms: *Cladodus*, *Lambdodus*, *Physonemus*.
Horizon: Upper Devonian to Upper Carboniferous.
Geographical distribution: Europe, North America.
Features: Middle-sized sharks with slender bodies. Head narrow. Snout pointed. In the dorsal mid line, immediately behind the head is a characteristic mushroom-shaped structure with a broad base. Upper margin of this structure expanded and with spines arranged to form a brush. Dorsal fin in the posterior half of the body, directly above the anal fin which is somewhat smaller. Pectoral fins narrow, each with a worm-like appendage arising from the base.
Remarks: Predatory fishes. The significance of the brush-like appendage uncertain.
Recent relatives: None. Died out in out in Upper Carboniferous.

Stethacanthus, reconstruction after Hunterian Museum.

CHONDRICHTHYES — Cartilaginous Fishes
Order: Eugeneodontiformes
Family: Agassizodontidae

Helicoprion bessonovi KARPINSKY (length c. 15 cm) from the Lower Permian of Russia. Original: Muséum National d'Histoire Naturelle, Paris, France. Photograph: Serette, Paris.

Genus: *Helicoprion* KARPINSKY, 1899.

Synonyms: *Lissoprion*.

Horizon: Lower Permian.

Geographical distribution: Europe, eastern Asia, Australia, North America.

Features: Nothing known of this fish except the very striking teeth. These are laterally very compressed and form a tight spiral which, when adult, may comprise three whorls with a total of up to 180 teeth. Adult animals must have been more than 1 m long.

Remarks: Predatory mode of life.

Recent relatives: None. Died out in Permian.

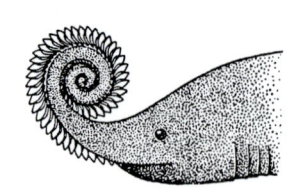

Helicoprion, after LONG.

CHONDRICHTHYES — Cartilaginous Fishes
Order: Eugeneodontiformes
Family: Edestidae

Edestus sp. (length c. 28 cm) from the Upper Devonian of St. Clair Co., Illinois, U.S.A. Original: Museum of Natural History, Lawrence, Kansas, U.S.A.

Genus: *Edestus* LEIDY, 1855.

Synonyms: *Edestes*, *Edestodus*, *Protospirata*.

Horizon: Upper Carboniferous.

Geographical distribution: North America, western and eastern Europe.

Features: Relatively large sharks preserved only as their characteristic dentitions. The teeth are in characteristic whorls and usually broader than long. Both sides of the teeth are sharply serrated. Arrangement of teeth alternating.

Remarks: Predatory fishes. Their teeth suggest that they could overpower even large prey.

Recent relatives: None. Died out in Upper Carboniferous.

CHONDRICHTHYES — Cartilaginous Fishes
Order: Eugeneodontiformes
Family: Edestidae

Unnamed shark (length c. 80 cm) from the Trias of Wapiti Lake, Canada. Original: Tyrell Museum of Paleontology, Drumheller, Alberta, Canada.

Genus: Unnamed.

Horizon: Trias.

Geographical distribution: North America.

Features: A still undescribed edestid with the body well preserved. Skull long and narrow. Pectoral fins slender and very large. Caudal fin forked and unusually large. Body slender.

Remarks: Probably very rapid and skillful swimmers.

Recent relatives: None. Died out in Triassic.

CHONDRICHTHYES — Cartilaginous Fishes
Order: Orodontiformes
Family: Orodontidae

Unnamed shark (length c. 12 cm) from the Lower Carboniferous of Bear Gulch, Montana, U.S.A. Original: Adelphi University, Garden City, N.J., U.S.A.

Genus: Not named.
Horizon: Lower Carboniferous.
Geographical distribution: North America.
Features: Genus not yet described. Evidently relatively small, plump sharks. Body laterally compressed. Head short. Fins small. Even the caudal fin has an "undeveloped" look.
Remarks: Probably more bottom-dwellers than free-swimming. Some members of the family Orodontidae, however, include members 3 m long.
Recent relatives: None. Died out in Lower Carboniferous.

CHONDRICHTHYES — Cartilaginous Fishes
Order: Petalodontiformes
Family: Petalidontidae

Janassa bituminosa von Schlotheim (length c. 54 cm) from the Permian of Bad Sachsa, Lauterberg, Harz, Germany. Original: private Possession.

Genus: *Janassa* Münster, 1839.
Synonyms: *Acrodus*, *Byzenos*, *Climaxodus*, *Dictea*, *Ianassa*, *Peltodus*, *Strigilina*, *Thoracodus*, *Trilobites*.
Horizon: Lower Carboniferous to Upper Permian.
Geographical distribution: Western and eastern Europe, North America, Greenland.
Features: Middle-sized fishes. Dorso-ventrally compressed and ray-like shape. Beak-like mouth on lower surface. Teeth arranged in longitudinal and transverse rows. Pectoral fins large, broad and semicircular. Anteriorly they surround about half the body. Small pelvic fins separated by a short distance from the pectoral fins. Dorsal fin situated above the pelvic fins. Body tapers to a point at the tail. Caudal fin rounded.
Remarks: Bottom-dwellers. Lived on hard food.
Recent relatives: None. Died out Upper Permian.

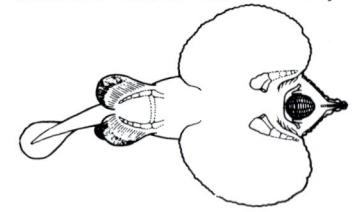

Janassa, reconstruction after Schaumberg.

CHONDRICHTHYES — Cartilaginous Fishes
Order: Petalodontiformes
Family: Belantseidae

Belantsea montana LUND (length c. 27 cm) from the Lower Carboniferous of Bear Gulch, Montana, U.S.A. Original: Adelphi University, Garden City, N.J., U.S.A.

Genus: *Belantsea* LUND, 1989.

Horizon: Lower Carboniferous.

Geographical distribution: North America.

Features: Middle-sized fishes of laterally flattened shape. Head deep. Mouth relatively small with strong dentition. Dorsal mid line with two humps carrying the two dorsal fins. Pectoral fins small. Pelvic fins very large. Caudal fin rounded. All fins give impression of being veil-like. Body covered with small denticles.

Remarks: Free-swimming, but nevertheless could only have been very lethargic swimmers.

Recent relatives: None. Died out in Lower Carboniferous. Lower Carboniferous.

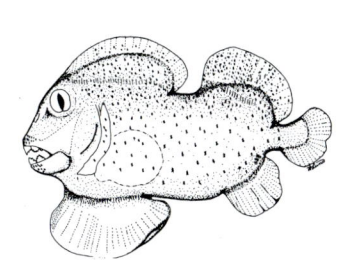

Belantsea, reconstruction after LUND.

CHONDRICHTHYES — Cartilaginous Fishes
Order: Ctenacanthiformes
Family: Hybodontidae

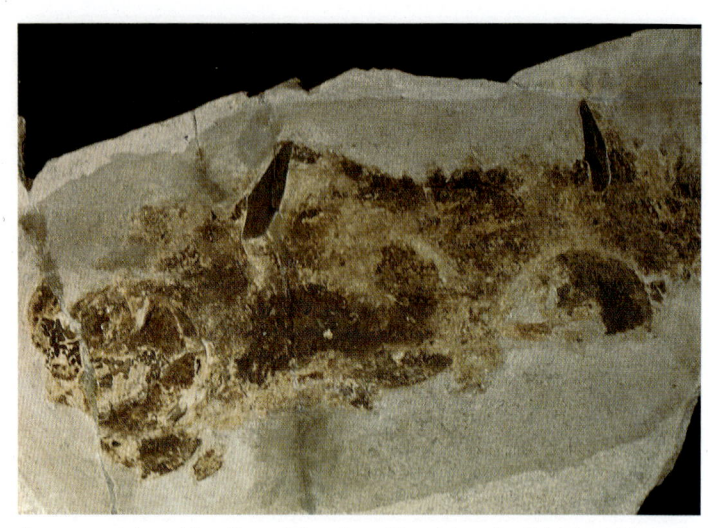

Acronemus tuberculatus (Bassani) (length c. 29 cm) from the Triassic of Monte San Giorgio, Switzerland. Original: Paläontologisches Museum, Zürich, Switzerland.

Genus: *Acronemus* Rieppel, 1982.

Synonyms: *Acrodus*, *Adiapneustes*, *Psilacanthus*, *Sphenonchus*, *Thectodus*.

Horizon: Lower Triassic to Upper Cretaceous.

Geographical distribution: Europe, North America, South America, southern Asia, Spitzbergen.

Features: Small to middle-sized sharks. Head large. Body tapers moderately rearwards. Two dorsal fins, both carried by a powerful spine. Pectoral fins relatively large. Ventral and anal fins small. Another spine located above pectoral fins.

Remarks: Predatory fishes.

Recent relatives: None. Died out in Upper Cretaceous.

Acronemus, reconstruction after Rieppel.

CHONDRICHTHYES   Cartilaginous Fishes
Order: Ctenacanthiformes
Family: Hybodontidae

Hamiltonichthys mapesi MAISEY (length c. 28 cm) from the Upper Carboniferous of Greenwood County, Kansas, U.S.A. Original: Museum of Natural History, Lawrence, Kansas, U.S.A.

Genus: *Hamiltonichthys* MAISEY, 1969.

Horizon: Upper Carboniferous.

Geographical distribution: North America.

Features: Small slim sharks. Body tapers to a pointed heterocercal caudal fin with a large lower lobe. Eyes small. Mouth slightly ventral. Teeth pointed and arranged spirally.

Remarks: Small predatory fish.

Recent relatives: None. Died out in Upper Carboniferous.

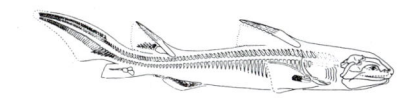

Hamiltonichthys, reconstruction after MAISEY.

CHONDRICHTHYES   Cartilaginous Fishes
Order: Ctenacanthiformes
Family: Hybodontidae

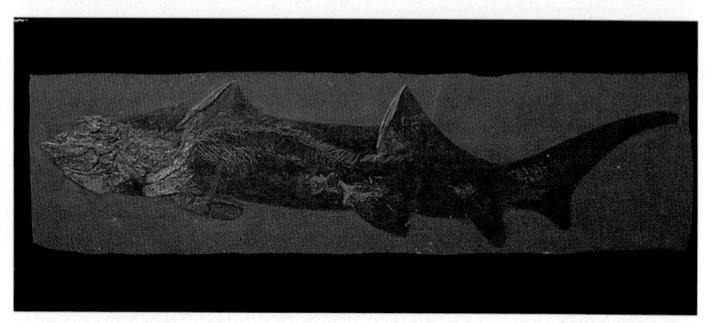

Hybodus hauffianus FRAAS (length c. 260 cm) from the Lower Jurassic of Holzmaden, Wurtemberg, Germany. Original: Staatliches Museum für Naturkunde, Stuttgart, Germany. Photograph: Lumpe, Stuttgart.

Genus: *Hybodus* AGASSIZ, 1837.

Synonyms: *Leiacanthus*, *Meristodon*, *Orthybodus*, *Parhybodus*, *Selachidea*.

Horizon: Upper Permian to Upper Cretaceous.

Geographical distribution: Europe, Spitzbergen, Greenland, North America, Eastern Asia, Australia.

Features: Large sharks with big head and massive body. Caudal fin heterocercal with an elongate upper lobe. Lower lobe relatively small. Two dorsal fins, each supported by a powerful spine. Pectoral fins elongate. Teeth elongate at the base with a main cusp and several subsidiary cusps and with striated surface. The males have hook-shaped head spines behind the eyes.

Remarks: Predatory fish. However, they can be shown to have taken not only fishes but also belemnites.

Recent relatives: None. Died out in Upper Cretaceous.

Hybodus, reconstruction after MAISEY.

CHONDRICHTHYES — Cartilaginous Fishes
Order: Ctenacanthiformes
Family: Hybodontidae?

Wodnika striatula MÜNSTER (length c. 12 cm) from the Upper Permian of Richelsdorf, Hesse, Germany. Original: Bürger Collection, Bad Hersfeld, Germany.

Genus: *Wodnika* MÜNSTER, 1843.

Synonyms: *Radamas*.

Horizon: Upper Permian.

Geographical distribution: Europe, North America.

Features: Middle-sized to large fishes, torpedo-shaped. Skull narrow. Snout pointed. Eyes relatively large. Mouth deeply incised. Lower jaw displaced rearwards. Both jaws set with bean-shaped teeth. Two dorsal fins, each supported by a furrowed spine. Anterior spine longer. Caudal fin with broad lower lobe. Anal fin small.

Remarks: The teeth suggest that these were not predators but that they fed on crustaceans and other invertebrates.

Recent relatives: None. Died out in Upper Permian.

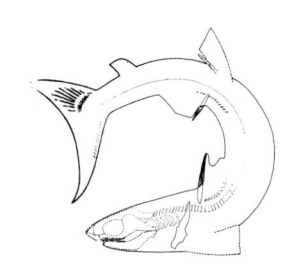

Wodnika, reconstruction after SCHAUMBERG.

CHONDRICHTHYES — Cartilaginous Fishes
Order: Ctenacanthiformes
Family: Unnamed

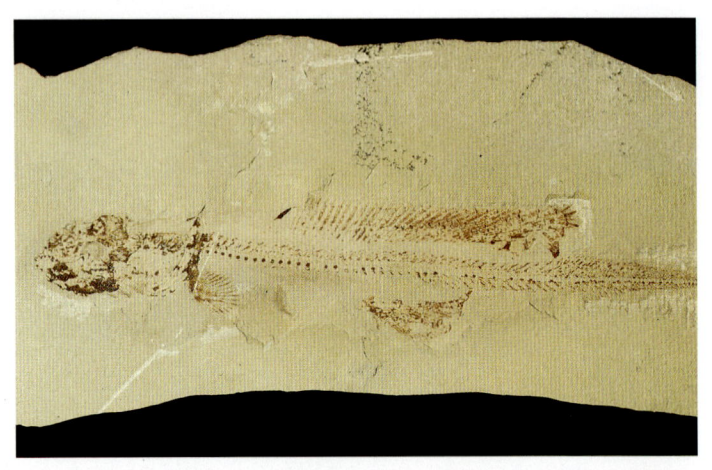

Heteropetalus elongatulus LUND (length c. 12 cm) from the Lower Carboniferous of Bear Gulch, Montana, U.S.A. Original: Carnegie Museum of Natural History, Pittsburgh, Penn., U.S.A.

Genus: *Heteropetalus* LUND, 1977.

Horizon: Lower Carboniferous.

Geographical distribution: North America.

Features: Elongate shape. Snout elongate but truncate at end. Long, almost fin-fold-like dorsal fin extends almost from the middle of the body into the posterior third. In front of it is a weak spine. Body tapers towards the caudal fin which is diphycercal with a broad lower lobe. Mouth slightly ventral. Teeth small but powerful. Dermal denticles present only along the lateral line.

Remarks: The teeth suggest a durophagous diet of snails, bivalves and other hard-shelled organisms.

Recent relatives: None. Died out in Lower Carboniferous.

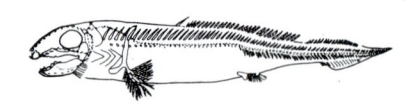

Heteropetalus, reconstruction after LUND.

CHONDRICHTHYES — Cartilaginous Fishes
Order: Galeiformes
Family: Heterodontidae
Suborder: Heterodontoidei

Heterodontus falcifer (WAGNER) (length c. 28 cm) from the Upper Jurassic of Solnhofen, (Eichstätt), Bavaria, Germany. Original: Jura-Museum, Eichstätt, Germany.

Genus: *Heterodontus* de BLAINVILLE, 1816.

Synonyms: *Cestracion*, *Drepanephorus*, *Gyropleurodus*, *Platyacrodus*, *Pseudacrodus*, *Tropidotus*.

Horizon: Upper Jurassic to recent.

Geographical distribution: Europe, South America, Africa, Australia, New Zealand.

Features: Relatively small slender sharks. Head relatively big. Two dorsal fins, each supported by a powerful spine. Spines smooth and smaller than the fins. Pectoral fins large. Caudal fin short with large lobes. Teeth pointed in anterior part of jaw but plate-like posteriorly.

Remarks: Small predatory fishes.

Recent relatives: Closely related to the recent bullhead shark *Heterodontus*.

Heterodontus sp., a recent bullhead shark.

CHONDRICHTHYES — Cartilaginous Fishes

Order: Galeiformes
Family: Heterodontidae
Suborder: Heterodontoidei

Paracestracion zitteli (WAGNER) (length c. 15 cm) from the Upper Jurassic of Solnhofen, (Eichstätt), Bavaria, Germany. Original: Carnegie Museum of Natural History, Pittsburgh, Penn. U.S.A.

Genus: *Paracestracion* KOKEN, 1911.

Horizon: Upper Jurassic.

Geographical distribution: Europe.

Features: *Paracestracion* differs from *Heterodontus* essentially in that the dorsal spines show a fine tuberculation on the sides. The teeth have a median keel.

Remarks: Some authors consider *Paracestracion* as a synonym of *Heterodontus*.

Recent relatives: Genus extinct. Distantly related to recent bullhead sharks of the family Heterodontidae which is represented in modern seas by one genus and eight species.

CHONDRICHTHYES
Cartilaginous Fishes
Order: Galeiformes
Family: Orectolobidae
Suborder: Orectoloboidei
Nurse Sharks

Corysodon cirinensis Saint-Seine from the Upper Jurassic of Cerin, France. Original: Musée Guimet d'Histoire Naturelle, Lyon, France. Photograph: Lyon Museum.

Genus: *Corysodon* Saint-Seine, 1949.

Horizon: Upper Jurassic.

Geographical distribution: Europe.

Features: Small sharks with two triangular dorsal fins, one approximately at middle of back and the other in the posterior third. Pelvic and anal fins obliquely beneath these. Teeth small and rather wide. Cutting edges not serrate.

Remarks: The genus *Corysodon* has recently been considered by some authors as a synonym of *Palaeoscyllium*.

Recent relatives: Genus extinct. Related to the recent nurse sharks.

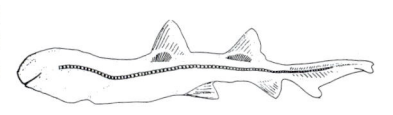

Corysodon, reconstruction after Saint-Seine.

173

CHONDRICHTHYES — Cartilaginous Fishes

Order: Galeiformes
Family: Orectolobidae

Suborder: Orectoloboidei
Nurse Sharks

Orectolobus jurassicus WOODWARD (length c. 30 cm) from the Upper Jurassic of Solnhofen (Eichstätt), Bavaria, Germany. Original: Krauss Collection, Weissenburg, Germany.

Genus: *Orectolobus* BONAPARTE, 1838.

Geological range: Upper Jurassic to recent.

Geographical distribution: Europe.

Features: Small to middle-sized sharks. Body somewhat dorsoventrally flattened. The rounded pectoral fins smaller than in *Palaeocarcharias*. Snout blunt. Caudal fin with large lower lobe and small upper one.

Remarks: This genus has recently been taken as doubtful and assigned to *Phorcynis*.

Recent relatives: Supposed to be closely related to the recent nurse shark *Orectolobus*.

Orectolobus wardi, a recent nurse shark.

CHONDRICHTHYES — Cartilaginous Fishes
Order: Galeiformes — Suborder: Orectoloboidei
Family: Orectolobidae — Nurse Sharks

Palaeocarcharias stromeri BEAUMONT (length c. 86 cm) from the Upper Jurassic of Solnhofen (Eichstätt), Bavaria, Germany. Original: Jura-Museum, Eichstätt, Germany.

Genus: *Palaeocarcharias* de BEAUMONT, 1960.

Geological range: Upper Jurassic.

Geographical distribution: Europe.

Features: Middle-sized sharks. Spindle-shaped bodies. Head short and rounded. Mouth almost terminal. Large triangular pectoral fins. Both dorsal fins and anal fin very posterior in position. Caudal fin long with rounded end. Teeth with broad bases, elongate and S-shaped if viewed from side.

Remarks: Predatory fishes.

Recent relatives: Genus extinct. Closely related to the recent nurse sharks of the family Orectolobidae which have 11 genera and about 28 species in recent seas.

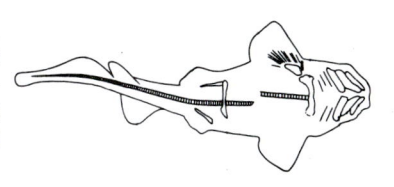

Palaeocarcharias, reconstruction after BEAUMONT.

CHONDRICHTHYES — Cartilaginous Fishes
Order: Galeiformes
Family: Orectolobidae
Suborder: Orectoloboidei
Nurse Sharks

Phorcynis catulina Thiollière from the Upper Jurassic of Cerin, France. Original: Musée Guimet d'Histoire Naturelle, Lyon, France.

Genus: *Phorcynis* Thiollière, 1854.

Synonyms: *Crossorhinus, Crossorhinops, Palaeocrossorhinus.*

Geological range: Upper Jurassic.

Geographical distribution: Europe.

Features: Small sharks with broad rounded pectoral fins and two dorsal fins. Pelvic fin obliquely opposite posterior dorsal fin and near to the pectoral fins. Head deep and with a short snout. Teeth small and asymmetrical. Maximum length c. 40 cm.

Remarks: The placing of this genus in the Orectolobidae is disputed.

Recent relatives: Genus extinct. Supposedly related to the recent nurse sharks.

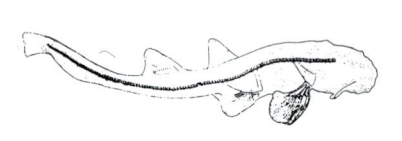

Phorcynis, reconstruction after Saint-Seine.

CHONDRICHTHYES
Order: Galeiformes
Family: Hemiscilliidae

Cartilaginous Fishes
Suborder: Orectoloboidei

Mesiteia emiliae KRAMBERGER (length c. 27 cm) from the Upper Cretaceous of the Lebanon. Original: Henne Collection, Stuttgart, Germany.

Genus: *Mesiteia* KRAMBERGER, 1885.

Geological range: Upper Cretaceous.

Geographical distribution: Middle East.

Features: Small sharks with elongate slender bodies. Head short and deep. Nose pointed. Two well developed dorsal fins in posterior half of body, the first lying obliquely opposite ventral fins. Pectoral fins rounded. Anal fin fin-fold-like, beginning opposite the first dorsal fin and continuing to end of second dorsal fin. Caudal fin similarly developed as a fin-fold on both sides. Anterior teeth narrow with two lateral cusps. More posterior teeth asymmetrical.

Remarks: Small sharks which probably lived near the bottom but could swim well.

Recent relatives: None. Extinct in the Upper Cretaceous.

CHONDRICHTHYES
Order: Galeiformes
Family: Otodontidae

Cartilaginous Fishes
Suborder: Lamnoidei

Carcharocles megalodon (AGASSIZ) from the Miocene. Original: Transvaal Museum, Pretoria, South Africa.

Genus: *Carcharocles* JORDAN & HANNIBAL, 1920.

Synonyms: *Carcharodon*, *Megaselachus*, *Procarcharodon*.

Geological range: Middle Eocene to Pliocene.

Geographical distribution: Europe, Africa, Australia, North America, southern Asia, South America, Indonesia, New Zealand.

Features: Known only from huge teeth which reach lengths of up to 15 cm. The crown is triangular, broad and high with finely serrate cutting edges.

Remarks: Judging by the teeth, *Carcharocles megalodon* may have reached a length of 30 m.

Recent relatives: None. Died out in the Pliocene.

CHONDRICHTHYES
Cartilaginous Fishes
Order: Galeiformes
Family: Mitsukurinidae
Suborder: Lamnoidei

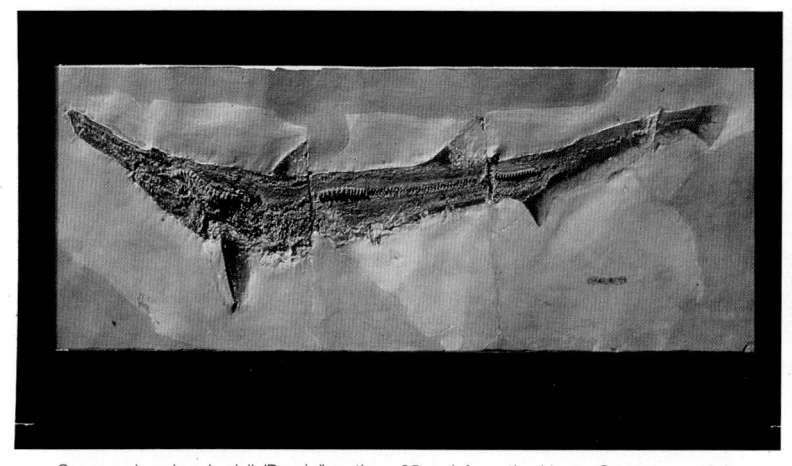

Scapanorhynchus lewisii (Davis) (length c. 65 cm) from the Upper Cretaceous of the Lebanon. Original: Muséum National d'Histoire Naturelle, Paris, France. Photograph: Serette, Paris.

Genus: *Scapanorhynchus lewisii* Woodward, 1889.

Geological range: Lower Cretaceous to Recent.

Geographical distribution: Europe, southwestern Asia, Australia, New Zealand, Africa, South America.

Features: Middle-sized sharks of slender shape. Snout greatly elongated. Mouth ventral. Dorsal fins triangular and relatively small. Caudal fin very long. Pectoral fins narrow and pointed. Pelvic fins small and angular. Anal fin elongate.

Remarks: Predatory fishes.

Recent relatives: Closely related to the recent goblin shark *Scapanorhynchus* (=*Mitsukurina*) which occurs as a great rarity in northern seas.

Scapanorhynchus, reconstruction after Macmillan.

CHONDRICHTHYES
Cartilaginous Fishes
Order: Galeiformes
Family: Anacoracidae
Suborder: Lamnoidei

Squalicorax sp. (length c. 188 cm) from the Upper Cretaceous of Kansas, U.S.A. Original: National Museum of Natural History, Smithsonian Institution, Washington, D.C., U.S.A.

Genus: *Squalicorax* WHITLEY, 1939.

Synonyms: *Anacorax*, *Corax*, *Xenolamia*.

Geological range: Upper Cretaceous to Paleocene.

Geographical distribution: Europe, North America.

Features: Large sharks. Snout pointed. Pectoral fins triangular. Teeth small or large according to species. Asymmetrically triangular. Cutting edges strongly serrated.

Remarks: Predatory fishes.

Recent relatives: None. Died out in Paleocene.

CHONDRICHTHYES — Cartilaginous Fishes
Order: Galeiformes
Family: Scyliorhinidae
Suborder: Carcharhinoidei
Cat Sharks

Macrourogaleus hassei (WOODWARD) (length c. 12 cm) from the Upper Jurassic of Solnhofen (Eichstätt), Bavaria, Germany. Original: Bayerische Staatssammlung für Paläontologie, Munich, Germany.

Genus: *Macrourogaleus* FOWLER, 1947.

Synonyms: *Pristiurus*

Geological range: Upper Jurassic.

Geographical distribution: Europe.

Features: Very small representatives of the cat shark family which at present are only known to a length of about 12 cm. The head is long and blunt-ended. Probably two dorsal fins, the second one located far posteriorly, almost at beginning of caudal fin. Anal fin relatively long. Well developed caudal fin takes up almost one-third of the length of fish. Teeth unknown.

Remarks: Probably the oldest and most primitive representative of the cat sharks.

Recent relatives: Possibly related to the recent cat sharks of the family Scyliorhinidae.

CHONDRICHTHYES   Cartilaginous Fishes
Order: Galeiformes   Suborder: Carcharhinoidei
Family: Scyliorhinidae   Cat Sharks

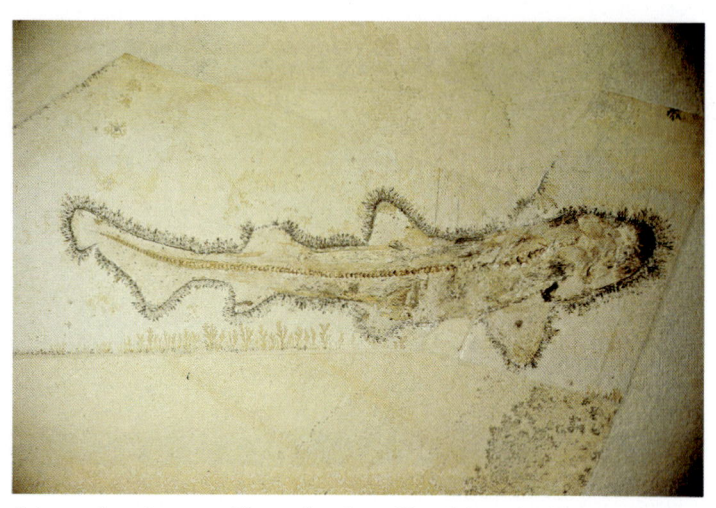

Palaeoscyllium formosum WAGNER (length c. 60 cm) from the Upper Jurassic of Solnhofen (Eichstätt), Bavaria, Germany. Original: Perner Collection, Bad Homburg, Germany.

Genus: *Palaeoscyllium* von der MARCK, 1860.

Geological range: Upper Jurassic to Upper Cretaceous.

Geographical distribution: Europe.

Features: Small slim sharks. Two triangular dorsal fins. Caudal fin elongate with the upper lobe larger. Mouth small. Teeth small, rather wide. Cutting edges not serrated.

Remarks: Like recent cat sharks, they may have fed mainly on bivalves and crustacea.

Recent relatives: Genus extinct. Distantly related to recent cat sharks of family Scylliorhinidae which are represented in modern seas by 17 genera and 86 species.

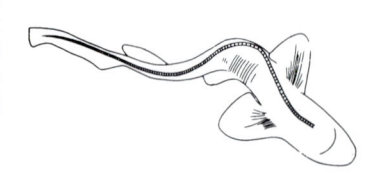

Palaeoscyllium, reconstruction after von der MARCK.

CHONDRICHTHYES
Order: Galeiformes
Family: Scyliorhinidae

Cartilaginous Fishes
Suborder: Carcharhinoidei
Cat Sharks

Scyliorhinus elongatus (DAVIS) (length c. 23 cm) from the Upper Cretaceous of the Lebanon. Original: Royal Museum of Scotland, Edinburgh, Scotland.

Genus: *Scyliorhingus* de BLAINVILLE, 1825.

Synonyms: *Scyllium*, *Thyellina*.

Geological range: Upper Cretaceous to recent.

Geographical distribution: Middle East, Africa, Europe.

Features: Small sharks. Body slim and elongate. Pectoral fins rounded. Two dorsal fins behind the middle of the body. Caudal fin long and narrow. Pelvic fins roughly in the middle of the body. Head long. Teeth pointed. Cutting edges not serrated.

Remarks: May have fed, like recent cat sharks, on crustacea, gastropods and bivalves.

Recent relatives: Closely related to the recent cat shark *Scyliorhinus*.

Scyliorhinus stellaris, a recent cat shark.

CHONDRICHTHYES — Cartilaginous Fishes
Order: Galeiformes
Family: Scyliorhinidae?
Suborder: Carcharhinoidei
Cat Sharks

Unknown shark (length c. 87 cm) from the Upper Cretaceous of the Lebanon. Original: Staatliches Museum für Naturkunde, Karlsruhe, Germany.

Genus: Unnamed.

Geological range: Upper Cretaceous.

Geographical distribution: Middle East.

Features: This middle-sized shark may perhaps represent a still-undescribed genus. Form slender. Head long. Two triangular dorsal fins. Caudal fin with a short lower lobe. Teeth small and pointed with two lateral cusps.

Remarks: Judging by its shape, this fish may have hunted free-swimming prey.

Recent relatives: Distantly, or perhaps even closely, related to the recent cat sharks of the family Scyliorhinidae which is represented in recent seas by 17 genera and about 86 species.

CHONDRICHTHYES
Order: Galeiformes
Family: Carcharhinidae

Cartilaginous Fishes
Suborder: Carcharhinoidei
Dog Sharks

Eogaleus bolcensis CAPETTA (length c. 110 cm) from the Eocene of Bolca, Italy. Original: Museo Civico di Storia Naturale, Verona, Italy.

Genus: *Eogaleus* CAPETTA, 1975.

Geological range: Middle Eocene.

Geographical distribution: Europe.

Features: Middle-sized shark with streamlined body. Head broad. Eyes small. Snout rounded. Mouth somewhat ventral. Gape long. Two pointed dorsal fins in the posterior third of the body. Caudal fin probably with the upper lobe larger. Pectoral fins long and pointed.

Remarks: Bottom-dwelling predatory fishes.

Recent relatives: Genus extinct. Possibly related to the recent cat sharks of the genus *Galeus*.

Galeus sp., a recent dog shark. Lithograph from COUGH.

185

CHONDRICHTHYES
Order: Galeiformes
Family: Triakidae

Cartilaginous Fishes
Suborder: Carcharhinoidei
Hound Sharks

Galeorhinus cuvieri (Agassiz) (length c. 78 cm) from the Middle Eocene of Bolca, Italy. Original: Museo Civico di Storia Naturale, Verona, Italy.

Genus: *Galeorhinus* de Blainville & Prevost, 1818.

Geological range: Upper Cretaceous to Recent.

Geographical distribution: Europe, northern Africa, northern Asia.

Features: Middle-sized slender sharks. Head long. Pectoral fins long and pointed. Two small dorsal fins. Long caudal fin with the upper lobe larger than the lower. Teeth short with the points directed rearwards. Lower part of posterior cutting edge coarsely serrated.

Remarks: Rapidly swimming predatory fishes.

Recent relatives: Closely related to recent representatives of the genus *Galeorhinus*.

Galeorhinus, reconstruction after Capetta.

CHONDRICHTHYES
Order: Galeiformes
Family: Triakidae

Cartilaginous Fishes
Suborder: Carcharhinoidei
Hound Sharks

Paratriakis curtirostris (DAVIS) (length c. 29 cm) from the Upper Cretaceous of the Lebanon. Original: The Natural History Museum, London, U.K.(P4022).

Genus: *Paratriakis* HERMAN, 1977.

Geological range: Upper Cretaceous.

Geographical distribution: Europe, Middle East.

Features: Small slender sharks. Head long. Snout somewhat pointed. Pectoral fins large, triangular. Caudal fin long, probably curved upward. Teeth small and pointed with the points directed rearwards. Cutting edges not serrated.

Remarks: Little predatory fishes which may mainly have fed on crustacea and other small organisms.

Recent relatives: Genus extinct. Closely related to the recent smooth dogfish *Triakis*.

Triakis semifasciatus, a recent smooth dogfish.

CHONDRICHTHYES
Cartilaginous Fishes
Order: Galeiformes
Family: Triakidae

Suborder: Hexanchoidei
Sand Sharks

Hexanchus gracilis (DAVIS) (length c. 29 cm) from the Upper Cretaceous of the Lebanon. Original: National Museum of Scotland, Edinburgh, U.K.

Genus: *Hexanchus* RAFINESQUE, 1810.

Synonyms: *Notidanus*.

Geological range: Upper Jurassic to recent.

Geographical distribution: Middle East, Australia, Europe.

Features: Small to middle-sized sharks with relatively short rounded head. One dorsal fin, located posteriorly. Caudal fin long with upper lobe larger than the lower. Teeth broad with one large cusp and five small ones directed rearwards.

Remarks: Rapidly swimming predators.

Recent relatives: Closely related to recent cow sharks of the genus *Hexanchus*. The family is represented by three genera and four species in recent seas.

Hexanchus griseus, the recent sand shark.

CHONDRICHTHYES — Cartilaginous Fishes
Order: Galeiformes?
Family: Unnamed

Unnamed shark (length c. 67 cm) from the Lower Jurassic of Holzmaden, Württemberg, Germany. Original: Staatliches Museum für Naturkunde, Stuttgart, Germany.

Genus: Not named.

Geological range: Lower Jurassic.

Geographical distribution: Europe.

Features: Middle-sized fishes with a slender body. Head long and shallow passing into a rostrum broad at the base and tapering forward. Eyes small. Two short but powerful spines dorsally, each supporting a dorsal fin. Vertebral column calcified.

Remarks: Systematic position uncertain. A rostrum is unusual in a shark from the Lower Jurassic. The calcified vertebral column shows that it belongs to the modern sharks (Neoselachii).

Recent relatives: None. Died out in Lower Jurassic.

CHONDRICHTHYES — Cartilaginous Fishes

Order: Squaliformes
Family: Squalidae

Suborder: Squaloidei
Spiny Dogfishes

Centrophoroides latidens DAVIS (length c. 37 cm) from the Upper Cretaceous of the Lebanon. Original: The Natural History Museum, London, U.K. (P4021).

Genus: *Centrophoroides* DAVIS, 1887.

Geological range: Upper Cretaceous.

Geographical distribution: Middle East.

Features: Slender sharks with pointed snout. Two dorsal fins. The first is supported by a powerful spine which projects above the fin. The second small dorsal fin is associated with a spine whose length is at most one-third of the height of the fin. Pectoral fins large and triangular. Caudal fin relatively short. Teeth broad with a short cusp directed rearwards.

Remarks: Predatory fishes that fed not only on smaller fishes but perhaps also, or even mainly, on crustaceans and other invertebrates.

Recent relatives: Genus extinct. Distantly related to recent dogfishes of the family Squalidae.

Squalus sp., a recent spiny dogfish. Lithograph from CUVIER.

CHONDRICHTHYES
Order: Squaliformes
Family: Squalidae

Cartilaginous Fishes
Suborder: Squaloidei
Spiny Dogfishes

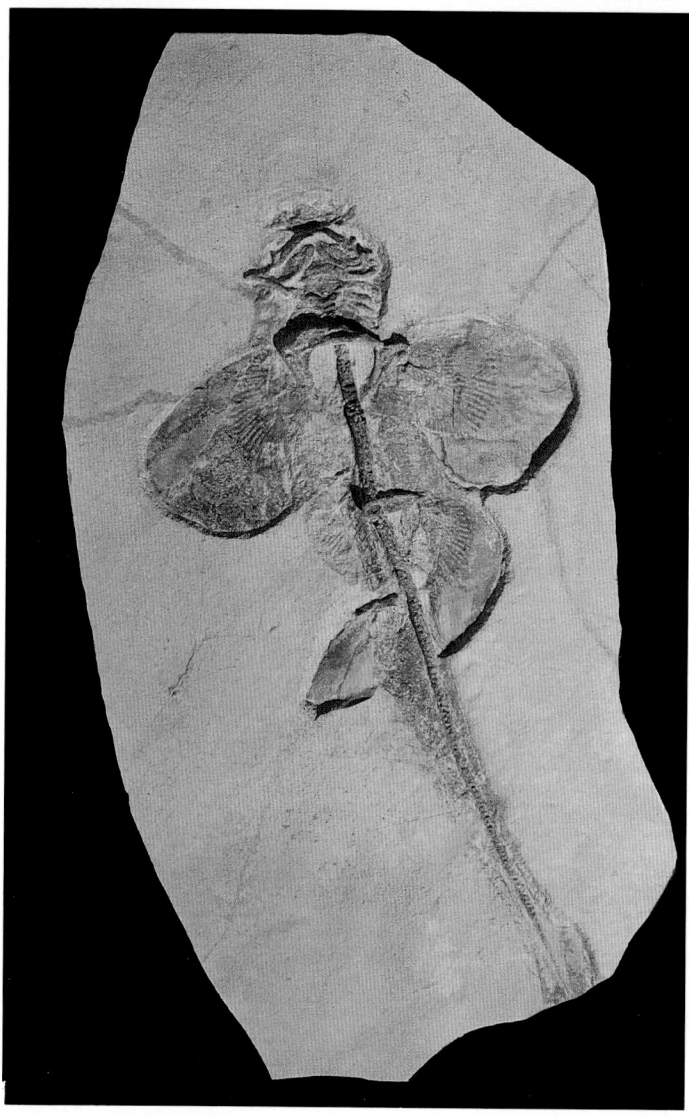

Protospinax annectens WOODWARD (length c. 146 cm) from the Upper Jurassic of Solnhofen (Eichstätt), Bavaria, Germany. Original: Bayerische Staatssammlung für Paläontologie, Munich, Germany.

CHONDRICHTHYES
Cartilaginous Fishes
Order: Squaliformes
Family: Squalidae
Suborder: Squaloidei
Spiny Dogfishes

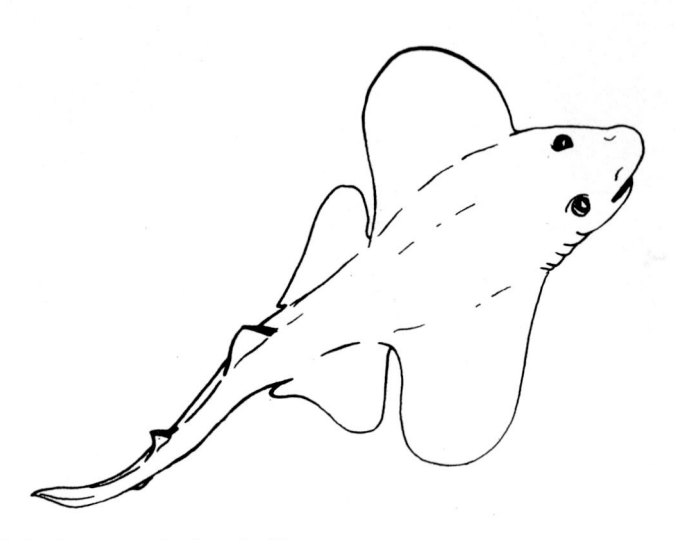

Protospinax, reconstruction after WOODWARD.

Genus: *Protospinax* WOODWARD, 1919.

Geological range: Upper Jurassic.

Geographical distribution: Europe.

Features: Middle-sized sharks with a dorso-ventrally flattened body. Head rounded. Gill slits latero-ventral. Very large pectoral fins. Pelvic fins also relatively large. Two small dorsal fins, each supported by a short spine. Caudal fin small and tapering to a point. Teeth broad and more or less flat.

Remarks: Probably more bottom-dwelling than free-swimming. Dentition suggests that they preferred shelly food.

Recent relatives: Genus extinct. Distantly related to recent dogfishes of the family Squalidae which are represented by 18 genera and 71 species in modern oceans.

CHONDRICHTHYES — Cartilaginous Fishes
Order: Squaliformes
Family: Squatinidae
Suborder: Squatinoidei
Angel Sharks

Pseudorhina alifera (Münster) (length c. 96 cm) from the Upper Jurassic of Solnhofen (Eichstätt), Bavaria, Germany. Original: Interfoss, Munich, Germany.

CHONDRICHTHYES — Cartilaginous Fishes

Order: Squaliformes
Family: Squatinidae
Suborder: Squatinoidei
Angel Sharks

Squatina australis, a recent angel shark.

Genus: *Pseudorhina* Jaekel, 1898.

Synonyms: *Squatina*, *Rhina*, *Thaumas*, *Trigenodus*.

Geological range: Upper Jurassic to Pleistocene.

Geographical distribution: Europe, Middle East, northern Africa, Australia.

Features: Middle-sized ray-like sharks. Head rounded. Gill slits lateral. Mouth ventral but at front end of head. Pectoral and pelvic fins large. Two small dorsal fins situated at narrow end of tail. Caudal fin small. Teeth broader than tall.

Remarks: Bottom-dwelling sharks.

Recent relatives: Genus extinct. Closely related to the angel sharks of the genus *Squatina* which is represented by 11 species in modern seas.

CHONDRICHTHYES
Order: Rajiformes
Family: Rhinobatidae

Cartilaginous Fishes
Suborder: Rhinobatoidei
Guitarfishes

Aellopos bugesiacus THIOLLIÉRE (length c. 110 cm) from the Upper Jurassic of Solnhofen (Eichstätt), Bavaria, Germany. Original: Museum Berger, Harthof bei Eichstätt, Germany.

Genus: *Aellopos* MÜNSTER, 1836.

Synonyms: *Euryarthra*, *Spathobatis*.

Geological range: Upper Jurassic.

Geographical distribution: Europe.

Features: Primitive rays, still somewhat like sharks in shape. Dorso-ventral body flattening is extreme only towards the pectoral fins. The latter are fused with the sides of the head and the mouth and gill slits are ventral, all of which are true ray characteristics. The long snout is a striking feature. Males with rod-like appendages on the pelvic fins. Teeth small, round and present in large numbers.

Remarks: Bottom-dwellers with durophagous diet.

Recent relatives: Genus extinct. Distantly related to recent guitarfishes of the family Rhinobatidae.

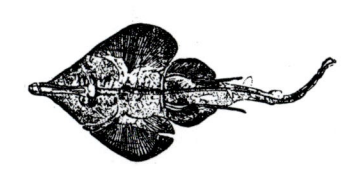

Aellopos, reconstruction after WOODWARD.

195

CHONDRICHTHYES
Order: Rajiformes
Family: Rhinobatidae

Cartilaginous Fishes
Suborder: Rhinobatoidei
Guitarfishes

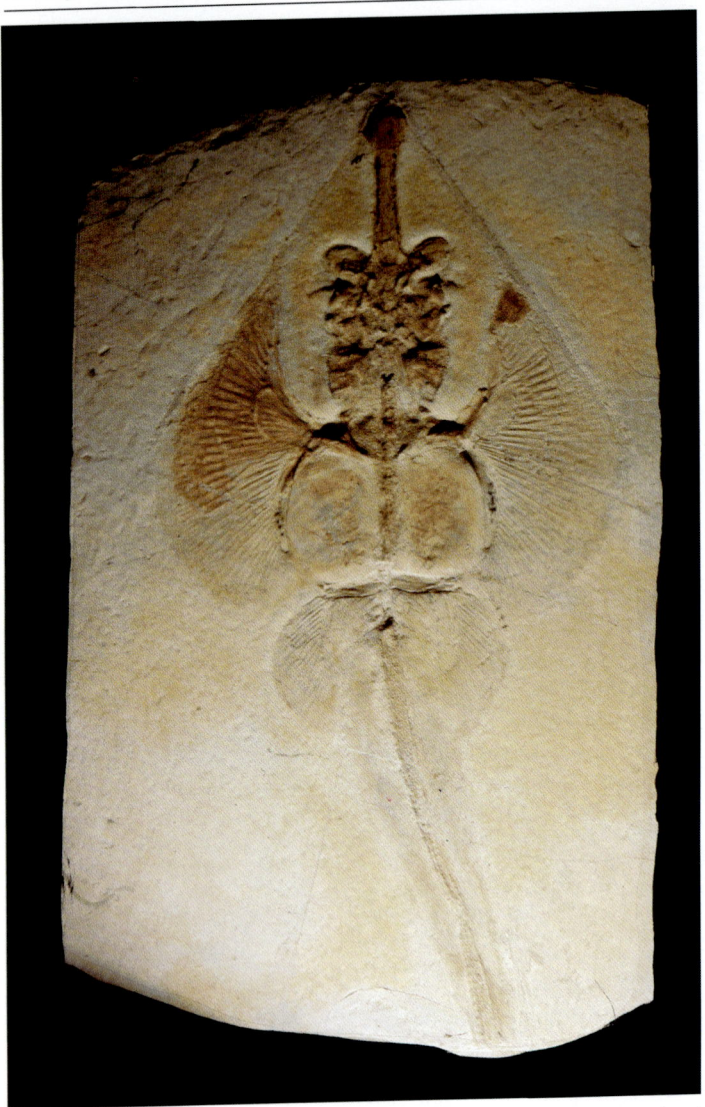

Asterodemus platypterus AGASSIZ (length c. 46 cm) from the Upper Jurassic of Solnhofen (Eichstätt), Bavaria, Germany. Original: Jura-Museum, Eichstätt.

CHONDRICHTHYES
Order: Rajiformes
Family: Rhinobatidae

Cartilaginous Fishes
Suborder: Rhinobatoidei
Guitarfishes

Aptychotrema vincentiana, a recent guitarfish.

Genus: *Asterodemus* AGASSIZ, 1843.

Geological range: Upper Jurassic.

Geographical distribution: Europe.

Features: Middle-sized rays. Like *Aellopos* but without the long snout. Pectoral fins broad. Pelvic fins rounded. Dorsal fins each with a small spine. Body not deep. Tail thin, with a small caudal fin. Skin covered with scales which carry star-shaped dermal denticles. Teeth not known.

Remarks: Bottom-dwellers.

Recent relatives: Genus extinct. Distantly related to recent guitarfishes of the family Rhinobatidae.

CHONDRICHTHYES — Cartilaginous Fishes
Order: Rajiformes
Suborder: Rhinobatoidei
Family: Rhinobatidae
Guitarfishes

Belemnobatis sismondae Thiollière (length c. 40 cm) from the Upper Jurassic of Cerin, France. Original: Naturhistoriska Riksmuseet, Stockholm, Sweden.

Genus: *Belemnobatis* Thiollière, 1854.

Geological range: Upper Jurassic.

Geographical distribution: Europe.

Features: Middle-sized rays. Disc wider than long. Pelvic fins long and rounded. Dorsal fins large, close together and with a protection of thorns. Tail (behind pelvic fins) shorter than rest of animal. Teeth wide with sharp crest.

Remarks: Bottom-dwellers.

Recent relatives: Genus extinct. Distantly related to recent guitarfishes of the family Rhinobatidae.

CHONDRICHTHYES — Cartilaginous Fishes
Order: Rajiformes
Family: Rhinobatidae
Suborder: Rhinobatoidei
Guitarfishes

Rhinobatos hakelensis CAPETTA (length c. 28 cm) from the Upper Cretaceous of the Lebanon. Original: Staatliches Museum für Naturkunde, Stuttgart, Germany.

CHONDRICHTHYES
Order: Rajiformes
Family: Rhinobatidae

Cartilaginous Fishes
Suborder: Rhinobatoidei
Guitarfishes

Rhinobatos granulatus, a recent guitarfish.

Genus: *Rhinobatos* LINCK, 1790.

Synonyms: *Rhinobatus*.

Geological range: Lower Cretaceous to recent.

Geographical distribution: Europe, northern Africa, Middle East.

Features: Middle-sized rays. Rostrum pointed. Dorsal fins located very posteriorly. Caudal fin lacks lower lobe. Skin covered with seed-like placoid scales. Teeth small, each with two lateral extensions, forming a pavement. Maximum length 2 m or more.

Remarks: Durophagous bottom-dweller.

Recent relatives: Closely related to recent members of the genus *Rhinobatos* of the family Rhinobatidae. The latter is represented in recent seas by seven genera and 45 species.

CHONDRICHTHYES — Cartilaginous Fishes
Order: Rajiformes
Suborder: Rhinobatoidei
Family: Rhinobatidae
Guitarfishes

Rhombopterygia rajoides CAPETTA (length c. 42 cm) from the Upper Cretaceous of the Lebanon. Original: Interfoss, Munich, Germany.

Genus: *Rhombopterygia* CAPETTA, 1980.

Geological range: Upper Cretaceous.

Geographical distribution: Middle East.

Features: Small rays. Disc quadrilateral. Only slightly broader than long. Tail about as long as disc. Nasal capsule elliptical. Teeth with a stout crown.

Remarks: Durophagous bottom-dweller.

Recent relatives: Genus extinct. Distantly related to recent guitarfishes of the family Rhinobatidae.

CHONDRICHTHYES
Order: Rajiformes
Family: Rhinobatidae

Cartilaginous Fishes
Suborder: Rhinobatoidei
Guitarfishes

Trigonorhina dezignii HECKEL (length c. 79 cm) from the Middle Eocene of Monte Bolca, Italy. Original: Naturhistorisches Museum, Vienna, Austria

Genus: *Trigonorhina* MÜLLER & HENLE, 1838.

Geological range: Eocene to recent.

Geographical distribution: Europe.

Features: Middle-sized rays. Disc oval, pointed anteriorly. Tail very powerful at base but pointed posteriorly, somewhat longer than the disc.

Remarks: Bottom-dwellers but probably also free-swimming.

Recent relatives: Closely related to recent members of the genus *Trigonorhina*.

Trigonorhina fasciata, a recent ray after WAITE.

CHONDRICHTHYES
Order: Rajiformes
Family: Rhinobatidae

Cartilaginous Fishes
Suborder: Rhinobatoidei
Guitarfishe

Zapteryx bichuti Sig (length c. 47 cm) from the Eocene of St. Vaas les Mello, Oise, France. Original: Muséum National d'Histoire Naturelle, Paris, France. Photograph: Serette, Paris.

Genus: *Zapteryx* Jordan & Gilbert, 1880.

Geological range: Eocene to recent.

Geographical distribution: Europe.

Features: Middle-sized relatively primitive rays with a short pointed rostrum. Disc almost circular. Pelvic fins small and rounded. Tail relatively short. No spines. Probably two dorsal fins.

Remarks: Bottom-dwelling.

Recent relatives: Closely related to recent members of the genus *Zapteryx*.

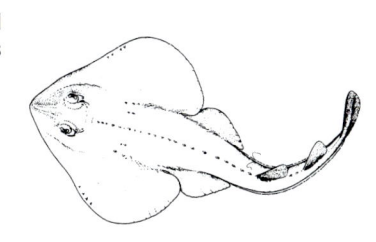

Zapteryx brevirostris, a recent ray after Bigelow.

CHONDRICHTHYES — Cartilaginous Fishes
Order: Rajiformes
Family: Platyrhinidae
Suborder: Rhinobatoidei

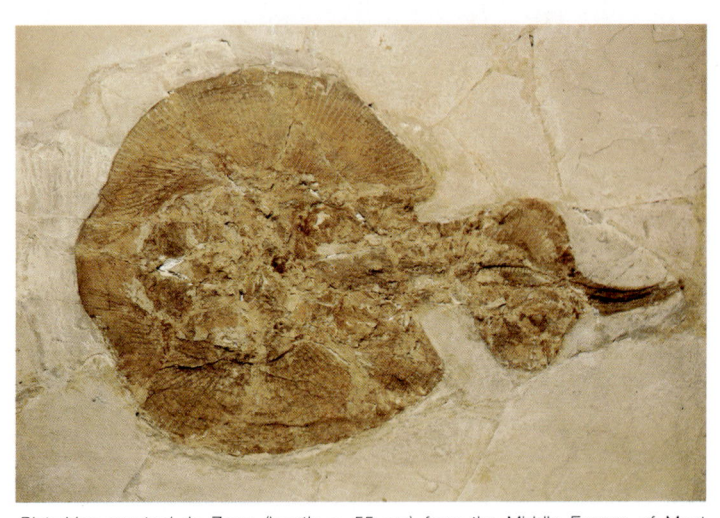

Platyrhina egertoni de Zigno (length c. 55 cm) from the Middle Eocene of Mont Bolca, Italy. Original: Museo Civica di Storia Naturale, Verona, Italy.

Genus: *Platyrhina* Müller & Henle, 1838.

Geological range: Eocene to recent.

Geographical distribution: Europe.

Features: Middle-sized rays. Disc large and round. Tail short, at most half as long as the disc. Two dorsal fins. Caudal fin small. Teeth unknown.

Remarks: Durophagous bottom-dweller.

Recent relatives: Closely related to recent members of the genus *Platyrhina*.

Platyrhina schoenleinii, a recent platyrhinid guitarfish.

CHONDRICHTHYES
Order: Rajiformes
Family: Rajidae

Cartilaginous Fishes
Suborder: Rajoidei
True Rays and Skates

Pararaja expansa (DAVIS) (c. 23 ∞ 23 cm) from the Upper Cretaceous of the Lebanon. Original: Siber & Siber Collection, Aathal, Switzerland.

Genus: *Pararaja* CAPETTA, 1980.

Geological range: Upper Cretaceous.

Geographical distribution: Middle East.

Features: Small skates. Disc broader than long. Tail shorter than disc. In males the pterygopodia (sexual appendages) almost as long as tail. Teeth small with flat crowns.

Remarks: Bottom-dwelling and free-swimming.

Recent relatives: Distant relatives of the recent skates (family Rajidae) which are represented in the oceans by 14 genera and about 190 species.

Raja batis, the recent common skate. Lithograph from BLOCH.

CHONDRICHTHYES — Cartilaginous Fishes
Order: Rajiformes
Family: Cyclobatidae
Suborder: Rajoidei

Cyclobatis major Davis (length c. 13 cm) from the Upper Cretaceous of the Lebanon. Original: Frickhinger Collection, Munich, Germany.

Genus: *Cyclobatis* Egerton, 1844.

Geological range: Lower Cretaceous.

Geographical distribution: Middle East.

Features: Little skates with a circular disc. Tail of medium length to very short, carrying two or three rows of angular spines. In dorsal aspect the pelvic fins completely covered by pectoral fins. No dorsal fins on the tail. Numerous very small teeth.

Remarks: Durophagous bottom-dwellers.

Recent relatives: Genus extinct. Perhaps distantly related to the skates (Rajidae).

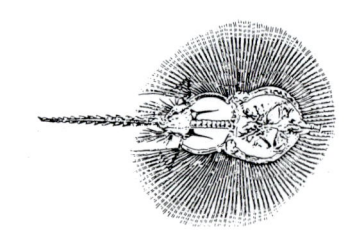

Cyclobatis, reconstruction after Arambourg & Bertin.

CHONDRICHTHYES
Cartilaginous Fishes
Order: Rajiformes
Family: Sclerorhynchidae
Suborder: Sclerorhynchoidei

Micropristis solomonis (HAY) (length c. 53 cm) from the Upper Cretaceous of the Lebanon. Original: Staatliches Museum für Naturkunde, Stuttgart, Germany.

Genus: *Micropristis* CAPETTA, 1980.

Geological range: Upper Cretaceous.

Geographical distribution: Middle East.

Features: Rostrum relatively short and blunt, carrying small teeth at the sides. Pectoral fins small, extending back to the pelvic fins. Tail broad at base but ending in a point. The anterior teeth are pointed and about 2.5 mm high while the posterior teeth are blunt.

Remarks: Probably bottom-dwelling and free-swimming.

Recent relatives: None. Died out in the Upper Cretaceous.

CHONDRICHTHYES — Cartilaginous Fishes
Order: Rajiformes
Family: Sclerorhynchidae
Suborder: Sclerorhynchoidei

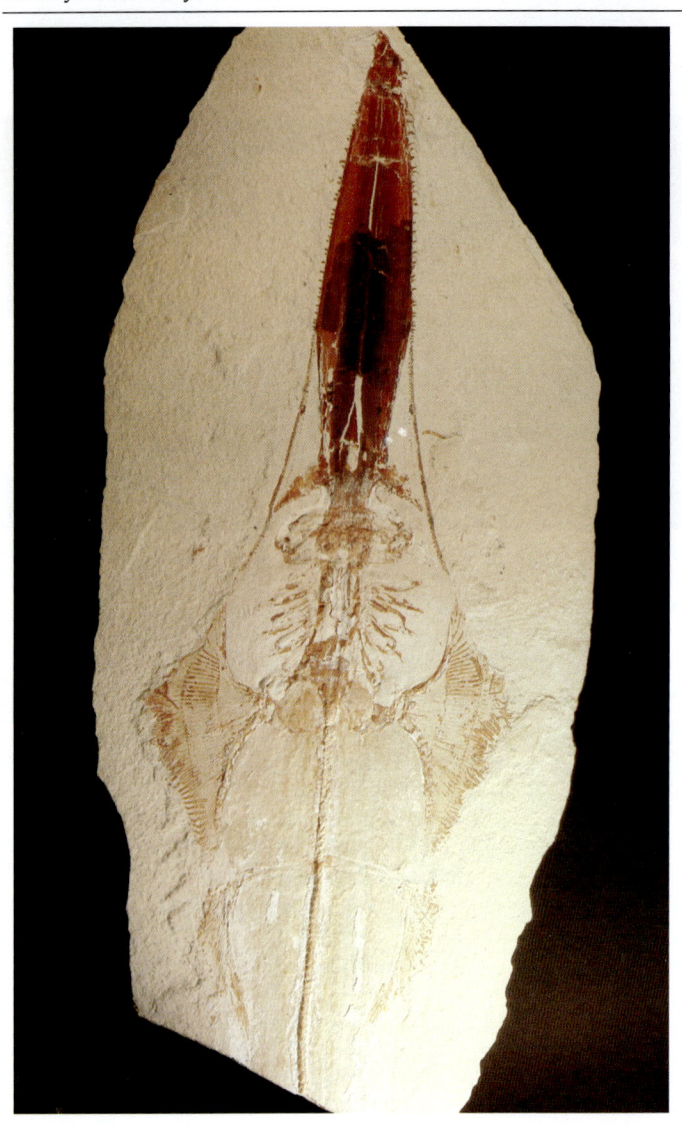

Sclerorhynchus atavus Woodward (length c. 68 cm) from the Upper Cretaceous of the Lebanon. Original: Staatliches Museum für Naturkunde, Karlsruhe, Germany.

CHONDRICHTHYES
Cartilaginous Fishes
Order: Rajiformes
Family: Sclerorhynchidae
Suborder: Sclerorhynchoidei

Sclerorhynchus, reconstruction after MACMILLAN.

Genus: *Sclerorhynchus* WOODWARD, 1889.

Synonym: *Ganopristis*

Geological range: Upper Cretaceous to Paleocene.

Geographical distribution: Europe, Africa, Middle East.

Features: Maximum length c. 1 m. Rostrum narrow and blunt anteriorly, with numerous small teeth at the sides. Pectoral fins not especially large and extending back to the pelvic fins. Tail broad at base but ending in a point. Two dorsal fins, close together. Anterior teeth pointed, becoming blunter posteriorly.

Remarks: Bottom-dwelling and free-swimming.

Recent relatives: None. Died out in Paleocene.

CHONDRICHTHYES — Cartilaginous Fishes
Order: Rajiformes
Family: Torpedinidae
Suborder: Torpedinoidei
Electric Rays

Torpedo sp.? (length c. 38 cm) from the Eocene of Bolca, Italy. Original: Museum für Naturkunde, Berlin, Germany.

Genus: *Torpedo* HOUTTUYN, 1764.

Synonym: *Narcobatus*

Geological range: Middle Eocene to recent.

Geographical distribution: Europe.

Features: Middle-sized fishes with strongly disc-shaped, anteriorly rounded bodies. Eyes small. Mouth ventral. Tail round in transverse section and relatively short. Two dorsal fins. Pectoral fins do not extend to the anterior end of the head. Skin naked. Teeth probably small.

Remarks: Bottom-dwelling genus with a predatory mode of life. Whether they already had an electric organ between the head and the pectoral fins is not established.

Recent relatives: Probably related to recent electric rays of the genus *Torpedo* which is represented by 13 species in modern seas.

Torpedo sp., a recent electric ray.

CHONDRICHTHYES
Cartilaginous Fishes
Order: Rajiformes
Family: Narcinidae
Suborder: Torpedinoidei

Narcine molini JAEKEL (length c. 90 cm) from the Middle Eocene of Bolca, Italy. Original: Università di Padova, Padua, Italy. Photograph: Università di Padova.

Genus: *Narcine* HENLE, 1834.

Geological range: Lower Eocene to recent.

Geographical distribution: Europe, northern and western Africa.

Features: Disc elongated. Well developed pelvic fins. Tail about as long as the rest of the body. One dorsal fin, approximately in middle of tail. Caudal fin narrow. Maximum length c. 1 m.

Remarks: Durophagous bottom-dweller.

Recent relatives: Closely related to the recent electric ray *Narcine*.

Narcine brunez, a recent electric ray.

211

CHONDRICHTHYES — Cartilaginous Fishes
Order: Rajiformes
Family: Dasyatidae
Suborder: Myliobatoidei
Stingrays

Heliobatis radians MARSH (length c. 40 cm) from the Eocene of Wyoming, U.S.A. Original: Frickhinger Collection, Munich, Germany.

CHONDRICHTHYES
Order: Rajiformes
Family: Dasyatidae

Cartilaginous Fishes
Suborder: Myliobatoidei
Stingrays

Dasyatis sp., a recent stingray. Lithograph from Cough.

Genus: *Heliobatis* Marsh, 1877.

Synonyms: *Dasybatis, Dasyatis, Palaeodasybatis, Xiphotrygus*.

Geological range: Upper Cretaceous to Pleistocene.

Geographical distribution: Europe, North America, northern Africa, Asia, Australia, Indonesia.

Features: Disc approximately circular. Tail very long and whip-like. Many small thorn-like spines along the dorsal mid line. No rostrum. Approximately in the middle of the tail three long, finely serrated spines. Maximum length c. 1 m.

Remarks: Inhabit fresh water.

Recent relatives: Can be seen as forerunners of the stingrays (see *Trygon*).

CHONDRICHTHYES
Order: Rajiformes
Family: Dasyatidae

Cartilaginous Fishes
Suborder: Myliobatoidei
Stingrays

Trygon muricata (VOLTA) (length c. 73 cm) from the Eocene of Bolca, Italy. Original: Museo Civico di Storia Naturale, Verona, Italy.

Genus: *Trygon* CUVIER, 1817.

Geological range: Middle Eocene.

Geographical distribution: Europe.

Features: Disc approximately circular. No rostrum. Tail long and thin. Long spine at end of tail. In dorsal aspect pelvic fins covered by the pectorals. Teeth blunt.

Remarks: Marine fishes.

Recent relatives: Can be seen as forerunners of the sting rays which are assigned to the same family (Dasyatidae) represented by five recent genera and more than 50 recent species. Most live in the sea, but some belong exclusively in fresh water.

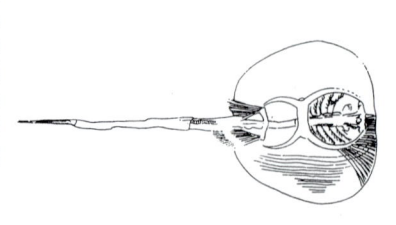

Trygon, reconstruction after JAEKEL.

CHONDRICHTHYES
Cartilaginous Fishes
Order: Rajiformes
Family: Myliobatidae
Suborder: Myliobatoidei
Eagle Rays

Promyliobatis gazolae (de Zigno) (length c. 45 cm) from the Eocene of Bolca, Italy. Original: Museo Civico di Storia Naturale, Verona, Italy.

Genus: *Promyliobatis* Jaekel, 1894.

Geological range: Middle Eocene.

Geographical distribution: Europe.

Features: Disc transversely rhombic. Pectoral fins extend to rostrum. One small dorsal fin. Teeth large, flat and hexagonal. Tail long and thin. Flat fin spine covered with denticles.

Remarks: Probably more free-swimming than bottom-dwelling.

Recent relatives: Can be seen as a forerunner of the eagle rays which, together with their closest relatives, have four genera and 24 species in recent seas.

Aetobatus sp., a recent eagle ray.

215

CHONDRICHTHYES — Cartilaginous Fishes
Order: Rajiformes
Family: Urolophidae
Suborder: Myliobatoidei
Round Rays

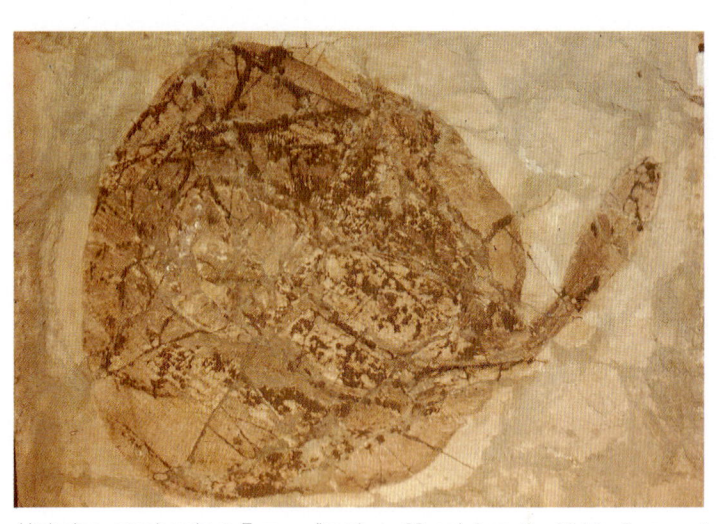

Urolophus crassicaudatus EASTMAN (length c. 80 cm) from the Middle Eocene of Bolca, Italy. Original: Museo Civico di Storia Naturale, Verona, Italy.

Genus: *Urolophus* MÜLLER & HENLE, 1838.

Geological range: Middle Eocene to recent.

Geographical distribution: Europe.

Features: Middle-sized rays. Disc circular, completely fused around the head. Eyes small. Mouth wide, situated on the lower surface. Tail stout and short. No dorsal fin. Caudal fin elongate and rounded.

Remarks: Bottom-dwelling fishes.

Recent relatives: Related to recent round rays of the genus *Urolophus*. The family Urolophidae is represented by two genera and 30 species in recent seas.

Urolophus halleri, a recent round ray.

CHONDRICHTHYES — Cartilaginous Fishes
Order: Chondrenchelyiformes
Family: Chondrenchelyidae

Chondrenchelys problematica Traquair (length c. 12 cm) from the Lower Carboniferous of Eskdale, Scotland. Original: National Museum of Scotland, Edinburgh, U.K.

Genus: *Chondrenchelys* Traquair, 1888.

Geological range: Lower Carboniferous.

Geographical distribution: Europe.

Features: Small cartilaginous fishes of elongate shape. Head elongate. Mouth slightly ventral. Eyes relatively large. Body tapers to a point posteriorly. Dorsal fin fin-fold-like, passes into the caudal fin which passes in turn into the anal fin. Pectoral fins biserial. Maximum length 15 cm.

Remarks: Probably free-swimming.

Recent relatives: None. Died out in Lower Carboniferous.

Chondrenchelys, reconstruction after Orlov.

CHONDRICHTHYES — Cartilaginous Fishes
Order: Chondrenchelyiformes
Family: Chondrenchelyidae

Harpagofututor volsellorhinus LUND (length c. 10 cm) from the Lower Carboniferous of Bear Gulch, Montana, U.S.A. Original: Carnegie Museum of Natural History, Pittsburgh, Penn., U.S.A.

Genus: *Harpagofututor* LUND, 1982.

Geological range: Lower Carboniferous.

Geographical distribution: North America.

Features: Small chondrichthyans with slender body tapering to a point posteriorly. Head elongated with a beak-like curve of the upper jaw. Mouth somewhat ventral. Dentition with strong rounded teeth. Eyes relatively large. Pectoral fins biserial. Maximum length scarcely more than 10 cm.

Remarks: Dentition suggests a durophagous diet.

Recent relatives: None. Died out in the Lower Carboniferous.

Harpagofututor, reconstruction after LUND.

CHONDRICHTHYES — Cartilaginous Fishes
Order: Iniopterygiiformes
Family: Iniopterygiidae

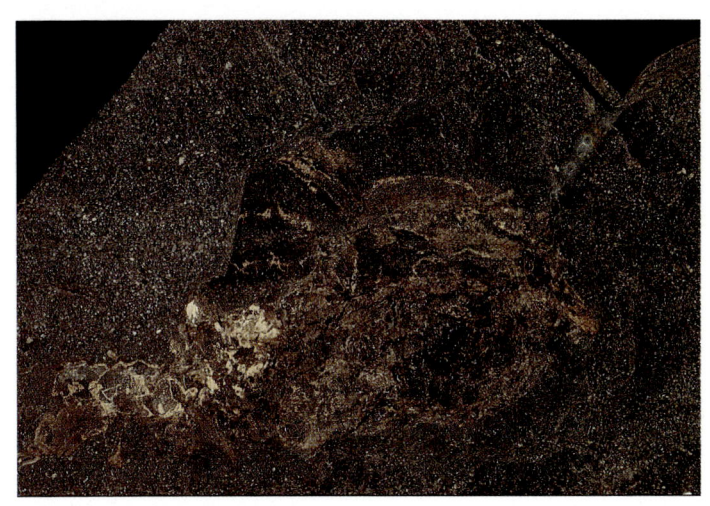

Iniopteryx rushlaui ZANGERL & CASE (length c. 24 cm) from the Upper Carboniferous of Nebraska, U.S.A. Original: American Museum of Natural History, New York, N.Y., U.S.A.

Genus: *Iniopteryx* ZANGERL & CASE, 1973.

Geological range: Upper Carboniferous.

Geographical distribution: North America.

Features: Plump middle-sized fishes. Head relatively large and massive. Nose extended somewhat anteriorly. Eyes large. Simple conical teeth. Pectoral fins small with the first fin ray elongated in males. A row of powerful spines mid-dorsally behind the head. Dorsal fin small. Caudal fin rounded. Pelvic fins with a rod-like jointed appendage (pterygopodium).

Remarks: Bottom dwellers, but probably also capable of free-swimming.

Recent relatives: None. Died out in the Upper Carboniferous.

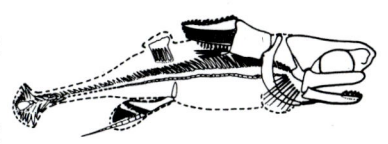

Iniopteryx, reconstruction after ZANGERL & CASE.

CHONDRICHTHYES — Cartilaginous Fishes
Order: Iniopterygiiformes
Family: Sibyrhynchidae

Iniopera richardsoni ZANGERL & CASE (length c. 24 cm) from the Upper Carboniferous of Pike County, Indiana, U.S.A. Original: Cleveland Museum of Natural History, Cleveland, Ohio, U.S.A.

Genus: *Iniopera* ZANGERL & CASE, 1973.

Geological range: Upper Carboniferous.

Geographical distribution: North America.

Features: Plump middle-sized fishes. Head small. Strong dentition of plate-like teeth. A row of pointed spines in the dorsal mid-line just behind the head. Dorsal fin small. Caudal fin probably rounded. Pelvic fin with a pointed rod-like posteriorly jointed appendage (pterygopodium).

Remarks: Bottom-dwellers, probably scarcely capable of free swimming.

Recent relatives: None. Died out in Upper Carboniferous.

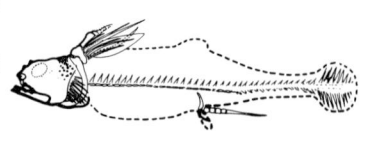

Iniopera, reconstruction after ZANGERL & CASE.

CHONDRICHTHYES — Cartilaginous Fishes
Order: **Iniopterygiiformes**
Family: **Sibyrhynchidae**

Sibirhynchus denisoni ZANGERL & CASE (length c. 20 cm) from the Upper Carboniferous of Pike County, Indiana, U.S.A. Original: Cleveland Museum of Natural History, Cleveland, Ohio, U.S.A.

Genus: *Sibirhynchus* ZANGERL & CASE, 1973.

Geological range: Upper Carboniferous.

Geographical distribution: North America.

Features: Plump middle-sized fishes. Head small. Lower jaw with a pointed anterior process. Dorsal fin small. Caudal fin probably rounded. Pectoral fins supported by spines of which the first is particularly strong and bears thorns on its upper surface. Pelvic fin small, with a rod-like jointed appendage (pterygopodium).

Remarks: Bottom dwellers, probably scarcely capable of free swimming.

Recent relatives: None. Died out in Upper Carboniferous.

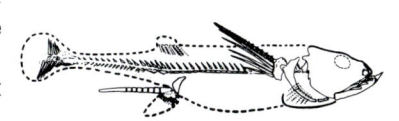

Sibirhynchus, reconstruction after ZANGERL & CASE

CHONDRICHTHYES — Cartilaginous Fishes
Order: Iniopterygiiformes
Family: Unnamed

Unnamed iniopterygiiform fish (length c. 10 cm) from the Lower Carboniferous of Bear Gulch, Montana, U.S.A. Original: Adelphi University, Garden City, N.J., U.S.A.

Genus: Unnamed.

Geological range: Lower Carboniferous.

Geographical distribution: North America.

Features: Small, still undescribed fishes. Head large, rounded anteriorly. Eyes very large, directed upwards. Pectoral fins unusually long, each with eight strong rays.

Remarks: The upward directed eyes suggest a bottom dweller.

Recent relatives: None. Died out in Lower Carboniferous.

CHONDRICHTHYES — Cartilaginous Fishes
Order: Iniopterygiiformes
Family: Unnamed

Unnamed iniopterygiiform fish (length c.10 cm) from the Lower Carboniferous of Bear Gulch, Montana. Original: Adelphi University, Garden City, N.J., U.S.A.

Genus: Unnamed.

Geological range: Lower Carboniferous.

Geographical distribution: North America.

Features: Small, still undescribed fishes. Body plump, drawn out into a point posteriorly. Head short. Just behind head, in mid-dorsal line, a branched antler-like outgrowth. One dorsal fin and small pelvic fins present.

Remarks: Probably free-swimming, but certainly not expert swimmers.

Recent relatives: None. Died out in Lower Carboniferous.

CHONDRICHTHYES — Cartilaginous Fishes
Order: Unnamed
Family: Unnamed
Suborder: Cochliodontoidei

Unnamed cochliodontoid fish (length c. 14 cm) from the Lower Carboniferous of Bear Gulch, Montana, U.S.A. Original: Adelphi University, Garden City, N.J., U.S.A.

Genus: Unnamed.

Geological range: Lower Carboniferous.

Geographical distribution: North America.

Features: Small, still undescribed fishes. Head small, snout pointed. Strong dentition. Eyes large. Two strong dorsal fins. The first with a long thorn anteriorly. Body pointed posteriorly. Males have a copulation hook on the ventral fin. Anal fin narrow and long.

Remarks: The strong dentition indicates a durophagous diet.

Recent relatives: None. Died out in Lower Carboniferous.

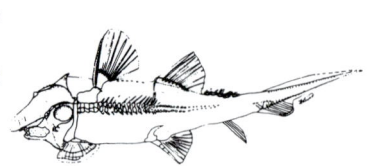

Reconstruction after LUND

CHONDRICHTHYES
Order: Unnamed
Family: Unnamed

Cartilaginous Fishes
Suborder: Cochliodontoidei

Unnamed cochliodontoid fish (length c. 11 cm) from the Lower Carboniferous of Bear Gulch, Montana, U.S.A. Original: Adelphi University, Garden City, N.J., U.S.A.

Genus: Unnamed.

Geological range: Lower Carboniferous.

Geographical distribution: North America.

Features: Small, still undescribed fishes. Head small with large eyes and strong dentition. Body rather plump. Short thorn in the nape. One dorsal fin very posterior.

Remarks: The strong dentition indicates a durophagous diet.

Recent relatives: None. Died out in Lower Carboniferous.

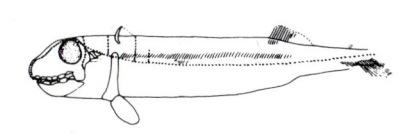

Reconstruction after Lund.

225

CHONDRICHTHYES — Cartilaginous Fishes
Order: Unnamed
Family: Unnamed
Suborder: Cochliodontoidei

Unnamed cochliodontoid fish (length c. 10 cm) from the Lower Carboniferous of Bear Gulch, Montana, U.S.A. Original: Adelphi University, Garden City, N.J., U.S.A

Genus: Unnamed.

Geological range: Lower Carboniferous.

Geographical distribution: North America.

Features: Small, still undescribed fishes. Head elongate. Snout pointed. Strong dentition. Two nasal spines. Many occipital spines, curved, directed rearwards and ending in sharp points.

Remarks: Probably free-swimming.

Recent relatives: None. Died out in Carboniferous.

CHONDRICHTHYES — Cartilaginous Fishes
Order: Unnamed
Family: Unnamed
Suborder: Cochliodontoidei

Unnamed cochliodontoid fish (length c. 9 cm) from the Lower Carboniferous of Bear Gulch, Montana, U.S.A. Original: Adelphi University, Garden City, N.J., U.S.A.

Genus: Unnamed.

Geological range: Lower Carboniferous.

Geographical distribution: North America.

Features: Small, still undescribed fish. Body rather plump. Head small. Snout flattened. Mouth ventral. Strong dentition. Two rows of pointed spines on the dorsal surface of the body. Probably two dorsal fins, with a weak spine at front of first one. Caudal fin with upper and lower lobes similar to each other and triangular. Male with claspers on pelvic fins.

Remarks: Probably free-swimming.

Recent relatives: None. Died out in Carboniferous.

Reconstruction after Lund.

CHONDRICHTHYES
Cartilaginous Fishes
Order: Unnamed
Family: Menaspidae
Suborder: Menaspoidei

Deltoptychius sp. (length c. 50 cm) from the Upper Carboniferous of Bearsden, Glasgow, Scotland, U.K. Original: The Natural History Museum, London, U.K.(P62092). Photograph: Hunterian Museum, Glasgow, U.K.

Genus: *Deltoptychius* MORRIS & ROBERTS, 1862.

Synonyms: *Listracanthus*, *Pnigeacanthus*, *Platacanthus*, *Platycanthus*, *Streblodus*.

Geological range: Lower to Upper Carboniferous.

Geographical distribution: Europe, North America.

Features: Middle-sized menaspoid fishes. Body wide anteriorly but tapering behind into the tail. Head narrow. Snout broadly pointed. On the dorsal surface anteriorly are two rows posteriorly pointing spines. More posteriorly is another row, in the dorsal mid line. The upper part of the end of the tail has a fin-fold-like fin. Pectoral fins rounded elongate and very large.

Remarks: Probably living near the bottom with a durophagous diet.

Recent relatives: None. Died out in Upper Carboniferous.

Deltoptychius, reconstruction after the Hunterian Museum.

228

CHONDRICHTHYES — Cartilaginous Fishes
Order: Unnamed
Suborder: Menaspoidei
Family: Menaspidae

Menaspis armata EICHWALD (length c. 16 cm) from the Upper Permian of Eisleben, Germany. Original: Museum für Naturkunde, Berlin, Germany.

CHONDRICHTHYES
Cartilaginous Fishes
Order: Unnamed
Family: Menaspidae
Suborder: Menaspoidei

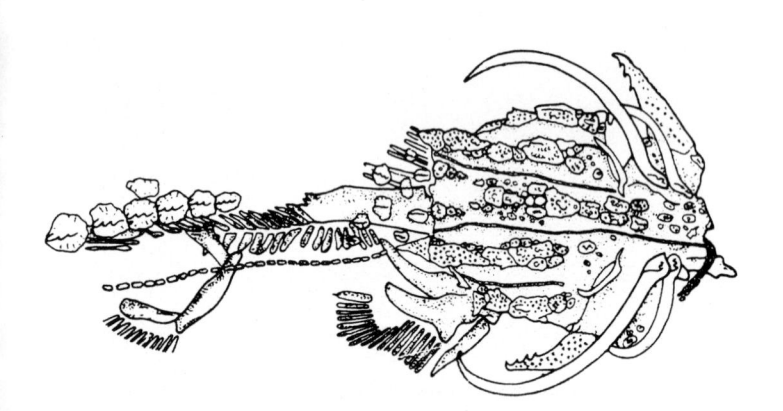

Menaspis, reconstruction after MOY-THOMAS & MILES.

Genus: *Menaspis* EICHWALD, 1848.

Synonyms: *Asima*, *Radamus*.

Geological range: Upper Permian.

Geographical distribution: Europe.

Features: Elongate body. On each side of the head a short thick triangular spine with a tuberculate surface. Behind come three thinner curved smooth spines, of which the second one is considerably longer than the two others. Head and trunk covered with longitudinally directed placoid scales which are partly covered with thorns or keeled and partly are seed-like. Dentition of small plates.

Remarks: Durophagous bottom dwellers.

Recent relatives: None. Died out in Upper Permian.

CHONDRICHTHYES — Cartilaginous Fishes
Order: Unnamed
Family: Menaspidae
Suborder: Menaspoidei

Acanthorhina jaekeli FRAAS (length c. 50 cm) from the Lower Jurassic of Holzmaden, Württemberg, Germany. Original: Staatliches Museum für Naturkunde, Stuttgart, Germany. Photograph: Lumpe, Stuttgart.

Genus: *Acanthorhina* FRAAS, 1911.

Geological range: Lower Jurassic.

Geographical distribution: Europe.

Features: Head tapering anteriorly to a long pointed rostral cartilage. Male with a small frontal spine. Strong fin spine in front of the first dorsal fin. Dentition is a pair of flat, undulating tooth plates in the upper jaw and three pairs in the lower jaw.

Remarks: Bottom-dwelling with durophagous diet.

Recent relatives: None. Died out in Lower Jurassic.

Acanthorhina, reconstruction after FRAAS.

CHONDRICHTHYES — Cartilaginous Fishes
Order: Chimaeriiformes
Suborder: Echinochimaeroidei
Family: Echinochimaeridae

Echinochimaera meltoni LUND (length c. 8 cm) from the Lower Carboniferous of Bear Gulch, Montana, U.S.A. Original: Carnegie Museum of Natural History, Pittsburgh, Penn., U.S.A.

Genus: *Echinochimaera* LUND, 1977.

Geological range: Lower Carboniferous.

Geographical distribution: North America.

Features: Dwarf chimaeras of depressed shape with long pointed tail. Head short. Eyes large. Mouth slightly ventral. On the dorsal surface of the head a few spines, some of them branched. Two dorsal fins, of which the first is upright and supported by a long, anteriorly serrated spine. On the tail is a row of rearward pointing thorns.

Remarks: Free-swimming, durophagous in diet.

Recent relatives: None. Died out in Lower Carboniferous.

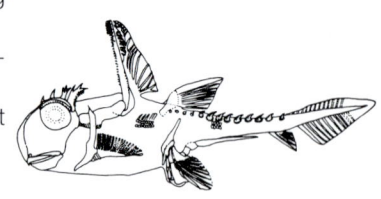

Echinochimaera, reconstruction after LUND.

CHONDRICHTHYES
Cartilaginous Fishes
Order: Chimaeriformes
Family: Chimaeridae
Order: Chimaeroidei
Chimaeras

Ischyodus quenstedti WAGNER (length c. 142 cm) from the Upper Jurassic of Solnhofen (Eichstätt), Bavaria, Germany. Original: Bayerische Staatssammlung für Paläontologie, Munich, Germany.

Genus: *Ischyodus* EGERTON, 1843.
Synonyms: *Auluxacanthus*, *Chimaeracanthus*.
Geological range: Middle Jurassic to Paleocene.
Geographical distribution: Europe, New Zealand.
Features: Large chimaeras with greatly elongate body tapering rearwards to a point. Head large. Nose probably pointed. Mouth slightly ventral. Lower jaw with two rhombic tooth plates. Palatal teeth small. Pectoral fins very large. First dorsal fin large and triangular, supported by a long projecting with denticles on the posterior surface. Second dorsal fin low and very long. The male has a short, slightly curved spine on the head.
Remarks: Probably bottom-dwellers but sometimes free-swimming. Durophagous diet.
Recent relatives: Genus extinct. Related to the recent chimaeras which are represented by six genera and about 30 species in the seas of the world.

Chimaera monstrosa, a recent chimaera. Lithograph from BLOCH.

233

CHONDRICHTHYES — Cartilaginous Fishes
Order: Chimaeriiformes
Family: Unnamed
Suborder: Unnamed

Delphyodontos dacriformis LUND (length c. 11 cm) from the Lower Carboniferous of Bear Gulch, Montana, U.S.A. Original: Adelphi University, Garden City, N.J., U.S.A.

Genus: *Delphyodontos* LUND, 1980.

Geological range: Lower Carboniferous.

Geographical distribution: North America.

Features: Small chimaeras of variable appearance. Plump in shape. Head large and not visibly distinct from the body. Eyes relatively large and pointing forwards. Mouth terminal. Tail end of body pointed. Skin covered with short spines.

Remarks: Bottom-dwelling and possibly clumsily free-swimming.

Recent relatives: None. Died out in Lower Carboniferous.

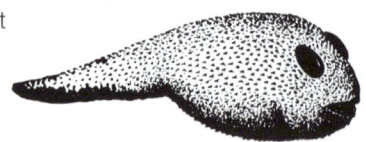

Delphyodontos, reconstruction after LUND.

CHONDRICHTHYES — Cartilaginous Fishes
Order: Unnamed
Family: Unnamed

Unnamed chondrichthyan (length c. 18 cm) from the Lower Carboniferous of Bear Gulch, Montana, U.S.A. Original: Adelphi University, Garden City, N.J., U.S.A

Genus: Unnamed.

Geological range: Lower Carboniferous.

Geographical distribution: North America.

Features: Small fishes of somewhat laterally compressed shape. Head deep. Eyes large. Snout elongate and pointed. Mouth probably large. Dorsal fin tall, beginning behind the head and continuing along the whole back as a fringe. Anal fins large and fan-shaped. Pectoral fins narrow. Caudal fin pointed, probably low and fringe-like.

Remarks: Lethargic fishes with a predatory mode of life.

Recent relatives: None. Died out in Carboniferous.

ACANTHODII — Acanthodians

The acanthodians are jaw-bearing fishes (Gnathostomata) but there is still no final agreement on their systematic position. They have a highly advanced, spindle-like body shape very similar to the normal conception of a fish. In general they are small, between 20 and 50 cm in length, but there are some real giants which reach up to 2.5 metres. Bony tissue occurs both in the exoskeleton and the endoskeleton. The body was covered with small scales arranged like a mosaic and, at least externally, these resemble those of "ganoid" fishes. Sometimes the scales continue onto the skin of the fins. From the evolutionary point of view, these scales are not dermal denticles, as in the sharks, for they have a bony base covered with dentine. This is why they recall the scales of "ganoids."

The snout region of the skull is strikingly small. The eyes are large and face laterally and the nostrils are high in the skull. Usually the little teeth are confined to the lower jaw, though in some species they are present on the upper jaw also. Other species are toothless.

A feature common to all of them is that every fin, except the caudal fin, is supported by a massive spine formed of dentine. This sometimes projects far beyond the fin. On the ventral surface, the series of spines may be continuous between the pectoral and pelvic fins consisting of one or several pairs of free spines. Perhaps these are vestiges of additional paired fins. The caudal fin is always heterocercal.

The acanthodians probably represent a blind side-branch whose ancestors gave rise to all other jaw-bearing fishes.

The acanthodians have been shown to exist in the Middle and Upper Silurian. They reached a maximum in the Lower Devonian and then the number of species continually declined. They died out in the Lower Permian without leaving any descendants. About 65 genera have been described and some of them are extremely well preserved.

ACANTHODII — Acanthodians

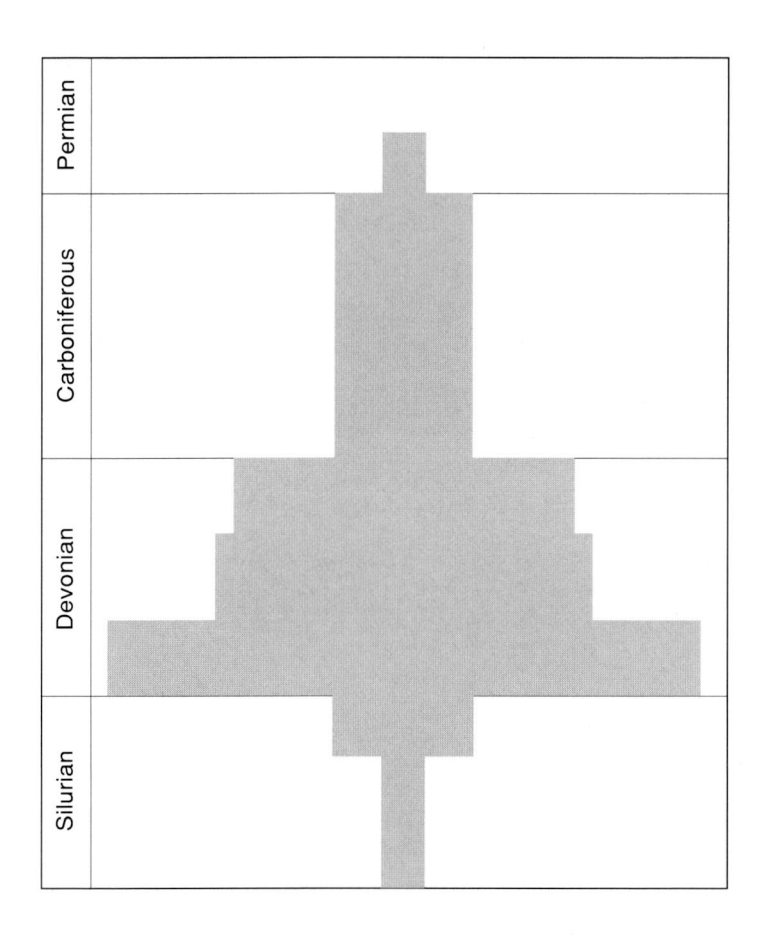

The approximate distribution of acanthodians in geological time, changed after MÜLLER

ACANTHODII — Acanthodians
Order: Climatiiformes
Family: Climatiidae

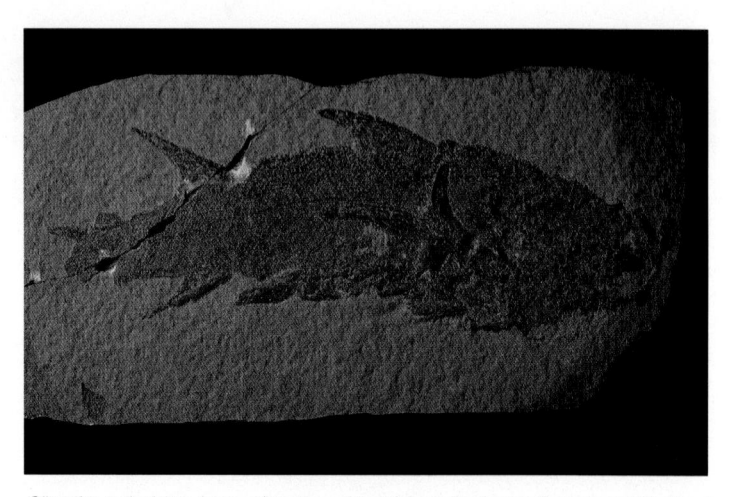

Climatius reticulatus AGASSIZ (length c. 14 cm) from the Lower Devonian of Scotland. Original: National Museum of Scotland, Edinburgh, U.K.

Genus: *Climatius* AGASSIZ, 1845.

Geological range: Upper Silurian to Lower Devonian.

Geographical distribution: Western and eastern Europe, North America.

Features: Elongated fishes with a rounded head. Eyes large. Mouth slightly ventral. Caudal fin tapering to a point in the upper lobe. Two short strong dorsal spines. On the ventral surface, between the pectoral and pelvic fins are four pairs of smaller spines which increase in size posteriorly. The teeth are flat, each one with a main cusp and two lateral cusps.

Remarks: Rapid swimmers.

Recent relatives: None. Died out in Lower Devonian.

Climatius, reconstruction after MACMILLAN.

ACANTHODII
Acanthodians

Order: Climatiiformes
Family: Climatiidae

Euthacanthus macnicolli POWRIE (length c. 14 cm) from the Lower Devonian of Angus, Scotland. Original: National Museum of Scotland, Edinburgh, U.K.

Genus: *Euthacanthus* POWRIE, 1864.

Geological range: Lower Devonian.

Geographical distribution: Europe.

Features: Elongate fishes with a relatively short caudal fin. Head rounded. Mouth slightly ventral. Five pairs of powerful ventral spines which become larger posteriorly. No teeth.

Remarks: Rapid swimmers.

Recent relatives: None. Died out in Lower Devonian.

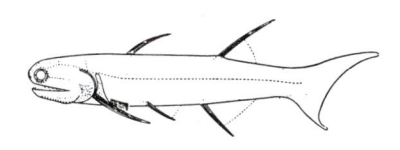

Euthacanthus, reconstruction after WATSON.

ACANTHODII
Acanthodians
Order: Climatiiformes
Family: Climatiidae

Parexus falcatus Powrie (length c. 14 cm) from the Lower Devonian of Angus, Scotland. Original: National Museum of Scotland, Edinburgh, U.K.

Genus: *Parexus* Agassiz, 1845.

Geological range: Lower Devonian.

Geographical distribution: Europe.

Features: Fishes with laterally compressed body shape. Head rounded. Mouth slightly ventral. Caudal fin relatively short and broad. Long teeth with a single point. Eyes large. Two dorsal spines, the first being extremely long. Posteriorly with two rows of denticle-like structures. On the ventral surface, between the pectoral and pelvic fins, there are three pairs of powerful spines which increase in size posteriorly.

Remarks: Probably somewhat clumsy swimmers.

Recent relatives: None. Died out in Lower Devonian.

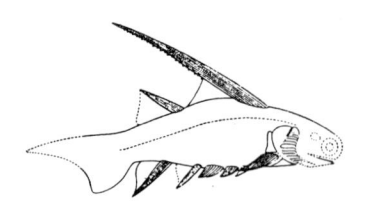

Parexus, reconstruction after Watson.

ACANTHODII
Acanthodians
Order: Climatiiformes
Family: Climatiidae

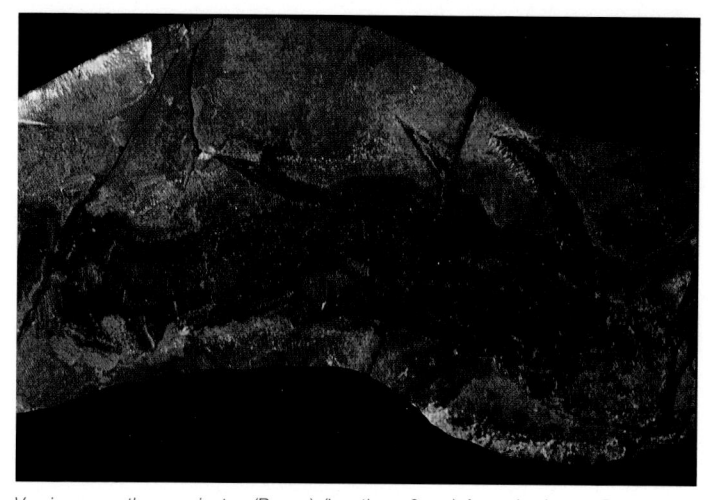

Vernicomacanthus uncinatus (Powrie) (length c. 8 cm) from the Lower Devonian of Forfar, Scotland, U.K. Original: National Museum of Scotland, Edinburgh, U.K.

Genus: *Vernicomacanthus* Miles, 1973.

Geological range: Lower Devonian.

Geographical distribution: Europe.

Features: Relatively small fishes with a somewhat laterally compressed body. Eyes large. Mouth ventral. Teeth flat. Two dorsal fins with powerful spines, the anterior spine being longer than the posterior. Four pairs of free ventral spines. Maximum length scarcely more than 15 cm.

Remarks: Nimble swimmers.

Recent relatives: None. Died out in Lower Devonian.

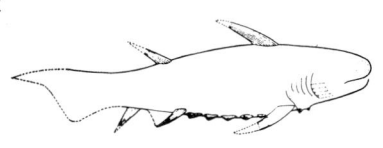

Vernicomacanthus, reconstruction after Miles.

241

ACANTHODII
Acanthodians
Order: Climatiiformes
Family: Diplacanthidae

Diplacanthus striatus AGASSIZ (length c. 5 cm) from the Devonian of Achanarras, Caithness, Scotland, U.K. Original: The Natural History Museum, London, U.K. (P22199).

Genus: *Diplacanthus* AGASSIZ, 1844.

Synonym: *Rhadinacanthus*

Geological range: Middle to Upper Devonian.

Geographical distribution: Western and eastern Europe, North America.

Features: Little fishes with somewhat laterally compressed body shape. Caudal fin relatively short. Mouth ventral. No teeth. Fin spines long and powerful. First dorsal fin very anterior in position. One pair of spines between the pectoral and pelvic fins.

Remarks: Probably not very good swimmers.

Recent relatives: None. Died out in Upper Devonian.

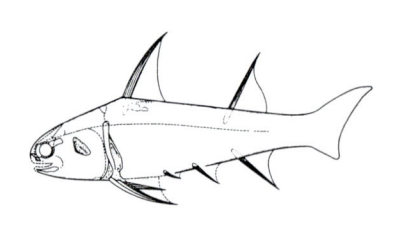

Diplacanthus, reconstruction after WATSON.

ACANTHODII — Acanthodians
Order: Climatiiformes
Family: Diplacanthidae

Rhadinacanthus longispinus TRAQUAIR (length c. 16 cm) from the Middle Devonian of Caithness, Scotland, U.K. Original: Tischlinger Collection, Stammham, Germany.

Genus: *Rhadinacanthus* TRAQUAIR, 1888.

Geological range: Middle Devonian.

Geographical distribution: Europe.

Features: Small to middle-sized, somewhat plump fishes. Head rounded. Eyes large. Mouth ventral. No teeth. Fin spines powerful and long. The first dorsal fin very anterior with a shorter, slightly curved spine. The second dorsal fin with a longer straight spine. One pair of spines between the pectoral and pelvic fins.

Remarks: The genus *Rhadinacanthus* is sometimes seen as a synonym of *Diplacanthus*.

Recent relatives: None. Died out in Devonian.

ACANTHODII
Acanthodians
Order: Ischnacanthiformes
Family: Ischnacanthidae

Ischnacanthus gracilis EGERTON (length c. 10 cm) from the Upper Devonian of Forfarshire, Scotland, U.K. Original: The Natural History Museum, London, U.K. (P132).

Genus: *Ischnacanthus* POWRIE, 1864.

Geological range: Lower Devonian.

Geographical distribution: Europe, North America.

Features: Elongate fishes with middle-sized caudal fin. Head rounded. Mouth slightly ventral. Eyes large. Two dorsal fins, each with a slender spine. First spine smaller and slightly curved. No free ventral spines. Teeth with broadly conical points. Maximum length scarcely more than 10 cm.

Remarks: Nimble swimmers.

Recent relatives: None. Died out in Upper Devonian.

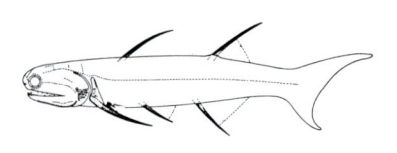

Ischnacanthus, reconstruction after WATSON.

ACANTHODII — Acanthodians
Order: Acanthodiformes
Family: Acanthodidae

Acanthodes bronni AGASSIZ (length c. 40 cm) from the Permian of Niederkirchen, Palatinate, Germany. Original: Staatliches Museum für Naturkunde, Stuttgart, Germany.

Genus: *Acanthodes* AGASSIZ, 1833.

Geological range: Upper Carboniferous to Lower Permian.

Geographical distribution: Europe, North America, Australia, South Africa, eastern Asia.

Features: Relatively large fishes, sometimes reaching a length of more than 50 cm. Laterally compressed body. Caudal fin clearly divided into an upper and a lower lobe. Head bluntly rounded. Eyes large. Mouth opening slightly ventral. No teeth. Only one dorsal fin, with a powerful spine which does not exceed the fin in height.

Remarks: Nimble swimmers.

Recent relatives: None. Died out in Lower Permian.

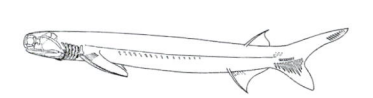

Acanthodes, after HEIDTKE.

ACANTHODII
Acanthodians
Order: Acanthodiformes
Family: Acanthodidae

Cheiracanthus latus EGERTON (length c. 14 cm) from the Upper Devonian of Banffshire, Scotland, U.K. Original: The Natural History Museum, London, U.K. (P15286).

Genus: *Cheiracanthus* AGASSIZ, 1835.

Geological range: Upper Devonian.

Geographical distribution: Western and eastern Europe.

Features: Rather large fishes with a somewhat laterally compressed body which may reach a length of about 30 cm. Caudal fin with greatly elongate upper lobe. Head rounded. Mouth somewhat ventral. Eyes large. No free ventral spines. Only one dorsal fin with a short spine which does not project beyond fin.

Remarks: Nimble swimmer.

Recent relatives: None. Died out in Upper Devonian.

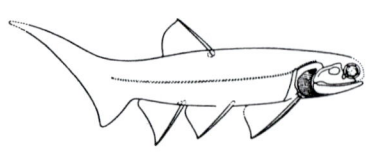

Cheiracanthus, reconstruction after WATSON.

ACANTHODII — Acanthodians
Order: Acanthodiformes
Family: Acanthodidae

Homalacanthus concinnus (Whiteaves) (length c. 8 cm) from the Upper Devonian of Miguasha, Gaspé Peninsula, Quebec, Canada. Original: Naturhistoriska Riksmuseet, Stockholm, Sweden.

Genus: *Homalacanthus* Russel, 1951.

Geological range: Upper Devonian to Lower Carboniferous.

Geographical distribution: North America, eastern Europe.

Features: Middle-sized fishes with a long slender body. Caudal fin extending into a point and with a long lower lobe. A single dorsal fin with a delicate short spine. Head rounded. Mouth slightly ventral. Eyes large. No free ventral spines. No teeth. Length scarcely more than 15 cm.

Remarks: Nimble swimmers.

Recent relatives: None. Died out in Lower Carboniferous.

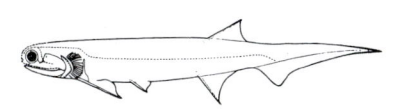

Homalacanthus, reconstruction after Miles.

ACANTHODII — Acanthodians
Order: Acanthodiformes
Family: Acanthodidae

Mesacanthus mitchelli EGERTON (length c. 6 cm) from the Lower Devonian of Scotland, U.K. Original: National Museum of Scotland, Edinburgh, U.K.

Genus: *Mesacanthus* TRAQUAIR, 1888.

Geological range: Lower Devonian to Middle Devonian.

Geographical distribution: Europe.

Features: Small fishes with a slender body. Head rounded. Mouth slightly ventral. Eyes large. Caudal fin relatively short. One pair of free ventral spines. No teeth. Only one dorsal fin, very posterior in position and supported by a spine which projects far above the fin. Length scarcely more than 15 cm.

Remarks: Nimble swimmers.

Recent relatives: None. Died out in Middle Devonian.

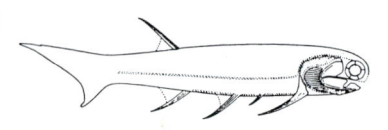

Mesacanthus, reconstruction after WATSON.

ACANTHODII
Acanthodians

Order: Acanthodiformes
Family: Acanthodidae

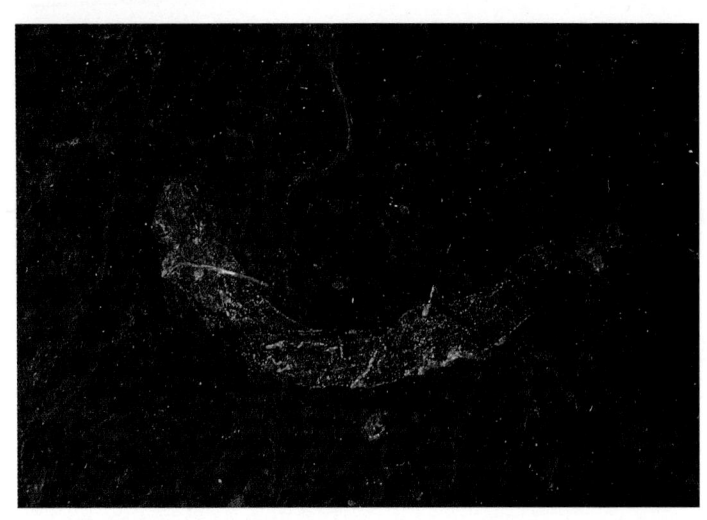

Traquairichthys pygmaeus (Fritsch) (length c. 6 cm) from the Lower Permian of Nursava, Czechoslovakia. Original: Naturhistorisches Museum, Vienna, Austria.

Genus: *Traquairichthys* Whitley, 1933.

Geological range: Upper Carboniferous to Lower Permian.

Geographical distribution: Europe, North America.

Features: Small, very slender fishes. The body ends in a caudal fin whose termination is curved slightly downwards. Head pointed. Eyes small. No teeth. Only one dorsal fin, located very posteriorly just in front of the caudal fin. No free ventral spines. No pelvic fins. Maximum length scarcely more than 10 cm.

Remarks: Nimble swimmers.

Recent relatives: None. Died out in Lower Permian.

Traquairichthys, reconstruction after Fritsch.

ACANTHODII — Acanthodians
Order: Acanthodiformes
Family: Acanthodidae

Triazeugacanthus affinis (Whiteaves) (length c. 3 cm) from the Upper Devonian of Miguasha, Gaspé Peninsula, Quebec, Canada. Original: Musée d'Histoire Naturelle, Miguasha, Canada.

Genus: *Triazeugacanthus* Miles, 1966.

Geological range: Upper Devonian.

Geographical distribution: North America.

Features: Small fishes with a very slender body. This ends in a caudal fin with the upper lobe tapering to a point and directed upwards. Head rounded. Eyes large. Mouth slightly ventral. No teeth. One pair of free ventral spines. Only one dorsal fin, with a delicate spine which does not project beyond the fin. Maximum length scarcely more than 10 cm.

Remarks: Nimble swimmers.

Recent relatives: None. Died out in Upper Devonian.

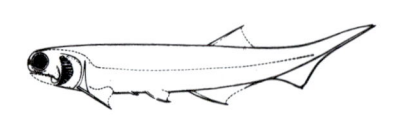

Triazeugacanthus, reconstruction after Miles.

ACANTHODII — Acanthodians
Order: Acanthodiformes
Family: Acanthodidae

Utahacanthus guntheri SCHULTZE (length c. 6 cm) from the Upper Carboniferous of Utah, U.S.A. Original: Brigham Young University, Provo, Utah, U.S.A.

Genus: *Utahacanthus* SCHULTZE, 1990.

Geological range: Upper Carboniferous.

Geographical distribution: North America.

Features: Very small fishes with a slender body. Head rounded. Eyes small. Mouth slightly ventral. Only one dorsal fin, posteriorly located with a delicate spine. Probably no teeth and no free ventral spines. Maximum length scarcely more than 10 cm.

Remarks: Nimble swimmers.

Recent relatives: None. Died out in Upper Carboniferous.

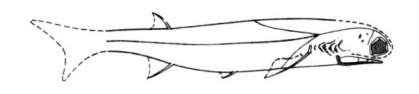

Utahacanthus, reconstruction after SCHULTZE.

CHONDROSTEI — Chondrosteans

Actinopterygians, or ray-finned fishes, include the true bony fishes or teleosts among others. They are characterized by paired fins supported by strong, radially arranged rays. The most primitive actinopterygians are referred to as chondrosteans (Chondrostei). The chondrosteans still have much cartilage in the endoskeleton —for example the centra of the vertebrae are not ossified. Moreover, with a few exceptions, the upper jaw and palate are rigidly attached to the anterior cover of the operculum, so that only the lower jaw is moveable. The eyes, which are usually large, are nearly always protected by a four-part sclerotic ring.

There is always only a single dorsal fin. With a few exceptions, the caudal fin is heterocercal. In the older representatives of this group, this fin is generally covered with scales up to the tip but in the course of evolution the scale-covered surface decreases.

Rhombic ganoid scales are the commonest type. They consist of ganoine, cosmine and bony tissue with the ganoine layer reaching a considerable thickness. Ganoine is very similar to tooth enamel and so these scales are referred to as enamel scales. The ganoine and cosmine layers, however, become more and more reduced in the course of evolution and in some cases the scales are almost completely lost. V-shaped keeled scales, called fulcral scales, commonly occur on the dorsal margins of the dorsal and anal fins and also on the anterior margin of the dorsal lobe of the caudal fin.

At first most chondrosteans may have lived in fresh water. Nevertheless, by the end of the Triassic almost all of them had taken to salt water. This fresh-water ancestry may be the reason why, as a sort of folk memory, some bony fishes live in the sea but return to fresh water to lay their eggs.

The first sparse occurrence of chondrosteans can be traced back to the Middle Devonian. They reached their first maximum in the Lower Carboniferous, then suffered a slight retreat to reach a second maximum in the Lower Triassic. In the Upper Jurassic they had already become very scarce and the only surviving fishes which are kin to them are the sturgeons and garpikes. More than 200 fossil genera have so far been described. They are often extremely well preserved.

CHONDROSTEI — Chondrosteans

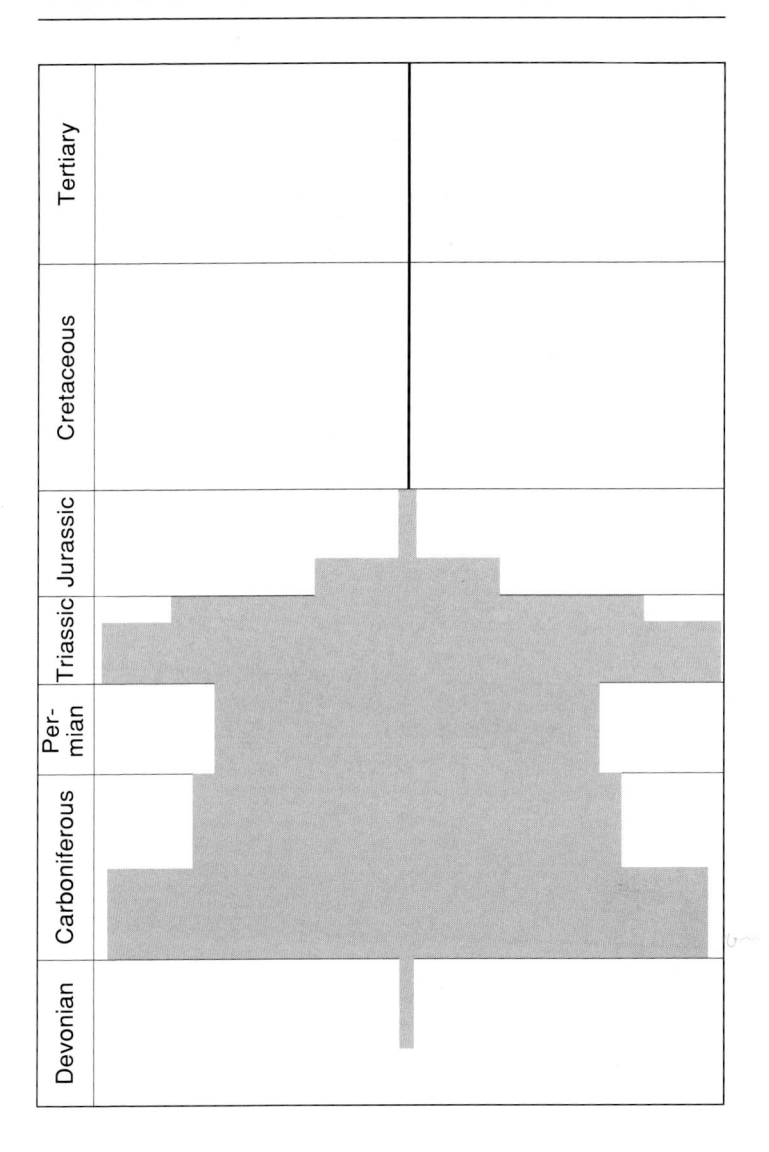

The approximate distribution of chondrosteans in geological time, changed after MÜLLER

CHONDROSTEI
Order: Palaeonisciformes
Family: Cheirolepididae

Chondrosteans
Suborder: Palaeoniscoidei

Cheirolepis trailli AGASSIZ (length c. 25 cm) from the Middle Devonian of Nairnshire, Scotland, U.K. Original: The Natural History Museum, London, U.K. (P453).

Genus: *Cheirolepis* AGASSIZ, 1835.

Geological range: Middle to Upper Devonian.

Geographical distribution: Europe, North America.

Features: Body shape elongate. Head rather deep. Pointed teeth on upper and lower jaws. Eyes relatively small, surrounded by sclerotic rings. Scales small and rhombic, with the bony layer projecting as an obtuse cone into the cosmine layer. Dorsal fin located very posteriorly, beginning behind the start of the opposing anal fin. Pelvic fins with a strikingly broad base. Pectoral fins with narrow lobes. Tail fin heterocercal with an axial lobe.

Remarks: Middle-sized predators.

Recent relatives: None. Died out in Upper Devonian.

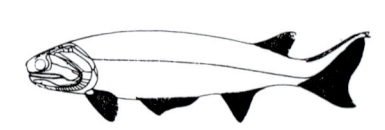

Cheirolepis, reconstruction after LEHMAN.

CHONDROSTEI
Order: Palaeonisciformes
Family: Stegotrachelidae

Chondrosteans
Suborder: Palaeoniscoidei

Kentuckia hlavini Dunkle (length c. 10 cm) from the Upper Devonian of Cleveland, Ohio, U.S.A. Original: Museum of Natural History, Cleveland, Ohio, U.S.A.

Genus: *Kentuckia* Rayner, 1951.

Geological range: Upper Devonian to Lower Carboniferous.

Geographical distribution: North America.

Features: Small to middle-sized fishes of spindle-like shape. Head large, somewhat elongate. Snout blunt. Mouth relatively wide. Teeth small, pointed. Scales thick and elongate. Dorsal fin in the posterior third of the body.

Remarks: Predatory fishes.

Recent relatives: None. Died out in Lower Carboniferous.

CHONDROSTEI
Order: Palaeonisciformes
Family: Stegotrachelidae

Chondrosteans
Suborder: Palaeoniscoidei

Moythomasia nitida Gross (length c. 7 cm) from the Middle Devonian of Bergisch Gladbach, Westphalia, Germany. Original: Geologisch-Paläontologisches Museum, Münster, Germany.

Genus: *Moythomasia* Gross, 1950.

Geological range: Middle to Upper Devonian.

Geographical distribution: Europe, Australia.

Features: Slender fishes. Head relatively short with a blunt snout. Upper and lower jaws with pointed teeth. Eyes strikingly large. Dorsal fin in the posterior half of the body, opposite the anal fin. Caudal fin heterocercal with an elongate upper lobe.

Remarks: Small predators.

Recent relatives: None. Died out in Upper Devonian.

Moythomasia, reconstruction after MacMillan.

CHONDROSTEI / Chondrosteans

Order: Palaeonisciformes
Family: Stegotrachelidae

Suborder: Palaeoniscoidei

Stegotrachelys finlayi (Woodward & White) (length c. 9 cm) from the Middle Devonian of Exnaboe, Shetland Islands, Scotland. Original: The Natural History Museum, London, U.K. (P 13408-9)

Genus: *Stegotrachelys* Woodward & White, 1926.

Geological range: Lower to Middle Devonian.

Geographical distribution: Europe, North America.

Features: Small fishes of somewhat laterally compressed shape. Dorsal fin pointed triangular, opposite the anal fin and equal in size. Caudal fin heterocercal. Upper lobe only slightly elongate. Pectoral and pelvic fins narrow. Scales square to rectangular.

Remarks: Small predators.

Recent relatives: None. Died out in Middle Devonian.

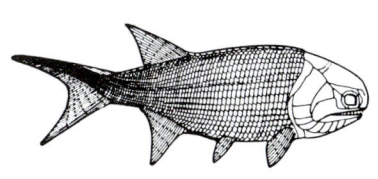

Stegotrachelys, reconstruction after White.

CHONDROSTEI
Chondrosteans
Order: Palaeonisciformes
Suborder: Palaeoniscoidei
Family: Tegeolepididae

Apateolepis australis Woodward (length c. 14 cm) from the Middle Triassic of Gosford, New South Wales, Australia. Original: The Natural History Museum, London, U.K. (P6268).

Genus: *Apateolepis* Woodward, 1890.

Geological range: Middle Triassic.

Geographical distribution: Australia.

Features: Small to middle-sized fishes with elongate, spindle-shaped bodies. Snout blunt. Scales small and thin. Dorsal fin located very posteriorly. Pectoral fins relatively broad with unsegmented bony fin rays (lepidotrichia).

Remarks: Predators.

Recent relatives: None. Died out in Middle Triassic.

Apateolepis, reconstruction after Woodward.

CHONDROSTEI
Order: Palaeonisciformes
Family: Tegeolepididae

Chondrosteans
Suborder: Palaeoniscoidei

Megapteriscus longicaudatus WADE (length c. 6 cm) from the Middle Triassic of Brookvale, New South Wales, Australia. Original: The Natural History Museum, London, U.K. (P16827)

Genus: *Megapteriscus* WADE, 1935.

Geological range: Middle Triassic.

Geographical distribution: Australia.

Features: Small fishes with spindle-shaped elongate bodies. Snout blunt. Dorsal fin very posterior. Strikingly broad pectoral and pelvic fins. Scales small and thin.

Remarks: Small fishes, probably predatory.

Recent relatives: None. Died out in Middle Triassic.

CHONDROSTEI
Order: Palaeonisciformes
Family: Rhabdolepididae

Chondrosteans
Suborder: Palaeoniscoidei

Rhabdolepis macropterus BRONN (length c. 25 cm) from the Lower Permian of the Palatinate, Germany. Original: Henne Collection, Stuttgart, Germany.

Genus: *Rhabdolepis* TROSCHEL, 1857.

Geological range: Lower Permian.

Geographical distribution: Europe.

Features: Small fishes with slender elongate bodies. Eyes relatively large. Dorsal fin in posterior half of the body. Anal fin large and triangular. Scales scalloped and divided by diagonal ridges. Upper and lower jaws with powerful conical teeth.

Remarks: Predators.

Recent relatives: None. Died out in Lower Permian.

Rhabdolepis, after AGASSIZ.

CHONDROSTEI
Order: Palaeonisciformes
Family: Rhabdolepididae

Chondrosteans
Suborder: Palaeoniscoidei

Aetheretmon valentiacum WHITE (length c. 6 cm) from the Lower Carboniferous of Berwickshire, Scotland, U.K. Original: The Natural History Museum, London, U.K. (P 13145)

Genus: *Aetheretmon* WHITE, 1927.

Geological range: Lower Carboniferous.

Geographical distribution: Europe.

Features: Small fishes of somewhat laterally compressed shape. Head relatively large with blunt snout. Eyes large. Dorsal fin in the posterior half of the body. Caudal fin heterocercal with elongate upper lobe. Pectoral fins narrow. Pelvic fins small. Anal fin of same size as dorsal fin. Scales square in the dorsal part of the body, elongate rectangular more ventrally, arranged in diagonal series.

Remarks: Small predators.

Recent relatives: None. Died out in Lower Carboniferous.

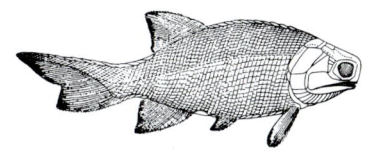

Aetheretmon, reconstruction after PIVETEAU.

CHONDROSTEI   Chondrosteans

Order: Palaeonisciformes   Suborder: Palaeoniscoidei
Family: Rhabdolepididae

Mentzichthys walshi JUBB (length c. 9 cm) from the Upper Devonian of Witteberg, South Africa. Original: Albany Museum, Grahamstown, South Africa.

Genus: *Mentzichthys* JUBB, 1965.

Geological range: Upper Devonian.

Geographical distribution: South Africa.

Features: Small slender fishes. Head narrow. Snout pointed. Eyes large. Dorsal fin located posteriorly, almost opposite the equally large anal fin. Caudal fin heterocercal with upper and lower lobes almost equal. Scales square and very small.

Remarks: Small predators.

Recent relatives: None. Died out in Upper Devonian.

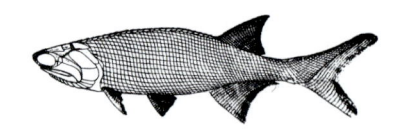

Mentzichthys, reconstruction after GARDINER.

CHONDROSTEI
Order: Palaeonisciformes
Family: Rhabdolepididae

Chondrosteans
Suborder: Palaeoniscoidei

Rhadinichthys carinatus (length c. 11 cm) from the Lower Carboniferous of Edinburgh, Scotland, U.K. Original: Henne Collection, Stuttgart, Germany.

Genus: *Rhadinichthys* TRAQUAIR, 1877.

Geological range: Upper Devonian to Upper Carboniferous.

Geographical distribution: Europe, South America, Africa, northern Asia.

Features: Small fishes with slender spindle-shaped bodies. Head elongate. Snout blunt. Dorsal fin in the posterior half of the body, obliquely opposite the almost equally large anal fin. Caudal fin heterocercal, with the upper lobe only slightly longer than the lower lobe. Scales square to rectangular, arranged in diagonal rows.

Remarks: Small predators.

Recent relatives: None. Died out in Upper Carboniferous.

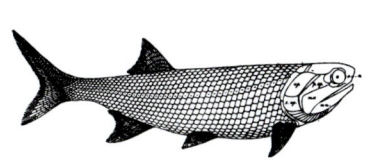

Rhadinichthys, reconstruction after GARDINER.

263

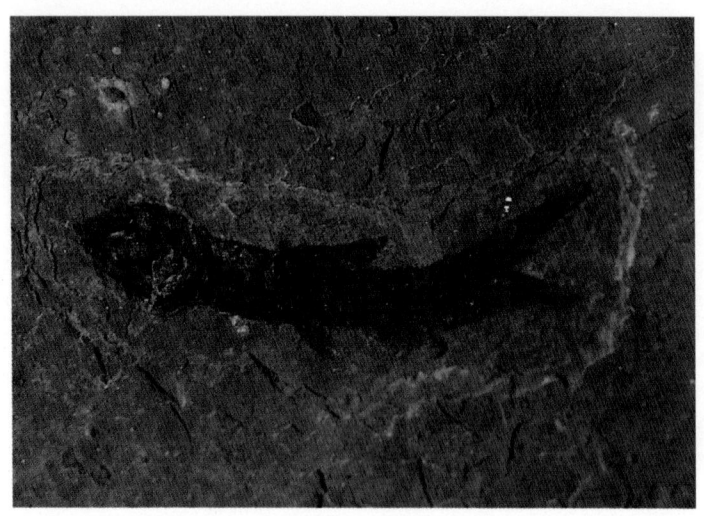

CHONDROSTEI
Order: Palaeonisciformes
Family: Carbovelidae

Chondrosteans
Suborder: Palaeoniscoidei

Phanerosteon pauper FRITSCH (length c. 6 cm) from the Lower Permian of Kostalov, Czechoslovakia. Original: Naturhistorisches Museum, Vienna, Austria.

Genus: *Phanerosteon* TRAQUAIR, 1881.

Synonyms: *Gymnoniscus*, *Sceletophorus*.

Geological range: Lower Carboniferous to Lower Permian.

Geographical distribution: Europe, North America.

Features: Small slender fishes. Head shallow. Snout rounded. Dorsal fin in the posterior half of the body, only slightly in front of the anal fin. Caudal fin heterocercal with long upper lobe. Pectoral and pelvic fins small.

Remarks: Small predatos.

Recent relatives: None. Died out in Lower Permian

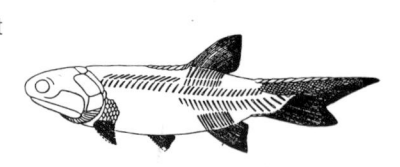

Phanerosteon, reconstruction after WHITE.

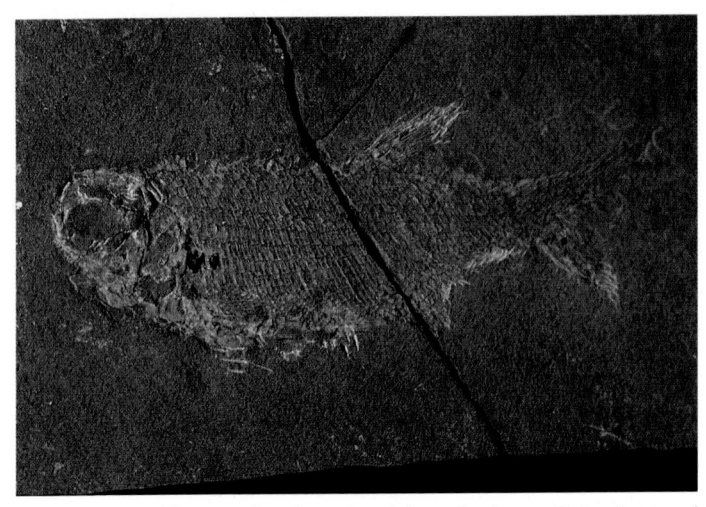

CHONDROSTEI
Order: Palaeonisciformes
Family: Canobiidae

Chondrosteans
Suborder: Palaeoniscoidei

Canobius ramsayi TRAQUAIR (length c. 6 cm) from the Lower Carboniferous of Dumfriesshire, Scotland, U.K. Original: Royal Museum of Scotland, Edinburgh, U.K.

Genus: *Canobius* TRAQUAIR, 1881.

Geological range: Lower Carboniferous.

Geographical distribution: Europe.

Features: Small fishes of somewhat laterally compressed shape. Head relatively deep. Snout rounded. Dorsal fin pointed triangular, situated in the posterior third of the body. Anal fin likewise triangular, slightly anterior to the dorsal fin. Pectoral and pelvic fins small.

Remarks: Small predators.

Recent relatives: None. Died out in Lower Carboniferous.

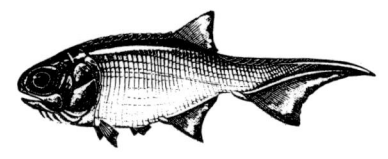

Canobius, reconstruction after MACMILLAN.

CHONDROSTEI / Chondrosteans

Order: Palaeonisciformes
Family: Canobiidae
Suborder: Palaeoniscoidei

Mesopoma politum TRAQUAIR (length c. 7 cm) from the Lower Carboniferous of Eskdale, Scotland, U.K. Original: The Natural History Museum, London, U.K. (P 4070a)

Genus: *Mesopoma* TRAQUAIR, 1890.

Geological range: Lower Carboniferous.

Geographical distribution: Europe.

Features: Small fishes of somewhat laterally compressed body shape. Head small, deep, with somewhat pointed snout. Eyes large. Dorsal fin in the posterior third of the body, opposite the anal fin. Scales square in the dorsal part of the body, rectangular more ventrally, arranged in diagonal rows.

Remarks: Small predators.

Recent relatives: None. Died out in Lower Carboniferous.

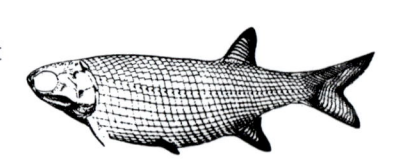

Mesopoma, reconstruction after the Hunterian Museum.

CHONDROSTEI — Chondrosteans
Order: Palaeonisciformes
Suborder: Palaeoniscoidei
Family: Canobiidae

Sundayichthys elegantulus GARDINER (length c. 25 cm) from the Upper Devonian of Witteberg, South Africa. Original: Albany Museum, Grahamstown, South Africa.

Genus: *Sundayichthys* GARDINER, 1969.

Geological range: Upper Devonian.

Geographical distribution: South Africa.

Features: Middle-sized fishes of somewhat compressed shape. Head deep with somewhat rounded snout. Eyes large. Dorsal fin relatively large and pointed, situated in the posterior half of the body. Anal fin very posterior. Caudal fin heterocercal, with the upper lobe longer than the lower. Pectoral and pelvic fins relatively broad. Scales square to rectangular.

Remarks: Middle-sized predators.

Recent relatives: None. Died out in Upper Devonian.

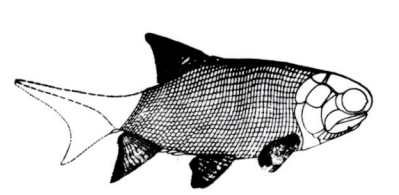

Sundayichthys, reconstruction after GARDINER.

267

CHONDROSTEI
Chondrosteans
Order: Palaeonisciformes
Suborder: Palaeoniscoidei
Family: Canobiidae

Cornuboniscus budensis WHITE (length c. 3 cm) from the Lower Carboniferous of Bude, Cornwall, England, U.K. Original: Geologisch Museum, Amsterdam, Netherlands.

Genus: *Cornuboniscus* WHITE, 1939.

Geological range: Lower Carboniferous.

Geographical distribution: Europe.

Features: Very small slender fishes with elongate head and rounded snout. Eyes large. Dorsal fin very posterior, opposite the smaller anal fin. Caudal fin heterocercal with projecting upper lobe. Pelvic fins small and pointed. Scales rectangular, arranged in diagonal rows.

Remarks: Very small predatory fishes.

Recent relatives: None. Died out in Lower Carboniferous.

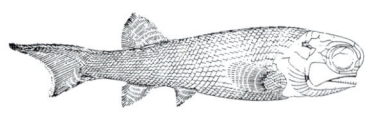

Cornuboniscus, reconstruction after WHITE.

CHONDROSTEI
Order: Palaeonisciformes
Family: Styracopteridae

Chondrosteans
Suborder: Palaeoniscoidei

Benedenius deneensis TRAQUAIR (length c. 22 cm) from the Lower Carboniferous of Denée, Belgium. Original: The Natural History Museum, London, U.K.

Genus: *Benedenius* TRAQUAIR, 1878.

Synonym: *Benedenichthys*

Geological range: Lower Carboniferous.

Geographical distribution: Europe.

Features: Middle-sized fishes of rather plump body shape. Head small and deep. Snout pointed. Eyes relatively small. Dorsal fin very posterior, almost at the beginning of the caudal fin, opposite the anal fin. Pectoral fins long and narrow. Pelvic fins very small. Scales small but thick.

Remarks: Probably relatively lethargic fishes.

Recent relatives: None. Died out in Lower Carboniferous.

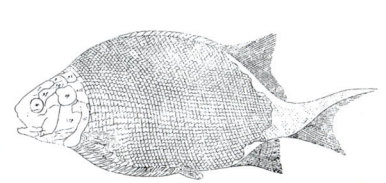

Benedenius, reconstruction after TRAQUAIR.

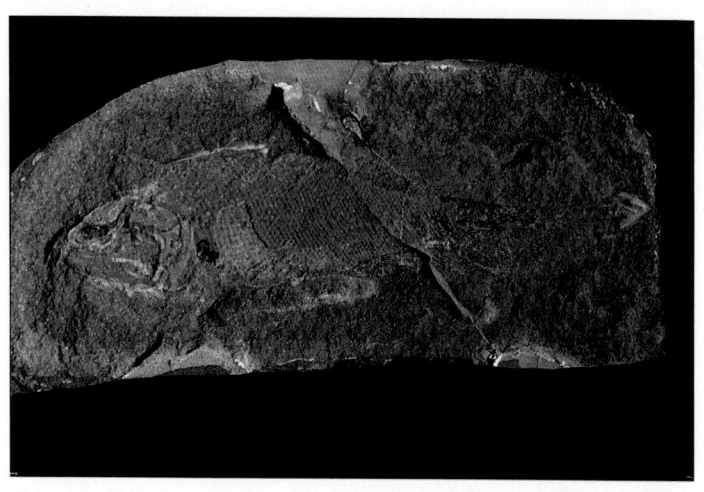

CHONDROSTEI
Order: Palaeonisciformes
Family: Holuriidae

Chondrosteans
Suborder: Palaeoniscoidei

Holurus parki TRAQUAIR (length c. 12 cm) from the Lower Carboniferous of Eskdale, Scotland, U.K. Original: Royal Museum of Scotland, Edinburgh, U.K.

Genus: *Holurus* TRAQUAIR, 1881.

Geological range: Lower Carboniferous.

Geographical distribution: Europe.

Features: Small fishes of somewhat laterally compressed body shape. Head elongate. Snout pointed. Eyes small. Dorsal fin broad and low, very posterior in position, opposite the smaller anal fin. Caudal fin not divided. Pectoral and pelvic fins small. Scales almost square, arranged in curved diagonal rows.

Remarks: Small predators.

Recent relatives: None. Died out in Lower Carboniferous.

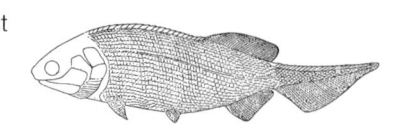

Holurus, reconstruction after TRAQUAIR.

CHONDROSTEI — Chondrosteans
Order: Palaeonisciformes
Family: Pygopteridae

Suborder: Palaeoniscoidei

Nematoptychius greenocki (AGASSIZ) (length c. 45 cm) from the Lower Carboniferous of Edinburgh, Scotland, U.K. Original: Henne Collection, Stuttgart, Germany.

Genus: *Nematoptychius* TRAQUAIR, 1875.

Geological range: Lower Carboniferous.

Geographical distribution: Europe.

Features: Relatively large fishes with slender streamlined bodies. Head elongate. Snout pointed. Eyes large. Dorsal fin pointed, opposite the likewise pointed anal fin. Caudal fin heterocercal with very elongate narrow lobes. Scales small and thin.

Remarks: Large predators.

Recent relatives: None. Died out in Lower Carboniferous.

CHONDROSTEI
Chondrosteans
Order: Palaeonisciformes
Suborder: Palaeoniscoidei
Family: Pygopteridae

Pygopterus humboldti AGASSIZ (length c. 48 cm) from the Upper Permian of Richelsdorf, Hesse, Germany. Original: Perner Collection, Bad Homburg, Germany.

Genus: *Pygopterus* AGASSIZ, 1833.

Geological range: Middle Permian to Lower Triassic.

Geographical distribution: Europe, Greenland, South Africa.

Features: Relatively large fishes with slender streamlined bodies. Head elongate. Snout pointed. Eyes large. Dorsal fin pointed, situated in the posterior half of the body, almost opposite the likewise pointed anal fin. Caudal fin heterocercal with long narrow lobes. Pectoral fins narrow. Pelvic fins small and pointed. Scales small and thin.

Remarks: Large predators.

Recent relatives: None. Died out in Lower Triassic.

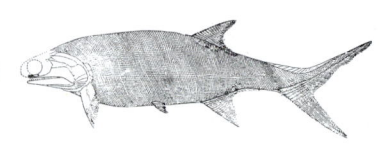

Pygopterus, reconstruction after ALDINGER.

CHONDROSTEI
Chondrosteans
Order: Palaeonisciformes
Family: Elonichthyidae

Suborder: Palaeoniscoidei

Drydenius insignis TRAQUAIR (length c. 10 cm) from the Lower Carboniferous of Edinburgh, Scotland, U.K. Original: National Museum of Scotland, Edinburgh, U.K.

Genus: *Drydenius* TRAQUAIR, 1890.

Geological range: Lower Carboniferous to Permian.

Geographical distribution: Europe.

Features: Small slender fishes. Head small and elongate. Snout pointed. Eyes small. Caudal fin heterocercal with narrow pointed lobes. Scales thick and rhombic.

Remarks: Small predators.

Recent relatives: None. Died out in Permian.

CHONDROSTEI — Chondrosteans
Order: Palaeonisciformes
Family: Elonichthyidae
Suborder: Palaeoniscoidei

Elonichthys punctatus ALDINGER (length c. 8 cm) from the Lower Permian of Palatinate, Germany. Original: Henne Collection, Stuttgart, Germany.

Genus: *Elonichthys* GIEBEL, 1848.

Synonyms: *Ganocrodus*, *Propalaeoniscus*.

Geological range: Lower Carboniferous to Upper Triassic.

Geographical distribution: South America, western Africa.

Features: Small to middle-sized fishes with somewhat laterally compressed bodies. Head elongate with slightly pointed snout. Eyes relatively small. Dorsal fin pointed triangular, in the posterior half of the body. Anal fin almost equal in size and somewhat more posterior. Pectoral and pelvic fins pointed and rather large. Scales square, arranged in diagonal rows.

Remarks: Predators. The species *punctatus* is not clear.

Recent relatives: None. Died out in Upper Triassic.

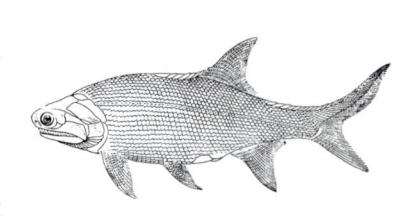

Elonichthys, after TRAQUAIR.

CHONDROSTEI — Chondrosteans
Order: Palaeonisciformes
Family: Elonichthyidae
Suborder: Palaeoniscoidei

Ganolepis gracilis WOODWARD (length c. 7 cm) from the Permian of Siberia, Russia, C.I.S. Original: Paleontologicheskii Muzei Russkoi Akademii Nauk, Moscow, Russia.

Genus: *Ganolepis* WOODWARD, 1893.

Geological range: Permian.

Geographical distribution: Northern Asia.

Features: Small fishes with slender elongate bodies. Head elongate. Snout rounded. Eyes large. Dorsal fin obtuse-triangular, situated in the posterior half of the body. Anal fin somewhat behind the dorsal fin. Pectoral and pelvic fins small. Scales square, arranged in regular rows.

Remarks: Predators.

Recent relatives: None. Died out in Permian.

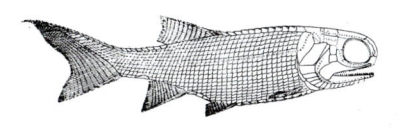

Ganolepis, reconstruction after ORLOV.

CHONDROSTEI
Order: Palaeonisciformes
Family: Elonichthyidae

Chondrosteans
Suborder: Palaeoniscoidei

Gonatodus punctatus Agassiz (length c. 17 cm) from the Lower Carboniferous of Edinburgh, Scotland, U.K. Original: National Museum of Scotland, Edinburgh, U.K.

Genus: *Gonatodus* Traquair, 1877.

Geological range: Lower to Upper Carboniferous.

Geographical distribution: Europe, North America.

Features: Middle-sized fishes with laterally compressed bodies. Head elongate. Snout rounded. Eyes large. Dorsal fin relatively large and pointed triangular, obliquely opposite the anal fin. Caudal fin heterocercal with almost equal-sized lobes. Pectoral and pelvic fins elongate and pointed. Scales rectangular, arranged in regular rows.

Remarks: Predatory fishes, probably with a somewhat lethargic mode of life.

Recent relatives: None. Died out

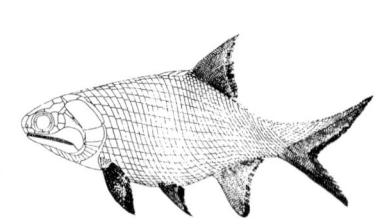

Gonatodus, reconstruction after Gardiner.

CHONDROSTEI / Chondrosteans

Order: Palaeonisciformes
Family: Elonichthyidae
Suborder: Palaeoniscoidei

Acrolepis ortholepis TRAQUAIR (length c. 30 cm) from the Lower Carboniferous of Eskdale, Scotland, U.K. Original: The Natural History Museum, London, U.K. (P4081).

Genus: *Acrolepis* AGASSIZ, 1833.

Geological range: Lower Carboniferous to Upper Permian.

Geographical distribution: Europe, North America, South America, northern Asia, Australia.

Features: Relatively large fishes with slender bodies. Head elongate. Snout rounded. Dorsal fin in the posterior half of the body. Pectoral, pelvic and anal fins large. Scales rhombic, overlapping.

Remarks: Large predatory fishes.

Recent relatives: None. Died out in Permian.

CHONDROSTEI
Order: Palaeonisciformes
Family: Acrolepididae

Chondrosteans
Suborder: Palaeoniscoidei

Acropholis stensioei ALDINGER (length c. 65 cm) from the Permian of Cape Stosch, Greenland. Original: Geologisk Museum, Copenhagen, Denmark.

Genus: *Acropholis* ALDINGER, 1935.

Geological range: Upper Permian.

Geographical distribution: Greenland.

Features: Large predatory fishes with elongate streamlined bodies. Head elongate. Snout pointed. Dorsal fin pointed triangular, very posterior in position, obliquely opposite the anal fin which is even more posterior. Caudal fin heterocercal, probably with narrow lobes of almost equal length. Scales very small and overlapping.

Remarks: Large predatory fishes.

Recent relatives: None. Died out in Upper Permian.

Acropholis, reconstruction after ALDINGER.

CHONDROSTEI
Order: Palaeonisciformes
Family: Acrolepididae

Chondrosteans
Suborder: Palaeoniscoidei

Boreosomus sp. (length c. 13 cm) from the Lower Triassic of Wapiti Lake, Canada. Original: Tyrell Museum of Paleontology, Drumheller, Alberta, Canada.

Genus: *Boreosomus* STENSIÖ, 1921.

Synonyms: *Diaphorognathus*

Geological range: Lower to Upper Triassic.

Geographical distribution: Greenland, Spitzbergen, Madagascar, North America.

Features: Small to middle-sized fishes with slender elongate bodies. Head deep. Snout pointed. Eyes relatively large. Dorsal fin at the hinder end of the anterior half of the body. Caudal fin heterocercal, with broad pointed lobes of equal length. Pectoral fins large and broad. Pelvic fins small. Anal fin triangular. Scales small, rectangular, arranged in diagonal rows.

Remarks: Predators.

Recent relatives: None. Died out in Upper Triassic.

Boreosomus, reconstruction after LEHMAN.

279

CHONDROSTEI
Order: Palaeonisciformes
Family: Acrolepididae

Chondrosteans
Suborder: Palaeoniscoidei

Mesembroniscus longisquamosus WADE (length c. 8 cm) from the Middle Triassic of Brookvale, New South Wales, Australia. Original: The Natural History Museum, London, U.K.

Genus: *Mesembroniscus* WADE, 1935.

Geological range: Middle Triassic.

Geographical distribution: Australia.

Features: Small fishes with elongate slender bodies. Head elongate. Snout rounded. Dorsal fin pointed triangular, situated in the posterior half of the body, obliquely opposite the more posterior anal fin. Caudal fin heterocercal with a long upper lobe. Scales small, rectangular.

Remarks: Small predators.

Recent relatives: None. Died out in Middle Triassic.

CHONDROSTEI
Order: Palaeonisciformes
Family: Acrolepididae

Chondrosteans
Suborder: Palaeoniscoidei

Reticulepis exsculpta (Kurtze) (length c. 57 cm) from the Upper Permian of Richelsdorf, Hesse, Germany. Original: Naturkundemuseum in Ottoneum, Kassel, Germany.

Genus: *Reticulepis* Westoll, 1934.

Geological range: Upper Permian.

Geographical distribution: Europe.

Features: Middle-sized fishes with slender bodies. Head relatively shallow. Snout probably rounded. Jaws set with pointed teeth. Dorsal fin triangular, in the posterior half of the body, obliquely opposite the smaller anal fin. Caudal fin heterocercal, with narrow pointed lobes of almost equal length. Scales finely sculptured. In the posterior part this sculpture appears reticulate because of transverse ridges.

Remarks: Predators.

Recent relatives: None. Died out in Upper Permian.

CHONDROSTEI — Chondrosteans
Order: Palaeonisciformes
Family: Acrolepididae
Suborder: Palaeoniscoidei

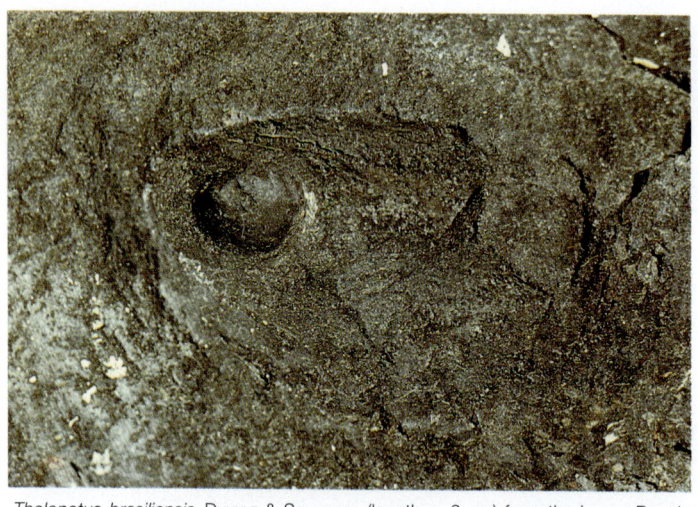

Tholonotus brasiliensis DUNKLE & SCHAEFFER (length c. 6 cm) from the Lower Permian of Brazil. Original: American Museum of Natural History, New York, N.Y., U.S.A.

Genus: *Tholonotus* DUNKLE & SCHAEFFER, 1956.

Geological range: Lower Permian.

Geographical distribution: South America.

Features: Small to middle-sized fishes. Head deep. Snout rounded. Eyes large. Scales thick and rhombic. Teeth small and pointed.

Remarks: Small to medium-sized predatory fishes.

Recent relatives: None. Died out in Lower Permian.

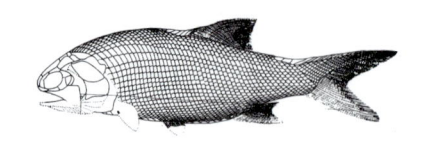

Tholonotus, reconstruction after DUNKLE & SCHAEFFER.

CHONDROSTEI / Chondrosteans
Order: Palaeonisciformes
Family: Amblypteridae
Suborder: Palaeoniscoidei

Amblypterus macropterus AGASSIZ (length c. 7 cm) from the Lower Permian of the Saar region, Germany. Original: Naturhistorisches Museum, Vienna, Austria.

Genus: *Amblypterus* AGASSIZ, 1833.

Geological range: Lower to Upper Permian.

Geographical distribution: Europe, North America.

Features: Small fishes with laterally compressed bodies. Head deep. Snout blunt. Eyes large. Dorsal fin relatively large, pointed triangular, situated in the posterior half of the body, obliquely opposite the likewise relatively large anal fin. Pectoral pelvic fins broadly pointed. Scales square to rectangular, arranged in diagonal rows.

Remarks: Small predators. Now reclassified Linto the genus *Paramblypterus*.

Recent relatives: None. Died out in Upper Permian.

Amblypterus, after AGASSIZ.

CHONDROSTEI
Chondrosteans
Order: Palaeonisciformes
Suborder: Palaeoniscoidei
Family: Amblypteridae

Lawnia sp. (length c. 14 cm) from the Lower Permian of Baylor County, Texas. Original: University of Alberta, Edmonton, Canada.

Genus: *Lawnia* WILSON, 1953.

Geological range: Lower Permian.

Geographical distribution: North America.

Features: Middle-sized fishes with elongate very slender bodies. Head elongate. Snout rounded. Eyes small. Dorsal fin triangular, situated in the posterior half of the body, opposite the smaller, but likewise triangular, anal fin. Pectoral fins elongate and narrow. Pelvic fins triangular. Scales thick and rectangular, arranged in diagonal rows.

Remarks: Middle-sized predators.

Recent relatives: None. Died out in Middle Permian.

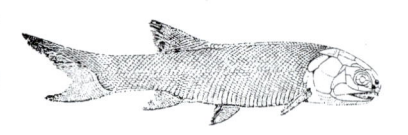

Lawnia, reconstruction after WILSON.

CHONDROSTEI / Chondrosteans
Order: Palaeonisciformes
Family: Aeduellidae
Suborder: Palaeoniscoidei

Aeduella blainvillei (AGASSIZ) (length c. 13 cm) from the Lower Permian of Palatinate, Germany. Original: Henne Collection, Stuttgart, Germany.

Genus: *Aeduella* WESTOLL, 1937.

Geological range: Lower Permian.

Geographical distribution: Europe.

Features: Middle-sized fishes with laterally compressed bodies. Head deep. Snout slightly pointed. Eyes unusually large. Dorsal fin pointed triangular, situated in the posterior half of the body, obliquely opposite the obtusely triangular anal fin. Pectoral fins small. Pelvic fins broad. Scales rectangular, arranged in regular rows.

Remarks: Middle-sized predators. The species *blainvillei* is still controversial.

Recent relatives: None. Died out in Lower Permian.

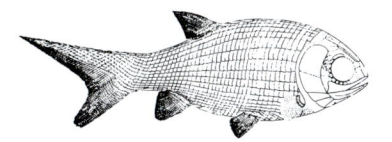

Aeduella, after PIVETEAU.

285

CHONDROSTEI
Chondrosteans
Order: Palaeonisciformes
Suborder: Palaeoniscoidei
Family: Aeduellidae

Bourbonella guilloti HEYLER (length c. 15 cm) from the Lower Permian of L'Archambault, France. Original: The Natural History Museum, London, U.K. (P 61120)

Genus: *Bourbonella* HEYLER, 1967.

Geological range: Lower Permian.

Geographical distribution: Europe.

Features: Middle-sized fishes with laterally compressed bodies. Head deep. Snout rounded. Eyes strikingly large. Dorsal fin pointed and elongate, situated in the posterior half of the body, obliquely opposite the anal fin which is likewise pointed. Pectoral fins small and triangular. Pelvic fins relatively long and broad. Scales square to rectangular, arranged in diagonal rows.

Remarks: Middle-sized predators.

Recent relatives: None. Died out in Lower Permian.

Bourbonella, reconstruction after HEYLER.

CHONDROSTEI
Chondrosteans
Order: Palaeonisciformes
Suborder: Palaeoniscoidei
Family: Commentryidae

Commentrya traquairi Sauvage (length c. 13 cm) from the Upper Carboniferous of Commentry, France. Original: The Natural History Museum, London, U.K. (P995).

Genus: *Commentrya* Sauvage, 1888.

Synonyms: *Elaveria*

Geological range: Upper Carboniferous.

Geographical distribution: Europe.

Features: Small to middle-sized fishes with somewhat laterally compressed bodies. Head deep. Snout rounded. Eyes relatively large. Dorsal fin triangular, very posterior in position, opposite the considerably larger anal fin. Pectoral and pelvic fins relatively large. Scales square to rectangular, arranged in regular rows.

Remarks: Predators.

Recent relatives: None. Died out in Upper Carboniferous.

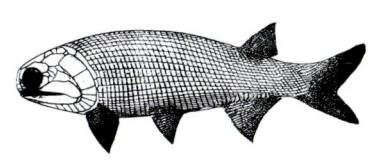

Commentrya, reconstruction after Piveteau.

CHONDROSTEI / Chondrosteans
Order: Palaeonisciformes — Suborder: Palaeoniscoidei
Family: Commentryidae

Paramblypterus gelberti (GOLDFUSS) (length c. 20 cm) from the Lower Permian of Odernheim, Palatinate, Germany. Original: Interfoss, Munich, Germany.

Genus: *Paramblypterus* SAUVAGE, 1888.

Synonyms: *Amblypterops, Cosmopoma, Dipteroma*.

Geological range: Lower Permian.

Geographical distribution: Europe.

Features: Middle-sized fishes with somewhat laterally compressed bodies. Head deep. Snout rounded. Eyes small. Dorsal fin triangular and pointed, posterior in position, obliquely opposite the equally pointed anal fin. Caudal fin heterocercal with the upper lobe longer than the lower. Pectoral fins elongate and pointed. Pelvic fins triangular. Scales rectangular to rhombic, arranged in diagonal rows.

Remarks: Predators.

Recent relatives: None. Died out in Lower Permian.

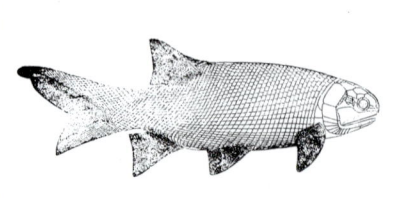

Paramblypterus, reconstruction after BLOT.

288

CHONDROSTEI
Chondrosteans
Order: Palaeonisciformes
Suborder: Palaeoniscoidei
Family: Palaeoniscidae

Gyrolepis albertii AGASSIZ (length c. 25 cm) from the Middle Triassic of Nußloch, Baden, Germany. Original: Staatliches Museum für Naturkunde, Karlsruhe, Germany.

Genus: *Gyrolepis* AGASSIZ, 1833.

Geological range: Lower to Upper Triassic.

Geographical distribution: Europe, North America, eastern Asia.

Features: Middle-sized fishes with slender bodies. Head shallow and elongate. Snout pointed. Dorsal fin pointed triangular, situated in the posterior half of the body, opposite the anal fin. Caudal fin heterocercal with narrow pointed lobes. Pectoral fins long and narrow. Pelvic fins triangular. Scales rhombic, arranged in diagonal rows.

Remarks: Predatory fishes.

Recent relatives: None. Died out in Upper Triassic.

CHONDROSTEI
Chondrosteans
Order: Palaeonisciformes
Suborder: Palaeoniscoidei
Family: Palaeoniscidae

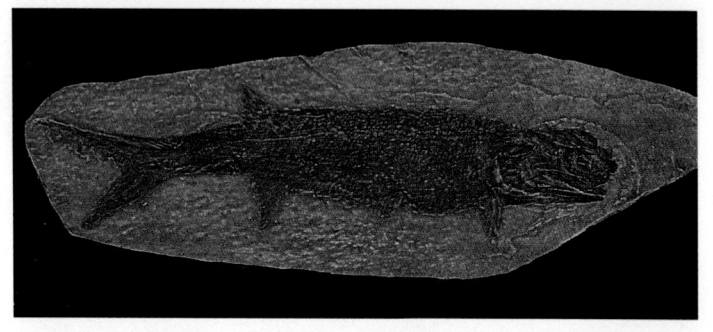

Howqualepis rostridens LONG (length c. 19 cm) from the Lower Carboniferous of Mansfield, Australia. Original: Bureau of Mineral Resources, Canberra, Australia.

Genus: *Howqualepis* LONG, 1988.

Geological range: Lower Carboniferous.

Geographical distribution: Australia.

Features: Middle-sized fishes with slender elongate bodies. Head elongate. Snout blunt. Eyes small. Dorsal fin triangular, situated in the posterior half of the body, opposite the likewise triangular anal fin. Caudal fin relatively large, heterocercal, with upper and lower lobes of almost equal length. Pectoral fins pointed. Pelvic fins broad at the base. Scales small, arranged in regular rows.

Remarks: Predatory fishes.

Recent relatives: None. Died out in Lower Carboniferous.

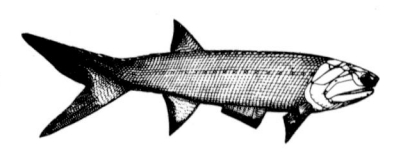

Howqualepis, after LONG.

CHONDROSTEI — Chondrosteans
Order: Palaeonisciformes
Family: Palaeoniscidae
Suborder: Palaeoniscoidei

Myriolepis clarki EGERTON (length c. 18 cm) from the Lower Triassic of Gosford, New South Wales, Australia. Original: The Natural History Museum, London, U.K. (P18069)

Genus: *Myriolepis* EGERTON, 1864.

Geological range: Lower Triassic.

Geographical distribution: Australia.

Features: Middle-sized fishes with slender elongate bodies. Head shallow and elongate. Snout pointed. Eyes small. Dorsal fin triangular, in the posterior half of the body. Anal fin lies considerably farther behind. Scales strong and dense.

Remarks: Predatory fishes.

Recent relatives: None. Died out in Lower Triassic.

CHONDROSTEI
Order: Palaeonisciformes
Family: Palaeoniscidae

Chondrosteans
Suborder: Palaeoniscoidei

Palaeoniscum freieslebeni de BLAINVILLE (length c. 28 cm) from the Upper Permian of Richelsdorf, Hesse, Germany. Original: Perner Collection, Bad Homburg, Germany.

Genus: *Palaeoniscum* de BLAINVILLE, 1818.

Synonyms: *Eupalaeouiscus, Palaeoniscus, Geomichthys, Palaeothrissum*

Geological range: Lower Permian to Upper Triassic.

Geographical distribution: Europe, North America, Greenland, Spitzbergen, Australia.

Features: Middle-sized fishes with elongate bodies. Head shallow and elongate. Snout blunt. Eyes large. Dorsal fin small and pointed. Pectoral fins also small. Scales small, arranged in regular rows.

Remarks: Predators.

Recent relatives: None. Died out in Upper Triassic.

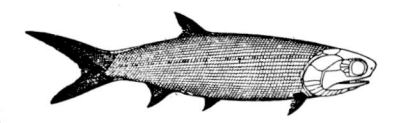

Palaeoniscum, reconstruction after TRAQUAIR.

CHONDROSTEI — Chondrosteans

Order: Palaeonisciformes
Family: Palaeoniscidae

Suborder: Palaeoniscoidei

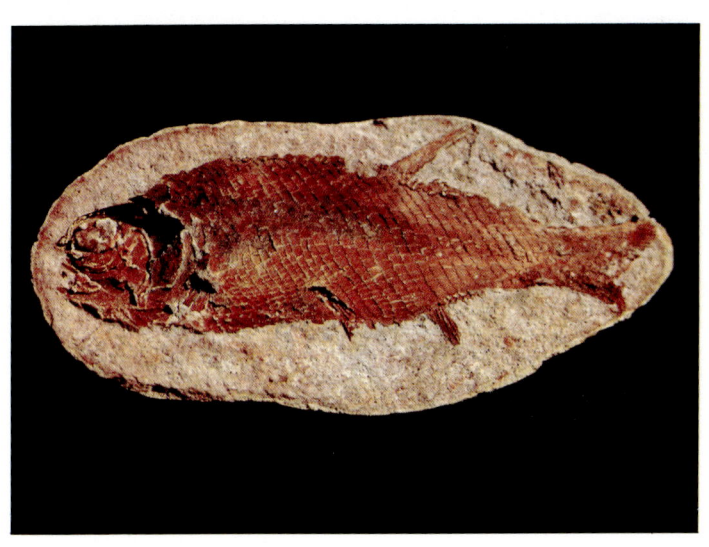

Pteronisculus cicatrosus WHITE (length c. 7 cm) from the Lower Triassic of Madagascar. Original: Interfoss, Munich, Germany.

Genus: *Pteronisculus* WHITE, 1933.

Synonym: *Glaucolepis*.

Geological range: Lower Triassic.

Geographical distribution: Spitzbergen, Greenland, Madagascar, Australia.

Features: Small fishes with somewhat laterally compressed bodies and elongate head. Snout pointed. Eyes large. Dorsal fin relatively small and triangular, obliquely opposite the more posteriorly placed anal fin. Pectoral fins long and broad. Pelvic fins small and pointed. Scales small and arranged in regular rows.

Remarks: Predators.

Recent relatives: None. Died out in Lower Triassic.

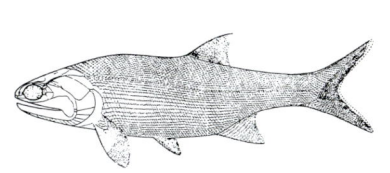

Pteronisculus, reconstruction after LEHMAN.

CHONDROSTEI
Order: Palaeonisciformes
Family: Palaeoniscidae

Chondrosteans
Suborder: Palaeoniscoidei

Turseodus acutus Leidy (length c. 19 cm) from the Upper Triassic of Firestone, U.S.A. Original: Peabody Museum of Natural History, New Haven, Connecticut, U.S.A.

Genus: *Turseodus* Leidy, 1857.

Synonyms: *Eurecana*, *Gwynnedichthys*.

Geological range: Upper Triassic.

Geographical distribution: North America.

Features: Middle-sized fishes with somewhat laterally compressed bodies. Head elongate. Snout rounded. Dorsal fin in the posterior half of the body. Caudal fin heterocercal with the upper lobe longer. Pectoral fins small and pointed. Scales small, arranged in regular rows.

Remarks: Probably predators.

Recent relatives: None. Died out in Upper Triassic.

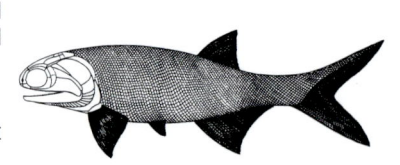

Turseodus, reconstruction after Schaeffer.

CHONDROSTEI
Chondrosteans
Order: Palaeonisciformes
Family: Dicellopygidae
Suborder: Palaeoniscoidei

Dicellopyge draperi (WOODWARD) (length c. 13 cm) from the Lower Triassic of Rouxville, South Africa. Original: The Natural History Museum, London, U.K. (P 6084)

Genus: *Dicellopyge* BROUGH, 1931.

Geological range: Lower Triassic.

Geographical distribution: South Africa.

Features: Middle-sized fishes with slender elongate bodies. Head deep. Snout rounded. Eyes large. Dorsal fin triangular, in the posterior half of the body, opposite the likewise triangular anal fin. Caudal fin heterocercal, deeply forked with relatively long, almost equal-sized lobes. Pectoral and pelvic fins small and pointed. Scales rectangular, arranged in diagonal rows.

Remarks: Predators.

Recent relatives: None. Died out in Lower Triassic.

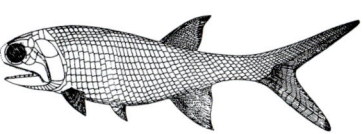

Dicellopyge, reconstruction after BROUGH.

295

CHONDROSTEI
Chondrosteans
Order: Palaeonisciformes
Suborder: Palaeoniscoidei
Family: Birgeriidae

Birgeria acuminata (AGASSIZ) (length c. 79 cm) from the Upper Triassic of Zogno, Bergamo, Italy. Original: Museo Civico Naturali Caffi, Bergamo, Italy.

Genus: *Birgeria* STENSIÖ, 1919.

Synonym: *Xenestes*.

Geological range: Lower to Upper Triassic.

Geographical distribution: Europe, Spitzbergen, Greenland, North America.

Features: Relatively large fishes with slender, elongate bodies. Head long and shallow. Snout blunt. Eyes small. Gape long. Dorsal fin triangular, very posterior in position, opposite the likewise triangular anal fin. Pectoral fins broad and pointed. Pelvic fins small. Scales sparse and thin.

Remarks: Predatory fishes.

Recent relatives: Some authors see the genus *Birgeria* as related to the order Acipenseriformes and thus as a forerunner of fossil sturgeons.

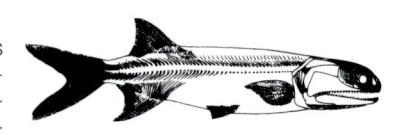

Birgeria, reconstruction after PIVETEAU.

CHONDROSTEI
Order: Palaeonisciformes
Family: Scanilepididae

Chondrosteans
Suborder: Palaeoniscoidei

Scanilepis dubia ALDINGER (length c. 65 cm) from the Triassic of Scania, Sweden. Original: Naturhistoriska Riksmuseet, Stockholm, Sweden.

Genus: *Scanilepis* ALDINGER, 1937.

Geological range: Lower to Upper Triassic.

Geographical distribution: Europe, Spitzbergen.

Features: Relatively large fishes with somewhat laterally compressed bodies. Skull deep. Snout blunt. Eyes small. Dorsal fin fringe-like, stretching along almost the whole of the back. Anal fin broad-based. Caudal fin heterocercal with narrow upper and broad lower lobes. Pectoral and pelvic fins small. Scales square to rectangular, arranged in diagonal rows.

Remarks: Large predators.

Recent relatives: None. Died out in Upper Triassic.

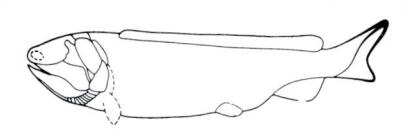

Scanilepis, reconstruction after LEHMAN.

CHONDROSTEI — Chondrosteans
Order: Palaeonisciformes
Family: Coccolepididae
Suborder: Palaeoniscoidei

Coccolepis bucklandi AGASSIZ (length c. 10 cm) from the Upper Jurassic of Solnhofen (Eichstätt), Bavaria, Germany. Original: Jura-Museum, Eichstätt, Germany.

Genus: *Coccolepis* AGASSIZ, 1874.

Geological range: Lower Jurassic to Lower Cretaceous.

Geographical distribution: Europe, Asia, Australia.

Features: Small fishes with somewhat laterally compressed bodies. Head deep. Snout rather blunt. Eyes small. Dorsal fin triangular, relatively large, situated in the posterior half of the body, obliquely opposite the anal fin. Caudal fin heterocercal with the upper lobe somewhat larger than the lower. Pelvic fins large and pectoral fins somewhat smaller. Scales round and delicate.

Remarks: The only chondrosteans in the Lithographic Stone of Solnhofen.

Recent relatives: None. Died out in Lower Cretaceous.

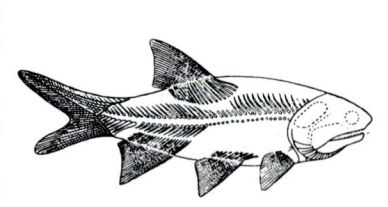

Coccolepis, reconstruction after TRAQUAIR

CHONDROSTEI
Chondrosteans
Order: Palaeonisciformes
Suborder: Palaeoniscoidei
Family: Unnamed

Acanthoniscus cracens LOWNEY (length c. 11 cm) from the Lower Carboniferous of Bear Gulch, Montana, U.S.A. Original: Field Museum of Natural History, Chicago, Illinois, U.S.A.

Genus: *Acanthoniscus* LOWNEY, 1980.

Geological range: Lower Carboniferous.

Geographical distribution: North America.

Features: Small fishes with slender elongate bodies. Head elongate. Snout pointed. Eyes small. Dorsal fin pointed, very posterior in position, almost opposite the relatively large anal fin. Pelvic fins small. Scales elongate, arranged in diagonal rows.

Remarks: Predators.

Recent relatives: None. Died out in Lower Carboniferous.

CHONDROSTEI
Order: Palaeonisciformes
Family: Unnamed

Chondrosteans
Suborder: Palaeoniscoidei

Atherstonia minor WOODWARD (length c. 14 cm) from the Permian of Plaatjesfontein, South Africa. Original: Albany Museum, Grahamstown, South Africa.

Genus: *Atherstonia* WOODWARD, 1889.

Synonym: *Hypterus*

Geological range: Upper Permian to Lower Triassic.

Geographical distribution: Europe, South Africa, Madagascar, North America.

Features: Middle-sized fishes with slender elongate bodies. Head elongate. Snout blunt. Eyes large. Dorsal fin with a broad base, posterior in position, obliquely opposite the anal fin. Pectoral fins elongate. Pelvic fins broad. Scales square to rectangular, arranged in diagonal rows.

Remarks: Predators.

Recent relatives: None. Died out in Lower Triassic.

Atherstonia, reconstruction after ORLOV.

CHONDROSTEI
Order: Palaeonisciformes
Family: Unnamed

Chondrosteans
Suborder: Palaeoniscoidei

Atracauda lundi LOWNEY (length c. 13 cm) from the Lower Carboniferous of Bear Gulch, Montana, U.S.A. Original: Tyrell Museum of Paleontology, Drumheller, Alberta, Canada.

Genus: *Atracauda* LOWNEY, 1980.

Geological range: Lower Carboniferous.

Geographical distribution: North America.

Features: Small to middle-sized fishes with slender elongate bodies. Head deep. Snout blunt. Dorsal fin relatively small, situated in the posterior half of the body, obliquely opposite the likewise small anal fin. Caudal fin heterocercal, deeply forked, upper lobe somewhat longer than the lower. Scales rhombic, arranged in diagonal rows.

Remarks: Predatory fishes.

Recent relatives: None. Died out in Lower Carboniferous.

CHONDROSTEI / Chondrosteans
Order: Palaeonisciformes — **Suborder: Palaeoniscoidei**
Family: Unnamed

Belichthys minimus WADE (length c. 5 cm) from the Middle Triassic of Brookvale, New South Wales, Australia. Original: The Natural History Museum, London, U.K. (P 24708-9)

Genus: *Belichthys* WADE, 1935.

Geological range: Middle Triassic.

Geographical distribution: Australia.

Features: Small fishes with slender elongate bodies. Head elongate. Snout rounded. Eyes large. Dorsal fin pointed, approximately in the middle of the body, opposite the small pelvic fins. Caudal fin heterocercal with narrow pointed lobes, the upper being longer than the lower. Scales small and rhombic.

Remarks: Small predators.

Recent relatives: None. Died out in Middle Triassic.

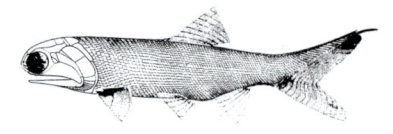

Belichthys, reconstruction after HUTCHINSON.

CHONDROSTEI / Chondrosteans
Order: Palaeonisciformes
Family: Unnamed
Suborder: Palaeoniscoidei?

Fubarichthys prolatus (length c. 10 cm) from the Lower Carboniferous of Bear Gulch, Montana, U.S.A. Original: Staatliches Museum für Naturkunde, Karlsruhe, Germany.

Genus: *Fubarichthys* Lowney

Geological range: Lower Carboniferous.

Geographical distribution: North America.

Features: Small fishes with somewhat laterally compressed bodies. Head deep. Snout rounded. Eyes large. Gape very long. Dorsal fin behind the middle of the body, obliquely opposite the pelvic fins. Caudal fin heterocercal, deeply forked, upper lobe somewhat longer than the lower. Anal fin pointed. Pelvic fins small. Pectoral fins somewhat broader. Scales small and square, arranged in diagonal rows.

Remarks: Small predators.

Recent relatives: None. Died out in Lower Carboniferous.

CHONDROSTEI / Chondrosteans
Order: Palaeonisciformes
Family: Unnamed
Suborder: Palaeoniscoidei

Gardineria akolkensis KAZANTSEVA (length c. 18 cm) from the Permian of eastern Europe. Original: Paleontologicheskii Muzei Russkoi Akademii Nauk, Moscow, Russia.

Genus: *Gardineria* KAZANTSEVA-SELENTEVA, 1981.

Geological range: Permian.

Geographical distribution: Eastern Europe.

Features: Slender, middle-sized fishes. Head narrow. Eyes small. Gape long. Dorsal fin pointed triangular, situated in the posterior third of the body, opposite the somewhat broader anal fin. Pelvic fins small. Scales arranged in diagonal rows.

Remarks: Small predators.

Recent relatives: None. Died out in Permian.

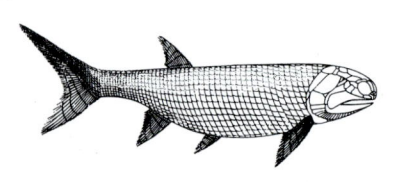

Gardineria, reconstruction after Akademia Nauk, Moscow.

CHONDROSTEI   Chondrosteans
Order: Palaeonisciformes   Suborder: Palaeoniscoidei
Family: Unnamed

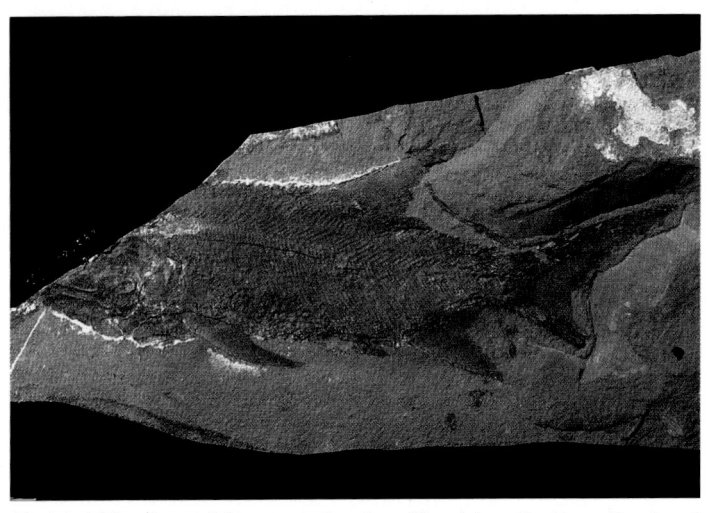

Muensterichthys buergeri SCHAUMBERG (length c. 32 cm) from the Upper Permian of Richelsdorf, Hesse, Germany. Original: Bürger Collection, Bad Hersfeld, Germany.

Genus: *Muensterichthys* SCHAUMBERG, 1989.

Geological range: Upper Permian.

Geographical distribution: Europe.

Features: Middle-sized spindle-shaped fishes. Head deep. Snout rounded. Eyes large. Gape long. Lower jaw set posteriorly. Dorsal fin large, triangular, situated in the posterior half of the body. Anal fin obliquely opposite, of the same shape but somewhat smaller. Caudal fin heterocercal, with the lower lobe shorter. Pectoral fins long, narrow and drawn out into a point. Pelvic fins short and pointed. Scales small.

Remarks: Probably predatory fishes.

Recent relatives: None. Died out in Upper Permian.

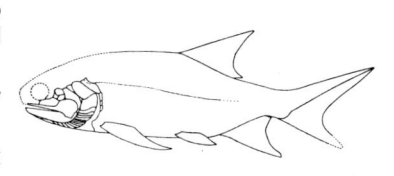

Muensterichthys, reconstruction after SCHAUMBERG.

CHONDROSTEI   Chondrosteans

Order: Palaeonisciformes   Suborder: Palaeoniscoidei
Family: Unnamed

Pteroniscus sp. (length c. 6 cm) from the Upper Jurassic of Karatau, Central Asia. Original: Museum für Geologie und Paläontologie, Tübingen, Germany.

Genus: *Pteroniscus* CHEKKER, 1848.

Geological range: Upper Jurassic.

Geographical distribution: Western and central Asia.

Features: Small fishes with slender elongate bodies. Head deep. Snout rounded. Eyes large. Dorsal fin broad at the base, obliquely opposite the posteriorly placed, likewise triangular, anal fins. Pectoral fins broad and pointed. Pelvic fins broad at the base. Scales small, arranged in regular rows.

Remarks: Small predators.

Recent relatives: None. Died out in Upper Jurassic.

Pteroniscus, reconstruction after ORLOV.

CHONDROSTEI — Chondrosteans
Order: Palaeonisciformes
Suborder: Palaeoniscoidei
Family: Unnamed

Willomorichthys striatulus Gardiner (length c. 15 cm) from the Upper Devonian of Witteberg, South Africa. Original: Albany Museum, Grahamstown, South Africa.

Genus: *Willomorichthys* Gardiner, 1969.

Geological range: Upper Devonian.

Geographical distribution: South Africa.

Features: Middle-sized fishes. Head narrow. Snout blunt. Dorsal fin very posterior in position, almost opposite the anal fin. Pectoral fins narrow. Scales small, arranged in regular rows.

Remarks: Predatory fishes.

Recent relatives: None. Died out in Upper Devonian.

CHONDROSTEI
Order: Palaeonisciformes
Family: Unnamed

Chondrosteans
Suborder: Palaeoniscoidei

Yogoniscus gulo LOWNEY (length c. 27 cm) from the Lower Carboniferous of Bear Gulch, Montana, U.S.A. Original: Adelphi University, Garden City, N.J., U.S.A.

Genus: *Yogoniscus* LOWNEY, 1980.

Geological range: Lower Carboniferous.

Geographical distribution: North America.

Features: Middle-sized fishes with elongated bodies. Head elongate. Snout pointed. Eyes large. Dorsal fin, triangular, pointed, situated in the posterior half of the body, obliquely opposite the anal fin which is likewise pointed. Caudal fin heterocercal, deeply forked with the upper lobe somewhat longer than the lower. Scales rhombic, arranged in diagonal rows.

Remarks: Predatory fishes.

Recent relatives: None. Died out in Lower Carboniferous.

CHONDROSTEI
Order: Palaeonisciformes
Family: Platysomidae

Chondrosteans
Suborder: Platysomoidei

Enzichthys aizenvergi SELEZNEVA (length c. 3.5 cm) from the Middle Carboniferous of the Donbass, Ukraine. Original: Paleontologicheskii Muzei Russkoi Akademii Nauk, Moscow, Russia.

Genus: *Enzichthys* SELEZNEVA, 1988.

Geological range: Middle Carboniferous.

Geographical distribution: Eastern Europe.

Features: Very small fishes of rounded rhombic outline. Head deep. Eyes large. Gape rather long. Dorsal fin pointed, situated behind the middle of the body opposite the anal fin. Caudal fin stalked, deeply divided, with narrow lobes. Scales in ventral part of body rod-shaped.

Remarks: Lived in still water and possibly fed on plants.

Recent relatives: None. Died out in Carboniferous.

CHONDROSTEI / Chondrosteans

Order: Palaeonisciformes
Family: Platysomidae
Suborder: Platysomoidei

Mesolepis scalaris TRAQUAIR (length c. 15 cm) from the Upper Carboniferous of Staffordshire, England, U.K. Original: The Natural History Museum, London, U.K. (P 8046)

Genus: *Mesolepis* YOUNG, 1866.

Synonyms: *Pododus*

Geological range: Lower to Upper Carboniferous.

Geographical distribution: Europe.

Features: Middle-sized, laterally compressed fishes with rhombic body outline. Head deep. Snout blunt. Dorsal fin pointed and elongate and fold-like posteriorly. Anal fin with a broad base, low, fold-like but passing into a narrow point. Pectoral and pelvic fins small. Scales rod-like ventrally.

Remarks: Probably lived in still water. Possibly fed, at least partly, on plants.

Recent relatives: None. Died out in Upper Carboniferous.

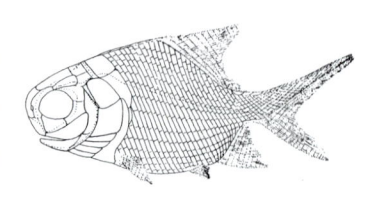

Mesolepis, reconstruction after MOY-THOMAS.

CHONDROSTEI — Chondrosteans
Order: Palaeonisciformes
Family: Platysomidae
Suborder: Platysomoidei

Platysomus striatus AGASSIZ (length c. 22 cm) from the Upper Permian of Richelsdorf, Hesse, Germany. Original: Interfoss, Munich, Germany.

Genus: *Platysomus* AGASSIZ, 1833.

Synonym: *Uropteryx*.

Geological range: Lower Carboniferous to Upper Triassic.

Geographical distribution: Europe, North America, Greenland, Spitzbergen, Australia.

Features: Middle-sized fishes with laterally compressed bodies and a rhombic outline. Head deep. Snout flattened. Dorsal fin anteriorly short and pointed, passing posteriorly into a low fringe-like fin. Anal fin of similar shape. Pectoral fins narrow and pointed. Pelvic fins very small. Scales rectangular, becoming more elongate ventrally, arranged in diagonal rows.

Remarks: Probably lived in still water. Perhaps fed, at least partly, on plants.

Recent relatives: None. Died out in Upper Triassic.

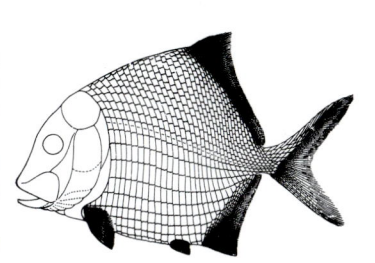

Platysomus, reconstruction after TRAQUAIR.

CHONDROSTEI — Chondrosteans
Order: Palaeonisciformes
Family: Chirodontidae
Suborder: Platysomoidei

Eurynothus crenatus AGASSIZ (length c. 17 cm) from the Lower Carboniferous of Edinburgh, Scotland, U.K. Original: National Museum of Scotland, Edinburgh, U.K.

Genus: *Eurynothus* AGASSIZ, 1834.

Synonyms: *Eurynotus Plectrolepis*

Geological range: Lower to Upper Carboniferous.

Geographical distribution: Europe, North America, northern Asia.

Features: Middle-sized, laterally compressed fishes of elongate oval outline. Head deep. Snout blunt. Eyes large. Dorsal fin large and pointed, running posteriorly into a low, fringe-like fin. Anal fin without a fringe. Pectoral fins narrowly elongate and ending in points. Pelvic fins small and pointed. Scales rectangular, arranged in regular rows.

Remarks: Lived in still water. Fed, at least partly, on plants.

Recent relatives: None. Died out in Upper Carboniferous.

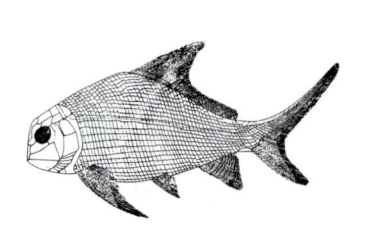

Eurynothus, reconstruction after TRAQUAIR.

CHONDROSTEI
Order: Palaeonisciformes
Family: Chirodontidae

Chondrosteans
Suborder: Platysomoidei

Eurysomus macrurus AGASSIZ (length c. 23 cm) from the Upper Permian of Richelsdorf, Hesse, Germany. Original: National Museum of Natural History, Smithsonian Institution, Washington, D.C., U.S.A.

Genus: *Eurysomus* YOUNG, 1866.

Synonym: *Globulodus*.

Geological range: Upper Permian.

Geographical distribution: Europe.

Features: Middle-sized, laterally compressed fishes, of rhombic outline. Head deep. Snout pointed. Dorsal fin short and pointed, running into a low fin fold. Anal fin of same shape. Pelvic fins very small. Scales rod-like, becoming longer ventrally. Teeth hemispherical (crushing dentition).

Remarks: Still-water fishes of durophagous diet.

Recent relatives: None. Died out in Upper Permian.

Eurysomus. Lithograph after DINKEL.

313

CHONDROSTEI
Order: **Palaeonisciformes**
Family: **Chirodontidae**

Chondrosteans
Suborder: **Platysomoidei**

Cheirodopsis geitziei TRAQUAIR (length c. 7 cm) from the Lower Carboniferous of Eskdale, Scotland, U.K. Original: The Natural History Museum, London, U.K. (P20221)

Genus: *Cheirodopsis* TRAQUAIR, 1881.

Geological range: Lower Carboniferous.

Geographical distribution: Europe.

Features: Small, laterally compressed fishes of rhombic body outline. Head deep. Snout flattened. Dorsal fin with a broad base and pointed, resembling the anal fin on the opposite side. Pectoral fins with a narrow base but expanding outwards and ending in a point. Pelvic fins very small. Scales rectangular and elongate.

Remarks: Still-water fishes. Probably fed, at least partly, on plants.

Recent relatives: None. Died out in Lower Carboniferous.

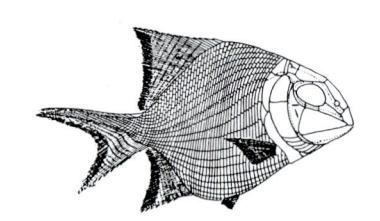

Cheirodopsis, reconstruction after MOY-THOMAS & DYNE.

314

CHONDROSTEI
Chondrosteans
Order: Palaeonisciformes
Family: Chirodontidae
Suborder: Platysomoidei

Chirodus sp. (length c. 9 cm) from the Upper Carboniferous of Springfield, Nebraska, U.S.A. Original: Henne Collection, Stuttgart, Germany.

Genus: *Chirodus* M'Coy, 1848.

Synonyms: *Amphicentrum, Cheirodus, Hemicladodus*.

Geological range: Lower to Upper Carboniferous.

Geographical distribution: Europe, North America.

Features: Small to middle-sized fishes, laterally compressed with rhombic body outline. Head deep. Snout pointed. Eyes large. Dorsal fin pointed, running into an elongate fin fold. Anal fin similar in shape. In front of the dorsal and anal fins there is a characteristic pointed apex on the body. Pectoral fins small. Pelvic fins absent. Scales elongate rectangular, arranged in curved rows.

Remarks: Still-water fishes. Probably fed, at least partly, on plants.

Recent relatives: None. Died out in Upper Carboniferous.

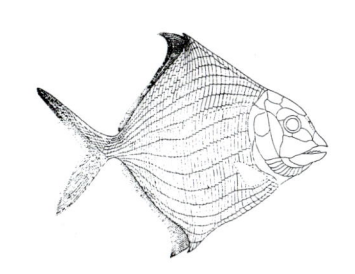

Chirodus, reconstruction after Traquair.

315

CHONDROSTEI
Order: Palaeonisciformes
Family: Bobasatraniidae

Chondrosteans
Suborder: Platysomoidei

Bobasatrania mahavavica WHITE (length c. 6 cm) from the Lower Triassic of Madagascar. Original: Frickhinger Collection, Munich, Germany.

Genus: *Bobasatrania* WHITE, 1932.

Geological range: Lower Triassic.

Geographical distribution: Madagascar, North America, Spitzbergen, Greenland.

Features: Small, laterally compressed fishes of rhombic body outline. Head deep. Snout blunt. Eyes large. Dorsal fin begins anteriorly with a little apex which passes into a low fringe. Pectoral fins narrow and pointed. Pelvic fins absent. Scales rhombic, becoming longer ventrally.

Remarks: Still-water fishes. Probably fed, at least partly, on plants.

Recent relatives: None. Died out in Lower Triassic.

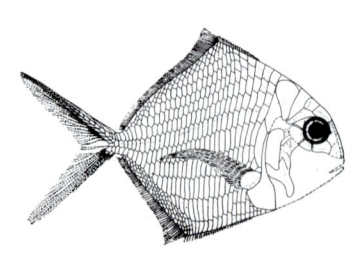

Bobasatrania, reconstruction after STENSIÖ.

CHONDROSTEI
Order: Palaeonisciformes
Family: Bobasatraniidae

Chondrosteans
Suborder: Platysomoidei

Ebenaqua ritchiei CAMPBELL (length c. 12 cm) from the Upper Permian of Queensland, Australia. Original: Interfoss, Munich, Germany.

Genus: *Ebenaqua* CAMPBELL & LE DUY PHUOC, 1983.

Geological range: Upper Permian.

Geographical distribution: Australia.

Features: Small to middle-sized, laterally compressed fishes of rhombic body outline. Head deep. Snout strongly pointed. Eyes large. Dorsal fin beginning with a long narrow point which passes into a fringe-like fin. Anal fin similar in shape. Scales long and rod-like ventrally.

Remarks: Still-water fishes. Probably fed, at least partly, on plants.

Recent relatives: None. Died out in Upper Permian.

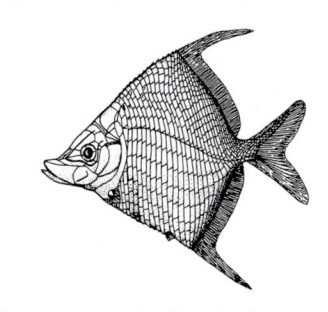

Ebenaqua, reconstruction after LONG.

CHONDROSTEI / Chondrosteans

Order: Palaeonisciformes
Family: Bobasatraniidae
Suborder: Platysomoidei

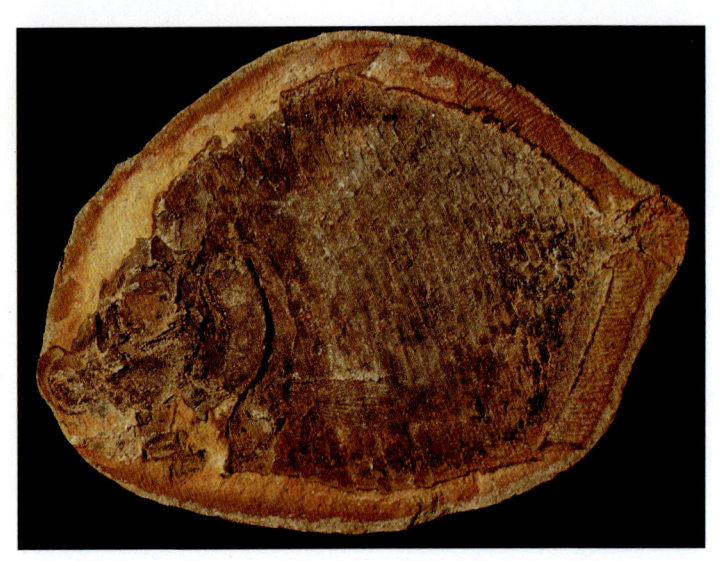

Ecrinesomus dixoni WOODWARD (length c. 12 cm) from the Lower Triassic of Madagascar. Original: Naturhistorisches Museum, Vienna, Austria.

Genus: *Ecrinesomus* WOODWARD, 1910.

Geological range: Lower Triassic.

Geographical distribution: Madagascar.

Features: Small to middle-sized, laterally compressed fishes of rhombic body outline. Head deep. Snout blunt. Eyes large. Dorsal fin with only a slight point at the anterior end, passing into a low fin fold. Anal fin of similar shape. Lepidotrichia (bony fin rays) packed densely together. Scales rhombic in shape, becoming longer ventrally.

Remarks: Still-water fishes. Probably fed, at least partly, on plants.

Recent relatives: None. Died out in Lower Triassic.

CHONDROSTEI
Order: Palaeonisciformes
Family: Guildaichthyidae

Chondrosteans
Suborder: Unnamed

Guildayichthys carnegiei LUND (length c. 6 cm) from the Lower Carboniferous of Bear Gulch, Montana, U.S.A. Original: Adelphi University, Garden City, N.J., U.S.A.

Genus: *Guildayichthys* LUND.

Geological range: Lower Carboniferous.

Geographical distribution: North America.

Features: Small, high-backed fishes with an oval body outline. Head deep. Snout pointed. Eyes large. Dorsal fin elongate, beginning somewhat anterior to the middle of the body and extending far posteriorly. Caudal fin not forked. Anal fin with a broad base. Pelvic fins elongate. Scales rod-shaped in the ventral part of the body, arranged in diagonal rows.

Remarks: Probably lethargic fishes, perhaps even living on plant food.

Recent relatives: None. Died out in Lower Carboniferous.

CHONDROSTEI
Chondrosteans
Order: Palaeonisciformes
Family: Unnamed

Discoserra pectinodon Lund (length c. 7 cm) from the Lower Carboniferous of Bear Gulch, Montana, U.S.A. Original: Adelphi University, Garden City, N.J., U.S.A.

Genus: *Discoserra* Lund.

Geological range: Lower Carboniferous.

Geographical distribution: North America.

Features: Small fishes of almost circular outline. Head deep. Snout pointed. Eyes large. Dorsal fin elongate, beginning in the middle of the body and reaching far posteriorly. Saw-like ridge scales on the anterior part of the back, on the mid line. Caudal fin not forked. Anal fin broad-based. Rod-like scales on ventral surface.

Remarks: Probably lethargic fishes, perhaps even living on plant food.

Recent relatives: None. Died out in Lower Carboniferous.

CHONDROSTEI
Chondrosteans
Order: Palaeonisciformes
Family: Unnamed

Haywardia jordani TANNER (length c. 11 cm) from the Upper Triassic of Bear Lake Co., Idaho, U.S.A. Original: Field Museum of Natural History, Chicago, Illinois, U.S.A.

Genus: *Haywardia* TANNER, 1936.

Geological range: Upper Triassic.

Geographical distribution: North America.

Features: Small to middle-sized fishes with elongate bodies. Head elongate. Snout pointed. Eyes small. Scales strikingly rod-like on the ventral surface of body.

Remarks: Not yet placed systematically.

Recent relatives: None. Died out in Upper Triassic.

CHONDROSTEI
Chondrosteans

Order: Palaeonisciformes
Family: Unnamed

Urosthenes latus WOODWARD (length c. 27 cm) from the Lower Permian of New South Wales, Australia. Original: The Natural History Museum, London, U.K.

Genus: *Urosthenes* DANA, 1848.

Geological range: Lower Permian.

Geographical distribution: Australia.

Features: Middle-sized fishes with laterally compressed bodies. Dorsal fin veil-like with a broad base, resembling the anal fin opposite. Pelvic fins elongate but expanded near the ends. Scales weak.

Remarks: Probably lethargic fishes, perhaps even feeding on plants.

Recent relatives: None. Died out in Lower Permian.

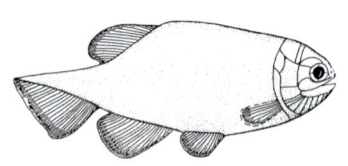

Urosthenes, after LE DUY PHUOC.

CHONDROSTEI   Chondrosteans
Order: Haplolepiformes
Family: Haplolepididae

Haplolepis sp. (length c. 4 cm) from the Upper Carboniferous of Mazon Creek, Illinois, U.S.A. Original: Field Museum of Natural History, Chicago, Illinois, U.S.A. P (22164)

Genus: *Haplolepis*   MILLER, 1982.

Synonyms: *Eurylepis*, *Mecolepis*, *Mekolepis*, *Parahaplolepis*.

Geological range: Upper Carboniferous.

Geographical distribution: North America.

Features: Small fishes with elongate slender bodies. Head deep. Snout rounded. Eyes very large. Dorsal fin long and narrow, in the posterior third of the body, almost opposite the very similar anal fin. Pelvic fins small. Pectoral fins somewhat longer and very narrow. Scales rectangular, appreciably longer than elsewhere along the longitudinal axis of the body, arranged in regular rows.

Remarks: Probably gregarious.

Recent relatives: None. Died out in Upper Carboniferous.

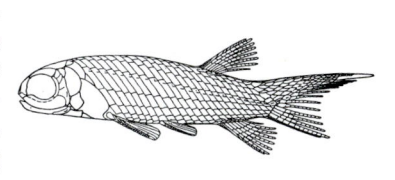

Haplolepis, reconstruction after WESTOLL.

CHONDROSTEI — Chondrosteans
Order: Haplolepiformes
Family: Haplolepididae

Microhaplolepis tuberculata LOWNEY (length c. 3 cm) from the Upper Carboniferous of Linton, Ohio, U.S.A. Original: Carnegie Museum of Natural History, Pittsburgh, Pennsylvania, U.S.A.

Genus: *Microhaplepis* LOWNEY, 1980.

Geological range: Upper Carboniferous.

Geographical distribution: North America.

Features: Very small fishes with slender bodies. Head massive. Snout rounded. Eyes very large. Dorsal fin very posterior in position, obliquely opposite the anal fin. Pectoral fins narrow. Scales rod-like.

Remarks: Probably gregarious.

Recent relatives: None. Died out in Upper Carboniferous.

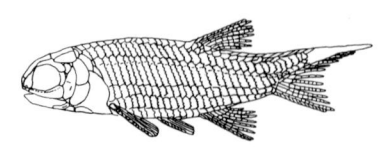

Microhaplolepis, reconstruction after LOWNEY.

CHONDROSTEI — Chondrosteans
Order: Haplolepiformes
Family: Haplolepididae

Pyritocephalus sculptus Fritsch (length c. 5 cm) from the Lower Permian of Nursava, Czechoslovakia. Original: Geologisk Museum, Copenhagen, Denmark.

Genus: *Pyritocephalus* Fritsch, 1894.

Synonym: *Teleopterina*.

Geological range: Upper Carboniferous to Lower Permian.

Geographical distribution: Europe, North America.

Features: Small fishes with elongate slender bodies. Head laterally compressed. Snout rounded. Dorsal fin very narrow, very posterior in position, opposite the somewhat broader anal fin. Caudal fin heterocercal. Posterior end of the vertebral column slightly curved. Pelvic fins small and narrow. Pectoral fins also narrow, but longer. Scales rectangular, arranged in diagonal rows.

Remarks: Probably gregarious.

Recent relatives: None. Died out in Lower Permian.

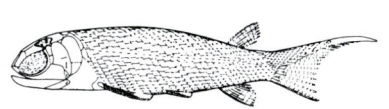

Pyritocephalus, reconstruction after Westoll.

325

CHONDROSTEI — Chondrosteans
Order: Dorypteriformes
Family: Dorypteridae

Dorypterus hoffmanni Germar (length c. 12 cm) from the Upper Permian of Richelsdorf, Hesse, Germany. Original: Munk Collection, Karlsruhe, Germany.

Genus: *Dorypterus* Germar, 1842.

Geological range: Lower to Upper Permian.

Geographical distribution: Europe, eastern Asia.

Features: Middle-sized laterally compressed fishes with oval body outline. Head deep. Snout rounded. Eyes large. Jaws toothless. Dorsal fin begins somewhat in front of the middle of the body with a narrow sail-like prolongation and continues as a fringe extending to the caudal fin. Anal fin similar but with a short point instead of the long sail. Pelvic fins small, unusually anterior in position. Body almost without scales.

Remarks: The toothless jaws suggest a peaceable disposition.

Recent relatives: None. Died out in Upper Permian.

Dorypterus, reconstruction after Westoll.

CHONDROSTEI — Chondrosteans
Order: Tarrasiiformes
Family: Tarrasiidae

Apholidotos ossna Lund (length c. 8 cm) from the Lower Carboniferous of Bear Gulch, Montana, U.S.A. Original: Tyrrell Museum of Paleontology, Drumheller, Alberta, Canada.

Genus: *Apholidotos* Lund.

Geological range: Lower Carboniferous.

Geographical distribution: North America.

Features: Small fishes with elongate lancet-shaped bodies. Head very small. Snout rounded. Fins probably joined into a fringe as in *Paratarrasius*. Scales sparse.

Remarks: Probably lived in crevices or burrowed into the sand.

Recent relatives: None. Died out in Lower Carboniferous.

CHONDROSTEI — Chondrosteans
Order: Tarrasiiformes
Family: Tarrasiidae

Paratarrasius hibbardi Lund & Melton (length c.12 cm) from the Lower Carboniferous of Bear Gulch, Montana, U.S.A. Original: Adelphi University, Garden City, N.J., U.S.A.

Genus: *Paratarrasius* Lund & Melton, 1982.

Geological range: Lower Carboniferous.

Geographical distribution: North America.

Features: Elongate lancet-shaped fishes. Head small. Snout rounded. Eyes relatively large. Dorsal fin in the form of a low fringe which begins behind the head and probably continues, *via* the pointed termination of the body, to the middle of the ventral surface. Scales delicate.

Remarks: Probably lived in crevices or burrowed into the sand.

Recent relatives: None. Died out in Lower Carboniferous.

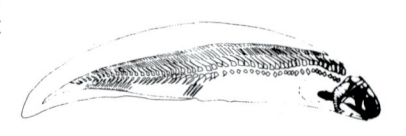

Paratarrasius, reconstruction after Lund.

CHONDROSTEI
Chondrosteans
Order: Ptycholepiformes
Family: Ptycholepididae

Ptycholepis bollensis AGASSIZ (length c. 32 cm) from the Lower Jurassic of Holzmaden, Württemberg, Germany. Original: Bayerische Staatssammlung für Paläontologie, Munich, Germany.

Genus: *Ptycholepis* AGASSIZ, 1833.

Geological range: Middle Triassic to Lower Jurassic.

Geographical distribution: Europe, North America.

Features: Middle-sized fishes with slender bodies. Head elongate. Snout pointed. Lower jaw strikingly long. Eyes large. Dorsal fin in the middle of the body. Caudal fin heterocercal, with the lower lobe somewhat shorter and broader than the upper lobe. Pectoral fins elongate. Anal and pelvic fins small. Scales denticulate at posterior edge of scale and with transverse furrows.

Remarks: Rapid swimmers.

Recent relatives: None. Died out in Lower Jurassic.

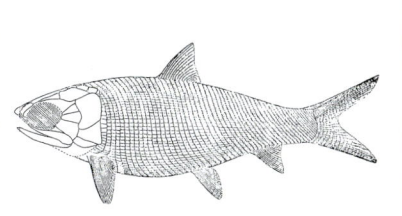

Ptycholepis, reconstruction after BROUGH.

CHONDROSTEI — Chondrosteans
Order: Pholidopleuriformes
Family: Pholidopleuridae

Australosomus merlei PRIEM (length c. 8 cm) from the Lower Triassic of Madagascar. Original: Museo Civico di Storia Naturale, Milan, Italy.

Genus: *Australosomus* PIVETEAU, 1930.

Geological range: Lower to Middle Triassic.

Geographical distribution: Africa, Madagascar, Greenland, Spitzbergen.

Features: Small to middle-sized fishes with elongate bodies. Head relatively less deep than the body. Snout blunt. Eyes large. Dorsal fin obtusely pointed. The anal fin opposite is broad-based. Caudal fin somewhat forked with two almost equal-sized lobes. Pectoral fins elongate and pointed. Pelvic fins very small. Scales long and rod-like, arranged in regular rows.

Remarks: Probably predators.

Recent relatives: None. Died out in Middle Triassic.

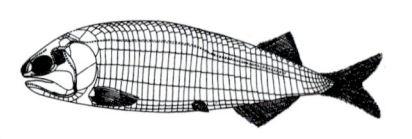

Australosomus, after LEHMAN.

CHONDROSTEI — Chondrosteans
Order: Pholidopleuriformes
Family: Pholidopleuridae

Macroaethes brookvalei WADE (length c. 30 cm) from the Middle Triassic of Hornsby Heights, Australia. Original: Australian Museum, Sydney, Australia.

Genus: *Macroaethes* WADE, 1932.

Geological range: Middle Triassic.

Geographical distribution: Australia.

Features: Middle-sized fishes with elongate streamlined bodies. Head shallow. Snout pointed. Eyes small. Dorsal fin small and pointed, very posterior in position, passing behind into a low fringe. Anal fin similar. Pelvic fins small. Long rod-like scales on the flanks.

Remarks: Probably very rapid swimmers.

Recent relatives: None. Died out in Middle Triassic.

CHONDROSTEI — Chondrosteans
Order: **Pholidopleuriformes**
Family: **Pholidopleuridae**

Pholidopleurus typus BRONN (length c. 9 cm) from the Middle Triassic of Carinthia, Austria. Original: The Natural History Museum, London, U.K. P (1099c)

Genus: *Pholidopleurus* BRONN, 1858.

Geological range: Middle to Upper Triassic.

Geographical distribution: Europe.

Features: Small fishes with elongate bodies. Head small. Snout blunt. Dorsal fin small, very posterior in position, passing into a low fringe. Anal fin similar in shape. Pectoral fins narrow and pointed. Characteristic long rod-shaped scales on the flanks.

Remarks: Probably gregarious.

Recent relatives: None. Died out in Upper Triassic.

Pholidopleurus, reconstruction after KNER.

CHONDROSTEI
Chondrosteans
Order: **Luganoiiformes**
Family: **Habroichthyidae**

Habroichthys sp. (length c. 3 cm) from the Middle Triassic of Perledo, Italy. Original: Paläontologisches Museum, Zürich, Switzerland.

Genus: *Habroichthys* BROUGH, 1939.

Geological range: Middle Triassic.

Geographical distribution: Europe.

Features: Small slender fishes. Head shallow. Snout pointed. Eyes large. Dorsal fin pointed, situated in the posterior half of the body, obliquely opposite the anal fin. Scales thick and shiny, rhombic on the dorsal surface and rod-like on flanks.

Remarks: Probably lethargic swimmers and gregarious.

Recent relatives: None. Died out in Middle Triassic.

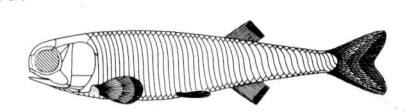

Habroichthys, reconstruction after GRIFFITH.

CHONDROSTEI — Chondrosteans
Order: Luganoiiformes
Family: Habroichthyidae

Nannolepis elegans GRIFFITH (length c. 7 cm) from the Upper Triassic of Polzberg, Lunz, Austria. Original: Naturhistorisches Museum, Vienna, Austria.

Genus: *Nannolepis* GRIFFITH, 1977.

Geological range: Upper Triassic.

Geographical distribution: Europe.

Features: Small slender fishes. Head relatively deep. Snout blunt. Dorsal fin very posterior in position, opposite the anal fin. Caudal fin forked, with almost equal-sized lobes. Pelvic fins small. Scales rhombic on the dorsal surface and rod-like on the anterior part of the flanks.

Remarks: Probably not very clever swimmers.

Recent relatives: None. Died out in Upper Triassic.

CHONDROSTEI — Chondrosteans
Order: Luganoiiformes
Family: Thoracopteridae

Thoracopterus magnificus Tintori (length c. 6 cm) from the Upper Triassic of Cene, Bergamo, Italy. Original: Naturmuseum Senckenberg, Frankfurt-am-Main, Germany.

Genus: *Thoracopterus* Bronn, 1858.

Synonyms: *Pterygopterus*.

Geological range: Lower to Upper Triassic.

Geographical distribution: Europe, North America, Australia.

Features: Small to middle-sized fishes with slender bodies. Head shallow. Snout pointed. Teeth small. Dorsal fin very small, very posterior in position. Anal fin even smaller than the dorsal fin. Caudal fin deeply forked, with the lower lobe longer than the upper. Pectoral fins greatly enlarged. Pelvic fins long and pointed. Scales square to rectangular, elongate on the flanks in the anterior part of the body.

Remarks: "Flying" fishes.

Recent relatives: None. Died out in Upper Triassic.

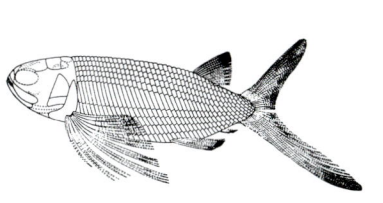

Thoracopterus, reconstruction after Lehman.

CHONDROSTEI — Chondrosteans
Order: Luganoiiformes
Family: Luganoiidae

Besania sp. (length c. 5 cm) from the Middle Triassic of Monte San Giorgio, Switzerland. Original: Paläontologisches Museum, Zürich.

Genus: *Besania* BROUGH, 1939.

Geological range: Middle to Upper Triassic.

Geographical distribution: Europe.

Features: Small fishes with slender bodies. Head small. Snout pointed. Eyes large. Scales thick, rhombic on the dorsal surface of the body, rod-like on the flanks.

Remarks: Probably gregarious little fishes but their thick "scale armour" suggests that they would not have been rapid swimmers.

Recent relatives: None. Died out in Upper Triassic.

CHONDROSTEI
Chondrosteans
Order: Luganoiiformes
Family: Luganoiidae

Luganoia lepidosteoides Brough (length c. 6 cm) from the Middle Triassic of Monte San Giorgio, Switzerland. Original: Paläontologisches Museum, Zürich, Switzerland.

Genus: *Luganoia* Brough, 1939.

Geological range: Middle to Upper Triassic.

Geographical distribution: Europe.

Features: Small fishes with slender bodies. Head shallow. Snout pointed. Teeth small. Dorsal fin in the posterior third of the body, obliquely opposite the anal fin. Pectoral fins probably narrow and rounded. Scales square to rectangular, elongate and rod-like on the anterior part of the flanks.

Remarks: Probably not rapid swimmers, in view of the thick "scale armour".

Recent relatives: None. Died out in Upper Triassic.

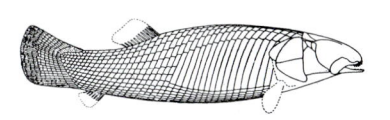

Luganoia, reconstruction after Brough.

337

CHONDROSTEI — Chondrosteans
Order: **Redfieldiiformes**
Family: **Redfieldiidae**

Atopocephala watsoni BROUGH (length c. 5 cm) from the Lower Triassic of Rouxville, South Africa. Original: The Natural History Museum, London, U.K. (P 16079)

Genus: *Atopocephala* BROUGH, 1934.

Geological range: Lower Triassic.

Geographical distribution: South Africa.

Features: Small fishes with a large head and very large eyes. Nose pointed. Gape very long. Upper and lower jaws set with small pointed teeth. Dorsal fin broad-based, shortly behind the middle of the body. Anal fin obliquely opposite. Pelvic fins small and pointed. Pectoral fins likewise pointed. Scales rhombic, arranged in regular rows.

Remarks: Probably gregarious.

Recent relatives: None. Died out in Lower Triassic.

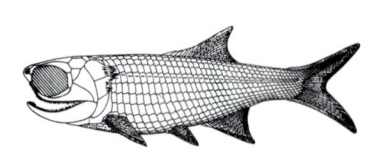

Atopocephala, reconstruction after PIVETEAU.

CHONDROSTEI — Chondrosteans
Order: Redfieldiiformes
Family: Redfieldiidae

Beaconia spinosa Wade (length c. 5 cm) from the Middle Triassic of New South Wales, Australia. Original: American Museum of Natural History, N.Y., U.S.A.

Genus: *Beaconia* Wade, 1935.

Geological range: Middle Triassic.

Geographical distribution: Australia.

Features: Small slender fishes. Head elongate. Eyes large. Dorsal fin in the posterior half of the body. Anal fin obliquely opposite. Dorsal and ventral mid lines carry a row of pointed spines in front of the caudal fin. Dorsal and anal fins both with two spines anteriorly. Caudal fin not strongly forked.

Remarks: By some authors the genus *Beaconia* is assigned to *Brookvalia*.

Recent relatives: None. Died out in Middle Triassic.

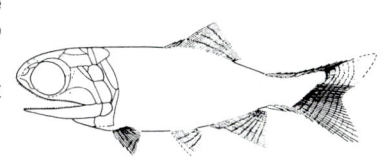

Beaconia, reconstruction after Hutchinson.

339

CHONDROSTEI   Chondrosteans
Order: Redfieldiiformes
Family: Redfieldiidae

Brookvalia gracilis WADE (length c. 9 cm) from the Middle Triassic of Brookvale, New South Wales, Australia. Original: The Natural History Museum, London, U.K. (P 15799-800)

Genus: *Brookvalia* WADE, 1935.

Geological range: Middle Triassic.

Geographical distribution: Australia.

Features: Small very slender fishes. Head elongate. Eyes very large. Gape very long. Small pointed teeth. Dorsal fin in the posterior half of the body, opposite the anal fin. Pointed spines in front of the caudal fin dorsally and ventrally, and also in front of the dorsal and anal fins. Pectoral and pelvic fins small. Scales square to rhombic.

Remarks: Probably rapidly swimming and gregarious.

Recent relatives: None. Died out in Middle Triassic.

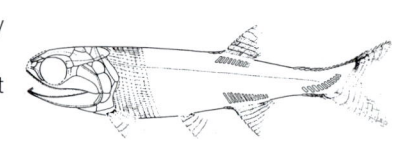

Brookvalia, reconstruction after HUTCHINSON.

CHONDROSTEI — Chondrosteans
Order: Redfieldiiformes
Family: Redfieldiidae

Cionichthys dunklei SCHAEFFER (length c. 15 cm) from the Upper Triassic of Montrose, Utah, U.S.A. Original: National Museum of Natural History, Smithsonian Institution, Washington, D.C., U.S.A.

Genus: *Cionichthys* SCHAEFFER, 1967.

Geological range: Upper Triassic.

Geographical distribution: North America.

Features: Middle-sized slender fishes. Head elongate. Snout somewhat pointed. Dorsal fin in the posterior half of the body, obliquely opposite the anal fin. Caudal fin relatively large, deeply forked. Scales rhombic, arranged in diagonal rows.

Remarks: Probably predators.

Recent relatives: None. Died out in Upper Triassic.

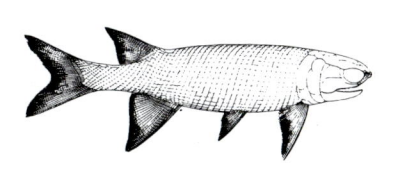

Cionichthys, reconstruction after SCHAEFFER.

CHONDROSTEI
Chondrosteans
Order: Redfieldiiformes
Family: Redfieldiidae

Dictyopyge illustrans Woodward (length c. 6 cm) from the Lower Triassic of Gosford, New South Wales. Original: The Natural History Museum, London, U.K. (P6269)

Genus: *Dictyopyge* Egerton, 1847.

Geological range: Lower Triassic.

Geographical distribution: Australia.

Features: Small slender fishes. Head elongate. Snout pointed. Dorsal fin very posterior in position, opposite the longer anal fin. Pectoral and pelvic fins likewise relatively long. Scales rectangular, arranged in diagonal rows.

Remarks: Probably predators.

Recent relatives: None. Died out in Lower Triassic.

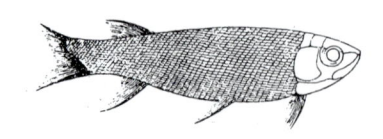

Dictyopyge, reconstruction after Struver.

CHONDROSTEI — Chondrosteans
Order: Redfieldiiformes
Family: Redfieldiidae

Helichthys browni BROOM (length c. 7) from the Lower Triassic of Rouxville, South Africa. Original: Museum für Geologie und Paläontologie, Tübingen, Germany.

Genus: *Helichthys* BROOM, 1909.

Geological range: Lower Triassic.

Geographical distribution: South Africa.

Features: Small slender fishes. Head elongate. Snout rounded. Eyes large. Jaws set with very small teeth. Dorsal fin triangular, pointed, very posterior in position, obliquely opposite the anal fin which is likewise triangular. Scales square to rhombic, arranged in diagonal rows.

Remarks: Probably gregarious.

Recent relatives: None. Died out in Lower Triassic.

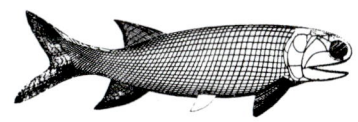

Helichthys, reconstruction after BROUGH.

CHONDROSTEI
Chondrosteans
Order: Redfieldiiformes
Family: Redfieldiidae

Ischnolepis bancrofti HAUGHTON (length c. 7 cm) from the Upper Triassic of Zimbabwe. Original: South African Museum, Cape Town, South Africa.

Genus: *Ischnolepis* HAUGHTON, 1934.

Geological range: Upper Triassic.

Geographical distribution: South Africa.

Features: Small slender fishes. Head elongate. Eyes very large. Gape very long. Upper and lower jaws set with small pointed teeth. Dorsal fin very posterior in position, opposite the broad-based anal fin. In front of the bases of every fin are one or several pointed spines. Scales rhombic, arranged in diagonal rows.

Remarks: Probably gregarious.

Recent relatives: None. Died out in Upper Triassic.

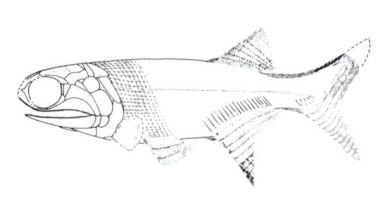

Ischnolepis, reconstruction after HUTCHINSON.

CHONDROSTEI — Chondrosteans
Order: Redfieldiiformes
Family: Redfieldiidae

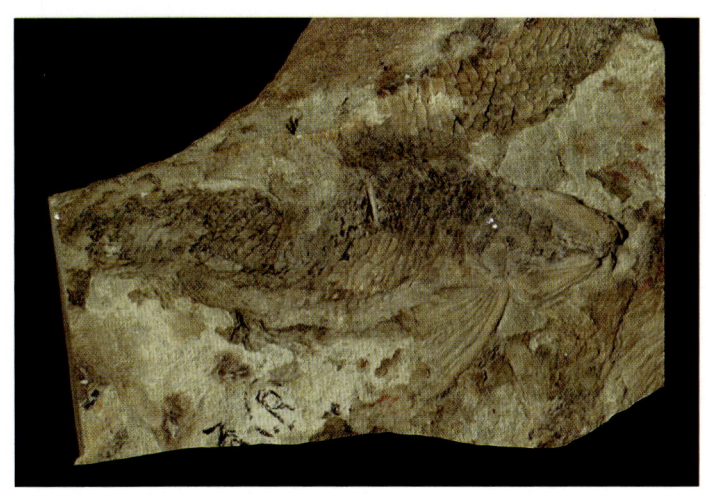

Lasalichthys hillsi SCHAEFFER (length c. 9 cm) from the Upper Triassic of Little Valley, Utah, U.S.A. Original: American Museum of Natural History, New York, N.Y., U.S.A.

Genus: *Lasalichthys* SCHAEFFER, 1967.

Geological range: Upper Triassic.

Geographical distribution: North America.

Features: Middle-sized slender fishes. Head elongate. Snout pointed. Pectoral fins triangular, strikingly large. Scales rhombic, arranged in diagonal rows.

Remarks: The large pectoral fins suggest that these fishes could "fly" for short distances.

Recent relatives: None. Died out in Upper Triassic.

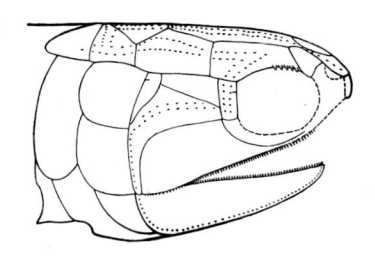

Lasalichthys, reconstruction after SCHAEFFER.

345

CHONDROSTEI
Chondrosteans
Order: Redfieldiiformes
Family: Redfieldiidae

Molybdichthys junior WADE (length c. 13 cm) from the Middle Triassic of Brookvale, New South Wales, Australia. Original: Australian Museum, Sydney, Australia.

Genus: *Molybdichthys* WADE, 1935.

Geological range: Middle Triassic.

Geographical distribution: Australia.

Features: Small to middle-sized slender fishes. Head elongate. Eyes very large. Dorsal fin very posterior in position, opposite the anal fin. Caudal fin only slightly divided. Pectoral fins small. Scales almost square, arranged in diagonal rows.

Remarks: Probably predators.

Recent relatives: None. Died out in Middle Triassic.

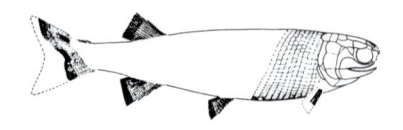

Molybdichthys, reconstruction after HUTCHINSON.

CHONDROSTEI
Chondrosteans
Order: Redfieldiiformes
Family: Redfieldiidae

Phlyctaenichthys pectinatus WADE (length c. 14 cm) from the Middle Triassic of Brookvale, New South Wales, Australia. Original: Australian Museum, Sydney, Australia.

Genus: *Phlyctaenichthys* WADE, 1935.

Geological range: Middle Triassic.

Geographical distribution: Australia.

Features: Middle-sized slender fishes. Head elongate. Snout rounded. Eyes very large. Gape very long. Dorsal fin in the posterior half of the body, almost opposite the small pelvic fins. In the dorsal mid line, in front of the beginning of the caudal fin, is a row of pointed spines. Scales arranged in diagonal rows.

Remarks: Probably gregarious.

Recent relatives: None. Died out in Middle Triassic.

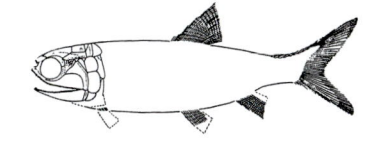

Phlyctaenichthys, reconstruction after WADE.

CHONDROSTEI — Chondrosteans
Order: Redfieldiiformes
Family: Redfieldiidae

Redfieldius gracilis (REDFIELD) (length c. 14 cm) from the Lower Triassic of Durham, Connecticut, U.S.A. Original: Carnegie Museum of Natural History, Pittsburgh, Pennsylvania, U.S.A.

Genus: *Redfieldius* HAY, 1899.

Synonyms: *Catopterus*.

Geological range: Lower Triassic.

Geographical distribution: North America.

Features: Medium-sized fishes with a somewhat stout body. Head broad. Snout rounded. Eyes large. Mandible with small teeth. Dorsal fin pointed, triangular, very posterior, almost opposite to the slightly larger anal fin. Ventral fins small. Pectoral fins somewhat broadened. Scales rectangular with sinuate fringes, arranged in diagonal rows.

Remarks: Predatory fishes.

Recent relatives: None. Died out in the Middle Triassic.

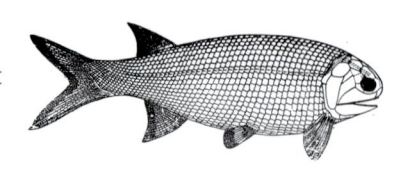

Redfieldius, reconstruction after BROUGH

CHONDROSTEI — Chondrosteans
Order: Redfieldiiformes
Family: Redfieldiidae

Schizurichthys pulcher Wade (length c. 20 cm) from the Middle Triassic of Brookvale, New South Wales, Australia. Original: Australian Museum, Sydney, Australia.

Genus: *Schizurichthys* Wade, 1935.

Geological range: Middle Triassic.

Geographical distribution: Australia.

Features: Medium-sized slender fishes. Head elongate. Snout pointed. Eyes large. Gape very long. Mandible with very small teeth. Dorsal fin on the posterior half of the body at a slant opposite to the broad anal fin. Pectoral and anal fins small. Scales thin.

Remarks: Predators.

Recent relatives: None. Died out in Middle Triassic.

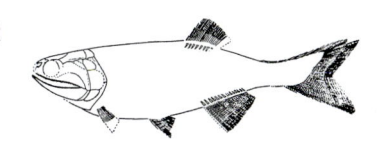

Schizurichthys, reconstruction after Hutchinson

349

CHONDROSTEI — Chondrosteans
Order: Redfieldiiformes
Family: Redfieldiidae

Synorichthys stewartii Schaeffer (length c. 17 cm) from the Upper Triassic of the U.S.A. Original: Peabody Museum of Natural History, New Haven, Connecticut, U.S.A.

Genus: *Synorichthys* Schaeffer, 1967.

Geological range: Upper Triassic.

Geographical distribution: North America.

Features: Middle-sized slender fishes. Head elongate. Snout rounded. Eyes large. Dorsal fin triangular, pointed, very posterior in position, opposite the somewhat larger but likewise triangular anal fin. Pectoral fins somewhat expanded. Pelvic fins small. Scales thick.

Remarks: Predatory fishes.

Recent relatives: None. Died out in Upper Triassic.

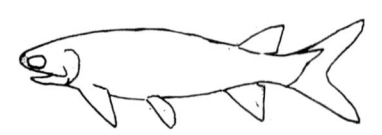

Synorichthys, reconstruction after Schaeffer.

CHONDROSTEI
Chondrosteans
Order: Perleidiformes
Family: Perleididae

Colobodus sp. (length c. 16 cm) from the Upper Triassic of Hirtenstein, Austria. Original: The Natural History Museum, London, U.K. (P 10944)

Genus: *Colobodus* AGASSIZ, 1844.

Synonyms: *Asterodon*, *Euplorodus*.

Geological range: Lower to Upper Triassic.

Geographical distribution: Europe, South Africa, eastern Africa, Australia, northern Asia.

Features: Middle-sized, broad-bodied fishes. Head deep. Snout pointed. Dorsal fin broad-based, situated in the posterior descending part of the dorsal mid line, obliquely opposite the small anal fin. Pectoral fins fan-like. Scales denticulate at posterior margin and ornamented with parallel ribs on the external surface. Teeth hemispherical, forming a pavement dentition.

Remarks: The dentition suggests a durophagous diet.

Recent relatives: None. Died out in Upper Triassic.

CHONDROSTEI   Chondrosteans
Order: Perleidiformes
Family: Perleididae

Manlietta crassa WADE (length c. 7 cm) from the Middle Triassic of Brookvale, New South Wales, Australia. Original: Australian Museum, Sydney, Australia.

Genus: *Manlietta* WADE, 1935.

Geological range: Middle Triassic.

Geographical distribution: Australia.

Features: Small fishes of somewhat compressed shape. Head elongate. Eyes large. Jaws set with small conical teeth. Mouth not deeply incised. Dorsal fin in the posterior third of the body, obliquely opposite the long broad anal fin. Caudal fin with a slightly concave posterior margin. Pectoral and pelvic fins small. Scales rhombic.

Remarks: Probably fed on crustacea and other small animals.

Recent relatives: None. Died out in Middle Triassic.

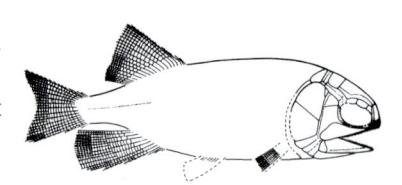

Manlietta, reconstruction after HUTCHINSON.

CHONDROSTEI
Chondrosteans
Order: Perleidiformes
Family: Perleididae

Meidiichthys browni (BROOM) (length c. 10 cm) from the Lower Triassic of Rouxville, South Africa. Original: The Natural History Museum, London, U.K. (P16073)

Genus: *Meidiichthys* BROUGH, 1931.

Geological range: Lower Triassic.

Geographical distribution: South Africa.

Features: Small slender fishes. Head deep. Eyes large. Gape not very long. Jaws set with conical teeth. Dorsal fin just behind the middle of the body, obliquely opposite the pointed anal fin. Pectoral and pelvic fins small. Scales square, with scalloped margins, arranged in diagonal rows.

Remarks: Probably fed on crustaceans and other small animals.

Recent relatives: None. Died out in Lower Triassic.

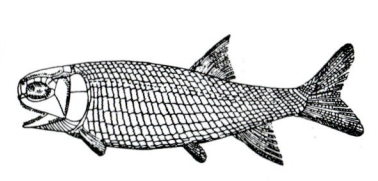

Meidiichthys, reconstruction after BROUGH.

353

CHONDROSTEI — Chondrosteans
Order: Perleidiformes
Family: Perleididae

Mendocinichthys brevis BORDAS (length c. 5 cm) from the Middle Triassic of Mendoza, Argentina. Original: American Museum of Natural History, New York, N.Y., U.S.A.

Genus: *Mendocinichthys* WHITLEY, 1953.

Synonym: *Mendocinia*.

Geological range: Middle Triassic.

Geographical distribution: South America.

Features: Small plump fishes. Head deep. Snout rounded. Jaws set with conical teeth. Dorsal fin very posterior in position, opposite the triangular anal fin. Scales square to rectangular, arranged in diagonal rows.

Remarks: Probably fed on crustaceans and other small animals.

Recent relatives: None. Died out in Middle Triassic.

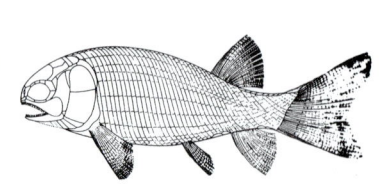

Mendocinichthys, reconstruction after SCHAEFFER.

CHONDROSTEI
Chondrosteans
Order: Perleidiformes
Family: Perleididae

Meridensia meridensis de ALESSANDRI (length c. 10 cm) from the Middle Triassic of Monte San Gorgio, Switzerland. Original: Paläontologisches Museum, Zürich, Switzerland.

Genus: *Meridensia* ANDERSSON, 1916.

Geological range: Middle to Upper Triassic.

Geographical distribution: Europe.

Features: Small elongate fishes. Head elongate. Snout pointed. Eyes large. Gape moderately long. Teeth small. Dorsal fin small, in the posterior third of the body, obliquely opposite the anal fin which is likewise small. Pectoral and pelvic fins pointed. Scales elongate, rounded.

Remarks: Probably gregarious.

Recent relatives: None. Died out in Upper Triassic.

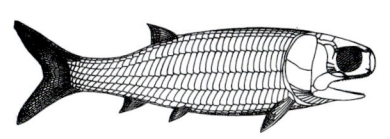

Meridensia, reconstruction after BROUGH.

CHONDROSTEI   Chondrosteans
Order: Perleidiformes
Family: Perleididae

Perleidus madagascariensis LEHMAN (length c. 23 cm) from the Lower Triassic of Madagascar. Original: Staatliches Museum für Naturkunde, Karlsruhe, Germany.

Genus: *Perleidus* de ALESSANDRI, 1910.

Geological range: Lower Triassic.

Geographical distribution: Madagascar.

Features: Middle-sized fishes with somewhat laterally compressed bodies. Head deep. Eyes large. Gape moderately long. Dorsal fin in the posterior third of the body, obliquely opposite the anal fin. Pectoral fins rounded. Pelvic fins small. Scales square to rectangular with scalloped edges, arranged in regular diagonal rows.

Remarks: Diet probably durophagous.

Recent relatives: None. Died out in Upper Triassic.

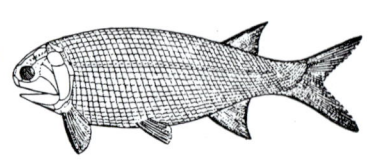

Perleidus, reconstruction after LEHMAN.

CHONDROSTEI
Chondrosteans
Order: Perleidiformes
Family: Perleididae

Pristisomus latus Woodward (length c. 11 cm) from the Lower Triassic of Gosford, New South Wales, Australia. Original: The Natural History Museum, London, U.K. (P 6274)

Genus: *Pristisomus* Woodward, 1890.

Geological range: Lower Triassic.

Geographical distribution: Australia, Madagascar.

Features: Small to middle-sized fishes of oval outline. Head deep. Dorsal fin in the posterior third of the body, opposite the somewhat larger anal fin. Caudal fin scarcely forked. Scales rod-shaped.

Remarks: Probably durophagous.

Recent relatives: None. Died out in Lower Triassic.

CHONDROSTEI — Chondrosteans
Order: Perleidiformes
Family: Perleididae

Procheirichthys ferox WADE (length c. 16 cm) from the Middle Triassic of Brookvale, New South Wales, Australia. Original: Australian Museum, Sydney, Australia.

Genus: *Procheirichthys* WADE, 1935.

Geological range: Middle Triassic.

Geographical distribution: Australia.

Features: Small slender fishes with laterally compressed bodies. Head deep. Snout rounded. Eyes large. Gape rather long. Teeth small. Dorsal fin large, situated in posterior third of the body, obliquely opposite the anal fin. Pectoral and pelvic fins small. Scales rectangular with smooth edges, arranged in diagonal rows.

Remarks: Probably fed on crustacea and other small animals.

Recent relatives: None. Died out in Middle Triassic.

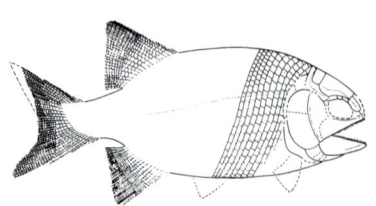

Procheirichthys, reconstruction after HUTCHINSON.

CHONDROSTEI — Chondrosteans
Order: Perleidiformes
Family: Perleididae

Tripelta dubia Woodward (length c. 6 cm) from the Lower Triassic of Gosford, New South Wales, Australia. Original: The Natural History Museum, London, U.K.
(P 6274 c)

Genus: *Tripelta* WADE, 1940.

Geological range: Lower Triassic.

Geographical distribution: Australia.

Features: Small slender fishes. Head elongate. Snout pointed. Dorsal fin very posterior in position, opposite the larger anal fin. Scales rectangular to rhombic.

Remarks: Probably fed on crustacea and other small animals.

Recent relatives: None. Died out in Lower Triassic.

CHONDROSTEI — Chondrosteans
Order: Perleidiformes
Family: Cleithrolepididae

Cleithrolepidina extoni (Woodward) (length c. 10 cm) from the Lower Triassic of Rouxville, South Africa. Original: National Museum, Bloemfontein, South Africa

Genus: *Cleithrolepidina* Berg, 1940.

Geological range: Lower Triassic.

Geographical distribution: South Africa.

Features: Small fishes, deep in the belly and with a sharp dorsal mid line. Head deep. Eyes large. Gape rather long. Jaws toothless. Dorsal and anal fins triangular, near the posterior end of the body. Pectoral and pelvic fins small. Scales elongate, each one curved to form a half-cylinder.

Remarks: The toothless jaws suggest a partly herbivorous diet.

Recent relatives: None. Died out in Lower Triassic.

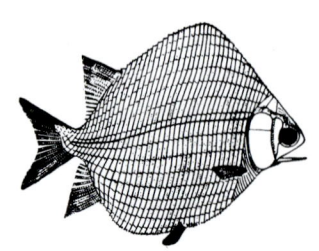

Cleithrolepidina, reconstruction after Jubb & Gardiner.

CHONDROSTEI — Chondrosteans
Order: Perleidiformes
Family: Cleithrolepididae

Cleithrolepis granulatus EGERTON (length c. 10 cm) from the Lower Triassic of Gosford, New South Wales. Original: The Natural History Museum, London, U.K. (P 1862)

Genus: *Cleithrolepis* EGERTON, 1864.

Geological range: Lower to Upper Triassic.

Geographical distribution: Europe, South Africa, Australia, South America.

Features: Small deep-bellied fishes with a sharp dorsal mid line. Laterally compressed. Head deep. Snout pointed. Eyes large. Gape rather long. Jaws toothless. Dorsal and anal fin very posterior in position. Pectoral and pelvic fins small. Scales elongate, rectangular, arranged in undulating diagonal rows.

Remarks: Probably partly herbivorous.

Recent relatives: None. Died out in Upper Triassic.

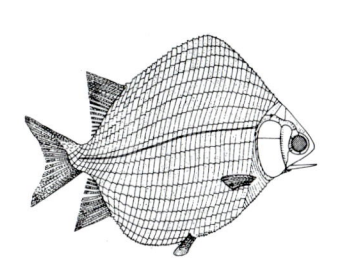

Cleithrolepis, reconstruction after BROUGH.

361

CHONDROSTEI   Chondrosteans
Order: Perleidiformes
Family: Cleithrolepididae

Dipteronotus olgiatii Tintori (length c. 7 cm) from the Middle Triassic of Ca'del Frate, Varese, Italy. Original: Museo Civico di Scienze Naturali d'Induno Olona, Varese, Italy.

Genus: *Dipteronotus* Egerton, 1854.

Geological range: Middle Triassic.

Geographical distribution: Europe.

Features: Small fishes of approximately oval outline with sharp dorsal mid line. Head elongate. Snout rounded. Eyes large. Dorsal fin fringe-like. Anal fin with long rays. Pectoral and pelvic fins small. Scales elongate rhombic.

Remarks: Probably still-water fishes, partly herbivorous in diet.

Recent relatives: None. Died out in Upper Triassic.

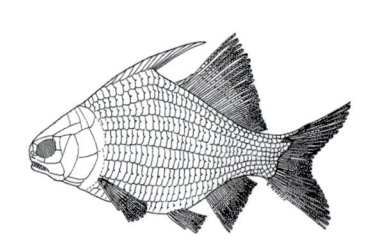

Dipteronotus, reconstruction after Tintori.

CHONDROSTEI — Chondrosteans
Order: Perleidiformes
Family: Aetheodontidae

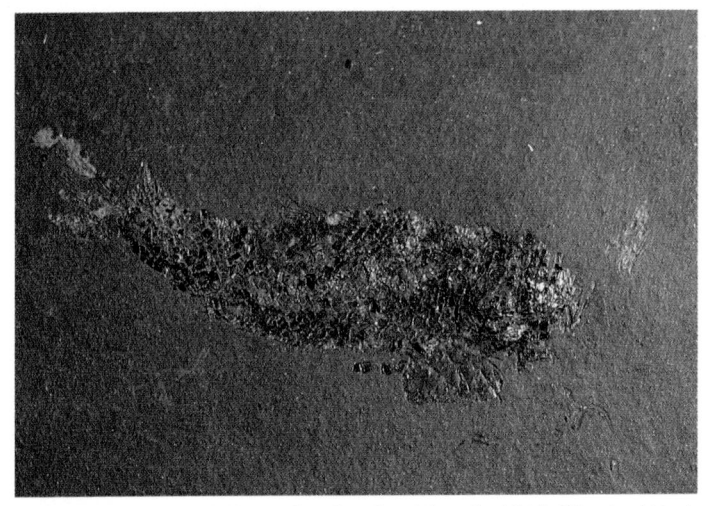

Aetheodontus besanensis BROUGH (length c. 5 cm) from the Middle Triassic of Monte San Giorgio, Switzerland. Original: Paläontologisches Museum, Zürich, Switzerland.

Genus: *Aetheodontus* BROUGH, 1939.

Geological range: Middle to Upper Triassic.

Geographical distribution: Europe.

Features: Small slender fishes. Head deep. Snout rounded. Eyes large. Dorsal fin in the posterior half of the body. Scales thick, rectangular to rhombic, arranged in diagonal rows.

Remarks: Probably fed on crustaceans and other small animals.

Recent relatives: None. Died out in Upper Triassic.

CHONDROSTEI   Chondrosteans
Order: Peltopleuriformes
Family: Peltopleuridae

Peltopleurus kneri WOODWARD (length c. 5 cm) from the Middle Triassic of Carinthia, Austria. Original: The Natural History Museum, London, U.K. (P1099a).

Genus: *Peltopleurus* KNER, 1866.

Geological range: Middle to Upper Triassic.

Geographical distribution: Europe, eastern Asia.

Features: Small slender fishes. Head deep. Eyes very large. Dorsal fin in the posterior third of the body, obliquely opposite the small anal fin. Pectoral and pelvic fins also small. Scales very thick, rod-like on the flanks but otherwise rectangular or square.

Remarks: Probably lived on crustaceans and other small animals.

Recent relatives: None. Died out in Upper Triassic.

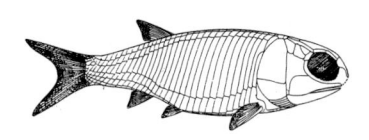

Peltopleurus, reconstruction after BROUGH.

CHONDROSTEI — Chondrosteans
Order: Peltopleuriformes
Family: Peltopleuridae

Placopleurus besanensis BROUGH (length c. 4 cm) from the Middle Triassic of Monte San Giorgio, Switzerland. Original: Paläontologisches Museum, Zürich, Switzerland.

Genus: *Placopleurus* BROUGH, 1939.

Geological range: Middle to Upper Triassic.

Geographical distribution: Europe.

Features: Small fishes of laterally compressed shape. Head deep. Snout rounded. Eyes very large. Dorsal fin small, situated in the middle of the body. Caudal fin deeply divided. Pectoral and pelvic fins small. Scales very thick, rod-like on the flanks, otherwise square or rectangular.

Remarks: Probably fed on crustaceans and other small animals.

Recent relatives: None. Died out in Upper Triassic.

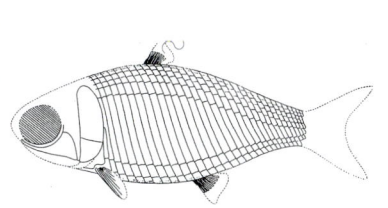

Placopleurus, reconstruction after BROUGH.

CHONDROSTEI — Chondrosteans
Order: Saurichthyiformes
Family: Saurichthyidae

Saurichthys sp. (length c. 35 cm) from the Middle Triassic of Monte San Giorgio, Switzerland. Original: Interfoss, Munich, Germany.

Genus: *Saurichthys* AGASSIZ, 1834.

Synonyms: *Acidorhynchus*, *Belonorhynchus*, *Gymnosaurichthys*, *Ichthyorhynchus*.

Geological range: Lower to Upper Triassic.

Geographical distribution: Western and eastern Europe, North America, Spitzbergen, Madagascar, Australia, Greenland, South Africa, southern, eastern and central Asia.

Features: Middle-sized fishes with elongate streamlined bodies. Head elongate, ending in a rostrum equally formed from upper and lower jaws which were of the same length. Dorsal fin almost at the posterior end of the body, opposite the fan-shaped anal fin. Pectoral and pelvic fins relatively small. Scales arranged in four longitudinal rows - dorsal, ventral and along each flank.

Remarks: Pike-like predators. Viviparous.

Recent relatives: None. Died out in Middle Triassic.

Saurichthys, after MacMillan.

CHONDROSTEI
Order: Saurichthyiformes
Family: Saurichthyidae

Chondrosteans

Saurorhynchus brevirostris WOODWARD (length c. 36 cm) from the Lower Jurassic of Holzmaden, Württemberg, Germany. Original: Staatliches Museum für Naturkunde, Stuttgart, Germany.

Genus: *Saurorhynchus* REIS, 1892.

Geological range: Lower Jurassic.

Geographical distribution: Europe.

Features: Middle-sized fishes of elongate streamlined shape. Head elongate, ending in a rostrum formed equally from upper and lower jaws. Teeth pointed conical. Caudal fin homocercal. Body almost scaleless.

Remarks: Eel-like predators.

Recent relatives: None. Died out in Lower Jurassic.

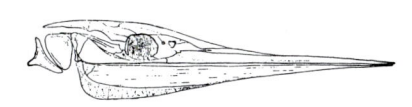

Saurorhynchus, reconstruction after GARDINER.

CHONDROSTEI — Chondrosteans
Order: Acipenseriformes
Family: Chondrosteidae

Chondrosteus hindenburgi (HENNIG) (length c. 300 cm) from the Lower Jurassic of Holzmaden, Württemberg, Germany. Original: Museum für Geologie und Paläontologie, Tübingen, Germany.

Genus: *Chondrosteus* EGERTON, 1858.

Geological range: Lower Jurassic.

Geographical distribution: Europe.

Features: Very large, rather plump fishes. Head deep. Snout pointed. Mouth ventral. Dorsal fin in the posterior third of the body, obliquely opposite the anal fin. Pectoral fins large. Pelvic fins pointed. Body largely scaleless.

Remarks: Marine.

Recent relatives: Genus and family extinct. Distantly related to the recent family Acipenseridae. Can be seen as forerunners of the true sturgeons.

Chondrosteus, reconstruction after WOODWARD.

CHONDROSTEI — Chondrosteans
Order: Acipenseriformes
Family: Chondrosteidae

Stichopterus popovi YAKOVLEV (length c. 56 cm) from the Lower Cretaceous of Mongolia. Original: Paleontologicheskii Musei Russkoi Akademii Nauk, Moscow, Russia.

Genus: *Stichopterus* YAKOVLEV, 1986.

Geological range: Lower Cretaceous.

Geographical distribution: Central Asia.

Features: Middle-sized fishes of rather laterally compressed shape. Head deep. Snout somewhat elongate. Dorsal fin triangular, obliquely opposite the anal fin. Body scaleless except for the axis of the caudal fin. Caudal fin heterocercal. The lower lobe concave in outline and considerably bigger than the upper, which carries ganoid scales.

Remarks: Predatory fishes.

Recent relatives: Genus and family extinct. Distantly related to recent sturgeons.

Acipenser sturio, a recent sturgeon. Lithograph from BLOCH.

CHONDROSTEI   Chondrosteans
Order: Acipenseriformes
Family: Polyodontidae

Crossopholis magnicaudatus COPE (length c. 39 cm) from the Eocene of Wyoming, U.S.A. Original: Field Museum of Natural History, Chicago, Illinois, U.S.A.

Genus: *Crossopholis* COPE, 1883.

Geological range: Eocene.

Geographical distribution: North America.

Features: Large fishes, laterally compressed. Head shallow, ending in a long rostrum formed from both upper and lower jaws. Dorsal fin relatively small, situated in the posterior third of the body, obliquely opposite the somewhat larger anal fin. Caudal fin heterocercal, lower lobe larger than the upper. Pectoral and pelvic fins triangular.

Remarks: Lived in fresh water.

Recent relatives: Genus extinct. Family still extant. Probably to be seen as forerunners of the paddlefish *Polyodon*.

Polyodon spathula, the recent paddlefish.

"HOLOSTEI" — Holosteans

The term "Holostei" is no longer used in modern systematics because the common features of this transitional group between the Chondrostei and the Teleostei are not enough to make a natural group. The few fishes that belong here are split into the divisions Ginglymodi and Halecostomi and the subdivision Halecomorphi. For clarity's sake I use the word "Holostei" in quotation marks.

Many skeletal parts represented by cartilage in the chondrosteans are ossified in the holosteans. The rigid contacts of the bones in the head are here lost so that the upper jaw becomes mobile relative to the skull. Teeth are usually present on upper as well as lower jaws. In semionotids and pycnodontids they are hemispherical and form a grinding dentition. The orbits of the eyes are more posterior and higher in the skull than in chondrosteans and generally are protected by a ring of bone. The gape is usually shorter.

There is only one dorsal fin. The hemiheterocercal caudal fin shortens, to a greater or lesser extent, and in the more advanced forms is externally almost symmetrical. The scaly upper lobe is usually greatly reduced. The unpaired fins, as in the chondrosteans, have bony keeled scales in front of them called fulcra. The ossification of the vertebral centra differs in different genera and is usually incomplete. Indeed, they are completely ossified only in the gars (family Lepisosteidae).

The scales are of ganoid type but can be circular or rhombic and sometimes very thick. The cosmine layer of chondrosteans is here lacking. Indeed, even the ganoine layer in many cases tends to reduction. Thin round scales occur in the bowfins (*Amia*). The first "holostei" appear in the Upper Permian. The group reached its absolute maximum in the Upper Jurassic. Its members were still common in the Cretaceous and a few genera remained even in the Tertiary. The only living survivors among holosteans are the gars and the bowfins.

More than one hundred fossil genera have so far been described. They are often very well preserved.

"HOLOSTEI"   Holosteans

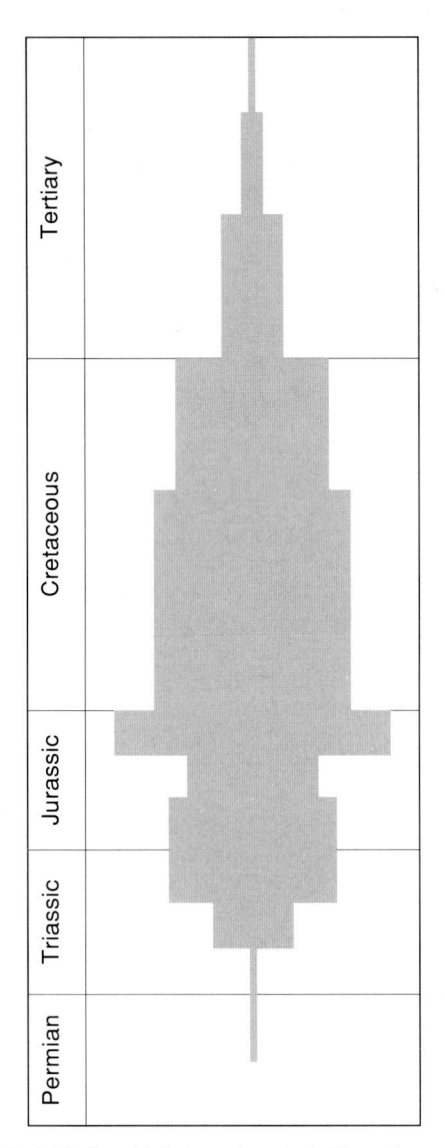

The approximate distribution of holosteans in geological time, changed after MÜLLER.

"HOLOSTEI" Ginglymodi   Holosteans
Order: Lepisosteiformes
Family: Lepisosteidae   Gars

Atractosteus strausi (KINKELIN) (length c. 25 cm) from the Eocene of Messel, Germany. Original: Frickhinger Collection, Munich, Germany.

Genus: *Atractosteus* RAFINESQUE, 1820.

Geological range: Upper Cretaceous to recent.

Geographical distribution: Europe, North America, western Africa.

Features: Middle-sized fishes with elongate slender bodies. Head narrow, ending in a rostrum formed from both upper and lower jaws. Teeth pointed. Eyes small. Dorsal fin very posterior in position, opposite the anal fin. Caudal fin not forked, rounded. Pectoral and pelvic fins small. Body covered with massive ganoid scales.

Remarks: Fresh-water fishes like their recent relatives.

Recent relatives: Closely related to the recent gars of the genus *Atractosteus* which occur in North America, Central America and Cuba.

Atractosteus spatula, a recent gar, after Yale University.

373

"HOLOSTEI" Ginglymodi — Holosteans
Order: Lepisosteiformes
Family: Lepisosteidae — Gars

Lepisosteus cuneatus (COPE) (length c. 65 cm) from the Eocene of Wyoming, U.S.A. Original: Field Museum of Natural History, Chicago, Illinois, U.S.A.

Genus: *Lepisosteus* de LACÉPÈDE, 1803.

Geological range: Upper Cretaceous to recent.

Geographical distribution: North America, southern Asia.

Features: Middle-sized to large fishes with elongate slender bodies. Head elongate, ending in a rostrum formed of upper and lower jaws which are nearly of equal length. Teeth pointed. Eyes small. Dorsal fin very posterior in position, opposite the large anal fin. Caudal fin not divided, rounded. Pectoral fins small and narrow. Pelvic fins somewhat broader. Body covered with thick ganoid scales.

Remarks: Fresh-water fishes, like their recent relatives.

Recent relatives: Closely related to the recent gars of the genus *Lepisosteus* which occur in North America, Central America and Cuba.

Lepisosteus osseus, the recent longnose gar.

"HOLOSTEI" Halecostomi   Holosteans
Order: Semionotiformes
Family: Semionotidae

Acentrophorus varians Kirkby (length c. 7 cm) from the Upper Permian of Durham, England. Original: The Natural History Museum, London, U.K. (P3481c).

Genus: *Acentrophorus* Traquair, 1877.

Geological range: Upper Permian to Upper Triassic.

Geographical distribution: Europe, North America.

Features: Small fishes with somewhat laterally compressed bodies. Head deep. Snout pointed. Eyes large. Teeth small and pointed. Dorsal fin attached behind the middle of the body, obliquely opposite the anal fin. Pectoral and pelvic fins broad. Body covered with rectangular ganoid scales.

Remarks: Probably herbivorous.

Recent relatives: None. Died out in Upper Triassic.

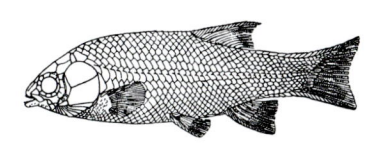

Acentrophorus, reconstruction after Gill.

375

"HOLOSTEI" Halecostomi — Holosteans
Order: Semionotiformes
Family: Semionotidae

Dandya ovalis GORJANOVIC - KRAMBERGER (length c. 5 cm) from the Upper Triassic of Cene, Bergamo, Italy. Original: Museo Civico di Scienze Naturali Caffi, Bergamo, Italy.

Genus: *Dandya* WHITE & MOY-THOMAS, 1940.

Geological range: Upper Triassic.

Geographical distribution: Europe.

Features: Small fishes with oval bodies. Head deep. Snout blunt. Eyes large. Teeth conical. Dorsal fin in the posterior half of the body, beginning with a point and continuing as a fringe. Anal fin similar in shape, opposite in position. Pectoral fins placed high on the body. Pelvic fins small. Scales thick, becoming longer ventrally.

Remarks: Still-water fishes which probably lived on crustaceans and other small animals.

Recent relatives: None. Died out in Upper Triassic.

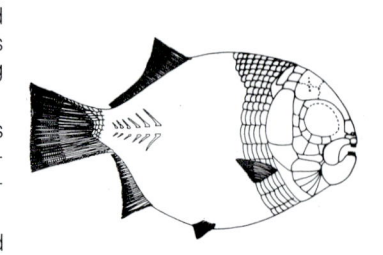

Dandya, after TINTORI.

376

"HOLOSTEI" Halecostomi Holosteans
Order: Semionotiformes
Family: Semionotidae

Dapedium punctatum Agassiz (length c. 34 cm) from the Lower Jurassic of Holzmaden, Württemberg, Germany. Original: Urweltmuseum Hauff, Holzmaden, Germany.

Genus: *Dapedium* Leach, 1832.

Synonyms: *Aeschmodus, Amblyurus, Dapedius, Omalopleurus, Pholidotus.*

Geological range: Upper Triassic to Lower Jurassic.

Geographical distribution: Europe, southern Asia.

Features: Middle-sized fishes of oval outline. Head deep. Snout rounded. Dorsal fin begins approximately in the middle of the body and reaches as a fringe to the base of the caudal fin. Anal fin likewise fringe-like but somewhat shorter. Pectoral and pelvic fins small. Teeth clavate. Thick ganoid scales, on the flanks longer than wide.

Remarks: Still-water herbivores that also fed on small animals.

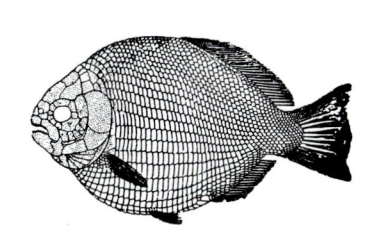

Dapedium, after Woodward.

Recent relatives: None. Died out in Lower Jurassic.

377

"HOLOSTEI" Halecostomi   Holosteans
Order: Semionotiformes
Family: Semionotidae

Enigmaichthys attenuatus WADE (length c. 5 cm) from the Middle Triassic of Hornsby, Sydney, Australia. Original: Australian Museum, Sydney, Australia.

Genus: *Enigmaichthys* WADE, 1935.

Geological range: Middle Triassic.

Geographical distribution: Australia.

Features: Small fishes of elongate fusiform shape. Head elongate. Snout pointed. Dorsal fin in posterior third of the body, opposite the anal fin. Caudal fin not forked. Pectoral and pelvic fins small. Body covered in ganoid scales.

Remarks: Probably fed on crustaceans and other small animals.

Recent relatives: None. Died out in Middle Triassic.

"HOLOSTEI" Halecostomi Holosteans
Order: Semionotiformes
Family: Semionotidae

Eosemionotus sp. (length c. 5 cm) from the Middle Triassic of Monte San Gorgio, Switzerland. Original: Paläontologisches Museum, Zürich, Switzerland.

Genus: *Eosemionotus* STOLLEY, 1920.

Geological range: Lower to Middle Triassic.

Geographical distribution: Europe.

Features: Small fishes with somewhat laterally compressed bodies. Head deep. Snout rather pointed. Dorsal fin just behind the middle of the body. Posterior margin of caudal fin slightly concave. Anal fin, pectoral fins and pelvic fins relatively small. Body covered with large, more or less rhombic, scales.

Remarks: Probably gregarious.

Recent relatives: None. Died out in Middle Triassic.

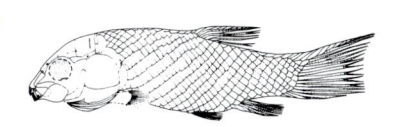

Eosemionotus, reconstruction after SCHULTZE.

"HOLOSTEI"   Halecostomi   Holosteans
Order: Semionotiformes
Family: Semionotidae

Hemicalypterus weiri Schaeffer (length c. 9 cm) from the Upper Triassic of San Juan County, Utah, U.S.A. Original: Museum of Natural History, Lawrence, Kansas, U.S.A.

Genus: *Hemicalypterus* Schaeffer, 1967.

Geological range: Upper Triassic.

Geographical distribution: North America.

Features: Small fishes of oval outline. Head deep. Snout blunt. Eyes relatively large. Dorsal fin tall, fringe-like, opposite the similarly shaped anal fin. Caudal fin not forked. Body covered with elongate to rod-shaped Scales.

Remarks: Still-water fishes which probably fed on crustaceans and other small animals.

Recent relatives: None. Died out in Upper Triassic.

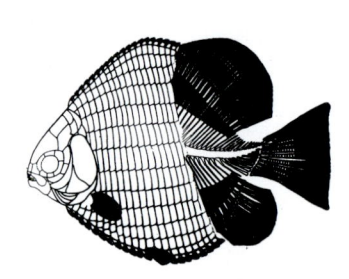

Hemicalypterus, reconstruction after Schaeffer.

"HOLOSTEI" Halecostomi — Holosteans
Order: Semionotiformes
Family: Semionotidae

Heterostrophus latus WAGNER (length c. 40 cm) from the Upper Jurassic of Solnhofen (Blumenberg), Bavaria, Germany. Original: Jura-Museum, Eichstätt, Germany.

Genus: *Heterostrophus* WAGNER, 1859.

Geological range: Upper Jurassic.

Geographical distribution: Europe.

Features: Middle-sized fishes of oval outline. Head deep. Snout rather pointed. Eyes relatively large. Dorsal fin in the posterior half of the body, with a point anteriorly but continuing posteriorly as a low fringe, opposite the anal fin which is also fringe-like. Pectoral and pelvic fins small. Scales square to rectangular, arranged in diagonal rows.

Remarks: This very rare fish is sometimes cited under the incorrect name of *Tetragonolepis*. Wagner's holotype has disappeared.

Recent relatives: None. Died out in Upper Jurassic.

"HOLOSTEI" Halecostomi — Holosteans
Order: Semionotiformes
Family: Semionotidae

Lepidotes elvensis (de BLAINVILLE) (length c. 47 cm) from the Lower Jurassic of Holzmaden, Württemberg, Germany. Original: Interfoss, Munich, Germany.

Genus: *Lepidotes* AGASSIZ, 1832.

Synonyms: *Lepidotus, Plesiodus, Prolepidotus, Scrobodus, Sphaerodus*.

Geological range: Upper Triassic to Lower Cretaceous.

Geographical distribution: Europe, Africa, North America, Asia, South America, Madagascar.

Features: Middle-sized to large fishes with laterally compressed bodies. Head elongate. Snout pointed. Eyes small. Teeth peg-shaped with rounded ends. Dorsal fin small and pointed, in the posterior half of the body. Anal fin more posterior. Posterior margin of caudal fin only moderately concave. Pelvic fins small. Pectoral fins somewhat larger. Scales very thick, rectangular, arranged in diagonal rows.

Remarks: Lethargic swimmers with durophagous diet.

Recent relatives: None. Died out in Lower Cretaceous.

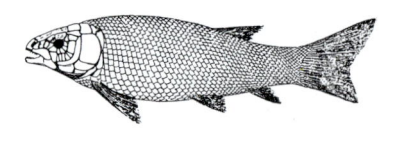

Lepidotes, reconstruction after JAEKEL.

"HOLOSTEI" Halecostomi Holosteans
Order: Semionotiformes
Family: Semionotidae

Paracentrophorus madagascariensis Piveteau (length c. 8 cm) from the Lower Triassic of Madagascar. Original: The Natural History Museum, London, U.K.

Genus: *Paracentrophorus* Piveteau, 1941.

Geological range: Lower Triassic.

Geographical distribution: Madagascar.

Features: Small fishes with laterally compressed bodies. Head deep. Snout rounded. Dorsal fin in the posterior third of the body, opposite the anal fin. Pectoral and pelvic fins small. Scales large, rectangular, arranged in diagonal rows.

Remarks: Probably of durophagous diet.

Recent relatives: None. Died out in Lower Triassic.

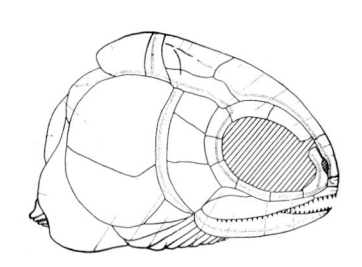

Paracentrophorus, reconstruction after Gardiner.

"HOLOSTEI"   Halecostomi   Holosteans
Order: Semionotiformes
Family: Semionotidae

Paralepidotus ornatus (AGASSIZ) (length c. 53 cm) from the Upper Triassic of Zogno, Bergamo, Italy. Original: Museo Brembano di Scienze Naturali, San Pellegrino, Bergamo, Italy.

Genus: *Paralepidotus* STOLLEY, 1920.

Geological range: Upper Permian to Upper Triassic.

Geographical distribution: Europe.

Features: Middle-sized to large fishes with somewhat corpulent bodies. Head elongate. Snout pointed. Eyes large. Dorsal fin relatively large, with a broad base, situated in the posterior half of the body. Anal fin opposite, considerably smaller. Caudal fin moderately concave behind. Scales thick and rectangular, arranged in diagonal rows.

Remarks: Still-water fishes with durophagous diet.

Recent relatives: None. Died out in Upper Triassic.

"HOLOSTEI" Halecostomi — Holosteans
Order: Semionotiformes
Family: Semionotidae

Pericentrophorus minimus JÖRG (length c. 3 cm) from the Lower Triassic of Durlach, Baden, Germany. Original: Staatliches Museum für Naturkunde, Karlsruhe, Germany.

Genus: *Pericentrophorus* JÖRG, 1969.

Geological range: Lower Triassic.

Geographical distribution: Europe.

Features: Very small slender fishes. Head elongate. Snout pointed. Teeth small. Dorsal fin pointed, triangular, broad-based, situated in the posterior half of the body, obliquely opposite the broadly elongate anal fin. Pectoral and pelvic fins relatively large. Scales quadrangular, becoming longer on the flanks.

Remarks: Probably fed on crustaceans and other small animals.

Recent relatives: None. Died out in Lower Triassic.

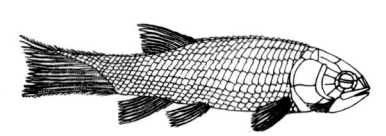

Pericentrophorus, reconstruction after JÖRG.

"HOLOSTEI" Halecostomi Holosteans
Order: Semionotiformes
Family: Semionotidae

Sargodon tomicus PLIENINGER (length c. 33 cm) from the Upper Triassic of Berbenno, Bergamo, Italy. Original: Museo Civico di Scienze Naturali Caffi, Bergamo, Italy.

Genus: *Sargodon* PLIENINGER, 1847.

Geological range: Upper Triassic.

Geographical distribution: Europe.

Features: Middle-sized fishes, broadly rhombic in outline. Head deep. Snout rounded. Teeth rod-like with rounded ends. Dorsal fin begins with a point at the place where the dorsal mid line turns downwards and continues as a fringe. Anal fin opposite and similar but shorter. Pectoral fins very high in the body. Pelvic fins very small. Scales square in the dorsal half of the body, becoming rod-shaped ventrally.

Remarks: Still-water fishes, probably with durophagous diet.

Recent relatives: None. Died out in Upper Triassic.

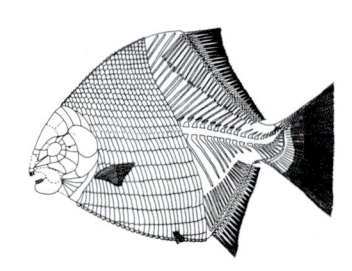

Sargodon, after TINTORI.

"HOLOSTEI" Halecostomi — Holosteans
Order: Semionotiformes
Family: Semionotidae

Semionotus bergeri AGASSIZ (length c. 17 cm) from the Upper Triassic of Weißenbrunn, Coburg, Bavaria, Germany. Original: Bayerische Staatssammlung für Paläontologie, Munich, Germany.

Genus: *Semionotus* AGASSIZ, 1832.

Synonyms: *Archaeosemionotus*, *Ischypterus*.

Geological range: Lower to Upper Triassic.

Geographical distribution: Europe, South Africa, Australia, North America, South America.

Features: Middle-sized slender fishes. Head elongate. Snout pointed. Dorsal fin relatively large, beginning with a row of keeled scales. Anal fin somewhat more posterior. Posterior margin of caudal fin straight to slightly concave. Pectoral and pelvic fins elongate. Teeth rod-like with rounded ends. Scales rhombic.

Remarks: Probably durophagous.

Recent relatives: None. Died out in Upper Triassic.

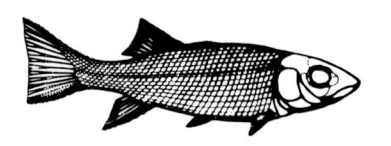

Semionotus, reconstruction after JUBB & GARDINER.

"HOLOSTEI" Halecostomi — Holosteans
Order: Semionotiformes
Family: Semionotidae

Tetragonolepis semicinctus (Bronn) (length c. 9 cm) from the Lower Jurassic of Sulzkirchen, Bavaria, Germany. Original: Tischlinger Collection, Stammham, Germany. Photograph: Tischlinger.

Genus: *Tetragonolepis* Bronn, 1830.

Synonyms: *Homoeolepis*, *Pleurolepis*.

Geological range: Lower Jurassic.

Geographical distribution: Europe, Asia.

Features: Small fishes with rounded oval outline and deep bellies. Laterally flattened. Head deep. Snout rounded. Dorsal fin beginning approximately in the middle of the body and continuing rearwards as a fringe. Anal fin similar. Posterior margin of caudal fin straight. Pectoral fins set high on the body. Scales rod-like, becoming longer ventrally.

Remarks: Still-water herbivores that also fed on small animals.

Recent relatives: None. Died out in Lower Jurassic.

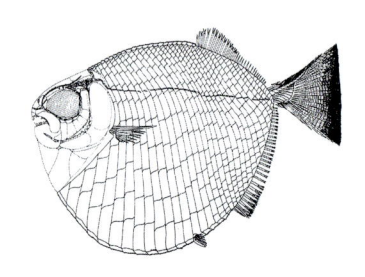

Tetragonolepis, after Thies.

"HOLOSTEI" Halecostomi — Holosteans
Order: Pycnodontiformes
Family: Brembodontidae

Brembodus ridens TINTORI (length c. 14 cm) from the Upper Triassic of Zogno, Bergamo, Italy. Original: Museo Civico di Scienze Naturali Caffi, Bergamo, Italy.

Genus: *Brembodus* TINTORI, 1980.

Geological range: Upper Triassic.

Geographical distribution: Europe.

Features: Small fishes of inflated-oval outline and laterally compressed bodies. Snout blunt. Eyes small. Gape directed downwards. Small rounded teeth. Dorsal mid line raised into a point in the anterior part of the body. Dorsal fin fringe-like, extending over the whole posterior half of the body. Anal fin considerably smaller. Caudal fin not forked.

Remarks: Probably durophagous.

Recent relatives: None. Died out in Upper Triassic.

"HOLOSTEI" Halecostomi   Holosteans
Order: Pycnodontiformes
Family: Brembodontidae

Gibbodon cenensis TINTORI (length c. 6 cm) from the Upper Triassic of Cene, Bergamo, Italy. Original: Museo Civico di Scienze Naturali Caffi, Bergamo, Italy.

Genus: *Gibbodon* TINTORI, 1980.

Geological range: Upper Triassic.

Geographical distribution: Europe.

Features: Small fishes of inflated-oval outline, laterally compressed. Head deep. Eyes relatively large. Gape directed downwards. Teeth rod-like with rounded ends. Anterior part of the dorsal mid line pointed. Dorsal fin low, with a very broad base, opposite the smaller anal fin. Caudal fin not subdivided. Scales massive.

Remarks: Probably durophagous.

Recent relatives: None. Died out in Upper Triassic.

"HOLOSTEI" Halecostomi Holosteans
Order: Pycnodontiformes
Family: Pycnodontidae

Arduafrons prominoris Böss (length c. 29 cm) from the Upper Jurassic of Solnhofen, Bavaria, Germany. Original: Bürgermeister Müller Museum, Solnhofen, Germany.

Genus: *Arduafrons* Böss.

Geological range: Upper Jurassic.

Geographical distribution: Europe.

Features: Middle-sized fishes with circular outline, laterally compressed. Head deep and narrow, with a relatively steep "forehead". Snout pointed. Gape short. Powerful rounded teeth. Anterior part of dorsal mid line pointed. Dorsal fin low, broad-based, very posterior, opposite the smaller anal fin which is drawn into a point at its anterior end. Caudal fin fan-shaped, not forked.

Remarks: Probably durophagous.

Recent relatives: None. Died out in Upper Jurassic.

"HOLOSTEI" Halecostomi Holosteans
Order: Pycnodontiformes
Family: Pycnodontidae

Coccodus insignis Pictet (length c. 12 cm) from the Upper Cretaceous of Lebanon. Original: Staatliches Museum für Naturkunde, Karlsruhe, Germany.

Genus: *Coccodus* Pictet, 1851.

Geological range: Upper Cretaceous.

Geographical distribution: Middle East.

Features: Small slender fishes with elongate oval bodies. Head elongate. Gape long. Mouth with strong hemispherical but laterally flattened teeth. There is a powerful dorsal spine and on left and right a thorn-shaped spike divided distally into two points.

Remarks: Durophagous.

Recent relatives: None. Died out in Upper Cretaceous.

"HOLOSTEI" Halecostomi Holosteans
Order: Pycnodontiformes
Family: Pycnodontidae

Coelodus costae HECKEL (length c. 36 cm) from the Lower Cretaceous of Pietraroia, Italy. Original: Interfoss, Munich.

Genus: *Coelodus* HECKEL, 1836.

Synonyms: *Anomiophthalmus, Cosmodus, Glossodus*.

Geological range: Upper Jurassic to Eocene.

Geographical distribution: Europe, North America, Madagascar, Asia.

Features: Middle-sized fishes with oval outline and laterally flattened bodies. Head deep. Snout pointed. Gape short. Mouth with rounded teeth. Dorsal fin in the posterior half of the body, broad-based and rising to a point near the anterior end. Anal fin opposite, similar in shape but much smaller. Caudal fin fan-shaped, with scalloped posterior margin.

Remarks: Durophagous.

Recent relatives: None. Died out in Eocene.

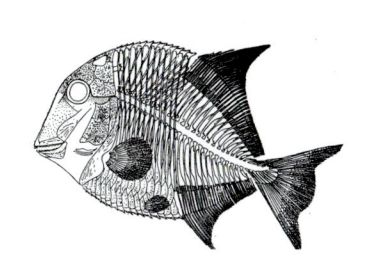

Coelodus, reconstruction after WOODWARD.

"HOLOSTEI" Halecostomi Holosteans
Order: Pycnodontiformes
Family: Pycnodontidae

Eomesodon gibbosus (WAGNER) (length c. 42 cm) from the Upper Jurassic of Solnhofen (Birkhof), Bavaria, Germany. Original: Jura-Museum, Eichstätt, Germany.

Genus: *Eomesodon* WOODWARD, 1918.

Geological range: Upper Triassic to Upper Jurassic.

Geographical distribution: Europe.

Features: Middle-sized fishes with oval outline, laterally compressed. Head deep. Gape directed downwards. Mouth with strong hemispherical teeth. "Forehead" steep. Dorsal mid line pointed in the anterior part. Dorsal fin in the posterior part of the dorsal mid line, broad-based and almost semicircular. Anal fin opposite, considerably smaller. Caudal fin not forked.

Remarks: Durophagous.

Recent relatives: None. Died out in Upper Jurassic.

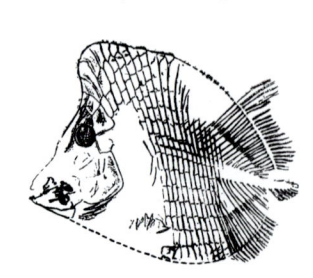

Eomesodon, reconstruction after WOODWARD.

"HOLOSTEI" Halecostomi — Holosteans
Order: Pycnodontiformes
Family: Pycnodontidae

Gyrodus hexagonus de BLAINVILLE (length c. 22 cm) from the Upper Jurassic of Solnhofen (Eichstätt), Bavaria, Germany. Original: Krauss Collection, Weißenburg, Germany.

Genus: *Gyrodus* AGASSIZ, 1833.

Synonym: *Strematodus*.

Geological range: Middle Jurassic to Upper Cretaceous.

Geographical distribution: Europe, Africa, Cuba.

Features: Body oval or almost circular in outline. Snout vertical. Rounded oval teeth with an obvious margin. In juvenile specimens the teeth pointed in the middle. Caudal fin large relative to the body, deeply forked with relatively narrow lobes. Dorsal fin narrow, almost opposite smaller anal fin. Maximum body length up to two metres.

Remarks: Fed on hard-shelled prey, possibly also on corals.

Recent relatives: None. Died out at end of Cretaceous.

Gyrodus, reconstruction after ZITTEL.

"HOLOSTEI" Halecostomi — Holosteans
Order: Pycnodontiformes
Family: Pycnodontidae

Gyronchus macropterus (WAGNER) (length c. 10 cm) from the Upper Jurassic of Solnhofen (Eichstätt), Bavaria, Germany. Original: Interfoss, Munich, Germany.

Genus: *Gyronchus* AGASSIZ, 1839.

Synonyms: *Mesodon, Macromesodon, Scaphozus, Typodus.*

Geological range: Middle Jurassic to Lower Cretaceous.

Geographical distribution: Europe.

Features: Small fishes with circular outline, laterally compressed. Head deep. Snout pointed. Eyes small. Gape directed downwards. Dorsal fin in the posterior half of the body, broad-based, with a point anteriorly. Anal fin opposite, of similar shape and likewise relatively large. Caudal fin short and unforked.

Remarks: Durophagous.

Recent relatives: None. Died out in Lower Cretaceous.

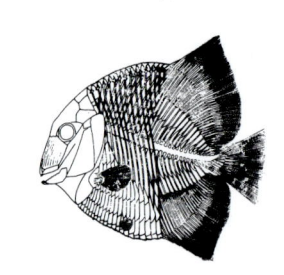

Gyronchys, reconstruction after WOODWARD.

"HOLOSTEI" Halecostomi   Holosteans
Order: Pycnodontiformes
Family: Pycnodontidae

Ichthyoceros spinosus GAYET (length c. 7 cm) from the Upper Cretaceous of the Lebanon. Original: Staatliches Museum für Naturkunde, Karlsruhe, Germany.

Genus: *Ichthyoceros* GAYET, 1984.

Geological range: Upper Cretaceous.

Geographical distribution: Middle East.

Features: Small fishes resembling coffer fishes in shape. Head deep, with a long and pointed snout. Teeth rod-like. Eyes large. Characteristic broad-based spine at the posterior end of the head. Dorsal fin fringe-like, situated in the posterior half of the body. Caudal fin with a stem-like base, unforked and rounded.

Remarks: Durophagous.

Recent relatives: None. Died out in Upper Cretaceous.

Mesturus, reconstruction after LEHMAN.

"HOLOSTEI" Halecostomi Holosteans
Order: Pycnodontiformes
Family: Pycnodontidae

Mesturus verrocosus WAGNER (length c. 28 cm) from the Upper Jurassic of Solnhofen (Eichstätt), Bavaria, Germany. Original: Krauss Collection, Weißenburg.

Genus: *Mesturus* WAGNER, 1859.

Geological range: Upper Jurassic.

Geographical distribution: Europe.

Features: Middle-sized fishes with oval outline, laterally compressed. Head deep. Snout pointed. Eyes large. Gape long with rounded teeth. Cheeks covered with a mosaic of bony plates. Dorsal fin low, broad-based. Anal fin opposite and similarly shaped. Caudal fin fan-shaped, not forked, with a concave posterior margin.

Remarks: Probably durophagous.

Recent relatives: None. Died out in Upper Jurassic.

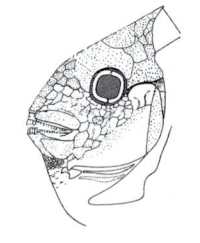

Mesturus, reconstruction after LEHMANN

"HOLOSTEI" Halecostomi Holosteans
Order: Pycnodontiformes
Family: Pycnodontidae

Neoproseinets penalvai (Silva Santos), length c. 37 cm, from the Lower Cretaceous of Ceará, Brazil. Original: Frickhinger Collection, Munich, Germany.

Genus: *Neoproscinetes* FIGUEIREDO & SILVA SANTOS, 1987

Synonym: *Microdon, Polysephus*.

Geological range: Lower Cretaceous.

Geographical distribution: South America.

Features: Middle-sized fishes of disc-shaped outline, laterally compressed. Head deep. Snout pointed and directed slightly downwards. Eyes large. Jaws with strong hemispherical teeth. Dorsal fin probably pointed, situated in the posterior third of the body, opposite the anal fin. Caudal fin very large, deeply forked, with narrow lobes.

Remarks: Fishes of durophagous diet.

Recent relatives: None. Died out in Lower Cretaceous.

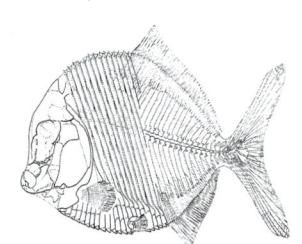

Neoproscinetes penalvai, after Maisey

"HOLOSTEI" Halecostomi Holosteans
Order: Pycnodontiformes
Family: Pycnodontidae

Nursallia veronae B<small>LOT</small> (length c. 31 cm) from the Middle Eocene of Bolca, Italy. Original: Museo Civico di Storia Naturale, Verona, Italy.

Genus: *Nursallia* B<small>LOT</small>, 1987.

Geological range: Middle Eocene.

Geographical distribution: Europe.

Features: Middle-sized fishes with elongate oval outline, laterally compressed. Head deep. Snout pointed. Eyes large. Gape rather long. Upper and lower jaws with a pavement of spherical teeth. Dorsal fin behind the highest point of the body. Caudal fin stalked, broadly expanded with pointed ends, the posterior margin concave but scalloped.

Remarks: Durophagous. Possibly bit pieces off corals. Possibly *Nursallia* is a synonym for *Pycnodus*.

Recent relatives: None. Died out in Eocene.

"HOLOSTEI"   Halecostomi   Holosteans
Order: Pycnodontiformes
Family: Pycnodontidae

Palaeobalistum goedeli HECKEL (length c. 20 cm) from the Upper Cretaceous of Lebanon. Original: Frickhinger Collection, Munich, Germany.

Genus: *Palaeobalistum* de BLAINVILLE, 1818.

Synonyms: *Palaeobalistes*.

Geological range: Upper Cretaceous to Eocene.

Geographical distribution: Middle East, South America, Europe, Africa.

Features: Middle-sized fishes with rounded oval outline, laterally compressed. Head deep. Gape directed downwards. Eyes small. Dorsal fin in the posterior half of the body, begins with a narrow point and passes into a low fringe. Anal fin opposite and similar in shape. Tail fin stalked, narrowly fan-shaped, with broadly scalloped posterior margin.

Remarks: Durophagous.

Recent relatives: None. Died out in Eocene.

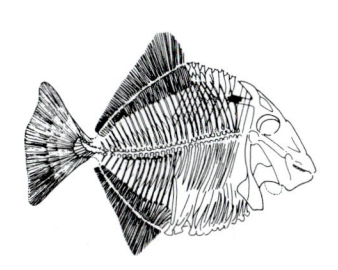

Palaeobalistum, reconstruction after HECKEL.

401

"HOLOSTEI" Halecostomi — Holosteans
Order: Pycnodontiformes
Family: Pycnodontidae

Proscinetes elegans AGASSIZ (length c. 24 cm) from the Upper Jurassic of Solnhofen, Bavaria, Germany. Original: Bayerische Staatssammlung für Paläontologie, Munich, Germany.

Genus: *Proscinetes* GISTL, 1848.

Synonyms: *Microdon*, *Polysephis*.

Geological range: Middle Jurassic to Lower Cretaceous.

Geographical distribution: Europe, Central America, South America, North America.

Features: Middle-sized fishes with circular outline, laterally compressed. Head deep. Gape directed downwards. Strong rounded teeth. Dorsal fin in the posterior half of the body, broad-based, beginning with a point but becoming lower posteriorly. Anal fin opposite, similar in shape. Caudal fin not forked but with a strongly concave posterior margin.

Remarks: Probably durophagous.

Recent relatives: None. Died out in Lower Cretaceous.

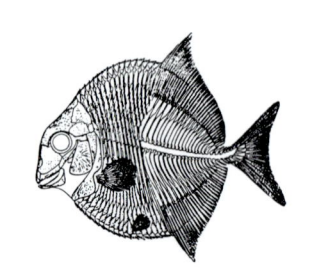

Proscinetes, reconstruction after WOODWARD.

"HOLOSTEI" Halecostomi — Holosteans
Order: Pycnodontiformes
Family: Pycnodontidae

Pycnodus platessus (de BLAINVILLE) (length c. 11 cm) from the Middle Eocene of Bolca, Italy. Original: Interfoss, Munich, Germany.

Genus: *Pycnodus* AGASSIZ, 1833.

Synonyms: *Periodus*, *Pychnodus*.

Geological range: Middle Jurassic to Eocene.

Geographical distribution: Europe, West Indies, Australia, North America, Africa, Asia.

Features: Small to middle-sized fishes with oval outline, laterally compressed. Head deep, with gape directed downwards. Rounded teeth. Eyes large. The dorsal mid line carries a small hump anteriorly. Behind this is the dorsal fin which has a point anteriorly but passes behind into a low fringe. Anal fin opposite and similarly shaped. Caudal fin stalked, with a concave posterior margin.

Remarks: Durophagous.

Recent relatives: None. Died out in Eocene.

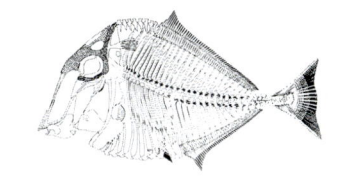

Pycnodus, reconstruction after BLOT.

"HOLOSTEI" Halecostomi — Holosteans
Order: Pycnodontiformes
Family: Pycnodontidae

Stemmatodus rhombus (AGASSIZ) (length c. 6 cm) from the Lower Cretaceous of Castellamare, Italy. Original: Frickhinger Collection, Munich, Germany.

Genus: *Stemmatodus* HECKEL, 1854.

Geological range: Upper Jurassic to Lower Cretaceous.

Geographical distribution: Europe.

Features: Small fishes with rounded oval outline, laterally compressed. Head deep. Snout pointed. Eyes large. Gape directed slightly downwards. Teeth small, rounded. Dorsal fin beginning behind the middle of the body, low, fringe-like. Anal fin opposite, similarly shaped. Caudal fin relatively small, deeply forked.

Remarks: Durophagous.

Recent relatives: None. Died out in Lower Cretaceous.

"HOLOSTEI" Halecostomi Holosteans
Order: Macrosemiiformes
Family: Macrosemiidae

Aphanepygus dorsalis Davis (length c. 7 cm) from the Upper Cretaceous of the Lebanon. Original: The Natural History Museum, London, U.K.

Genus: *Aphanepygus* Bassani, 1879.

Geological range: Upper Cretaceous.

Geographical distribution: Middle East.

Features: Small fishes with elongate slender bodies. Head shallow. Gape short. Mouth terminal. Dorsal fin extends as a long low fringe along almost all of the back. Caudal fin not forked. Scales arranged in diagonal rows.

Remarks: *Aphanepygus* is often assigned to the genus *Petalopteryx*.

Recent relatives: None. Died out in Upper Cretaceous.

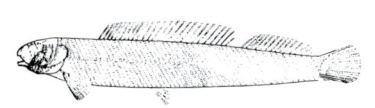

Aphanepygus, reconstruction after Bartram.

405

"HOLOSTEI" Halecostomi — Holosteans

Order: Macrosemiiformes
Family: Macrosemiidae

Disticholepis dumortieri THIOLLIERE (length c. 15 cm) from the Upper Jurassic of Cerin, France. Original: Musée Guimet d'Histoire Naturelle, Lyon, France.

Genus: *Disticholepis* THIOLLIERE, 1873.

Geological range: Upper Jurassic.

Geographical distribution: Europe.

Features: Small fishes with slender bodies. Head long and shallow. Snout pointed. Mouth terminal. Dorsal fin stretches like a sail along the whole of the back. Anal fin rounded. Caudal fin not forked. Pectoral fins rounded. Pelvic fins small.

Remarks: The genus *Disticholepis* is considered by some authors as a synonym of *Macrosemius*.

Recent relatives: None. Died out in Upper Jurassic.

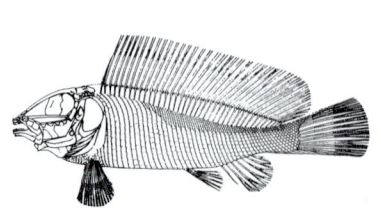

Disticholepis, reconstruction after BARTRAM.

"HOLOSTEI"   Halecostomi   Holosteans
Order: Macrosemiiformes
Family: Macrosemiidae

Histionotus oberndorferi WAGNER (length c. 13 cm) from the Upper Jurassic of Solnhofen (Eichstätt), Bavaria, Germany. Original: Museum Berger, Harthof bei Eichstätt, Germany.

Genus: *Histionotus* EGERTON, 1854.

Geological range: Upper Jurassic to Lower Cretaceous.

Geographical distribution: Europe.

Features: Small fishes with somewhat laterally compressed bodies. Head deep. Mouth terminal. Two dorsal fins, the first sail-like, high and pointed, the second starting immediately behind the first, low triangular. Anal, pectoral and pelvic fins small. Caudal fin forked. Scales elongate rectangular to rhombic.

Remarks: Probably reef dwellers.

Recent relatives: None. Died out in Lower Cretaceous.

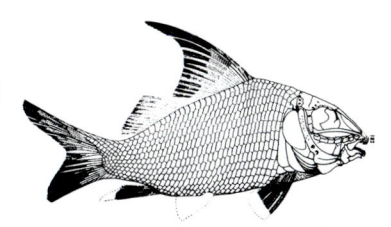

Histionotus, reconstruction after BARTRAM.

"HOLOSTEI" Halecostomi — Holosteans
Order: Macrosemiiformes
Family: Macrosemiidae

Legnonotus krambergeri BARTRAM (length c. 9 cm) from the Upper Triassic of Cene, Bergamo, Italy. Original: Museo Civico di Scienze Naturali Caffi, Bergamo, Italy.

Genus: *Legnonotus* EGERTON, 1854.

Geological range: Upper Triassic.

Geographical distribution: Europe.

Features: Small slender fishes. Head elongate and shallow. Mouth terminal. Dorsal fin broad-based, approximately in the middle of the body, anteriorly tall and sail-like but decreasing in height posteriorly. Anal and pelvic fins small. Caudal fin small and moderately forked. Pectoral fins somewhat broader than the pelvic fins. Scales small and elongate rectangular.

Remarks: Probably reef dwellers.

Recent relatives: None. Died out in Upper Triassic.

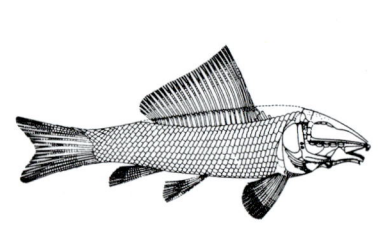

Legnonotus, reconstruction after BARTRAM.

"HOLOSTEI" Halecostomi — Holosteans

Order: Macrosemiiformes
Family: Macrosemiidae

Macrosemius rostratus AGASSIZ (length c. 12 cm) from the Upper Jurassic of Solnhofen (Eichstätt), Bavaria, Germany. Original: Krauss Collection, Weißenburg, Germany.

Genus: *Macrosemius* AGASSIZ, 1844.

Geological range: Upper Jurassic.

Geographical distribution: Europe, western Africa.

Features: Small to middle-sized fishes with elongate bodies. Head relatively large. Mouth small and terminal. Dorsal fin very broad-based, extending almost the whole length of the back. Caudal fin not forked, narrow and rounded. Anal fin rounded. Pectoral fins fan-like. Pelvic fins small.
Scales small.

Remarks: Probably reef dwellers.

Recent relatives: None. Died out in Upper Jurassic.

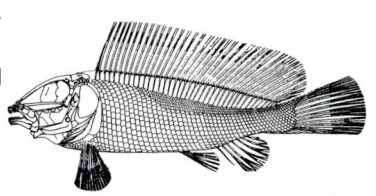

Macrosemius, reconstruction after BARTRAM.

"HOLOSTEI" Halecostomi — Holosteans
Order: **Macrosemiiformes**
Family: **Macrosemiidae**

Notagogus denticulatus AGASSIZ (length c. 9 cm) from the Upper Jurassic of Solnhofen (Kelheim), Bavaria, Germany. Original: Bayerische Staatssammlung für Paläontologie, Munich, Germany.

Genus: *Notagogus* AGASSIZ, 1835.

Synonyms: *Blenniomogius*, *Callignathus*.

Geological range: Upper Jurassic to Lower Cretaceous.

Geographical distribution: Europe.

Features: Small fishes with elongate bodies. Head relatively large. Snout pointed. Gape not very long. Two dorsal fins, the first tall anteriorly and decreasing in height posteriorly, the second small and approximately quadrilateral. Caudal fin moderately forked. Anal fin and pelvic fins small. Pectoral fins fan-shaped. Scales small, serrate at the longitudinal margins.

Remarks: Probably reef dwellers.

Recent relatives: None. Died out in Lower Cretaceous.

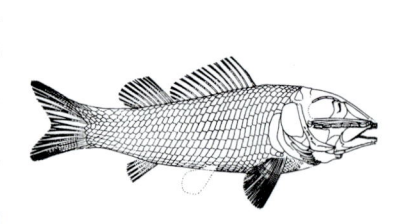

Notagogus, reconstruction after BARTRAM.

"HOLOSTEI" Halecostomi — Holosteans
Order: Macrosemiiformes
Family: Macrosemiidae

Petalopteryxs syriacus PICTET (length c. 24 cm) from the Upper Cretaceous of the Lebanon. Original: Naturmuseum Senckenberg, Frankfurt-am-Main, Germany.

Genus: *Petalopteryx* PICTET, 1851.

Geological range: Lower to Upper Cretaceous.

Geographical distribution: Europe, Middle East.

Features: Middle-sized fishes with elongate bodies. Head relatively large. Gape moderately long. Two dorsal fins—the first begins in the anterior part of the body and is anteriorly tall and pointed, becoming lower posteriorly with a concave upper margin; the second is in the posterior third of the body and triangular. Anal fin and pelvic fins small and pointed. Pectoral fins fan-shaped. Caudal fin forked. Scales thick and quadrangular.

Remarks: Rapid swimmers, probably living near reefs.

Recent relatives: None. Died out in Upper Cretaceous.

"HOLOSTEI" Halecostomi   Holosteans
Order: **Macrosemiiformes**
Family: **Macrosemiidae**

Propterus microstomus AGASSIZ (length c. 10 cm) from the Upper Jurassic of Solnhofen (Eichstätt), Bavaria, Germany. Original: Krauss Collection, Weißenburg, Germany.

Genus: *Propterus*   AGASSIZ, 1834.

Geological range: Upper Jurassic to Lower Cretaceous.

Geographical distribution: Europe.

Features: Small fishes with somewhat laterally compressed bodies. Head deep. Mouth very small. Two dorsal fins—the first, in the anterior half of the body, is tall and pointed, with the first fin ray forming a long spine; the second is low and small. Anal fin pointed. Pelvic fins small. Pectoral fins fan-shaped. Caudal fin deeply forked. Scales weakly serrated along the longitudinal margins.

Remarks: Probably reef dwellers.

Recent relatives: None. Died out in the Lower Cretaceous.

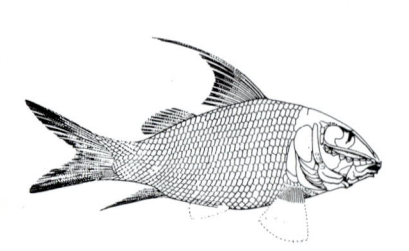

Propterus, reconstruction after BARTRAM.

"HOLOSTEI" Halecostomi   Holosteans
Order: Macrosemiiformes
Family: Uarbryichthyidae

Uarbryichthys latus WADE (length c. 32 cm) from the Lower Jurassic of Talbragar, New South Wales, Australia. Original: Australian Museum, Sydney, Australia.

Genus: *Uarbryichthys* WADE, 1941.

Geological range: Lower Jurassic.

Geographical distribution: Australia.

Features: Middle-sized fishes with somewhat laterally compressed bodies. Head large. Snout pointed. Mouth terminal. Gape not very long. Dorsal fin extending like a sail over almost the whole of the back, very tall anteriorly, becoming lower posteriorly. Anal and pelvic fins small. Pectoral fins fan-shaped. Caudal fin forked. Scales small.

Remarks: Still-water herbivores that also fed on small animals.

Recent relatives: None. Died out in Lower Jurassic.

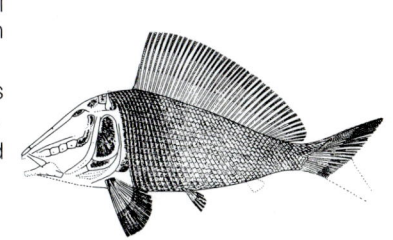

Uarbryichthys, after BARTRAM.

"HOLOSTEI" Halecostomi — Holosteans
Order: Macrosemiiformes
Family: Unnamed

Ophiopsis procera AGASSIZ (length c. 26 cm) from the Upper Jurassic of Solnhofen (Eichstätt), Bavaria, Germany. Original: Schwegler Museum, Langenaltheim near Solnhofen, Germany.

Genus: *Ophiopsis* AGASSIZ, 1834.

Geological range: Middle Triassic to Lower Cretaceous.

Geographical distribution: Europe, western Africa.

Features: Middle-sized fishes with slender elongate bodies. Head shallow. Snout pointed. Gape rather long. Dorsal fin broad-based, begins in the anterior half of the body and anteriorly is tall and pointed but decreases in height posteriorly, with a concave upper margin. Anal fin small. Pelvic fins somewhat larger. Pectoral fins fan-shaped. Thick quadrangular scales.

Remarks: Probably lived near reefs.

Recent relatives: None. Died out in Lower Cretaceous.

Ophiopsis, reconstruction after WOODWARD.

"HOLOSTEI"   Halecomorphi   Holosteans
Order: Amiiformes
Family: Parasemionotidae

Albertonia cupidinia (Lambe) (length c. 36 cm) from the Lower Triassic of Wapiti Lake, Alberta, Canada. Original: Bayerische Staatssammlung für Paläontologie, Munich, Germany.

Genus: *Albertonia* Gardiner, 1966.

Geological range: Lower Triassic.

Geographical distribution: North America.

Features: Middle-sized fishes with laterally compressed bodies. Head elongate. Snout rounded. Gape rather long. Eyes small. Dorsal fin very large, flag- or veil-like and situated in the posterior third of the body, opposite the rounded anal fin. Pelvic fins small. Pectoral fins strikingly long and veil-like. Scales strong and quadrangular.

Remarks: Still-water fishes that probably fed on plants.

Recent relatives: None. Died out in Lower Triassic.

"HOLOSTEI" Halecomorphi Holosteans
Order: Amiiformes
Family: Parasemionotidae

Jacobulus novus Lehman (length c. 8 cm) from the Lower Triassic of Madagascar. Original: Muséum National d'Histoire Naturelle, Paris, France. Photograph: Serette Paris.

Genus: *Jacobulus* Lehman, 1952.

Geological range: Lower Triassic.

Geographical distribution: Madagascar.

Features: Small fishes with rather deep bodies. Head deep. Snout rounded. Eyes small. Gape long. Mouth with powerful dentition. Dorsal fin triangular, situated in the posterior half of the body. Pectoral fins narrow. Pelvic fins fan-like. Caudal fin probably emarginate of slightly forked. Scales quadrangular, sometimes rectangular.

Remarks: Probably predators.

Recent relatives: None. Died out in Triassic.

"HOLOSTEI" Halecomorphi Holosteans

Order: Amiiformes
Family: Parasemionotidae

Parasemiontus labordei PIVETEAU (length c. 13 cm) from the Lower Triassic of Madagascar. Original: Hennlye Collection, Stuttgart, Germany.

Genus: *Parasemionotus* PIVETEAU, 1929.

Geological range: Lower Triassic.

Geographical distribution: Madagascar, Greenland.

Features: Small to middle-sized fishes with rather laterally compressed bodies. Head deep. Snout rounded. Eyes large. Mouth small. Dorsal fin triangular, very posterior in position. Anal fin likewise triangular. Pelvic and pectoral fins narrow. Caudal fin slightly concave posteriorly. Scales square to rectangular, arranged in diagonal rows.

Remarks: Probably fed on crustaceans and other small animals.

Recent relatives: None. Died out in Lower Triassic.

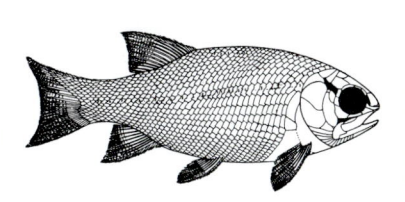

Parasemionotus, reconstruction after LEHMAN.

"HOLOSTEI" Halecomorphi Holosteans
Order: Amiiformes
Family: Parasemionotidae

Phaidrosoma lunzensis GRIFFITH (length c. 12 cm) from the Upper Triassic of Polzberg, Austria. Original: Naturhistorisches Museum, Vienna, Austria.

Genus: *Phaidrosoma* GRIFFITH, 1977.

Geological range: Upper Triassic.

Geographical distribution: Europe,.

Features: Small fishes with elongate fusiform bodies. Head elongate. Snout pointed. Dorsal fin acute triangular, located in the posterior third of the body. Anal and pelvic fins elongate. Caudal fin deeply forked. Pectoral fins.

Remarks: Probably fed on crustaceans and other small animals. Has been reclassed into the genus *Dipteronotus*.

Recent relatives: None. Died out in Upper Triassic.

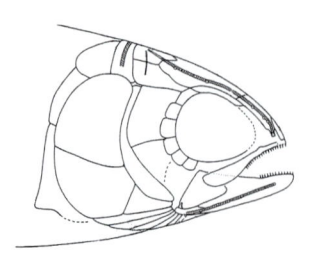

Phaidrosoma, reconstruction after GRIFFITH

"HOLOSTEI" Halecomorphi Holosteans
Order: Amiiformes
Family: Parasemionotidae

Praesemionotus sp. (length c. 3 cm) from the Lower Triassic of Durlach, Baden, Germany. Original: Staatliches Museum für Naturkunde, Karlsruhe, Germany.

Genus: *Praesemionotus* JÖRG, 1969.

Geological range: Lower Triassic.

Geographical distribution: Europe.

Features: Very small fishes with somewhat laterally compressed bodies. Head relatively large. Snout rounded. Gape rather long. Small pointed teeth. Eyes relatively large. Dorsal fin triangular, located very posteriorly. Anal fin long and narrow. Pelvic fins elongate. Pectoral fins similar and inserted very low on the body. Caudal fin large, deeply forked.

Remarks: Probably fed on crustaceans and other small animals. Has been reclassified into the genus *Dipteronotus*.

Recent relatives: None. Died out in Lower Triassic.

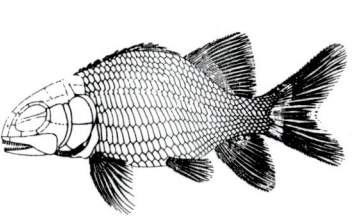

Praesemionotus, after JÖRG.

419

"HOLOSTEI" Halecomorphi Holosteans
Order: **Amiiformes**
Family: **Parasemionotidae**

Promecosomina beaconensis WADE (length c. 26 cm) from the Middle Triassic of Gosford, New South Wales, Australia. Original: Australian Museum, Sydney, Australia.

Genus: *Promecosomina* WADE, 1935.

Geological range: Middle to Upper Triassic.

Geographical distribution: Australia.

Features: Middle-sized fishes with rather laterally compressed bodies. Head elongate. Snout pointed. Gape short. Eyes small. Dorsal fin broad-based, situated in the posterior third of the body, opposite the anal fin. Anal fin, pelvic fins and pectoral fins narrow. Caudal fin strongly concave posteriorly. Scales arranged in diagonal rows.

Remarks: Probably fed on crustaceans and other small animals and perhaps also on plants.

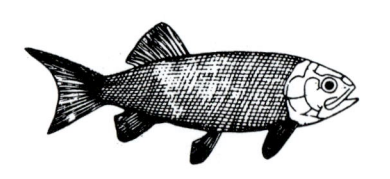

Recent relatives: None. Died out in Upper Triassic.

Promecosomina, after WADE.

"HOLOSTEI" Halecomorphi Holosteans
Order: Amiiformes
Family: Parasemionotidae

Watsonulus eugnathoides (PIVETEAU) (length c. 11 cm) from the Upper Triassic of Madagascar. Original: Carnegie Museum of Natural History, Pittsburgh, Pennsylvania, U.S.A.

Genus: *Watsonulus* BROUGH, 1939.

Geological range: Lower Triassic.

Geographical distribution: Madagascar, North America.

Features: Small to middle-sized fishes with rather laterally compressed bodies. Head deep. Snout rounded. Eyes small. Gape rather long. Dorsal fin in the posterior third of the body, opposite the anal fin. Pelvic and pectoral fins elongate. Caudal fin concave posteriorly. Scales arranged in diagonal rows.

Remarks: Probably fed on crustaceans and other small animals and perhaps also on plants.

Recent relatives: None. Died out in Upper Triassic.

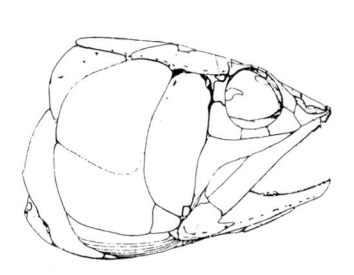

Watsonulus, reconstruction after OLSEN.

"HOLOSTEI" Halecomorphi Holosteans
Order: Amiiformes
Family: Parasemionotidae?

Unnamed fish (length c. 32 cm) from the Triassic of Wapiti Lake, British Columbia, Canada. Original: Staatliches Museum für Naturkunde, Karlsruhe, Germany.

Genus: Not named.

Geological range: Lower Triassic.

Geographical distribution: North America.

Features: Middle-sized fishes with streamlined bodies. Head shallow. Snout rounded. Small pointed teeth. Dorsal fin just behind the middle of the body, obliquely opposite the anal fin. Pectoral fins strikingly long, almost veil-like. Caudal fin deeply forked. Scales circular.

Remarks: This fish has not yet been described. Possibly a new species of the genus *Albertonia* or perhaps some other genus.

Recent relatives: None. Died out in Lower Triassic.

"HOLOSTEI" Halecomorphi   Holosteans
Order: Amiiformes?
Family: Parasemionotidae?

Unnamed fish (length c. 50 cm) from the Lower Jurassic of Holzmaden. Original: Urweltmuseum Hauff, Holzmaden, Württemberg, Germany.

Genus: Unknown.

Geological range: Lower Jurassic.

Geographical distribution: Europe.

Features: Middle-sized fishes of slender shape. Head deep. Snout pointed. Gape long. Upper and lower jaws set with pointed teeth. Dorsal fin triangular, located just behind the middle of the body, opposite the narrow pectoral fins. Anal fin small. Pectoral fins large, fan-shaped. Caudal fin heterocercal, with a narrow upper and a broad lower lobe. Body covered with thick, diagonally arranged scales.

Remarks: Predators.

Recent relatives: None. Probably died out in Lower Jurassic.

"HOLOSTEI" Halecomorphi Holosteans
Order: Amiiformes
Family: Caturidae

Caturus furcatus AGASSIZ (length c. 28 cm) from the Upper Jurassic of Solnhofen (Eichstätt), Bavaria, Germany. Original: Interfoss, Munich, Germany.

Genus: *Caturus* AGASSIZ, 1834.

Synonyms: *Conocus, Ditaxiodus, Endactis, Thlattodus, Uraeus.*

Geological range: Lower Jurassic to Lower Cretaceous.

Geographical distribution: Europe, west Africa.

Features: Middle-sized fishes of slender salmon-like shape. Head short, with powerful, strongly toothed jaws. Eyes relatively small. Dorsal fin pointed, located shortly behind the middle of the body. Anal fin likewise pointed, attached more posteriorly. Pelvic and pectoral fins narrow. Caudal fin large, deeply forked. Scales small, rounded, almost cycloid. Vertebral column incompletely ossified.

Remarks: Rapidly swimming predators.

Recent relatives: None. Died out in Lower Cretaceous.

Caturus, reconstruction after WOODWARD.

"HOLOSTEI" Halecomorphi Holosteans
Order: Amiiformes
Family: Caturidae

Eoeugnathus megalepis BROUGH (length c. 9 cm) from the Middle Triassic of Monte San Giorgio, Switzerland. Original: Paläontologisches Museum, Zürich, Switzerland.

Genus: *Eoeugnathus* BROUGH, 1939.

Geological range: Middle to Upper Triassic.

Geographical distribution: Europe.

Features: Small fishes of rather laterally compressed shape. Head deep. Snout rounded. Gape rather long. Jaws with small pointed teeth. Eyes large. Dorsal fin triangular, shortly behind the anterior half of the body, obliquely opposite the anal fin which is smaller but likewise triangular. Pelvic fins small and pointed. Pectoral fins rounded. Caudal fin posteriorly strongly concave. Scales relatively thick.

Remarks: Predators.

Recent relatives: None. Died out in Upper Triassic.

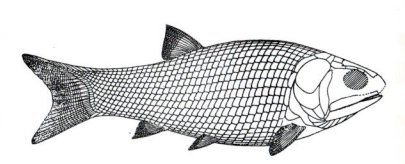

Eoeugnathus, reconstruction after BROUGH.

425

"HOLOSTEI" Halecomorphi Holosteans
Order: Amiiformes
Family: Caturidae

Amblysemius bellicianus THIOLLIERE (length c. 23 cm) from the Upper Jurassic of Solnhofen (Zandt), Bavaria, Germany. Original: Bayerische Staatssammlung für Paläontologie, Munich, Germany.

Genus: *Amblysemius* AGASSIZ, 1844.

Geological range: Upper Jurassic.

Geographical distribution: Europe.

Features: Middle-sized fishes with elongate slender bodies. Head elongate and shallow. Snout somewhat rounded. Gape long. Mouth with powerful jaws and very strong dentition. Dorsal fin triangular, located in the posterior third of the body. Anal fin likewise triangular but located more posteriorly. Pectoral fins narrow and somewhat fan-like. Caudal fin deeply forked.

Remarks: Rapidly swimming predators.

Recent relatives: None. Died out in Upper Jurassic.

HOLOSTEI" Halecomorphi Holosteans
Order: Amiiformes
Family: Caturidae

Furo longimanus (AGASSIZ) (length c. 15 cm) from the Upper Jurassic of Solnhofen, Bavaria, Germany. Original: Bürgermeister Müller Museum, Solnhofen, Germany.

Genus: *Furo* GISTL, 1848.

Synonyms: *Isopholis, Lissolepis*.

Geological range: Upper Jurassic.

Geographical distribution: Europe, Asia.

Features: Small to middle-sized fishes with elongate slender bodies. Head elongate and shallow. Gape long. Mouth powerful jaws and strong teeth. Dorsal fin acutely triangular, located shortly behind the middle of the body. Anal fin small and triangular, situated more posteriorly. Pelvic and pectoral fins narrow. Scales quadrangular, relatively thick.

Remarks: Rapidly swimming predators.

Recent relatives: None. Died out in Upper Jurassic.

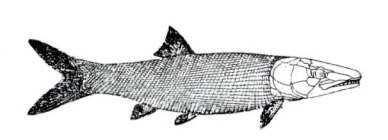

Furo, reconstruction after WOODWARD.

"HOLOSTEI" Halecomorphi Holosteans
Order: Amiiformes
Family: Caturidae

Heterolepidotus dorsalis KNER (length c. 17 cm) from the Upper Triassic of Adnet, Hallein, Austria. Original: Bayerische Staatssammlung für Paläontologie, Munich, Germany.

Genus: *Heterolepidotus* EGERTON, 1872.

Synonyms: *Brachyichthys*, *Eulepidotus*.

Geological range: Upper Triassic to Upper Jurassic.

Geographical distribution: Europe, Central Asia.

Features: Small to middle-sized fishes with rather laterally compressed bodies. Head elongate and shallow. Snout pointed. Gape rather long. Jaws with small pointed teeth. Dorsal fin rounded, located in the posterior third of the body, obliquely opposite the smaller anal fin. Pelvic fins elongate and rounded. Pectoral fins similar, but considerably larger. Caudal fin only slightly forked, with broad lobes. Scales thick and quadrangular.

Remarks: Predators.

Recent relatives: None. Died out in Upper Jurassic.

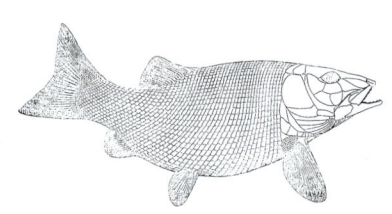

Heterolepidotus, reconstruction after BROUGH.

"HOLOSTEI" Halecomorphi Holosteans
Order: Amiiformes
Family: Caturidae

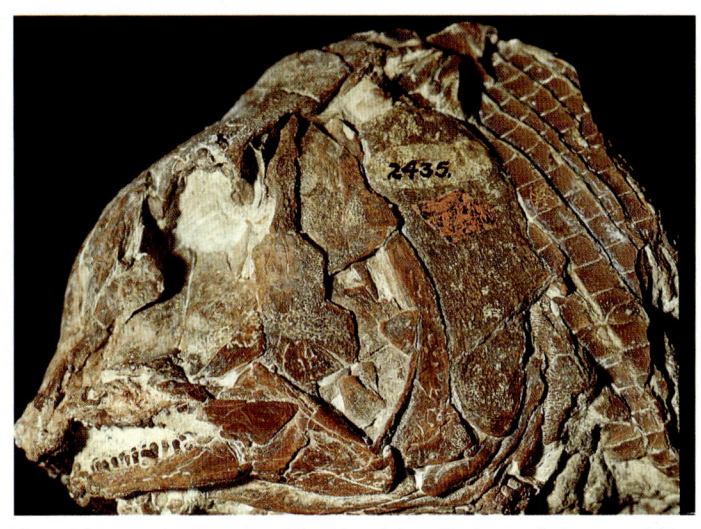

Macrepistius arenatus COPE (length c. 11 cm) from the Lower Cretaceous of Glen Rose, Texas. Original: American Museum of Natural History, New York, N.Y., U.S.A.

Genus: *Macrepistius* COPE, 1895.

Geological range: Lower Cretaceous.

Geographical distribution: North America.

Features: Middle-sized to large fishes with slender bodies. Head deep. Snout pointed. Gape rather long. Jaws with powerful peg-shaped teeth. Eyes relatively large. Scales quadrangular, thick and shiny. Very similar to fishes of the order Semionotiformes.

Remarks: The teeth suggest a durophagous diet.

Recent relatives: None. Died out in Lower Cretaceous.

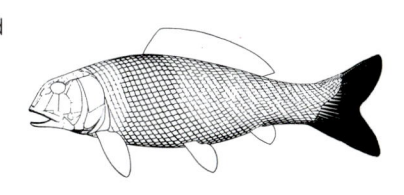

Macrepistius, reconstruction after SCHAEFFER.

429

"HOLOSTEI"   Halecomorphi   Holosteans
Order: Amiiformes
Family: Caturidae

Strobilodus giganteus WAGNER (length c. 177 cm) from the Upper Jurassic of Solnhofen (Eichstätt), Bavaria, Germany. Original: Jura-Museum, Eichstätt, Germany.

Genus: *Strobilodus* WAGNER, 1851.

Geological range: Upper Jurassic.

Geographical distribution: Europe.

Features: Large fishes with slender bodies. Head short. Snout pointed. Eyes relatively small. Jaws very powerful and strongly toothed. Dorsal fin narrow and pointed, located shortly behind the middle of the body. Anal fin acutely triangular. Pelvic and pectoral fins narrow. Caudal fin very large, deeply forked.

Remarks: Large predators, often placed in the genus *Caturus*.

Recent relatives: None. Died out in Upper Jurassic.

"HOLOSTEI" Halecomorphi Holosteans
Order: Amiiformes
Family: Amiidae

Bowfins

Amia kehreri ANDREAE (length c. 25 cm) from the Eocene of Messel, Hesse, Germany. Original: Frickhinger Collection, Munich, Germany.

Genus: *Amia* LINNAEUS, 1766.

Synonyms: *Amiatus, Paramiatus, Protamia*.

Geological range: Upper Cretaceous to Recent.

Geographical distribution: Europe, North America, Asia, Spitzbergen.

Features: Middle-sized to large fishes of deep but elongate shape. Head elongate. Snout pointed. Eyes small. Teeth small and pointed. Dorsal fin extended like a fringe, long and low. Anal fin broadly elongate and rounded. Pelvic and pectoral fins relatively small. Caudal fin rounded. Scales thin, overlapping, without a ganoin layer and approaching the cycloid type.

Remarks: Freshwater fishes. Probably cryptic predators.

Recent relatives: The genus is recent. This fossil fish is closely related to the recent bowfin *Amia calva*.

Amia calva, the recent bowfin.

"HOLOSTEI" Halecomorphi Holosteans
Order: Amiiformes
Family: Amiidae

Bowfins

Amiopsis dolloi Traquair (length c. 14 cm) from the Lower Cretaceous of Bernissart, Belgium. Original: Musée Royale des Sciences Naturelles de Belgique, Brussels, Belgium.

Genus: *Amiopsis* Kner, 1863.

Geological range: Upper Jurassic to Lower Cretaceous.

Geographical distribution: Europe.

Features: Small fishes with somewhat laterally compressed bodies. Head elongate. Snout pointed. Gape long. Eyes small. Dorsal fin triangular, located in the posterior half of the body, opposite the narrow elongate anal fin. Pelvic and pectoral fins small. Caudal fin forked, rounded.

Remarks: Probably cryptic predators.

Recent relatives: Genus extinct. Family recent. Closely related to the recent bowfin *Amia calva*.

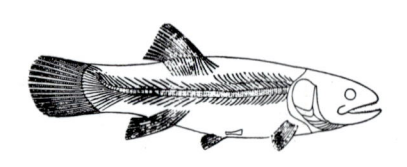

Amiopsis, reconstruction after Woodward.

"HOLOSTEI" Halecomorphi Holosteans
Order: Amiiformes
Family: Amiidae

Bowfins

Calamopleurus cylindricus AGASSIZ (length c. 84 cm) from the Cretaceous of Ceará, Brazil. Original: Frickhinger Collection, Munich, Germany.

Genus: *Calamopleurus* AGASSIZ, 1841.

Synonyms: *Enneles*

Geological range: Lower Cretaceous.

Geographical distribution: South America.

Features: Middle-sized to large fishes of elongate shape. Head elongate. Snout somewhat rounded. Eyes small. Gape long. Jaws powerful, with long pointed teeth. Dorsal fin triangular, located shortly behind the middle of the body, obliquely opposite the elongate anal fin. Pelvic and pectoral fins small. Caudal fin not forked, rounded. Large and thick quadrangular scales.

Remarks: Predators living in salt water.

Recent relatives: Genus extinct. Family recent. Closely related to the recent bowfin *Amia calva*.

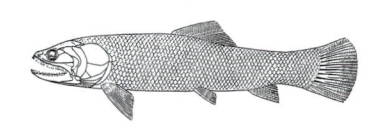

Calamapleurus, reconstruction after MAISEY.

"HOLOSTEI" Halecomorphi Holosteans
Order: Amiiformes
Family: Amiidae

Bowfins

Liodesmus sprattiformis WAGNER (length c. 12 cm) from the Upper Jurassic of Solnhofen (Schernfeld), Bavaria, Germany. Original: Jura-Museum, Eichstätt, Bavaria, Germany.

Genus: *Liodesmus* WAGNER, 1859.

Synonyms: *Lophiurus*.

Geological range: Upper Jurassic.

Geographical distribution: Europe.

Features: Small fishes of elongate shape which, at first sight, are not obvious members of the Amiidae. Head elongate. Snout slightly pointed. Dorsal fin triangular, situated just behind the anterior half of the body, obliquely opposite the anal fin which is likewise triangular. Pelvic fins small. Pectoral fins elongate and broad. Caudal fin forked, with broad lobes. Scales thin.

Remarks: Small marine predators.

Recent relatives: None. Died out in Upper Jurassic.

"HOLOSTEI" Halecomorphi Holosteans
Order: Amiiformes
Family: Amiidae

Bowfins

Sinamia zdanskyi STENSIÖ (length 4.5 cm) from the Lower Cretaceous of Ning-Khia-Kou, Shantung Province, China. Original: Paleontologiska Museet, Uppsala, Sweden.

Genus: *Sinamia* STENSIÖ, 1936.

Geological range: Lower Cretaceous.

Geographical distribution: Eastern Asia.

Features: Middle-sized fishes with slender elongate bodies. Head elongate. Snout rounded. Eyes large. Gape long. Upper and lower jaws bearing teeth. Overall structure very similar to *Amia*. Scales rhombic and covered with ganoin.

Remarks: Freshwater fishes.

Recent relatives: Genus extinct. Closely related to the recent bowfin *Amia* which lives in fresh-water in North America.

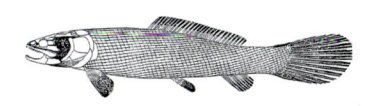

Sinamia, after LIN.

435

"HOLOSTEI" Halecomorphi Holosteans
Order: Amiiformes
Family: Amiidae

Bowfins

Urocles altivelus WAGNER (length c. 44 cm) from the Upper Jurassic of Solnhofen (Eichstätt), Bavaria, Germany. Original: Interfoss, Munich.

Genus: *Urocles* JORDAN, 1919.

Synonyms: *Megalurus*, *Synergus*.

Geological range: Upper Jurassic.

Geographical distribution: Europe.

Features: Middle-sized fishes of rather deep-bodied but elongate shape. Head elongate. Snout slightly rounded. Gape long. Jaws with pointed teeth. Dorsal fin broad-based, beginning tall and approximately in the middle of the body and diminishing in height posteriorly. The small anal fin lies opposite. Pelvic fins also small. Pectoral fins fan-like. Caudal fin not forked, convex behind.

Remarks: Marine predatory fishes.

Recent relatives: Genus extinct. Family recent. Closely related to the bowfin *Amia calva*.

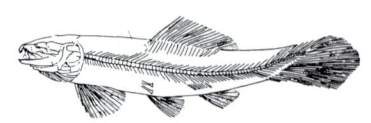

Urocles, reconstruction after WOODWARD.

"HOLOSTEI" Halecomorphi Holosteans
Order: Amiiformes?
Family: Unnamed

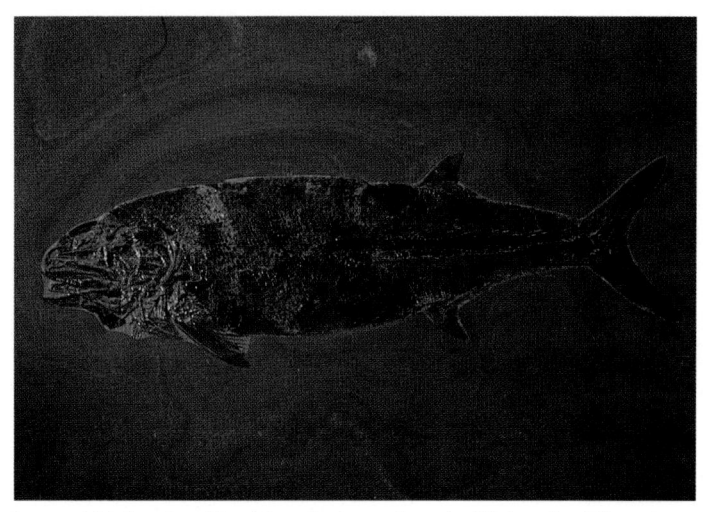

Unnamed fish (length c. 50 cm) from the Lower Jurassic of Holzmaden, Württemberg, Germany. Original: Urweltmuseum Hauff, Holzmaden, Germany.

Genus: Not named.

Geological range: Lower Jurassic.

Geographical distribution: Europe.

Features: Middle-sized fishes with elongate streamlined bodies. Head deep. Snout slightly protrusive. Eyes small. Upper and lower jaws with teeth. Dorsal fin small, located in the posterior third of the body, opposite the anal fin which is likewise small. Pectoral fins elongate and fan-shaped. Caudal fin deeply forked, with narrow lobes.

Remarks: Predators.

Recent relatives: None. Probably died out in Lower Jurassic.

"HOLOSTEI" Halecomorphi Holosteans
Order: **Pachycormiformes**
Family: **Pachycormidae**

Asthenocormus titanicus (WAGNER) (length c. 216 cm) from the Upper Jurassic of Solnhofen (Eichstätt) Bavaria, Germany. Original: Jura-Museum, Eichstätt, Germany.

Genus: *Asthenocormus* WOODWARD, 1895.

Synonyms: *Agassizia*.

Geological range: Upper Jurassic.

Geographical distribution: Europe.

Features: Large to very large fishes with elongate bodies. Head long and shallow. Snout pointed. Eyes small. Caudal fin very large, forked even at the base, with almost vertically diverging long narrow lobes. Pelvic fins absent. Pectoral fins unusually long. Vertebral centra almost unossified.

Remarks: Rapidly swimming predators which probably lived in the open sea.

Recent relatives: None. Died out in Upper Jurassic.

"HOLOSTEI" Halecomorphi Holosteans
Order: Pachycormiformes
Family: Pachycormidae

Euthynotus intermedius (AGASSIZ) (length c. 31 cm) from the Lower Jurassic of Werther, Westphalia, Germany. Original: Bayerische Staatssammlung für Paläontologie, Munich, Germany.

Genus: *Euthynotus* WAGNER, 1860.

Synonyms: *Cyclospondylus*, *Heterothrissops*, *Parathrissops*, *Pseudothrissops*.

Geological range: Lower Jurassic.

Geographical distribution: Europe.

Features: Middle-sized fishes of elongate slender shape. Head long and shallow. Snout slightly pointed. Eyes large. Gape long. Dorsal fin very small, located in the posterior third of the body. Anal and pelvic fins also small. Pectoral fins pointed, somewhat larger. Caudal fin relatively short, moderately forked. Scales small.

Remarks: Rapidly swimming predators.

Recent relatives: None. Died out in Lower Jurassic.

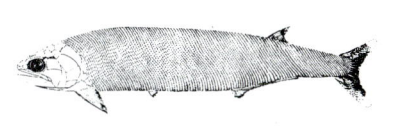

Euthynotus, reconstruction after WENZ.

"HOLOSTEI"   Halecomorphi   Holosteans
Order: Pachycormiiformes
Family: Pachycormidae

Hypsocormus insignis W<small>AGNER</small> (length c. 70 cm) from the Upper Jurassic of Solnhofen (Eichstätt), Bavaria, Germany. Original: Staatliches Museum für Naturkunde, Stuttgart, Germany.

Genus: *Hypsocormus* W<small>AGNER</small>, 1860.

Geological range: Upper Triassic to Upper Jurassic.

Geographical distribution: Europe.

Features: Middle-sized to large fishes with slender bodies somewhat deepened anteriorly. Head long and shallow. Snout slightly pointed. Gape long. Jaws with pointed teeth. Dorsal fin in the posterior half of the body, anteriorly with a point but decreasing in height posteriorly with a concave upper margin. Anal fin obliquely opposite with a broad base. Pelvic fins small. Pectoral fins long and narrow. Caudal fin deeply forked, with long narrow lobes.

Remarks: Rapidly swimming predators, probably living in coastal regions.

Recent relatives: None. Died out in Upper Jurassic.

Hypsocormus, reconstruction after W<small>OODWARD</small>.

440

"HOLOSTEI" Halecomorphi Holosteans
Order: Pachycormiformes
Family: Pachycormidae

Orthocormus cornutus W<small>EITZEL</small> (length c. 113 cm) from the Upper Jurassic of Solnhofen (Eichstätt), Bavaria, Germany. Original: Jura-Museum, Eichstätt.

Genus: *Orthocormus* W<small>EITZEL</small>, 1930.

Geological range: Upper Jurassic.

Geographical distribution: Europe.

Features: Middle-sized to large fishes with elongate slender bodies. Head long and shallow. Snout slightly pointed. Gape long. Jaws with pointed teeth. Dorsal fin behind the middle of the body, narrow and pointed, obliquely opposite the narrow anal fin. Pelvic and pectoral fins likewise long and narrow. Caudal fin deeply divided, with narrow lobes diverging almost vertically from each other.

Remarks: Rapidly swimming predators which probably lived in coastal regions or in the open ocean.

Recent relatives: None. Died out in Upper Jurassic.

"HOLOSTEI" Halecomorphi Holosteans
Order: Pachycormiformes
Family: Pachycormidae

Pachycormus curtus AGASSIZ (length c. 30 cm) from the Lower Jurassic of Holzmaden, Württemberg, Germany. Original: Urwelt-Museum Hauff, Holzmaden, Germany.

Genus: *Pachycormus* AGASSIZ, 1833.

Synonyms: *Cephenoplosus*.

Geological range: Lower Jurassic.

Geographical distribution: Europe.

Features: Middle-sized fishes with rather laterally compressed bodies. Head deep. Snout pointed. Eyes small. Jaws with pointed teeth. Dorsal fin only slightly behind the middle of the body, small and triangular. Anal fin likewise small and triangular, located more posteriorly. Pectoral fins pointed and relatively long. Caudal fin large, deeply forked, with strongly divergent narrow lobes.

Remarks: Rapidly swimming predators.

Recent relatives: None. Died out in Lower Jurassic.

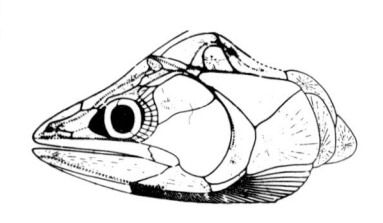

Pachycormus, reconstruction after LEHMAN.

"HOLOSTEI" Halecomorphi Holosteans
Order: Pachycormiformes
Family: Pachycormidae

Protosphyraena sp. (length c. 47 cm) from the Upper Cretaceous of Kansas, U.S.A. Original: Sternberg Memorial Museum, Fort Hays, Kansas, U.S.A. Photograph: Bennett, Lawrence, Kansas, U.S.A.

Genus: *Protosphyraena* Leidy, 1857.

Synonyms: *Erisichthe*, *Pelecopterus*.

Geological range: Upper Cretaceous.

Geographical distribution: Europe, Asia, North America, South America.

Features: Large fishes with long shallow skulls extending into a strong very elongate rostrum. Gape very long. Mouth with strong forward-directed teeth which are exceptionally long in the anterior parts of the jaws. Eyes relatively large. Pectoral fins large and very narrow, their anterior margins set with tooth-like processes.

Remarks: Obviously dangerous predators which could overpower even large prey. The significance of the rostrum is uncertain.

Recent relatives: None. Died out in Upper Cretaceous.

"HOLOSTEI" Halecomorphi Holosteans
Order: Pachycormiformes
Family: Pachycormidae

Sauropsis longimanus AGASSIZ (length c. 32 cm) from the Upper Jurassic of Solnhofen (Eichstätt), Bavaria, Germany. Original: Bayerische Staatssammlung für Paläontologie, Munich, Germany.

Genus: *Sauropsis* AGASSIZ, 1832.

Synonyms: *Diplolepis*.

Geological range: Lower to Upper Jurassic.

Geographical distribution: Europe, North America.

Features: Middle-sized fishes with somewhat compressed bodies. Head large and deep. Snout rounded. Gape long. Jaws with powerful teeth. Dorsal fin behind the middle of the body, narrow and pointed. Anal fin opposite, of similar shape. Pectoral fins long and narrow. Caudal fin deeply forked, with narrow lobes.

Remarks: Rapidly swimming predators.

Recent relatives: None. Died out in Upper Jurassic.

"HOLOSTEI"   Halecomorphi   Holosteans
Order: Pachycormiformes
Family: Pachycormidae

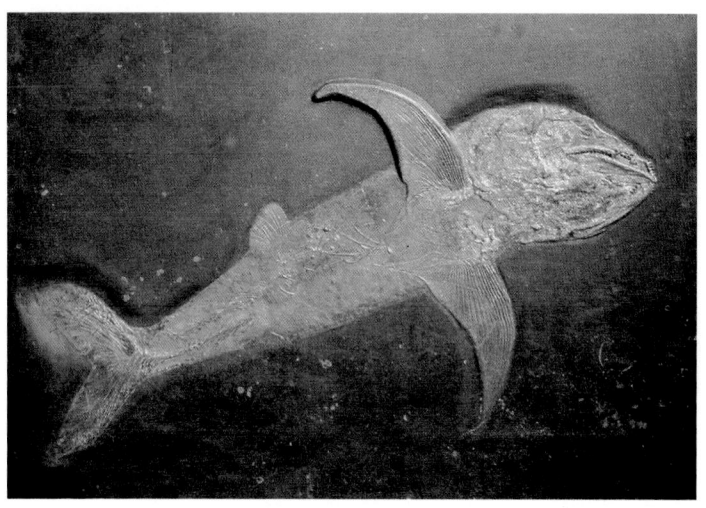

Saurostomus esocinus AGASSIZ (length c. 94 cm) from the Lower Jurassic of Holzmaden, Württemberg, Germany. Original: Interfoss, Munich, Germany.

Genus: *Saurostomus* AGASSIZ, 1833.

Synonyms: *Pachycormus*, *Protosauropsis*, *Prosauropsis*.

Geological range: Lower Jurassic.

Geographical distribution: Europe.

Features: Middle-sized to large fishes with rather laterally compressed bodies. Head deep. Snout slightly pointed. Gape long. Jaws with pointed teeth. Dorsal fin shortly behind the middle of the body, very small. Anal fin likewise very small, somewhat more posterior. Pectoral fins strikingly large, almost wing-like. Caudal fin deeply forked, with relatively broad lobes. Scales small and rhombic.

Remarks: Rapidly swimming predators which probably lived in the open sea.

Recent relatives: None. Died out in Lower Jurassic.

"HOLOSTEI" Halecomorphi Holosteans
Order: Aspidorhynchiformes
Family: Aspidorhynchidae

Aspidorhynchus acutirostris (de BLAINVILLE) (length c. 60 cm) from the Upper Jurassic of Solnhofen (Eichstätt), Bavaria, Germany. Original: Interfoss, Munich, Germany.

Genus: *Aspidorhynchus* AGASSIZ, 1833.

Geological range: Upper Jurassic to Upper Cretaceous.

Geographical distribution: Europe, North America, Asia, Australia, north Africa.

Features: Middle-sized, very slender, elongate pike-like fishes. Head elongate. Snout with a long and pointed rostrum formed from the upper jaw. Eyes large. Jaws with small pointed teeth. Dorsal fin small, situated in the posterior third of the body, opposite the small triangular anal fin. Pelvic fins very small. Pectoral fins somewhat longer. Caudal fin deeply forked, with narrow lobes. Characteristic rod-like scales on the flanks.

Remarks: Rapidly swimming predators. The rostrum probably served for deflecting gregarious fishes and hitting prey from the side.

Recent relatives: None. Died out in Upper Cretaceous.

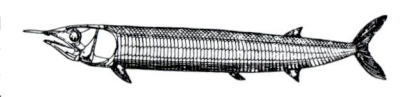

Aspidorhynchus, after ASSMANN.

446

"HOLOSTEI" Halecomorphi Holosteans
Order: Aspidorhynchiformes
Family: Aspidorhynchidae

Belonostomus tenuirostris AGASSIZ (length c. 34 cm) from the Upper Jurassic of Solnhofen (Zandt), Bavaria, Germany. Original: Bayerische Staatssammlung für Paläontologie, Munich, Bavaria, Germany.

Genus: *Belonostomus* AGASSIZ, 1834.
Synonyms: *Belonostmus, Dichelospondylus, Hemirhynchus, Ophirachis*.
Geological range: Upper Jurassic to Upper Cretaceous.
Geographical distribution: Europe, North America, Middle East, Australia.
Features: Middle-sized fishes but smaller than *Aspidorhynchus*. Of slender almost eel-like shape. Head shallow. Snout pointed, with a rostrum formed from upper and lower jaws—the lower jaw extending into the rostrum is only slightly shorter than the upper. Teeth pointed. Dorsal fin small, opposite the anal fin which is likewise small. Caudal fin forked, with narrow but powerful lobes. Characteristic rod-like scales on the flanks.
Remarks: Predators. The rostrum probably had the same significance as in *Aspidorhynchus*.
Recent relatives: None. Died out in Upper Cretaceous.

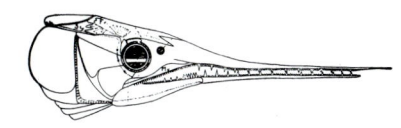

Belonostomus, after SAINT-SEINE.

"HOLOSTEI" Halecomorphi — Holosteans
Order: Aspidorhynchiformes
Family: Aspidorhynchidae

Vinctifer comptoni AGASSIZ (length c. 80 cm) from the Lower Cretaceous of Ceará, Brazil. Original: Frickhinger Collection, Munich, Germany.

Genus: *Vinctifer* JORDAN, 1920.

Synonyms: *Aspidorhynchus*, *Belonostomus*.

Geological range: Lower Cretaceous.

Geographical distribution: South America.

Features: Middle-sized fishes with slender, elongate, pike-like bodies. Head long and shallow. Upper jaw projecting to form a long narrow rostrum. Teeth probably small. Dorsal fin located very posteriorly opposite the small anal fin. Pelvic fins very small, pectoral fins somewhat larger. Caudal fin deeply forked, with strong lobes. Characteristic rod-like scales on the flanks.

Remarks: Rapidly swimming predators that probably hunted small gregarious fishes.

Recent relatives: None. Died out in Lower Cretaceous.

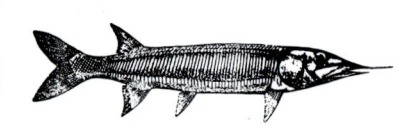

Vinctifer, reconstruction after SILVA SANTOS.

TELEOSTEI — True Bony Fishes

The first teleosts retain some primitive features, such as a thin ganoin layer on the scales or the vertebral column bent strongly upwards near the caudal fin. Such features no longer occur in the advanced teleosts (Euteleostei). These two groups are treated separately in what follows.

The internal skeleton of teleosts is completely ossified. The scales are mostly cycloid (with rounded posterior margins) or ctenoid (with denticulate posterior margins). Some fishes, however, have lost the scales completely. The pelvic fins tend to migrate forwards and so are sometimes sited in a pectoral position, or even under the throat or the chin. With a few exceptions the caudal fin is homocercal. There may be one, two, or sometimes even three, dorsal fins. In some genera there is an additional adipose fin on the back. It lacks fin rays and is, of course, very seldom preserved in fossils. The jaws may be toothless or the teeth may be of any type, whether small and pointed, or carnassial-like tearing teeth or the crushing teeth of the Tetraodontiformes. Length varies from a few centimetres to several metres.

The Pholidophoriformes used to be placed in the "Holostei" on account of their enamel-covered scales. Now, however, they are put at the beginning of the Teleostei as clearly indicated by their head skeleton. In consequence the origin of the true bony fishes goes back to the Lower Triassic. The sprat-shaped *Leptolepis* also has great evolutionary importance. It used often to be regarded as the latest common ancestor of true bony fishes. Now, however, it seems certain that other Holostei have contributed to this evolution which is still continuing today.

In the Jurassic true bony fishes were by no means common. There were very few genera apart from *Pholidophorus* and *Leptolepis*. The irresistible expansion of the group began slowly in the Lower Cretaceous and became rapid in the Upper Cretaceous. The first high point of the group was in the Miocene, but this has been surpassed by the 25,000 species which live today. About 1100 genera have been described fossil. Many of them, but not all, are preserved complete.

TELEOSTEI — True Bony Fishes

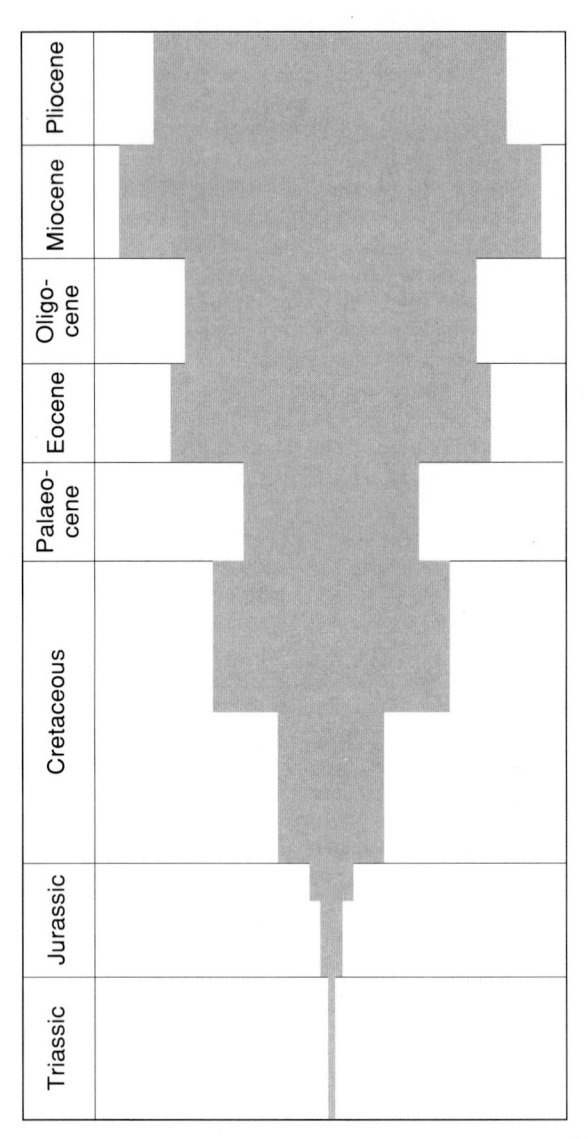

The approximate stratigraphical distribution of bony fishes, changed after MÜLLER.

TELEOSTEI
Order: Pholidophoriformes
Family: Pholidophoridae

True Bony Fishes

Baleiichthys sp. (length c. 6.5 cm) from the Jurassic of Balei, Siberia, Russia. Original: Museum für Naturkunde, Berlin, Germany.

Genus: *Baleiichthus* Rohon, 1890.

Geological range: Jurassic.

Geographical distribution: East Asia.

Features: Small fishes with very slender elongate bodies. Head shallow. Eyes small. Gape rather long. Dorsal fin approximately in the middle of the body, obliquely opposite the small triangular anal fin. Pectoral fins small and rather fan-like. Caudal fin rather deeply forked. Body covered with diagonally arranged, relatively thick scales.

Remarks: Predators.

Recent relatives: None. Died out in Jurassic.

TELEOSTEI
True Bony Fishes
Order: Pholidophoriformes
Family: Pholidophoridae

Eurycormus speciosus WAGNER (length c. 30 cm) from the Upper Jurassic of Solnhofen (Eichstätt), Bavaria, Germany. Original: Jura-Museum, Eichstätt, Germany.

Genus: *Eurycormus* WAGNER, 1859.

Geological range: Upper Jurassic.

Geographical distribution: Europe.

Features: Middle-sized fishes with rather laterally compressed bodies. Head deep. Snout pointed. Eyes strikingly large. Mouth rather long. Dorsal fin small, behind the middle of the body. Caudal fin deeply forked, with narrow lobes. Scales thin.

Remarks: Probably predators.

Recent relatives: None. Died out in Upper Jurassic.

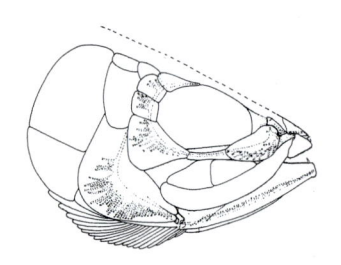

Eurycormus, reconstruction after PATTERSON

TELEOSTEI
Order: Pholidophoriformes
Family: Pholidophoridae

True Bony Fishes

Parapholidophorus caffii (AIRAGHI) (length c. 6 cm) from the Upper Triassic of San Pellegrino, Italy. Original: Museo Civico Scienze Naturali Caffi, Bergamo, Italy.

Genus: *Parapholidophorus* ZAMBELLI, 1975.

Geological range: Upper Triassic.

Geographical distribution: Europe.

Features: Small fishes of slender shape. Head elongate. Snout pointed. Eyes large. Gape rather long. Dorsal fin small, approximately in the middle of the body, opposite the elongate pelvic fins. Anal fin small. Pectoral fins fan-shaped. Caudal fin moderately forked, with lobes broad at the base and pointed at the ends. Scales thick.

Remarks: Probably gregarious.

Recent relatives: None. Died out in Upper Triassic.

TELEOSTEI
True Bony Fishes
Order: Pholidophoriformes
Family: Pholidophoridae

Pholidoctenus serianus ZAMBELLI (length c. 9 cm) from the Upper Triassic of Cene, Bergamo, Italy. Original: Museo Civico Scienze Naturali Caffi, Bergamo, Italy.

Genus: *Pholidoctenus* ZAMBELLI, 1977.

Geological range: Upper Triassic.

Geographical distribution: Europe.

Features: Small fishes of rather laterally compressed shape. Head short and large. Snout rounded. Eyes large. Dorsal fin pointed, located approximately in the middle of the body. Pectoral fins fan-shaped. Caudal fin forked, with narrow pointed lobes. Thick scales arranged in diagonal rows.

Remarks: Probably gregarious.

Recent relatives: None. Died out in Upper Triassic.

TELEOSTEI
True Bony Fishes
Order: Pholidophoriformes
Family: Pholidophoridae

Pholidolepis dorsetensis NYBELIN (length c. 11 cm) from the Lower Jurassic of Lyme Regis, England, U.K. Original: The Natural History Museum, London, U.K. (P 39862)

Genus: *Pholidolepis* NYBELIN, 1966.

Geological range: Lower Jurassic.

Geographical distribution: Europe.

Features: Small fishes of elongate, generally slender shape. Head elongate. Snout pointed. Dorsal fin pointed, located approximately in the middle of the body. Pectoral fins narrow. Caudal fin moderately forked, with narrow lobes.

Remarks: Probably gregarious.

Recent relatives: None. Died out in Lower Jurassic.

TELEOSTEI
Order: Pholidophoriformes
Family: Pholidophoridae

True Bony Fishes

Pholidophorus macrocephalus AGASSIZ (length c. 33 cm) from the Upper Jurassic of Solnhofen (Eichstätt), Bavaria, Germany. Original: Bayerische Staatssammlung für Paläontologie, Munich, Bavaria, Germany.

Genus: *Pholidophorus* AGASSIZ, 1832.
Synonyms: *Phelidophorus*.
Geological range: Lower Triassic to Upper Jurassic.
Geographical distribution: Europe, North America, South America, west Africa, Asia.
Features: Middle-sized fishes of slender shape. Head deep. Snout rather pointed. Eyes large. Gape rather long. Dorsal fin with a tall point anteriorly, decreasing in height posteriorly and with the upper margin concave, opposite the pelvic fins. Anal fin located more posteriorly. Caudal fin rather forked, with broad lobes. Scales thin and with a thin ganoin layer.
Remarks: Swift fishes, probably predatory.
Recent relatives: The order Pholidophoriformes shows the first definite steps in the direction of the true bony fishes. Distantly related to the Leptolepiformes but also to the Osteoglossiformes and to the tarpons.

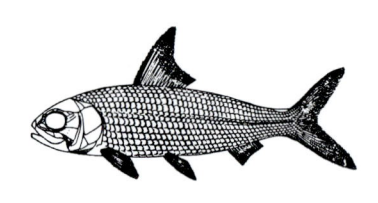

Pholidophorus, after WOODWARD.

TELEOSTEI
Order: Pholidophoriformes
Family: Pholidophoridae

True Bony Fishes

Pholidorhynchodon malzanni ZAMBELLI (length c. 7 cm) from the Upper Triassic of Cene, Bergamo, Italy. Original: Museo Civico Scienze Naturali Caffi, Bergamo, Italy.

Genus: *Pholidorhynchodon* ZAMBELLI, 1980.

Geological range: Upper Triassic.

Geographical distribution: Europe.

Features: Small fishes with rather laterally compressed bodies. Head elongate. Snout pointed. Eyes large. Gape long. Dorsal fin small, approximately in the middle of the body, opposite the pelvic fins. Anal fin located more posteriorly. Pectoral fins fan-shaped. Caudal fin forked, with narrow lobes. Scales thick.

Remarks: Probably gregarious.

Recent relatives: None. Died out in Upper Triassic.

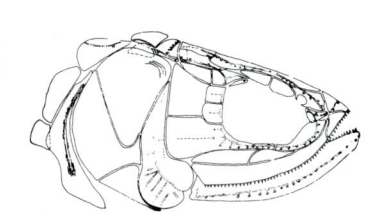

Pholidorhynchodon, reconstruction after ZAMBELLI.

457

TELEOSTEI
Order: Pholidophoriformes
Family: Pholidophoridae

True Bony Fishes

Prohalecites porroi BELOTTI (length c. 3 cm) from the Middle Triassic of ca del Frate, Varese, Italy. Original: Museo Civico Scienze Naturali, Induno Olona, Varese, Italy.

Genus: *Prohalecites* DEECKE, 1889.

Geological range: Middle to Upper Triassic.

Geographical distribution: Europe.

Features: Very small fishes of slender shape. Head large. Gape long. Jaws with small pointed teeth. Dorsal fin in the posterior third of the body, opposite the anal fin. Pelvic fins small, pectoral fins somewhat longer. Caudal fin posteriorly concave rather than forked.

Remarks: Probably gregarious.

Recent relatives: None. Died out in Upper Triassic.

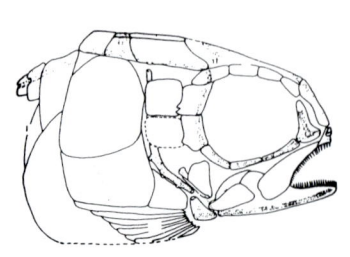

Prohalecites, after TINTORI.

TELEOSTEI
Order: Pholidophoriformes
Family: Ichthyokentemidae

True Bony Fishes

Catervariolus hornemani SAINT SEINE (length c. 6 cm) from the Upper Jurassic of Zaire. Original: Rijksmuseum van Geologie en Mineralogie, Leiden, Netherlands.

Genus: *Catervariolus* SAINT SEINE, 1955.

Geological range: Upper Jurassic.

Geographical distribution: West Africa.

Features: Small fishes of slender shape. Head shallow. Snout rounded. Eyes small. Dorsal fin in the posterior half of the body, obliquely opposite the anal fin. Caudal fin strongly concave posteriorly, with pointed lobes. Scales thick.

Remarks: Probably gregarious.

Recent relatives: None. Died out in Upper Jurassic.

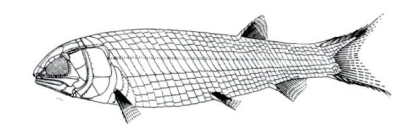

Catervariolus, reconstruction after SAINT SEINE.

TELEOSTEI
Order: Pholidophoriformes
Family: Ichthyokentenidae

True Bony Fishes

Ichthyokentema purbeckensis DAVIES (length c. 4 cm) from the Upper Jurassic of Wiltshire, England, U.K. Original: The Natural History Museum, London, U.K. (P7640).

Genus: *Ichthyokentema* WOODWARD, 1941.

Geological range: Upper Jurassic.

Geographical distribution: Europe.

Features: Very small fishes of slender shape. Head elongate. Snout somewhat pointed. Eyes large. Dorsal fin pointed, shortly behind the middle of the body, obliquely opposite the somewhat more posterior anal fin. Caudal fin divided. Scales very thick, quadrangular, almost rod-shaped on the anterior part of the flanks.

Remarks: Probably gregarious.

Recent relatives: None. Died out in Upper Jurassic.

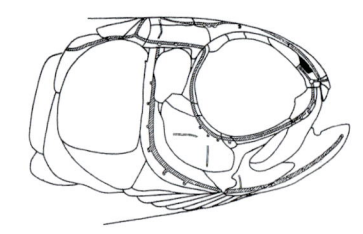

Ichthyokentema, after PATTERSON

460

TELEOSTEI
Order: Pholidophoriformes
Family: Pleuropholidae

True Bony Fishes

Pleuropholis laevissimus AGASSIZ (length c. 6 cm) from the Upper Jurassic of Solnhofen (Kelheim), Bavaria, Germany. Original: The Natural History Museum, London, U.K. (P1100)

Genus: *Pleuropholis* EGERTON, 1858.

Geological range: Upper Triassic to Lower Cretaceous.

Geographical distribution: Europe, western Africa.

Features: Small fishes of slender shape. Head elongate. Snout rounded. Eyes large. Gape moderately long. Dorsal fin in the posterior third of the body, opposite the anal fin. Pelvic fins small. Pectoral fins elongate. Caudal fin forked, with broad lobes. Scales with serrated margins, quadrangular on the back and belly, but strikingly rod-shaped on the flanks.

Remarks: Probably predators.

Recent relatives: None. Died out in Lower Cretaceous.

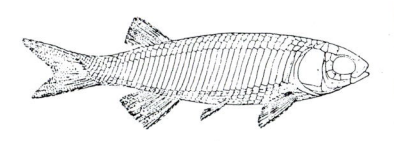

Pleuropholis, reconstruction after WOODWARD.

TELEOSTEI
Order: Pholidophoriformes
Family: Archaeomaenidae

True Bony Fishes

Aphnelepis sp. (length c. 8 cm) from the Lower Jurassic of Talbragar, New South Wales, Australia. Original: Australian Museum, Sydney, Australia.

Genus: *Aphnelepis* WOODWARD, 1895.

Geological range: Lower Jurassic.

Geographical distribution: Australia.

Features: Small fishes of slender shape. Head elongate. Snout pointed. Eyes large. Gape long. Dorsal fin in the posterior half of the body, anteriorly with a point but decreasing in height posteriorly and with a concave dorsal margin, obliquely opposite the anal fin. Pectoral fins narrow. Caudal fin slightly forked, with relatively broad lobes.

Remarks: Probably gregarious.

Recent relatives: None. Died out in Lower Jurassic.

TELEOSTEI
Order: Pholidophoriformes
Family: Archaeomaenidae

True Bony Fishes

Archaeomaene tenuis WOODWARD (length c. 12 cm) from the Lower Jurassic of Talbragar, NSW. Original: The Natural History Museum, London, U.K. (P40498).

Genus: *Archaeomene* WOODWARD, 1895.

Geological range: Lower Jurassic.

Geographical distribution: Australia.

Features: Small fishes of elongate shape. Head short and deep. Snout rounded. Eyes large. Gape rather long. Dorsal fin small, located very posteriorly, obliquely opposite the larger anal fin. Pelvic fins elongate, rounded at the ends. Pectoral fins narrow. Caudal fin small, forked, with broad lobes. Scales rounded.

Remarks: Probably gregarious.

Recent relatives: None. Died out in Lower Jurassic.

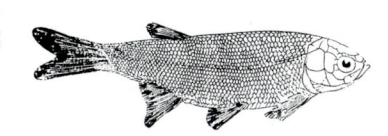

Archaeomenae, after WADE.

463

TELEOSTEI
Order: **Pholidophoriformes**
Family: **Archaeomaenidae**

True Bony Fishes

Wadeichthys oxyops WALDMAN (length c. 16 cm) from the Lower Cretaceous of Australia. Original: Field Museum of Natural History, Chicago, Illinois, U.S.A.

Genus: *Wadeichthys* WALDMAN, 1971.

Geological range: Lower Cretaceous.

Geographical distribution: Australia.

Features: Small fishes with elongate bodies. Head short and deep. Snout rounded. Gape long, with the lower jaw projecting. Eyes small. Dorsal fin behind the middle of the body, obliquely opposite the triangular anal fin. Pelvic fins small. Pectoral fins somewhat longer. Caudal fin forked, with relatively broad lobes. Scales arranged in diagonal rows.

Remarks: Probably predators.

Recent relatives: None. Died out in Lower Cretaceous.

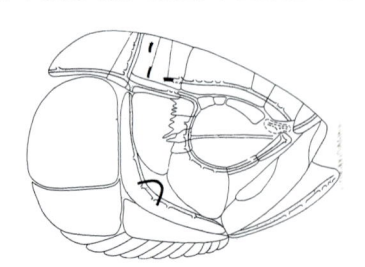

Wadeichthys, reconstruction after WADE.

TELEOSTEI
Order: Pholidophoriformes
Family: Oligopleuridae

True Bony Fishes

Callopterus agassizi Thiollière (length c. 55 cm) from the Upper Jurassic of Solnhofen (Eichstätt), Bavaria, Germany. Original: Jura-Museum, Eichstätt, Bavaria, Germany.

Genus: *Callopterus* Thiollière, 1854.

Geological range: Upper Jurassic.

Geographical distribution: Europe.

Features: Middle-sized fishes of slender, rather laterally compressed shape. Head short and deep. Snout rounded. Gape relatively long. Eyes large. Dorsal fin located very posteriorly, large and triangular, obliquely opposite the anal fin which is also triangular. Pectoral fins fan-like. Caudal fin large, strongly concave posteriorly.

Remarks: Probably predatory fishes.

Recent relatives: None. Died out in Upper Jurassic.

TELEOSTEI
Order: Pholidophoriformes
Family: Oligopleuridae

True Bony Fishes

Ionoscopus cyprinoides WAGNER (length c. 44 cm) from the Upper Jurassic of Solnhofen (Eichstätt), Bavaria, Germany. Original: Kraus Collection, Weißenburg, Germany.

Genus: *Ionoscopus* COSTA, 1853.

Synonyms: *Opsigonus*.

Geological range: Upper Jurassic to Lower Cretaceous.

Geographical distribution: Europe.

Features: Middle-sized fishes of rather laterally compressed shape. Head elongate. Snout pointed. Gape long. Jaws with pointed teeth. Dorsal fin acute triangular, situated behind the middle of the body, obliquely opposite the anal fin which is likewise an acute triangle. Pectoral fins elongate. Caudal fin rather deeply forked, with lobes broad at the base and pointed at the ends.

Remarks: Probably predators.

Recent relatives: None. Died out in Lower Cretaceous.

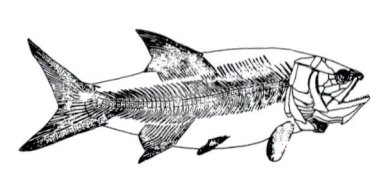

Ionoscopus, reconstruction after WAGNER.

TELEOSTEI
Order: Pholidophoriformes
Family: Oligopleuridae

True Bony Fishes

Oshunia brevis WENZ & KELLNER (length c. 40 cm) from the Lower Cretaceous of Ceará, Brazil. Original: American Museum of Natural History, New York, N.Y., U.S.A.

Genus: *Oshunia* WENZ & KELLNER, 1986.

Geological range: Lower Cretaceous.

Geographical distribution: South America.

Features: Middle-sized fishes with deep bodies and a convex dorsal margin. Head shallow. Snout pointed. Gape long with powerful teeth. Eyes small. Dorsal fin behind the middle of the body, almost opposite the pelvic fins. Pectoral fins small. Scales thick.

Remarks: Still-water predatory fishes.

Recent relatives: None. Died out in Lower Cretaceous.

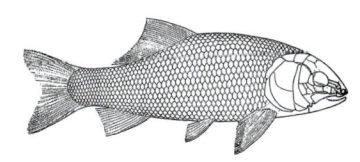

Oshunia, after MAISEY

TELEOSTEI
Order: **Pholidophoriformes**
Family: **Unnamed**

True Bony Fishes

Hulettia americana EASTMAN (length c. 10 cm) from the Lower Jurassic of New Mexico, U.S.A. Original: Frickhinger Collection, Munich, Germany.

Genus: *Hulettia* SCHAEFFER & PATTERSON, 1984.

Geological range: Lower Jurassic.

Geographical distribution: North America.

Features: Small fishes of slender shape. Head deep. Snout rounded. Gape rather long. Dorsal fin in the posterior third of the body. Anal fin pointed, located more posteriorly. Pelvic and pectoral fins small. Caudal fin forked, with broad lobes. Scales thick and shiny.

Remarks: Probably predatory fishes.

Recent relatives: None. Died out in Lower Jurassic.

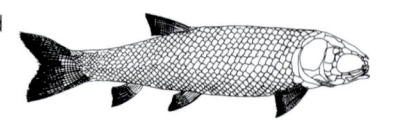

Hulettia, reconstruction after SCHAEFFER & PATTERSON.

468

TELEOSTEI
Order: Leptolepiformes
Family: Leptolepididae

True Bony Fishes

Ascalabos voithii MÜNSTER (length c. 10 cm) from the Upper Jurassic of Solnhofen (Eichstätt), Bavaria, Germany. Original: Museum of Natural History, Lawrence, Kansas, U.S.A.

Genus: *Ascalabos* MÜNSTER, 1839.

Geological range: Upper Jurassic.

Geographical distribution: Europe.

Features: Small fishes of slender shape. Head elongate. Snout pointed. Eyes strikingly large. Dorsal fin opposite the pelvic fins. Anal fin small. Pectoral fins narrow, fan-shaped. Caudal fin. Fewer vertebral centra than *Leptolepides*.

Remarks: Probably gregarious fishes.

Recent relatives: None. Died out in Upper Jurassic.

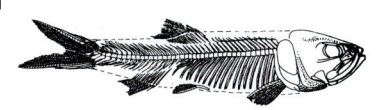

Ascalabos, reconstruction after TAVERNE.

TELEOSTEI
Order: Leptolepiformes
Family: Leptolepididae

True Bony Fishes

Clupavus neocomiensis (BASSANI) (length c. 6 cm) from the Lower Cretaceous of Tselfat, Morocco. Original: Muséum National d'Histoire Naturelle, Paris, France. Photograph: Serette, Paris.

Genus: *Clupavus* ARAMBOURG, 1950.

Geological range: Upper Jurassic to Lower Cretaceous.

Geographical distribution: Europe, northern Africa, North America.

Features: Small fishes with slender elongate bodies. Head elongate. Snout pointed. Gape long. Eyes large. Dorsal fin small, triangular, attached at the anterior end of the posterior half of the body. Anal fin small and elongate. Pelvic and pectoral fins fanlike. Pelvic fins opposite the dorsal fin. Caudal fin forked.

Remarks: Gregarious fishes.

Recent relatives: None. Died out in the Cretaceous.

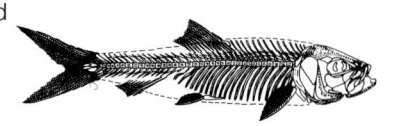

Clupavus, reconstruction after TAVERNE.

470

TELEOSTEI
True Bony Fishes
Order: Leptolepiformes
Family: Leptolepididae

Leptolepides sprattiformis (AGASSIZ) (length c. 8 cm) from the Upper Jurassic of Solnhofen, Bavaria, Germany. Original: Frickhinger Collection, Munich, Germany.

Genus: *Leptolepides* NYBELIN, 1974.

Synonyms: *Leptolepis*.

Geological range: Upper Jurassic.

Geographical distribution: Europe.

Features: Small fishes with slender bodies. Head shallow. Snout slightly pointed. Jaws with minute teeth. Dorsal fin approximately in the middle of the body, opposite the pelvic fins. Anal fin small. Caudal fin forked. Scales thin, cycloid and overlapping, with a thin ganoin layer.

Remarks: Gregarious fishes which occurred in huge numbers and served as food for many other fishes in the Jurassic seas.

Recent relatives: The genus *Leptolepides* and other genera of the Leptolepiformes already show predominantly the features of true bony fishes. They may represent early stages on the route towards herrings (Clupeiformes).

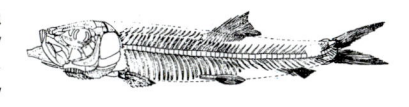

Leptolepides, reconstruction after TAVERNE.

471

TELEOSTEI
Order: Leptolepiformes
Family: Leptolepididae

True Bony Fishes

Leptolepis talbragarensis W<small>OODWARD</small> (length c. 12 cm) from the Lower Jurassic of Talbragar, New South Wales, Australia. Original: Australian Museum, Sydney, Australia.

Genus: *Leptolepis* A<small>GASSIZ</small>, 1832.

Synonyms: *Liassolepis*, *Megastoma*, *Sarginites*.

Geological range: Lower Jurassic to Lower Cretaceous.

Geographical distribution: Europe, North America, Spitzbergen, Australia, Asia, South America, Africa.

Features: Small fishes of rather laterally compressed shape. Head shallow. Snout slightly truncate. Eyes relatively large. Dorsal fin opposite the relatively large pelvic fins. Pectoral fins narrow, fan-shaped. Caudal fin forked.

Remarks: Probably gregarious fishes.

Recent relatives: None. Died out in Lower Cretaceous.

TELEOSTEI
Order: Leptolepiformes
Family: Leptolepididae

True Bony Fishes

Orthogonikleithrus leichi ARRATIA (length c. 6 cm) from the Upper Jurassic of Solnhofen, Bavaria, Germany. Original: Field Museum of Natural History, Chicago, Ill., U.S.A.

Genus: *Orthogonikleithrus* ARRATIA, 1987.

Geological range: Upper Jurassic.

Geographical distribution: Europe.

Features: Small to very small fishes of slender elongate shape. Head elongate. Snout pointed. Eyes large. Dorsal fin approximately in the middle of the body, opposite the pelvic fins. Caudal fin forked, with the lobes broad at the base and narrow terminally. Scales thin.

Remarks: Probably gregarious.

Recent relatives: None. Died out in Upper Jurassic.

TELEOSTEI
Order: Leptolepiformes
Family: Leptolepididae

True Bony Fishes

Proleptolepis elongata Nybelin (length c. 12 cm) from the Lower Jurassic of Lyme Regis, England, U.K. Original: The Natural History Museum, London, U.K. (P 7801)

Genus: *Proleptolepis* Nybelin, 1974.

Geological range: Lower Jurassic.

Geographical distribution: Europe.

Features: Small fishes with very slender elongate bodies. Head shallow. Snout rounded. Eyes small. Dorsal fin opposite the pelvic fins. Caudal fin forked.

Remarks: Probably gregarious.

Recent relatives: None. Died out in Lower Jurassic.

TELEOSTEI
Order: Leptolepiformes
Family: Leptolepididae

True Bony Fishes

Tharsis dubius (de BLAINVILLE) (length c. 20 cm) from the Upper Jurassic of Solnhofen (Eichtstätt), Bavaria, Germany. Original: Interfoss, Munich, Germany

Genus: *Tharsis* GIEBEL, 1847.

Geological range: Upper Jurassic.

Geographical distribution: Europe.

Features: Middle-sized fishes with slender, rather laterally compressed bodies. Head elongate. Snout pointed. Eyes relatively large. Dorsal fin behind the middle of the body, opposite the small narrow pelvic fins. Caudal fin forked with narrow lobes.

Remarks: Probably gregarious.

Recent relatives: None. Died out in Upper Jurassic.

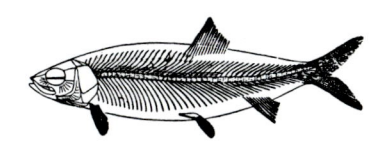

Tharsis, after WOODWARD.

TELEOSTEI
True Bony Fishes
Order: Leptolepiformes
Family: Leptolepididae

Tharrhias araripis JORDAN & BRANNER (length c. 30 cm) from the Lower Cretaceous of Ceará, Brazil. Original: Frickhinger Collection, Munich, Germany.

Genus: *Tarrhias* JORDAN & BRANNER, 1908.

Geological range: Lower Cretaceous.

Geographical distribution: South America.

Features: Middle-sized fishes with slender bodies. Head elongate. Snout pointed. Eyes small. Dorsal fin opposite the pelvic fins. Anal fin triangular. Caudal fin forked, with broad lobes. Scales quadrangular.

Remarks: Probably gregarious.

Recent relatives: None. Died out in Lower Cretaceous.

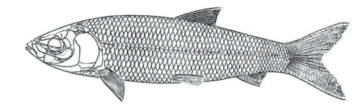

Tharrhias araripis, reconstruction after MAISEY.

TELEOSTEI
Order: Leptolepiformes
Family: Leptolepididae

True Bony Fishes

Todiltia schoewi (Dunkle) (length c. 6 cm) from the Lower Jurassic of New Mexico, U.S.A. Original: Museum of Natural History, Lawrence, Kansas, U.S.A.

Genus: *Todiltia* Schaeffer & Patterson, 1981.

Geological range: Lower Jurassic.

Geographical distribution: North America.

Features: Small or very small fishes with slender bodies. Head short and deep. Snout truncate. Eyes relatively large. Dorsal fin in the posterior half of the body, obliquely opposite the pelvic fins. Caudal fin deeply forked. Scales somewhat thicker than in related forms.

Remarks: Probably gregarious.

Recent relatives: None. Died out in Lower Jurassic.

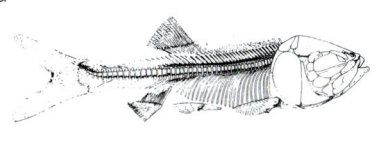

Todiltia, reconstruction after Schaeffer & Patterson.

TELEOSTEI
Order: Leptolepiformes
Family: Varasichthyidae

True Bony Fishes

Varasichthys ariasi ARRATIA (length c. 19 cm) from the Upper Jurassic of northern Chile. Original: Universidad de Chile, Santiago, Chile.

Genus: *Varasichthys* ARRATIA, 1981.

Geological range: Upper Jurassic.

Geographical distribution: South America.

Features: Small fishes to middle-sized fishes with slender elongate bodies. Head elongate. Snout somewhat rounded. Eyes relatively small. Dorsal fin approximately in the middle of the body, obliquely opposite the pelvic fins. Caudal fin forked.

Remarks: Probably gregarious.

Recent relatives: None. Died out in Upper Jurassic.

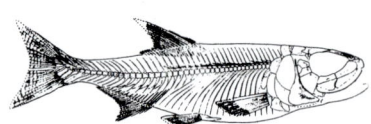

Varasichthys, reconstruction after ARRATIA.

478

TELEOSTEI
Order: Ichthyodectiformes
Family: Allothrissopidae

True Bony Fishes

Allothrissops salmoneus (de BLAINVILLE) (length c. 28 cm) from the Upper Jurassic of Solnhofen (Eichstätt), Bavaria, Germany. Original: Bayerische Staatssammlung für Paläontologie, Munich, Germany.

Genus: *Allothrissops* NYBELIN, 1964.

Geological range: Upper Jurassic to Lower Cretaceous.

Geographical distribution: Europe.

Features: Middle-sized fishes with very slender elongate bodies. Head small. Gape rather long. Eyes middle-sized. Dorsal fin small, situated very posteriorly, opposite the anal fin. Pelvic fins very small. Pectoral fins narrow and somewhat longer. Caudal fin small, moderately forked, with short lobes.

Remarks: Rapidly swimming predators.

Recent relatives: None. Died out in Lower Cretaceous.

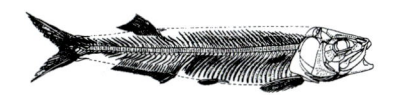

Allothrissops, reconstruction after TAVERNE.

TELEOSTEI
True Bony Fishes
Order: Ichthyodectiformes
Family: Ichthyodectidae

Chirocentrites coroninii HECKEL (length c. 33 cm) from the Lower Cretaceous of Komen, Jugoslavia. Original: Naturhistorisches Museum, Vienna, Austria.

Genus: *Chirocentrites* HECKEL, 1849.

Geological range: Lower Cretaceous.

Geographical distribution: Europe.

Features: Middle-sized fishes with slender elongate bodies. Head shallow. Gape long and directed upwards. Eyes large. Dorsal fin located very posteriorly, obliquely opposite the anal fin. Pelvic fins very small. Pectoral fins narrow and somewhat longer. Caudal fin deeply forked, with long narrow lobes.

Remarks: Rapidly swimming predators.

Recent relatives: Genus extinct. Perhaps closely related to the wolf herrings of the genus *Chirocentrus*.

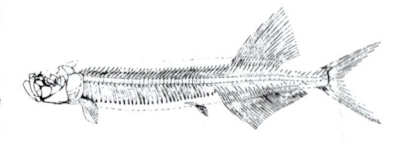

Chirocentrites, reconstruction after HECKEL.

TELEOSTEI
True Bony Fishes
Order: Ichthyodectiformes
Family: Ichthyodectidae

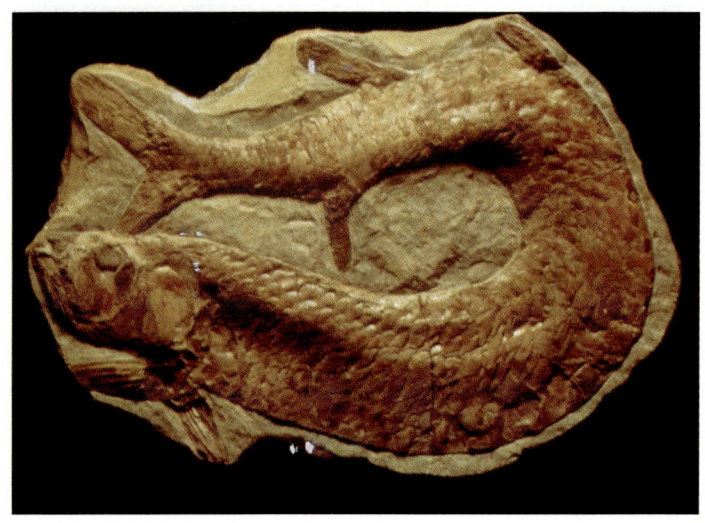

Cladocyclus GARDNERI AGASSIZ (length c. 125 cm) from the Lower Cretaceous of Ceará, Brazil. Original: Interfoss, Munich, Germany.

Genus: *Cladocyclus* AGASSIZ, 1841.

Geological range: Lower Cretaceous.

Geographical distribution: South America.

Features: Middle-sized to large fishes with slender elongate bodies. Head long and shallow. Gape long and directed upward. Eyes middle-sized. Jaws with powerful teeth. Dorsal fin relatively small, located very posteriorly, obliquely opposite the narrow anal fin. Pelvic fins small and narrow. Pectoral fins somewhat longer. Caudal fin deeply forked with long narrow lobes.

Remarks: Predatory fishes.

Recent relatives: Genus and family extinct. Perhaps distantly related to the wolf herrings of the family Chirocentridae.

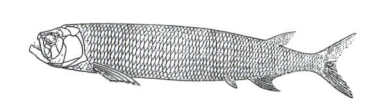

Cladocyclus, after MAISEY.

TELEOSTEI
Order: Ichthyodectiformes
Family: Ichthyodectidae

True Bony Fishes

Cooyoo australis BARTHOLOMAI & LEES (length c. 16 cm) from the Lower Cretaceous of Richmond, Queensland, Australia. Original: Queensland Museum, Brisbane, Queensland, Australia.

Genus: *Cooyoo* BARTHOLOMAI & LEES, 1987.

Geological range: Lower Cretaceous.

Geographical distribution: Australia.

Features: Middle-sized to large fishes with a big deep head. Snout rounded. Gape long and directed upward. Eyes large. Jaws with pointed teeth of differing shapes, anteriorly developed as grasping teeth. Characteristic horn-shaped process on the head.

Remarks: Formidable predators.

Recent relatives: None. Died out in Lower Cretaceous.

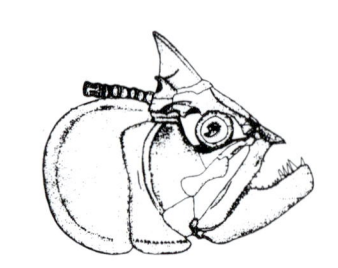

Cooyoo, reconstruction after BARTHOLOMAI & LEES.

482

TELEOSTEI
Order: Ichthyodectiformes
Family: Ichthyodectidae

True Bony Fishes

Eubiodectes libanicus (Pictet & Humbert) (length c. 58 cm) from the Upper Cretaceous of the Lebanon. Original: Interfoss, Munich, Germany

Genus: *Eubiodectes* Hay, 1903.

Geological range: Upper Cretaceous.

Geographical distribution: Middle East.

Features: Middle-sized fishes of slender elongate shape. Head shallow. Gape long and directed upwards. Eyes relatively large. Jaws with pointed teeth. Dorsal fin small, located in the posterior third of the body, opposite the pelvic fins which are likewise small. Pectoral fins narrow and somewhat longer. Caudal fin deeply forked with slender lobes.

Remarks: Predators.

Recent relatives: Genus extinct. Perhaps related to wolf herrings of the family Chirocentridae.

TELEOSTEI
True Bony Fishes
Order: Ichthyodectiformes
Family: Ichthyodectidae

Gillicus arcuatus (COPE) (length c. 157 cm) from the Upper Cretaceous of Kansas, U.S.A. Original: Siber & Siber Collection, Aathal, Switzerland.

Genus: *Gillicus* HAY, 1898.

Geological range: Lower to Upper Cretaceous.

Geographical distribution: Europe, North America.

Features: Large fishes with elongate bodies. Head long and shallow. Gape long and directed upwards. Eyes relatively small. Jaws with pointed teeth. Dorsal fin pointed, located very posteriorly, opposite the anal fin which is likewise pointed. Pelvic fins small and narrow. Pectoral fins strikingly long and pointed. Caudal fin large, deeply forked, with long narrow lobes.

Remarks: Large predators.

Recent relatives: None. Died out in Upper Cretaceous.

TELEOSTEI
True Bony Fishes
Order: Ichthyodectiformes
Family: Ichthyodectidae

Ichthyodectes ctenodon COPE (length c. 220 cm) from the Upper Cretaceous of Kansas, U.S.A. Original: Museum of Natural History, Lawrence, Kansas, U.S.A.

Genus: *Ichthyodectes* COPE, 1870.

Geological range: Lower to Upper Cretaceous.

Geographical distribution: Europe, North America.

Features: Large fishes with slender elongate bodies. Head relatively small. Gape long. Dorsal fin small, in the posterior half of the body, opposite the somewhat larger anal fin. Pelvic fins small and narrow. Pectoral fins narrow and somewhat longer. Caudal fin very large, deeply forked, with long narrow lobes.

Remarks: Large predators.

Recent relatives: None. Died out in Upper Cretaceous.

TELEOSTEI
Order: Ichthyodectiformes
Family: Ichthyodectidae

True Bony Fishes

Proportheus sp. (length c. 16 cm) from the Lower Cretaceous of Lesina, Yugoslavia. Original: Museum für Naturkunde, Berlin.

Genus: *Proportheus* JAEKEL, 1909.

Geological range: Lower Cretaceous.

Geographical distribution: Europe.

Features: Middle-sized fishes with massive heads. Eyes relatively small. Gape long and directed upwards. Upper and lower jaws with long pointed teeth of varying sizes, the anterior ones developed as grasping teeth. Pectoral fins very long and pointed.

Remarks: Dangerous predators.

Recent relatives: None. Died out in Lower Cretaceous.

TELEOSTEI
Order: Ichthyodectiformes
Family: Ichthyodectidae

True Bony Fishes

Prymnites longiventer COPE (length c. 52 cm) from the Tertiary of Chiapas, Mexico. Original: National Museum of Natural History, Smithsonian Institution, Washington D.C., U.S.A.

Genus: *Prymnites* COPE, 1871.

Geological range: Tertiary.

Geographical distribution: Central America.

Features: Middle-sized fishes with slender elongate bodies. Head deep. Snout slightly rounded. Eyes relatively large. Dorsal fin small, located very posteriorly. Anal fin small and narrow. Pectoral fins long and narrow. Caudal fin forked.

Remarks: Predators.

Recent relatives: Genus extinct. Perhaps distantly related to wolf herrings of the family Chirocentridae.

TELEOSTEI
True Bony Fishes
Order: Ichthyodectiformes
Family: Ichthyodectidae

Thrissops formosus AGASSIZ (length c. 28 cm) from the Upper Jurassic of Solnhofen (Schernfeld) Bavaria, Germany. Original: Jura-Museum, Eichstätt, Germany.

Genus: *Thrissops* AGASSIZ, 1883.

Geological range: Upper Jurassic to Upper Cretaceous.

Geographical distribution: Europe.

Features: Middle-sized fishes with rather laterally compressed bodies. Head small. Gape rather long. Jaws with small pointed teeth. Dorsal fin small and triangular, in the posterior third of the body, opposite the anal fin which is anteriorly pointed but more posteriorly forms a fringe. Pelvic fins very small. Pectoral fins long and narrow. Caudal fin large, deeply forked, with long narrow lobes.

Remarks: Rapidly swimming predators.

Recent relatives: Genus extinct, perhaps distantly related to wolf herrings of the family Chirocentridae.

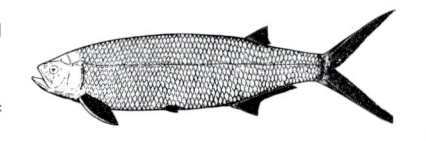

Thrissops, reconstruction after TAVERNE.

TELEOSTEI
Order: Ichthyodectiformes
Family: Ichthyodectidae

True Bony Fishes

Xiphactinus audax Leidy (length c. 430 cm) from the Upper Cretaceous of Kansas, U.S.A. Cast: Tetra-Werke, Melle, Germany.

Genus: *Xiphactinus* Leidy, 1870.

Synonyms: *Portheus*.

Geological range: Lower to Upper Cretaceous.

Geographical distribution: North America, Australia, Europe.

Features: Very large fishes with elongate bodies. Head elongate and shallow, with a horn-like process. Gape long, directed upwards, with long pointed teeth of various shapes, the anterior ones being developed as grasping teeth. Dorsal fin relatively small, somewhat behind the middle of the body. Anal and pelvic fins likewise small. Pectoral fins long, carried by a strong bony ray. Caudal fin very large, deeply forked, with the lobes broad at the base and pointed at the ends.

Remarks: Formidable predators.

Recent relatives: None. Died out in Lower Cretaceous.

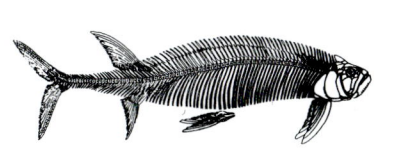

Xiphactinus, reconstruction after Osborn.

TELEOSTEI
Order: Ichthyodectiformes
Family: Saurodontidae

True Bony Fishes

Saurodon leanus Hays (length c. 20 cm) from the Upper Cretaceous of Kansas, U.S.A. Original: Field Museum of Natural History, Chicago, Illinois, U.S.A.

Genus: *Saurodon* Hays, 1829.

Synonyms: *Daptinus*.

Geological range: Upper Cretaceous.

Geographical distribution: North America, Europe.

Features: Middle-sized fishes with shallow elongate heads. Snout elongate and somewhat rounded. Gape very long, with many pointed conical teeth. Lower jaw projecting.

Remarks: Formidable predators.

Recent relatives: None. Died out in Upper Cretaceous.

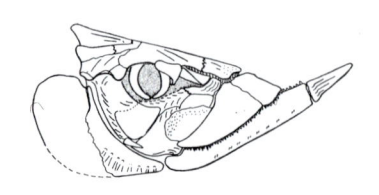

Saurodon, reconstruction after Bardack.

TELEOSTEI
Order: Ichthyodectiformes
Family: Thryptodontidae

True Bony Fishes

Bananogmius evolutus (COPE) (length c. 76 cm) from the Upper Cretaceous of Kansas, U.S.A. Original: Museum of Natural History, Lawrence, Kansas, U.S.A.

Genus: *Bananogmius* WHITLEY, 1940.

Synonyms: *Ananogmius*, *Anogmius*.

Geological range: Upper Cretaceous.

Geographical distribution: North America, Europe.

Features: Large fishes with elongate, relatively shallow heads. Snout rounded. Gape rather long. Eyes middle-sized. Jaws with small teeth. Dorsal fin small, located shortly behind the head.

Remarks: Probably sluggish swimmers.

Recent relatives: None. Died out in Upper Cretaceous.

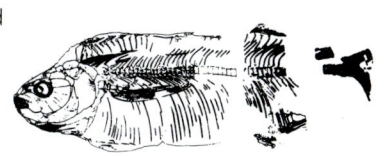

Bananogmius, reconstruction after HAY.

TELEOSTEI
Order: Ichthyodectiformes
Family: Thryptodontidae

True Bony Fishes

Zanclites xenurus JORDAN (length c. 60 cm) from the Upper Cretaceous of Kansas. Original: Museum of Natural History, Lawrence, Kansas, U.S.A.

Genus: *Zanclites* JORDAN, 1925.

Geological range: Upper Cretaceous.

Geographical distribution: North America.

Features: Middle-sized fishes of elliptical outline. Head long and shallow. Snout pointed. Dorsal fin in the middle of the body, anteriorly with a point but running rearwards as a fringe, obliquely opposite the anal fin which is likewise fringe-like. Pelvic fins small. Pectoral fins located high on the body. Caudal fin large, deeply forked, with long lobes.

Remarks: Predators.

Recent relatives: None. Died out in the Upper Cretaceous.

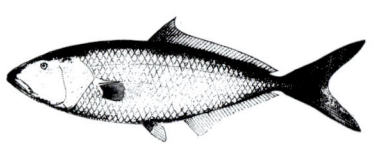

Zanclites, reconstruction after JORDAN.

TELEOSTEI
Order: Ichthyodectiformes?
Family: Unnamed

True Bony Fishes

Unnamed fish (length c. 95 cm) from the Upper Jurassic of Solnhofen (Langenaltheim), Bavaria, Germany. Original: Bayerische Staatssammlung für Paläontologie, Munich, Germany.

Genus: Not named.

Geological range: Upper Jurassic.

Geographical distribution: Europe.

Features: Middle-sized to large fishes of elongate but nevertheless somewhat plump shape. Head relatively small and shallow. Snout pointed. Gape long and directed upwards. Powerful teeth. Dorsal fin small, located very posteriorly, obliquely opposite the anal fin which is also small. Pelvic fins narrow and pointed. Pectoral fins strikingly long and narrow.

Remarks: This fish may belong to the family Pachycormidae.

Recent relatives: None. Died out in Upper Jurassic.

TELEOSTEI
Order: Unnamed
Family: Tselfattiidae

True Bony Fishes

Protobrama avus WOODWARD (length c. 7 cm) from the Upper Cretaceous of the Lebanon. Original: Naturhistoriska Riksmuseet, Stockholm, Sweden.

Genus: *Protobrama* WOODWARD, 1942.

Geological range: Upper Cretaceous.

Geographical distribution: Middle East.

Features: Small fishes of approximately elliptical outline. Head shallow. Snout pointed. Eyes large. Dorsal fin low, beginning anteriorly in front of the middle of the body and running rearwards as a fringe, opposite the anal fin which is similarly constructed. Pectoral fins rounded elongate and set high on the body. Caudal fin stalked, deeply concave posteriorly with broad lobes.

Remarks: Probably rather sluggish fishes, perhaps plant-eating.

Recent relatives: None. Died out in Upper Cretaceous.

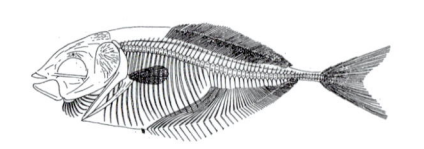

Protobrama, reconstruction after PATTERSON.

TELEOSTEI
True Bony Fishes
Order: Unnamed
Family: Tselfatiidae

Tselfatia formosa ARAMBOURG (length c. 13 cm) from the Lower Cretaceous of Tselfat, Morocco. Original: Muséum National d'Histoire Naturelle, Paris, France. Photograph: Serette, Paris.

Genus: *Tselfatia* ARAMBOURG, 1958.

Geological range: Lower Cretaceous.

Geographical distribution: North Africa.

Features: Small to middle-sized fishes with bodies deep anteriorly and tapering strongly behind. Head rounded. Eyes large. Gape rather long. Dorsal fin beginning just behind the head, anteriorly increasing strongly in height and then decreasing to the end of the body. Anal fin very large and similar in shape to the dorsal fin. Pelvic and pectoral fins very small. Caudal fin relatively small and forked.

Remarks: Probably not aggressive fishes.

Recent relatives: None. Died out in Cretaceous.

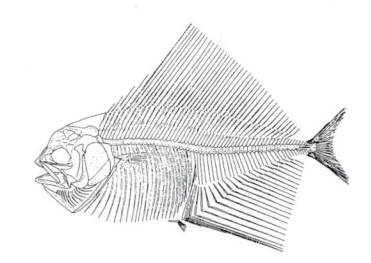

Tselfatia, reconstruction after PATTERSON.

TELEOSTEI
Order: Osteoglossiformes
Family: Osteoglossidae

True Bony Fishes
Suborder: Osteoglossoidei
Bony Tongues

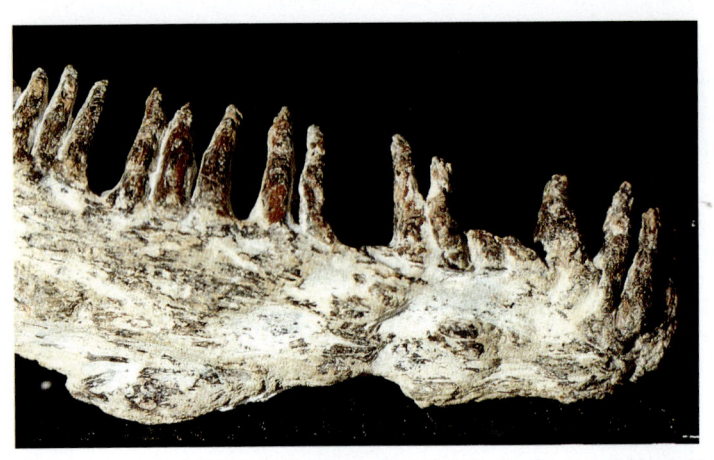

Brychaetus muelleri WOODWARD (length c. 19 cm) from the Eocene of Maryland, U.S.A. Original: National Museum of Natural History, Smithsonian Institution, Washington, D.C., U.S.A.

Genus: *Brychaetus* AGASSIZ, 1845.

Synonyms: *Platops*, *Pomphractus*.

Geological range: Upper Cretaceous to Paleocene.

Geographical distribution: Europe, North America, North Africa.

Features: Middle-sized to large fishes with powerful jaws. Teeth extremely long and not very pointed.

Remarks: Fresh-water fishes, probably predators.

Recent relatives: None. Died out in Paleocene.

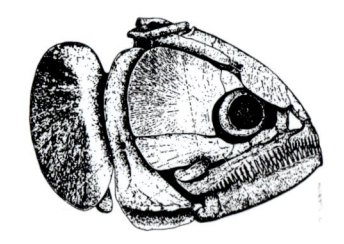

Brychaetus, reconstruction after TAVERNE.

TELEOSTEI
Order: Osteoglossiformes
Family: Osteoglossidae

True Bony Fishes
Suborder: Osteoglossoidei
Bony Tongues

Phareodus testis (COPE) (length c. 31 cm) from the Eocene of Wyoming, U.S.A. Original: Frickhinger Collection, Munich, Germany.

Genus: *Phareodus* LEIDY, 1873.

Synonyms: *Dapedoglossus*.

Geological range: Middle Eocene to Oligocene.

Geographical distribution: North America, Australia.

Features: Middle-sized fishes of oval outline. Head small. Snout slightly pointed. Gape rather long. Eyes relatively large. Dorsal fin broad at the base, posterior in position, opposite the anal fin which is larger. Pelvic fins small. Pectoral fins longer and narrow. Caudal fin slightly forked, with broad lobes.

Remarks: Fresh-water fishes.

Recent relatives: Genus extinct. Related to recent bony tongues of the family Osteoglossidae, such as *Arapaima* and *Osteoglossum*. The butterfly fish *Pantodon* is also a distant relative.

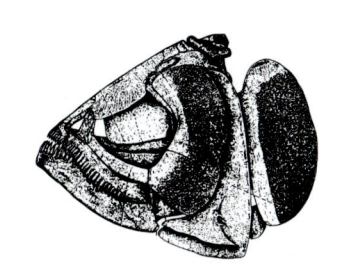

Phareodus, reconstruction after TAVERNE.

TELEOSTEI
Order: Osteoglossiformes
Family: Lycopteridae

True Bony Fishes
Suborder: Notopteroidei

Lycoptera davidi Sauvage (length c. 8 cm) from the Upper Jurassic of Manchuria. Original: Staatliches Museum für Naturkunde, Stuttgart, Germany.

Genus: *Lycoptera* Müller, 1848.

Synonyms: *Asiatolepis*.

Geological range: Upper Jurassic.

Geographical distribution: East Asia.

Features: Small fishes with slender elongate bodies. Head shallow. Snout rounded. Gape rather long and directed upwards. Dorsal fin in the posterior half of the body, opposite the anal fin. Pelvic fins short and narrow. Pectoral fins long and narrow. Caudal fin slightly forked with pointed lobes.

Remarks: Probably gregarious.

Recent relatives: None. Died out in Upper Jurassic.

Lycoptera, reconstruction after Reis.

TELEOSTEI
Order: Osteoglossiformes
Family: Hiodontidae

True Bony Fishes
Suborder: Notopteroidea
Moon Eyes

Eohiodon falcatus GRANDE (length c. 17 cm) from the Eocene of Wyoming, U.S.A. Original: Field Museum of Natural History, Chicago, Illinois.

Genus: *Eohiodon* CAVENDER, 1966.

Geological range: Paleocene to Eocene.

Geographical distribution: North America.

Features: Small to middle-sized fishes of rather laterally compressed shape. Head short and deep. Snout rounded. Gape rather long, with small pointed teeth. Eyes very large. Dorsal fin shortly behind the middle of the body, anteriorly pointed but decreasing in height posteriorly with a concave postero-dorsal margin, obliquely opposite the anal fin which is similar in shape but broader. Pelvic fins small. Pectoral fins somewhat larger. Caudal fin strongly forked with pointed lobes.

Remarks: Fresh-water fishes.

Recent relatives: Genus extinct. Closely related to the recent genus *Hiodon* and more distantly related to knife fishes of the family Notopteridae.

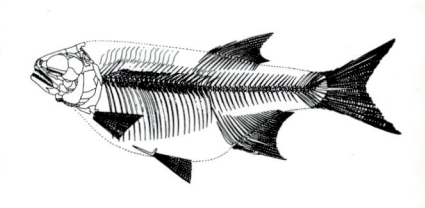

Eohiodon, reconstruction after GRANDE.

TELEOSTEI
True Bony Fishes
Order: Elopiformes
Family: Anaethalionidae

Anaethalion knorri (de BLAINVILLE) (length c. 17 cm) from the Upper Jurassic of Solnhofen (Eichstätt), Bavaria, Germany. Original: Tischlinger Collection, Stammham, Germany. Photo: Tischlinger

Genus: *Anaethalion* WHITE, 1938.

Synonyms: *Aethalion*.

Geological range: Upper Jurassic to Lower Cretaceous.

Geographical distribution: Europe.

Features: Small to middle-sized fishes of slender shape. Head elongate and relatively shallow. Snout pointed. Gape rather long. Eyes large. Dorsal fin pointed, approximately in the middle of the body, opposite the very narrow pelvic fins. Pectoral fins likewise narrow. Anal fin anteriorly with a point but broad-based and decreasing in height posteriorly. Caudal fin deeply forked with rather broad lobes.

Remarks: Probably gregarious.

Recent relatives: Genus extinct. Related to the tenpounders and probably also to the herrings.

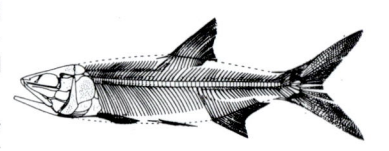

Anaethalion, after FOREY.

TELEOSTEI
Order: Elopiformes
Family: Crossognathidae

True Bony Fishes

Apsopelix agilis (STEWART) (length c. 31 cm) from the Upper Cretaceous of Kansas, U.S.A. Original: The Natural History Museum, London, U.K. (P 9184)

Genus: *Apsopelix* COPE, 1871.

Synonyms: *Helmintholepis, Leptichthys, Palaeoclupea, Pelecorapis, Syllaemus*.

Geological range: Upper Cretaceous.

Geographical distribution: Europe, North America.

Features: Middle-sized fishes of slender shape. Head long and shallow. Snout pointed. Eyes small. Dorsal fin triangular, opposite the pointed pelvic fins. Anal fin low, broad-based. Pectoral fins long and narrow. Caudal fin forked, with broad lobes. Scales rhombic.

Remarks: Probably gregarious.

Recent relatives: Genus extinct. Probably related to recent tarpons.

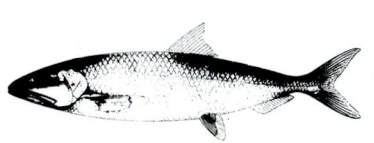

Apsopelix, reconstruction after JORDAN.

TELEOSTEI
True Bony Fishes
Order: Elopiformes
Family: Crossognathidae

Crossognathus sabaudianus P<small>ICTET</small> (length c. 22 cm) from the Lower Cretaceous of Westphalia, Germany. Original: Museum für Geologie und Paläontologie, Tübingen, Germany.

Genus: *Crossognathus* P<small>ICTET</small>, 1858.

Geological range: Lower Cretaceous.

Geographical distribution: Europe.

Features: Middle-sized fishes of slender shape. Head long and shallow. Snout pointed. Gape relatively long. Dorsal fin slightly in front of the middle of the body. Caudal fin deeply forked, with narrow lobes.

Remarks: Probably gregarious.

Recent relatives: Genus extinct. Possibly related to recent tenpounders.

Crossognathus, reconstruction after T<small>AVERNE</small>.

TELEOSTEI
Order: Elopiformes
Family: Elopidae

True Bony Fishes
Suborder: Elopoidei
Tenpounders

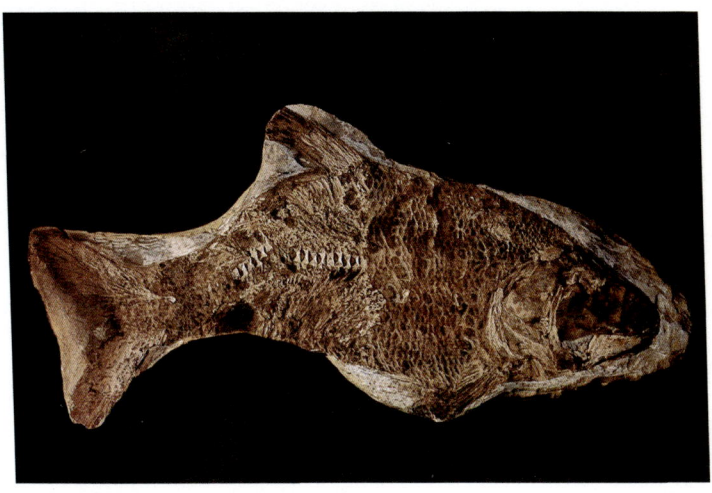

Brannerion vestitum JORDAN & BRANNER (length c. 33 cm) from the Lower Cretaceous of Ceará, Brazil. Original: Interfoss, Munich, Germany.

Genus: *Brannerion* JORDAN, 1919.

Geological range: Lower Cretaceous.

Geographical distribution: South America.

Features: Middle-sized fishes with somewhat compressed bodies. Head deep. Snout rounded. Dorsal fin tall and pointed, in the posterior half of the body, opposite the anal fin which is likewise pointed. Pectoral fins long and narrow. Caudal fin forked, with broad lobes.

Remarks: Probably fed partly on plants.

Recent relatives: None. Died out in Lower Cretaceous.

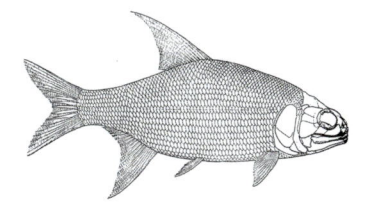

Brannerion, reconstruction after MAISEY.

TELEOSTEI
Order: Elopiformes
Family: Elopidae

True Bony Fishes
Suborder: Elopoidei
Tenpounders

Dastilbe elongatus SILVA SANTOS (length c. 6 cm) from the Lower Cretaceous of Ceará, Brazil. Original: American Museum of Natural History, New York, N.Y., U.S.A.

Genus: *Dastilbe* JORDAN, 1910.

Geological range: Lower Cretaceous.

Geographical distribution: South America.

Features: Small to very small fishes with slender elongate bodies. Head shallow. Snout pointed. Eyes middle-sized. Dorsal fin approximately in the middle of the body, opposite the pelvic fins. Caudal fin deeply forked, with relatively broad lobes.

Remarks: Gregarious.

Recent relatives: None. Died out in Lower Cretaceous.

Dastile, after MAISEY

TELEOSTEI
Order: Elopiformes
Family: Elopidae

True Bony Fishes
Suborder: Elopoidei
Tenpounders

Davichthys gardneri FOREY (length c. 9 cm) from the Upper Cretaceous of Lebanon. Original: Field Museum of Natural History, Chicago, Illinois, U.S.A.

Genus: *Davichthys* FOREY, 1973.

Geological range: Upper Cretaceous.

Geographical distribution: Middle East.

Features: Small fishes with slender bodies. Head deep. Gape rather long. Dorsal fin long and pointed, somewhat behind the middle of the body, obliquely opposite the very small pelvic fins. Anal fin small and pectoral fins narrow. Caudal fin forked, with relatively broad lobes.

Remarks: Probably gregarious.

Recent relatives: Genus extinct. Distantly related to recent tenpounders of the family Elopidae.

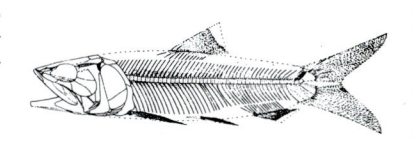

Davichthys, reconstruction after FOREY.

TELEOSTEI
Order: Elopiformes
Family: Elopidae

True Bony Fishes
Suborder: Elopoidei
Tenpounders

Paraelops cearensis SILVA SANTOS (length c. 70 cm) from the Lower Cretaceous of Ceará, Brazil. Original: Kandler collection, Augsburg, Germany.

Genus: *Paraelops* SILVA SANTOS, 1971.

Geological range: Lower Cretaceous.

Geographical distribution: South America.

Features: Middle-sized to large fishes with slender elongate bodies. Head shallow. Snout slightly pointed. Gape rather long. Eyes middle-sized. Dorsal fin in the posterior half of the body, obtusely triangular, scaly, approximately opposite the small pelvic fins. Anal fin likewise obtusely triangular. Caudal fin deeply forked, with broad lobes.

Remarks: Rapidly swimming predators.

Recent relatives: None. Died out in Lower Cretaceous.

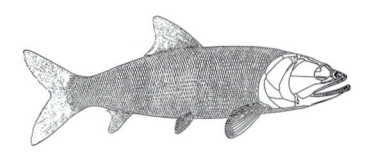

Paraelops, after MAISEY.

TELEOSTEI
Order: Elopiformes
Family: Elopidae

True Bony Fishes
Suborder: Elopoidei
Tenpounders

Parasyllaemus gracilis STERNBERG (length c. 31 cm) from the Upper Cretaceous of Manitoba, Canada. Original: Royal Ontario Museum, Toronto, Canada.

Genus: *Parasyllaemus*.

Geological range: Upper Cretaceous.

Geographical distribution: North America.

Features: Middle-sized fishes with slender elongate bodies. Head long and shallow. Gape long. Eyes large. Dorsal fin approximately in the middle of the body, opposite the pelvic fins. Anal fin pointed. Pectoral fins long and narrow. Caudal fin deeply divided with narrow lobes. Scales rounded.

Remarks: The pointed mouth suggests that it fed on worms and other burrowing animals.

Recent relatives: Genus extinct. Possibly distantly related to tenpounders of the family Elopidae.

TELEOSTEI
Order: Elopiformes
Family: Elopidae

True Bony Fishes
Suborder: Elopoidei
Tenpounders

Spaniodon elongatus PICTET (length c. 18 cm) from the Upper Cretaceous of the Lebanon. Original: Field Museum of Natural History, Chicago, Illinois, U.S.A.

Genus: *Spaniodon* PICTET, 1851.

Geological range: Upper Cretaceous.

Geographical distribution: Middle East.

Features: Small to middle-sized fishes with slender bodies. Head long and shallow. Snout somewhat rounded. Gape rather long. Eyes large. Dorsal fin triangular, slightly behind the middle of the body, obliquely opposite the very small pelvic fins. Anal fin somewhat larger. Pectoral fins fan-shaped. Caudal fin divided with broad lobes.

Remarks: Probably gregarious.

Recent relatives: Genus extinct. Possibly related to recent tenpounders of the family Elopidae.

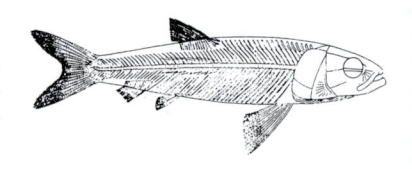

Spaniodon, reconstruction after WOODWARD.

508

TELEOSTEI
Order: Elopiformes
Family: Elopidae?

True Bony Fishes
Suborder: Elopoidei
Tenpounders

Unnamed fish (length c. 21 cm) from the Cretaceous of Nardo, Italy. Original: Museo Civico di Storia Naturale, Verona, Italy.

Genus: Unnamed.

Geological range: Cretaceous.

Geographical distribution: Europe.

Features: Small to middle-sized fishes of slender shape. Head long and shallow. Snout pointed. Gape relatively long. Eyes small. Jaws with pointed teeth. Dorsal fin pointed, somewhat anterior to the middle of the body, opposite the small fan-shaped pelvic fins. Anal fin very small. Caudal fin deeply forked, with the lobes broad at the base and narrow towards the tips.

Remarks: Probably gregarious.

Recent relatives: Genus extinct. Possibly related to recent tenpounders of the genus *Elops*.

Elops hawaiiensis, a recent tenpounder.

TELEOSTEI
Order: Elopiformes
Family: Unnamed

True Bony Fishes

Daitingichthys tischlingeri ARRATIA (length c. 30 cm) from the Upper Jurassic of Solnhofen (Daiting), Bavaria, Germany. Original: Tischlinger Collection, Stammham, Germany.

Genus: *Daitingichthys* ARRATIA, 1987.

Geological range: Upper Jurassic.

Geographical distribution: Europe.

Features: Slender fishes with elongate bodies. Head shallow. Gape rather long. Eyes small. Dorsal fin triangular, in the posterior half of the body. Anal fin likewise small and somewhat more posterior. Pelvic fins very small and approximately in the middle of the body. Body covered with relatively large cycloid scales.

Remarks: Probably gregarious.

Recent relatives: None. Died out in Jurassic.

TELEOSTEI
Order: Elopiformes
Family: Megalopidae

True Bony Fishes
Suborder: Elopoidei
Tarpons

Pachythrissops propterus WAGNER (length c. 38 cm) from the Upper Jurassic of Solnhofen (Painten), Bavaria, Germany. Original: Bayerische Staatssammlung für Paläontologie, Munich, Germany.

Genus: *Pachythrissops* WOODWARD, 1919.

Geological range: Upper Jurassic to Lower Cretaceous.

Geographical distribution: Europe.

Features: Middle-sized fishes with rather laterally compressed bodies. Head deep. Gape rather long. Dorsal fin acute-triangular, somewhat behind the middle of the body, opposite small pelvic fins. Anal fin likewise acute-triangular. Pectoral fins narrow. Caudal fin deeply forked with relatively broad lobes.

Remarks: Probably rather slow swimmers which fed partly on plants.

Recent relatives: Genus extinct. Possibly related to recent tarpons of the family Megalopidae.

TELEOSTEI
Order: Elopiformes
Family: Megalopidae

True Bony Fishes
Suborder: Elopoidei
Tarpons

Sendenhorstia granulata (von der Marck) (length c. 9 cm) from the Upper Cretaceous of Sendenhorst, Westphalia, Germany. Original: Geologisch-Paläontologisches Museum, Münster, Westphalia, Germany.

Genus: *Sendenhorstia* White & Moy-Thomas, 1941.

Synonyms: *Microcoelia*.

Geological range: Upper Cretaceous.

Geographical distribution: Europe.

Features: Small fishes with somewhat laterally compressed bodies. Head large and deep. Gape rather long. Dorsal fin triangular, approximately in the middle of the body. Anal fin likewise triangular. Pelvic fins small. Pectoral fins narrow. Caudal fin forked with broad lobes.

Remarks: Probably gregarious.

Recent relatives: Genus extinct. Related to tarpons of the family Megalopidae.

Megalops cyprinoides, a recent tarpon.

TELEOSTEI
Order: Elopiformes
Family: Osmeroididae

True Bony Fishes
Suborder: Albuloidei

Osmeroides sardinoides Pictet (length c. 8 cm) from the Upper Cretaceous of the Lebanon. Original: Naturmuseum Senckenberg, Frankfurt-am-Main, Germany.

Genus: *Osmeroides* Agassiz, 1834.

Synonym: *Dermatoptychus*.

Geological range: Lower to Upper Cretaceous.

Geographical distribution: Europe, Middle East.

Features: Small fishes with elongate streamlined bodies. Head long and shallow. Snout pointed. Eyes large. Dorsal fin triangular, approximately in the middle of the body, opposite the short and narrow pelvic fins. Anal fin small. Pectoral fins narrow. Caudal fin forked, lobes broad at the base and pointed at the ends. Scales rounded.

Remarks: Probably gregarious.

Recent relatives: Genus extinct. Perhaps distantly related to recent bonefishes of the family Albulidae.

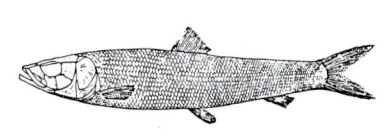

Osmeroides, reconstruction after Arambourg.

TELEOSTEI
True Bony Fishes
Order: Elopiformes
Family: Pterothrissidae
Suborder: Albuloidei

Hajulia multidens Woodward (length c. 7 cm) from the Upper Cretaceous of the Lebanon. Original: The Natural History Museum, London, U.K. (P 13906)

Genus: *Hajulia* Woodward, 1942.

Geological range: Upper Cretaceous.

Geographical distribution: Middle East.

Features: Small fishes with slender bodies. Head long and shallow. Snout pointed. Gape long. Dorsal fin approximately in the middle of the body, opposite the pelvic fins. Anal fin short. Caudal fin forked, with relatively broad lobes.

Remarks: Probably fed on worms and other small animals.

Recent relatives: Genus extinct. Possibly related to the recent genus *Pterothrissus*.

TELEOSTEI
Order: Elopiformes
Family: Pterothrissidae

True Bony Fishes
Suborder: Albuloidei

Istieus macrocephalus AGASSIZ (length c. 33 cm) from the Upper Cretaceous of Sendenhorst, Westphalia, Germany. Original: Geologisch-Paläontologisches Museum, Münster, Germany.

Genus: *Istieus* AGASSIZ, 1844.

Geological range: Upper Cretaceous.

Geographical distribution: Europe.

Features: Middle-sized fishes with slender elongate bodies. Head long and shallow. Gape short. Eyes large. Dorsal fin elongate and fringe-like, beginning in the anterior third of the body and decreasing in height posteriorly. Anal fin elongate and rounded. Pelvic fins small. Pectoral fins narrow. Caudal fin deeply forked, with broad lobes.

Remarks: These fishes, like their recent relatives, may have fed mainly on worms snails and other small animals.

Recent relatives: Genus extinct. Related to the recent genus *Pterothrissus*.

Istieus, reconstruction after FOREY.

515

TELEOSTEI
True Bony Fishes
Order: Elopiformes
Family: Pterothrissidae
Suborder: Albuloidei

Thrissopteroides elongatus von der Marck (length c. 20 cm) from the Upper Cretaceous of Sendenhorst, Westphalia, Germany. Original: Geologisch-Paläontologisches Museum, Münster, Westphalia, Germany.

Genus: *Thrissipteroides* Woodward, 1898.

Geological range: Upper Cretaceous.

Geographical distribution: Europe, Middle East.

Features: Small to middle-sized fishes with elongate, very slender bodies. Head shallow and elongate. Snout pointed. Dorsal fin in the posterior half of the body, opposite the narrow pelvic fins. Anal fin likewise narrow. Caudal fin deeply forked, with very narrow lobes.

Remarks: Probably fed on worms and other small animals living in the sea bottom.

Recent relatives: None. Died out in the Upper Cretaceous.

TELEOSTEI
Order: Elopiformes
Family: Albulidae

True Bony Fishes
Suborder: Albuloidei
Bonefishes

Lebonichthys lewisi (DAVIS) (length c. 30 cm.) from the Upper Cretaceous of the Lebanon. Original: The Natural History Museum, London, U.K. (P 6024)

Genus: *Lebonichthys* FOREY, 1973.

Geological range: Upper Cretaceous.

Geographical distribution: Middle East.

Features: Small to middle-sized fishes of very slender elongate outline. Head long and shallow. Snout pointed. Gape rather long. Eyes large. Dorsal fin broad-based, beginning in the anterior half of the body and decreasing in height posteriorly, opposite the very narrow pelvic fins. Anal fin triangular. Pectoral fins long and narrow. Caudal fin forked with relatively broad lobes.

Remarks: Probably gregarious.

Recent relatives: Genus extinct. Possibly related to recent bonefishes of the family Albulidae.

Albula sp., a recent bonefish. Lithograph from CUVIER.

517

TELEOSTEI
True Bony Fishes
Order: Elopiformes
Family: Pachyrhizodontidae
Suborder: Pachyrhizodontoidei

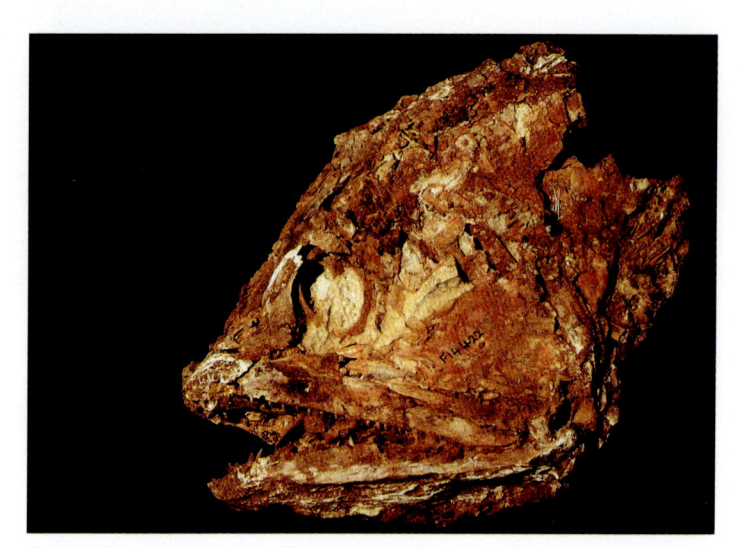

Pachyrhizodus marathonensis (ETHERIDGE) (length c. 22 cm) from the Lower Cretaceous of Queensland, Australia. Original: Queensland Museum, Brisbane, Australia.

Genus: *Pachyrhizodus* AGASSIZ, 1850.

Synonym: *Thrissopater*.

Geological range: Lower Cretaceous.

Geographical distribution: Europe, North America, Australia.

Features: Middle-sized to large fishes with deep heads. Snout pointed. Gape long, with pointed teeth. Eyes large.

Remarks: Predators.

Recent relatives: None. Died out in Lower Cretaceous.

TELEOSTEI
Order: Elopiformes
Family: Pachyrhizodontidae

True Bony Fishes
Suborder: Pachyrhizodontoidei

Rhacolepis buccalis AGASSIZ (length c. 14 cm) from the Lower Cretaceous of Ceará, Brazil. Original: Frickhinger Collection, Munich, Germany.

Genus: *Rhacolepis* AGASSIZ, 1841.

Geological range: Lower Cretaceous.

Geographical distribution: South America.

Features: Small to middle-sized fishes with slender, very streamlined bodies. Head long and shallow. Snout pointed. Gape long. Eyes relatively large. Dorsal fin in the posterior half of the body. Anal fin small. Pelvic fins very small. Pectoral fins narrow and somewhat longer. Caudal fin deeply forked, with narrow pointed lobes. Scales rhombic.

Remarks: Probably gregarious.

Recent relatives: None. Died out in Lower Cretaceous.

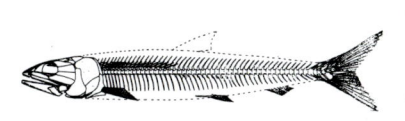

Rhacolepis, reconstruction after FOREY.

TELEOSTEI
True Bony Fishes
Order: Elopiformes
Family: Notelopidae
Suborder: Pachyrhizodontoidei

Notelops brama AGASSIZ (length c. 73 cm) from the Lower Cretaceous of Ceará, Brazil. Original: Frickhinger Collection, Munich, Germany.

Genus: *Notelops* WOODWARD, 1901.

Geological range: Lower Cretaceous.

Geographical distribution: South America.

Features: Middle-sized fishes with elongate streamlined bodies. Head elongate and shallow. Snout pointed. Gape very long. Eyes large. Dorsal fin relatively tall, probably ending distally in a point, obliquely opposite the narrow anal fin. Pelvic fins very small. Pectoral fins long and narrow. Caudal fin strikingly large, deeply forked, with narrow, strongly divergent lobes.

Remarks: Rapidly swimming predators.

Recent relatives: None. Died out in Lower Cretaceous.

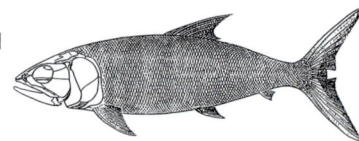

Notelops, after MAISEY.

TELEOSTEI
Order: Notacanthiformes
Family: Halosauridae

True Bony Fishes
Halosaurs

Echidnocephalus troscheli (von der Marck) (length c. 30 cm) from the Upper Cretaceous of Sendenhorst, Westphalia, Germany. Original: Geologisch-Paläontologisches Museum, Münster, Westphalia, Germany.

Genus: *Echidnocephalus* von der Marck, 1858.

Geological range: Upper Cretaceous.

Geographical distribution: Europe, North Africa.

Features: Middle-sized very slender fishes of eel-like shape. Head long and shallow. Dorsal fin very small, somewhat in front of the middle of the body. Anal fin fringe-like, reaching from the point of the tail to the middle of the body. Fins without spines.

Remarks: Predators.

Recent relatives: Genus extinct. Related to recent halosaurs of the family Halosauridae.

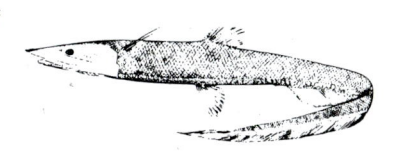

Halosauropsis macrochir, a recent halosaur (after Smith).

TELEOSTEI
Order: Notacanthiformes
Family: Notacanthidae

True Bony Fishes

Spiny Eels

Pronotacanthus sahelalmae DAVIS (length c. 14 cm) from the Upper Cretaceous of the Lebanon. Original: The Natural History Museum, London, U.K. (49542)

Genus: *Pronotacanthus* WOODWARD, 1900.

Geological range: Upper Cretaceous to Oligocene.

Geographical distribution: Europe, Middle East.

Features: Small to middle-sized fishes of elongate eel-like shape. Body ending posteriorly in a point. Head long and shallow. Snout rounded. Gape directed downwards. Eyes large. Dorsal fin replaced by a row of disconnected spines. Anal fin fringe-like.

Remarks: Predators.

Recent relatives: Genus extinct. Related to the recent spiny eel *Notacanthus*, now found living in the deep sea.

Notacanthus sp., a recent spiny eel. Lithograph from BLOCH.

TELEOSTEI
Order: Anguilliformes
Family: Anguillidae

True Bony Fishes
Suborder: Anguilloidei
True Eels

Anguilla pachyura AGASSIZ (length c. 87 cm) from the Miocene of Öhningen, Württemberg, Germany. Original: Teylers Museum, Haarlem, Netherlands.

Genus: *Anguilla* SHAW, 1803.

Geological range: Miocene to recent.

Geographical distribution: Europe.

Features: Middle-sized to large fishes with powerful eel-like bodies. Head shallow. Snout pointed. Eyes small. Dorsal and anal fins fused to form a fringe which reaches to the posterior pointed end of the body. Pectoral fins small and rounded.

Remarks: Predators.

Recent relatives: Closely related to recent eels of the genus *Anguilla*.

Anguilla anguilla, the European eel.

TELEOSTEI
True Bony Fishes
Order: Anguilliformes
Family: Anguillavidae
Suborder: Anguilloidei

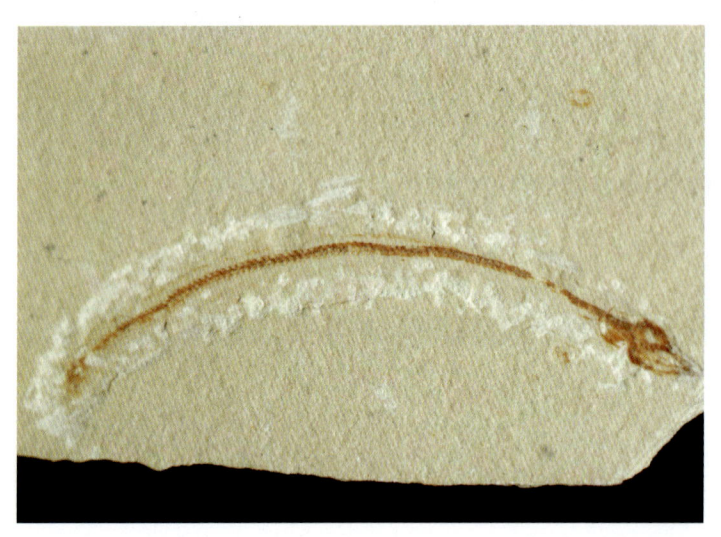

Anguillavus quadripinnis Hay (length c. 6.5 cm) from the Upper Cretaceous of the Lebanon. Original: American Museum of Natural History, New York, N.Y., U.S.A.

Genus: *Anguillavus* Hay, 1903.

Geological range: Upper Cretaceous.

Geographical distribution: Middle East.

Features: Small fishes with narrow eel-like bodies. Head shallow. Snout pointed. Eyes small. Dorsal and anal fins joined to form a low fringe running to the pointed posterior end of the body. Pectoral fins with eight rays.

Remarks: Probably fed on worms, crustaceans and other small animals.

Recent relatives: One of the earliest eels. Genus extinct. Perhaps nevertheless distantly related to recent eels.

TELEOSTEI
Order: **Anguilliformes**
Family: **Paranguillidae**

True Bony Fishes
Suborder: **Anguilloidei**

Dalpiaziella brevicauda CADROBBI (length c. 30 cm) from the Middle Eocene of Bolca, Italy. Original: Università di Padova, Padua, Italy.

Genus: *Dalpiaziella* CADROBBI, 1962.

Geological range: Middle Eocene.

Geographical distribution: Europe.

Features: Middle-sized to large fishes with elongate moray-eel-like bodies. Head shallow. Gape very long. Eyes small. Dorsal fin begins just behind the head and runs around the posterior end of the body into the anal fin which reaches to the middle of the ventral surface. Pectoral fins small.

Remarks: Predators. Probably lived like moray eels.

Recent relatives: None. Died out in the Eocene.

Dalpiazielliya, reconstruction after BLOT.

525

TELEOSTEI
Order: Anguilliformes
Family: Paranguillidae

True Bony Fishes
Suborder: Anguilloidei

Paranguilla tigrina (AGASSIZ) (length c. 30 cm) from the Middle Eocene of Bolca, Italy. Original: Bayerische Staatssammlung für Paläontologie, Munich, Germany.

Genus: *Paranguilla* BLEEKER, 1864.

Geological range: Middle Eocene.

Geographical distribution: Europe.

Features: Middle-sized fishes with rather broad eel-shaped bodies. Head deep. Snout pointed. Eyes small. Dorsal and anal fins joined to form a relatively tall fringe which begins immediately behind the head and runs to the pointed posterior end of the body. Pectoral fins small and rounded, located somewhat behind the beginning of the fringing fin.

Remarks: Predators.

Recent relatives: Genus extinct. Perhaps distantly related to recent moray eels.

Muraena helena, the Mediterranean moray eel.

TELEOSTEI
Order: Anguilliformes
Family: Xenocongridae

True Bony Fishes
Suborder: Anguilloidei
False Morays

Eomyrophis latispinus AGASSIZ (length c. 18 cm) from the Middle Eocene of Bolca, Italy. Original: Bayerische Staatssammlung für Paläontologie, Munich, Germany.

Genus: *Eomyrophis* WHITLEY, 1950.

Synonyms: *Eomyrus*.

Geological range: Middle Eocene.

Geographical distribution: Europe.

Features: Small to middle-sized fishes with slender eel-like bodies. Head shallow. Snout pointed. Eyes small. Dorsal fin and anal fins run together to form a low fringe which begins shortly behind the head and extends to the pointed posterior end of the body. Pectoral fins small.

Remarks: Probably fed on crustaceans and other small animals.

Recent relatives: Genus extinct. Probably related to recent false morays of the family Xenocongridae.

Kaupichthys sp., a recent false moray.

527

TELEOSTEI
Order: Anguilliformes
Family: Xenocongridae

True Bony Fishes
Suborder: Anguilloidei
False Morays

Mylomyrus frangens WOODWARD (length c. 31 cm) from the Eocene of Tura, Egypt. Original: The Natural History Museum, London, U.K. (P14484).

Genus: *Mylomyrus* WOODWARD, 1910.

Geological range: Eocene.

Geographical distribution: Northern Africa.

Features: Middle-sized fishes with slender elongate eel-shaped bodies. Head shallow. Snout pointed. Eyes small. Dorsal and anal fins run together as a fringe which is broad anteriorly but becomes narrower towards the pointed posterior end of the body. Jaws with obvious teeth. Pectoral fins small.

Remarks: Probably fed on worms, crustaceans and other small animals.

Recent relatives: Genus extinct. Possibly related to recent false morays.

TELEOSTEI
Order: Anguilliformes
Family: Xenocongridae

True Bony Fishes
Suborder: Anguilloidei
False Morays

Whitapodus breviculus (AGASSIZ) (length c. 7 cm) from the Middle Eocene of Bolca, Italy. Original: The Natural History Museum, London, U.K. (P24406a).

Genus: *Whitapodus* BLOT, 1980.

Geological range: Middle Eocene.

Geographical distribution: Europe.

Features: Small fishes of narrow eel-like shape. Head shallow. Snout pointed. Eyes small. Dorsal and anal fins join to form a fringe which is low anteriorly, broadens posteriorly, and then tapers again toward the pointed posterior end of the body.

Remarks: Probably fed on worms, crustaceans and other small animals.

Recent relatives: Genus extinct. Probably related to recent false morays.

Whitapodus, reconstruction after BLOT.

TELEOSTEI
Order: Anguilliformes
Family: Proteomyridae

True Bony Fishes
Suborder: Anguilloidei

Proteomyris ventralis (AGASSIZ) (length c. 20 cm) from the Middle Eocene of Bolca, Italy. Original: Teylers Museum, Haarlem, Netherlands.

Genus: *Proteomyris* CADROBBI, 1962.

Geological range: Middle Eocene.

Geographical distribution: Europe.

Features: Small to fishes with very slender, elongate, eel-shaped bodies. Head shallow. Snout pointed. Eyes small. Dorsal and anal fins run together as a low fringe which begins shortly behind the head and runs to the pointed posterior end of the body. Pectoral fins very small, located just beneath the anterior end of the fringe.

Remarks: Probably fed on worms, crustaceans and other small animals.

Recent relatives: None. Died out in Eocene.

Proteomyrus, reconstruction after BLOT.

TELEOSTEI
Order: Anguilliformes
Family: Anguilloididae

True Bony Fishes
Suborder: Anguilloidei

Anguilloides branchiostegalis (Eastman) (length c. 38 cm) from the Middle Eocene of Bolca, Italy. Original: Museo Civico di Storia Naturale, Verona, Italy.

Genus: *Anguilloides* Cadrobbi, 1962.

Geological range: Middle Eocene.

Geographical distribution: Europe.

Features: Middle-sized fishes with narrow eel-shaped bodies. Head shallow. Snout pointed. Eyes small. Dorsal and anal fins run together as a low fringe which begins shortly behind the head and runs to the pointed posterior end of the body. Pectoral fins very small and rounded.

Remarks: Probably fed on worms, crustaceans and other small animals.

Recent relatives: None. Died out in Middle Eocene.

Anguilloides, reconstruction after Blot.

531

TELEOSTEI
Order: Anguilliformes
Family: Anguilloididae

True Bony Fishes
Suborder: Anguilloidei

Veronanguilla ruffoi BLOT (length c. 30 cm) from the Middle Eocene of Bolca, Italy. Original: Museo Civico di Storia Naturale, Verona, Italy.

Genus: *Veronanguilla* BLOT, 1978.

Geological range: Middle Eocene.

Geographical distribution: Europe.

Features: Small to middle-sized fishes with very slender eel-shaped bodies. Head shallow. Snout pointed. Gape long. Dorsal fin low and fringe-like, begins in front of the middle of the body and continuous with the caudal and anal fins. Ventrally the fringe begins approximately in the middle of the body. Pelvic fins absent. Pectoral fins small.

Remarks: Predators.

Recent relatives: None. Died out in Eocene.

Veronanguilla, reconstruction after BLOT.

TELEOSTEI
Order: Anguilliformes
Family: Milananguillidae

True Bony Fishes
Suborder: Anguilloidei

Milananguilla lehmani BLOT (length c. 15 cm) from the Middle Eocene of Bolca, Italy. Original: Museo Civico di Storia Naturale, Verona, Italy.

Genus: *Milananguilla* BLOT, 1978.

Geological range: Middle Eocene.

Geographical distribution: Europe.

Features: Small fishes with very slender eel-shaped bodies. Head shallow. Snout pointed. Eyes small. Dorsal, caudal and anal fins form a continuous fringe. End of body pointed.

Remarks: Probably fed on worms, crustaceans and other small animals.

Recent relatives: None. Died out in Middle Eocene.

Milananguilla, reconstruction after BLOT.

TELEOSTEI
Order: **Anguilliformes**
Family: **Ophichthidae**

True Bony Fishes
Suborder: **Anguilloidei**
Snake Eels

Goslinophis acuticaudus (AGASSIZ) (length c. 32 cm) from the Middle Eocene of Bolca, Italy. Original: Museo Civico di Storia Naturale, Verona, Italy.

Genus: *Goslinophis* BLOT, 1980.

Synonyms: *Ophisurus*, *Ophichthys*.

Geological range: Middle Eocene.

Geographical distribution: Bolca, Italy.

Features: Middle-sized, extremely slender, eel-like fishes. Head shallow. Snout pointed. Eyes small. Dorsal and anal fins run together as a low fringe which begins shortly behind the head and runs to the pointed posterior end of the body. Pectoral fins very small.

Remarks: Probably fed on worms, crustaceans and other small animals.

Recent relatives: Genus extinct. Related to recent snake eels of the family Ophichthidae.

Myrichthys colubrinus, a recent snake eel.

TELEOSTEI
Order: Anguilliformes
Family: Congridae

True Bony Fishes
Suborder: Anguilloidei
Conger Eels

Bolcyrus bajai BLOT (length c. 24 cm) from the Middle Eocene of Bolca, Italy. Original: Museo Civico di Storia Naturale, Verona, Italy.

Genus: *Bolcyrus* BLOT, 1978.

Geological range: Middle Eocene.

Geographical distribution: Europe.

Features: Middle-sized fishes of slender eel-like shape. Head shallow. Snout pointed. Eyes small. Dorsal and anal fins run together as a low fringe to the pointed posterior end of the body. Pectoral fins very small and rounded.

Remarks: Probably predators.

Recent relatives: Genus extinct. Closely related to recent congers of the family Congridae.

Bolcyrus, reconstruction after BLOT.

TELEOSTEI
Order: Anguilliformes
Family: Congidae

True Bony Fishes
Suborder: Anguilloidei
Conger Eels

Conger sp. (length c. 30 cm) from the Pliocene of Fiume Marecchia, Italy. Original: Museo Civico di Storia Naturale, Verona, Italy.

Genus: *Conger* OKEN, 1817.

Geological range: Eocene to recent.

Geographical distribution: Europe, North America, New Zealand.

Features: Middle-sized fishes of very slender eel-like shape. Head shallow. Snout pointed. Gape rather long. Eyes small. Dorsal, caudal and anal fins form a continuous fringe which begins just behind the head and ends ventrally near the middle of the body. Pectoral fins small. Skin without scales.

Remarks: Predators.

Recent relatives: Closely related to recent congers of the genus *Conger* which occur in almost all oceans of the world.

Conger sp., a recent conger eel. Lithograph from BLOCH.

TELEOSTEI
Order: Anguilliformes
Family: Congridae

True Bony Fishes
Suborder: Anguilloidei
Conger Eels

Enchelion montium Hay (length c. 13 cm) from the Upper Cretaceous of Lebanon. Original: Siber & Siber Collection, Aathal, Switzerland.

Genus: *Enchelion* Hay, 1903.

Geological range: Upper Cretaceous.

Geographical distribution: Middle East.

Features: Small fishes with extremely slender bodies. Head small. Snout pointed. Fins probably formed a fringe.

Remarks: Probably fed on worms, crustaceans and other small animals.

Recent relatives: None. Died out in Upper Cretaceous.

TELEOSTEI
Order: Anguilliformes
Family: Congridae

True Bony Fishes
Suborder: Anguilloidei
Conger Eels

Pavelichthys daniltschenkoi BANNIKOV & FEDOTOV (length c. 9 cm) from the Lower Oligocene of the northern Caucasus. Original: Paleontologicheskii Musei Russkoi Akademii Nauk, Moscow, Russia.

Genus: *Pavelichthys* BANNIKOV & FEDOTOV, 1984.

Geological range: Lower Oligocene.

Geographical distribution: Eastern Europe.

Features: Small fishes with very slender elongate bodies. Head shallow. Snout pointed. Gape long. Eyes small. Dorsal caudal and anal fins continuous as a fringe which begins in the second third of the body and ends ventrally in the middle of the body. Skin without scales.

Remarks: Predators.

Recent relatives: None. Died out in Oligocene.

TELEOSTEI
Order: Anguilliformes
Family: Congridae

True Bony Fishes
Suborder: Anguilloidei
Conger Eels

Voltaconger latispinus (AGASSIZ) (length c. 25 cm) from the Middle Eocene of Bolca, Italy. Original: Museo Civico di Storia Naturale, Verona, Italy.

Genus: *Voltaconger* BLOT, 1978.

Geological range: Middle Eocene.

Geographical distribution: Europe.

Features: Middle-sized fishes of rather broad eel-like shape. Snout pointed. Eyes small. Dorsal, caudal and anal fins form a continuous fringe.

Remarks: Predators.

Recent relatives: Genus extinct. Closely related to recent congers of the family Congridae.

Voltaconger, reconstruction after BLOT.

TELEOSTEI
Order: Anguilliformes
Family: Serrivomeridae

True Bony Fishes
Suborder: Anguilloidei

Proserrivomer mecquenemi (PRIEM) from the Lower Oligocene of Iran. Original: Muséum National d'Histoire Naturelle, Paris, France. Photograph: Serette, Paris.

Genus: *Proserrivomer* ARAMBOURG, 1939.

Geological range: Oligocene.

Geographical distribution: Middle East.

Features: Small fishes with very slender eel-like bodies. Head shallow. Eyes large. Both jaws elongated to form a rostrum. Dorsal, caudal and anal fins form a continuous low fringe which begins dorsally in the second third of the body and extends ventrally to the anterior third of the body. Pectoral fins very small.

Remarks: Bottom-dwelling predators.

Recent relatives: Genus extinct. Perhaps related to recent eels of the genus *Serrivomer*.

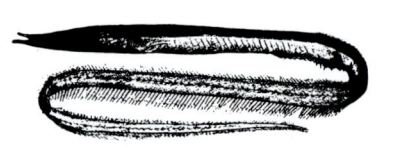

Serrivomer beanii. A recent serrivomerid eel.

540

TELEOSTEI
Order: Anguilliformes
Family: Patavichthyidae

True Bony Fishes
Suborder: Anguilloidei

Bolcanguilla brachycephala BLOT (length c. 26 cm) from the Middle Eocene of Bolca, Italy. Original: Muséum National d'Histoire Naturelle, Paris, France. Photograph: Serette, France.

Genus: *Bolcanguilla* BLOT, 1980.

Geological range: Eocene.

Geographical distribution: Europe.

Features: Middle-sized fishes with slender eel-like bodies. Head deep. Snout pointed-triangular. Dorsal, caudal and anal fins united to form a continuous fringe which reaches to the middle of the ventral surface. Pectoral fins very small.

Remarks: Predators feeding on small organisms.

Recent relatives: None. Died out in Eocene.

Bolcanguilla, reconstruction after BLOT.

TELEOSTEI
Order: Anguilliformes
Family: Patavichthyidae

True Bony Fishes
Suborder: Anguilloidei

Patavichthys bolcensis (BASSANI) (length c. 13 cm) from the Middle Eocene of Bolca, Italy. Original: Università di Padova, Padua, Italy. Photograph: Università di Padova.

Genus: *Patavichthys* BLOT, 1980.

Geological range: Middle Eocene.

Geographical distribution: Europe.

Features: Small fishes with slender elongate bodies. Head shallow, ending in a rostrum formed from upper and lower jaws with the ends of both slightly divergent. Dorsal fin fringe-like, extending from the middle of the body to shortly before the pointed posterior end of the body. Anal fin similar but begins more posteriorly. Pectoral fins very small.

Remarks: Bottom-dwellers. Probably fed on worms and other animals living in the bottom.

Recent relatives: None. Died out in Eocene.

Patavichthys, reconstruction after BLOT.

TELEOSTEI
Order: Anguilliformes
Family: Urenchelyidae

True Bony Fishes
Suborder: Anguilloidei

Urenchelys germanus Hay (length c. 16 cm) from the Upper Cretaceous of Lebanon. Original: Frickhinger Collection, Munich, Germany.

Genus: *Urenchelys* Woodward, 1900.

Geological range: Upper Cretaceous.

Geographical distribution: Europe, North Africa, Middle East.

Features: Fishes with slender eel-like bodies. Head shallow. Snout pointed. Dorsal and anal fins probably fringe-like, but the caudal fin is nevertheless clearly distinct.

Remarks: Probably predators.

Recent relatives: One of the earliest eels. Perhaps distantly related to recent eels.

TELEOSTEI
Order: Anguilliformes
Family: Unnamed

True Bony Fishes
Suborder: Anguilloidei

Unnamed eel (length c. 45 cm) from the Miocene of St. Margarethen, Austria. Original: Weiss Collection, Vienna, Austria. Photograph: Weiss, Vienna.

Genus: Not named.

Geological range: Middle Miocene.

Geographical distribution: Europe.

Features: Middle-sized fishes with slender eel-like bodies. Head small. Gape rather long. Eyes small. Jaws with very small, pointed, backwardly curved teeth. Dorsal, caudal and anal fins form a continuous fringe which begins dorsally shortly behind the head and extends ventrally over the posterior third of the body.

Remarks: Predators.

Recent relatives: Probably related to recent eels.

TELEOSTEI
Order: Ellimmichthyiformes
Family: Ellimmichthyidae

True Bony Fishes

Diplomystus dentatus COPE (length c. 28 cm) from the Eocene of Wyoming, U.S.A. Original: Frickhinger Collection, Munich, Germany.

Genus: *Diplomystus* COPE, 1877.

Synonyms: *Copeichthys*, *Histiurus*, *Hyperlophus*.

Geological range: Upper Cretaceous to Miocene.

Geographical distribution: Europe, South America, Africa.

Features: Middle-sized fishes with laterally compressed bodies and moderately deep bellies. Ventral keel with saw-tooth-like scales. Head short and deep. Snout slightly pointed. Gape rather long, directed upwards. Dorsal fin approximately in the middle of the body, small and pointed. Anal fin fringe-like. Caudal fin deeply divided.

Remarks: Fresh-water fishes feeding at least partly on plants.

Recent relatives: None. Died out in Miocene.

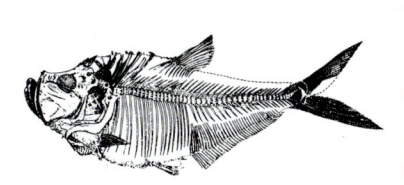

Diplomystus, reconstruction after JORDAN.

545

TELEOSTEI
True Bony Fishes

Order: Ellimmichthyiformes
Family: Ellimmichthyidae

Ellimma branneri JORDAN (length c. 9 cm) from the Upper Eocene of Alagos, Brazil. Original: American Museum of Natural History, New York, N.Y., U.S.A.

Genus: *Ellimma* JORDAN, 1913.

Geological range: Upper Eocene.

Geographical distribution: South America.

Features: Small fishes with laterally compressed bodies and deep bellies. Head deep. Snout somewhat pointed. Dorsal fin approximately in the middle of the body, small and pointed. Anal fin likewise small, more posterior. Small saw-tooth-like scales on the ventral keel. Caudal fin deeply divided with narrow lobes.

Remarks: Still-water fishes. Probably fed, at least partly, on plants.

Recent relatives: None. Died out in Upper Eocene.

TELEOSTEI
Order: Ellimmichthyiformes
Family: Ellimmichthyidae

True Bony Fishes

Ellimmichthys longicostatus (COPE) (length c. 15 cm) from the Lower Cretaceous of Itacaranha, Brazil. Original: The Natural History Museum, London, U.K. (P 7109)

Genus: *Ellimmichthys* JORDAN, 1919.

Geological range: Lower Cretaceous.

Geographical distribution: South America.

Features: Small fishes of laterally compressed shape, with a deep belly. Head short and deep. Snout rounded. Eyes small. The body rises to a point in the dorsal mid line and has sawtooth-like scales on the ventral keel. Dorsal fin immediately behind the dorsal apex, tall and pointed. Caudal fin deeply forked, with narrow lobes.

Remarks: Probably still-water fishes which fed, at least partly, on plants.

Recent relatives: None. Died out in Lower Cretaceous.

TELEOSTEI
True Bony Fishes
Order: Ellimmichthyiformes?
Family: Not named

Unnamed fish (length c. 8.5 cm) from the Upper Cretaceous of Lebanon. Original: The Natural History Museum, London, U.K.

Genus: Not named.

Geological range: Upper Cretaceous.

Geographical distribution: Middle East.

Features: Small fishes with deep belly. Head short and deep. Eyes large. Dorsal fin tall and pointed. Caudal fin very large, deeply forked with narrow lobes. Anal fin low and fringe-like. Saw-tooth-like scales on the ventral keel and on the posterior part of the dorsal mid line.

Remarks: Probably still-water fishes.

Recent relatives: None. Died out in Upper Cretaceous.

TELEOSTEI
Order: Ellimmichthyiformes?
Family: Unnamed

True Bony Fishes

Unnamed fish (length c. 10 cm) from the Upper Cretaceous of Bethel, Israel. Original: Staatliches Museum für Naturkunde, Karlsruhe, Germany.

Genus: Not named.

Geological range: Upper Cretaceous.

Geographical distribution: Middle East.

Features: Small fishes with very deep bellies. Dorsal mid line rises to an obtuse point. Head deep and short. Eyes large. Dorsal fin with a tall point anteriorly, but steeply decreasing in height and passing into a low fringe. Caudal fin divided with narrow lobes. Saw-tooth-like scales on the ventral keel.

Remarks: Probably still-water fishes.

Recent relatives: None. Died out in Upper Cretaceous.

TELEOSTEI
Order: Clupeiformes
Family: Denticipitidae

True Bony Fishes
Suborder: Denticipitoidei
Denticle Herrings

Palaeodenticeps tanganyikae GREENWOOD (length c. 3 cm) from the Miocene of Zingida, Tanzania. Original: The Natural History Museum, London, U.K. (P42616).

Genus: *Palaeodenticeps* GREENWOOD, 1960.

Geological range: Miocene.

Geographical distribution: Eastern Africa.

Features: Very small fishes of elongate slender shape. Head long and shallow. Eyes large. Dorsal fin in the posterior half of the body. Pectoral fins narrow. Caudal fin with concave posterior margin. Anal fin fringe-like. Spines on some scales and on the head.

Remarks: Gregarious freshwater fishes.

Recent relatives: Genus extinct. Related to recent denticle herrings of the genus *Denticeps*.

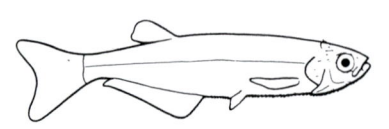

Denticeps clupeoides, the recent denticle herring (after NELSON).

TELEOSTEI
Order: Clupeiformes
Family: Clupeidae

True Bony Fishes
Suborder: Clupeoidei
Herrings

Alosa elongata AGASSIZ (length c. 31 cm) from the Upper Miocene of Oran, Algeria. Original: Muséum National d'Histoire Naturelle, Paris, France. Photograph: Serette, Paris.

Genus: *Alosa* LINCK, 1790.

Synonyms: *Alausa, Caspiolus, Clupeonella.*

Geological range: Miocene to recent.

Geographical distribution: Europe, northern Africa, western Asia.

Features: Middle-sized fishes of slender shape. Head short and deep. Gape short. Eyes small. Dorsal fin approximately in the middle of the body. Pectoral fins pointed. Pelvic fins very small. Caudal fin forked, with relatively broad lobes.

Remarks: *Alosa* has recently been considered as a synonym of *Pomolobus*.

Recent relatives: Closely related to fishes of the recent genus *Alosa*.

Alosa sp., the recent blueback.

551

TELEOSTEI
Order: Clupeiformes
Family: Clupeidae

True Bony Fishes
Suborder: Clupeoidei
Herrings

Clupea humilis Meyer (length c. 8 cm) from the Upper Miocene of Unterkirchberg, Württemberg, Germany. Original: Staatliches Museum für Naturkunde, Stuttgart, Germany.

Genus: *Clupea* Linnaeus, 1758.

Synonyms: *Alonsina, Clupeops, Sahelinia*.

Geological range: Eocene to recent.

Geographical distribution: Europe, South America, western Asia, East Indies, northern Africa.

Features: Small fishes of slender elongate shape. Head shallow and elongate. Gape rather long. Eyes large. Dorsal fin approximately in the middle of the body, opposite the small pelvic fins. Anal fin low and fringe-like. Caudal fin forked with broad lobes.

Remarks: This fish has recently been assigned to the genus *Clupeonella*.

Recent relatives: Closely related to the recent herring *Clupea harengus*.

Clupea harengus, the herring. Lithograph from Bloch.

TELEOSTEI
Order: Clupeiformes
Family: Clupeidae

True Bony Fishes
Suborder: Clupeoidei
Herrings

Domeykos profetaensis ARRATIA & SCHULTZE (length c. 13 cm) from the Upper Jurassic of northern Chile. Original: Universidad de Chile, Santiago, Chile.

Genus: *Domeykos* ARRATIA & SCHULTZE, 1985.

Geological range: Upper Jurassic.

Geographical distribution: South America.

Features: Small fishes with slender elongate bodies. Head shallow and elongate. Dorsal fin approximately in the middle of the body, opposite the small fan-shaped pelvic fins. Caudal fin forked.

Remarks: Probably gregarious.

Recent relatives: None. Died out in Upper Jurassic.

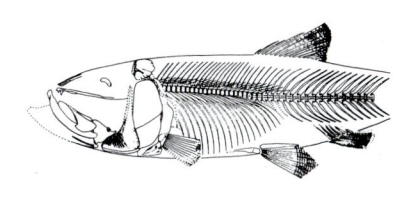

Domeykos, reconstruction after ARRATIA.

TELOSTEI
Order: Clupeiformes
Family: Clupeidae

True Bony Fishes
Suborder: Clupeoidei
Herrings

Erichalcis arcta FOREY (length c. 11 cm) from the Cretaceous of Hay River, Canada. Original: University of Alberta, Edmonton, Alberta, Canada.

Genus: *Erichalcis* FOREY, 1975.

Geological range: Cretaceous.

Geographical distribution: North America.

Features: Small fishes with slender bodies. Head long and shallow. Snout rounded. Dorsal fin opposite the pelvic fins. Caudal fin forked.

Remarks: Probably gregarious.

Recent relatives: None. Died out in Cretaceous. Belongs among the oldest known herrings.

TELEOSTEI
Order: Clupeiformes
Family: Clupeidae

True Bony Fishes
Suborder: Clupeoidei
Herrings

Etrumeus teres (de Kay) (length c. 14 cm) from the Pliocene of Fiume Marecchia, Italy. Original: Museo Civico di Storia Naturale, Verona, Italy.

Genus: *Etrumeus* Bleeker, 1853.

Synonyms: *Halecula*, *Parahalecula*.

Geological range: Oligocene to recent.

Geographical distribution: Western Asia, Europe, northern Africa.

Features: Small to middle-sized fishes of slender shape, but somewhat protruding ventrally. Head shallow. Gape rather long. Eyes large. Dorsal fin in the middle of the body, opposite the small pelvic fins. Anal fin low, broad-based. Pectoral fins narrow. Caudal fin deeply forked.

Remarks: Gregarious.

Recent relatives: Closely related to recent round herrings of the genus *Etrumeus*.

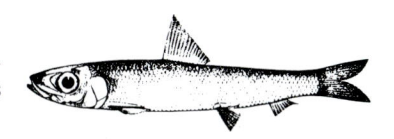

Etrumeus teres, a recent round herring, after Smith.

555

TELEOSTEI
Order: Clupeiformes
Family: Clupeidae

True Bony Fishes
Suborder: Clupeoidei
Herrings

Gosiutichthys parvus G<small>RANDE</small> (length c. 5 cm) from the Eocene of Wyoming, U.S.A. Original: Frickhinger Collection, Munich, Germany.

Genus: *Gosiutichthys* G<small>RANDE</small>, 1982.

Geological range: Eocene.

Geographical distribution: North America.

Features: Small to very small fishes with short, laterally compressed bodies. Head short and deep. Gape rather long and directed upwards. Eyes large. Dorsal fin pointed, somewhat anterior to the middle of the body, opposite the small pelvic fins. Anal fin rather broader at the base. Caudal fin divided with broad lobes.

Remarks: Gregarious freshwater fishes.

Recent relatives: None. Died out in Eocene.

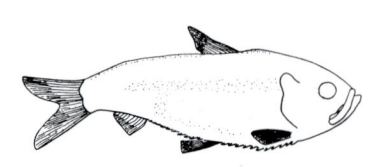

Gosiutichthys, reconstruction after G<small>RANDE</small>.

556

TELEOSTEI
Order: Clupeiformes
Family: Clupeidae

True Bony Fishes
Suborder: Clupeoidei
Herrings

Hilsa sp. (length c. 16 cm) from the Lower Pliocene of Transcaucasia. Original: Paleontologicheskii Muzei Russkoi Akademii Nauk, Moscow, Russia.

Genus: *Hilsa* REGAN, 1917.

Geological range: Lower Pliocene to recent.

Geographical distribution: Western Asia.

Features: Small to middle-sized fishes with elongate but nevertheless somewhat laterally compressed shape. Head shallow. Eyes moderately large. Snout rounded. Dorsal fin narrow, approximately in the middle of the body, obliquely opposite the small anal fin. Pelvic fins small. Pectoral fins somewhat fan-shaped. Caudal fin sharply forked.

Remarks: Probably gregarious. Lived in coastal areas and probably also in the fresh water of large rivers.

Recent relatives: Closely related to recent shads of the genus *Hilsa*.

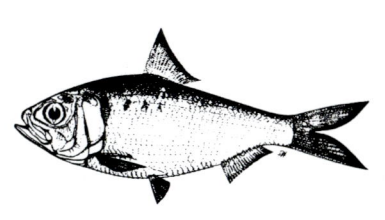

Hilsa kelee, a recent shad. After SMITH.

557

TELEOSTEI
Order: Clupeiformes
Family: Clupeidae

True Bony Fishes
Suborder: Clupeoidei
Herrings

Histiothrissa macrodactyla (von der MARCK) (length c. 25 cm) from the Upper Cretaceous of Sendenhorst, Westphalia, Germany. Original: Geologisch-Paläontologisches Museum, Münster, Germany.

Genus: *Histiothrissa* WOODWARD, 1901.

Geological range: Upper Cretaceous.

Geographical distribution: Europe, Middle East.

Features: Middle-sized fishes with relatively broad bodies. Head deep and elongate. Snout rounded. Dorsal fin large, triangular, opposite the pelvic fins which are likewise triangular. Anal fin low triangular. Pectoral fins very large, fan-shaped. Caudal fin forked, with broad lobes.

Remarks: Probably still-water fishes.

Recent relatives: None. Died out in Upper Cretaceous.

Histiothrissa, reconstruction after von der MARCK.

TELEOSTEI
Order: Clupeiformes
Family: Clupeidae

True Bony Fishes
Suborder: Clupeoidei
Herrings

Knightia alta (LEIDY) (length c. cm) from the Eocene of Wyoming, U.S.A. Original: Frickhinger Collection, Munich, Germany.

Genus: *Knightia* JORDAN, 1907.

Synonyms: *Ellimma*, *Ellipos*.

Geological range: Eocene.

Geographical distribution: North America, South America.

Features: Small to middle-sized fishes with slender, somewhat laterally compressed bodies. Head deep and short. Gape rather long. Dorsal fin triangular, approximately in the middle of the body, opposite the pelvic fins which are likewise triangular. Anal fin low triangular. Caudal fin forked, with broad lobes.

Remarks: Gregarious fresh-water fishes.

Recent relatives: None. Died out in Eocene.

TELEOSTEI
Order: Clupeiformes
Family: Clupeidae

True Bony Fishes
Suborder: Clupeoidei
Herrings

Ornategulum sardinioides (PICTET) (length c. 17 cm) from the Upper Cretaceous of Lebanon. Original: Field Museum of Natural History, Chicago, Illinois, U.S.A.

Genus: *Ornategulum* FOREY, 1973.

Geological range: Upper Cretaceous.

Geographical distribution: Middle East.

Features: Middle-sized fishes with slender elongate bodies. Head long and shallow. Gape rather long. Dorsal fin opposite the small pelvic fins. Pectoral fins narrow.

Remarks: The assignment to the family Clupeidae is uncertain.

Recent relatives: None. Died out in Upper Cretaceous.

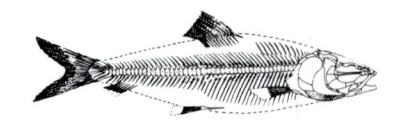

Ornategulum, reconstruction after FOREY.

TELEOSTEI
Order: Clupeiformes
Family: Clupeidae

True Bony Fishes
Suborder: Clupeoidei
Herrings

Pateroperca libanica GAUDANT (length c. 10 cm) from the Upper Cretaceous of the Lebanon. Original: Muséum National d'Histoire Naturelle, Paris, France. Photograph: Serette, Paris.

Genus: *Pateroperca* WOODWARD, 1942.

Geological range: Upper Cretaceous.

Geographical distribution: Middle East.

Features: Small to middle-sized fishes with rather slender bodies. Head deep. Snout rounded. Gape short. Eyes large. Dorsal fin tall, sail-like, in the middle of the body. Anal fin small, obliquely opposite the end of the dorsal fin. Pelvic fins long and narrow, almost opposite the pelvic fins which are likewise narrow but somewhat broader. Caudal fin broad, not forked.

Remarks: Probably not aggressive.

Recent relatives: None. Died out in Cretaceous.

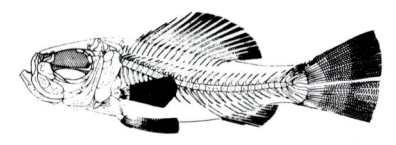

Pateroperca, reconstruction after GAYET.

TELEOSTEI
True Bony Fishes
Order: Clupeiformes
Family: Clupeidae
Suborder: Clupeoidei
Herrings

Pomolobus antiquus (SMIRNOV) (length c. 6 cm) from the Lower Oligocene of the Caucasus, C.I.S. Original: Paleontologicheskii Musei Russkoi Akademii Nauk, Moscow, Russia (Bannikov Collection).

Genus: *Pomolobus* RAFINESQUE, 1820.

Geological range: Miocene to recent.

Geographical distribution: Western and eastern Europe.

Features: Small fishes with elongate bodies, somewhat deeper anteriorly. Head deep. Snout rounded. Eyes small. Dorsal fin narrow, slightly anterior to the middle of the body, obliquely opposite the broad and ventrally located anal fin. Pelvic fins small. Pectoral fins somewhat longer. Caudal fin forked.

Remarks: Gregarious fishes which lived in the sea but probably sometimes entered the fresh water of large rivers.

Recent relatives: Closely related to recent river herrings of the genus *Pomolobus*.

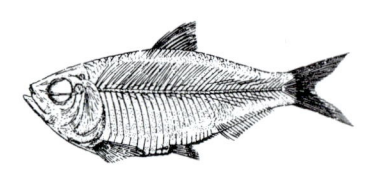

Pomolobus, reconstruction after Akademia Nauk, Moscow.

TELEOSTEI
Order: Clupeiformes
Family: Clupeidae

True Bony Fishes
Suborder: Clupeoidei
Herrings

Protoclupea chilensis ARRATIA, CHANG & CHONG (length c. 11 cm) from the Upper Jurassic of northern Chile. Original: Universidad de Chile, Santiago, Chile.

Genus: *Protoclupea* ARRATIA, CHANG & CHONG, 1975.

Geological range: Upper Jurassic.

Geographical distribution: South America.

Features: Small fishes of slender elongate shape. Head long and shallow. Eyes large. Dorsal fin approximately in the middle of the body, opposite the fan-like pelvic fins. Pectoral fins likewise fan-shaped. Caudal fin forked.

Remarks: Probably gregarious.

Recent relatives: None. Died out in Upper Jurassic. Belongs among the oldest herrings yet known.

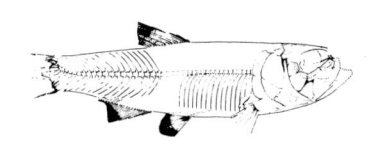

Protoclupea, reconstruction after ARRATIA & SCHULTZE.

TELEOSTEI
Order: Clupeiformes
Family: Clupeidae

True Bony Fishes
Suborder: Clupeoidei
Herrings

Pseudoberyx syriacus PICTET & HUMBERT (length c. 5.5 cm) from the Upper Cretaceous of Lebanon. Original: Museum für Naturkunde, Berlin, Germany.

Genus: *Pseudoberyx* PICTET & HUMBERT, 1866.

Geological range: Upper Cretaceous.

Geographical distribution: Middle East.

Features: Very small to small fishes with somewhat laterally compressed bodies. Head deep and short. Snout pointed. Eyes large. Dorsal fin opposite the pelvic fins. Caudal fin forked. Scales elongate rhombic and thick.

Remarks: Gregarious.

Recent relatives: None. Died out in Upper Cretaceous.

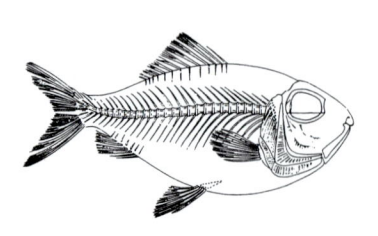

Pseudoberyx, reconstruction after PICTET & HUMBERT.

TELEOSTEI
Order: **Clupeiformes**
Family: **Clupeidae**

True Bony Fishes
Suborder: **Clupeoidei**
Herrings

Sardina pilchardus (WALBAUM) (length c. 13 cm) from the Pliocene of Fiume Marecchia, Italy. Original: Museo Civico di Storia Naturale, Verona, Italy.

Genus: *Sardina* ANTIPA, 1906.

Geological range: Pliocene to recent.

Geographical distribution: Europe.

Features: Small fishes of slender outline but ventrally slightly protruding. Head shallow. Gape rather long. Eyes large. Dorsal fin in the middle of the body, opposite the small pelvic fins. Anal fin low, broad-based. Pectoral fins narrow. Caudal fin deeply forked.

Remarks: Gregarious.

Recent relatives: The fossil and recent species are identical.

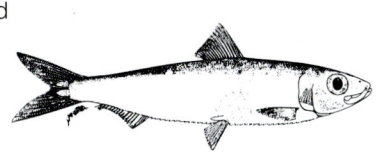

Sardina pilchardus. A recent sardine, after WHITEHEAD.

TELEOSTEI
Order: Clupeiformes
Family: Clupeidae

True Bony Fishes
Suborder: Clupeoidei
Herrings

Sardinella sardinites (Heckel) (length c. 8 cm) from the Middle Oligocene of the Caucasus, C.I.S. Original: Paleontologicheskii Musei Russkoi Akademii Nauk, Moscow, Russia.

Genus: *Sardinella* Valenciennes, 1847.

Geological range: Miocene to recent.

Geographical distribution: Western and eastern Europe.

Features: Small fishes with slender elongate bodies. Head shallow. Snout slightly pointed. Gape rather long. Eyes large. Dorsal fin small, in the middle of the body, opposite the pelvic fins which are likewise small. Pectoral fins fan-shaped. Caudal fin forked.

Remarks: Gregarious.

Recent relatives: Closely related to recent sardines of the genus *Sardinella*.

Sardinella sp., a recent sardine. Lithograph from Cuvier.

TELEOSTEI
Order: Clupeiformes
Family: Clupeidae

True Bony Fishes
Suborder: Clupeoidei
Herrings

Scombroclupea macrophthalma Heckel (length c. 12 cm) from the Upper Cretaceous of Lebanon. Original: Staatliches Museum für Naturkunde, Stuttgart, Germany.

Genus: *Scombroclupea* Kner, 1863.

Geological range: Upper Cretaceous.

Geographical distribution: Middle East.

Features: Small fishes with laterally compressed, elongate bodies. Head elongate. Snout pointed. Eyes large. Dorsal fin in the middle of the body, opposite the pelvic fins. Caudal fin rather deeply divided with lobes broad at the base and pointed at the ends.

Remarks: Probably gregarious.

Recent relatives: None. Died out in Upper Cretaceous.

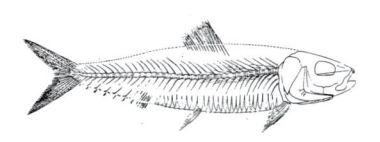

Scombroclupea, reconstruction after Piveteau.

567

TELEOSTEI
Order: Clupeiformes
Family: Clupeidae

True Bony Fishes
Suborder: Clupeoidei
Herrings

Spratelloides gracilis SCHLEGEL (length c. 6.5 cm) from the Pliocene of Fiume Marecchia, Italy. Original: Museo Civico di Storia Naturale, Verona, Italy.

Genus: *Spratelloides* de LACÉPÈDE, 1803.

Synonym: *Stolephorus*.

Geological range: Miocene to recent.

Geographical distribution: Europe, northern Africa, North America.

Features: Small fishes of slender shape. Head shallow. Gape rather long. Eyes large. Dorsal fin in the middle of the body, opposite the small pelvic fins. Anal fin low and broad-based. Caudal fin deeply forked.

Remarks: Gregarious.

Recent relatives: Closely related to recent round herrings of the genus *Spratelloides*.

Spratelloides sp., a recent sprat. Lithograph after CUVIER.

TELEOSTEI
Order: Clupeiformes
Family: Clupeidae

True Bony Fishes
Suborder: Clupeoidei
Herrings

Sprattus crenatus (length c. 9 cm) from the Oligocene of Flörsheim, Hesse, Germany. Original: Naturmuseum Senckenberg, Frankfurt-am-Main, Germany.

Genus: *Sprattus* GIRGENSOHN, 1846.

Synonym: *Meletta*.

Geological range: Oligocene to recent.

Geographical distribution: Europe.

Features: Small fishes with slender elongate bodies. Head long and shallow. Eyes large. Dorsal fin approximately in the middle of the body, opposite the small pelvic fins. Pectoral fins narrow. Caudal fin forked. Scales rounded.

Remarks: Gregarious.

Recent relatives: Closely related to recent sprats of the genus *Sprattus*.

Sprattus sprattus, the sprat. Lithograph from BLOCH.

569

TELEOSTEI
Order: Clupeiformes
Family: Clupeidae

True Bony Fishes
Suborder: Clupeoidei
Herrings

Xyne grex JORDAN & GILBERT (length c. 16 cm) from the Miocene of Lompoc, California, U.S.A. Original: Field Museum of Natural History, Chicago, Illinois, U.S.A.

Genus: *Xyne* JORDAN & GILBERT, 1919.

Geological range: Miocene.

Geographical distribution: North America.

Features: Middle-sized fishes of slender elongate shape. Head shallow. Dorsal fin opposite the small pelvic fins. Caudal fin forked.

Remarks: Probably gregarious.

Recent relatives: None. Died out in Miocene.

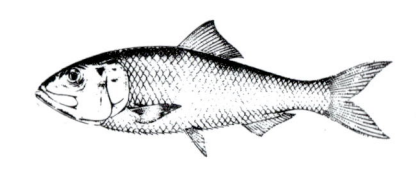

Xyne, reconstruction after JORDAN.

TELEOSTEI
Order: Clupeiformes
Family: Engraulidae

True Bony Fishes
Suborder: Clupeoidei
Anchovies

Engraulis tethensis GRANDE & NELSON (length c. 7 cm) from the Miocene of Lyssie, Cyprus. Original: The Natural History Museum, London, U.K. (P61224b).

Genus: *Engraulis* CUVIER, 1817.

Geological range: Miocene to recent.

Geographical distribution: Europe.

Features: Small fishes with slender elongate bodies. Head shallow and elongate. Gape long. Eyes large. Dorsal fin somewhat anterior to the middle of the body, opposite the pelvic fins. Pectoral fins narrow. Caudal fin forked, with broad lobes.

Remarks: Gregarious.

Recent relatives: Closely related to the recent anchovy *Engraulis*.

Engraulis encrasicholus, the European anchovy. Lithograph from BLOCH.

TELEOSTEI
Order: Clupeiformes
Family: Chirocentridae

True Bony Fishes
Suborder: Clupeoidei
Wolf Herrings

Platinx catulli HECKEL (length c. 90 cm) from the Middle Eocene of Bolca, Italy. Original: Museo Civico di Storia Naturale, Verona, Italy.

Genus: *Platinx* AGASSIZ, 1835.

Geological range: Middle Eocene.

Geographical distribution: Europe.

Features: Middle-sized to large fishes with elongate streamlined bodies. Head shallow. Gape long. Eyes large. Dorsal fin in the posterior third of the body, opposite the anal fin. Pectoral fins strikingly long and narrow.

Remarks: Rapidly swimming predators.

Recent relatives: Genus extinct. Perhaps distantly related to recent wolf herrings of the genus *Chirocentrus*.

Chirocentrus dorab, the wolf herring. Lithograph from BLEEKER.

EUTELEOSTEI
Order: Gonorhynchiformes
Family: Chanidae

Higher Bony Fishes
Suborder: Chanoidei
Milkfishes

Chanos zignii KNER & STEINDACHNER (length c. 39 cm) from the Oligocene of Chiavon, Italy. Original: Naturhistorisches Museum, Vienna, Austria. Photograph: Serette, Paris.

Genus: *Chanos* de LACÉPÈDE, 1803.

Geological range: Eocene to recent.

Geographical distribution: Europe.

Features: Middle-sized fishes with herring-shaped bodies. Head shallow. Snout slightly pointed. Eyes relatively large. Dorsal fin pointed, approximately in the middle of the body, opposite the small pelvic fins. Pectoral fins fan-shaped. Caudal fin large, deeply forked.

Remarks: Gregarious and probably herbivorous like their recent relatives.

Recent relatives: Closely related to the recent milk fish *Chanos*.

Chanos chanos, the milkfish.

EUTELEOSTEI
Order: Gonorhynchiformes
Family: Chanidae

Higher Bony Fishes
Suborder: Chanoidei
Milkfishes

Parachanos aethiopicus WEILER (length c. 22 cm) from the Upper Cretaceous of Gabon, Africa. Original: Muséum National d'Histoire Naturelle, Paris, France.

Genus: *Parachanos* ARAMBOURG, 1935.

Geological range: Lower to Upper Cretaceous.

Geographical distribution: Africa, South America, Europe.

Features: Small to middle-sized fishes of slender shape. Head deep. Snout pointed. Mouth small. Eyes small. Dorsal fin narrow, approximately in the middle of the body. Anal, pelvic and pectoral fins likewise small.

Remarks: Gregarious and probably plant eaters.

Recent relatives: Genus extinct. Distantly related to other milk fishes of the family Chanidae.

EUTELEOSTEI
Order: Gonorhynchiformes?
Family: Unnamed

Higher Bony Fishes
Suborder: Chanoidei?

Chanoides macropoma Woodward (length c. 12 cm) from the Middle Eocene of Bolca, Italy. Original: Museo Civico di Storia Naturale, Verona, Italy.

Genus: *Chanoides* Woodward, 1901.

Geological range: Middle Eocene.

Geographical distribution: Europe.

Features: Small fishes with slender herring-shaped bodies. Head shallow and elongate. Snout rather pointed. Eyes large. Dorsal fin pointed triangular, approximately in the middle of the body. Caudal fin forked.

Remarks: Probably gregarious.

Recent relatives: Genus extinct. Systematic position unclear. Sometimes assigned to the family Albulidae.

EUTELEOSTEI
Order: Gonorhynchiformes
Family: Gonorhynchidae

Higher Bony Fishes
Suborder: Gonorhynchoidei

Charitosomus hakelensis DAVIS (length c. 14 cm) from the Upper Cretaceous of Lebanon. Original: Museum für Geologie und Paläontologie, Tübingen, Germany.

Genus: *Charitosomus* von der MARCK, 1885.

Synonym: *Solenognathus*.

Geological range: Upper Cretaceous.

Geographical distribution: Europe, Middle East, North America.

Features: Small fishes with very slender elongate bodies. Head shallow and elongate. Gape rather long, directed slightly downwards. Dorsal fin small, approximately in the middle of the body, opposite the pelvic fins which are also small. Pectoral fins fan-shaped. Caudal fin only slightly forked.

Remarks: Probably bottom dwellers which fed on prey animals living in the sand.

Recent relatives: Genus extinct. Perhaps distantly related to recent members of the family Goniorhynchidae.

Charitosomus, reconstruction after PICTET & HUMBERT.

EUTELEOSTEI
Higher Bony Fishes
Order: Gonorhynchiformes
Family: Gonorhynchidae
Suborder: Gonorhynchoidei

Notogoneus osculus COPE (length c. 58 cm) from the Eocene of Wyoming, U.S.A. Original: Pabst Collection, Zürich, Switzerland.

Genus: *Notogoneus* COPE, 1885.

Synonyms: *Colpopholis*, *Phalacropholis*, *Protocarostomus*, *Sphenolepis*.

Geological range: Paleocene to Oligocene.

Geographical distribution: Europe, North America, Australia.

Features: Middle-sized fishes of slender elongate shape. Head shallow. Mouth opening ventrally. Eyes large. Dorsal fin small, somewhat behind the middle of the body, opposite the pelvic fins which are likewise small and rather fan-shaped. Anal fin elongate. Pectoral fins rounded and somewhat broader. Caudal fin slightly concave posteriorly.

Remarks: Fed on prey animals living in sand. Unlike their recent relatives, they inhabited fresh-water.

Recent relatives: Distantly related to recent members of the family Gonorhynchidae.

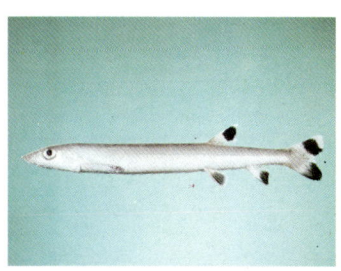

Gonorhynchus, a recent gonorhynchid.

EUTELEOSTEI
Higher Bony Fishes
Order: Gonorhynchiformes
Suborder: Gonorhynchoidei
Family: Unnamed

Aethalionopsis robusta (Traquair) (length c. 17 cm) from the Cretaceous of Bernissart, Belgium. Original: Musée Royal des Sciences Naturelles de Belgique, Brussels, Belgium.

Genus: *Aethalionopsis* Gaudant, 1966.

Geological range: Cretaceous.

Geographical distribution: Europe.

Features: Small fishes with a somewhat stout body. Head short. Snout area slightly pointed. Eyes small. Dorsal fin pointed, slightly behind the midpoint of the body. Anal and ventral fins small. Pectoral fins slightly fan-shaped. Caudal fin moderately forked.

Remarks: Probably schooling fishes.

Recent relatives: None, became extinct in the Cretaceous.

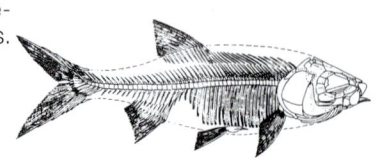

Aethalionopsis, reconstruction after Taverne

EUTELEOSTEI
Order: Cypriniformes
Family: Cyprinidae

Higher Bony Fishes

Minnows and Carps

Aspius gracilis AGASSIZ (length c. 8 cm) from the Miocene of Öhningen, Württemberg, Germany. Original: Paläontologisches Museum, Zürich, Switzerland.

Genus: *Aspius* AGASSIZ, 1832.

Geological range: Miocene to recent.

Geographical distribution: Europe.

Features: Small fishes of slender shape. Head elongate. Eyes large. Dorsal fin somewhat behind the anterior half of the body, opposite the small pelvic fins. Anal fin rather broader-based. Caudal fin moderately forked.

Remarks: Fossil fishes assigned to the genus *Aspius* have recently been considered as juveniles of the genus *Leuciscus*.

Recent relatives: Perhaps closely related to recent members of the genus *Aspius*.

Aspius aspius, the recent asp.

EUTELEOSTEI
Order: Cypriniformes
Family: Cyprinidae

Higher Bony Fishes

Minnows and Carps

Cyprinus priscus MEYER (length c. 17 cm) from the Miocene of Unterkirchberg, Allgäu, Germany. Original: Staatliches Museum für Naturkunde, Stuttgart, Germany.

Genus: *Cyprinus* LINNAEUS, 1758.

Geological range: Miocene to recent.

Geographical distribution: Europe.

Features: Middle-sized fishes with arched backs. Head short and deep. Dorsal fin behind the anterior convexity of the back, opposite the small pelvic fins. Anal fin narrow and fan-shaped. Caudal fin moderately forked.

Remarks: Lived in stagnant fresh water.

Recent relatives: Closely related to recent carps.

Cyprinus carpio, the carp. Lithograph from BLOCH (next page).

Rex Cyprinorum.
Der Spiegelkarpfen.
La Reine des Carpes.
The Royal Carp.

EUTELEOSTEI
Order: Cypriniformes
Family: Cyprinidae

Higher Bony Fishes

Minnows and Carps

Gobio analis AGASSIZ (length c. 5 cm) from the Miocene of Öhningen, Württemberg, Germany. Original: Teyler's Museum, Haarlem, Netherlands.

Genus: *Gobio* CUVIER, 1792.

Geological range: Miocene to recent.

Geographical distribution: Europe.

Features: Small fishes of slender shape. Head short. Eyes small. Dorsal fin triangular, somewhat behind the middle of the body, opposite the small pelvic fins. Anal fin likewise triangular. Caudal fin moderately forked.

Remarks: Fresh-water fishes. It has recently been suggested that fossil fishes of the genus *Gobio* are juveniles of the genus *Tinca*.

Recent relatives: Perhaps closely related to recent gudgeons of the genus *Gobio*.

Gobio gobio, a recent gudgeon.

EUTELEOSTEI
Order: Cypriniformes
Family: Cyprinidae

Higher Bony Fishes

Minnows and Carps

Leuciscus oeningensis AGASSIZ (length c. 9 cm) from the Miocene of Öhningen, Württemberg, Germany. Original: Staatliches Museum für Naturkunde, Stuttgart, Germany.

Genus: *Leuciscus* CUVIER, 1817.

Geological range: Oligocene to recent.

Geographical distribution: Europe.

Features: Small fishes of slender shape. Head elongate and flat. Gape relatively long. Dorsal fin triangular, approximately in the middle of the body, opposite the small pelvic fins. Anal fin triangular, broad-based. Caudal fin moderately forked.

Remarks: Fresh-water fishes.

Recent relatives: Genus extinct. Closely related to recent bitterling of the genus *Leuciscus*.

Leuciscus idus, the recent ide.

583

EUTELEOSTEI
Order: Cypriniformes
Family: Cyprinidae

Higher Bony Fishes

Minnows and Carps

Pseudorasbora macrocephala YOUNG & CHANG (length c. 4 cm) from the Miocene of Shantung, China. Original: The Natural History Museum, London, U.K. (P20972).

Genus: *Pseudorasbora* BLEEKER, 1860.

Geological range: Miocene to recent.

Geographical distribution: Asia.

Features: Small fishes with slender bodies. Head shallow and elongate. Dorsal fin in the posterior half of the body, opposite the narrow anal fin. Caudal fin forked.

Remarks: Fresh-water fishes.

Recent relatives: Genus extinct. Closely related to recent false rasboras of the genus *Pseudorasbora*.

Pseudorasbora parva, a recent barb.

EUTELEOSTEI
Order: Cypriniformes
Family: Cyprinidae

Higher Bony Fishes

Minnows and Carps

Rhodeus elongatus (length c. 5 cm) from the Miocene of Öhningen, Württemberg, Germany. Original: Paläontologisches Museum, Zürich, Switzerland.

Genus: *Rhodeus* AGASSIZ, 1832.

Geological range: Miocene to recent.

Geographical distribution: Europe.

Features: Small fishes with somewhat laterally compressed bodies. Head short and deep. Dorsal fin in the posterior half of the body, approximately opposite the anal fin. Pectoral and pelvic fins small. Caudal fin moderately forked.

Remarks: Fresh-water fishes. A new interpretation is that the fossil genus *Rhodius* may represent juveniles of the genus *Leuciscus*.

Recent relatives: Perhaps closely related to the bitterling *Rhodeus sericeus amarus*.

Rhodeus sericeus amarus, the recent bitterling.

585

EUTELEOSTEI
Order: Cypriniformes
Family: Cyprinidae

Higher Bony Fishes

Minnows and Carps

Richardsonius turneri (Lucas) (length c. 9 cm) from the Pliocene of the U.S.A. Original: National Museum of Natural History, The Smithsonian Institution, Washington, D.C., U.S.A.

Genus: *Richardsonius* Steindachner, 1866.

Geological range: Pliocene to recent.

Geographical distribution: North America.

Features: Small fishes with slender bodies. Head elongate. Snout pointed. Gape rather long. Dorsal fin in the middle of the body, approximately opposite the pelvic fins. Pectoral fins small and narrow. Anal fin somewhat broader.

Remarks: Fresh-water fishes.

Recent relatives: Closely related to recent members of the genus *Richardsonius*.

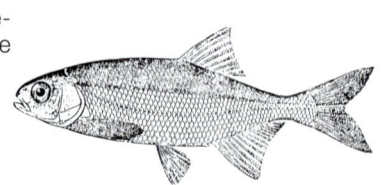

Recent *Richardsonius*, after Jordan.

EUTELEOSTEI
Order: Cypriniformes
Family: Cyprinidae

Higher Bony Fishes
Minnows and Carps

Rutilus rubilio (BP) (length c. 5 cm) from the Pleistocene of Riano, Italy. Original: The Natural History Museum, London, U.K. (P44671).

Genus: *Rutilus* RAFINESQUE, 1820.

Geological range: Eocene to recent.

Geographical distribution: Europe.

Features: Small fishes with elongate bodies. Head deep. Gape rather long. Dorsal fin low triangular, opposite the small pelvic fins. Caudal fin forked.

Remarks: Fresh-water fishes.

Recent relatives: Closely related to recent roaches of genus *Rutilus*.

Rutilus rutilus, the recent roach.

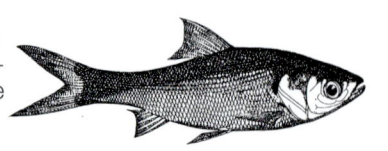

EUTELEOSTEI
Order: Cypriniformes
Family: Cyprinidae

Higher Bony Fishes
Minnows and Carps

Thynnichthys amblystoma (von der Marck) (length c. 14 cm) from the Tertiary of Panchung, Sumatra. Original: The Natural History Museum, London, U.K. (47522).

Genus: *Thynnichthys* Giglioli, 1880.

Geological range: Tertiary.

Geographical distribution: Indonesia.

Features: Small to middle-sized fishes with slender bodies. Head deep. Snout slightly rounded. Gape relatively long, directed somewhat upwards. Dorsal fin approximately in the middle of the body, opposite the small and narrow pelvic fins. Caudal fin forked.

Remarks: Probably predators.

Recent relatives: Closely related to recent members of the genus *Thynnichthys*.

Recent *Thynnichthys thynnoides*, after Weber.

588

EUTELEOSTEI
Order: Cypriniformes
Family: Cyprinidae

Higher Bony Fishes

Minnows and Carps

Tinca micropygoptera AGASSIZ (length c. 18 cm) from the Upper Miocene of Steinheim, Württemberg, Germany. Original: Staatliches Museum für Naturkunde, Stuttgart, Germany.

Genus: *Tinca* CUVIER, 1817.

Synonyms: *Tarsichthys*.

Geological range: Oligocene to recent.

Geographical distribution: Europe.

Features: Small to middle-sized fishes with relatively slender bodies. Head shallow and elongate. Snout slightly pointed. Dorsal fin approximately in the middle of the body. Pelvic fins and anal fin rounded. Pectoral fins small and somewhat narrower. Caudal fin moderately forked.

Remarks: Fresh-water fishes. Probably fed on plants and invertebrates.

Recent relatives: Genus extinct. Closely related to recent tenches of the genus *Tinca*.

Tinca tinca, the tench. Lithograph after BLOCH (see next page).

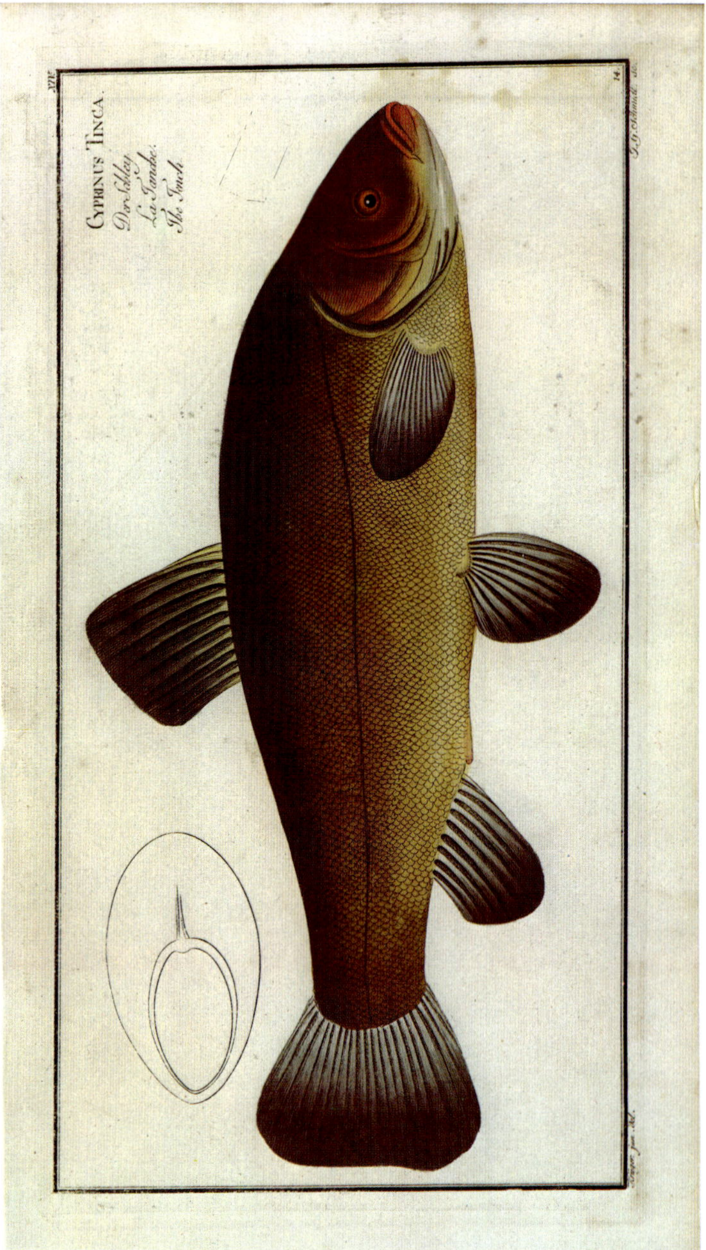
XIV.
Cyprinus Tinca.
Der Schley.
La Tanche.
The Tench.
14.

EUTELEOSTEI
Order: Cypriniformes
Family: Cobititidae

Higher Bony Fishes

Loaches

Cobitis centrochir Agassiz (length c. 10 cm) from the Miocene of Öhningen, Württemberg, Germany. Original: Teylers Museum, Haarlem, Netherlands.

Genus: *Cobitis* Linnaeus, 1758.

Synonyms: *Acanthopsis*.

Geological range: Oligocene to recent.

Geographical distribution: Europe.

Features: Small fishes with very slender elongate bodies. Head shallow and elongate. Mouth opening downwards. Eyes small. Dorsal fin approximately in the middle of the body, opposite the pelvic fins. Anal fin small and rounded. Pectoral fins long and somewhat fan-shaped. Caudal fin rounded.

Remarks: Bottom-dwelling fresh-water fishes.

Recent relatives: Closely related to recent loaches of the genus *Cobitis*.

Cobitis taenia, a recent loach.

EUTELEOSTEI
Higher Bony Fishes
Order: Cypriniformes
Family: Cobititidae

Loaches

Nemacheilus musceli PAUCA (length c. 5 cm) from the Oligocene of Muscel, Romania. Original: The Natural History Museum, London, U.K. (P16793).

Genus: *Nemacheilus* van HASSELT, 1823.

Geological range: Oligocene to recent.

Geographical distribution: Europe.

Features: Small fishes with exceedingly slender bodies. Head long and narrow. Eyes small. Mouth opening downwards. Dorsal fin rounded, slightly behind the middle of the body, opposite the elongate pelvic fins. Caudal fin forked.

Remarks: Bottom dwellers.

Recent relatives: Closely related to recent loaches of the genus *Nemacheilus*.

Nemacheilus barbatulus, the recent brook loach.

EUTELEOSTEI — Higher Bony Fishes

Order: Cypriniformes
Family: Catostomidae — Suckers

Amyzon aggregatum WILSON (length c. 22 cm) from the Middle Eocene of British Columbia, Canada. Original: Royal Ontario Museum, Toronto, Ontario, Canada

Genus: *Amyzon* COPE, 1872.

Geological range: Eocene to Oligocene.

Geographical distribution: North America.

Features: Middle-sized fishes with laterally compressed carp-like bodies. Head deep and short. Dorsal fin with a point anteriorly, running rearwards into a fringe. Pectoral fins slightly rounded, like the pelvic fins. Anal fin somewhat broader. Caudal fin large, somewhat concave behind.

Remarks: Probably fed on plants and invertebrates. Freshwater fishes.

Recent relatives: Genus extinct. Nevertheless related to recent suckers of the family Catostomidae.

Catostomus commersonii, a recent sucker.

593

EUTELEOSTEI
Higher Bony Fishes
Order: Characiformes
Family: Clupavidae

Lusitanichthys sp. (length c. 5 cm) from the Cretaceous of Nardo, Italy. Original: Museo Civico di Storia Naturale, Verona, Italy.

Genus: *Lusitanichthys* GAYET, 1981.

Geological range: Cretaceous.

Geographical distribution: Europe.

Features: Small fishes of slender, streamlined shape. Head relatively deep. Eyes large. Gape rather long. Snout rounded. Dorsal fin narrow, approximately in the middle of the body, opposite the pelvic fins which are likewise narrow. Anal fin short. Pectoral fins long and narrow. Caudal fin forked.

Remarks: Probably gregarious.

Recent relatives: None. Died out in the Cretaceous.

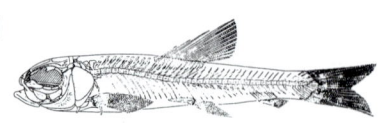

Lusitanichthys, reconstruction after GAYET.

EUTELEOSTEI
Higher Bony Fishes
Order: Characiformes
Family: Characidae

True Characins

Brycon avus WOODWARD (length c. 11 cm) from the Miocene of Taubaté, Brazil. Original: The Natural History Museum, London, U.K. (P9224).

Genus: *Brycon* MÜLLER & TROSCHEL, 1844.

Geological range: Oligocene to recent.

Geographical distribution: South America.

Features: Small fishes of slender shape. Head shallow. Dorsal fin relatively tall, approximately in the middle of the body, opposite the small pelvic fins. Pectoral fins narrow. Anal fin running off into a fringe. Caudal fin forked.

Remarks: Fresh-water fishes.

Recent relatives: Closely related to recent members of the genus *Brycon* and to other characins of the subfamily Bryconinae.

Brycon falcatus, a recent characin.

EUTELEOSTEI

Higher Bony Fishes

Order: Characiformes
Family: Characidae

True Characins

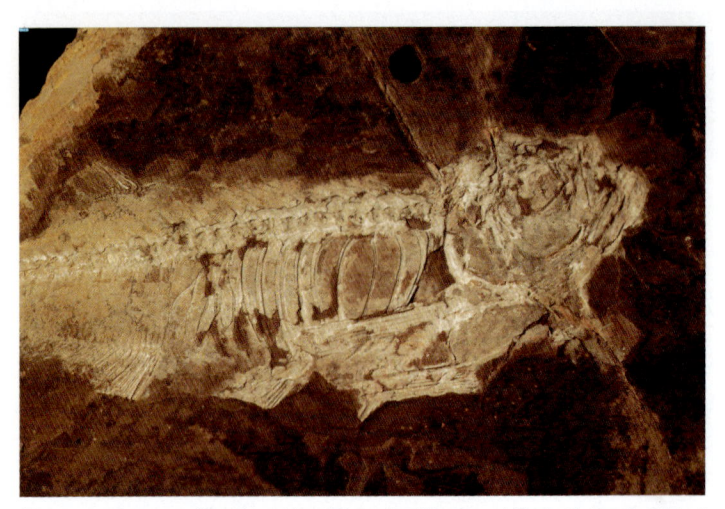

Tetragonopterus sp. (length c. 11 cm) from the Miocene of Taubaté, Brazil. Original: Naturhistorisches Museum Vienna, Austria.

Genus: *Tetragonopterus* CUVIER, 1817.

Geological range: Miocene to recent.

Geographical distribution: South America.

Features: Small fishes with slender bodies. Head elongate. Dorsal fin shortly behind the middle of the body, opposite the somewhat fringe-like anal fin. Pelvic fins small. Pectoral fins elongate. Caudal fin forked.

Remarks: Fresh-water fishes.

Recent relatives: Closely related to recent members of the genus *Tetragonopterus* and to many characins of the subfamily Tetragonopterinae.

Tetragonopterus argenteus, the recent silver tetra.

EUTELEOSTEI
Order: Characiformes
Family: Characidae

Higher Bony Fishes
True Characins

Triportheus ligniticus (WOODWARD) (length c. 9 cm) from the Miocene of Taubaté, Brazil. Original: The Natural History Museum, London, U.K. (P25001).

Genus: *Triportheus* COPE, 1872.

Synonym: *Lignobrycon*

Geological range: Miocene to recent.

Geographical distribution: South America.

Features: Small fishes of slender, almost herring-like shape. Head shallow. Dorsal fin shortly behind the anterior half of the body, opposite the small pelvic fins. Pectoral fins very long and very powerful. Caudal fin forked.

Remarks: Fresh-water fishes. In view of their powerful pectoral fins, they could presumably "fly" like their recent relatives.

Recent relatives: Closely related to the recent members of the genus *Triportheus* and to other characins of the subfamily Tryconinae.

Triportheus angulatus, the recent narrow hatchetfish.

EUTELEOSTEI — Higher Bony Fishes
Order: Siluriformes
Family: Hypsidoridae

Hypsidoris farsonensis LUNDBERG & CASE (length c. 26 cm) from the Eocene of Wyoming, U.S.A. Original: Field Museum of Natural History, Chicago, Illinois, U.S.A.

Genus: *Hypsidoris* LUNDBERG & CASE, 1970.

Geological range: Eocene.

Geographical distribution: North America.

Features: Middle-sized fishes with laterally compressed bodies, ventrally slightly flattened. Head broad and flat. Dorsal fin immediately behind the head, carried by a powerful spine. Pelvic fins small. Pectoral fins elongate. Anal fin broad-based. Caudal fin slightly concave posteriorly.

Remarks: Fresh-water fishes, mainly bottom-dwelling but partly also free-swimming.

Recent relatives: Distantly related to recent catfishes of the family Ictaluridae.

Ictalurus melas, a recent catfish.

EUTELEOSTEI

Order: Siluriformes
Family: Ictaluridae

Higher Bony Fishes

Bullhead Catfishes

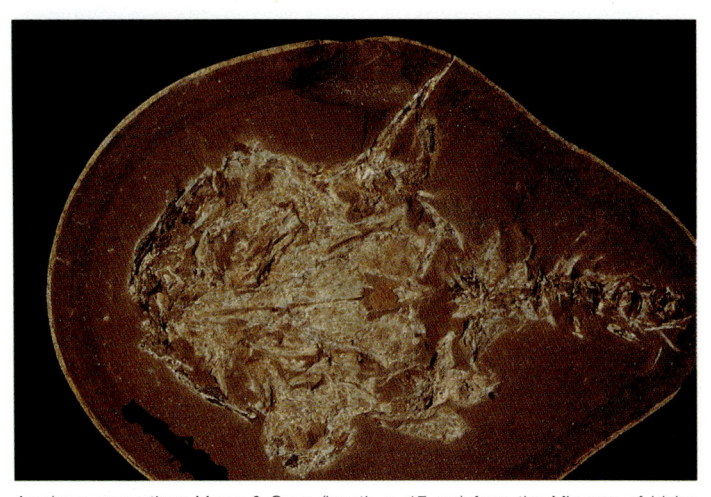

Ameiurus vespertinus MILLER & SMITH (length c. 17 cm) from the Miocene of Idaho, U.S.A. Original: Field Museum of Natural History, Chicago, Illinois, U.S.A.

Genus: *Ameiurus* RAFINESQUE, 1820.

Synonym: *Ictalurus*.

Geological range: Oligocene to recent.

Geographical distribution: Asia, North America.

Features: Middle-sized fishes with laterally compressed bodies. Head powerful and broad. In the neck region, immediately behind the head, is a powerful spine carrying the dorsal fin. Caudal fin deeply concave posteriorly.

Remarks: Fresh-water fishes, mainly bottom-dwelling but sometimes also free-swimming.

Recent relatives: Closely related to North American fresh-water catfishes of the genus *Ameirus*.

Ictalurus (*Ameiurus*) *nebulosus*, the recent brown bullhead.

EUTELEOSTEI
Order: Siluriformes
Family: Ictaluridae

Higher Bony Fishes
Bullhead Catfishes

Astephas antiquus (LEIDY) (length c. 14 cm) from the Eocene of Wyoming, U.S.A. Original: Field Museum of Natural History, Chicago, Illinois, U.S.A.

Genus: *Astephas* COPE, 1873.

Synonym: *Rhineastes*.

Geological range: Eocene to recent.

Geographical distribution: North America.

Features: Small to middle-sized fishes with cylindrical bodies. Head large, broad and flat. Gape long and broad. Dorsal fin and pectoral fins each borne by a powerful spine. Caudal fin deeply forked.

Remarks: Fresh-water fishes, mostly bottom-dwelling but sometimes free-swimming.

Recent relatives: Related to recent cat fishes of the family Ictaluridae.

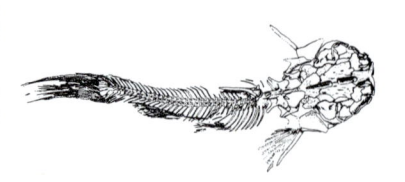

Astephas, reconstruction after GRANDE.

EUTELEOSTEI
Order: Siluriformes
Family: Bagridae

Higher Bony Fishes

Bagrid Catfishes

Aoria saropteryx (von der Marck) (length c. 28 cm) from the Oligocene of Sipang, Sumatra. Original: Museum für Geologie und Paläontologie, Tübingen, Germany.

Genus: *Aoria* Jordan, 1919.

Geological range: Oligocene.

Geographical distribution: Southeastern Asia.

Features: Middle-sized fishes with laterally compressed bodies. Head large and broad. A powerful spine in the neck region carries the dorsal fin. Pectoral fins also with spines. Caudal fin forked.

Remarks: Fresh-water fishes, bottom-dwelling and free-swimming.

Recent relatives: Related to recent spiny catfishes of the family Bagridae.

Bagrus sp., a recent bagrid catfish. Lithograph from Bloch.

601

EUTELEOSTEI
Order: Siluriformes
Family: Pangasiidae

Higher Bony Fishes

Shark Catfishes

Pangasius indicus (von der MARCK) (length c. 35 cm) from the Oligocene of Sipang, Sumatra. Original: Museum für Geologie und Paläontologie, Tübingen, Germany.

Genus: *Pangasius* BLEEKER, 1846.

Geological range: Oligocene to recent.

Geographical distribution: Southeastern Asia.

Features: Middle-sized fishes with elongate bodies, approximately circular in section. Head large and broad, flattened towards the snout. A powerful spine in the rear part of the head. Dorsal fin approximately in the middle of the body. Caudal fin strongly forked.

Remarks: Bottom-dwelling and free-swimming. Perhaps ate plants, like many of its recent relatives.

Recent relatives: Closely related to recent pangasiid catfishes of the genus *Pangasius*.

Pangasius sutchi, a recent shark catfish.

EUTELEOSTEI
Order: Siluriformes
Family: Pimelodidae

Higher Bony Fishes
Antenna Catfishes

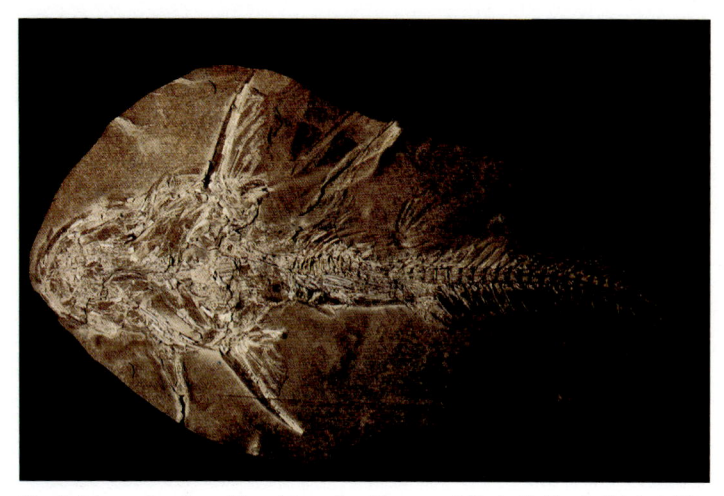

Pimelodus sp. (length c. 27 cm) from the Miocene of Taubaté, Brazil. Original: The Natural History Museum, London, U.K. (P9010).

Genus: *Pimelodus* de Lacépède, 1803.

Geological range: Miocene to recent.

Geographical distribution: South America, Africa.

Features: Middle-sized fishes with laterally compressed but ventrally flattened bodies. Head broad and flat. Pectoral fins small, with a spine. Dorsal fin approximately in the middle of the body. Pelvic fins very small. Caudal fin moderately forked.

Remarks: Bottom-dwelling fresh-water fishes.

Recent relatives: Closely related to the recent antenna catfish *Pimelodus*.

Pimelodus, a recent antenna catfish.

603

EUTELEOSTEI
Order: Siluriformes
Family: Callichthyidae

Higher Bony Fishes
Armoured Catfishes

Corydoras revelatus COCKERELL (length c. 3 cm) from the Miocene of Sunchal, Argentina. Original: The Natural History Museum, London, U.K. (P136179).

Genus: *Corydoras* de LACÉPÈDE, 1803.

Geological range: Miocene to recent.

Geographical distribution: South America.

Features: Small fishes with laterally compressed but ventrally flattened bodies. Dorsal surface armoured with V-shaped plates of bone. Ventral surface unarmoured. Head short and deep. Eyes small. In the nape region there is a powerful spine which carries the dorsal fin. Caudal fin relatively large, moderately forked.

Remarks: Bottom-dwelling fresh-water fishes.

Recent relatives: Closely related to the recent corycats of the genus *Corydoras*.

Corydoras arcuatus, a recent armoured catfish.

EUTELEOSTEI
Order: Unnamed
Family: Unnamed

Higher Bony Fishes

Pharmacichthys venenifer WOODWARD (length c. 4 cm) from the Upper Cretaceous of Lebanon. Original: The Natural History Museum, London, U.K.

Genus: *Pharmacichthys* WOODWARD, 1942.

Geological range: Upper Cretaceous.

Geographical distribution: Middle East.

Features: Small fishes with broadly oval outline, laterally compressed. Head deep. Snout slightly pointed. On the highest point of the body is a long thin spine which probably carried the very tall dorsal fin. Pelvic and pectoral fins small. Anal fin. Caudal fin strongly forked.

Remarks: Probably still-water fishes. The name suggests a poisonous fish, referring to the first ray of the dorsal fin. The poisonous nature of this spine, however, is not proven. Systematic position uncertain.

Recent relatives: None. Died out in Upper Cretaceous.

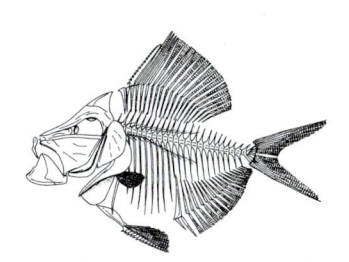

Pharmacichthys, reconstruction after PATTERSON.

EUTELEOSTEI
Order: Salmoniformes
Family: Palaeosocidae

Higher Bony Fishes
Suborder: Esocoidei

Boltyshia brevicauda SYTCHEVSKAYA & DANILTCHENKO (length c. 8 cm) from the Upper Paleocene of C.I.S. Original: Paleontologicheskii Muzei Russkoi Akademii Nauk, Moscow, Russia.

Genus: *Boltyshia* SYTCHEVSKAYA & DANILTCHENKO, 1975.

Geological range: Upper Palaeocene.

Geographical distribution: Eastern Europe.

Features: Small fishes with slender elongate bodies. Head shallow. Eyes small. Snout very pointed. Gape long. Dorsal fin pointed, in the posterior third of the body, opposite the anal fin. Pelvic fins small. Pectoral fins somewhat fan-shaped. Anal fin. Caudal fin not forked, probably emarginate.

Remarks: Fresh-water predators.

Recent relatives: None. Died out in Paleocene.

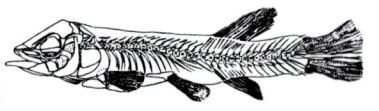

Boltyshia, reconstruction after Akademia Nauk, Moscow.

EUTELEOSTEI
Order: Salmoniformes
Family: Esocidae

Higher Bony Fishes
Suborder: Esocoidei
Pikes

Esox lepidotus AGASSIZ (length c. 70 cm) from the Miocene of Öhningen, Württemberg, Germany. Original: Staatliches Museum für Naturkunde, Karlsruhe, Germany.

Genus: *Esox* LINNAEUS, 1758.

Synonyms: *Trematina*.

Geological range: Paleocene to recent.

Geographical distribution: Europe, Asia, North America.

Features: Middle-sized fishes with slender streamlined bodies. Head elongate. Snout flattened. Eyes small. Dorsal fin very posterior, opposite the anal fin which is of the same size. Pelvic fins small. Pectoral fins obliquely fan-shaped. Caudal fin strongly forked.

Remarks: Fresh-water predators.

Recent relatives: Closely related to the recent pike.

Esox lucius, the pike. Lithograph from BLOCH (see next page).

XXXII
ESOX LUCIO.
Der Hecht.
Le Brochet.
The Pike.
Krüger jun. del.

EUTELEOSTEI — Higher Bony Fishes

Order: Salmoniformes
Family: Umbridae

Suborder: Esocoidei
Mud Minnows

Umbra perpusilla (AGASSIZ) (length c. 3 cm) from the Miocene of Öhningen, Württemberg, Germany. Original: Teylers Museum, Haarlem, Netherlands.

Genus: *Umbra* GRONOV, 1763.

Geological range: Oligocene to recent.

Geographical distribution: Europe.

Features: Very small fishes of slender shape. Head shallow. Snout pointed. Eyes small. Mouth opening downwards. Dorsal fin rounded, very posterior, opposite the elongate anal fin. Caudal fin with a convex margin.

Remarks: Fresh-water fishes which fed on small animals.

Recent relatives: Closely related to the recent mud minnows.

Umbra pygmaea, the recent mud minnow.

EUTELEOSTEI
Order: Salmoniformes
Family: Argentinidae?

Higher Bony Fishes
Suborder: Argentinoidei
Herring Smelts

Unnamed fish (length c. 7.5 cm) from the Eocene of Fuur, Denmark. Original: Paleontologiska Muséet, Uppsala, Sweden.

Genus: Not named.

Geological range: Eocene.

Geographical distribution: Europe.

Features: Small, very slender fishes with streamlined bodies. Head shallow. Eyes large. Snout pointed. Dorsal fin small and pointed, opposite the fan-shaped pelvic fins. Caudal fin deeply forked, with narrow lobes.

Remarks: Gregarious.

Recent relatives: Genus probably extinct. Perhaps closely related to recent herring smelts of the family Argentinidae.

EUTELEOSTEI   Higher Bony Fishes
Order: Salmoniformes   Suborder: Argentinoidei
Family: Bathylagidae   Deep-Sea Smelts

Bathylagus angelensis JORDAN & GILBERT (length c. 8 cm) from the Miocene of California, U.S.A. Original: Siber & Siber Collection, Aathal, Switzerland.

Genus: *Bathylagus* GÜNTHER, 1878.

Geological range: Miocene to recent.

Geographical distribution: North America.

Features: Small fishes of slender elongate shape. Head shallow. Eyes large. Gape rather long. Dorsal fin pointed, approximately in the middle of the body, opposite the elongate pelvic fins. Anal fin rounded. Caudal fin slightly forked.

Remarks: Probably lived in the upper layers of the sea.

Recent relatives: Closely related to recent deep sea smelts of the genus *Bathylagus*.

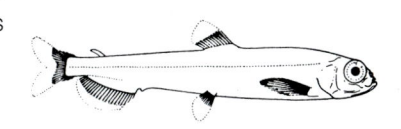

Bathylagus berycoides, a recent deep sea smelt, after NORMAN.

EUTELEOSTEI
Order: Salmoniformes
Family: Unnamed

Higher Bony Fishes
Suborder: Argentinoidei

Gaudryella gaudryi (PICTET & HUMBERT) (length c. 11 cm) from the Upper Cretaceous of Lebanon. Original: Henne Collection, Stuttgart, Germany.

Genus: *Gaudryella* PATTERSON, 1970.

Synonyms: *Eoclupea*.

Geological range: Upper Cretaceous.

Geographical distribution: Middle East.

Features: Small fishes with elongate bodies. Head elongate. Snout pointed. Gape long. Dorsal fin in the anterior half of the body. Caudal fin deeply forked.

Remarks: Probably gregarious.

Recent relatives: None. Died out in Upper Cretaceous.

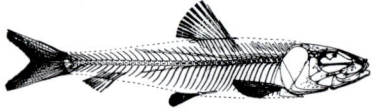

Gaudryella, reconstruction after PICTET & HUMBERT.

EUTELEOSTEI
Order: Salmoniformes
Family: Unnamed

Higher Bony Fishes
Suborder: Argentinoidei

Humbertia operta PATTERSON (length c. 10 cm) from the Eocene of Bolca, Italy. Original: American Museum of Natural History, New York, N.Y., U.S.A..

Genus: *Humbertia* PATTERSON, 1970.

Geological range: Upper Cretaceous to Eocene.

Geographical distribution: Europe, Middle East.

Features: Small fishes of elongate shape. Head elongate. Eyes large. Dorsal fin somewhat anterior to the middle of the body. Pectoral fins fan-shaped. Caudal fin forked.

Remarks: Probably gregarious.

Recent relatives: None. Died out in Eocene.

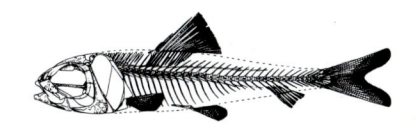

Humbertia, reconstruction after PATTERSON.

613

EUTELEOSTEI
Order: Salmoniformes
Family: Osmeridae

Higher Bony Fishes
Suborder: Osmeroidei
Smelts

Mallotus villosus Cuvier (length c. 12 cm) from the Pleistocene of Canada. Original: The Natural History Museum, London, U.K. (P58863a, b).

Genus: *Mallotus* Cuvier, 1829.

Geological range: Pleistocene to recent.

Geographical distribution: Europe, North America, Greenland.

Features: Small fishes of slender streamlined shape. Head shallow. Snout slightly rounded. Gape rather long. Dorsal fin approximately in the middle of the body, opposite the small pelvic fins. Pectoral fins elongate. Anal fin broad-based, almost fringe-like. Caudal fin forked.

Remarks: Gregarious.

Recent relatives: The fossil species is identical to the recent one.

Mallotus villosus, the recent capelin. Lithograph from Cuvier.

EUTELEOSTEI
Order: Salmoniformes
Family: Osmeridae

Higher Bony Fishes
Suborder: Osmeroidei
Smelts

Osmerus mordax (MITCHILL) (length c. 14 cm) from the Pleistocene of Canada. Original: National Museum of Natural Sciences, Ottawa, Canada.

Genus: *Osmerus* FORSKÅL, 1775.

Geological range: Miocene to recent.

Geographical distribution: Europe, North America.

Features: Small fishes with elongate bodies. Head elongate. Eyes large. Gape long. Jaws set with small teeth. Dorsal fin approximately in the middle of the body, opposite the small fan-shaped pelvic fins. Anal fin broad-based. Caudal fin slightly forked, with broad lobes.

Remarks: Gregarious.

Recent relatives: Closely related to recent smelts of the genus *Osmerus*.

Osmerus eperlanus, the recent stint. Lithograph from BLOCH.

EUTELEOSTEI
Higher Bony Fishes

Order: Salmoniformes
Family: Salmonidae

Suborder: Salmonoidei
Salmonids

Coregonus artedii Lesueur (length c. 6 cm) from the Pleistocene of Canada. Original: National Museum of Natural Sciences, Ottawa, Canada.

Genus: *Coregonus* de Lacépède, 1803.

Geological range: Pleistocene to recent.

Geographical distribution: Europe, North America.

Features: Small fishes of slender streamlined shape. Head elongate. Eyes large. Snout pointed. Gape long. Jaws with small teeth. Dorsal fin pointed, approximately in the middle of the body. Pectoral and pelvic fins elongate. Anal fin broad-based. Caudal fin rather deeply forked.

Remarks: Probably gregarious.

Recent relatives: Closely related to recent whitefishes and ciscos.

Coregonus sp., a recent whitefish. Lithograph from Cuvier.

EUTELEOSTEI
Order: Salmoniformes
Family: Salmonidae

Higher Bony Fishes
Suborder: Salmonoidei
Salmonids

Eosalmo driftwoodensis WILSON (length c. 18 cm) from the Middle Eocene of Driftwood Creek, Canada. Original: University of Alberta, Edmonton, Canada.

Genus: *Eosalmo* WILSON, 1977.

Geological range: Middle Eocene.

Geographical distribution: North America.

Features: Small to middle-sized fishes of slender elongate shape. Head elongate. Snout pointed. Gape rather long. Jaws with small teeth. Dorsal fin small, at the posterior end of the anterior half of the body, opposite the small pelvic fins. Pectoral fins narrow. Anal fin with a somewhat broader base. Caudal fin somewhat emarginate.

Remarks: Gregarious, fresh-water fishes.

Recent relatives: Closely related to recent salmon of the genus *Salmo*.

Salmo salar, the recent salmon. Lithograph from BLOCH (see next page).

Salmo Salar Mas.
Der Vasenlachs.
Le Saumon Bécard.
The Male Salmon.

EUTELEOSTEI
Order: Salmoniformes
Family: Salmonidae

Higher Bony Fishes
Suborder: Salmonoidei
Salmonids

Thaumaturus intermedius WEITZEL (length c. 6 cm) from the Middle Eocene of Messel, Hesse, Germany. Original: Frickhinger Collection, Munich, Germany.

Genus: *Thaumaturus* REUSS, 1844.

Geological range: Middle Eocene to Lower Miocene.

Geographical distribution: Europe.

Features: Small fishes with elongate bodies. Head shallow. Eyes large. Snout pointed. Jaws with small teeth. Dorsal fin low, broad-based, very posterior in position. Pectoral and pelvic fins small. Anal fin opposite the dorsal fin, likewise broad-based. Caudal fin rather emarginate.

Remarks: Small fresh-water predators.

Recent relatives: Distantly related to recent salmon.

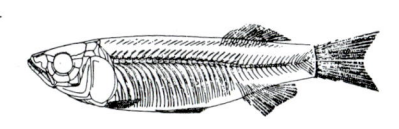

Thaumaturus, reconstruction after WEITZEL.

EUTELEOSTEI — Higher Bony Fishes
Order: Salmoniformes
Family: Unnamed

Gharbouria libanica GAYET (length c. 3.5 cm) from the Upper Cretaceous of Lebanon. Original: Muséum National d'Histoire Naturelle, Paris, France. Photograph: Serette, Paris.

Genus: *Gharbouria* GAYET, 1988.

Geological range: Upper Cretaceous.

Geographical distribution: Middle East.

Features: Very small fishes of slender shape. Head shallow. Eyes large. Snout pointed. Gape rather long. Dorsal fin small, approximately in the middle of the body, opposite the narrow pelvic fins. Pectoral fins small and fan-shaped. Caudal fin forked.

Remarks: Probably gregarious.

Recent relatives: None. Died out in Cretaceous.

EUTELEOSTEI
Order: Stomiiformes
Family: Gonostomatidae

Higher Bony Fishes
Suborder: Gonostomatoidei
Bristlemouths

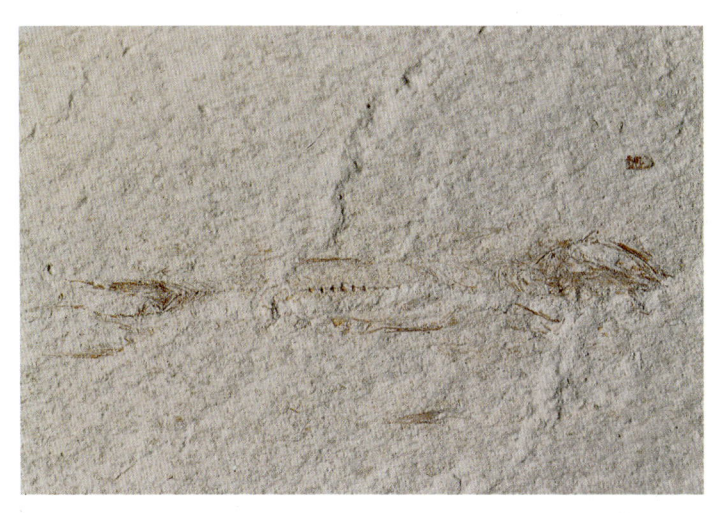

Cyclothone sp. (length c. 4 cm) from the Upper Miocene of California, U.S.A. Original: Peabody Museum of Natural History, New Haven, Connecticut, U.S.A.

Genus: *Cyclothone* GOODE & BEAN, 1883.

Synonyms: *Regenius*.

Geological range: Miocene to recent.

Geographical distribution: North America.

Features: Very small fishes with slender elongate bodies. Head elongate. Eyes large. Snout pointed. Jaws with sharp teeth. Dorsal fin in the posterior half of the body. Caudal fin deeply forked.

Remarks: Probably gregarious.

Recent relatives: Closely related to recent bristlemouths of the genus *Cyclothone*. This has twelve species in modern seas and is perhaps the most abundant genus of all fishes.

Cyclothone, a recent bristlemouth, after BADCOCK.

EUTELEOSTEI
Order: Stomiiformes
Family: Gonostomatidae

Higher Bony Fishes
Suborder: Gonostomatoidei
Bristlemouths

Gonostoma albyi Sauvage (length c. 9 cm) from the Upper Miocene of Licata, Sicily, Italy. Original: Muséum National d'Histoire Naturelle, Paris, France. Photograph: Serette, Paris.

Genus: *Gonostoma* Rafinesque, 1810.

Geological range: Miocene to recent.

Geographical distribution: Europe, North Africa.

Features: Small fishes with slender elongate bodies. Head relatively large. Eyes small. Snout pointed. Gape long. Dorsal fin approximately in the middle of the body. Anal fin begins opposite the dorsal fin. Pectoral and pelvic fins small.

Remarks: Predators. The group probably had light organs even at that early date.

Recent relatives: Closely related to recent bristlemouths of the genus *Gonostoma*.

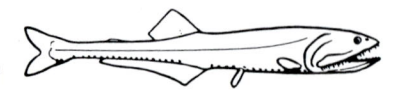

Gonostoma sp., a recent bristlemouth, after Nelson.

EUTELEOSTEI
Order: Stomiiformes
Family: Gonostomatidae

Higher Bony Fishes
Suborder: Gonostomatoidei
Bristlemouths

Idrissia jubae ARAMBOURG (length c. 6 cm) from the Lower Cretaceous of Tselfat, Morocco. Original: Muséum National d'Histoire Naturelle, Paris, France. Photograph: Serette, Paris.

Genus: *Idrissia* ARAMBOURG, 1954.

Geological range: Lower Cretaceous.

Geographical distribution: Northern Africa.

Features: Small fishes of slender shape, tapering rearwards. Head large. Eyes large. Snout slightly pointed. Gape long. Dorsal fin approximately in the middle of the body, opposite the pelvic fins. Pectoral fins small. Caudal fin deeply forked.

Remarks: Probably bottom-dwelling.

Recent relatives: None. Died out in Cretaceous.

EUTELEOSTEI
Order: Stomiiformes
Family: Gonostomatidae

Higher Bony Fishes
Suborder: Gonostomatoidei
Bristlemouths

Protostomias maroccanus ARAMBOURG (length c. 17 cm) from the Lower Cretaceous of Tselfat, Morocco. Original: Muséum National d'Histoire Naturelle, Paris, France. Photograph: Serette, Paris.

Genus: *Protostomias* ARAMBOURG, 1943.

Geological range: Lower Cretaceous.

Geographical distribution: Northern Africa.

Features: Small fishes with slender elongate, anteriorly deepened bodies. Head relatively large. Eyes small. Snout rounded. Gape long. Dorsal fin probably in the posterior half of the body. Caudal fin relatively small and deeply forked.

Remarks: Probably bottom dwellers.

Recent relatives: None. Died out in the Cretaceous.

EUTELEOSTEI
Order: **Stomiiformes**
Family: **Gonostomatidae**

Higher Bony Fishes
Suborder: **Gonostomatoidei**
Bristlemouths

Scopeloides glarisianus Agassiz (length c. 7 cm) from Middle Eocene of Litencice, Czechoslovakia. Original: Frickhinger Collection, Munich, Germany.

Genus: *Scopeloides* Wettstein, 1887.

Geological range: Middle Eocene to Miocene.

Geographical distribution: Europe, western Asia.

Features: Small fishes with elongated bodies. Head shallow. Eyes large. Snout pointed. Gape long. Dorsal fin pointed, behind the middle of the body. Pectoral fins elongate. Pelvic fins small. Anal fin pointed, with a fringe-like posterior extension. Caudal fin deeply forked. Light organs on the flanks of the body.

Remarks: Probably deep-sea fishes.

Recent relatives: Genus extinct. Distantly related to extant bristlemouths of the family Gonostomatidae.

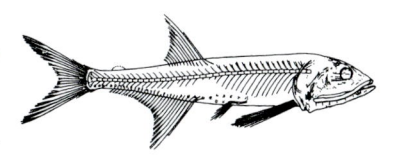

Scopeloides, reconstruction after Danilchenko.

EUTELEOSTEI
Order: Stomiiformes
Family: Sternoptychidae

Higher Bony Fishes
Suborder: Gonostomatoidei
Marine Hatchetfishes

Argyropelecus sp. (length c. 5 cm) from the Miocene of California, U.S.A. Original: Peabody Museum of Natural History, New Haven, Connecticut, U.S.A.

Genus: *Argyropelecus* Cocco, 1829.

Geological range: Oligocene to recent.

Geographical distribution: Europe, northern Africa, North America.

Features: Small fishes of almost circular outline, laterally compressed and deep-bellied. Head deep. Eyes large. Gape rather long, directed upwards. Dorsal fin somewhat behind the middle of the body, divided into two parts. Pectoral fins obliquely fan-shaped. Anal fin rounded. Pelvic fins small. Caudal fin not forked.

Remarks: Probably still-water fishes which fed near the surface of the water.

Recent relatives: Closely related to recent hatchet fishes of the genus *Argyropelecus*, which are ubiquitous in the pelagic waters of the oceans.

Argyropelecus aculeatus, a recent hatchetfish.

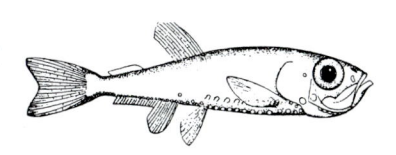

EUTELEOSTEI
Order: Stomiiformes
Family: Sternoptychidae

Higher Bony Fishes
Suborder: Gonostomatoidei
Marine Hatchetfishes

Maurolicus muelleri GMELIN (length c. 4 cm) from the Pliocene of Fiume Marecchia, Italy. Original: Museo Civico di Storia Naturale, Verona, Italy.

Genus: *Maurolicus* Cocco, 1838.

Geological range: Pliocene to recent.

Geographical distribution: Europe.

Features: Very small fishes of slender shape. Head shallow. Eyes large. Snout pointed. Gape directed upwards. Dorsal fin behind the middle of the body, obliquely opposite the narrow pelvic fins. Anal fin is tall anteriorly, but low in its posterior continuation. Caudal fin rather deeply forked.

Remarks: Probably had light organs even at that time.

Recent relatives: The fossil species is identical with the recent one.

Maurolicus muelleri, a recent lightfish.

627

EUTELEOSTEI
Order: Stomiiformes
Family: Photichthyidae

Higher Bony Fishes
Suborder: Photichthyoidei
Lightfishes

Photichthys larteti SAUVAGE (length c. 19 cm) from the Upper Miocene of Licata, Sicily, Italy. Original: Muséum National d'Histoire Naturelle, Paris, France. Photograph: Serette, Paris.

Genus: *Photichthys* HUTTON & HECTOR, 1872.

Geological range: Miocene to recent.

Geographical distribution: Europe.

Features: Small to middle-sized fishes of slender shape. Head relatively large, elongate. Eyes small. Snout pointed. Dorsal fin narrow, shortly in front of the middle of the body. Anal fin broad-based. Pectoral fins elongate.

Remarks: Possess light organs.

Recent relatives: Closely related to recent lightfishes of the genus *Photichthys*.

Photichthys argenteus, a recent lightfish.

EUTELEOSTEI
Order: Stomiiformes
Family: Photichthyidae

Higher Bony Fishes
Suborder: Photichthyoidei
Lightfishes

Vinciguerria sp. (length c. 6 cm) from the Pliocene of Fiume Marecchia, Italy. Original: Museo Civico di Storia Naturale, Verona, Italy.

Genus: *Vinciguerria* JORDAN & EVERMANN, 1896.

Synonym: *Zalarges*.

Geological range: Oligocene to recent.

Geographical distribution: Europe.

Features: Small fishes with slender bodies. Head shallow. Eyes large. Snout pointed. Dorsal fin triangular, very posterior in position, obliquely opposite the anal fin which is likewise triangular. Pelvic fins small. Pectoral fins elongate. Caudal fin forked. Light organs in the ventral part of the posterior part of the body.

Remarks: Probably pelagic even at that period.

Recent relatives: Closely related to recent lightfishes of the genus *Vinciguerria*.

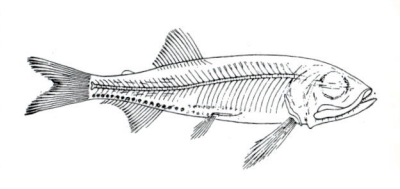

Vinciguerria, reconstruction after ORLOV.

EUTELEOSTEI
Higher Bony Fishes
Order: Aulopiformes
Suborder: Enchodontoidei
Family: Enchodontidae

Enchodus macropterus von der MARCK (length c. 23 cm) from the Upper Cretaceous of Sendenhorst, Westphalia, Germany. Original: Geologisch-Paläontologisches Museum, Münster, Germany.

Genus: *Enchodus* AGASSIZ, 1835.

Synonyms: *Eurygnathus, Holcodon, Ischyrecephalus, Isodon, Solenodon, Tetheodus*.

Geological range: Upper Cretaceous to Eocene.

Geographical distribution: Middle East, North America, Europe, Africa, South America.

Features: Middle-sized fishes with somewhat laterally compressed bodies. Head large and deep. Gape long, directed upwards. Predatory dentition. Dorsal fin triangular, approximately in the middle of the body. Pectoral fins disproportionately large. Anal fin triangular. Caudal fin large and forked.

Remarks: Formidable predators.

Recent relatives: None. Died out in Eocene.

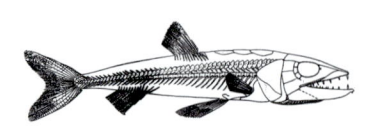

Enchodus, reconstruction after GOODY.

EUTELEOSTEI
Order: Aulopiformes
Family: Enchodontidae

Higher Bony Fishes
Suborder: Enchodontoidei

Leptecodon rectus WILLISTON (length c. 23 cm) from the Upper Cretaceous of Kansas, U.S.A. Original: Museum of Natural History, Lawrence, Kansas, U.S.A.

Genus: *Leptecodon* WILLISTON, 1899.

Geological range: Upper Cretaceous.

Geographical distribution: North America.

Features: Middle-sized fishes of slender shape. Head shallow with projecting snout running into a point. Eyes large. Jaws set with sharp teeth. Body covered with bony plates arranged in rows.

Remarks: Predators.

Recent relatives: None. Died out in Upper Cretaceous.

EUTELEOSTEI
Order: Aulopiformes
Family: Enchodontidae

Higher Bony Fishes
Suborder: Enchodontoidei

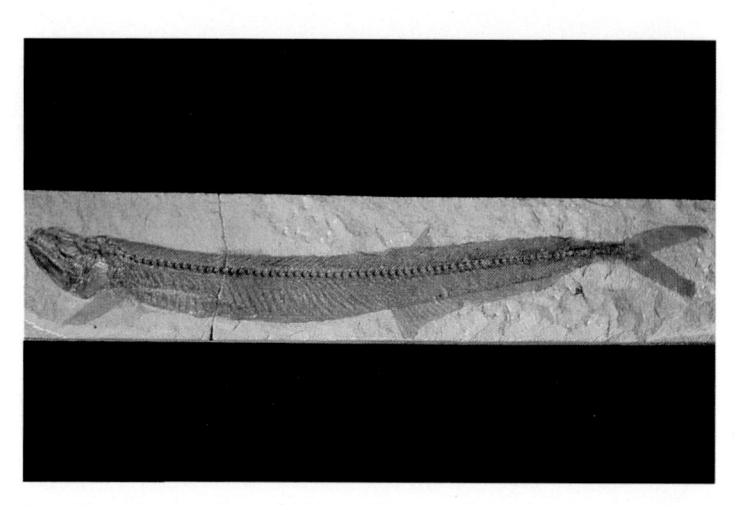

Palaeolycus dregenensis von der MARCK (length c. 40 cm) from the Upper Cretaceous of Sendenhorst, Westphalia, Germany. Original: Geologisch-Paläontologisches Museum, Münster, Germany.

Genus: *Palaeolycus* von der MARCK, 1863.

Geological range: Upper Cretaceous.

Geographical distribution: Europe.

Features: Middle-sized fishes of very slender eel-like shape. Head elongate. Jaws with powerful teeth. Eyes large. Dorsal fin strikingly small, shortly behind the middle of the body. Pectoral fins fan-shaped. Anal fin begins anteriorly opposite the dorsal fin and runs rearwards, as a fringe, almost to the caudal fin. Caudal fin forked.

Remarks: Predators.

Recent relatives: None. Died out in Upper Cretaceous.

Palaeolycus, reconstruction after GOODY.

EUTELEOSTEI
Order: Aulopiformes
Family: Eurypholidae

Higher Bony Fishes
Suborder: Enchodontoidei

Eurypholis boissieri PICTET (length c. 21 cm) from the Upper Cretaceous of Lebanon. Original: Frickhinger Collection, Munich, Germany.

Genus: *Eurypholis* PICTET, 1831.

Geological range: Upper Cretaceous.

Geographical distribution: Europe, northern Africa, Middle East.

Features: Middle-sized fishes of slender shape. Head large, and broad in dorsal aspect. Eyes large. Snout pointed. Gape long. Dorsal fin pointed triangular, in the anterior half of the body. Caudal fin deeply forked. The dorsal mid-line and the flanks each carry a row of large bony scales.

Remarks: Predators.

Recent relatives: None. Died out in the Upper Cretaceous.

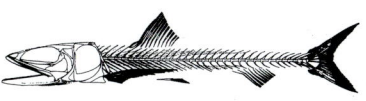

Eurypholis, reconstruction after ORLOV.

633

EUTELEOSTEI
Order: Aulopiformes
Family: Halecidae

Higher Bony Fishes
Suborder: Halecoidei

Halec microlepis (DAVIS) (length c. 18 cm) from the Upper Cretaceous of Lebanon. Original: Muséum National d'Histoire Naturelle, Paris, France. Photograph: Serette, Paris.

Genus: *Halec* AGASSIZ, 1834.

Synonyms: *Archaeogadus*, *Pomognathus*.

Geological range: Upper Cretaceous.

Geographical distribution: Europe, Middle East.

Features: Small to middle-sized fishes with slender elongate or somewhat broadened bodies. Head shallow. Eyes large. Snout pointed. Gape long. Dorsal fin in the anterior half of the body, opposite the small pelvic fins. Anal fin likewise small. Pectoral fins rather widened. Caudal fin relatively large, slightly forked.

Remarks: Rapid swimmer.

Recent relatives: None. Died out in the Cretaceous.

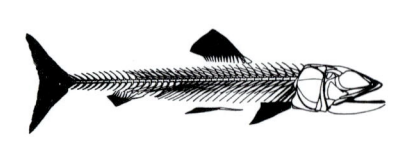

Halec, reconstruction after GOODY.

EUTELEOSTEI
Order: Aulopiformes
Family: Halecidae

Higher Bony Fishes
Suborder: Enchodontoidei

Hemisaurida hakelensis Goody (length c. 5 cm) from the Upper Cretaceous of Lebanon. Original: Field Museum of Natural History, Chicago, Illinois, U.S.A.

Genus: *Hemisaurida* Kner, 1867.

Geological range: Upper Cretaceous.

Geographical distribution: Europe, Middle East.

Features: Small fishes of slender shape. Head long and shallow. Eyes large. Snout pointed. Gape long. Dorsal fin small, in the anterior half of the body, opposite the pelvic fins. Caudal fin moderately forked, with narrow lobes.

Remarks: Probably gregarious.

Recent relatives: None. Died out in the Upper Cretaceous.

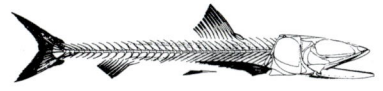

Hemisaurida, reconstruction after Goody.

EUTELEOSTEI
Order: Aulopiformes
Family: Halecidae

Higher Bony Fishes
Suborder: Halecoidei

Phylactocephalus microlepis Davis (length c. 15 cm) from the Upper Cretaceous of Lebanon. Original: Naturmuseum Senckenberg, Frankfurt-am-Main, Germany.

Genus: *Phylactocephalus* Davis, 1887.

Geological range: Upper Cretaceous.

Geographical distribution: Middle East.

Features: Middle-sized fishes with somewhat laterally compressed bodies. Head deep. Gape long, directed upwards. Dorsal fin triangular, in the anterior half of the body. Pectoral fins long and narrow. Pelvic and anal fins small. Caudal fin moderately forked. Strong scales.

Remarks: Certainly rather slow swimmers. Probably fed partly on plants.

Recent relatives: None. Died out in the Upper Cretaceous.

Phylactocephalus, reconstruction after Goody.

EUTELEOSTEI
Order: Aulopiformes
Family: Synodontidae

Higher Bony Fishes
Suborder: Alepisauroidei
Lizardfishes

Sardinius cordieri AGASSIZ (length c. 14 cm) from the Upper Cretaceous of Baumberge, Westphalia, Germany. Original: Geologisches-Paläontologisches Museum, Münster, Germany.

Genus: *Sardinius* von der MARCK, 1858.

Geological range: Upper Cretaceous.

Geographical distribution: Europe.

Features: Small to middle-sized fishes of rather laterally compressed shape. Head short and deep. Gape long, directed upwards. Dorsal fin triangular, approximately in the middle of the body. Pectoral fins broadly fan-shaped. Pelvic fins likewise broad. Anal fin with a point near the anterior end but becoming lower posteriorly. Caudal fin forked.

Remarks: Probably gregarious.

Recent relatives: Distantly related to recent lizard fishes of the family Synodontidae.

Sardinius, reconstruction after von der MARCK.

EUTELEOSTEI
Order: Aulopiformes
Family: Synodontidae

Higher Bony Fishes
Suborder: Alepisauroidei
Lizardfishes

Synodus saurus (length c. 5 cm) from the Pliocene of Fiume Marecchia, Italy. Original: Museo Civico di Storia Naturale, Verona, Italy.

Genus: *Synodus* GRONOV, 1763.

Synonyms: *Xystodus*.

Geological range: Pliocene to recent.

Geographical distribution: Europe.

Features: Small fishes of elongate outline. Head elongate. Snout pointed. Dorsal fin pointed triangular, in the anterior half of the body. Pectoral fins narrow. Points on the ventral surface of the body were probably light organs.

Remarks: Probably solitary fishes which, like their recent relatives, lurked for prey supporting themselves on their pectoral fins.

Recent relatives: Related to recent lizard fishes of the genus *Synodus*.

Synodus sp., a lizardfish.

EUTELEOSTEI
Order: Aulopiformes
Family: Paralepididae

Higher Bony Fishes
Suborder: Alepisauroidei
Barracudinas

Lestidiops sphyraenoides Risso (length c. 17 cm) from the Pliocene of Fiume Marecchia, Italy. Original: Museo Civico di Storia Naturale, Verona, Italy.

Genus: *Lestidiops* Hubbs, 1916.

Geological range: Pliocene to recent.

Geographical distribution: Europe.

Features: Middle-sized fishes of slender streamlined outline. Head shallow and elongate. Dorsal fin very posterior in position. Pectoral fins elongate and expanding forwards. Pelvic fins small. Caudal fin forked.

Remarks: Predators.

Recent relatives: Closely related to recent barracudinas of the genus *Lestidiops*.

Lestidiops similis, a recent barracudina, after Smith.

EUTELEOSTEI
Order: Aulopiformes
Family: Paralepididae

Higher Bony Fishes
Suborder: Alepisauroidei
Barracudinas

Paralepis albyi (SAUVAGE) (length c. 23 cm) from the Oligocene of southern France. Original: Interfoss, Munich, Germany.

Genus: *Paralepis* CUVIER, 1817.

Synonyms: *Anapterus*, *Tydeus*.

Geological range: Oligocene to recent.

Geographical distribution: Europe, northern Africa.

Features: Small to middle-sized fishes of very slender elongate shape. Head long and shallow. Eyes relatively large. Snout elongated to form a short pike-like rostrum. Gape long. Dorsal fin small, in the posterior half of the body, opposite the small pelvic fins. Pectoral fins narrow. Caudal fin small, deeply forked.

Remarks: Rapidly swimming predators.

Recent relatives: Closely related to recent barracudinas of the genus *Paralepis*.

Paralepis sp., a recent barracudina. Lithograph from CUVIER.

EUTELEOSTEI
Order: Aulopiformes
Family: Paralepididae

Higher Bony Fishes
Suborder: Alepisauroidei
Barracudinas

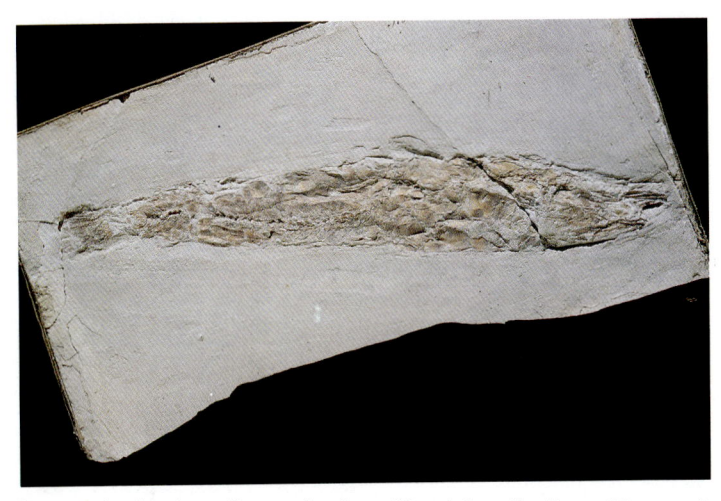

Parascopelus lacertosus SAUVAGE (length c. 22 cm) from the Upper Miocene of Licata, Sicily, Italy. Original: Muséum National d'Histoire Naturelle, Paris, France. Photograph: Serette, Paris.

Genus: *Parascopelus* SAUVAGE, 1873.

Geological range: Miocene to Pliocene.

Geographical distribution: Europe.

Features: Middle-sized fishes with slender streamlined bodies. Head elongate. Eyes small. Snout pointed. Gape long. Dorsal fin small, approximately in the middle of the body. Caudal fin likewise relatively small and moderately deeply forked.

Remarks: Predators.

Recent relatives: None. Died out in the Pliocene.

EUTELEOSTEI
Order: Aulopiformes
Family: Paralepididae

Higher Bony Fishes
Suborder: Alepisauroidei
Barracudinas

Sudis sphecodes (SAUVAGE) (length c. 19 cm) from the Upper Miocene of Licata, Sicily, Italy. Original: Muséum National d'Histoire Naturelle, Paris, France. Photo: Serette, Paris, France.

Genus: *Sudis* RAFINESQUE, 1810.

Geological range: Miocene to recent.

Geographical distribution: Europe, northern Africa.

Features: Middle-sized fishes with elongate streamlined bodies. Head elongate. Eyes small. Snout pointed. Dorsal fin behind the middle of the body. Pectoral fins fan-shaped. Anal fin elongate. Pelvic fins small.

Remarks: Predators.

Recent relatives: Closely related to recent members of the genus *Sudis*.

Sudis hyalina, a recent barracudina.

EUTELEOSTEI
Order: Aulopiformes
Family: Ichthyotringidae

Higher Bony Fishes
Suborder: Ichthyotringoidei

Apateopholis laniatus (DAVIS) (length c. 31 cm) from the Upper Cretaceous of Lebanon. Original: Staatliches Museum für Naturkunde, Karlsruhe, Germany.

Genus: *Apateopholis* WOODWARD, 1890.

Geological range: Upper Cretaceous.

Geographical distribution: Middle East.

Features: Middle-sized fishes of slender outline. Head elongate and shallow. Upper and lower jaws set with small teeth and elongated to form a rostrum. Eyes large. Dorsal fin low, broad-based. Caudal fin deeply forked, with broad lobes.

Remarks: Predators. The rostrum was presumably used to strike prey from the side.

Recent relatives: None. Died out in the Upper Cretaceous.

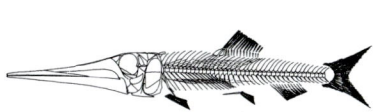

Apateopholis, reconstruction after GOODY.

EUTELEOSTEI
Order: Aulopiformes
Family: Ichthyotringidae

Higher Bony Fishes
Suborder: Ichthyotringoidei

Ichthyotringa furcata (AGASSIZ) (length c. 15 cm) from the Upper Cretaceous of Bethel, Israel. Original: Staatliches Museum für Naturkunde, Karlsruhe, Germany.

Genus: *Ichthyotringa* COPE, 1878.

Synonym: *Rhinellus*.

Geological range: Upper Cretaceous.

Geographical distribution: Europe, Middle East, North America, northern Africa.

Features: Small to middle-sized fishes of slender shape. Head shallow and elongate. Upper and lower jaws extended to form a rostrum. Eyes large. Dorsal fin approximately in the middle of the body. Pectoral fins narrow, obliquely fan-shaped. Pelvic fins small. Anal fin low, broad-based. Caudal fin forked.

Remarks: Predators. The rostrum presumably served to strike prey from the side.

Recent relatives: None. Died out in the Upper Cretaceous.

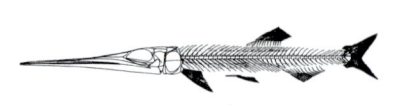

Ichthyotringa, reconstruction after GOODY.

EUTELEOSTEI
Higher Bony Fishes
Order: Aulopiformes
Family: Cheirothricidae
Suborder: Ichthyotringoidei

Cheirothrix libanicus PICTET & HUMBERT (length c. 15 cm) from the Upper Cretaceous of the Lebanon. Original: Muséum National d'Histoire Naturelle, Paris, France. Photo: Serette, Paris.

Genus: *Cheirothrix* PICTET & HUMBERT, 1866.

Synonyms: *Chirothrix*, *Megapus*, *Megistopuspholis*.

Geological range: Upper Cretaceous.

Geographical distribution: Middle East, Europe.

Features: Small fishes with slender bodies. Head elongate and shallow. Eyes large. Gape rather long. Pelvic fins broad and extremely elongate, wing-shaped. Dorsal fin narrow and long, very anterior, opposite the pelvic fins. Caudal fin forked.

Remarks: "Flying" fishes.

Recent relatives: None. Died out in the Upper Cretaceous.

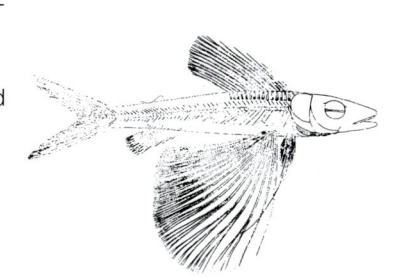

Cheirothrix, reconstruction after WOODWARD.

EUTELEOSTEI — Higher Bony Fishes
Order: Aulopiformes — **Suborder: Ichthyotringoidei**
Family: Chirothricidae

Exocoetoides minor DAVIS (length c. 5 cm) from the Upper Cretaceous of Lebanon. Original: Frickhinger Collection, Munich, Germany.

Genus: *Exocoetoides* DAVIS, 1887.

Geological range: Upper Cretaceous.

Geographical distribution: Middle East.

Features: Small fishes with slender bodies. Head elongate and shallow. Snout pointed. Pectoral fins narrow and very elongate. Pelvic fins rounded and expanded.

Remarks: "Flying" fishes.

Recent relatives: Genus extinct. Perhaps distantly related to recent "flying fishes" of the genus *Exocoetes*.

Exocoetus volitans, a flying fish. Lithograph from BLOCH.

EUTELEOSTEI — Higher Bony Fishes
Order: Aulopiformes
Suborder: Ichthyotringoidei
Family: Cheirothricidae

Telepholis tenuis DAVIS (length c. 15 cm) from the Upper Cretaceous of Lebanon. Original: Field Museum of Natural History, Chicago, Illinois, U.S.A.

Genus: *Telepholis* von der MARCK, 1868.

Geological range: Upper Cretaceous.

Geographical distribution: Europe, Middle East.

Features: Small to middle-sized fishes of slender shape. Head elongate and shallow. Snout slightly pointed. Pectoral fins greatly expanded. Dorsal fin very posterior, opposite the low anal fin.

Remarks: Could probably "fly" short distances.

Recent relatives: None. Died out in the Upper Cretaceous.

EUTELEOSTEI
Higher Bony Fishes
Order: Aulopiformes
Family: Cheirothricidae
Suborder: Ichthyotringoidei

Unnamed fish (length c. 18 cm) from the Lower Cretaceous of Hughenden, Queensland, Australia. Original: Queensland Museum, Brisbane, Australia.

Genus: Not named.

Geological range: Lower Cretaceous.

Geographical distribution: Australia.

Features: Small fishes of slender shape. Head elongate and shallow. Pectoral fins strongly expanded into "wings". Pelvic fins very small.

Remarks: "Flying" fishes.

EUTELEOSTEI
Order: Aulopiformes
Family: Dercetidae

Higher Bony Fishes
Suborder: Ichthyotringoidei

Dercetis triqueter PICTET (length c. 27 cm) from the Upper Cretaceous of Lebanon. Original: National Museum of Scotland, Edinburgh, U.K.

Genus: *Dercetis* AGASSIZ, 1834.

Synonyms: *Leptotrachelus*, *Benthesikyme*.

Geological range: Upper Cretaceous.

Geographical distribution: Europe, Middle East.

Features: Middle-sized fishes with very slender elongate bodies. Head elongate and very shallow. Eyes large. Upper and lower jaws produced to form a short rostrum. Dorsal fin low, broad-based, approximately in the middle of the body. Pectoral and pelvic fins narrow. Caudal fin moderately forked. Bony shields arranged in rows on the body.

Remarks: Predators.

Recent relatives: None. Died out in the Upper Cretaceous.

Dercetis, reconstruction after GOODY.

649

EUTELEOSTEI
Order: Aulopiformes
Family: Dercetidae

Higher Bony Fishes
Suborder: Ichthyotringoidei

Pelargorhynchus dercetiformis von der MARCK (length c. 48 cm) from the Upper Cretaceous of Sendenhorst, Westphalia. Original: Geologisch-Paläontologisches Museum, Münster, Germany.

Genus: *Pelargorhynchus* von der MARCK, 1858.

Geological range: Upper Cretaceous.

Geographical distribution: Europe.

Features: Middle-sized fishes with elongate, very narrow bodies. Head elongate and shallow. Upper and lower jaws lengthened to form a rostrum. Dorsal fin approximately in the middle of the body. Caudal fin stalked and unforked. Bony shields arranged in rows on the body.

Remarks: Predators.

Recent relatives: None. Died out in the Upper Cretaceous.

EUTELEOSTEI
Order: Aulopiformes
Family: Dercetidae

Higher Bony Fishes
Suborder: Ichthyotringoidei

Rhynchodercetis hakelensis PICTET & HUMBERT (length c. 32 cm) from the Upper Cretaceous of Lebanon. Original: Naturhistorisches Museum, Vienna, Austria.

Genus: *Rhynchodercetis* ARAMBOURG, 1944.

Geological range: Upper Cretaceous.

Geographical distribution: Europe, Middle East.

Features: Middle-sized fishes of very slender shape. Head elongate and shallow. Upper and lower jaws lengthened to form a rostrum, with upper jaw projecting only slightly beyond the lower. Dorsal fin in the anterior half of the body, opposite the small pelvic fins. Anal fin likewise small. Caudal fin forked, with relatively narrow lobes.

Remarks: Predators.

Recent relatives: None. Died out in the Upper Cretaceous.

Rhynchodercetis, reconstruction after GOODY.

EUTELEOSTEI
Order: Aulopiformes
Family: Cimolichthyidae

Higher Bony Fishes
Suborder: Ichthyotringoidei

Cimolichthys nepaholica (COPE) (length c. 147 cm) from the Upper Cretaceous of Kansas, U.S.A. Original: Museum of Natural History, Lawrence, Kansas, U.S.A.

Genus: *Cimolichthys* LEIDY, 1857.

Synonym: *Empo*.

Geological range: Upper Cretaceous to Paleocene.

Geographical distribution: North America, South America, Europe, northern Africa.

Features: Large fishes of slender streamlined shape. Head shallow and relatively long. Snout pointed. Upper and lower jaws set with sharp teeth. On the back a row of large bony shields extends from the head to the dorsal fin. Smaller bony shields along the lateral line. Caudal fin disproportionately large, deeply forked, with narrow lobes.

Remarks: Predators.

Recent relatives: None. Died out in the Paleocene.

EUTELEOSTEI
Order: Aulopiformes
Family: Prionolepididae

Higher Bony Fishes
Suborder: Ichthyotringoidei

Prionolepis cataphractus (PICTET & HUMBERT) (length c. 21 cm) from the Upper Cretaceous of Lebanon. Original: Frickhinger Collection, Munich, Germany.

Genus: *Prionolepis* EGERTON, 1850.

Synonym: *Aspidopleurus*.

Geological range: Upper Cretaceous.

Geographical distribution: Europe, Middle East.

Features: Middle-sized fishes of slender shape. Head elongate and shallow. Gape rather long. Dorsal fin broad-based, in the anterior half of the body. Anal fin likewise broad-based. Caudal fin forked. Serrated scales arranged in rows.

Remarks: Probably predators.

Recent relatives: None. Died out in the Upper Cretaceous.

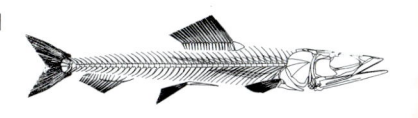

Prionolepis, reconstruction after GOODY.

653

EUTELEOSTEI
Order: Myctophiformes
Family: Sardinioididae

Higher Bony Fishes

Sardinioides monasterii AGASSIZ (length c. 18 cm) from the Upper Cretaceous of Sendenhorst, Westphalia, Germany. Original: Geologisch-Paläontologisches Museum, Münster, Westphalia, Germany.

Genus: *Sardinioides* von der MARCK, 1858.

Geological range: Upper Cretaceous.

Geographical distribution: Europe, Middle East.

Features: Small to middle-sized fishes with rather laterally compressed bodies. Head short and deep. Eyes large. Gape long, directed upwards. Dorsal fin in the middle of the body. Pelvic fins very anterior in position, almost vertically beneath the small pectoral fins. Caudal fin forked, with broad lobes. Body covered with large scales.

Remarks: Probably predators.

Recent relatives: None. Died out in the Upper Cretaceous.

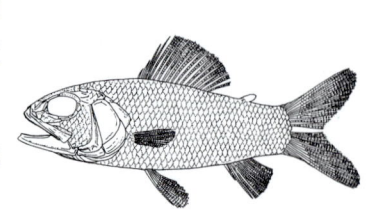

Sardinioides, reconstruction after PATTERSON.

EUTELEOSTEI — Higher Bony Fishes
Order: Myctophiformes
Family: Myctophidae — Lanternfishes

Ceratoscopelus maderensis LOWE (length c. 8 cm) from the Pliocene of Fiume Marecchia, Italy. Original: Museo Civico di Storia Naturale, Verona, Italy.

Genus: *Ceratoscopelus* GÜNTHER 1864.

Geological range: Pliocene to recent.

Geographical distribution: Europe.

Features: Small fishes of slender shape. Head deep. Eyes large. Gape long, directed upwards. Dorsal fin in the middle of the body, opposite the small and narrow pelvic fins. Anal fin broad-based. Pectoral fins narrow. Caudal fin deeply forked.

Remarks: Probably already possessed light organs.

Recent relatives: Closely related to recent lantern fishes of the genus *Ceratoscopelus*.

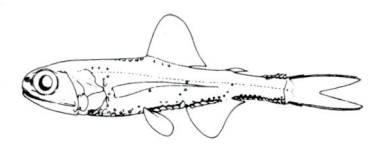

Ceratoscopelus warmingii, a recent lanternfish (after SMITH).

655

EUTELEOSTEI
Order: Myctophiformes
Family: Myctophidae

Higher Bony Fishes
Lanternfishes

Dactylopogon grandis von der MARCK (length c. 44 cm) from the Upper Cretaceous of Sendenhorst, Westphalia, Germany. Original: Geologisch-Paläontologisches Museum, Münster, Germany.

Genus: *Dactylopogon* von der MARCK, 1868.

Geological range: Upper Cretaceous.

Geographical distribution: Europe.

Features: Middle-sized fishes with rather laterally compressed bodies. Head short and deep. Gape long, directed upwards. Dorsal fin triangular, approximately in the middle of the body. Pectoral fins unusually large, long and narrow. Pelvic fins small. Anal fin with a point anteriorly, becoming lower posteriorly. Caudal fin forked, with relatively narrow lobes.

Remarks: Probably predators.

Recent relatives: None. Died out in the Upper Cretaceous.

EUTELEOSTEI
Order: Myctophiformes
Family: Myctophidae

Higher Bony Fishes

Lanternfishes

Eomyctophum koraense DANILTCHENKO (length c. 5 cm) from the Oligocene of Georgia. Original: Paleontologicheskii Muzei Russkoi Akademii Nauk, Moscow, Russia.

Genus: *Eomyctophum* DANILTCHENKO 1947.

Geological range: Oligocene to Miocene.

Geographical distribution: Western and eastern Europe, western Asia.

Features: Small sized fishes of somewhat laterally compressed shape. Head short and relatively deep. Snout rounded. Gape long. Dorsal fin approximately in the middle of the body. Pectoral and pelvic fins small. Anal fin larger. Light organs probably present.

Remarks: Probably fed on small organisms.

Recent relatives: Genus extinct. Closely related to recent lantern fishes of the genus *Myctophum*.

Myctophum sp. a recent lanternfish. Lithograph from BLEEKER.

EUTELEOSTEI
Order: Myctophiformes
Family: Myctophidae

Higher Bony Fishes
Lanternfishes

Hakelia laticauda (PICTET) (length c. 9 cm) from the Upper Cretaceous of Lebanon. Original: American Museum of Natural History, New York, N.Y., U.S.A.

Genus: *Hakelia* WOODWARD, 1942.

Geological range: Upper Cretaceous.

Geographical distribution: Middle East.

Features: Small fishes with slender bodies. Head elongate. Snout pointed. Gape long, directed upwards. Dorsal fin small, approximately in the middle of the body. Caudal fin unusually large, deeply forked.

Remarks: Probably fed on small organisms.

Recent relatives: Genus extinct. Distantly related to other lantern fishes of the family Myctophidae.

EUTELEOSTEI
Order: Myctophiformes
Family: Myctophidae

Higher Bony Fishes
Lanternfishes

Hygophum sp. (length c. 5 cm) from the Pliocene of Fiume Marecchia, Italy. Original: Museo Civico di Storia Naturale, Verona, Italy.

Genus: *Hygophum* Bolin, 1939.

Geological range: Pliocene.

Geographical distribution: Europe.

Features: Small fishes of slender shape. Head deep. Eyes relatively large. Snout produced, pointed. Gape rather long, directed upwards. Dorsal fin approximately in the middle of the body. Caudal fin forked.

Remarks: Probably predators.

Recent relatives: Closely related to recent lantern fishes of the genus *Hygophum*.

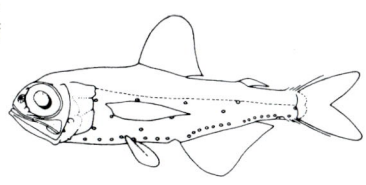

Hygophum hygomii, a recent lanternfish, after Smith.

EUTELEOSTEI
Order: Myctophiformes
Family: Myctophidae

Higher Bony Fishes
Lanternfishes

Lampanyctus sp. (length c. 6 cm) from the Miocene of California, U.S.A. Original: American Museum of Natural History, New York, N.Y., U.S.A.

Genus: *Lampanyctus* BONAPARTE, 1840.

Geological range: Miocene to recent.

Geographical distribution: New Zealand, North America, Europe.

Features: Small fishes of slender shape. Head short and deep. Eyes large. Gape long. Dorsal fin in the middle of the body, obliquely opposite the somewhat larger and probably rather fringe-like anal fin.

Remarks: Probably fed on small organisms.

Recent relatives: Closely related to recent lantern fishes of the genus *Lampanyctus*.

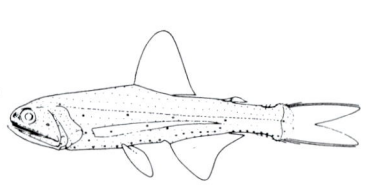

Lampanyctus alatus, a recent lanternfish, after SMITH.

EUTELEOSTEI
Order: **Myctophiformes**
Family: **Myctophidae**

Higher Bony Fishes

Lanternfishes

Leptosomus elongatus von der MARCK (length c. 8 cm) from the Upper Cretaceous of Sendenhorst, Westphalia, Germany. Original: Geologisch-Paläontologisches Museum, Münster, Germany.

Genus: *Leptosomus* AGASSIZ, 1846.

Synonym: *Cassandra*.

Geological range: Upper Cretaceous.

Geographical distribution: Europe, Asia.

Features: Small fishes of slender shape. Head elongate. Snout pointed. Gape long. Dorsal fin triangular, in the anterior half of the body. Pectoral and pelvic fins small, set close together. Anal fin low. Caudal fin deeply forked.

Remarks: Predators.

Recent relatives: Genus extinct. Closely related to recent lantern fishes of the family Myctophidae.

Leptosomus, reconstruction after PICTET & HUMBERT.

661

EUTELEOSTEI
Order: Myctophiformes
Family: Myctophidae

Higher Bony Fishes

Lanternfishes

Nematonotus longispinus PICTET & HUMBERT (length c. 14 cm) from the Upper Cretaceous of Lebanon. Original: Frickhinger Collection, Munich, Germany.

Genus: *Nematonotus* WOODWARD, 1899.

Geological range: Upper Cretaceous.

Geographical distribution: Middle East.

Features: Small to middle-sized fishes with rather laterally compressed bodies. Head short and deep. Eyes large. Gape long, directed upwards. Dorsal fin slightly anterior to the middle of the body, with the first fin ray elongated to form a spine. Pectoral fins elongate, likewise with a projecting first fin ray. Pelvic and anal fins small.

Remarks: Predators.

Recent relatives: None. Died out in the Upper Cretaceous.

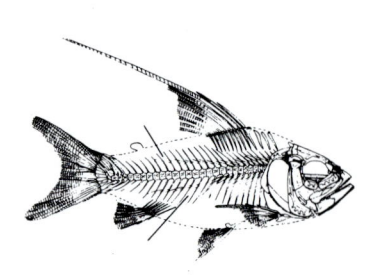

Nematonotus, reconstruction after ROSEN & PATTERSON.

EUTELEOSTEI
Order: Myctophiformes
Family: Myctophidae

Higher Bony Fishes

Lanternfishes

Nyctophus vexillifer (length c. 4 cm) from the Miocene of Forli, Italy. Original: Museo Civico di Storia Naturale, Milan, Italy.

Genus: *Nyctophus* Cocco, 1829.

Geological range: Miocene to Pliocene.

Geographical distribution: Europe, northern Africa.

Features: Small fishes of slender shape. Head elongate. Snout rounded. Dorsal fin in the middle of the body, opposite the pelvic fins. Caudal fin forked.

Remarks: Probably fed on small organisms.

Recent relatives: Distantly related to recent lantern fishes of the family Myctophidae.

EUTELEOSTEI
Order: Myctophiformes
Family: Myctophidae

Higher Bony Fishes

Lanternfishes

Opistopteryx gracilis PICTET & HUMBERT (length c. 12 cm) from the Upper Cretaceous of Lebanon. Original: National Museum of Natural History, Smithsonian Institution, Washington, D.C., U.S.A.

Genus: *Opistopteryx* WOODWARD, 1901.

Geological range: Upper Cretaceous.

Geographical distribution: Middle East.

Features: Small fishes of very slender shape. Head elongate. Eyes large. Gape rather long. Dorsal fin approximately in the middle of the body. Pelvic and pectoral fins long and narrow. Anal fin broad-based. Caudal fin deeply forked, with narrow lobes.

Remarks: Probably predators.

Recent relatives: Genus extinct. Distantly related to recent lantern fishes of the family Myctophidae.

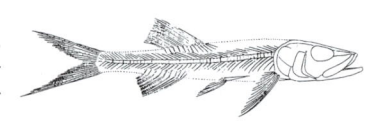

Opistopteryx, reconstruction after PICTET & HUMBERT.

EUTELEOSTEI
Order: Myctophiformes
Family: Myctophidae

Higher Bony Fishes

Lanternfishes

Tachynectes longipes von der Marck (length c. 27 cm) from the Upper Cretaceous of Sendenhorst, Westphalia, Germany. Original: Geologisch-Paläontologisches Museum, Münster, Germany.

Genus: *Tachynectes* von der Marck, 1863.

Geological range: Upper Cretaceous.

Geographical distribution: Europe.

Features: Middle-sized fishes of slender shape. Head elongate. Snout rounded like a pike. Dorsal fin approximately in the middle of the body. Pectoral fins unusually large, broad and rounded. Caudal fin forked.

Remarks: Probably bottom-dwelling fishes which lurked, waiting for prey, supported on their pectoral fins.

Recent relatives: None. Died out in the Upper Cretaceous.

EUTELEOSTEI — Higher Bony Fishes
Order: Pattersonichthyiformes
Family: Pattersonichthyidae

Humilichthys orientalis GAUDANT (length c. 4.5 cm) from the Upper Cretaceous of Lebanon. Original: Muséum National d'Histoire Naturelle, Paris, France. Photograph: Serette, Paris.

Genus: *Humilichthys* GAUDANT, 1978.

Geological range: Upper Cretaceous.

Geographical distribution: Middle East.

Features: Very small fishes with slender bodies. Head elongate. Eyes large. Dorsal fin approximately in the middle of the body, narrow and strikingly long, obliquely opposite the anal fin. Pectoral fins fan-shaped. Pelvic fins long and likewise fan-shaped. Caudal fin slightly forked, with broad lobes.

Remarks: Probably coral-reef fishes.

Recent relatives: None. Died out in the Cretaceous.

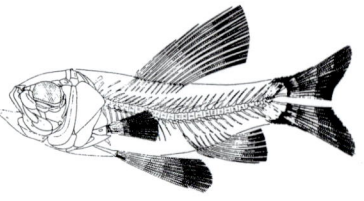

Humilichthys, reconstruction after GAUDANT.

EUTELEOSTEI — Higher Bony Fishes
Order: Pattersonichthyiformes
Family: Pattersonichthyidae

Pattersonichthys delicatus Goody (length c. 4 cm) from the Upper Cretaceous of Lebanon. Original: American Museum of Natural History, New York, N.Y., U.S.A.

Genus: *Pattersonichthys* Goody, 1969.

Geological range: Upper Cretaceous.

Geographical distribution: Middle East.

Features: Small fishes with slender bodies. Head elongate. Eyes large. Gape long. Dorsal fin in the anterior half of the body, pointed triangular. Pectoral fins narrow, with the very narrow pelvic fins immediately behind them. Anal fin triangular. Caudal fin forked.

Remarks: Probably coral-reef fishes.

Recent relatives: None. Died out in the Upper Cretaceous.

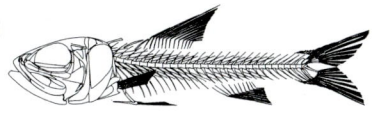

Pattersonichthys, reconstruction after Goody.

EUTELEOSTEI
Order: Pattersonichthyiformes
Family: Pattersonichthyidae

Higher Bony Fishes

Phoenicolepis arcuatus GAUDANT (length c. 5 cm) from the Upper Cretaceous of Lebanon. Original: Muséum National d'Histoire Naturelle, Paris, France. Photograph: Serette, Paris.

Genus: *Phoenicolepis* GAUDANT, 1978.

Geological range: Upper Cretaceous.

Geographical distribution: Middle East.

Features: Small fishes of squat shape. Head deep. Eyes large. Snout rounded. Gape rather long. Dorsal fin inserted anterior to the middle of the body, narrow and strikingly long. Pectoral and pelvic fins small. Anal fin somewhat longer. Caudal fin forked.

Remarks: Probably coral-reef fishes.

Recent relatives: None. Died out in the Upper Cretaceous.

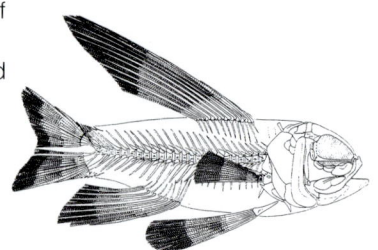

Phoenicolepis, reconstruction after GAYET.

EUTELEOSTEI
Higher Bony Fishes
Order: Ctenothrissiformes
Family: Ctenothrissidae

Ctenothrissa vexillifer PICTET (length c. 9 cm) from the Upper Cretaceous of Lebanon. Original: Frickhinger Collection, Munich, Germany.

Genus: *Ctenothrissa* WOODWARD, 1899.

Synonym: *Aeothrissa*.

Geological range: Upper Cretaceous.

Geographical distribution: Europe, Middle East.

Features: Small fishes of laterally compressed shape. Head deep. Eyes large. Snout pointed. Dorsal fin in the middle of the body, very broad-based, expanded like a fan. Pectoral fins very small. Pelvic fins long and narrow. Anal fin broad and low. Caudal fin rather deeply forked.

Remarks: Probably coral-reef fishes.

Recent relatives: None. Died out in the Upper Cretaceous.

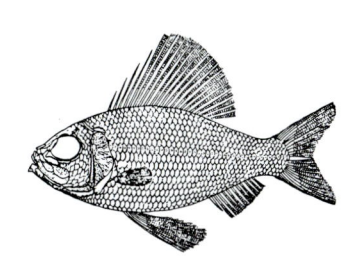

Ctenothrissa, reconstruction after PATTERSON.

EUTELEOSTEI — Higher Bony Fishes
Order: Ctenothrissiformes
Family: Ctenothrissidae

Heterothrissa signeuxae GAUDANT (length c. 5.5 cm) from the Upper Cretaceous of Lebanon. Original: Muséum National d'Histoire Naturelle, Paris, France. Photograph: Serette, Paris.

Genus: *Heterothrissa* GAUDANT, 1978.

Geological range: Upper Cretaceous.

Geographical distribution: Middle East.

Features: Small fishes with bodies deeper anteriorly than posteriorly. Head deep. Eyes large. Gape short. Dorsal fin beginning slightly anterior to the middle of the body, tall and arcuate. Anal fin large, pointed triangular. Pectoral fins small, fan-shaped. Pelvic fins likewise fan-shaped and strikingly large. Caudal fin forked.

Remarks: Probably gregarious.

Recent relatives: None. Died out in the Cretaceous.

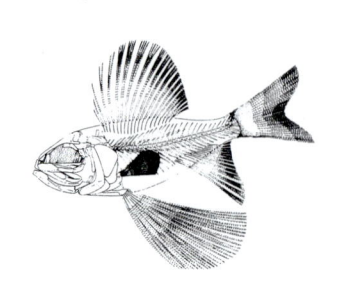

Heterothrissa, reconstruction after GAYET.

670

EUTELEOSTEI — Higher Bony Fishes
Order: Not Named.
Family: Mcconichthyidae

Mcconichthys longipinnis GRANDE (length c. 33 cm) from the Paleocene of Montana, U.S.A. Original: Field Museum of Natural History, Chicago, Illinois, U.S.A.

Genus: *Mcconichthys* GRANDE, 1988.

Geological range: Paleocene.

Geographical distribution: North America.

Features: Middle-sized fishes of slender shape. Head shallow. Eyes large. Snout pointed. Gape rather long. Dorsal fin low triangular, in the middle of the body, immediately behind the highest point of the back. Pelvic and pectoral fins close together. Anal fin rounded. Caudal fin rather deeply forked.

Remarks: Probably fed, at least partly, on plants.

Recent relatives: None. Died out in the Paleocene.

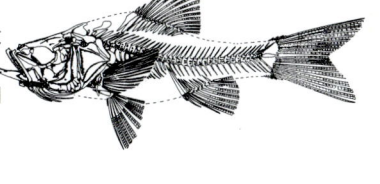

Mcconichthys, reconstruction after GRANDE.

671

EUTELEOSTEI
Higher Bony Fishes
Order: Percopsiformes
Family: Sphenocephalidae
Suborder: Sphenocephaloidei

Sphenocephalus fissicaudus (AGASSIZ) (length c. 11 cm) from the Upper Cretaceous of Baumberge, Westphalia, Germany. Original: Bayerische Staatssammlung für Paläontologie, Munich, Germany.

Genus: *Sphenocephalus* AGASSIZ, 1838.

Geological range: Upper Cretaceous.

Geographical distribution: Europe.

Features: Small fishes of laterally compressed shape. Head deep. Eyes large. Gape rather long. A horn-like spine mid-dorsally at the posterior end of the head. Dorsal fin approximately in the middle of the body, tall anteriorly but decreasing in height posteriorly. Pectoral fins very small, close to the fan-shaped pelvic fins. Anal fin broad-based, decreasing in height posteriorly. Caudal fin rather concave posteriorly.

Remarks: Fresh-water predators.

Recent relatives: None. Died out in the Eocene.

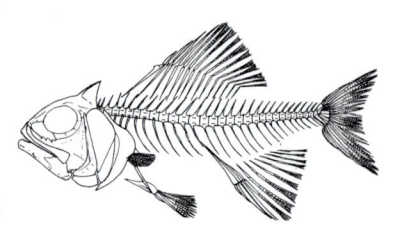

Spnenocephalus, reconstruction after PATTERSON.

EUTELEOSTEI
Order: Percopsiformes
Family: Percopsidae

Higher Bony Fishes
Suborder: Percopsoidei
Trout Perches

Libotonius pearsoni WILSON (length c. 3 cm) from the Eocene of Washington State, U.S.A. Original: University of Alberta, Edmonton, Alberta, Canada.

Genus: *Libotonius* WILSON, 1977.

Geological range: Eocene.

Geographical distribution: North America.

Features: Very small fishes of slender shape. Head rather deep. Gape not very long. Dorsal fin obtusely triangular, slightly anterior to the middle of the body. Pectoral and pelvic fins close together. Anal fin triangular, obliquely opposite the dorsal fin.

Remarks: Fresh-water fishes.

Recent relatives: None. Died out in Eocene.

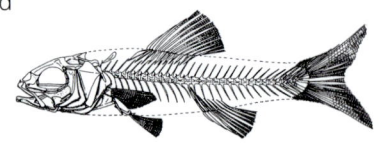

EUTELEOSTEI
Order: Percopsiformes
Family: Aphredoderidae

Higher Bony Fishes
Suborder: Aphredoderoidei
Pirate Perches

Amphiplaga brachyptera Cope (length c. 7 cm) from the Eocene of Wyoming, U.S.A. Original: The Natural History Museum, London, U.K. (P61236).

Genus: *Amphiplaga* Cope, 1877.

Geological range: Middle Eocene.

Geographical distribution: North America.

Features: Small fishes of slender shape. Head elongate. Eyes large. Gape rather long. Dorsal fin slightly anterior to the middle of the body, relatively tall and rounded. Pectoral and pelvic fins close together. Anal fin long and rounded. Caudal fin deeply emarginate.

Remarks: Fresh-water fishes.

Recent relatives: None. Died out in Eocene.

Amphiplaga, reconstruction after Grande.

EUTELEOSTEI
Order: Percopsiformes
Family: Aphredoderidae

Higher Bony Fishes
Suborder: Aphredoderoidei
Pirate Perches

Asineops squamifrons COPE (length c. 13 cm) from the Middle Eocene of Wyoming, U.S.A. Original: Frickhinger Collection, Munich, Germany.

Genus: *Asineops* COPE, 1870.

Geological range: Middle Eocene.

Geographical distribution: North America.

Features: Small fishes with laterally compressed bodies. Head deep. Eyes large. Gape rather long. Dorsal fin rounded, with nine spines anterior to it. Anal fin broad and rounded. Pectoral and pelvic fins close together. Caudal fin not forked, rounded.

Remarks: Fresh-water fishes.

Recent relatives: Genus extinct. Probably related to the recent pirate perch *Aphredoderus*.

Aphredoderus sayanus, the recent pirate perch.

675

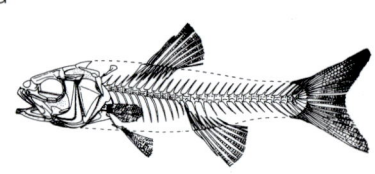

EUTELEOSTEI
Order: Percopsiformes
Family: Aphredoderidae

Higher Bony Fishes
Suborder: Aphredoderoidei
Pirate Perches

Erismatopterus levatus (COPE) (length c. 7 cm) from the Eocene of Wyoming, U.S.A. Original: Field Museum of Natural History, Chicago, Illinois, U.S.A.

Genus: *Erismatopterus* COPE, 1871.

Geological range: Middle Eocene.

Geographical distribution: North America.

Features: Small fishes of slender shape. Head elongate. Eyes large. Snout pointed. Dorsal fin slightly anterior to the middle of the body, relatively tall and rounded. Anal fin broad and rounded. Pectoral and pelvic fins close together. Caudal fin deeply forked.

Remarks: Fresh-water fishes.

Recent relatives: None. Died out in Eocene.

Erismatopterus, reconstruction after ROSEN & PATTERSON.

EUTELEOSTEI — Higher Bony Fishes

Order: Percopsiformes
Family: Aphredoderidae
Suborder: Aphredoderoidei
Pirate Perches

Trichophanes foliarum (Cope) (length c. 11 cm) from the Oligocene of Florissant, Colorado, U.S.A. Original: Field Museum of Natural History, Chicago, Illinois, U.S.A.

Genus: *Trichophanes* Cope, 1872.

Geological range: Oligocene to Miocene.

Geographical distribution: North America.

Features: Small fishes of slender shape. Head elongate. Gape rather long. Dorsal fin obtusely triangular, approximately in the middle of the body. Anal fin small. Pectoral and pelvic fins close together. Caudal fin emarginate.

Remarks: Fresh-water fishes.

Recent relatives: None. Died out in the Miocene.

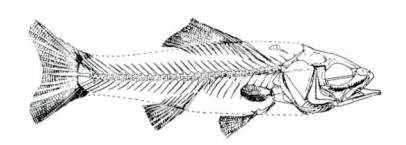

Trichophanes, reconstruction after Rosen & Patterson.

EUTELEOSTEI
Order: Gadiformes
Family: Moridae

Higher Bony Fishes
Suborder: Gadoidei
Flatnose Cods

Gadella sp. (length c. 10 cm) from the Pliocene of Fiume Marecchia, Italy. Original: Museo Civico di Storia Naturale, Verona, Italy.

Genus: *Gadella* Lowe, 1843.

Geological range: Pliocene to recent.

Geographical distribution: Europe.

Features: Small fishes of slender shape. Head deep. Eyes large. Snout rounded. Gape rather long. Three dorsal fins, the most posterior of which is somewhat fringe-like, resembling the bipartite anal fin opposite. Pelvic fins situated on the throat. Pectoral fins narrow. Caudal fin slightly forked.

Remarks: Gregarious.

Recent relatives: Closely related to recent members of the genus *Gadella*.

Gadella sp., a recent codlet. Lithograph from Bloch.

678

EUTELEOSTEI
Order: Gadiformes
Family: Bregmacerotidae

Higher Bony Fishes
Suborder: Gadoidei
Codlets

Bregmaceros albyi (SAUVAGE) (length c. 7 cm) from the Pliocene of Fiume Marecchia, Italy. Original: Frickhinger Collection, Munich, Germany.

Genus: *Bregmaceros* THOMPSON, 1840.

Synonym: *Podopteryx.*

Geological range: Eocene to recent.

Geographical distribution: New Zealand, North America, Europe, western Asia, northern Africa.

Features: Small fishes of slender shape. Head shallow. Eyes large. Snout pointed. Anterior dorsal fin consists of one ray on the posterior part of the head. Posterior dorsal fin fringe-like. Pectoral fins very long. Caudal fin not forked, rounded.

Remarks: Fed on small organisms.

Recent relatives: Closely related to recent codlets of the genus *Bregmaceros*.

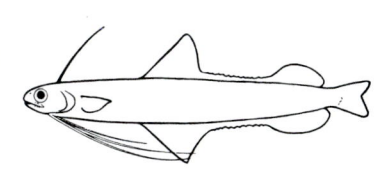

Bregmaceros atlanticus, the recent antenna codlet, after NELSON.

EUTELEOSTEI
Higher Bony Fishes
Order: Gadiformes
Suborder: Gadoidei
Family: Bregmatocerotidae
Codlets

Bregmacerina antiqua (SMIRNOV) (length c. 11 cm) from the Lower Miocene of the northern Caucasus, C.I.S. Original: Paleontologicheskii Muzei Russkoi Akademii Nauk, Moscow, Russia.

Genus: *Bregmacerina* DANILTCHENKO, 1957.

Geological range: Miocene.

Geographical distribution: Western and eastern Europe.

Features: Small fishes of slender shape. Head shallow. Eyes large. Snout pointed. Posterior dorsal fin an upwardly arcuate fringe extending almost the whole length of the back. Anterior dorsal fin a single ray on the posterior part of the head. Anal fin fringe-like and similar to the posterior dorsal fin. Pectoral and pelvic fins relatively long. Caudal fin not forked, rounded.

Remarks: Probably fed on small organisms.

Recent relatives: Genus extinct. Possibly related to recent codlets of the genus *Bregmaceros*.

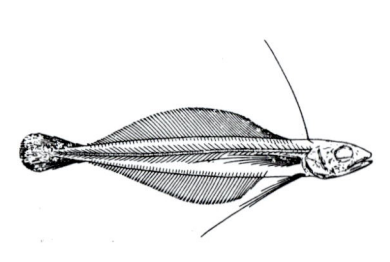

Bregmacerina, reconstruction after DANILCHENKO.

EUTELEOSTEI
Order: **Gadiformes**
Family: **Gadidae**

Higher Bony Fishes
Suborder: **Gadoidei**
Cods

Gadus sp. (length c. 18 cm) from the Pliocene of Fiume Marecchia, Italy. Original: Royal Ontario Museum, Toronto, Canada.

Genus: *Gadus* LINNAEUS, 1758.

Synonym: *Morhus*.

Geological range: Paleocene to recent.

Geographical distribution: Europe, Australia, Greenland.

Features: Middle-sized fishes of slender shape. Head shallow, conical. Eyes large. Snout pointed. Three dorsal fins, the first being pointed and the other two low and rounded. Two anal fins. Pectoral and pelvic fins small, close together. Caudal fin slightly forked.

Remarks: Predators.

Recent relatives: Closely related to recent cods of the genus *Gadus*.

Gadus morhua, the cod. Lithograph from BLOCH.

681

EUTELEOSTEI
Higher Bony Fishes
Order: Gadiformes
Family: Gadidae
Suborder: Gadoidei
Cods

Lota sp. (length c. 25 cm) from the Pleistocene of Münster-Brehloh, Lower Saxony, Germany. Original: Stöbener Collection, Staufenberg, Germany.

Genus: *Lota* OKEN, 1817.

Geological range: Pliocene to recent.

Geographical distribution: Europe.

Features: Middle-sized fishes of elongate slender shape. Head long and shallow. Eyes small. Gape long. First dorsal fin small. Second dorsal fin fringe-like. Anal fin likewise fringe-like. Pectoral fins rounded. Pelvic fins fan-shaped, anterior to the pectoral fins. Caudal fin rounded.

Remarks: Predators.

Recent relatives: Related to the recent burbot *Lota lota*.

Lota lota, the recent burbot. Lithograph from BLOCH.

682

EUTELEOSTEI
Higher Bony Fishes
Order: Gadiformes
Family: Gadidae
Suborder: Gadoidei
Cods

Micromesistius poutassou Risso (length c. 12 cm) from the Pliocene of Fiume Marecchia, Italy. Original: Museo Civico di Storia Naturale, Verona, Italy.

Genus: *Micromesistius* Gill, 1864.

Geological range: Pliocene to recent.

Geographical distribution: Europe.

Features: Middle-sized fishes of slender shape. Head shallow. Eyes large. Snout pointed. Gape long. First and second dorsal fins acute-triangular. Third dorsal fin rounded, like the anal fin opposite whose second part has a broad base. Pelvic fins much reduced, located on the throat. Pectoral fins pointed. Caudal fin emarginate.

Remarks: Gregarious.

Recent relatives: Closely related to the recent cods of the genus *Micromesistius*, which lives in enormous shoals in northern seas.

Micromesistius poutassou, a cod.

EUTELEOSTEI
Order: Gadiformes
Family: Gadidae

Higher Bony Fishes
Suborder: Gadoidei
Cods

Nemopteryx crassus (AGASSIZ) (length c. 27 cm) from the Lower Oligocene of Glarus, Switzerland. Original: British Museum (Natural History), London, U.K.(P15361).

Genus: *Nemopteryx* RATH, 1859.

Synonyms: *Lotimorpha, Megalolepis, Palaeobrosmius*

Geological range: Eocene to Miocene.

Geographical distribution: Europe, western Asia.

Features: Middle-sized fishes of slender shape. Head shallow. Snout pointed. Dorsal fin fringe-like. Pectoral and pelvic fins relatively long. Anal fin likewise fringe-like. Pectoral and pelvic fins close together. Caudal fin not forked, rounded.

Remarks: *Nemopteryx* is sometimes considered a synonym of *Palaeogadus*.

Recent relatives: Genus extinct. Distantly related to recent cods.

EUTELEOSTEI
Order: Gadiformes
Family: Gadidae

Higher Bony Fishes
Suborder: Gadoidei
Cods

Onobrosmius oligocenicus (BOGATCHOV) (length c. 5 cm) from the Lower Miocene of the northern Caucasus, C.I.S. Original: Paleontologicheskii Muzei Russkoi Akademii Nauk, Moscow, Russia.

Genus: *Onobrosmius* BOGATCHOV, 1938.

Geological range: Miocene to Pliocene.

Geographical distribution: Western and eastern Europe, western Asia.

Features: Small fishes of slender shape. Head rather deep. Snout pointed. Gape not very long. Eyes large. Dorsal fin a low fringe beginning in the anterior half of the body. Caudal fin not forked.

Remarks: Probably fed on small organisms.

Recent relatives: None. Died out in the Pliocene.

EUTELEOSTEI
Order: Gadiformes
Family: Gadidae

Higher Bony Fishes
Suborder: Gadoidei
Cods

Palaeogadus intergerinus DANILTCHENKO (length c. 18 cm) from the Lower Oligocene of the northern Caucasus, C.I.S. Original: Paleontologicheskii Muzei Rucckoi Akademii Nauk, Moscow, Russia.

Genus: *Palaeogadus* RATH, 1859.

Synonyms: *Lotimorpha*, *Megalolepis*, *Palaeobrosmius*, *Pseudolota*, *Ruppelianus*.

Geological range: Eocene to Oligocene.

Geographical distribution: Western and eastern Europe.

Features: Small to middle-sized fishes. Head shallow. Eyes large. Snout pointed. Anterior dorsal fin short. Posterior dorsal fin fringe-like. Anal fin likewise fringe-like. Caudal fin elongate, not forked.

Remarks: Probably fed on small organisms.

Recent relatives: Genus extinct. Related to recent cods of the genus *Gadus*.

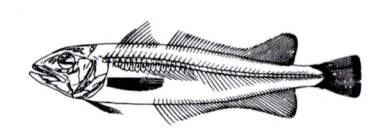

Palaeogadus, reconstruction after DANILTCHENKO.

EUTELEOSTEI
Order: Gadiformes
Family: Gadidae

Higher Bony Fishes
Suborder: Gadoidei
Cods

Palaeomolva monstrata FEDOTOV (length c. 6 cm) from the Lower Miocene of the Caucasus. Original: Paleontologicheskii Muzei Russkoi Academii Nauk, Moscow, Russia (Bannikov Collection).

Genus: *Palaeomolva* DANILTCHENKO, 1947.

Geological range: Lower Miocene.

Geographical distribution: Western and eastern Europe.

Features: Small fishes of slender shape. Head shallow. Snout pointed. Dorsal fin in two parts, fringe-like. Anal fin likewise fringe-like. Caudal fin not forked, rounded.

Remarks: Probably fed on small organisms.

Recent relatives: Genus extinct. Nevertheless related to recent hakes of the genus *Molva*.

Molva molva, a recent hake. Lithograph from BLOCH.

EUTELEOSTEI
Order: Gadiformes
Family: Gadidae

Higher Bony Fishes
Suborder: Gadoidei
Cods

Pseudoraniceps sagus FEDOTOV (length c. 8.5 cm) from the Upper Oligocene of the northern Caucasus, C.I.S. Original: Paleontologicheskii Muzei Russkoi Akademii Nauk, Moscow, Russia (Bannikov Collection).

Genus: *Pseudoraniceps* FEDOTOV, 1974.

Geological range: Upper Oligocene.

Geographical distribution: Eastern Europe.

Features: Small fishes of slender shape. Head shallow. Eyes large. Snout pointed. Dorsal fin fringe-like. Pectoral fins small. Pelvic fins modified as feelers. Anal fin likewise fringe-like. Caudal fin not forked, rounded.

Remarks: Probably fed on small organisms. *Pseudoraniceps* is occasionally considered a synonym of *Onobrosmius*.

Recent relatives: Genus extinct. Perhaps distantly related to recent hakes of the genus *Raniceps*.

Raniceps sp., a recent hake. Lithograph from COUGH.

EUTELEOSTEI
Order: Gadiformes
Family: Merlucciidae

Higher Bony Fishes
Suborder: Gadoidei
Merlucoid Hakes

Merluccius errans (SMIRNOV) (length c. 19 cm) from the Oligocene of the Caucasus. Original: The Natural History Museum, London, U.K. (P22036).

Genus: *Merluccius* RAFINESQUE, 1810.

Synonym: *Spinogadus*.

Geological range: Eocene to recent.

Geographical distribution: Europe, Australia, New Zealand.

Features: Middle-sized fishes of slender shape. Head shallow. Snout pointed. The anterior dorsal fin short and pointed. Posterior dorsal fin fringe-like but dorsally concave, opposite the anal fin which is fringe-like and ventrally concave. Pectoral and pelvic fins narrow and close together. Caudal fin not forked, slightly emarginate.

Remarks: Predators.

Recent relatives: Closely related to recent merluccid hakes of the genus *Merluccius*.

Merluccius sp., a recent merlucoid hake.

689

EUTELEOSTEI
Order: Ophidiiformes
Family: Ophidiidae

Higher Bony Fishes

Cusk-Eels

Eolamprogrammus senectus DANILTCHENKO (length c. 5 cm) from the Lower Eocene of Turkmenistan, C.I.S. Original: Paleontologicheskii Muzei Russkoi Akademii Nauk, Moscow, Russia (Bannikov Collection).

Genus: *Eolamprogrammus* DANILTCHENKO, 1968.

Geological range: Lower Eocene.

Geographical distribution: Western Asia.

Features: Small fishes of slender shape. Head deep. Eyes small. Gape rather long. Dorsal fin soft-rayed, extending as a fringe over two-thirds of the back. Anal fin somewhat shorter, likewise fringe-like. Pelvic fins very narrow, on the throat. Pectoral fins small, rounded. Caudal fin fused with the dorsal and anal fins as a fringe.

Remarks: Probably fed on small organisms.

Recent relatives: Genus died out in Eocene. Distantly related to recent cusk eels of the family Ophidiidae.

EUTELEOSTEI
Order: Ophidiiformes
Family: Ophidiidae

Higher Bony Fishes
Cusk-Eels

Ophidion voltianum MASSALONGO (length c. 17 cm) from the Middle Eocene of Bolca, Italy. Original: Museo Civico di Storia Naturale, Verona, Italy.

Genus: *Ophidion* LINNAEUS, 1758.

Synonym: *Ophidium*.

Geological range: Paleocene to recent.

Geographical distribution: Europe, West Indies, Australia.

Features: Small fishes with slender bodies. Head shallow. Eyes small. Snout slightly pointed. Mouth small. Dorsal fin begins shortly behind the head and continues as a fringe, running into the caudal and anal fins and ending in the middle of the ventral surface. Pectoral fins small. Pelvic fins on the throat. Probably scaleless.

Remarks: Probably fed on small organisms.

Recent relatives: Probably related to recent cusk-eels of the genus *Ophidion*.

Ophidion barbatum, the recent cusk eel. Lithograph from BLOCH.

EUTELEOSTEI
Order: Ophidiiformes
Family: Ophidiidae

Higher Bony Fishes
Cusk-Eels

Propteridium douvillei ARAMBOURG (length c. 14 cm) from the Lower Oligocene of Iran. Original: Muséum National d'Histoire Naturelle, Paris, France. Photograph: Serette, Paris.

Genus: *Propteridium* PRIEM, 1908.

Geological range: Lower Oligocene.

Geographical distribution: Middle East.

Features: Small fishes with very slender elongate bodies. Head elongate. Eyes small. Snout pointed. Gape short. Dorsal fin low, beginning shortly behind the head and running as a fringe which continues into the caudal and anal fin to end in the middle of the ventral surface. Pectoral fins small.

Remarks: Bottom-dwellers.

Recent relatives: None. Died out in the Oligocene.

EUTELEOSTEI
Order: Batrachoidiformes
Family: Batrachoididae

Higher Bony Fishes
Toadfishes

Batrachoides didactylus BLOCH & SCHNEIDER (length c. 18 cm) from the Miocene of Oran, Algeria. Original: Muséum National d'Histoire Naturelle, Paris, France. Photograph: Serette, Paris.

Genus: *Batrachoides* de LACÉPÈDE, 1798.

Geological range: Miocene to recent.

Geographical distribution: Northern Africa.

Features: Small to middle-sized fishes of plump shape. Head flat and broad. Mouth terminal and very large. Jaws with strong pointed teeth. Gill cover spiny. Anterior dorsal fin reduced to a few spines. Posterior dorsal fin elongate and soft-rayed, like the anal fin. Pelvic fins on the throat. Caudal fin not forked.

Remarks: Predators.

Recent relatives: Closely related to recent toadfishes of the genus *Batrachoides*.

Batrachoides sp., a recent toadfish. Lithograph from CUVIER.

EUTELEOSTEI
Order: Lophiiformes
Family: Lophiidae

Higher Bony Fishes
Suborder: Lophioidei
Anglerfishes

Lophius brachysomus AGASSIZ (length c. 15 cm) from the Middle Eocene of Bolca, Italy. Original: Museo Civico di Storia Naturale, Verona, Italy.

Genus: *Lophius* LINNAEUS, 1758.

Geological range: Eocene to recent.

Geographical distribution: Europe.

Features: Small to middle-sized fishes of plump, dorso-ventrally flattened shape, becoming narrower posteriorly. Head disproportionately large, with strongly toothed mouth. The first ray of the dorsal fin modified to form a lure on the head. Pectoral fins very broad and rounded. Caudal fin not forked, rounded.

Remarks: Bottom-dwelling fishes which, like their recent relatives, attracted prey by means of their lure.

Recent relatives: Closely related to recent angler fishes of the genus *Lophius*.

Lophius piscatorius, the recent anglerfish. Lithograph from BLOCH.

EUTELEOSTEI
Order: **Lophiiformes**
Family: **Antennariidae**

Higher Bony Fishes
Suborder: **Antennarioidei**
Anglerfishes

Histionotophorus bassani (de Zigno) (length c. 3 cm) from the Middle Eocene of Bolca, Italy. Original: The Natural History Museum, London, U.K. (P19060-1).

Genus: *Histionotophorus* Eastman, 1904.

Synonym: *Histiocephalus*.

Geological range: Middle Eocene.

Geographical distribution: Europe.

Features: Small fishes of laterally compressed shape. Head deep. Eyes large. Mouth very large. Two lures on the head. The dorsal fin hard-rayed and running along the whole of the back. Anal fin broadly elongate. Caudal fin not forked.

Remarks: Bottom-dwelling fishes which attracted prey by means of their lures, as their recent relatives still do.

Recent relatives: Genus extinct. Distantly related to recent anglerfishes of the family Antennariidae.

Antennarius moluccensis, a recent anglerfish.

695

EUTELEOSTEI — Higher Bony Fishes

Order: Cyprinodontiformes
Family: Exocoetidae?
Suborder: Exocoetoidei
Flying Fishes

Rhamphexocoetus volans BANNIKOV et al. (length c. 15 cm) from the Middle Eocene of Bolca, Italy. Museo Civico di Storia Naturale, Milan, Italy.

Genus: *Rhamphexocoetus* BANNIKOV, PARIN & PINNA, 1985.

Geological range: Middle Eocene.

Geographical distribution: Europe.

Features: Small to middle-sized fishes of slender shape. Head shallow. Upper jaw short. Lower jaw produced to form a pointed rostrum. Pectoral fins long and wing-like. Pelvic fins broad and long, with a narrow base. Dorsal fin very small, very posterior in position, opposite the anal fin which is likewise very small.

Remarks: Probably had the ability to fly for short distances.

Recent relatives: Perhaps distantly related to recent flying fishes.

Rhamphexocoetus, after BANNIKOV.

EUTELEOSTEI
Order: Cyprinodontiformes
Family: Hemirhamphidae

Higher Bony Fishes
Suborder: Exocoetoidei
Halfbeaks

Cobitopsis acutus (length c. 7 cm) from the Oligocene of Puy de Dome, France. Original: The Natural History Museum, London, U.K. (P61500).

Genus: *Cobitopsis* POMEL, 1853.

Geological range: Upper Cretaceous to Oligocene.

Geographical distribution: Europe, Middle East.

Features: Small fishes of very slender shape. Head elongate. Eyes large. Both jaws elongated to form a short rostrum. Dorsal fin in the posterior third of the body, opposite the considerably larger anal fin. Pectoral and pelvic fins small. Caudal fin emarginate.

Remarks: Fresh-water fishes.

Recent relatives: Genus extinct. Distantly related to recent halfbeaks of the family Hemirhamphidae.

Cobitopsis, reconstruction after WOODWARD.

EUTELEOSTEI
Order: Cyprinodontiformes
Family: Hemirhamphidae

Higher Bony Fishes
Suborder: Exocoetoidei
Halfbeaks

"Brachyrhamphus" bolcensis de Zigno (length c. 6 cm) from the Middle Eocene of Bolca, Italy. Original: Università di Padova, Padua, Italy.

Genus: *Brachyrhamphus*.

Geological range: Middle Eocene.

Geographical distribution: Europe.

Features: Small fishes of slender shape. Head shallow. Eyes middle-sized. Both jaws elongated to form a pointed rostrum, with the lower jaw slightly shorter than the upper. Dorsal fin broad-based, relatively tall, carried by strong rays. Pectoral fins narrow.

Remarks: The name *Rhamphyrhynchus* is invalid and must be replaced since it is pre-occupied by a bird and an insect.

Recent relatives: None. Died out in Eocene.

EUTELEOSTEI
Order: Cyprinodontiformes
Family: Hemirhamphidae

Higher Bony Fishes
Suborder: Exocoetoidei
Halfbeaks

Hemirhamphus edwardsi Bassani (length c. 7 cm) from the Middle Eocene of Bolca, Italy. Original: Carnegie Museum of Natural History, Pittsburgh, Pennsylvania, U.S.A.

Genus: *Hemirhamphus* Voigt, 1832.

Geological range: Middle Eocene to recent.

Geographical distribution: Europe.

Features: Small fishes of slender shape. Head shallow. Eyes large. Lower jaw elongated to form a long and pointed rostrum. Dorsal fin very posterior, opposite the anal fin. Caudal fin not forked, rounded.

Remarks: Marine fishes. Even today some halfbeaks live in fresh water and others in sea water.

Recent relatives: Closely related to recent halfbeaks of the genus *Hemirhamphus*.

Hemirhamphus brasiliensis, a halfbeak. Lithograph from Bloch.

EUTELEOSTEI — Higher Bony Fishes

Order: Cyprinodontiformes
Family: Hemirhamphidae

Suborder: Exocoetoidei
Halfbeaks

Hyporhamphus sp. (length c. 13 cm) from the Pliocene of Fiume Marecchia, Italy. Original: Museo Civico di Storia Naturale, Verona, Italy.

Genus: *Hyporhamphus* GILL, 1859.

Synonym: *Reporhamphus*.

Geological range: Pliocene to recent.

Geographical distribution: Europe.

Features: Small fishes of slender shape. Head shallow. Eyes large. Snout elongated to form a rostrum with the lower jaw much longer than the upper. Dorsal fin in the posterior third of the body, opposite the similarly shaped anal fin. Pectoral and pelvic fins small. Caudal fin rather deeply forked.

Remarks: Probably fed mainly on floating foods.

Recent relatives: Genus extinct. Closely related to recent marine halfbeaks of the genus *Hyporhamphus*.

Hyporhamphus acutus, a recent marine halfbeak.

EUTELEOSTEI — Higher Bony Fishes

Order: Cyprinodontiformes
Family: Belonidae

Suborder: Exocoetoidei
Needlefishes

Belone sp. (length c. 25 cm) from the Pliocene of Fiume Marecchia, Italy. Original: Staatliches Museum für Naturkunde, Karlsruhe, Germany.

Genus: *Belone* Cuvier, 1817.

Geological range: Miocene to recent.

Geographical distribution: Europe, northern Africa.

Features: Middle-sized fishes with very slender bodies. Head elongate. Eyes large. Both jaws elongated to an equal extent to form a rostrum set with small pointed teeth. Dorsal fin in the posterior third of the body, Opposite the anal fin. Pectoral and pelvic fins small. Caudal fin forked.

Remarks: Predators. The rostrum served to deflect the prey and to strike it from the side.

Recent relatives: Closely related to recent needlefishes of the genus *Belone*.

Belone belone, the recent needlefish. Lithograph from Bloch.

701

EUTELEOSTEI — Higher Bony Fishes
Order: Cyprinodontiformes — Suborder: Cyprinodontoidei
Family: Cyprinodontidae — Killifishes

Aphanius crassicaudus (AGASSIZ) (length c. 4 cm) from the Pliocene of Castellaro, Italy. Original: Museo Civico di Storia Naturale, Verona, Italy.

Genus: *Aphanius* NARDO, 1827.

Geological range: Miocene to recent.

Geographical distribution: Europe.

Features: Very small fishes of laterally compressed shape. Head short. Eyes large. Gape short. Dorsal fin in the posterior third of the body, opposite the rounded anal fin. Pelvic fins narrow. Pectoral fins broader. Caudal fin not forked, rounded.

Remarks: Probably lived in brackish water and fed on plants.

Recent relatives: Closely related to recent killifishes of the genus *Aphanius*.

Aphanius sirhani, a recent killifish.

702

EUTELEOSTEI — Higher Bony Fishes

Order: Cyprinodontiformes
Family: Cyprinodontidae

Suborder: Cyprinodontoidei
Killifishes

Brachylebias persicus Priem (length c. 4 cm) from the Miocene of northwestern Iran. Original: The Natural History Museum, London, U.K. (P47944/5).

Genus: *Brachylebias* Priem, 1908.

Geological range: Miocene.

Geographical distribution: Western Asia.

Features: Very small fishes with rather laterally compressed bodies. Head short. Eyes large. Dorsal fin in the posterior half of the body, opposite the anal fin. Pectoral and pelvic fins small. Caudal fin small, not forked, rounded.

Remarks: Fresh-water fishes.

Recent relatives: Genus extinct. Related to recent killifishes of the family Cyprinodontidae.

EUTELEOSTEI
Higher Bony Fishes
Order: Cyprinodontiformes
Family: Cyprinodontidae
Suborder: Cyprinodontoidei
Killifishes

Carrionellus diumortuus WHITE (length c. 5 cm) from the Miocene of Loja, Ecuador. Original: The Natural History Museum, London, U.K. (P47944/5).

Genus: *Carrionellus* WHITE, 1927.

Geological range: Lower Miocene.

Geographical distribution: South America.

Features: Small fishes with rather deep bodies anteriorly, becoming shallower behind. Head deep. Eyes large. Gape short. Dorsal fin in the posterior half of the body, opposite the larger anal fin.

Remarks: Fresh-water fishes.

Recent relatives: Genus extinct. Related to recent killifishes of the family Cyprinodontidae.

Cyprinodon variegatus, a recent killifish

EUTELEOSTEI
Order: Cyprinodontiformes
Family: Cyprinodontidae

Higher Bony Fishes
Suborder: Cyprinodontoidei
Killifishes

Fundulus sp. (length c. 6 cm) from the Pliocene of Kansas, U.S.A. Original: Museum of Natural History, Cleveland, Ohio, U.S.A.

Genus: *Fundulus* de Lacépède, 1803.

Synonyms: *Gephyrura*, *Parafundulus*.

Geological range: Pliocene to recent.

Geographical distribution: North America.

Features: Small fishes of slender shape. Head elongate. Eyes large. Gape short. Dorsal fin in the posterior third of the body, opposite the larger anal fin. Pelvic fins narrow. Pectoral fins fan-shaped. Caudal fin not forked.

Remarks: Fresh-water fishes.

Recent relatives: Genus extinct. Closely related to recent killi-fishes of the genus *Fundulus*.

Fundulus pulvereus, a recent killifish.

705

EUTELEOSTEI
Higher Bony Fishes
Order: Cyprinodontiformes
Family: Cyprinodontidae
Suborder: Cyprinodontoidei
Killifishes

Lebias perpusillus (AGASSIZ) (length c. 5 cm) from the Miocene of Öhningen, Württemberg, Germany. Original: Paläontologisches Museum, Zürich, Switzerland.

Genus: *Lebias* OKEN, 1817.

Geological range: Miocene.

Geographical distribution: Europe.

Features: Very small fishes with somewhat laterally compressed bodies. Head short. Eyes large. Gape short. Dorsal fin approximately in the middle of the body. Caudal fin slightly emarginate.

Remarks: Fresh-water fishes. There is some doubt whether this fish is a killifish.

Recent relatives: Genus extinct. Perhaps related to recent killifishes of the family Cyprinodontidae.

Lebias, reconstruction after ZITTEL.

EUTELEOSTEI — Higher Bony Fishes
Order: Cyprinodontiformes — Suborder: Cyprinodontoidei
Family: Cyprinodontidae — Killifishes

Lithofundulus brouweri de BEAUFORT (length c. 6 cm) from the Miocene of Gimpoe, Celebes. Original: Geologisch Museum, Amsterdam, Netherlands.

Genus: *Lithofundulus*.

Geological range: Miocene.

Geographical distribution: Indonesia.

Features: Small fishes of slender shape. Head elongate. Eyes large. Snout somewhat pointed. Dorsal fin small, in the posterior half of the body, opposite the considerably larger anal fin.

Remarks: Fresh-water fishes.

Recent relatives: Genus extinct. Related to recent killifishes of the family Cyprinodontidae.

EUTELEOSTEI
Order: Cyprinodontiformes
Family: Cyprinodontidae

Higher Bony Fishes
Suborder: Cyprinodontoidei
Killifishes

Pachylebias crassicaudus (AGASSIZ) (length c. 8 cm) from the Miocene of San Vittorio d'Alba, Italy. Original: Interfoss, Munich, Germany.

Genus: *Pachylebias* WOODWARD, 1901.

Synonyms: *Anelia*, *Physocephalus*.

Geological range: Oligocene to Miocene.

Geographical distribution: Europe.

Features: Small fishes of slender shape. Head short. Eyes large. Gape very short. Dorsal fin behind the middle of the body, obliquely opposite the anal fin. Pelvic fins small. Pectoral fins fan-shaped. Caudal fin not forked, elongate and rounded.

Remarks: Fresh-water fishes.

Recent relatives: Genus extinct. Related to recent killifishes of the family Cyprinodontidae.

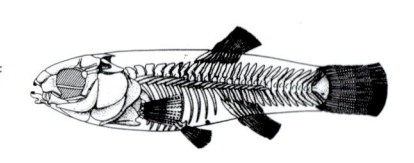

Pachylebias, reconstruction after GAUDANT.

EUTELEOSTEI
Order: Cyprinodontiformes
Family: Cyprinodontidae

Higher Bony Fishes
Suborder: Cyprinodontoidei
Killifishes

Prolebias cephalotus AGASSIZ (length c. 3 cm) from the Oligocene of Aix-en-Provence, France. Original: The Natural History Museum, London, U.K.

Genus: *Prolebias* SAUVAGE, 1874.

Synonyms: *Ismene*, *Pachystetus*.

Geological range: Oligocene to Miocene.

Geographical distribution: Europe.

Features: Very small fishes with somewhat laterally compressed bodies. Head short and relatively deep. Eyes large. Gape short. Dorsal fin small, in the posterior half of the body, opposite the considerably larger anal fin.
Caudal fin not forked, rounded.

Remarks: Fresh-water fishes.

Recent relatives: Genus extinct. Related to recent killifishes of the family Cyprinodontidae.

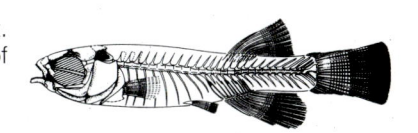

Prolebias, reconstruction after GAUDANT.

709

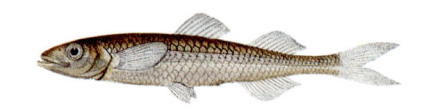

EUTELEOSTEI
Order: Atheriniformes
Family: Atherinidae

Higher Bony Fishes

Silversides

Atherina verdonis SAUVAGE (length c. 8 cm) from the Oligocene of Gard, France. Original: Royal Ontario Museum, Toronto, Canada.

Genus: *Atherina* LINNAEUS, 1758.

Geological range: Middle Eocene to recent.

Geographical distribution: Europe, Asia, North America.

Features: Small fishes with slender bodies. Head shallow. Eyes large. Gape long. Two dorsal fins, the posterior one opposite the anal fin. Caudal fin rather forked.

Remarks: Fresh-water fishes.

Recent relatives: Closely related to recent silversides of the family Atherinidae.

Atherina sp., a recent silverside. Lithograph from BLOCH.

EUTELEOSTEI
Order: Atheriniformes
Family: Atherinidae

Higher Bony Fishes

Silversides

Rhamphognathus sphyraenoides (AGASSIZ) (length c. 12 cm) from the Middle Eocene of Bolca, Italy. Original: The Natural History Museum, London, U.K.

Genus: *Rhamphognathus* AGASSIZ, 1835.

Synonym: *Mesogaster*.

Geological range: Middle Eocene.

Geographical distribution: Europe.

Features: Small to middle-sized fishes of very slender shape. Head shallow and elongate. Eyes large. Gape relatively long. Two dorsal fins, the posterior opposite the anal fin. Pectoral fins small and fan-shaped. Caudal fin large and deeply forked.

Remarks: Predators.

Recent relatives: Genus extinct. Related to recent silversides of the family Atherinidae.

EUTELEOSTEI
Order: Lampridiformes
Family: Lampridae

Higher Bony Fishes
Suborder: Lampridoidei
Opah

Bajaichthys elegans Sorbini (length c. 4 cm) from the Middle Eocene of Bolca, Italy. Original: Museo Civico di Storia Naturale, Verona, Italy.

Genus: *Bajaichthys* Sorbini, 1983.

Geological range: Middle Eocene.

Geographical distribution: Europe.

Features: Very small fishes with bodies deep anteriorly and becoming less deep posteriorly. Head deep. Eyes large. Snout pointed. Gape short. Dorsal fin narrow, greatly elongated, situated just behind the head. Pectoral fins very long and narrow. Pelvic fins broad-based. Anal fin small.

Remarks: Probably coral-reef fishes.

Recent relatives: None. Died out in Eocene.

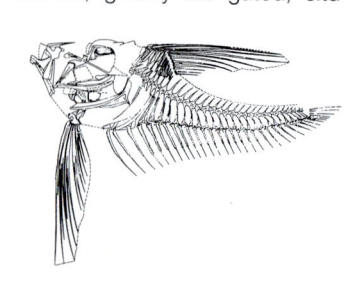

Bajaichthys, reconstruction after Sorbini.

712

EUTELEOSTEI
Order: Lampridiformes
Family: Turkmenidae

Higher Bony Fishes
Suborder: Lampridoidei

Analectis pala DANILTCHENKO (length c. 5 cm) from the Lower Oligocene of northern Caucasus. Original: Paleontologicheskii Muzei Russkoi Akademii Nauk, Moscow, Russia.

Genus: *Analectis*   DANILTCHENKO, 1980.

Geological range: Lower Oligocene.

Geographical distribution: Eastern Europe.

Features: Small fishes with a deep belly. Head deep. Eyes large. Snout pointed. Dorsal fin very posterior, shortly in front of the caudal fin. Anal fin opposite, fringe-like, broad-based and rather rounded. Pelvic fins narrow, attached to the lowest part of the body. Pectoral fins immediately above them, fan-shaped. Caudal fin broad, not forked.

Remarks: Fresh-water fishes, probably predators.

Recent relatives: Genus extinct. Perhaps related to the recent opah *Lampris*.

Analectis, reconstruction after Akademia Nauk, Moscow.

EUTELEOSTEI
Order: Lampridiformes
Family: Turkmenidae

Higher Bony Fishes
Suborder: Lampridoidei

Turkmene finitimus DANILTCHENKO (length c. 11 cm) from the Lower Eocene of Turkmenistan. Original: Paleontologicheskii Muzei Russkoi Akademii Nauk, Moscow, Russia (Bannikov Collection).

Genus: *Turkmene* DANILTCHENKO, 1968.

Geological range: Lower Eocene.

Geographical distribution: Western Asia.

Features: Small fishes of oval outline, laterally flattened. Head small. Eyes large. Gape short. Dorsal fin tall and hard-rayed anteriorly but continuing posteriorly as a fringe. Anal fin similar. Pelvic fins long and narrow. Caudal fin forked.

Remarks: Probably fed on crustaceans and small organisms.

Recent relatives: Genus extinct in Eocene. Distantly related to the recent opah *Lampris regius* which lives in the oceans as the only species of its suborder.

Lampris regius, the recent opah. Lithograph from CUVIER.

EUTELEOSTEI
Order: Lampridiformes
Family: Lophotidae

Higher Bony Fishes
Suborder: Trachipteroidei
Crestfishes

Protolophotus elami (ARAMBOURG) (length c. 42 cm) from the Lower Oligocene of Iran. Original: Muséum National d'Histoire Naturelle, Paris, France. Photograph: Serette, Paris.

Genus: *Protolophotus* WALTERS, 1957.

Geological range: Oligocene.

Geographical distribution: Middle East.

Features: Middle-sized fishes of somewhat laterally compressed shape. Head deep. Eyes small. A comb-like outgrowth on the upper part of the head. Dorsal fin begins shortly behind the head and runs as a fringe which includes the caudal and anal fins and reaches to the middle of the belly.

Remarks: Predators.

Recent relatives: Distantly related to recent crestfishes of the genus *Lophotus*.

Lophotus cepedianus, a recent crestfish. Lithograph from CUVIER.

EUTELEOSTEI — Higher Bony Fishes
Order: Beryciformes
Suborder: Berycoidei
Family: Trachichthyidae
Slimeheads

Acrogaster heckeli (PICTET) (length c. 7 cm) from the Upper Cretaceous of Lebanon. Original: Staatliches Museum für Naturkunde, Stuttgart, Germany.

Genus: *Acrogaster* AGASSIZ, 1834.

Synonyms: *Acanthophoria*.

Geological range: Upper Cretaceous.

Geographical distribution: Middle East.

Features: Small fishes of almost disc-shaped outline, laterally flattened. Head disproportionately deep. Eyes large. Gape rather long. Dorsal fin with low hard rays anteriorly but rounded and decreasing in height posteriorly. Anal fin likewise with hard rays anteriorly. Pelvic fins fan-shaped, attached immediately opposite the pectoral fins. Caudal fin somewhat forked, with broad lobes.

Remarks: Probably fed partly on plants.

Recent relatives: None. Died out in Upper Cretaceous.

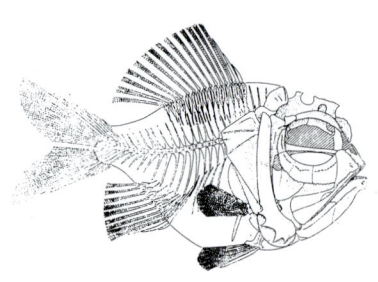

Acrogaster, reconstruction after PATTERSON.

EUTELEOSTEI
Order: Beryciformes
Family: Trachichthyidae

Higher Bony Fishes
Suborder: Berycoidei
Slimeheads

Gephyroberyx robustus (BOGACHOV) (length c. 6 cm) from the Lower Oligocene of northern Caucasus, C.I.S. Original: Paleontologicheskii Muzei Russkoi Akademii Nauk, Moscow, Russia (Bannikov Collection).

Genus: *Gephyroberyx* BOULENGER, 1902.

Geological range: Lower Oligocene to recent.

Geographical distribution: Eastern Europe.

Features: Small fishes with deep oval outline, laterally flattened. Head deep. Eyes large. Gape long. Dorsal fin begins approximately in the middle of the body and runs far posteriorly. Anal fin obliquely opposite, likewise broad. Pelvic and pectoral fins narrow, opposite each other. Caudal fin rather deeply forked.

Remarks: Probably predators.

Recent relatives: Closely related to recent slimeheads of the genus *Gephyroberyx*.

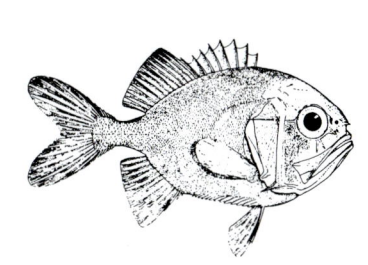

Gephyroberyx orbiculatus, a recent slimehead, after SMITH.

EUTELEOSTEI
Order: Beryciformes
Family: Trachichthyidae

Higher Bony Fishes
Suborder: Berycoidei
Slimeheads

Hoplopteryx antiquus (AGASSIZ) (length c. 13 cm) from the Upper Cretaceous of Baumberge, Westphalia, Germany. Original: Bayerische Staatssammlung für Paläontologie, Munich, Germany.

Genus: *Hoplopteryx* AGASSIZ, 1838.
Synonyms: *Goniolepis*, *Hemicyclolepis*, *Hemigonolepis*, *Priconolepis*.
Geological range: Upper Cretaceous.
Geographical distribution: Europe, Middle East, northern Africa, North America.
Features: Small to middle-sized fishes with oval outline, laterally flattened. Head deep. Eyes large. Gape rather long. Dorsal fin with hard rays anteriorly, decreasing in height more posteriorly. Anal fin likewise with hard rays anteriorly. Pectoral fins small, vertically above the pelvic fins which are likewise small. Caudal fin of great height, concave posteriorly.
Remarks: Fed partly on plants.
Recent relatives: Possibly related to the recent genus *Centroberyx* (= *Hoplopteryx*).

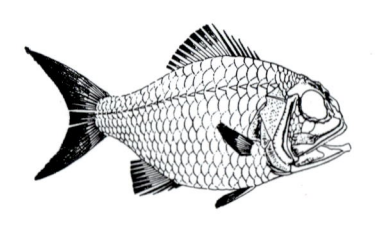

Hoplopteryx, reconstruction after WOODWARD.

EUTELEOSTEI — Higher Bony Fishes
Order: Beryciformes — Suborder: Berycoidei
Family: Trachyichthyidae — Slimeheads

Libanoberyx spinosus GAYET (length c. 5.5 cm) from the Upper Cretaceous of Lebanon. Original: Muséum National d'Histoire Naturelle, Paris. Photograph: Serette, Paris.

Genus: *Libanoberyx* GAYET, 1980.

Geological range: Upper Cretaceous.

Geographical distribution: Middle East.

Features: Small fishes with oval outline, laterally flattened. Head deep. Eyes large. Gape long. Dorsal fin in the posterior half of the body, hard-rayed anteriorly. Anal fin similar. Pectoral fins fan-shaped. Pelvic fins vertically below them, carried by a spine-like thick ray. Caudal fin slightly forked, with broad lobes.

Remarks: Probably predators.

Recent relatives: None. Died out in the Cretaceous.

EUTELEOSTEI
Order: Beryciformes
Family: Trachichthyidae

Higher Bony Fishes
Suborder: Berycoidei
Slimeheads

Lissoberyx arambourgi GAUDANT (length c. 6 cm) from the Upper Cretaceous of Lebanon. Original: Muséum National d'Histoire Naturelle, Paris, France. Photograph: Serette, Paris.

Genus: *Lissoberyx* PATTERSON, 1967.

Geological range: Lower to Upper Cretaceous.

Geographical distribution: North Africa, Middle East.

Features: Small to middle-sized fishes with plump bodies. Head deep. Eyes large. Gape rather long. Dorsal fin approximately in the middle of the body, obliquely opposite the anal fin. Both dorsal and anal fins hard-rayed anteriorly and soft-rayed more posteriorly. Pelvic and pectoral fins fan-shaped, close together. Caudal fin forked, with broad lobes.

Remarks: Probably fed at least partly on plants.

Recent relatives: None. Died out in the Cretaceous.

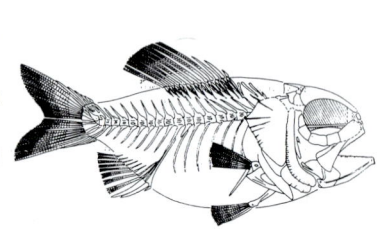

Lissoberyx, reconstruction after GAYET.

EUTELEOSTEI
Order: Beryciformes
Family: Trachichthyidae

Higher Bony Fishes
Suborder: Berycoidei
Slimeheads

Stichopteryx lewisi (DAVIS) (length c. 7 cm) from the Upper Cretaceous of Lebanon. Original: The Natural History Museum, London, U.K.

Genus: *Stichopteryx* GAUDANT, 1969.

Geological range: Upper Cretaceous.

Geographical distribution: Middle East.

Features: Small fishes with oval outline, laterally flattened. Head deep. Eyes large. Gape rather long. Dorsal fin with hard rays anteriorly and ending rather tall near the root of the tail. Pelvic fins small, vertically beneath the fan-shaped pectoral fins. Caudal fin moderately forked, with broad lobes.

Remarks: Probably predators.

Recent relatives: None. Died out in the Cretaceous.

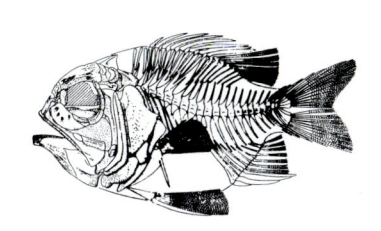

Stichopteryx, reconstruction after GAYET.

721

EUTELEOSTEI
Higher Bony Fishes
Order: Beryciformes
Family: Trachichthyidae
Suborder: Berycoidei
Slimeheads

Tubantia cataphractus von der Marck (length c. 16 cm) from the Upper Cretaceous of Baumberge, Westphalia. Original: The Natural History Museum, London, U.K. (P21984).

Genus: *Tubantia* Patterson, 1964.

Geological range: Upper Cretaceous.

Geographical distribution: Europe.

Features: Middle-sized fishes with elongate, somewhat laterally compressed bodies. Head deep. Eyes large. Gape long. Dorsal fin approximately in the middle of the body, tall and with hard rays anteriorly and decreasing in height more posteriorly. Anal fin likewise with hard rays anteriorly. Pelvic fins fan-shaped. Caudal fin emarginate.

Remarks: Predators.

Recent relatives: None. Died out in the Upper Cretaceous.

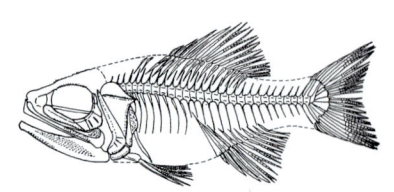

Tubantia, reconstruction after Patterson.

EUTELEOSTEI
Higher Bony Fishes
Order: Beryciformes
Family: Trachichthyidae
Suborder: Berycoidei
Slimeheads

Berycomorus firdoussi ARAMBOURG (length c. 12 cm) from the Lower Oligocene of Iran. Original: Muséum National d'Histoire Naturelle, Paris, France. Photograph: Serette.

Genus: *Berycomorus* ARAMBOURG, 1939.

Geological range: Oligocene.

Geographical distribution: Middle East.

Features: Small to middle-sized fishes with oval outline, laterally flattened. Head deep. Eyes large. Snout rounded. Gape rather long. Dorsal fin hard-rayed, pointed, approximately in the middle of the body. Anal fin with a broader base. Pectoral fins fan-shaped. Caudal fin rather forked.

Remarks: Probably predators.

Recent relatives: Genus extinct. Perhaps related to recent slime-heads of the family Berycidae.

Beryx decadactylus, a recent slimehead.

723

EUTELEOSTEI — Higher Bony Fishes

Order: Beryciformes
Family: Holocentridae

Suborder: Berycoidei
Squirrelfishes

Berybolcensis leptacanthus (AGASSIZ) (length c. 13 cm) from the Middle Eocene of Bolca, Italy. Original: Bayerische Staatssammlung für Paläontologie, Munich, Germany.

Genus: *Berybolcensis* SORBINI, 1979.

Geological range: Middle Eocene.

Geographical distribution: Europe.

Features: Small fishes with rather laterally compressed bodies. Head deep. Eyes large. Gape long. Two Dorsal fins, the posterior being triangular and the anterior one supported by strong rays. Anal fin triangular, with a broad base. Pectoral fins small, pelvic fins vertically beneath them, fan-shaped. Caudal fin rather deeply forked.

Remarks: Gregarious predators.

Recent relatives: None. Died out in the Eocene.

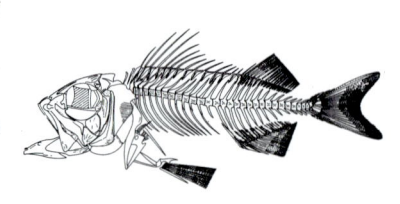

Berybolcensis, reconstruction after SORBINI.

EUTELEOSTEI
Order: Beryciformes
Family: Holocentridae

Higher Bony Fishes
Suborder: Berycoidei
Squirrelfishes

Ctenocephalichthys loreti GAUDANT (length c. 5 cm) from the Upper Cretaceous of Lebanon. Original: Muséum National d'Histoire Naturelle, Paris, France. Photograph: Serette, Paris.

Genus: *Ctenocephalichthys* GAUDANT, 1969.

Geological range: Upper Cretaceous.

Geographical distribution: Middle East.

Features: Small fishes with rather broad bodies. Head deep. Eyes large. Gape rather long. Snout rather pointed. Anterior portion of dorsal fin hard-rayed and beginning anterior to the middle of the body. Posterior portion of fin soft-rayed, arcuate dorsally and declining in height rearwards. Anal fin likewise hard-rayed anteriorly and soft-rayed more posteriorly. Pectoral fins long and narrow. Caudal fin deeply emarginate.

Remarks: Probably fed, at least partly, on plants.

Recent relatives: Genus extinct. Perhaps distantly related to other squirrelfishes of the family Holocentridae.

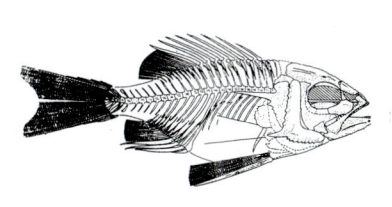

Ctenocephalichthys, reconstruction after GAYET.

EUTELEOSTEI
Order: Beryciformes
Family: Holocentridae

Higher Bony Fishes
Suborder: Berycoidei
Squirrelfishes

Eoholocentrum macrocephalum (de BLAINVILLE) (length c. 11 cm) from the Middle Eocene of Bolca, Italy. Original: Museo Civico di Storia Naturale, Verona, Italy.

Genus: *Eoholocentrum* SORBINI & TIRAPELLE, 1974.

Geological range: Middle Eocene.

Geographical distribution: Europa.

Features: Small fishes with slenderly oval bodies. Head deep. Eyes large. Gape rather long. Two dorsal fins, the posterior triangular, the anterior supported by strong rays. Anal fin likewise triangular. Pectoral fins vertically above pelvic fins. Caudal fin forked, with rounded lobes.

Remarks: Gregarious predators.

Recent relatives: Genus extinct. Related to recent squirrelfishes of the genus *Holocentrus*.

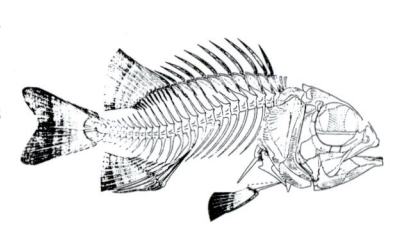

Eoholocentrum, reconstruction after SORBINI & TIRAPELLE.

EUTELEOSTEI
Higher Bony Fishes
Order: Beryciformes
Family: Holocentridae
Suborder: Berycoidei
Squirrelfishes

Unknown *Holocentrid* (length c. 18 cm) from the Middle Eocene of Bolca, Italy. Original: Paleontologiska Muséet, Uppsala, Sweden.

Genus: *Holocentrus* Scopoli, 1777.

Geological range: Eocene to recent.

Geographical distribution: Europe.

Features: Small to middle-sized fishes with elongate oval, laterally flattened bodies. Head deep. Eyes large. Gape rather long. Dorsal fin begins with hard rays in the anterior half of the body and probably rises to a tall point just anterior to the root of the tail. Anal fin opposite the posterior portion of the dorsal fin. Pelvic in the anterior third of the body. Pectoral fins narrow. Caudal fin on a stalk, deeply forked.

Remarks: Probably gregarious.

Recent relatives: Closely related to recent squirrelfishes of the genus *Holocentrus*.

Holocentrus rufus, a recent squirrelfish.

EUTELEOSTEI
Order: Beryciformes
Family: Holocentridae

Higher Bony Fishes
Suborder: Berycoidei
Squirrelfishes

Myripristis homopterygius AGASSIZ (length c. 11 cm) from the Middle Eocene of Bolca, Italy. Original: Staatliches Museum für Naturkunde, Karlsruhe, Germany.

Genus: *Myripristis* CUVIER, 1827.

Geological range: Eocene to Miocene.

Geographical distribution: Europe.

Features: Small fishes with slender, somewhat laterally compressed bodies. Head deep. Eyes large. Gape long. Two dorsal fins, the anterior hard-rayed, the posterior low and fringe-like, opposite the anal fin. Pectoral fins almost vertically above the pelvic fins. Caudal fin forked.

Remarks: Gregarious predators. Possibly the fossiled fish belongs to the genus *Berybolcensis*.

Recent relatives: Closely related to recent squirrelfishes of the genus *Myripristis*.

Myripristis murdjan, a recent squirrelfish.

728

EUTELEOSTEI
Order: Beryciformes
Family: Holocentridae

Higher Bony Fishes
Suborder: Berycoidei
Squirrelfishes

Paraspinus cupulus GAYET (length c. 16 cm) from the Upper Cretaceous of Lebanon. Original: Muséum National d'Histoire Naturelle, Paris, France. Photograph: Serette, Paris.

Genus: *Paraspinus* GAYET, 1981.

Geological range: Upper Cretaceous.

Geographical distribution: Middle East.

Features: Middle-sized fishes with elongate oval, laterally flattened bodies. Head deep, somewhat elongate. Eyes large. Gape long. Jaws set with sharp teeth. Snout slightly pointed. Dorsal fin hard-rayed anteriorly, soft-rayed posteriorly, begins approximately in the middle of the body. Anal fin begins anteriorly with a spine-like hard ray, as also do the pelvic fins. Pectoral fins fan-shaped. Caudal fin slightly forked, with broad lobes.

Remarks: Probably predators.

Recent relatives: None. Died out in the Cretaceous.

EUTELEOSTEI
Order: Beryciformes
Family: Holocentridae

Higher Bony Fishes
Suborder: Berycoidei
Squirrelfishes

Sargocentron rubrum FORSKÅL (length c. 3.5 cm) from the Pliocene of Fiume Marecchia, Italy. Original: Museo Civico di Storia Naturale, Verona, Italy.

Genus: *Sargocentron* FOWLER, 1904.

Synonym: *Sargocentrum*.

Geological range: Pliocene to recent.

Geographical distribution: Europe.

Features: Small fishes with rather laterally compressed bodies. Head deep. Eyes large. Gape rather long. Two dorsal fins. The anterior one hard-rayed and tall anteriorly, decreasing in height posteriorly. The more posterior soft-rayed and opposite the anal fin, which is likewise hard-rayed anteriorly and soft-rayed posteriorly. Pelvic fins vertically beneath the pectoral fins. Caudal fin forked.

Remarks: Gregarious.

Recent relatives: Closely related to recent squirrlefishes of the genus *Sargocentrum*.

Sargocentrum diadema, a recent squirrelfish.

EUTELEOSTEI
Order: Beryciformes
Family: Holocentridae

Higher Bony Fishes
Suborder: Berycoidei
Squirrelfishes

Stichoberyx polydesmus (ARAMBOURG) (length c. 8 cm) from the Lower Cretaceous of Tselfat, Morocco. Original: Museum National d'Histoire Naturelle, Paris, France. Photograph: Serette, Paris.

Genus: *Stichoberyx* GAUDANT, 1978.

Geological range: Lower Cretaceous.

Geographical distribution: Northern Africa.

Features: Small to middle-sized fishes with rather plump, laterally flattened bodies. Head deep. Eyes large. Dorsal fins broad-based, begins just anterior to the middle of the body and consists of hard rays anteriorly and soft rays posteriorly. Anal fin opposite the posterior end of the dorsal fin. Pectoral fins fan-shaped, vertically above the pelvic fins which are likewise fan-shaped. Caudal fin forked, with relatively broad lobes.

Remarks: Probably predators.

Recent relatives: None. Died out in the Cretaceous.

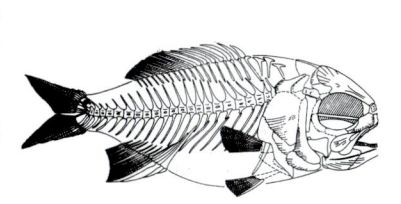

Stichoberyx, reconstruction after GAYET.

EUTELEOSTEI
Order: Beryciformes
Family: Holocentridae

Higher Bony Fishes
Suborder: Berycoidei
Squirrelfishes

Tenuicentrum lanceolatum (BASSANI) (length c. 14 cm) from the Middle Eocene of Bolca, Italy. Original: The Natural History Museum, London, U.K. (P19063).

Genus: *Tenuicentrum* SORBINI, 1975.

Geological range: Middle Eocene.

Geographical distribution: Europe.

Features: Small to middle-sized fishes with oval bodies. Head deep. Eyes large. Gape rather long. Two dorsal fins, the posterior being triangular and the anterior hard-rayed. Anal fin tall anteriorly, but then decreasing in height and forming a fringe. Pectoral fins rounded. Pelvic fins vertically beneath them, narrow and relatively long. Caudal fin rather deeply forked.

Remarks: Probably predators.

Recent relatives: Genus extinct. Possibly related to recent squirrelfish of the family Holocentridae.

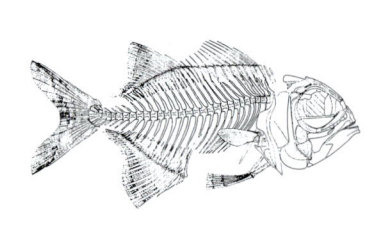

Tenuicentrum, reconstruction after SORBINI.

EUTELEOSTEI
Order: Beryciformes
Family: Unnamed

Higher Bony Fishes
Suborder: Berycoidei

Cryptoberyx minimus GAUDANT (length c. 3 cm) from the Upper Cretaceous of Lebanon. Original: Muséum National d'Histoire Naturelle, Paris, France. Photograph: Serette, Paris.

Genus: *Cryptoberyx* GAUDANT, 1978.

Geological range: Upper Cretaceous.

Geographical distribution: Middle East.

Features: Small fishes of rather plump shape. Head deep. Eyes large. Gape rather long. Dorsal fin begins shortly in front of the middle of the body, hard-rayed anteriorly and soft-rayed posteriorly. Anal fin similar but shorter. Pectoral fins small, fan-shaped. Pelvic fins almost vertically below. Caudal fin slightly forked.

Remarks: Probably gregarious.

Recent relatives: None. Died out in the Cretaceous.

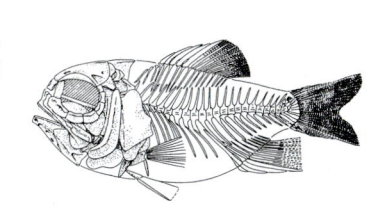

Cryptoberyx, reconstruction after GAYET.

EUTELEOSTEI — Higher Bony Fishes
Order: Beryciformes — **Suborder: Berycoidei**
Family: Not named

Plesioberyx maximus GAYET (length c. 9 cm) from the Upper Cretaceous of Lebanon. Original: Muséum National d'Histoire Naturelle, Paris, France. Photograph: Serette Paris.

Genus: *Plesioberyx* GAYET, 1980.

Geological range: Upper Cretaceous.

Geographical distribution: Middle East.

Features: Small fishes with oval, laterally flattened bodies. Head deep. Eyes large. Gape long. Snout slightly pointed. Dorsal fin begins shortly behind the head with hard rays. Anal and pelvic fins likewise carried by hard rays. Pectoral fins small and fan-shaped. Caudal fin slightly forked, with relatively broad lobes.

Remarks: Probably predators.

Recent relatives: None. Died out in the Cretaceous.

EUTELEOSTEI
Order: Beryciformes
Family: Dinopterygidae

Higher Bony Fishes
Suborder: Dinopterygoidei

Dinopteryx spinosus DAVIS (length c. 14 cm) from the Upper Cretaceous of Lebanon. Original: The Natural History Museum, London, U.K. (P4761).

Genus: *Dinopteryx* WOODWARD, 1901.

Geological range: Upper Cretaceous.

Geographical distribution: Middle East.

Features: Middle-sized fishes with deep bodies which taper sharply toward the tail root. Head shallow. Eyes large. Snout slightly pointed. Dorsal fin with numerous strong rays anteriorly, extending over the whole back. Anal fin similar but smaller. Pelvic fins narrow, fan-shaped. Pectoral fins. Caudal fin emarginate.

Remarks: Probably predators.

Recent relatives: None. Died out in the Upper Cretaceous.

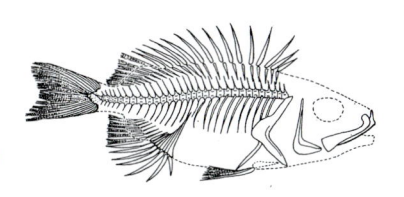

Dinopteryx, reconstruction after PATTERSON.

EUTELEOSTEI
Order: Beryciformes
Family: Dinopterygidae

Higher Bony Fishes
Suborder: Dinopterygoidei

Aipichthys velifer WOODWARD (length c. 8 cm) from the Upper Cretaceous of Lebanon. Original: Frickhinger Collection, Munich, Germany.

Genus: *Aipichthys* STEINDACHNER, 1859.

Geological range: Upper Cretaceous.

Geographical distribution: Middle East.

Features: Small fishes with almost circular, laterally flattened bodies. Head deep. Eyes small. Gape rather long, directed upwards. Snout slightly pointed. Dorsal fin begins anteriorly with a tall point, but decreases in height posteriorly, with an arcuate upper margin. Anal fin fringe-like. Pectoral fins small. Pelvic fins elongate and pointed. Caudal fin forked.

Remarks: Probably predators.

Recent relatives: None. Died out in the Upper Cretaceous.

Aipichthys, reconstruction after WOODWARD.

EUTELEOSTEI
Order: Beryciformes
Family: Pycnosteroididae

Higher Bony Fishes
Suborder: Dinopterygoidei

Pycnosteroides laevispinosus (HAY) (length c. 7 cm) from the Upper Cretaceous of Lebanon. Original: Field Museum of Natural History, Chicago, Illinois, U.S.A.

Genus: *Pycnosteroides* WOODWARD, 1942.

Geological range: Upper Cretaceous.

Geographical distribution: Middle East.

Features: Small fishes with circular, laterally flattened bodies. Head deep. Eyes large. Gape rather long. Dorsal fins with hard rays anteriorly but continuing as a tall fringe to the root of the tail. Anal fin similar but smaller. Pectoral fins small. Pelvic fins obliquely fan-shaped. Caudal fin strongly emarginate.

Remarks: Probably fed partly on plants.

Recent relatives: None. Died out in the Cretaceous.

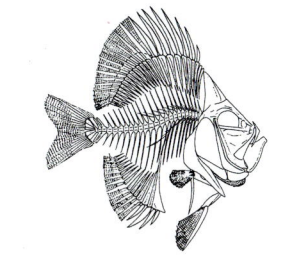

Pycnosteroides, reconstruction after PATTERSON.

EUTELEOSTEI
Order: **Beryciformes**
Family: **Stichocentridae**

Higher Bony Fishes
Suborder: **Dinopterygoidei**

Stichocentrus livatus PATTERSON (length c. 6 cm) from the Upper Cretaceous of Lebanon. Original: The Natural History Museum, London, U.K. (P5/681).

Genus: *Stichocentrus* PATTERSON, 1967.

Geological range: Upper Cretaceous.

Geographical distribution: Middle East.

Features: Small fishes with oval, laterally flattened bodies. Head deep. Eyes large. Gape rather long. Dorsal fins with hard rays anteriorly and then decreasing in height towards the tail root. Anal fin likewise with hard rays anteriorly. Pelvic fins fan-shaped. Caudal fin rather deeply forked.

Remarks: Probably predators.

Recent relatives: None. Died out in the Upper Cretaceous.

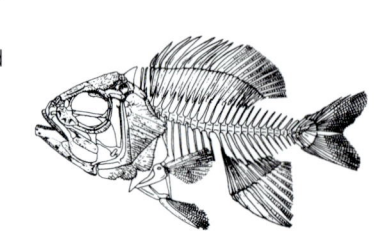

Stichocentrus, reconstruction after PATTERSON.

EUTELEOSTEI
Order: **Beryciformes**
Family: **Digoriidae**

Higher Bony Fishes
Suborder: **Dinopterygoidei**

Digoria ambigua DANILTCHENKO (length c. 7 cm) from the Lower Oligocene of northern Caucases. Original: Paleontologicheskii Muzei Russkoi Akademii Nauk, Moscow, Russia.

Genus: *Digoria* DANILTCHENKO, 1980.

Geological range: Lower Oligocene.

Geographical distribution: Eastern Europe.

Features: Small fishes with rather laterally compressed bodies. Head deep. Eyes large. Gape rather long. Dorsal fin hard-rayed and rather tall anteriorly, lower and soft-rayed posteriorly. Anal fin low, broad-based. Pelvic fins small. Pectoral fins fan-shaped. Caudal fin deeply forked.

Remarks: Probably predators.

Recent relatives: None. Died out in Oligocene.

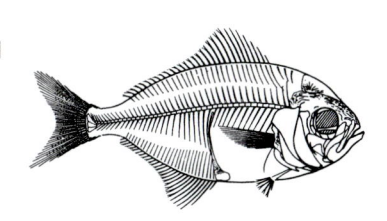

Digoria, reconstruction after Akademia Nauk, Moscow.

EUTELEOSTEI
Order: Beryciformes
Family: Polymixiidae

Higher Bony Fishes
Suborder: Polymixoidei
Beardfishes

Omosoma sahelalmae (COSTA) (length c. 8 cm) from the Upper Cretaceous of Lebanon. Original: The Natural History Museum, London, U.K. (P 4862)

Genus: *Omosoma* COSTA, 1857.

Geological range: Upper Cretaceous.

Geographical distribution: Europe, North Africa, Middle East.

Features: Small fishes with laterally compressed bodies. Head deep. Eyes large. Gape rather long. Dorsal fin begins anterior to the middle of the body, fringe-like, decreasing in height posteriorly. Anal fin similar but smaller. Pelvic and pectoral fins small. Caudal fin forked, with relatively narrow lobes.

Remarks: Probably predators.

Recent relatives: None. Died out in the Upper Cretaceous.

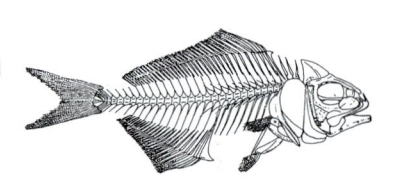

Omosoma, reconstruction after PATTERSON.

EUTELEOSTEI
Order: Beryciformes
Family: Polymixiidae

Higher Bony Fishes
Suborder: Polymyxoidei
Beardfishes

Omosomopsis simum (ARAMBOURG) (length c. 6 cm) from the Lower Cretaceous of Tselfat, Morocco. Original: Muséum National d'Histoire Naturelle, Paris, France. Photograph: Serette, Paris.

Genus: *Omosomopsis* GAUDANT, 1978.

Geological range: Lower Cretaceous.

Geographical distribution: Northern Africa.

Features: Small to middle-sized fishes with rather plump bodies. Head deep. Eyes large. Gape rather long. Snout rounded. Dorsal fin approximately in the middle of the body, opposite the low, broad-based anal fin. Pelvic fins small, fan-shaped. Pectoral fins elongate, rounded. Caudal fin small, deeply forked, with narrow lobes.

Remarks: Probably fed at least partly on plants.

Recent relatives: None. Died out in the Cretaceous.

Omosomopsis, reconstruction after GAYET.

EUTELEOSTEI
Order: **Beryciformes**
Family: **Polymixiidae**

Higher Bony Fishes
Suborder: **Polymixoidei**
Beardfishes

Platycormus germanus AGASSIZ (length c. 20 cm) from the Upper Cretaceous of Baumberge, Westphalia, Germany. Original: Geologisch-Paläontologisches Museum, Münster, Germany.

Genus: *Platycormus* von der MARCK, 1858.
Synonym: *Berycopsis*.
Geological range: Upper Cretaceous.
Geographical distribution: Europe.
Features: Middle-sized fishes with almost disc-shaped, laterally flattened bodies. Head deep. Eyes large. Gape rather long. Snout slightly pointed. Dorsal fin beginning in the middle of the body with a few hard rays, rising to a point in the anterior part and then decreasing in height towards the root of the tail. Anal fin fringe-like. Pelvic and pectoral fins small. Caudal fin deeply forked, with narrow lobes.
Remarks: Still-water fishes. Probably fed partly on plants.
Recent relatives: None. Died out in the Upper Cretaceous.

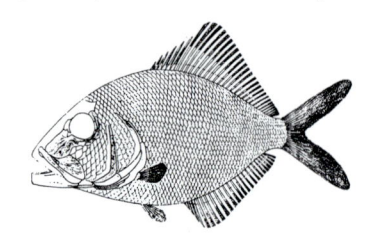

Platycormus, reconstruction after WOODWARD.

EUTELEOSTEI
Order: Beryciformes
Family: Polymixiidae

Higher Bony Fishes
Suborder: Polymixoidei
Beardfishes

Pycnosterinx russeggeri HECKEL (length c. 5 cm) from the Upper Cretaceous of Lebanon. Original: National Museum of Scotland, Edinburgh, U.K.

Genus: *Pycnosterinx* HECKEL, 1849.

Geological range: Upper Cretaceous.

Geographical distribution: Middle East.

Features: Small fishes with broad bodies. Head deep. Eyes large. Gape rather long. Dorsal fin begins in the middle of the body, opposite the somewhat smaller anal fin. Pelvic and pectoral fins small. Caudal fin forked, with relatively narrow lobes.

Remarks: Probably predators.

Recent relatives: Genus extinct. Possibly related to the recent genus *Polymixia*.

Polymixia berndti, a recent beardfish.

EUTELEOSTEI — Higher Bony Fishes

Order: Beryciformes?
Family: Araripichthyidae
Suborder: Araripichthyoidei

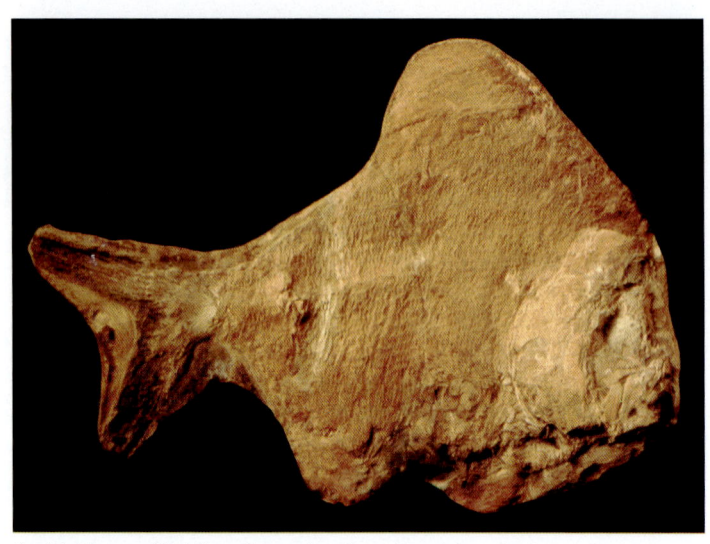

Araripichthys castilhoi Silva Santos (length c. 42 cm) from the Lower Cretaceous of Cearà, Brazil. Original: Herrmann Collection, Büchenbach, Germany.

Genus: *Araripichthys* Silva Santos, 1985.

Geological range: Lower Cretaceous.

Geographical distribution: South America.

Features: Middle-sized fishes with disc-shaped, laterally flattened bodies. Head deep. Eyes large. Gape rather long. Dorsal fin in the middle of the body, rising to a point, partly covered with scales. Anal fin likewise partly covered with scales. Caudal fin deeply forked, with narrow lobes.

Remarks: Still-water fishes.

Recent relatives: None. Died out in the Lower Cretaceous.

Araripichthys, reconstruction after Silva Santos.

EUTELEOSTEI
Higher Bony Fishes
Order: Beryciformes?
Family: Not named

Unnamed fish (length c. 12 cm) from the Upper Cretaceous of Lebanon. Original: Beyrouthy Collection, Toulouse, France.

Genus: Not named.

Geological range: Upper Cretaceous.

Geographical distribution: Middle East.

Features: Middle-sized fishes with disc-shaped, laterally flattened bodies. Head deep. Eyes large. Gape rather long. Dorsal fin beginning anterior to the middle of the body, tall and pointed. It is obliquely opposite to the anal fin which is likewise tall anteriorly but then decreases in height and becomes fringe-like. Pectoral fins long and fan-shaped. Caudal fin rather deeply forked.

Remarks: Still-water fishes which probably fed partly on plants.

Recent relatives: None. Died out in the Upper Cretaceous.

EUTELEOSTEI
Order: Beryciformes
Family: Not named

Higher Bony Fishes

Unnamed fish (length c. 9 cm) from the Upper Cretaceous of Lebanon. Original: Beyrouthy Collection, Toulouse, France.

Genus: Not named.

Geological range: Upper Cretaceous.

Geographical distribution: Middle East.

Features: Small fishes with disc-shaped outline, laterally flattened. Head deep. Eyes small. Gape rather long. Dorsal fin in the middle of the body, long and flag-like. Anal fin tall anteriorly, but running back into a low fringe. Pelvic fins very anterior in position, long and narrow. Caudal fin rather deeply forked, with slightly rounded lobes.

Remarks: Still-water fishes which probably fed partly on plants.

Recent relatives: None. Died out in the Upper Cretaceous.

EUTELEOSTEI
Order: Beryciformes?
Family: Not named

Higher Bony Fishes

Unnamed fish (length c. 8 cm) from the Upper Cretaceous of Lebanon. Original: Beyrouthy Collection, Toulouse, France.

Genus: Not named.

Geological range: Upper Cretaceous.

Geographical distribution: Middle East.

Features: Small fishes with deeply oval outline, laterally flattened. Head deep. Eyes large. Gape long. Dorsal fin begins shortly behind the head and runs as a tall fringe along the whole of the back, borne by hard thick spines which become thinner posteriorly. Anal fin triangular. Caudal fin moderately forked, with broad lobes.

Remarks: Probably predators.

Recent relatives: None. Died out in the Upper Cretaceous.

EUTELEOSTEI
Higher Bony Fishes
Order: Zeiformes
Family: Zeidae

Dories

Zenopsis clarus DANILTCHENKO (length c. 9 cm) from the Lower Oligocene of the northern Caucasus. Original: Paleontologicheskii Muzei Russkoi Akademii Nauk, Moscow, Russia.

Genus: *Zenopsis* GILL, 1862.

Geological range: Oligocene to recent.

Geographical distribution: Western and eastern Europe.

Features: Small fishes with almost circular outline, laterally flattened. Head deep. Gape long, directed upwards. Snout pointed. Dorsal fin approximately in the middle of the body, carried by hard rays. Anal fin broad-based. Pectoral fins small. Pelvic fins very anterior in position. Caudal fin not forked. Jaws set with small teeth.

Remarks: Open-water predators.

Recent relatives: Closely related to recent dories of the genus *Zenopsis*.

Zenopsis conchifer, a recent dory.

748

EUTELEOSTEI
Order: Zeiformes
Family: Zeidae

Higher Bony Fishes

Dories

Zeus sp. (length c. 9 cm) from the Pliocene of Fiume Marecchia, Italy. Original: Interfoss, Munich, Germany.

Genus: *Zeus* Linnaeus, 1758.

Geological range: Oligocene to recent.

Geographical distribution: Europe, North Africa.

Features: Small to middle-sized fishes with oval outline, laterally flattened. Head deep. Eyes large. Gape long, directed upwards. Snout pointed. Dorsal fin approximately in the middle of the body, anteriorly with strong, elongate rays but continuing posteriorly as a fringe. Anal fin similar. Pelvic fins elongate, very anterior in position. Pectoral fins small. Caudal fin not forked.

Remarks: Probably open-water predators.

Recent relatives: Closely related to recent dories of the genus *Zeus*.

Zeus faber, the recent John dory. Lithograph from Bloch.

EUTELEOSTEI
Order: Zeiformes
Family: Caproidae

Higher Bony Fishes

Boarfishes

Antigonia veronensis Sorbini (length c. 3 cm) from the Middle Eocene of Bolca, Italy. Original: Museo Civico di Storia Naturale, Verona, Italy.

Genus: *Antigonia* Lowe, 1843.

Geological range: Middle Eocene to recent.

Geographical distribution: Europe.

Features: Small to middle-sized fishes with rounded lozenge-shaped outline, laterally flattened. Head deep. Eyes large. Snout pointed. Dorsal fin begins at the highest point of the body, hard-rayed anteriorly but continuing rearward as a soft-rayed fringe. Anal fin similar. Pelvic fins very anterior. Pectoral fins small. Caudal fin not forked.

Remarks: Predators.

Recent relatives: Closely related to recent boarfishes of the genus *Antigonia*.

Antigonia steindachneri, a recent boarfish.

EUTELEOSTEI
Order: Zeiformes
Family: Caproidae

Higher Bony Fishes

Boarfishes

Capros radobojanus (KRAMBERGER) (length c. 3 cm) from the Oligocene of Wiesloch, Baden, Germany. Original: Staatliches Museum für Naturkunde, Karlsruhe, Germany.

Genus: *Capros* de LACÉPÈDE, 1802.

Synonyms: *Glyphisoma*, *Metapomichthys*, *Proantigonia*.

Geological range: Oligocene to recent.

Geographical distribution: Western and eastern Europe, North Africa.

Features: Very small fishes with almost circular outline, laterally flattened. Head deep. Eyes large. Dorsal fin begins with hard rays just behind the head and continues rearwards as a soft-rayed fringe. Anal fin similar. Pelvic fins very anterior in position. Pectoral fins small. Caudal fin not forked.

Remarks: Predators.

Recent relatives: Closely related to recent boarfishes of the genus *Capros*.

Capros aper, a recent boarfish.

EUTELEOSTEI — Higher Bony Fishes

Order: Gasterosteiformes
Family: Gasterosteidae — Sticklebacks

Gasterosteus doryssus JORDAN (length c. 6 cm) from the Miocene of California, U.S.A. Original: National Museum of Natural History, Smithsonian Institution, Washington, D.C., U.S.A.

Genus: *Gasterosteus* LINNAEUS, 1758.

Synonym: *Meriamella*.

Geological range: Upper Miocene to recent.

Geographical distribution: North America, Europe, Asia, North Africa.

Features: Small fishes of slender shape. Head shallow. Eyes large. Snout pointed. Dorsal fin with spines anteriorly, continuing rearwards as a fringe decreasing in height. Pectoral fins large. Pelvic fins consist of a powerful and obvious spine. Caudal fin slightly emarginate. Flanks of body armoured with bony plates.

Remarks: Fresh-water predators.

Recent relatives: Closely related to recent sticklebacks of the genus *Gasterosteus*.

Gasterosteus aculeatus, a recent stickleback.

EUTELEOSTEI
Order: **Pegasiformes**
Family: **Pegasidae**

Higher Bony Fishes

Seamoths

Pegasus volans VOLTA (length c. 8 cm) from the Middle Eocene of Bolca, Italy. Original: Muséum National d'Histoire Naturelle, Paris, France. Photograph: Serette, Paris.

Genus: *Pegasus* LINNAEUS, 1758.

Geological range: Eocene.

Geographical distribution: Europe.

Features: Small fishes of unusual shape. Head small. Eyes small. Gape long. Snout produced as a broad rostrum. Mouth toothless. Pectoral fins transformed into long many-rayed "wings".

Remarks: Fed on small free-swimming organisms.

Recent relatives: Probably related to seamoths of the genus *Pegasus*.

Pegasus volans, a recent seamoth. Lithograph from CUVIER.

EUTELEOSTEI — Higher Bony Fishes
Order: Syngnathiformes
Family: Aulostomidae
Suborder: Aulostomoidei
Trumpetfishes

Aulostomoides tyleri BLOT (length c. 7 cm) from the Middle Eocene of Bolca, Italy. Original: Muséum National d'Histoire Naturelle, Paris, France. Photograph: Serette, Paris.

Genus: *Aulostomoides* BLOT, 1980.

Geological range: Eocene.

Geographical distribution: Europe.

Features: Small fishes with elongate, very slender bodies. Head shallow. Eyes relatively large. Snout produced to form a tube-shaped rostrum. Dorsal fin very posterior.

Remarks: Fed on free-swimming organisms.

Recent relatives: None. Died out in Eocene.

EUTELEOSTEI
Order: **Syngnathiformes**
Family: **Aulostomidae**

Higher Bony Fishes
Suborder: **Aulostomoidei**
Trumpetfishes

Eoaulostomus bolcensis (AGASSIZ) (length c. 10 cm) from the Middle Eocene of Bolca, Italy. Original: Museo Civico di Storia Naturale, Verona, Italy.

Genus: *Eoaulostomus* BLOT, 1980.

Synonym: *Aulostoma*.

Geological range: Middle Eocene.

Geographical distribution: Europe.

Features: Small fishes with elongate, very thin bodies. Head shallow. Eyes large. A powerful, rather long, tube-shaped snout with a terminal mouth. Caudal fin small and not forked.

Remarks: Fed on microscopic organisms.

Recent relatives: Related to recent trumpetfishes of the genus *Aulostomus*.

Aulostomus sinensis, a recent trumpetfish.

755

EUTELEOSTEI
Higher Bony Fishes
Order: Syngnathiformes
Family: Aulostomidae
Suborder: Aulostomoidei
Trumpetfishes

Macraulostomus veronensis Blot (length c. 18 cm) from the Middle Eocene of Bolca, Italy. Original: Museo Civico di Storia Naturale, Verona, Italy.

Genus: *Macraulostomus* Blot, 1980.

Geological range: Middle Eocene.

Geographical distribution: Europe.

Features: Small fishes with elongate slender bodies. Head shallow. Eyes relatively large. Upper and lower jaws fused to form a rather long tube. Mouth relatively large. Dorsal fin in the posterior third of the body, opposite the anal fin. Pectoral fins small. Caudal fin not forked, rounded. Body covered with small ctenoid scales.

Remarks: Fed on microscopic prey.

Recent relatives: Genus extinct. Perhaps distantly related to recent trumpetfishes of the genus *Aulostomus*.

EUTELEOSTEI
Order: Syngnathiformes
Family: Urosphenidae

Higher Bony Fishes
Suborder: Aulostomoidei

Urosphen dubia (BLAINVILLE) (length c. 18 cm) from the Middle Eocene of Bolca, Italy. Original: Museo Civico di Storia Naturale, Verona, Italy.

Genus: *Urosphen* AGASSIZ, 1835.

Geological range: Middle Eocene.

Geographical distribution: Europe.

Features: Small fishes with thin, very slender bodies. Head shallow. Eyes large. Snout elongated to form a narrow tube. Mouth opening very small, terminal. Dorsal fin in the posterior third of the body, opposite the anal fin. Caudal fin not forked, rounded.

Remarks: In view of the small mouth, fed only on microscopic organisms.

Recent relatives: None. Died out in Oligocene.

EUTELEOSTEI
Higher Bony Fishes
Order: Syngnathiformes
Suborder: Aulostomoidei
Family: Urosphenidae

Urosphenopsis sagitta Daniltchenko (length c. 16 cm) from the Eocene of Turkmenistan, C.I.S. Original: Paleontologicheskii Muzei Akademii Nauk Russkoi Akademii Nauk, Moscow, Russia, C.I.S.

Genus: *Urospehopsis* Daniltchenko, 1968.

Geological range: Lower Eocene.

Geographical distribution: Western Asia.

Features: Small fishes with very narrow, elongate bodies. Head shallow. Eyes small. Massive tubular snout with terminal mouth. Body covered with bony armour.

Remarks: Fed on microscopic organisms.

Recent relatives: None. Died out in Eocene.

Urosphenopsis, reconstruction after Akademia Nauk, Moscow.

EUTELEOSTEI
Order: Syngnathiformes
Family: Fistulariidae

Higher Bony Fishes
Suborder: Aulostomoidei
Cornetfishes

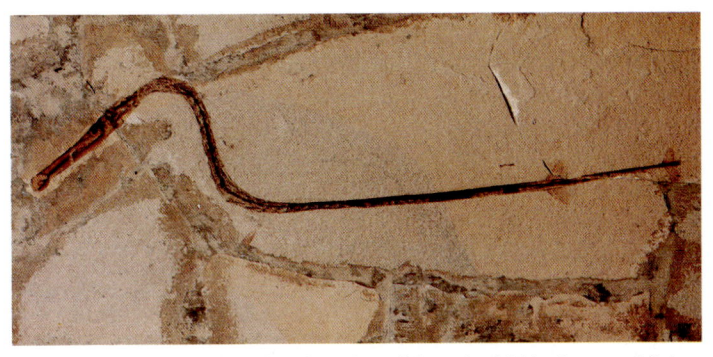

Fistularioides veronensis BLOT (length c. 21 cm) from the Middle Eocene of Bolca, Italy. Original: Museo Civico di Storia Naturale, Verona, Italy.

Genus: *Fistularioides* BLOT, 1980.

Geological range: Middle Eocene.

Geographical distribution: Europe.

Features: Small to middle-sized fishes with elongate very thin bodies. Head shallow. Eyes small. Snout rather long, massive and tube-shaped with a small terminal mouth. Dorsal fin opposite anal fin. Caudal fin forked, with a filamentous appendage.

Remarks: Fed on microscopic organisms.

Recent relatives: Related to recent cornetfishes of the genus *Fistularia*.

Fistularia tabaccaria, a recent cornetfish. Lithograph from BLOCH.

759

EUTELEOSTEI — Higher Bony Fishes
Order: Syngnathiformes
Family: Parasynarcualidae
Suborder: Aulostomoidei

Parasynarcualis longirostris (de BLAINVILLE) (length c. 22 cm) from the Middle Eocene of Bolca, Italy. Original: Museo Civico di Storia Naturale, Verona, Italy.

Genus: *Parasynarcualis* BLOT, 1980.

Synonym: *Fistularia*.

Geological range: Middle Eocene.

Geographical distribution: Europe.

Features: Small to middle-sized fishes with elongate, very narrow bodies. Head shallow. Eyes large. Snout powerful, rather long and tubular with a terminal mouth. Dorsal fin bipartite. Anal fin fringe-like. Caudal fin not forked.

Remarks: Fed on microscopic organisms.

Recent relatives: Genus extinct. Possibly related to recent cornetfishes of the family Fistulariidae.

Parasynarcualis, reconstruction after Akademia Nauk, Moscow.

EUTELEOSTEI
Order: Syngnathiformes
Family: Macrorhamphosidae

Higher Bony Fishes
Suborder: Aulostomoidei
Snipefishes

Aulorhamphus bolcensis (STEINDACHNER) (length c. 6 cm) from the Middle Eocene of Bolca, Italy. Original: Naturhistorisches Museum, Vienna, Austria.

Genus: *Aulorhamphus* de ZIGNO, 1890.

Geological range: Middle Eocene.

Geographical distribution: Europe.

Features: Small fishes with relatively deep, laterally flattened bodies. Head shallow. Eyes small. Snout short and tubular, with a small terminal mouth. Dorsal fin with hard rays anteriorly. Anal fin broad-based. Caudal fin not forked, rounded.

Remarks: Fed on microscopic animals.

Recent relatives: Possible related to recent snipefishes of the family Macrorhamphosidae.

Macrorhamphosus scolopax, a recent snipefish.

EUTELEOSTEI
Order: **Syngnathiformes**
Family: **Macrorhamphosidae**

Higher Bony Fishes
Suborder: **Aulostomoidei**
Snipefishes

Gasterorhamphosus zuppichini Sorbini (length c. 6 cm) from the Upper Cretaceous of Nardo, Italy. Original: Museo Civico di Storia Naturale, Verona, Italy.

Genus: *Gasterorhamphosus* Sorbini, 1981.

Geological range: Upper Cretaceous.

Geographical distribution: Europe.

Features: Small fishes with laterally flattened, relatively deep bodies. Head shallow. Eyes large. Snout tubular. Body partly armoured. Dorsal fin very posterior, the first ray very thick, denticulate on the dorsal surface and very long, projecting far behind the body. Anal fin small. Caudal fin not forked.

Remarks: Fed on microorganisms.

Recent relatives: Genus extinct. Related to recent snipefishes of the genus *Macrorhamphosus*.

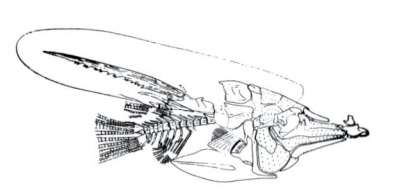

Gasterorhamphosus, reconstruction after Sorbini.

EUTELEOSTEI
Higher Bony Fishes
Order: Syngnathiformes
Family: Centriscidae
Suborder: Aulostomoidei
Shrimpfishes

Aeoliscus apsheronicus (LEDNEV) (length c. 10 cm) from the northern Caucasus, C.I.S. Original: Paleontologicheskii Muzei Russkoi Akademii Nauk, Moscow, Russia.

Genus: *Aeoliscus* JORDAN & STARKS, 1902.

Geological range: Oligocene to recent.

Geographical distribution: Western and eastern Europe.

Features: Small fishes with elongate, very laterally compressed bodies. Head shallow. Snout long and tubular, with small terminal mouth. Body covered with bony armour. Mid-ventral line sharp. Trunk extends rearwards into a long powerful spine. Tail region bent downwards. Caudal fin anterior to the spine, which represents the posterior end of the animal.

Remarks: Probably swam head-downwards, like their recent relatives.

Recent relatives: Related to recent shrimpfishes of the genus *Aeoliscus*.

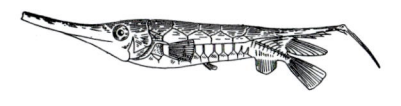

Aeoliscus, reconstruction after ORLOV.

763

EUTELEOSTEI
Order: Syngnathiformes
Family: Centriscidae

Higher Bony Fishes
Suborder: Aulostomoidei
Shrimpfishes

Centriscus strigatus GÜNTHER (length c. 14 cm) from the Pliocene of Fiume Marecchia, Italy. Original: Frickhinger Collection, Munich, Germany.

Genus: *Centriscus* LINNAEUS, 1758.

Synonym: *Amphisile*.

Geological range: Oligocene to recent.

Geographical distribution: Western Asia, Europe.

Features: Small fishes with slender, laterally very compressed bodies and sharp ventral edge. Head shallow. Eyes large. Rather long tubular snout with small terminal mouth. A long rearward-pointing spine projects beyond the posterior end of the body. Caudal fin small, rounded and turned downwards.

Remarks: Fed on microorganisms.

Recent relatives: Closely related to recent shrimpfishes of the genus *Centriscus*.

Centriscus scutatus, a recent shrimpfish. Lithograph from BLOCH.

EUTELEOSTEI
Order: Syngnathiformes
Family: Centriscidae

Higher Bony Fishes
Suborder: Aulostomoidei
Shrimpfishes

Paramphisile weileri BLOT (length c. 7 cm) from the Middle Eocene of Bolca, Italy. Original: Museo Civico di Storia Naturale, Verona, Italy.

Genus: *Paramphisile* BLOT, 1980.

Geological range: Middle Eocene.

Geographical distribution: Europe.

Features: Small fishes with slender, laterally very compressed bodies with sharp ventral edge. Head shallow. Eyes large. Snout long, tubular, with small terminal mouth. Powerful spine projects beyond the posterior end of the body. Caudal fin small, rounded and turned downwards.

Remarks: Fed on microorganisms.

Recent relatives: Genus extinct. Distantly related to recent shrimpfishes of the genus *Centriscus*.

EUTELEOSTEI
Order: Syngnathiformes
Family: Paraeoliscidae

Higher Bony Fishes
Suborder: Aulostomoidei
Shrimpfishes

Aeoliscoides longirostris (AGASSIZ) (c. 4 cm) from the middle Eocene of Bolca, Italy. Original: Museo Civico di Storia Naturale, Verona, Italy.

Genus: *Aeoliscoides* BLOT, 1980.

Geological range: Middle Eocene.

Geographical distribution: Europe.

Features: Small fishes with slender, compressed bodies. Sharp ventral edge. Snout elongated into a slender, tubular rostrum. Mouth small and terminal. The posterior end of the body terminates in a spine.

Remarks: Due to the small mouth these fishes could only feed on the smallest prey organisms.

Recent relatives: Genus extinct. There is a possible relation to recent shrimpfishes of the genus *Aeoliscus*.

EUTELEOSTEI
Order: Syngnathiformes
Family: Paraeoliscidae

Higher Bony Fishes
Suborder: Aulostomoidei
Shrimpfishes

Paraeoliscus robinetae BLOT (length c. 10 cm) from the Middle Eocene of Bolca, Italy. Original: Museo Civico di Storia Naturale, Verona, Italy.

Genus: *Paraeoliscus* BLOT, 1980.

Geological range: Middle Eocene.

Geographical distribution: Europe.

Features: Small fishes with narrow, very laterally compressed bodies. Head slender. Eyes large. Long tubular snout with small terminal mouth. A spine points posteriorly, extending far beyond the posterior end of the body which turns downwards, together with the caudal fin.

Remarks: Fed on microorganisms.

Recent relatives: Genus extinct. Related to recent shrimpfishes of the genus *Aeoliscus*.

Aeoliscus punctulatus, a recent shrimpfish.

EUTELEOSTEI
Order: Syngnathiformes
Family: Solenostomidae

Higher Bony Fishes
Suborder: Aulostomoidei
Ghost Pipefishes

Calamostoma breviculum AGASSIZ (length c. 12 cm) from the Middle Eocene of Bolca, Italy. Original: Museo Civico di Storia Naturale, Verona, Italy.

Genus: *Calamostoma* AGASSIZ, 1833.

Geological range: Middle Eocene.

Geographical distribution: Europe.

Features: Small fishes of slender shape. Head shallow. Eyes relatively large. Snout extended to form a tube.

Mouth small. Two dorsal fins. Anal fin and pelvic fins small. Pectoral fins somewhat larger. Caudal fin relatively large, not forked. Body armoured with bony plates.

Remarks: Could only have fed on very small organisms in view of the narrow tubular mouth.

Recent relatives: Genus extinct. Perhaps distantly related to the recent genus *Solenostomus*.

Solenostomus cyanopterus, a recent ghost pipefish.

EUTELEOSTEI
Order: Syngnathiformes
Family: Solenostomidae

Higher Bony Fishes
Suborder: Syngnathoidei
Ghost Pipefishes

Prosolenostomus lessinii BLOT (length c. 4 cm) from the Middle Eocene of Bolca, Italy. Original: Carnegie Museum of Natural History, Pittsburgh, Penn., U.S.A.

Genus: *Prosolenostomus* BLOT, 1980.

Geological range: Middle Eocene.

Geographical distribution: Europe.

Features: Very small fishes of narrow elongate shape. Head shallow. Eyes small. Short tubular snout. Body armoured with quadrangular plates arranged in rows. Caudal fin not forked, rounded.

Remarks: Fed on microorganisms.

Recent relatives: Genus extinct. Related to recent ghost pipefishes of the family Solenostomidae.

EUTELEOSTEI
Order: Syngnathiformes
Family: Syngnathidae

Higher Bony Fishes
Suborder: Syngnathoidei
Pipefishes and Seahorses

Hippocampus ramulosus Leach (length c. 5 cm) from the Pliocene of Fiume Marecchia, Italy. Original: Museo Civico di Storia Naturale, Verona, Italy.

EUTELEOSTEI
Order: Syngnathiformes
Family: Syngnathidae

Higher Bony Fishes
Suborder: Syngnathoidei
Pipefishes and Seahorses

Hippocampus cuda, a recent seahorse.

Genus: *Hippocampus* Rafinesque, 1810.

Geological range: Pliocene to recent.

Geographical distribution: Europe.

Features: Small fishes with elongate, angularly curved bodies, scaleless and surrounded by bony dermal shields. Head shallow. Eyes small. Rather long tubular snout with small terminal mouth. Dorsal fin shortly anterior to the beginning of the tail. Pectoral fins fan-shaped. Caudal fin absent.

Remarks: Fed on microorganisms.

Recent relatives: Closely related to recent seahorses of the genus *Hippocampus*.

EUTELEOSTEI — Higher Bony Fishes
Order: Syngnathiformes — Suborder: Syngnathoidei
Family: Syngnathidae — Pipefishes and Seahorses

Pseudosyngnathus opisthopterus (AGASSIZ) (length c. 30 cm) from the Middle Eocene of Bolca, Italy. Original: Muséum National d'Histoire Naturelle, Paris, France. Photograph: Serette, Paris.

Genus: *Pseudosyngnathus* KNER, 1863.

Geological range: Eocene.

Geographical distribution: Europe.

Features: Middle-sized fishes with very slender elongate bodies. Head small and elongate. Eyes small. Snout produced to form a long thin tubular rostrum. Dorsal fin small, very posterior. Caudal fin elongate, not forked, with a rounded end.

Remarks: Fed on free-swimming microorganisms.

Recent relatives: None. Died out in Eocene.

EUTELEOSTEI
Order: Syngnathiformes
Family: Syngnathidae

Higher Bony Fishes
Suborder: Syngnathoidei
Pipefishes and Seahorses

Syngnathus heckeli de Zigno (length c. 9 cm) from the Middle Eocene of Bolca, Italy. Original: Museo Civico di Storia Naturale, Verona, Italy.

Genus: *Syngnathus* Linnaeus, 1758.

Synonym: *Siphonostoma*

Geological range: Middle Eocene to recent.

Geographical distribution: Europe, North America, northern Africa.

Features: Small to middle-sized fishes with elongate, very narrow bodies. Head shallow. Eyes small. Short tubular snout with small terminal mouth. Body covered with bony quadrangular plates arranged in rows. Caudal fin not forked, rounded.

Remarks: Fed on microorganisms.

Recent relatives: Genus extinct. Closely related to recent pipefishes of the genus *Syngnathus*.

Syngnathus sp., a recent pipefish.

773

EUTELEOSTEI
Order: Syngnathiformes
Family: Syngnathidae

Higher Bony Fishes
Suborder: Syngnathoidei
Pipefishes and Seahorses

Unnamed fish (length c. 22 cm) from the Pliocene of Fiume Marecchia, Italy. Original: Frickhinger Collection, Munich, Germany.

Genus: Not named.

Geological range: Pliocene.

Geographical distribution: Europe.

Features: Middle-sized fishes with elongate, very narrow bodies. Head shallow. Eyes large. Rather long tubular snout with small terminal mouth. Body armoured with rounded plates of bone. Body tapers to a much narrower tail stem with a small unforked caudal fin.

Remarks: Fed on microorganisms.

Recent relatives: Related to recent pipefishes.

EUTELEOSTEI
Order: Dactyliopteriformes
Family: Dactyliopteridae

Higher Bony Fishes

Flying Gurnards

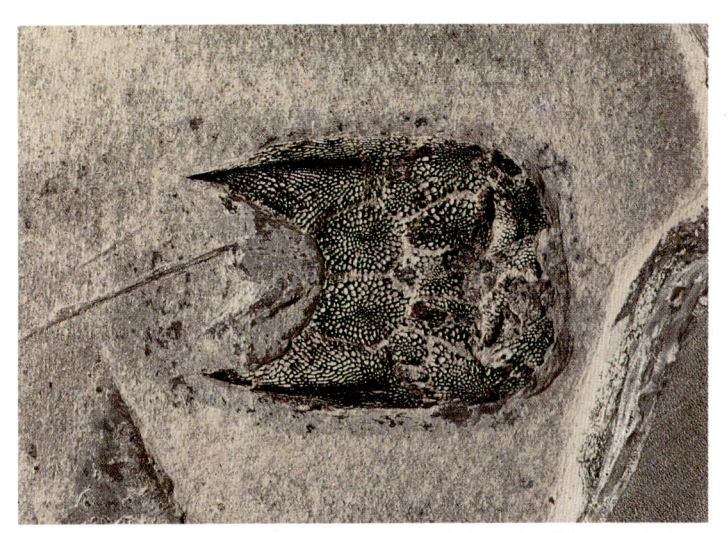

Dactylopterus volitans (LINNAEUS) (length c. 3.5cm) from the Pliocene of Fiume Marecchia, Italy. Original: Museo Civico di Storia Naturale, Verona, Italy.

Genus: *Dactylopterus* de LACÉPÈDE, 1801.

Geological range: Pliocene to recent.

Geographical distribution: Europe.

Features: Small to middle-sized fishes with slender bodies. Head broad. Eyes large. Upper surface of skull flat, fused with the first three vertebrae, armoured with bony plates. Snout falling away steeply. First dorsal fin hard-rayed, shorter than the soft-rayed second dorsal fin. Pectoral fins on the throat. Caudal fin not forked. Scales fused firmly together.

Remarks: Probably bottom-dwelling fishes. Their "flying ability" is greatly in doubt.

Recent relatives: Closely related to recent flying gurnards of the genus *Dactylopterus*.

Dactylopterus sp., a recent flying gurnard.

775

EUTELEOSTEI
Order: Scorpaeniformes
Family: Scorpaenidae

Higher Bony Fishes
Suborder: Scorpaenoidei
Scorpionfishes

Scorpaena prior HECKEL (length c. 19 cm) from the Miocene of St. Margarethen, Austria. Original: Weiss Collection, Vienna, Austria. Photograph: Weiss, Vienna.

Genus: *Scorpaena* LINNAEUS, 1758.

Geological range: Miocene to recent.

Geographical distribution: Europe.

Features: Small to middle-sized fishes of plump shape. Head large. Eyes large. Gape very long. Anterior part of the dorsal fin carried by hard rays, the posterior part soft-rayed. Anal fin opposite the posterior part. Pelvic fins under the broad pectoral fins. Caudal fin not forked, rounded.

Remarks: Bottom-dwelling predators. Even at that time the hard fin rays were probably poisonous.

Recent relatives: Closely related to recent scorpionfishes of the genus *Scorpaena*.

Scorpaena notata, a recent scorpionfish.

EUTELEOSTEI
Order: Scorpaeniformes
Family: Pterygocephalidae

Higher Bony Fishes
Suborder: Scorpaenoidei

Pterygocephalus paradoxus AGASSIZ (length c. 5 cm) from the Middle Eocene of Bolca, Italy. Original: Museo Civico di Storia Naturale, Verona, Italy.

Genus: *Pterygocephalus* AGASSIZ, 1835.

Geological range: Middle Eocene.

Geographical distribution: Europe.

Features: Small fishes of rather broad shape. Head shallow. Eyes large. Gape rather long. First head spine longer than second. First dorsal fin of powerful spines. Second dorsal fin rounded, opposite the anal fin which likewise begins with spines. Pectoral fins relatively large. Caudal fin large, not forked, rounded.

Remarks: Predators.

Recent relatives: None. Died out in Eocene

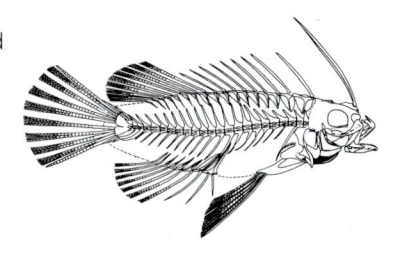

Pterygocephalus, reconstruction after BLOT.

EUTELEOSTEI
Order: **Syngnathiformes**
Family: **Rhamphosidae**

Higher Bony Fishes
Suborder: **Scorpaenoidei**

Rhamphosus aculeatus (de BLAINVILLE) (length c. 6 cm) from the Middle Eocene of Bolca, Italy. Original: Museo Civico di Storia Naturale, Verona, Italy.

Genus: *Rhamphosus* AGASSIZ, 1835.

Geological range: Middle Eocene.

Geographical distribution: Europe.

Features: Small fishes of slender shape. Head shallow. Eyes small. Snout produced to form a pointed rostrum. Long, posteriorly directed spine approximately in the middle of the body. Dorsal fin very posterior, opposite the anal fin. Caudal fin not forked.

Remarks: Probably fed on microorganisms.

Recent relatives: None. Died out in Eocene.

EUTELEOSTEI
Order: Scorpaeniformes
Family: Triglidae

Higher Bony Fishes
Suborder: Scorpaenoidei
Searobins

Trigla licatae SAUVAGE (length c. 7 cm) from the Upper Miocene of Licata, Sicily, Italy. Original: Muséum National d'Histoire Naturelle, Paris, France. Photograph: Serette, Paris.

Genus: *Trigla* LINNAEUS, 1758.

Geological range: Eocene to recent.

Geographical distribution: Europe, western Asia, North America, northern Africa.

Features: Small fishes of rather plump shape. Head large. Eyes large. Snout pointed. Gape long. Two dorsal fins, the anterior hard-rayed. Anal fin broad-based. Pectoral fins greatly enlarged. Caudal fin slightly emarginate.

Remarks: Bottom-dwellers.

Recent relatives: Closely related to recent searobins of the genus *Trigla*.

Trigla sp., a recent searobin. Lithograph from BLOCH.

EUTELEOSTEI
Higher Bony Fishes

Order: Scorpaeniformes
Family: Cottidae

Suborder: Cottoidei
Sculpins

Cottopsis gaudryi (Priem) (length c. 10 cm) from the Lower Oligocene of Iran. Original: Muséum National d'Histoire Naturelle, Paris, France. Photograph: Serette, Paris.

Genus: *Cottopsis* Priem, 1908.

Geological range: Oligocene.

Geographical distribution: Middle East.

Features: Small fishes of rather laterally compressed shape. Head large. Eyes large. Two dorsal fins, the first in anterior half of body and the second in posterior half. The pectoral fins obliquely opposite the first dorsal fin. The broad-based anal fin opposite the second dorsal fin. Pelvic fins beneath the pectoral fins. Caudal fin forked.

Remarks: Bottom-dwelling predators.

Recent relatives: Genus extinct. Perhaps distantly related to recent sculpins of the family Cottidae.

EUTELEOSTEI
Order: **Scorpaeniformes**
Family: **Cottidae**

Higher Bony Fishes
Suborder: **Cottoidei**
Sculpins

Cottus brevis AGASSIZ (length c. 5 cm) from the Upper Miocene of Unterkirchberg, Württemberg, Germany. Original: Frickhinger Collection, Munich, Germany.

Genus: *Cottus* LINNAEUS, 1758.

Geological range: Oligocene to recent.

Geographical distribution: Asia, New Zealand, Europe, North America.

Features: Small fishes with rather laterally compressed shape. Head relatively wide. Two dorsal fins, the anterior being shorter than the posterior. Anal fin opposite the posterior dorsal fin. Pectoral fins large. Caudal fin not forked, rounded.

Remarks: Bottom-dwelling predators.

Recent relatives: Genus extinct. Closely related to recent sculpins of the genus *Cottus*.

Cottus gobio, a recent sculpin.

EUTELEOSTEI
Order: Scorpaeniformes
Family: Cottidae

Higher Bony Fishes
Suborder: Cottoidei
Sculpins

Eocottus veronensis VOLTA (length c. 9 cm) from the Middle Eocene of Bolca, Italy. Original: The Natural History Museum, London, U.K., (P16131).

Genus: *Eocottus* WOODWARD, 1901.

Geological range: Middle Eocene.

Geographical distribution: Europe.

Features: Small fishes of slender outline. Head shallow. Eyes large. Gape long. Two dorsal fins with the anal fin opposite the more posterior. Caudal fin large, not forked, rounded.

Remarks: Probably bottom-dwelling predators.

Recent relatives: Genus extinct. Related to recent sculpins of the genus *Cottus*.

EUTELEOSTEI
Order: Scorpaeniformes
Family: Cottidae

Higher Bony Fishes
Suborder: Cottoidei
Sculpins

Lepidocottus aries (AGASSIZ) (length c. 8 cm) from the Lower Oligocene of Aix en Provence, France. Original: The Natural History Museum, London, U.K. (P27442).

Genus: *Lepidocottus* SAUVAGE, 1875.

Geological range: Lower Oligocene.

Geographical distribution: Europe.

Features: Small fishes of elongate shape. Head shallow. Eyes large. Snout pointed. Gape long, directed upwards. Two dorsal fins, the first in the anterior and the second in the posterior half of the body. Anal fin opposite the second dorsal fin. Pectoral fins relatively broad. Caudal fin not forked, rounded.

Remarks: Bottom-dwelling predators.

Recent relatives: Genus extinct. Related to recent sculpins of the family Cottidae.

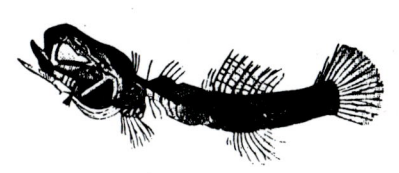

Lepidocottus, reconstruction after ZITTEL.

783

EUTELEOSTEI
Higher Bony Fishes
Order: Scorpaeniformes
Family: ?

Unnamed fish (length c. 3.5 cm) from the Eocene of Fuur, Denmark. Original: Paleontologiska Muséet, Uppsala, Sweden.

Genus: Not named.

Geological range: Eocene.

Geographical distribution: Europe.

Features: Small fishes of slender shape. Head shallow. Eyes large. Gape long. Upper and lower jaws set with small pointed teeth. Dorsal fin beginning shortly behind the head. Pectoral fins fan-shaped. Pelvic fins opposite them and preceded by free spines. Caudal fin not forked, rounded. A few barbels on the chin.

Remarks: Probably bottom-dwellers.

Recent relatives: Genus presumably extinct. Possibly related to recent fishes of the order Scorpaeniformes.

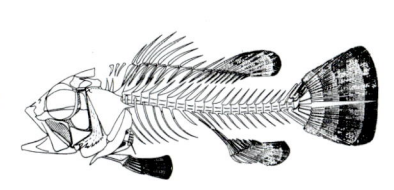

EUTELEOSTEI
Order: Perdiformes
Family: Centropomidae

Higher Bony Fishes
Suborder: Percoidei
Snooks

Cyclopoma gigas AGASSIZ (length c. 40 cm) from the Middle Eocene of Bolca, Italy. Original: Rijksmuseum van Geologie en Mineralogie, Leiden, Netherlands.

Genus: *Cyclopoma* AGASSIZ, 1833.

Geological range: Middle Eocene.

Geographical distribution: Europe.

Features: Middle-sized fishes of rather laterally compressed shape. Head shallow. Eyes small. Snout pointed. Gape rather long. Two dorsal fins, the anterior consisting of a few hard rays, the posterior rounded and soft-rayed. Anal fin with three hard rays anteriorly, continuing posteriorly with an elongate, rounded soft-rayed portion. Pelvic fins fan-shaped. Caudal fin, large, rounded, not forked.

Remarks: Predators.

Recent relatives: None. Died out in Eocene.

Cyclopoma, reconstruction after SORBINI.

785

EUTELEOSTEI
Order: Perciformes
Family: Centropomidae

Higher Bony Fishes
Suborder: Percoidei
Snooks

Eolates gracilis (AGASSIZ) (length c. 16 cm) from the Middle Eocene of Bolca, Italy. Original: Krauss Collection, Weißenburg, Germany.

Genus: *Eolates* SORBINI, 1970.

Geological range: Eocene.

Geographical distribution: Europe, Africa.

Features: Middle-sized fishes, very laterally compressed in shape. Head shallow. Anterior dorsal fin of hard rays. Second dorsal fin tall, rounded and soft-rayed. Anal fin with a few hard rays anteriorly, continuing posteriorly as an elongate, rounded, soft-rayed portion. Pectoral fins fan-shaped. Caudal fin large, rounded, not forked.

Remarks: Predators.

Recent relatives: Genus extinct. Closely related to recent perches of the genus *Lates*, to which the large Nile perch and the well known Australian food fish barramundi belong. Seven species of this genus live in fresh water and one in the sea.

Lates calcarifer, the barramundi.

EUTELEOSTEI
Order: Perciformes
Family: Percichthyidae

Higher Bony Fishes
Suborder: Percoidei
Temperate Basses

Blotichthys coleanus (AGASSIZ) (length c. 4 cm) from the Middle Eocene of Bolca, Italy. Original: The Natural History Museum, London, U.K. (P5513921).

Genus: *Blotichthys* SORBINI, 1979.

Geological range: Middle Eocene.

Geographical distribution: Europe.

Features: Very small fishes of oval outline, laterally flattened. Head deep. Eyes large. Snout somewhat pointed. Dorsal fins with short hard rays anteriorly, becoming taller and soft-rayed posteriorly. Anal fin shorter but otherwise similar. Pectoral fins small. Pelvic fins rather elongate. Caudal fin rounded, not forked.

Remarks: Predators living in littoral zones.

Recent relatives: None. Died out in Eocene.

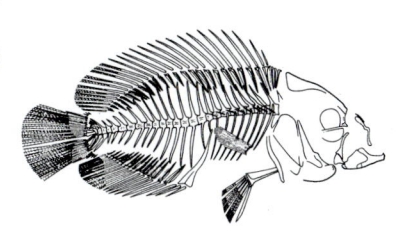

Blotichthys, reconstruction after SORBINI.

787

EUTELEOSTEI
Order: Perciformes
Family: Percichthyidae

Higher Bony Fishes
Suborder: Percoidei
Temperate Basses

Morone sp. (length c. 23 cm) from the Oligocene of Wiesbaden, Hesse, Germany. Original: Bürger Collection, Bad Hersfeld, Germany.

Genus: *Morone* MITCHILL, 1814.

Geological range: Oligocene to recent.

Geographical distribution: Europe, North America.

Features: Small to middle-sized fishes of slender shape. Head shallow. Eyes relatively small. Snout slightly pointed. Gape rather long. Anterior dorsal fin consisting of hard-rays, beginning approximately in the middle of the body. Posterior dorsal fin considerably smaller, soft-rayed. Anal fin opposite the posterior dorsal fin, elongate and rounded, with hard rays anteriorly. Pelvic fins beneath the pectoral fins. Caudal fin deeply forked.

Remarks: Fresh-water predators.

Recent relatives: Closely related to recent perches and bass of the genus *Morone* (*Roccus*). This lives in North America and Europe, partly in fresh water and partly in the sea, but it always seeks fresh water to lay its eggs.

Morone americana, the recent white perch.

EUTELEOSTEI
Order: Perciformes
Family: Percichthyidae

Higher Bony Fishes
Suborder: Percoidei
Temperate Basses

Percalates sp. (length c. 5 cm) from the Eocene of Queensland, Australia. Original: Queensland Museum, Brisbane, Australia.

Genus: *Percalates* RAMSAY & OGILBY, 1887.

Geological range: Eocene to recent.

Geographical distribution: Australia.

Features: Very small fishes with rather laterally compressed bodies. Head shallow. Eyes small. Snout pointed. Dorsal fin hard-rayed anteriorly, soft-rayed posteriorly. Anal fin similarly with hard rays anteriorly. Pelvic fins vertically beneath the pectoral fins. Caudal fin not forked, slightly emarginate.

Remarks: Bottom-dwellers.

Recent relatives: Genus extinct. Closely related to the recent genus *Percalates* which lives in Australia.

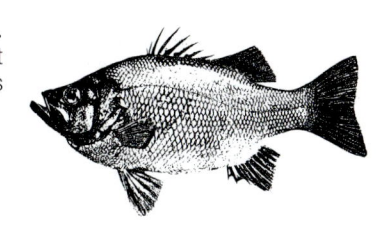

Percalates colonorum, a recent bass.

EUTELEOSTEI
Order: Perciformes
Family: Percichthyidae

Higher Bony Fishes
Suborder: Percoidei
Temperate Basses

Percichthys antiquus (length c. 8 cm) from the Miocene of Taubaté, Brazil. Original: Interfoss, Munich, Germany.

Genus: *Percichthys* Girard, 1834.

Geological range: Paleocene to recent.

Geographical distribution: South America.

Features: Small fishes with rather laterally compressed bodies. Head deep. Eyes large. Gape rather long. Dorsal fin in the middle of the body, with hard rays anteriorly and soft rays posteriorly. Obliquely opposite the anal fin, which likewise has hard rays anteriorly. Pectoral and pelvic fins small.

Remarks: Predators. *Percichthys* is probably identical with the genus *Santosius*.

Recent relatives: Genus extinct, but closely related to recent basses of the genus *Percichthys*.

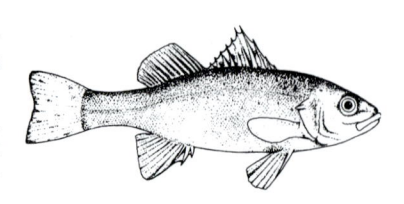

Percichthys trucha, a recent bass after Arratia.

EUTELEOSTEI
Order: Perciformes
Family: Percichthyidae

Higher Bony Fishes
Suborder: Percoidei
Temperate Basses

Santosius antiquus WOODWARD (length c. 12 cm) from the Miocene of Taubaté, Brazil. Original: Naturmuseum Senckenberg, Frankfurt-am-Main, Germany.

Genus: *Santosius* ARRATIA, 1982.

Geological range: Miocene.

Geographical distribution: South America.

Features: Small fishes of slender shape. Head shallow. Eyes large. Snout pointed. Dorsal fin with hard rays anteriorly and posteriorly continuing as a soft-rayed fringe. Pectoral fins very small. Pelvic and anal fins somewhat larger. Caudal fin not forked.

Remarks: Fresh-water predators.

Recent relatives: Genus extinct. Perhaps related to recent basses of the *Percichthys* which live in South America.

EUTELEOSTEI
Higher Bony Fishes
Order: Perciformes
Family: Serranidae
Suborder: Percoidei
Sea Basses

Acanus gracilis AGASSIZ (length c. 18 cm) from the Lower Oligocene of Glarus, Switzerland. Original: Tischlinger Collection, Stammham, Germany. Photo: Tischlinger.

Genus: *Acanus* AGASSIZ, 1834.

Geological range: Oligocene.

Geographical distribution: Europe.

Features: Small fishes of oval outline, laterally flattened. Head deep. Eyes very large. Snout rather pointed. Gape rather long. Dorsal fin hard-rayed anteriorly and soft-rayed posteriorly. Anal fin likewise with hard rays anteriorly. Pectoral fins small. Pelvic fins somewhat elongate. Caudal fin not forked.

Remarks: Predators. Probably lived in the littoral zones. Recently assigned to the genus *Priacanthus*.

Recent relatives: None. Died out in Oligocene.

EUTELEOSTEI — Higher Bony Fishes

Order: Perciformes
Family: Serranidae
Suborder: Percoidei
Sea Basses

Amphiperca multiformis WEITZEL (length c. 20 cm) from the Eocene of Messel, Germany. Original: Frickhinger Collection, Munich, Germany.

Genus: *Amphiperca* WEITZEL, 1933.

Geological range: Eocene to Miocene.

Geographical distribution: Europe.

Features: Middle-sized fishes with deep, laterally compressed bodies. Head short and deep. Eyes large. Snout pointed. Gape rather long. Anterior dorsal fin consisting of hard rays. Posterior dorsal fin soft-rayed. Anal fin shorter, likewise hard-rayed anteriorly and soft-rayed posteriorly. Pectoral fins small. Pelvic fins vertically beneath and rather broader. Caudal fin rounded, elongate, not forked.

Remarks: Fresh-water predators.

Recent relatives: None. Died out in Miocene.

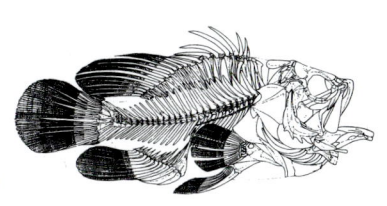

Amphiperca, reconstruction after MICKLICH.

793

EUTELEOSTEI
Order: Perciformes
Family: Serranidae

Higher Bony Fishes
Suborder: Percoidei
Sea Basses

Blabe crawleyi WHITE (length c. 5 cm) from the Miocene of Tourah, Egypt. Original: The Natural History Museum, London, U.K. (P14486).

Genus: *Blabe* WHITE, 1936.

Geological range: Miocene.

Geographical distribution: Northern Africa.

Features: Very small fishes with oval outline, laterally flattened. Head deep. Eyes large. Snout somewhat pointed. Gape rather long. Dorsal fin with hard rays anteriorly, continuing as a soft-rayed fringe posteriorly. Anal fin shorter, but otherwise similar. Pectoral fins small. Pelvic fins elongate. Caudal fin rounded, not forked.

Remarks: Probably predators.

Recent relatives: None. Died out in Miocene.

Blabe, reconstruction after WHITE.

EUTELEOSTEI
Higher Bony Fishes
Order: Perciformes
Family: Serranidae
Suborder: Percoidei
Sea Basses

Dapalis macrurus (AGASSIZ) (length c. 21 cm) from the Oligocene of Cereste, France. Original: Frickhinger Collection, Munich, Germany.

Genus: *Dapalis* GISTLY, 1848.

Synonym: *Smerdis*.

Geological range: Paleocene to Miocene.

Geographical distribution: Europe, northern Africa.

Features: Middle-sized fishes of rather laterally compressed shape. Head deep. Eyes large. Gape rather long. Anterior dorsal fin tall, hard-rayed. Posterior dorsal fin low, triangular and soft-rayed. Anal and pelvic fins triangular. Pectoral fins small. Caudal fin rather deeply forked, with broad lobes.

Remarks: Fresh-water predators.

Recent relatives: None. Died out in Miocene.

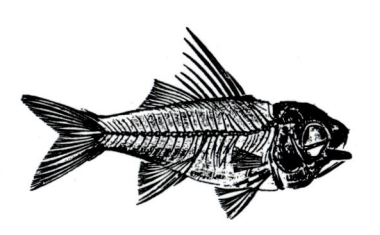

Dapalis, reconstruction after WOODWARD.

795

EUTELEOSTEI
Higher Bony Fishes

Order: Perciformes
Family: Serranidae

Suborder: Percoidei
Sea Basses

Epinephelus sp. (length c. 21 cm) from the Miocene of Oran, Algeria. Original: Muséum National d'Histoire Naturelle, Paris, France. Photograph: Serette, Paris.

Genus: *Epinephelus* BLOCH, 1793.

Synonym: *Emmachaere*.

Geological range: Miocene to recent.

Geographical distribution: Northern Africa.

Features: Small fishes with rather deep bodies anteriorly, becoming less deep rearwards. Head elongate. Eyes small. Gape rather long. Dorsal fin begins just behind head with hard rays and continues, with soft rays, to near the end of the body. Anal fin likewise hard-rayed anteriorly. Pectoral fins vertically above the pelvic fins. Caudal fin not forked.

Remarks: Predators.

Recent relatives: Closely related to recent groupers of the genus *Epinephelus*.

Epinephelus sp., a recent grouper. Lithograph from BLOCH.

EUTELEOSTEI
Order: Perciformes
Family: Serranidae

Higher Bony Fishes
Suborder: Percoidei
Sea Basses

Palaeoperca proxima MICKLICH (length c. 21 cm) from the Eocene of Messel, Hesse, Germany. Original: Staatliches Museum für Naturkunde, Karlsruhe, Germany.

Genus: *Palaeoperca* MICKLICH, 1978.

Geological range: Eocene.

Geographical distribution: Europe.

Features: Middle-sized fishes of rather laterally compressed shape. Head deep. Eyes small. Snout pointed. Gape long. Anterior dorsal fin hard-rayed. Posterior dorsal fin triangular and soft-rayed. Anal fin with hard rays anteriorly and soft rays posteriorly. Caudal fin not forked, slightly emarginate.

Remarks: Fresh-water predators.

Recent relatives: None. Died out in Eocene.

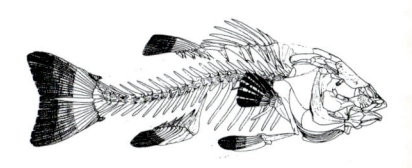

Palaeoperca, reconstruction after MICKLICH.

EUTELEOSTEI — Higher Bony Fishes
Order: Perciformes — **Suborder: Percoidei**
Family: Serranidae — **Sea Basses**

Priacanthopsis crassispinus ARAMBOURG (length c. 2 cm) from the Lower Oligocene of Iran. Original: Muséum National d'Histoire Naturelle, Paris, France. Photograph: Serette, Paris.

Genus: *Priacanthopsis* ARAMBOURG, 1967.

Geological range: Lower Oligocene to recent.

Geographical distribution: Middle East.

Features: Very small fishes with oval bodies. Head deep. Eyes large. Snout slightly pointed. Gape rather long. Dorsal fin tall and hard-rayed anteriorly, but posteriorly low and soft-rayed. Anal fin similar. Pelvic fins long and narrow. Caudal fin not forked.

Remarks: Probably predators.

Recent relatives: None. Died out in Oligocene.

EUTELEOSTEI
Order: **Perciformes**
Family: **Serranidae**

Higher Bony Fishes
Suborder: **Percoidei**
Sea Basses

Prolates heberti GERVAIS (length c. 6 cm) from the Upper Cretaceous of Monte Aimée, France. Original: The Natural History Museum, London, U.K.

Genus: *Prolates* PRIEM, 1899.

Synonym: *Pseudolates*.

Geological range: Upper Cretaceous to Paleocene.

Geographical distribution: Europe.

Features: Small fishes of rather laterally compressed shape. Head shallow. Eyes large. Gape rather long. Dorsal fin hard-rayed anteriorly and soft-rayed posteriorly. Anal fin similar. Pelvic fins likewise with hard rays. Caudal fin rounded, not forked.

Remarks: Predators.

Recent relatives: None. Died out in Paleocene.

EUTELEOSTEI — Higher Bony Fishes

Order: Perciformes
Family: Serranidae
Suborder: Percoidei
Sea Basses

Properca angusta (length c. 17 cm) from the Middle Miocene of Puy de Dome, France. Original: The Natural History Museum, London, U.K. (P27736).

Genus: *Properca* Sauvage, 1880.

Geological range: Eocene to Miocene.

Geographical distribution: Europe.

Features: Middle-sized fishes with rather laterally compressed bodies. Head shallow. Eyes small. Gape rather long. Dorsal fin low and hard-rayed anteriorly, triangular and soft-rayed posteriorly. Anal fin opposite the posterior part of the dorsal fin. Pelvic fins rounded. Caudal fin not forked, slightly emarginate.

Remarks: Fresh-water fishes.

Recent relatives: None. Died out in Miocene.

EUTELEOSTEI   **Higher Bony Fishes**
Order: **Perciformes**   Suborder: **Percoidei**
Family: **Serranidae**   **Sea Basses**

Serranus rugosus Heckel (length c. 14 cm) from the Middle Eocene of Bolca, Italy. Original: Museo Civico di Storia Naturale, Verona, Italy.

Genus: *Serranus* Cuvier, 1817.

Geological range: Middle Eocene to recent.

Geographical distribution: Europe, northern Africa.

Features: Small fishes of somewhat laterally compressed shape. Anterior dorsal fin hard-rayed. Posterior dorsal fin rounded, soft-rayed. Anal fin with a few hard rays. Pectoral and pelvic fins rounded. Pelvic fins vertically beneath pectorals. Caudal fin forked.

Remarks: Predators.

Recent relatives: Closely related to recent sea basses of the genus *Serranus*.

Serranus baldwini, a recent sea bass.

801

EUTELEOSTEI
Order: Perciformes
Family: Serranidae?

Higher Bony Fishes
Suborder: Percoidei
Sea Basses

Unnamed bass (length c. 3 cm) from the Eocene of Mors, Denmark. Original: Paleontologiska Muséet, Uppsala, Sweden.

Genus: Not named.

Geological range: Eocene.

Geographical distribution: Europe.

Features: Very small fishes of elongate oval outline, laterally flattened. Head deep. Eyes large. Gape short. Anterior dorsal fin hard-rayed, approximately in the middle of the body. Posterior dorsal fin soft-rayed, in the posterior third of the body, opposite the broad-based anal fin. Pectoral fins narrow. Caudal fin slightly emarginate.

Remarks: Fed on small animals.

Recent relatives: Genus presumably extinct. Possibly related to recent basses of the family Serranidae.

EUTELEOSTEI
Order: **Perciformes**
Family: **Centrarchidae**

Higher Bony Fishes
Suborder: **Percoidei**
Sunfishes

Boreocentrarchus sp. (length c. 13 cm) from the Miocene of Nevada, U.S.A. Original: Field Museum of Natural History, Chicago, Illinois, U.S.A.

Genus: *Boreocentrarchus* SCHLAIKJER, 1937.

Geological range: Miocene.

Geographical distribution: North America.

Features: Small fishes with deep, laterally flattened bodies. Head deep. Eyes large. Gape rather long. Dorsal fin hard-rayed anteriorly but low and soft-rayed posteriorly. Anal fin similar. Pelvic fins vertically beneath pectoral fins. Caudal fin rather deeply forked.

Remarks: Fresh-water fishes.

Recent relatives: Genus extinct. Possibly related to other sunfishes, living in North America, of the family Centrarchidae.

EUTELEOSTEI

Higher Bony Fishes

Order: Perciformes
Family: Centrarchidae

Suborder: Percoidei
Sunfishes

Chaenobryttus kansasensis HIBBARD (length c. 8 cm) from the Miocene of Kansas, U.S.A. Original: Museum of Natural History, Lawrence, Kansas, U.S.A.

Genus: *Chaenobryttus* COPE, 1865.

Geological range: Miocene to recent.

Geographical distribution: North America.

Features: Small fishes of rather laterally compressed shape. Head shallow. Eyes large. Gape rather long. Dorsal fin hard-rayed anteriorly, soft-rayed posteriorly. Anal fin similar. Pelvic fins short, lying vertically beneath the likewise short pectoral fins. Caudal fin not forked, emarginate.

Remarks: Fresh-water fishes.

Recent relatives: Related to recent sunfishes of the genus *Chaenobryttus*.

Chaenobryttus gulosus, a recent sunfish.

EUTELEOSTEI
Higher Bony Fishes
Order: Perciformes
Suborder: Percoidei
Family: Centrarchidae
Sunfishes

Oligoplarchus squamipinnis COPE (length c. 9 cm) from the Oligocene of South Dakota, U.S.A. Original: National Museum of Natural History, Smithsonian Institution, Washington, D.C., U.S.A.

Genus: *Oligoplarchus* COPE, 1891.

Synonym: *Lepomis*.

Geological range: Oligocene.

Geographical distribution: North America.

Features: Small fishes of oval outline, laterally flattened. Head deep. Eyes large. Gape rather long. Dorsal fin hard-rayed anteriorly and soft-rayed posteriorly. Anal fin similar. Pelvic and pectoral fins small. Caudal fin not forked.

Remarks: Fresh-water fishes.

Recent relatives: None. Died out in Oligocene.

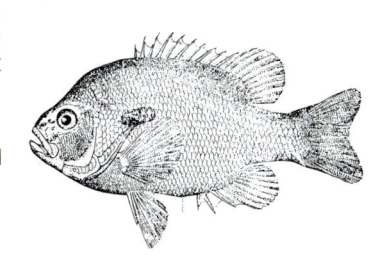

Oligoplarchus, reconstruction after JORDAN.

EUTELEOSTEI / Higher Bony Fishes

Order: Perciformes
Suborder: Percoidei
Family: Centrarchidae
Sunfishes

Pomoxis lanei HIBBARD (length c. 5 cm) from the Miocene of Kansas, U.S.A. Original: Museum of Natural History, Lawrence, Kansas, U.S.A.

Genus: *Pomoxis* RAFINESQUE, 1818.

Geological range: Miocene to recent.

Geographical distribution: North America.

Features: Very small fishes of rather laterally compressed shape. Head deep. Eyes large. Gape short. Anterior dorsal fin hard-rayed. Posterior dorsal fin soft-rayed. Anal fin similar. Pelvic fins small, vertically beneath the pectoral fins which are likewise small. Caudal fin not forked, emarginate.

Remarks: Fresh-water fishes.

Recent relatives: Closely related to the recent sunfishes named crappies and placed in the genus *Pomoxis*. These fishes live in the fresh waters of North America.

Pomoxis nigromaculatus, a recent sunfish.

EUTELEOSTEI
Order: Perciformes
Family: Percidae

Higher Bony Fishes
Suborder: Percoidei
Perches

Dules temnopterus AGASSIZ (length c. 11 cm) from the Middle Eocene of Bolca, Italy. Original: Rijksmuseum van Geologie en Mineralogie, Leiden, Netherlands.

Genus: *Dules* AGASSIZ, 1844.

Geological range: Middle Eocene.

Geographical distribution: Europe.

Features: Small fishes of rather laterally compressed shape. Head deep. Eyes large. Gape rather long. Dorsal fin begins shortly behind the head and continues posteriorly as a fringe. Anal fin considerably shorter, but likewise fringe-like. Caudal fin short and broad, not forked, slightly emarginate.

Remarks: Probably predators.

Recent relatives: None. Died out in Eocene.

EUTELEOSTEI
Order: Perciformes
Family: Percidae

Higher Bony Fishes
Suborder: Percoidei
Perches

Mioplosus labracoides COPE (length c. 27 cm) from the Eocene of Wyoming, U.S.A. Original: Interfoss, Munich, Germany.

Genus: *Mioplosus* COPE, 1877.

Geological range: Eocene.

Geographical distribution: North America.

Features: Middle-sized fishes of slender shape. Head shallow. Eyes large. Gape long. Anterior dorsal fin hard-rayed. Posterior dorsal fin soft-rayed, triangular, opposite the anal fin which is likewise triangular. Caudal fin deeply emarginate.

Remarks: Fresh-water predators.

Recent relatives: Genus extinct. Perhaps distantly related to recent pike perches of the genus *Stizostedion*.

Stizostedion lucioperca, the recent pike perch. Lithograph from BLOCH (see next page).

PERCA LUCIOPERCA.
Der Zander.
Le Sandre.
The Pirke-Perch.

EUTELEOSTEI
Higher Bony Fishes
Order: Perciformes
Family: Percidae
Suborder: Percoidei
Perches

Perca fluviatilis LINNAEUS (length c. 21 cm) from the Upper Pliocene of Willershausen, Lower Saxony, Germany. Original: Staatliches Museum für Naturkunde, Stuttgart, Germany.

Genus: *Perca* LINNAEUS, 1758.

Synonyms: *Coeloperca, Eoperca, Percostoma*.

Geological range: Eocene to recent.

Geographical distribution: Europe, North America, western Asia.

Features: Small to middle-sized fishes of slender shape. Head shallow. Eyes large. Gape long. Anterior dorsal fin hard-rayed, arcuate. Posterior dorsal fin soft-rayed. Anal fin narrow. Pectoral fins rounded. Pelvic fins elongate. Caudal fin deeply emarginate.

Remarks: Predators.

Recent relatives: The fossil species is identical to the recent one.

Perca fluviatilis, the recent perch. Lithograph from BLOCH (see next page).

PERCA FLUVIATILIS.
Der Barsch.
La Perche.
The Perch.

EUTELEOSTEI
Higher Bony Fishes
Order: Perciformes
Family: Percidae
Suborder: Percoidei
Perches

Plioplarchus whitei COPE (length c. 7 cm) from the Oligocene of North Dakota, U.S.A. Original: National Museum of Natural History, Smithsonian Institution, Washington, D.C., U.S.A.

Genus: *Plioplarchus* COPE, 1883.

Geological range: Eocene to recent.

Geographical distribution: Europe, North America.

Features: Small fishes with rather laterally compressed bodies. Head deep. Eyes large. Gape rather long. Dorsal fin hard-rayed anteriorly and soft-rayed posteriorly. Anal fin similar but shorter. Pelvic and pectoral fins elongate. Caudal fin not forked, rather emarginate.

Remarks: Predators.

Recent relatives: Closely related to recent perches of the genus *Plioplarchus*.

EUTELEOSTEI
Order: Perciformes
Family: Priacanthidae

Higher Bony Fishes
Suborder: Percoidei
Bigeyes

Pristigenys substriatus EASTMAN (length c. 6 cm) from the Middle Eocene of Bolca, Italy. Original: Museo Civico di Storia Naturale, Verona, Italy.

Genus: *Pristigenys* AGASSIZ, 1835.

Synonyms: *Pseudopriacanthos*

Geological range: Eocene to recent.

Geographical distribution: Europe.

Features: Small fishes of oval outline, laterally flattened. Head deep. Eyes large. Gape rather long. Dorsal and anal fins very large, hard-rayed anteriorly and soft-rayed posteriorly. Pectoral fins small. Pelvic fins long and narrow. Caudal fin not forked.

Remarks: Probably lived near reefs.

Recent relatives: Closely related to recent bigeyes of the genus *Pristigenys* which live in modern oceans.

Pristigenys altus, a recent bigeye.

EUTELEOSTEI

Higher Bony Fishes

Order: Perciformes
Family: Apogonidae

Suborder: Percoidei
Cardinalfishes

Apogon spinosus AGASSIZ (length c. 4 cm) from the Middle Eocene of Bolca, Italy. Original: Museo Civico di Storia Naturale, Verona, Italy.

Genus: *Apogon* de LACÉPÈDE, 1802.

Synonym: *Eretima*.

Geological range: Middle Eocene to recent.

Geographical distribution: Europe, North America.

Features: Small fishes of rather laterally compressed shape. Head deep. Eyes large. Gape rather long. Anterior dorsal fin hard-rayed. Posterior dorsal fin soft-rayed. Both relatively tall. Anal fin expanded on a narrow base. Rounded pectoral and pelvic fins. Caudal fin not forked.

Remarks: Lived in coral reefs like their recent relatives.

Recent relatives: None. Died out in Miocene. Genus extinct. Closely related to cardinalfishes of the genus *Apogon*.

Apogon maculatus, a recent cardinalfish.

EUTELEOSTEI
Order: Perciformes
Family: Apogonidae

Higher Bony Fishes
Suborder: Percoidei
Cardinalfishes

Eosphaeramia margaritae Sorbini (length c. 4 cm) from the Middle Eocene of Bolca, Italy. Original: Museo Civico di Storia Naturale, Verona, Italy.

Genus: *Eosphaeramia* Sorbini, 1983.

Geological range: Middle Eocene.

Geographical distribution: Europe.

Features: Small fishes of oval outline, laterally flattened. Head deep. Eyes large. Gape rather long. Anterior dorsal fin very tall, hard-rayed. Posterior dorsal fin considerably lower, soft-rayed. Anal fin hard-rayed anteriorly and soft-rayed posteriorly. Pectoral fins small. Pelvic fins very long. Caudal fin forked with broad lobes.

Remarks: Reef-dwellers.

Recent relatives: Genus extinct. Possibly related to recent cardinalfishes of the genus *Apogon*.

Apogon nematopterus, a recent cardinalfish.

EUTELEOSTEI
Order: Perciformes
Family: Acropomatidae

Higher Bony Fishes
Suborder: Percoidei

Acropoma lepidotus (AGASSIZ) (length c. 3 cm) from the Middle Eocene of Bolca, Italy. Original: Museo Civico di Storia Naturale, Verona, Italy.

Genus: *Acropoma* TEMMINCK & SCHLEGEL, 1843.

Synonym: *Labrax*.

Geological range: Middle Eocene.

Geographical distribution: Europe.

Features: Very small fishes of oval outline, rather rounded in transverse section. Head deep. Eyes large. Gape short. Two dorsal fins, the posterior one opposite the anal fin. Caudal fin rather deeply forked, with broad lobes.

Remarks: The genus *Acropoma* is placed by some authors in the family Percichthyidae.

Recent relatives: Closely related to recent members of the genus *Acropoma*.

Acropoma sp., a recent representative.

EUTELEOSTEI
Order: Perciformes
Family: Pomatomidae

Higher Bony Fishes
Suborder: Percoidei
Bluefishes

Lednevia oligocenica (SMIRNOV) (length c. 5 cm) from the Lower Miocene of the northern Caucasus, C.I.S. Original: Paleontologicheskii Muzei Russkoi Akademii Nauk, Moscow, Russia (Bannikov Collection).

Genus: *Lednevia* DANILTCHENKO, 1960.

Geological range: Miocene.

Geographical distribution: Western and eastern Europe.

Features: Small fishes of slender shape. Head deep. Eyes large. Gape long, directed slightly upwards. Dorsal fins begin approximately in the middle of the body, the first being hard-rayed and the second soft-rayed. Anal fin opposite the second dorsal fin. Caudal fin relatively large, emarginate.

Remarks: Predators.

Recent relatives: Genus died out in Miocene. Perhaps related to recent bluefishes of the family Pomatomidae.

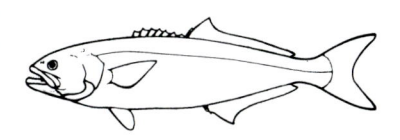

Pomatomus saltatrix, a recent bluefish, after NELSON.

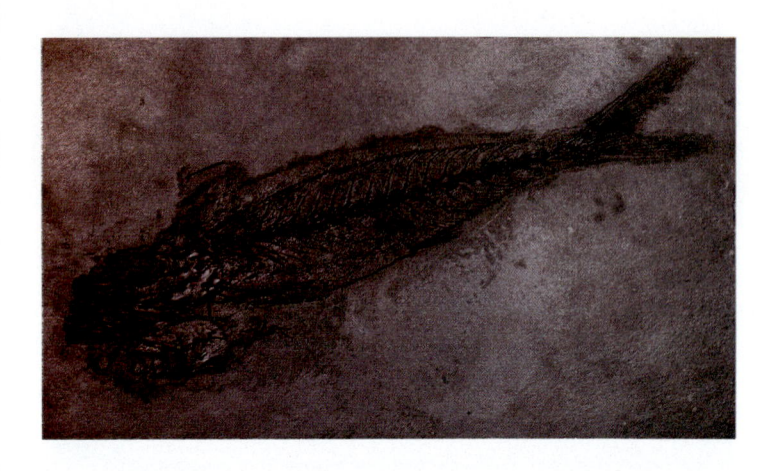

EUTELEOSTEI
Order: Perciformes
Family: Echeneidae

Higher Bony Fishes
Suborder: Percoidei
Remoras

Echineis glaronensis WETTSTEIN (length c. 28 cm) from the Lower Oligocene of Glarus, Switzerland. Original: Paläontologisches Museum, Zürich, Switzerland.

Genus: *Echineis* LINNAEUS, 1758.

Geological range: Oligocene to recent.

Geographical distribution: Europe.

Features: Middle-sized fishes of slender elongate shape. Head shallow. Eyes small. Gape rather long. A characteristic oval sucker on the head. Dorsal fin in the posterior half of the body, fringe-like. Anal fin likewise fringe-like. Caudal fin rather deeply forked.

Remarks: Probably attached itself to larger fishes, even at that time.

Recent relatives: Closely related to recent remoras of the genus *Echineis* which live nowadays in the oceans.

Echineis sp., a recent remora.

818

EUTELEOSTEI

Order: Perciformes
Family: Carangidae

Higher Bony Fishes

Suborder: Percoidei
Jacks and Pompanos

Archaeus sp. (length c. 7 cm) from the Oligocene of Wiesloch, Baden, Germany. Original: Staatliches Museum für Naturkunde, Karlsruhe, Germany.

Genus: *Archaeus* AGASSIZ, 1834.

Synonym: *Archaeoides*.

Geological range: Oligocene to Miocene.

Geographical distribution: Europe.

Features: Small fishes of elongate oval outline, laterally flattened. Head deep. Eyes large. Gape rather long. Anterior dorsal fin hard-rayed. Posterior dorsal fin soft-rayed. Anal fin low and fringe-like. Caudal fin rather deeply forked.

Remarks: Probably gregarious.

Recent relatives: None. Died out in Miocene.

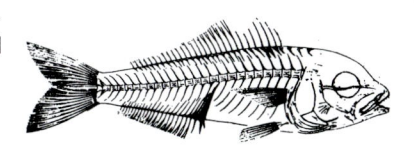

Archaeus, reconstruction after Akademia Nauk, Moscow.

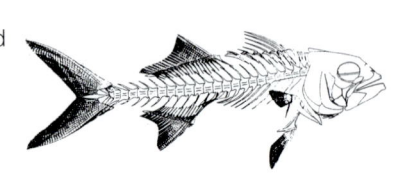

EUTELEOSTEI
Order: Perciformes
Family: Carangidae

Higher Bony Fishes
Suborder: Percoidei
Jacks and Pompanos

Carangopsis dorsalis AGASSIZ (length c. 32 cm) from the Middle Eocene of Bolca, Italy. Original: Museo Civico di Storia Naturale, Verona, Italy.

Genus: *Carangopsis* AGASSIZ, 1844.

Geological range: Middle Eocene.

Geographical distribution: Europe.

Features: Small fishes with slender outline, deeper anteriorly than posteriorly. Head shallow. Eyes small. Gape rather long. Anterior dorsal fin hard-rayed. Posterior dorsal fin soft-rayed, rather fringe-like. Pectoral fins pointed. Caudal deeply forked, with narrow lobes.

Remarks: Predators.

Recent relatives: None. Died out in Eocene.

Carangopsis, reconstruction after BLOT.

EUTELEOSTEI
Order: Perciformes
Family: Carangidae

Higher Bony Fishes
Suborder: Percoidei
Jacks and Pompanos

Caranx ovalis HECKEL (length c. 11 cm) from the Oligocene of Chiavon, Italy. Original: Naturhistorisches Museum, Vienna, Austria.

Genus: *Caranx* de LACÉPÈDE, 1802.

Synonyms: *Citula*, *Perequula*.

Geological range: Middle Eocene to recent.

Geographical distribution: Europe, North America, northern Africa.

Features: Small fishes of oval outline, laterally flattened. Head deep. Eyes large. Gape rather long. Dorsal fins small, the first hard-rayed and the second soft-rayed. Anal fin low and fringe-like. Caudal fin forked, with narrow lobes.

Remarks: Probably gregarious.

Recent relatives: Closely related to recent jacks of the genus *Caranx*, the most important of which is the yellow jack.

Caranx bartholomaei, the recent yellow jack.

EUTELEOSTEI
Order: Perciformes
Family: Carangidae

Higher Bony Fishes
Suborder: Percoidei
Jacks and Pompanos

Ceratoichthys pinnatiformis de Blainville (length c. 50 cm) from the Middle Eocene of Bolca, Italy. Original: Museo Civico di Storia Naturale, Verona, Italy.

EUTELEOSTEI
Order: Perciformes
Family: Carangidae

Higher Bony Fishes
Suborder: Percoidei
Jacks and Pompanos

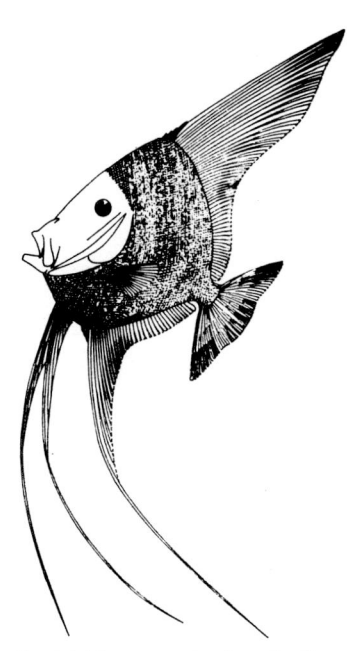

Ceratoichthys, reconstruction after BLOT.

Genus: *Ceratoichthys* BLOT, 1969.

Geological range: Middle Eocene.

Geographical distribution: Europe.

Features: Middle-sized fishes, broadly oval in outline and laterally flattened. Head deep. Eyes small. Gape short. Dorsal fin begins with a few hard rays and rises steeply to a high point, then decreases in height with a posteriorly convex curve and continues rearwards as a low fringe. Anal fin with a long first ray, but then becoming rapidly less tall in a posteriorly concave curve and likewise passing into a low fringe. Pelvic fins drawn out into two long filaments. Pectoral fins small. Caudal fin not forked, with an undulating posterior margin.

Remarks: Probably open-water fishes.

Recent relatives: None. Died out in Eocene.

EUTELEOSTEI — Higher Bony Fishes
Order: Perciformes
Family: Carangidae
Suborder: Percoidei
Jacks and Pompanos

Ductor vestenae VOLTA (length c. 11 cm) from the Middle Eocene of Bolca, Italy. Original: Museo Civico di Storia Naturale, Verona, Italy.

Genus: *Ductor* AGASSIZ, 1844.

Geological range: Middle Eocene.

Geographical distribution: Europe.

Features: Small fishes of slender elongate shape. Head shallow. Eyes small. Snout pointed. Gape rather long. Jaws set with small teeth. Anterior dorsal fin of a few hard rays. Posterior dorsal fin soft-rayed and fairly high, running off into a fringe. Anal fin similar. Pectoral and pelvic fins narrow, set close together. Caudal fin rather deeply forked, with broad lobes.

Remarks: Gregarious.

Recent relatives: None. Died out in Eocene.

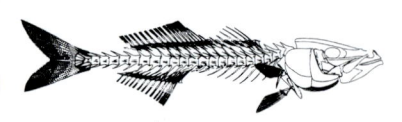

Ductor, reconstruction after BLOT.

824

EUTELEOSTEI
Order: Perciformes
Family: Carangidae

Higher Bony Fishes
Suborder: Percoidei
Jacks and Pompanos

Paratrachinotus tenuiceps AGASSIZ (length c. 9 cm) from the Middle Eocene of Bolca, Italy. Original: Bayerisches Staatssammlung für Paläontologie, Munich, Germany.

Genus: *Paratrachinotus* BLOT, 1969.

Geological range: Middle Eocene.

Geographical distribution: Europe.

Features: Small fishes of approximately lozenge-shaped outline, laterally flattened. Head deep. Eyes large. Gape rather long. Dorsal fin with a few hard rays anteriorly, rises to a point approximately in the middle of the body and then continues rearwards as a low fringe. Anal fin similarly constructed and of same length. Pectoral fins rounded. Caudal fin rather deeply forked.

Remarks: Probably fed partly on plants.

Recent relatives: Related to recent pompanos of the genus *Trachinotus*.

Trachinotus carolinus, the recent Florida pompano.

825

EUTELEOSTEI
Order: Perciformes
Family: Carangidae

Higher Bony Fishes
Suborder: Percoidei
Jacks and Pompanos

Seriola prisca AGASSIZ (length c. 22 cm) from the Middle Eocene of Bolca, Italy. Original: Interfoss, Munich, Germany.

Genus: *Seriola* CUVIER, 1817.

Synonyms: *Carangopsis*, *Lichia*, *Micropteryx*.

Geological range: Middle Eocene to recent.

Geographical distribution: Europe, North America, northern Africa.

Features: Middle-sized fishes of slender elongate shape. Head elongate. Eyes small. Gape rather long. Dorsal fin begins shortly behind the head with hard rays, but more posteriorly is soft-rayed, at first rising to a point and then continuing as a low fringe. Anal fin likewise fringe-like. Pectoral and pelvic fins elongate and pointed. Caudal fin forked, with broad lobes.

Remarks: Gregarious.

Recent relatives: Closely related to recent amberjacks of the genus *Seriola*.

Seriola dumerilii, a recent amberjack.

EUTELEOSTEI
Order: Perciformes
Family: Carangidae

Higher Bony Fishes
Suborder: Percoidei
Jacks and Pompanos

Trachurus primaevus EASTMAN (length c. 7 cm) from the Middle Eocene of Bolca, Italy. Original: The Natural History Museum, London, U.K. (P 17493)

Genus: *Trachyurus* de LACÉPÈDE, 1802.

Geological range: Middle Eocene.

Geographical distribution: Europe, northern Africa.

Features: Small fishes with elongate, rather laterally compressed bodies. Head shallow. Eyes small. Snout pointed. Gape rather long. Dorsal fin hard-rayed anteriorly and soft-rayed posteriorly. Pelvic fins small and fan-shaped. Caudal fin rather deeply forked.

Remarks: Predators. Has been reclassified into the genus *Eastmanalepes*.

Recent relatives: Closely related to recent jack mackerels of the genus *Trachurus*.

Trachurus trachurus, a recent jack mackerel. Lithograph from BLOCH.

EUTELEOSTEI
Order: Perciformes
Family: Carangidae

Higher Bony Fishes
Suborder: Percoidei
Jacks and Pompanos

Vomeropsis triurus VOLTA (length c. 20 cm) from the Middle Eocene of Bolca, Italy. Original: Museo Civico di Storia Naturale, Verona, Italy.

Genus: *Vomeropsis* HECKEL, 1854.

Geological range: Middle Eocene.

Geographical distribution: Europe.

Features: Middle-sized fishes of oval outline, laterally flattened. Head deep. Eyes small. Gape rather long. Dorsal fin begins approximately in the middle of the body at a tall point and continues posteriorly as a low fringe. Anal fin likewise low and fringe-like. Pectoral fins small, obliquely fan-shaped. Pelvic fins with long and short hard rays. Caudal fin broad, not forked, with an obtuse point in the middle and emarginate above and below the point.

Remarks: Probably durophagous.

Recent relatives: None. Died out in Eocene.

Vomeropsis, reconstruction after BLOT.

EUTELEOSTEI
Order: Perciformes
Family: Menidae

Higher Bony Fishes
Suborder: Percoidei
Moonfishes

Mene rhombea VOLTA (length c. 31 cm) from the Middle Eocene of Bolca, Italy. Original: Interfoss, Munich, Germany.

EUTELEOSTEI
Order: Perciformes
Family: Menidae

Higher Bony Fishes
Suborder: Percoidei
Moonfishes

Mene maculata, a recent moonfish. Lithograph from CUVIER.

Genus: *Mene* de LACÉPÈDE, 1803.

Synonym: *Gasteronemus.*

Geological range: Paleocene to recent.

Geographical distribution: Europe, northern Africa.

Features: Middle-sized fishes of rounded, deep-bellied outline, laterally flattened. Head deep. Eyes large. Gape rather long. Dorsal fin begins with a point at the highest part of the body and continues rearwards as a very low fringe. Pectoral fins narrow. Pelvic fins transformed into two long filaments. Caudal fin narrow, not forked, very slightly emarginate.

Remarks: Probably open-water fishes.

Recent relatives: Closely related to the recent of *Mene maculata*, which lives today as a pelagic fish in the Pacific Ocean.

EUTELEOSTEI
Order: Perciformes
Family: Leiognathidae

Higher Bony Fishes
Suborder: Percoidei
Slipmouths

Leiognathus altapinnus (WEILER) (length c. 9 cm) from the Lower Oligocene of northern Caucasus C.I.S. Original: Paleontologicheskii Muzei Russkoi Akademii Nauk, Moscow, Russia.

Genus: *Leiognathus* de LACÉPÈDE, 1803.

Synonym: *Equula*.

Geological range: Oligocene to recent.

Geographical distribution: Western and eastern Europe.

Features: Small fishes with rather high-backed bodies. Head short and deep. Eyes large. Anterior dorsal fin beginning at the highest point of the body, hard-rayed. Posterior dorsal fin soft-rayed, almost fringe-like, opposite the anal fin which is likewise hard-rayed anteriorly. Caudal fin large, deeply forked.

Remarks: Predators.

Recent relatives: Closely related to recent slipmouths of the genus *Leiognathus*.

Leiognathus sp., a recent slipmouth.

831

EUTELEOSTEI
Order: Perciformes
Family: Bramidae

Higher Bony Fishes
Suborder: Percoidei
Pomfrets

Brama sp. (length c. 19 cm) from the Pliocene of Fiume Marecchia, Italy. Original: Museo Civico di Storia Naturale, Verona, Italy.

Genus: *Brama* BLOCH & SCHNEIDER, 1801.

Geological range: Pliocene to recent.

Geographical distribution: Europe.

Features: Middle-sized fishes of rounded outline, laterally flattened. Head deep. Eyes large. Snout pointed. Gape short. Dorsal fin hard-rayed anteriorly and rising to a point, continuing posteriorly as a low fringe. Anal fin similar. Pectoral fins long and narrow. Caudal fin forked.

Remarks: Fed on plants.

Recent relatives: Closely related to recent pomfrets of the genus *Brama*.

Brama sp., a recent pomfret. Lithograph from BLOCH.

EUTELEOSTEI
Order: Perciformes
Family: Haemulidae

Higher Bony Fishes
Suborder: Percoidei
Grunts

Parapristipoma prohumile ARAMBOURG (length c. 20 cm) from the Miocene of Oran, Algeria. Original: Muséum National d'Histoire Naturelle, Paris, France. Photograph: Serette, Paris.

Genus: *Parapristipoma* BLEEKER, 1872.

Geological range: Miocene to recent.

Geographical distribution: Northern Africa.

Features: Small fishes with rather deep bodies anteriorly. Head deep. Eyes large. Gape rather long. Dorsal fin beginning shortly behind the head, hard-rayed anteriorly, soft-rayed posteriorly and continuing almost to the end of the body. Anal fin opposite the posterior end of the dorsal fin. Pectoral fins elongate. Pelvic fins hard-rayed. Caudal fin forked.

Remarks: Predators.

Recent relatives: Closely related to recent grunts of the genus *Parapristipoma*.

Parapristipoma pumile, a recent grunt, after WHITEHEAD.

EUTELEOSTEI — Higher Bony Fishes

Order: Perciformes
Family: Haemulidae
Suborder: Percoidei
Grunts

Pomadasys furcatus (AGASSIZ) (length c. 10 cm) from the Middle Eocene of Bolca, Italy. Original: Naturhistorisches Museum, Vienna, Austria.

Genus: *Pomadasys* de LACÉPÈDE, 1802.

Synonym: *Pristipoma*.

Geological range: Eocene to recent.

Geographical distribution: Europe, northern Africa.

Features: Small fishes with oval outline, laterally flattened. Head deep. Eyes large. Gape rather long. Jaws set with pointed teeth. Dorsal fin hard-rayed anteriorly, soft-rayed and fringe-like posteriorly. Anal fin similar, but smaller. Caudal fin broad, not forked.

Remarks: Probably gregarious.

Recent relatives: Closely related to recent grunts of the genus *Pomadasys*, which now live in the oceans.

Pomadasys kaakan, a recent grunt.

EUTELEOSTEI
Order: Perciformes
Family: Sparidae

Higher Bony Fishes
Suborder: Percoidei
Porgies

Boops sp. (length c. 12 cm) from the Pliocene of Fiume Marecchia, Italy. Original: Museo Civico di Storia Naturale, Verona, Italy.

Genus: *Boops* Cuvier, 1814.

Synonym: *Box*.

Geological range: Pliocene to recent.

Geographical distribution: Europe.

Features: Middle-sized fishes of elongate outline but rather plump. Head deep. Eyes large. Snout rounded. Gape short. Dorsal fin hard-rayed anteriorly, soft-rayed posteriorly. Anal fin similar, but considerably smaller. Pelvic fins vertically beneath the narrow pectoral fins. Caudal fin deeply forked.

Remarks: Probably fed essentially on plants.

Recent relatives: None. Died out in Miocene. Genus extinct. Closely related to recent porgies of the genus *Boops*.

Boops boops, a recent porgy.

EUTELEOSTEI
Order: Perciformes
Family: Sparidae

Higher Bony Fishes
Suborder: Percoidei
Porgies

Ctenodentex laekeniensis (van BENEDEN) (length c. 30 cm) from the Upper Eocene of Heembeek, Belgium. Original: Musée Royal des Sciences Naturelles de Belgique, Brussels, Belgium.

Genus: *Ctenodentex* STORMS, 1897.

Geological range: Eocene.

Geographical distribution: Europe, northern Africa.

Features: Middle-sized fishes of high-backed outline, laterally flattened. Head short and deep. Eyes large. Snout pointed. Gape rather long. Jaws set with powerful teeth. Dorsal fin low, hard-rayed anteriorly and soft-rayed and fringe-like posteriorly. Anal fin similar but shorter. Pelvic fins long and pointed. Caudal fin somewhat forked, with broad lobes.

Remarks: Probably gregarious.

Recent relatives: None. Died out in Eocene.

EUTELEOSTEI — Higher Bony Fishes

Order: Perciformes
Family: Sparidae
Suborder: Percoidei
Porgies

Dentex microdon AGASSIZ (length c. 16 cm) from the Middle Eocene of Bolca, Italy. Original: Bayerische Staatssammlung für Paläontologie, Munich, Germany.

Genus: *Dentex* CUVIER, 1815.

Geological range: Eocene to recent.

Geographical distribution: Europe, northern Africa, New Zealand.

Features: Small to middle-sized fishes with laterally compressed bodies. Head deep. Eyes large. Gape rather long. Jaws set with powerful teeth. Dorsal fin hard-rayed anteriorly, soft-rayed and fringe-like posteriorly. Anal fin similar but smaller. Pectoral fins long and fan-shaped. Caudal fin deeply forked, with broad lobes.

Remarks: Probably gregarious.

Recent relatives: None. Died out in Miocene. Genus extinct. Closely related to recent porgies of the genus *Dentex*.

Dentex sp., a recent porgy. Lithograph from BLOCH.

837

EUTELEOSTEI
Higher Bony Fishes

Order: Perciformes
Family: Sparidae

Suborder: Percoidei
Porgies

Diplodus oranensis (WOODWARD) (length c. 14 cm) from the Miocene of Oran, Algeria. Original: Muséum National d'Histoire Naturelle, Paris, France. Photograph: Serette, Paris.

Genus: *Diplodus* RAFINESQUE, 1810.

Synonym: *Sargus*.

Geological range: Eocene to recent.

Geographical distribution: Europe, northern Africa, Australia, North America.

Features: Small to middle-sized fishes of broadly oval outline, laterally flattened. Head deep. Eyes small. Gape rather long. Jaws with teeth. Snout slightly pointed. Dorsal fin begins shortly behind the head, hard-rayed anteriorly, soft-rayed posteriorly and continuing almost to the end of the body. Most anterior ray of the anal fin spine-like. Pectoral fins elongate. Pelvic fins small. Caudal fin forked.

Remarks: Gregarious.

Recent relatives: Closely related to recent porgies of the genus *Diplodus*.

Diplodus sargus, a recent porgy.

EUTELEOSTEI
Order: Perciformes
Family: Sparidae

Higher Bony Fishes
Suborder: Percoidei
Porgies

Pagellus microdon AGASSIZ (length c. 24 cm) from the Middle Eocene of Bolca, Italy. Original: Interfoss, Munich, Germany.

Genus: *Pagellus* GRIFFITH & SMITH, 1834.

Geological range: Paleocene to recent.

Geographical distribution: Europe, New Zealand.

Features: Middle-sized fishes with rather laterally compressed bodies. Head deep. Eyes large. Gape rather long. Dorsal fin begins at the highest point of the body, hard-rayed anteriorly, soft-rayed posteriorly. Anal fin likewise hard-rayed anteriorly. Pelvic fins small. Pectoral fins long and narrow. Caudal fin deeply forked, with narrow lobes.

Remarks: Gregarious.

Recent relatives: Closely related to recent porgies of the genus *Pagellus* which live in the oceans.

Pagellus sp., a recent porgy. Lithograph from BLOCH.

EUTELEOSTEI
Higher Bony Fishes

Order: Perciformes
Family: Sparidae

Suborder: Percoidei
Porgies

Pagrus mauretanicus ARAMBOURG (length c. 33 cm) from the Miocene of Oran, Algeria. Original: Muséum National d'Histoire Naturelle, Paris, France. Photograph: Serette, Paris.

Genus: *Pagrus* CUVIER, 1817.

Geological range: Paleocene to recent.

Geographical distribution: Europe, northern Africa.

Features: Middle-sized fishes of elongate oval outline, laterally flattened. Head deep. Eyes large. Snout pointed. Jaws set with conical teeth. Anal fin small. Pelvic fins elongate. Pectoral fins fan-shaped. Caudal fin forked, with broad lobes.

Remarks: Gregarious.

Recent relatives: Closely related to recent porgies of the genus *Pagrus*.

Pagrus sp., a recent porgy. Lithograph from BLOCH.

EUTELEOSTEI
Order: Perciformes
Family: Sparidae

Higher Bony Fishes
Suborder: Percoidei
Porgies

Rythmias starrii JORDAN & GILBERT (length c. 18 cm) from the Miocene of California, U.S.A. Original: National Museum of Natural History, Smithsonian Institution, Washington, D.C., U.S.A.

Genus: *Rythmias* JORDAN & GILBERT, 1920.

Geological range: Miocene.

Geographical distribution: North America.

Features: Small to middle-sized fishes of laterally compressed shape. Head deep. Eyes large. Dorsal fin hard-rayed anteriorly and soft-rayed posteriorly. Anal fin similar. Pectoral fins long and pointed. Caudal fin rather deeply forked.

Remarks: Probably gregarious.

Recent relatives: None. Died out in Miocene.

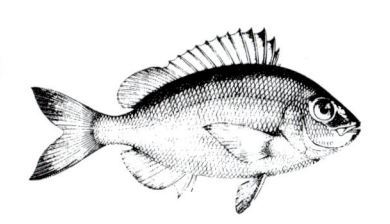

Rhythmias, reconstruction after JORDAN.

EUTELEOSTEI
Order: Perciformes
Family: Sparidae

Higher Bony Fishes
Suborder: Percoidei
Porgies

Sparnodus vulgaris AGASSIZ (length c. 14 cm) from the Middle Eocene of Bolca, Italy. Original: Museo Civico di Storia Naturale, Verona, Italy.

Genus: *Sparnodus* AGASSIZ, 1835.

Geological range: Eocene to Miocene.

Geographical distribution: Europe.

Features: Small to middle-sized fishes of rather laterally compressed shape. Head deep. Eyes large. Gape short. Jaws set with powerful teeth. Dorsal fin low, hard-rayed anteriorly, soft-rayed and fringe-like posteriorly. Anal fin similar, but considerably shorter. Pectoral fins fan-shaped. Caudal fin rather deeply forked with broad lobes.

Remarks: Probably gregarious.

Recent relatives: Genus extinct. Related to porgies of the family Sparidae.

EUTELEOSTEI
Order: Perciformes
Family: Sparidae

Higher Bony Fishes
Suborder: Percoidei
Porgies

Sparus sp. (length c. 43 cm) from the Miocene of Overland Corner, South Australia. Original: South Australian Museum, Adelaide, Australia.

Genus: *Sparus* LINNAEUS, 1758.

Synonyms: *Aurata, Chrysophrys*.

Geological range: Eocene to recent.

Geographical distribution: West Indies, Europe, northern Africa, Australia.

Features: Middle-sized fishes with rather laterally compressed bodies. Head deep. Eyes large. Gape short. Dorsal fin hard-rayed anteriorly, low and soft-rayed anteriorly. Pectoral fins long and pointed. Caudal fin rather forked, with relatively broad lobes.

Remarks: Gregarious.

Recent relatives: Related to recent porgies of the genus *Sparus* which live in oceans.

Sparus auratus, the recent golden porgy. Lithograph from BLOCH.

843

EUTELEOSTEI
Order: Perciformes
Family: Sciaenidae

Higher Bony Fishes
Suborder: Percoidei
Croakers

Lompoquia retropes JORDAN & GILBERT (length c. 27 cm) from the Miocene of California, U.S.A. Original: National Museum of Natural History, Smithsonian Institution, Washington, D.C., U.S.A.

Genus: *Lompoquia* JORDAN & GILBERT, 1919.

Geological range: Miocene.

Geographical distribution: North America.

Features: Middle-sized fishes of elongate slender shape. Head shallow. Eyes small. Snout pointed. Anterior dorsal fin hard-rayed. Posterior dorsal fin soft-rayed, opposite the anal fin. Pelvic and pectoral fins elongate. Caudal fin slightly emarginate.

Remarks: Gregarious.

Recent relatives: Genus extinct. Possibly related to recent croakers of the family Sciaenidae.

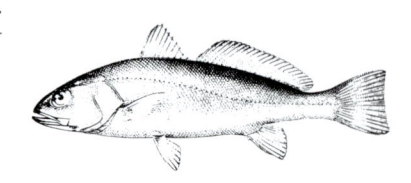

Lompoquia, reconstruction after JORDAN.

EUTELEOSTEI
Order: Perciformes
Family: Sciaenidae

Higher Bony Fishes
Suborder: Percoidei
Croakers

Sciaena knyrkoi DANILTCHENKO (length c. 14 cm) from the Upper Miocene of the northern Caucasus, C.I.S. Original: Paleontologicheskii Muzei Russkoi Akademii Nauk, Moscow, Russia (Bannikov Collection).

Genus: *Sciaena* LINNAEUS, 1758.

Synonym: *Sciaenops*.

Geological range: Upper Miocene to recent.

Geographical distribution: Western and eastern Europe, North America.

Features: Middle-sized fishes of slender outline, rather deeper in middle of body. Head shallow. Snout slightly pointed. Gape rather long. Anterior dorsal fin low and hard-rayed. Posterior dorsal fin soft-rayed and likewise low. Anal fin small, opposite the posterior dorsal fin. Caudal fin, not forked, rhombic.

Remarks: Predators.

Recent relatives: Related to recent croakers of the genus *Sciaena*.

Sciaena sp., a recent croaker. Lithograph from BLOCH.

845

EUTELEOSTEI
Higher Bony Fishes
Order: Perciformes
Family: Mullidae
Suborder: Percoidei
Goatfishes

Mullus moldavicus SVITCHENSKAYA (length c. 8 cm) from the Upper Miocene of Moldavia, C.I.S. Original: Paleontologicheskii Muzei Russkoi Akademii Nauk, Moscow, Russia (Bannikov Collection).

Genus: *Mullus* LINNAEUS, 1758.

Geological range: Miocene to recent.

Geographical distribution: Europe, western Asia.

Features: Small fishes of slender elongate shape. Head shallow. Eyes large. Snout pointed. Anterior dorsal fin hard-rayed, situated in the anterior half of the body. Posterior dorsal fin soft-rayed, opposite the anal fin. Pectoral and pelvic fins narrow. Caudal fin rather deeply forked.

Remarks: Gregarious.

Recent relatives: Related to recent goatfishes of the genus *Mullus* which live in the oceans.

Mullus surmuletus, a recent goatfish.

EUTELEOSTEI
Order: Perciformes
Family: Monodactylidae

Higher Bony Fishes
Suborder: Percoidei
Fingerfishes

Pasaichthys pleuronectiformes BLOT (length c. 6 cm) from the Middle Eocene of Bolca, Italy. Original: Museo Civico di Storia Naturale, Verona, Italy.

Genus: *Pasaichthys* BLOT, 1969.
Geological range: Middle Eocene.
Geographical distribution: Europe.
Features: Small fishes of rounded oval outline, laterally compressed. Head deep. Eyes large. Gape short. Dorsal fin begins in the anterior half of the body, increases gently in height and then passes rearwards into a fringe which extends to the root of the tail. Anal fin similar, but shorter. Pectoral fins rounded. Pelvic fins small. Caudal fin large, not forked, posterior margin regularly concave.
Remarks: Fed partly on plants.
Recent relatives: Genus extinct. Perhaps related to recent fingerfishes of the family Monodactylidae which are represented by three genera and five species in modern oceans.

Monodactylus argenteus, the recent mono.

EUTELEOSTEI
Order: Perciformes
Family: Monodactylidae

Higher Bony Fishes
Suborder: Percoidei
Fingerfishes

Psettopsis subarcuatus de BLAINVILLE (length c. 45 cm) from the Eocene of Bolca, Italy. Original: Museo Civico di Storia Naturale, Verona, Italy.

Genus: *Psettopsis* BLOT, 1969.

Geological range: Middle Eocene.

Geographical distribution: Europe.

Features: Middle-sized fishes of rounded oval outline, laterally flattened. Head deep. Eyes large. Gape short. Dorsal fin tall, extending in an arc over the whole of the back. Anal fin likewise tall and arcuate. Caudal fin large, triangular and not forked.

Remarks: Fed at least partly on plants.

Recent relatives: Genus extinct. Perhaps related to recent fingerfishes of the family Monodactylidae which are represented by three genera and about five species in modern oceans.

Psettopsis, reconstruction after BLOT.

EUTELEOSTEI
Order: Perciformes
Family: Toxotidae

Higher Bony Fishes
Suborder: Percoidei
Archerfishes

Toxotes antiquus (AGASSIZ) (length c. 11 cm) from the Middle Eocene of Bolca, Italy. Original: Naturhistorisches Museum, Vienna, Austria.

Genus: *Toxotes* EASTMAN, 1914.

Geological range: Middle Eocene.

Geographical distribution: Europe.

Features: Small fishes of elongate oval outline. Head deep. Eyes large. Snout pointed. Gape long. Dorsal fin approximately in the middle of the body, hard-rayed anteriorly. Soft-rayed part lower, opposite the anal fin. Caudal fin somewhat forked, with broad lobes.

Remarks: The generic name *Toxotes* is disputed, but the ascription to the family Toxotidae nevertheless seems certain.

Recent relatives: Perhaps related to recent archerfishes of the genus *Toxotes* which is represented by six species, mainly in warm brackish waters.

Toxotes jaculatrix, a recent archerfish.

EUTELEOSTEI
Higher Bony Fishes
Order: Perciformes
Family: Amphistiidae
Suborder: Percoidei

Amphistium paradoxum AGASSIZ (length c. 6 cm) from the Middle Eocene of Bolca, Italy. Original: Interfoss, Munich, Germany.

Genus: *Amphistium* AGASSIZ, 1844.

Synonyms: *Macrostoma, Woodwardichthys*.

Geological range: Middle Eocene.

Geographical distribution: Europe.

Features: Small fishes of rounded oval outline, laterally flattened. Head deep. Eyes small. Snout pointed. Dorsal fin extending in an arc over the whole of the back. Anal fin similar. Pelvic and pectoral fins very small. Caudal fin large, elongate, unforked and rounded.

Remarks: Probably predators.

Recent relatives: None. Died out in Eocene.

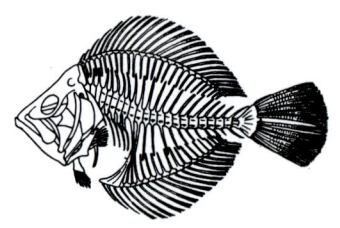

Amphistium, reconstruction after EASTMAN.

EUTELEOSTEI
Order: Perciformes
Family: Ephippidae

Higher Bony Fishes
Suborder: Percoidei
Spadefishes

Archaephippus asper VOLTA (length c. 38 cm) from the Middle Eocene of Bolca, Italy. Original: Naturhistorisches Museum, Vienna, Austria.

Genus: *Archaephippus* BLOT, 1969.

Synonym: *Ephippus*.

Geological range: Middle Eocene.

Geographical distribution: Europe.

Features: Middle-sized fishes of rounded oval outline, laterally flattened. Head deep. Eyes large. Gape short. Anterior dorsal fin hard-rayed. Posterior dorsal fin soft-rayed, at first increasing in height and then decreasing in a gentle curve. Anal fin similar to the posterior dorsal fin and opposite. Pectoral fins narrow and pointed. Pelvic fins long and pointed. Caudal fin not forked.

Remarks: Fed at least partly on plants.

Recent relatives: Genus extinct. Perhaps related to recent spadefishes of the family Ephippidae which is represented by three genera and twelve species in modern oceans.

Archaephippus, reconstruction after BLOT.

EUTELEOSTEI
Higher Bony Fishes
Order: Perciformes
Suborder: Percoidei
Family: Ephippidae
Spadefishes

Ephippus longipennis AGASSIZ (length c. 11 cm) from the Middle Eocene of Bolca, Italy. Original: Bayerische Staatssammlung für Paläontologie, Munich, Germany.

Genus: *Ephippus* CUVIER, 1817.

Geological range: Middle Eocene.

Geographical distribution: Europe.

Features: Small fishes of almost circular outline, laterally flattened. Head deep. Eyes small. Gape short. Anterior dorsal fin hard-rayed. Posterior dorsal fin soft-rayed, in its anterior part taller than the anterior dorsal fin. Anal fin opposite, with hard spines. Caudal fin not forked.

Remarks: Predators.

Recent relatives: Related to recent spadefishes of the genus *Ephippus* which live in warm seas.

Ephippus faber, a recent spadefish.

852

EUTELEOSTEI
Order: Perciformes
Family: Ephippidae

Higher Bony Fishes
Suborder: Percoidei
Spadefishes

Exellia velifer (VOLTA) (length c. 14 cm) from the Middle Eocene of Bolca, Italy. Original: Museo Civico di Storia Naturale, Verona, Italy.

Genus: *Exellia* WHITE & MOY-THOMAS, 1941.
Synonym: *Semiophorus*.
Geological range: Middle Eocene.
Geographical distribution: Europe.
Features: Middle-sized fishes of oval outline, laterally flattened. Head deep. Eyes large. Gape short. Dorsal fin begins anteriorly with a few hard rays, becomes rapidly taller and flag-like, reaching double the height of the body, then sharply decreases again in height, extending as a fringe to the root of the tail. Anal fin fringe-like, with a short point anteriorly. Pectoral fins small. Pelvic fins long, narrow and tapering to a point. Caudal fin not forked, narrow and slightly emarginate.
Remarks: Fed, at least partly, on plants.
Recent relatives: None. Died out in Eocene.

Exellia, reconstruction after BLOT.

853

EUTELEOSTEI — Higher Bony Fishes
Order: Perciformes — Suborder: Percoidei
Family: Platacidae — Batfishes

Eoplatax papilio (Volta) (length c. 62 cm) from the Middle Eocene of Bolca, Italy. Original: Museo Civico di Storia Naturale, Verona, Italy.

EUTELEOSTEI
Order: Perciformes
Family: Platacidae

Higher Bony Fishes
Suborder: Percoidei
Batfishes

Platax orbicularis, the recent orbiculate batfish.

Genus: *Eoplatax* BLOT, 1969.

Synonym: *Platax*.

Geological range: Middle Eocene.

Geographical distribution: Europe.

Features: Middle-sized fishes almost circular in outline, laterally flattened. Head deep. Eyes small. Gape short. Dorsal fin begins with short hard rays, increases in height to more than the height of the body, then decreases steeply in height to near the root of the tail. Anal fin similar in size and shape. Pelvic and pectoral fins small. Caudal fin small, not forked, somewhat rounded.

Remarks: Open-water predators.

Recent relatives: Genus extinct. Related to recent batfishes of the genus *Platax*, three species of which live in warm seas.

EUTELEOSTEI
Order: Perciformes
Family: Scatophagidae

Higher Bony Fishes
Suborder: Percoidei
Scats

Scatophagus frontalis AGASSIZ (length c. 12 cm) from the Middle Eocene of Bolca, Italy. Original: Interfoss, Munich, Germany.

Genus: *Scatophagus* CUVIER & VALENCIENNES, 1830.

Geological range: Eocene to recent.

Geographical distribution: Europe.

Features: Small high-backed fishes, laterally flattened. Head deep and short. Eyes large. Anterior dorsal fin begins at highest point of the body, hard-rayed. Posterior dorsal fin soft-rayed, opposite the anal fin which has hard rays anterior to it. Pectoral fins rounded. Pelvic fins small, with two hard rays.

Remarks: Probably already lived partly on live prey and partly on detritus.

Recent relatives: Closely related to recent scats of the genus *Scatophagus* which live in warm seas and brackish water.

Scatophagus argus, a recent scat.

856

EUTELEOSTEI
Order: Perciformes
Family: Chaetodontidae

Higher Bony Fishes
Suborder: Percoidei
Butterflyfishes

Chaetodon ficheuri ARAMBOURG (length c. 18 cm) from the Upper Miocene of Oran, Algeria. Original: Muséum National d'Histoire Naturelle, Paris, France. Photograph: Serette, Paris.

Genus: *Chaetodon* LINNAEUS, 1758.

Geological range: Oligocene to recent.

Geographical distribution: Europe.

Features: Small fishes of oval outline, laterally flattened. Head short and deep. Eyes small. Snout pointed. Gape rather long. Dorsal fin fringe-like, with hard rays anteriorly and soft rays posteriorly. Anal fin similar but shorter. Pelvic and pectoral fins small. Caudal fin not forked.

Remarks: The systematic position of this fish in the family Chaetodontidae is disputed.

Recent relatives: Perhaps closely related to recent butterflyfishes.

Chaetodon semilarvatus, a recent butterflyfish.

EUTELEOSTEI — Higher Bony Fishes

Order: Perciformes
Suborder: Percoidei
Family: Chaetodontidae
Butterflyfishes

Pygaeus gazolai (MASSALONGO) (length c. 8 cm) from the Middle Eocene of Bolca, Italy. Original: Museo Civico di Storia Naturale, Verona, Italy.

Genus: *Pygaeus* AGASSIZ, 1838.

Geological range: Middle Eocene.

Geographical distribution: Europe.

Features: Small fishes of circular outline, laterally flattened. Head deep. Eyes large. Upper and lower jaws produced to form an obvious rostrum. Anterior dorsal fin begins at the highest part of the body with a point formed from hard rays, contiguous with the posterior dorsal fin which is soft-rayed and likewise pointed. Anal fin with hard rays anteriorly, running off into a soft-rayed fringe. Pectoral fins small. Pelvic fins elongate. Caudal fin not forked.

Remarks: Probably fed on corals and associated small organisms.

Recent relatives: None. Died out in Eocene.

EUTELEOSTEI
Order: Perciformes
Family: Enoplosidae

Higher Bony Fishes
Suborder: Percoidei

Enoplosus pygopterus AGASSIZ (length c. 4 cm) from the Middle Eocene of Bolca, Italy. Original: Museum National d'Histoire Naturelle, Paris, France. Photograph: Serette, Paris, France.

Genus: *Enoplosus* de LACÉPÈDE, 1803.

Geological range: Eocene to recent.

Geographical distribution: Europe.

Features: Small fishes with rather laterally compressed bodies. Head deep. Eyes large. Snout slightly pointed. Gape rather long. Two separate dorsal fins, the first hard-rayed entirely and the second hard-rayed anteriorly. Anal fin broad-based. Pelvic fins fan-shaped. Pectoral fins rounded. Caudal fin broad, slightly forked.

Remarks: Probably fed mainly on plants.

Recent relatives: Related to recent fishes of the genus *Enoplosus*.

Enoplosus armatus, the oldwife fish.

EUTELEOSTEI — Higher Bony Fishes

Order: Perciformes
Family: Pentacerotidae

Suborder: Percoidei
Armourheads

Pentaceros sakhalinicus GRETCHINA (length c. 8 cm) from the Miocene of Sakhalin, Siberia, C.I.S. Original: Paleontologicheskii Muzei Russkoi Akademii Nauk, Moscow, Russia.

Genus: *Pentaceros* CUVIER, 1829.

Geological range: Miocene to recent.

Geographical distribution: Eastern Asia.

Features: Small fishes of rounded oval outline, laterally flattened. Head deep. Eyes large. Snout pointed. Anterior dorsal fin tall, hard-rayed. Posterior dorsal fin soft-rayed, rounded. Anal fin likewise accompanied by hard rays.

Remarks: Predators.

Recent relatives: Closely related to recent armourheads of the genus *Pentaceros*.

Pentaceros sp., a recent armourhead. Lithograph from CUVIER.

EUTELEOSTEI   Higher Bony Fishes
Order: Perciformes   Suborder: Percoidei
Family: Cichlidae   Cichlids

Geophagus priscus (WOODWARD) (length c. 12 cm) from the Miocene of Maranhao, Brazil. Original: The Natural History Museum, London, U.K. (P25258).

Genus: *Geophagus* HECKEL, 1840.

Synonym: *Macracara*.

Geological range: Miocene.

Geographical distribution: South America, northern Africa.

Features: Small fishes with rather laterally compressed bodies. Head deep. Eyes small. Snout pointed. Dorsal fin anteriorly tall and fringe-like, more posteriorly projecting into a point. Anal fin large, with the middle ray elongated. Pectoral and pelvic fins long and narrow. Caudal fin not forked or weakly emarginate.

Remarks: Like their recent relatives, probably chewed through the bottom mud looking for food.

Recent relatives: Closely related to recent members of the genus *Geophagus*.

Geophagus sp., a recent "earth eater".

EUTELEOSTEI
Higher Bony Fishes
Order: Perciformes
Suborder: Percoidei
Family: Cichlidae
Cichlids

Tilapia fossilis WHITE (length c. 10 cm) from the Pleistocene of Askati, Kenya. Original: The Natural History Museum, London, U.K. (P19089-4).

Genus: *Tilapia* SMITH, 1840.

Geological range: Pliocene to recent.

Geographical distribution: Africa.

Features: Small fishes with laterally compressed bodies. Head large. Eyes large. Gape short. Dorsal fin low and fringe-like anteriorly but becoming taller posteriorly. Anal fin likewise decreasing in height posteriorly. Pectoral fins narrow. Caudal fin not forked.

Remarks: Probably fed on plants.

Recent relatives: Closely related to the recent African cichlids of the genus *Tilapia*.

Tilapia buttikoferi, the recent zebra tilapia.

862

EUTELEOSTEI

Order: Perciformes
Family: Cichlidae

Higher Bony Fishes

Suborder: Percoidei
Cichlids

Unnamed cichlid (length c. 8 cm) from the Pliocene of Castellaro, Italy. Original: Museo Civico di Storia Naturale, Verona, Italy.

Genus: Not named.

Geological range: Pliocene.

Geographical distribution: Europe.

Features: Small fishes of oval outline, laterally flattened. Head deep. Eyes large. Snout rounded. Gape short. Dorsal fin hard-rayed anteriorly, soft-rayed posteriorly. Anal fin similar but shorter. Pelvic fins narrow, vertically beneath the broader pectoral fins. Caudal fin rounded, not forked.

Remarks: Probably lived in brackish water and fed on plants.

Recent relatives: Related to recent members of the family Cichlidae.

EUTELEOSTEI
Order: Perciformes
Family: Cichlidae?

Higher Bony Fishes
Suborder: Percoidei
Cichlids

Unnamed fish (length c. 16 cm) from the Eocene of Vicenza, Italy. Original: Leonhardt Interfoss, Munich, Germany.

Genus: Not named.

Geological range: Eocene.

Geographical distribution: Europe.

Features: Small to middle-sized fishes of oval outline, laterally flattened. Head deep. Eyes small. Gape short. Dorsal fin begins shortly behind the head, hard-rayed anteriorly, soft-rayed posteriorly. Anal fin large and rounded. Pelvic fins narrow. Pectoral fins small. Caudal fin broad, not forked.

Remarks: Probably fed on plants.

Recent relatives: None. Died out in Eocene.

EUTELEOSTEI
Order: Perciformes
Family: Pomacentridae

Higher Bony Fishes
Suborder: Percoidei
Damselfishes

Odonteus pygmaeus de Zigno (length c. 5 cm) from the Middle Eocene of Bolca, Italy. Original: Museo Civico di Storia Naturale, Verona, Italy.

Genus: *Odonteus* Agassiz, 1835.

Geological range: Middle Eocene.

Geographical distribution: Europe.

Features: Small fishes of circular outline, laterally flattened. Head deep. Eyes large. Gape rather long. Anterior dorsal fin of powerful spines, the first one being disproportionately long. Posterior dorsal fin soft-rayed and fringe-like. Anal fin likewise accompanied by powerful spines. Caudal fin, not forked, slightly rounded.

Remarks: Lived in coral reefs and probably fed on small animals.

Recent relatives: Related to recent damselfishes of the family Pomacentridae which are represented by 28 genera and about 335 species in the reefs of tropical seas.

Dascyllus melanurus, a recent damselfish.

865

EUTELEOSTEI — Higher Bony Fishes

Order: Perciformes
Suborder: Percoidei
Family: Priscacaridae

Priscacara liops COPE (length c. 13 cm) from the Eocene of Wyoming, U.S.A. Original: Pabst Collection, Zürich, Switzerland.

Genus: *Priscacara* COPE, 1877.

Geological range: Eocene.

Geographical distribution: North America.

Features: Small to middle-sized fishes of oval outline, laterally flattened. Head deep. Eyes large. Gape rather long. Anterior dorsal fin hard-rayed. Posterior dorsal fin soft-rayed and rounded. Anal fin rounded, associated with hard rays. Caudal fin not forked, slightly rounded.

Remarks: The genus *Priscacara* is placed by some authors in the family Percichthyidae and by others in the family Cichlidae. They were fresh-water fishes.

Recent relatives: None. Died out in Miocene. Genus extinct. Perhaps related to cichlids (family Cichlidae).

EUTELEOSTEI
Order: Perciformes
Family: Dipterichthyidae

Higher Bony Fishes
Suborder: Percoidei

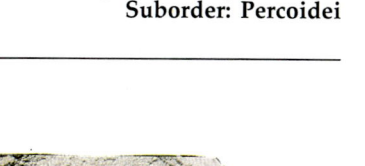

Dipterichthys leptosomus ARAMBOURG (length c. 11 cm) from the Lower Oligocene of Iran. Original: Muséum National d'Histoire Naturelle, Paris, France. Photograph: Serette, Paris.

Genus: *Dipterichthys* ARAMBOURG, 1939.

Geological range: Oligocene.

Geographical distribution: Middle East.

Features: Small fishes of elongate slender outline. Head shallow and elongate. Eyes large. Snout pointed. Gape long. The two dorsal fins relatively far apart from each other. Anal fin opposite the posterior dorsal fin. Pectoral fin narrow, almost vertically above the pelvic fins. Caudal fin forked.

Remarks: Predators.

Recent relatives: None. Died out in Oligocene.

EUTELEOSTEI
Order: Perciformes
Family: Arambourgellidae

Higher Bony Fishes
Suborder: Percoidei

Arambourgella cephala (HECKEL) (length c. 16 cm) from the Middle Eocene of Bolca, Italy. Original: Museo Civico di Storia Naturale, Verona, Italy.

Genus: *Arambourgella* BLOT, 1981.

Synonym: *Carangodes*.

Geological range: Middle Eocene.

Geographical distribution: Europe.

Features: Small to middle-sized fishes with laterally compressed bodies. Head large. Eyes large. Gape long. Dorsal fin with steep anterior slope and rounded posterior slope. Anal fin and pectoral fins large. Caudal fin stalked and deeply forked, with relatively broad lobes.

Remarks: Predators.

Recent relatives: None. Died out in Eocene.

EUTELEOSTEI
Order: Perciformes
Family: Not named

Higher Bony Fishes
Suborder: Percoidei

Ottaviania mariae SORBINI (length c. 14 cm) from the Middle Eocene of Bolca, Italy. Original: Museo Civico di Storia Naturale, Verona, Italy.

Genus: *Ottaviania* SORBINI, 1983.

Geological range: Middle Eocene.

Geographical distribution: Europe.

Features: Small fishes with slender bodies. Head deep. Eyes rather large. Gape long. Anterior dorsal fin begins just behind the head, fringe-like, consisting of powerful spines. Posterior dorsal fin small, soft-rayed. Caudal fin deeply forked, with narrow lobes.

Remarks: Predators.

Recent relatives: None. Died out in Eocene.

EUTELEOSTEI
Order: Perciformes
Family: Not named

Higher Bony Fishes
Suborder: Percoidei

Ruffoichthys spinosus SORBINI (length c. 6 cm) from the Middle Eocene of Bolca, Italy. Original: Museo Civico di Storia Naturale, Verona, Italy.

Genus: *Ruffoichthys* SORBINI, 1983.

Geological range: Middle Eocene.

Geographical distribution: Europe.

Features: Small fishes of slender outline, rather deep in the middle of the body but less so posteriorly. Head shallow. Eyes small. Gape rather long. Anterior dorsal fin consisting of well separated hard spines. Posterior dorsal fin small and soft-rayed. Caudal fin stalked.

Remarks: Predators.

Recent relatives: None. Died out in Eocene.

EUTELEOSTEI
Order: Perciformes
Family: Not named

Higher Bony Fishes
Suborder: Percoidei

Unnamed fish (length c. 9 cm) from the Middle Eocene of Bolca, Italy. Original: Paläontologisches Museum Zürich, Switzerland.

EUTELEOSTEI
Higher Bony Fishes
Order: Perciformes
Family: Not named
Suborder: Percoidei

Picture on the previous page.

Genus: Not named.

Geological range: Eocene to recent.

Geographical distribution: Europe.

Features: Small fishes of almost lozenge-shaped outline, laterally flattened. Head deep. Eyes large. Snout pointed. First ray of the dorsal fin disproportionately elongate, as also the first ray of the pelvic fins. Caudal fin stalked, triangular, slightly forked.

Remarks: Probably still-water predators.

Recent relatives: None. Died out in Eocene.

EUTELEOSTEI
Order: Perciformes
Family: Mugilidae

Higher Bony Fishes
Suborder: Mugiloidei
Mullets

Mugil princeps AGASSIZ (length c. 8 cm) from the Oligocene of Sodom, Israel. Original: Naturhistoriska Riksmuseet, Stockholm, Sweden.

Genus: *Mugil* LINNAEUS, 1758.

Geological range: Eocene to recent.

Geographical distribution: Europe, northern Africa, western Asia.

Features: Small fishes of elongate, but nevertheless rather plump, shape. Head shallow. Eyes small. Snout pointed. Anterior dorsal fin pointed, hard-rayed. Posterior dorsal fin soft-rayed, approximately triangular. Pelvic fins elongate and broad. Pectoral fins pointed. Caudal fin deeply forked.

Remarks: Gregarious.

Recent relatives: Closely related to recent mullets of the genus *Mugil*.

Mugil cephalus, a recent mullet. Lithograph from BLOCH.

EUTELEOSTEI
Order: Perciformes
Family: Sphyraenidae

Higher Bony Fishes
Suborder: Mugiloidei
Barracudas

Parasphyraena apsheronica SVITCHENSKA (length c. 11 cm) from the Upper Miocene of Azerbaijan, C.I.S. Original: Paleontologicheskii Muzei Russkoi Akademii Nauk, Moscow, Russia.

Genus: *Parasphyraena* SVITCHENSKA, 1968.

Geological range: Upper Miocene.

Geographical distribution: Western Asia.

Features: Small to middle-sized fishes of slender streamlined shape. Head shallow. Eyes small. Snout pointed. Two relatively small dorsal fins. Anterior dorsal fin hard-rayed, in the anterior half of the body. Posterior dorsal fin soft-rayed, in the posterior half of the body, opposite the similarly shaped anal fin. Pelvic fins very small. Caudal fin forked.

Remarks: Predators.

Recent relatives: Genus extinct but nevertheless related to recent barracudas of the genus *Sphyraena* which is represented by 18 species in tropical seas.

Parasphyraena, reconstruction after Akademia Nauk, Moscow.

EUTELEOSTEI
Order: Perciformes
Family: Sphyraenidae

Higher Bony Fishes
Suborder: Sphyraenoidei
Barracudas

Sphyraena bolcensis AGASSIZ (length c. 18 cm) from the Middle Eocene of Bolca, Italy. Original: Interfoss, Munich, Germany.

Genus: *Sphyraena* ARTEDI, 1792.

Geological range: Eocene to recent.

Geographical distribution: Europe, Africa, Indonesia, Asia, North America.

Features: Middle-sized fishes of slender streamlined shape. Head shallow. Eyes small. Upper and lower jaws set with powerful teeth and elongated to form a broad rostrum. Two relatively small dorsal fins. Anterior dorsal fin hard-rayed. Posterior dorsal fin soft-rayed, opposite the similarly shaped anal fin. Pectoral and pelvic fins small. Caudal fin deeply forked, with narrow lobes.

Remarks: Predators.

Recent relatives: Closely related to recent barracudas of the genus *Sphyraena*, represented by 18 species in tropical seas.

Sphyraena barracuda, a recent barracuda. Lithograph from BLOCH.

875

EUTELEOSTEI
Order: Perciformes
Family: Labridae

Higher Bony Fishes
Suborder: Labroidei
Wrasses

Eolabroides szajnochae (de Zigno) (length c. 10 cm) from the Middle Eocene of Bolca, Italy. Original: Università di Padova, Padua, Italy.

Genus: *Eolabroides* Eastman, 1914.

Geological range: Middle Eocene.

Geographical distribution: Europe.

Features: Small fishes with elongate bodies. Head relatively shallow. Eyes small. Dorsal fin extends over almost the whole length of the back, divided into a long hard-rayed and a short soft-rayed portion. Anal fin with a few hard rays anteriorly, soft-rayed more posteriorly. Caudal fin rounded, not forked.

Remarks: Fed on small animals and also on bivalves and snails.

Recent relatives: Genus extinct. Nevertheless related to recent wrasses.

EUTELEOSTEI
Order: Perciformes
Family: Labridae

Higher Bony Fishes
Suborder: Labroidei
Wrasses

Labrus agassizi MÜNSTER (length c. 17 cm) from the Miocene of St. Margarethen, Austria. Original: Naturhistorisches Museum, Vienna, Austria.

Genus: *Labrus* LINNAEUS, 1758.

Geological range: Eocene to recent.

Geographical distribution: Europe.

Features: Small to middle-sized fishes with rather laterally compressed bodies. Head shallow. Eyes relatively small. Gape short. Dorsal fin divided into a long hard-rayed and a short soft-rayed portion. Caudal fin strongly emarginate.

Remarks: Fed on small animals and also on bivalves and snails.

Recent relatives: Closely related to recent wrasses of the genus *Labrus*.

Labrus sp., a recent wrasse.

EUTELEOSTEI — Higher Bony Fishes
Order: Perciformes
Family: Labridae

Suborder: Labroidei
Wrasses

Pseudovomer minutus S<small>AUVAGE</small> (length c. 5 cm) from the Upper Miocene of Licata, Sicily, Italy. Original: Muséum National d'Histoire Naturelle, Paris, France. Photograph: Serette, Paris.

Genus: *Pseudovomer* S<small>AUVAGE</small>, 1873.

Geological range: Miocene to Pliocene.

Geographical distribution: Europe.

Features: Small fishes of oval outline, laterally flattened. Head deep. Eyes large. Snout somewhat protruding. Dorsal fin beginning shortly behind the head with hard rays. Pectoral fins fan-shaped. Anal fin with a spine-like first ray. Pelvic fins narrow.

Remarks: Fed on small animals.

Recent relatives: None. Died out in Pliocene.

EUTELEOSTEI
Order: Perciformes
Family: Labridae

Higher Bony Fishes
Suborder: Labroidei
Wrasses

Symphodus salvus BANNIKOV (length c. 9 cm) from the Upper Miocene of Moldavia, C.I.S. Original: Paleontologicheskii Muzei Russkoi Akademii Nauk, Moscow, Russia (Bannikov Collection).

Genus: *Symphodus* RAFINESQUE, 1810.

Geological range: Miocene to Pliocene.

Geographical distribution: Western and eastern Europe, northern Africa.

Features: Small fishes of elongate oval outline. Head short and deep. Eyes large. Dorsal fin beginning just behind the head, anteriorly hard-rayed but with a soft-rayed, posteriorly arcuate portion. Anal fin with a few hard rays anteriorly, soft-rayed posteriorly. Caudal fin not forked.

Remarks: Probably fed mainly on small animals but also on bivalves and snails.

Recent relatives: Closely related to recent wrasses the genus *Symphodus*.

Symphodus melops, the mermaid.

EUTELEOSTEI
Order: Perciformes
Family: Labridae

Higher Bony Fishes
Suborder: Labroidei
Wrasses

Tortonesia esilis SORBINI (length c. 7 cm) from the Middle Eocene of Bolca, Italy. Original: Museo Civico di Storia Naturale, Verona, Italy.

Genus: *Tortonesia* SORBINI, 1983.

Geological range: Middle Eocene.

Geographical distribution: Europe.

Features: Small fishes with elongate slender bodies. Head shallow. Snout pointed. Dorsal fin broad-based, divided into a long hard-rayed and a short soft-rayed portion. Anal fin relatively long. Pectoral fins rounded. Caudal fin not forked, with a rounded end.

Remarks: Fed mainly on small animals but also on bivalves and snails.

Recent relatives: Related to recent wrasses of the family Labridae which is represented by 57 genera and about 500 species in warm seas.

Bodianus izuensis, a recent wrasse.

EUTELEOSTEI
Order: Perciformes
Family: Pholididae

Higher Bony Fishes
Suborder: Zoarcoidei
Gunnels

Pholis gunellus LINNAEUS (length c. 12 cm) from the Pleistocene of Greenland. Original: Naturhistoriska Riksmuseet, Stockholm, Sweden.

Genus: *Pholis* GRONOV, 1760.

Geological range: Pleistocene to recent.

Geographical distribution: Greenland.

Features: Small fishes with elongate slender, laterally compressed bodies. Head shallow. Eyes small. Gape short, directed upwards. Dorsal fin long, hard-rayed. Caudal fin rounded, not forked.

Remarks: Fed on small animals.

Recent relatives: The fossil species is identical to the recent one. The genus *Pholis* is represented by ten species in northern seas.

Pholis gunellus, a recent gunnel. Lithograph from BLOCH.

881

EUTELEOSTEI
Order: Perciformes
Family: Trachinidae

Higher Bony Fishes
Suborder: Zoarcoidei
Weeverfishes

Callipterys speciosus AGASSIZ (length c. 36 cm) from the Middle Eocene of Bolca, Italy. Original: Field Museum of Natural History, Chicago, Illinois, U.S.A.

Genus: *Callipterys* AGASSIZ, 1835.

Geological range: Middle Eocene.

Geographical distribution: Europe.

Features: Middle-sized fishes with elongate, rather laterally compressed bodies. Head shallow. Snout pointed. Dorsal fin divided into a short, relatively hard-rayed and a long soft-rayed portion. Anal fin fringe-like, beginning in the middle of the body. Caudal fin elongate, rounded posteriorly.

Remarks: Probably lived mainly near the bottom.

Recent relatives: Genus extinct. Perhaps distantly related to weeverfishes of the genus *Trachinus*, represented by four species in the Mediterranean and other temperate seas.

Trachinus draco, the recent greater weever. Lithograph from BLOCH.

EUTELEOSTEI
Order: Perciformes
Family: Mugiloididae

Higher Bony Fishes
Suborder: Trachinoidei
Sandperches

Neopercis mesogea ARAMBOURG (length c. 18 cm) from the Miocene of Oran, Algeria. Original: Muséum National d'Histoire Naturelle, Paris, France. Photograph: Serette, Paris.

Genus: *Neopercis* STEINDACHNER, 1884.

Synonym: *Parapercis*.

Geological range: Miocene to recent.

Geographical distribution: Northern Africa.

Features: Small, rather plump fishes. Head deep. Eyes small. Snout pointed. Gape long. Dorsal fin begins just behind the head and runs as a fringe to near the posterior end of the body. Anal fin likewise fringe-like. Pectoral fins small. Pelvic fins vertically beneath the pectorals and very elongate. Caudal fin not forked, rounded.

Remarks: Lived near the bottom.

Recent relatives: Closely related to recent sandperches of the genus *Neopercis (Parapercis)*.

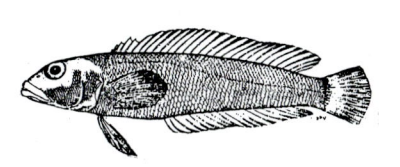

Parapercis multifasciata, a recent sandperch. (After SMITH).

883

EUTELEOSTEI
Order: Perciformes
Family: Clinidae

Higher Bony Fishes
Suborder: Trachinoidei
Clinids

Clinitrachus gratus BANNIKOV (length c. 4.5 cm) from the Upper Miocene of Moldavia, C.I.S. Original: Paleontologicheskii Muzei Russkoi Akademii Nauk, Moscow, Russia (Bannikov Collection).

Genus: *Clinitrachus* SWAINSON, 1839.

Geological range: Upper Miocene to recent.

Geographical distribution: Eastern Europe.

Features: Very Small fishes of slender shape. Head short and deep. Eyes small. Gape short. Dorsal fin extending over the whole of the back. Anal fin fringe-like. Pectoral fins broad. Pelvic fins small. Caudal fin rounded, not forked.

Remarks: Fed on small organisms and lived near the bottom.

Recent relatives: Closely related to recent clinids of the genus *Clinitrachus* which live in the Mediterranean.

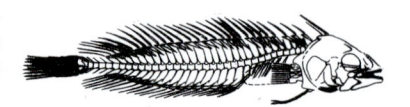

Clinitrachus, reconstruction after BANNIKOV.

EUTELEOSTEI
Order: Perciformes
Family: Clinidae

Higher Bony Fishes
Suborder: Blennioidei
Clinids

Clinus gracilis STEINDACHNER (length c. 7 cm) from the Upper Miocene of Hernals, near Vienna, Austria. Original: Naturhistorisches Museum, Vienna, Austria.

Genus: *Clinus* CUVIER, 1817.

Geological range: Miocene to recent.

Geographical distribution: Europe, norther Africa.

Features: Small fishes with elongate slender bodies. Head shallow. Eyes small. Snout pointed. Dorsal fin extends as a fringe over the whole of the back. Anal fin likewise fringe-like. Caudal fin not forked, rounded.

Remarks: Fed on small organisms and lived near the bottom.

Recent relatives: Closely related to recent clinids of the genus *Clinus* which live in temperate eastern seas.

Clinus sp., a clinid. Lithograph from CUVIER.

EUTELEOSTEI
Order: Perciformes
Family: Ammodytidae

Higher Bony Fishes
Suborder: Blennioidei
Sandlances

Ammodytes antipai PAUCA (length c. 4 cm) from the Middle Oligocene of Rumania. Original: Naturhistorisches Museum, Vienna, Austria.

Genus: *Ammodytes* LINNAEUS, 1758.

Geological range: Oligocene to recent.

Geographical distribution: Europe.

Features: Very small fishes with elongate eel-like bodies. Head long and shallow. Snout pointed. Dorsal fin low, extending over almost the whole of the back. Anal fin likewise low, but considerably shorter. Caudal fin rather deeply forked.

Remarks: Fed on small organisms and lived on a sandy bottom.

Recent relatives: Closely related to recent sandlances of the genus *Ammodytes* which live in the oceans.

Ammodytes sp. a recent sand lance. Lithograph from BLOCH.

886

EUTELEOSTEI
Order: Perciformes
Family: Gobiidae

Higher Bony Fishes
Suborder: Blennioidei
Gobies

Gobius microcephalus AGASSIZ (length c. 5 cm) from the Middle Eocene of Bolca, Italy. Original: Museo Civico di Storia Naturale, Verona, Italy.

Genus: *Gobius* LINNAEUS, 1758.

Geological range: Middle Eocene to recent.

Geographical distribution: Europe, North America, western Asia, northern Africa.

Features: Very small fishes with laterally compressed bodies. Head deep. Eyes large. Gape short. Two dorsal fins, the anterior short, the posterior broad-based. Anal fin opposite the second dorsal fin. Pelvic fins small. Pectoral fins relatively broad. Caudal fin rounded, not forked.

Remarks: Fed on small organisms and lived near the bottom.

Recent relatives: Closely related to recent gobies of the genus *Gobius*.

Gobius sp., a recent goby. Lithograph from CUVIER.

887

EUTELEOSTEI
Order: Perciformes
Family: Acanthuridae

Higher Bony Fishes
Suborder: Blennioidei
Surgeonfishes

Acanthonemus subaureus (de BLAINVILLE) (length c. 14 cm) from the Middle Eocene of Bolca, Italy. Original: The Natural History Museum, London, U.K. (P16201).

Genus: *Acanthonemus* AGASSIZ, 1834.

Geological range: Middle Eocene.

Geographical distribution: Europe.

Features: Small fishes of oval outline and laterally flattened bodies. Head short and deep. Eyes small. Anterior dorsal fin hard rayed, very tall and prominent. Posterior dorsal fin soft-rayed, low and extending to the root of the tail. Anal fin likewise with long hard rays anteriorly and soft rays posteriorly. Pectoral fins short and pointed. Pelvic fins somewhat longer and tapering. Caudal fin broad, not forked.

Remarks: Probably fed at least partly on plants.

Recent relatives: None. Died out in Eocene.

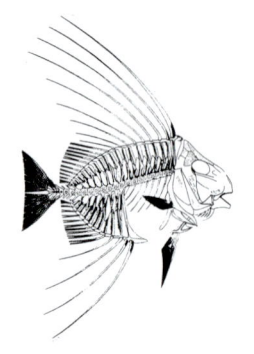

Acanthonemus, reconstruction after de BLAINVILLE.

EUTELEOSTEI
Order: Perciformes
Family: Acanthuridae

Higher Bony Fishes
Suborder: Blennioidei
Surgeonfishes

Acanthurus ovalis AGASSIZ (length c. 14 cm) from the Middle Eocene of Bolca, Italy. Original: Museo Civico di Storia Naturale, Verona, Italy.

Genus: *Acanthurus* FORSKÅL, 1775.

Geological range: Middle Eocene to recent.

Geographical distribution: Europe.

Features: Middle-sized fishes of oval outline, laterally flattened. Head short and deep. Eyes large. Snout slightly pointed. Dorsal fin begins shortly behind the head with hard rays and continues as a soft-rayed fringe to the root of the tail. Anal fin similar and fringe-like. Pectoral and pelvic fins small. Caudal fin not forked, emarginate.

Remarks: Fed at least partly on plants. Has been reclassified into the genus *Proacanthurus*

Recent relatives: Closely related to recent surgeonfishes of the genus *Acanthurus* which live in all tropical seas.

Acanthurus leucosternon, the powder-blue surgeonfish.

EUTELEOSTEI
Order: Perciformes
Family: Acanthuridae

Higher Bony Fishes
Suborder: Blennioidei
Surgeonfishes

Eozanclus brevirostris AGASSIZ (length c. 12 cm) from the Middle Eocene of Bolca, Italy. Original: Museum National d'Histoire Naturelle, Paris, France. Photograph: Serette, Paris.

Genus: *Eozanclus* BLOT & VORUZ, 1974.
Geological range: Middle Eocene.
Geographical distribution: Europe.
Features: Small fishes of almost circular outline, laterally flattened. Head deep. Eyes small. Snout somewhat produced. Dorsal fin hard-rayed anteriorly, projects upward from the highest part of the body and ends in a tall point, then descends in a curve and extends as a fringe to the root of the tail. Anal fin similarly fringe-like and beginning with a few hard rays. Pectoral fins small. Pelvic fins pointed. Caudal fin rounded, not forked.
Remarks: Probably fed, at least partly, on plants.
Recent relatives: Closely related to recent surgeonfishes of the genus *Zanclus*, represented by a few species in tropical seas.

Zanclus cornutus, the recent Moorish idol.

890

EUTELEOSTEI
Order: Perciformes
Family: Acanthuridae

Higher Bony Fishes
Suborder: Blennioidei
Surgeonfishes

Naseus rectifrons AGASSIZ (length c. 10 cm) from the Middle Eocene of Bolca, Italy. Original: Museo Civico di Storia Naturale, Verona, Italy.

Genus: *Naseus* de LACÉPÈDE, 1802.

Synonym: *Naso*.

Geological range: Middle Eocene to recent.

Geographical distribution: Europe.

Features: Small fishes of rounded outline, laterally flattened. Head short and deep. Upper and lower jaws form a projecting snout. Dorsal fin begins at the highest part of the body, is hard-rayed anteriorly and continues as a soft-rayed portion rounded posteriorly. Anal fin similar and extending as a fringe to the root of the tail. Pectoral fins small. Pelvic fins hard-rayed. Caudal fin, not forked, emarginate.

Remarks: Fed partly on plants. Has been reclassified into the genus *Eorandallius*.

Recent relatives: Closely related to recent unicornfishes of the genus *Naso* which live in tropical seas.

Naso lituratus, a recent unicornfish.

891

EUTELEOSTEI
Order: Perciformes
Family: Acanthuridae

Higher Bony Fishes
Suborder: Blennioidei
Surgeonfishes

Parapygaeus polyacanthus PELLEGRIN (length c. 7 cm) from the Middle Eocene of Bolca, Italy. Original: Muséum National d'Histoire Naturelle, Paris, France. Photograph: Serette, Paris.

Genus: *Parapygaeus* PELLEGRIN, 1907.

Geological range: Eocene.

Geographical distribution: Europe.

Features: Small fishes of elongate oval outline, laterally flattened. Head deep. Eyes large. Snout somewhat produced. Dorsal fin hard-rayed anteriorly and fringe-like and soft-rayed posteriorly. Anal fin similar but shorter. Pelvic and pectoral fins small.

Remarks: Predators.

Recent relatives: None. Died out in Eocene.

EUTELEOSTEI
Order: Perciformes
Family: Acanthuridae

Higher Bony Fishes
Suborder: Blennioidei
Surgeonfishes

Tylerichthys nuchalis (AGASSIZ) (length c. 21 cm) from the Middle Eocene of Bolca, Italy. Original: Field Museum of Natural History, Chicago, Illinois, U.S.A.

Genus: *Tylerichthys* BLOT, 1980.

Synonym: *Naseus*.

Geological range: Middle Eocene.

Geographical distribution: Europe.

Features: Middle-sized fishes of oval outline, laterally flattened. Head deep. Eyes small. Gape rather long. Dorsal fin in the posterior half of the body, anteriorly with a few hard rays, posteriorly soft-rayed. Anal fin opposite, fringe-like. Caudal fin not forked, deeply emarginate.

Remarks: Probably lived partly on hard-shelled food.

Recent relatives: None. Died out in Eocene.

EUTELEOSTEI
Order: Perciformes
Family: Caprovesposidae

Higher Bony Fishes
Suborder: Acanthuroidei

Caprovesposus parvus DANILTCHENKO (length c. 3 cm) from the Lower Oligocene of northern Caucasus, C.I.S. Original: Paleontologicheskii Muzei Russkoi Akademii Nauk, Moscow, Russia.

Genus: *Caprovesposus* DANILTCHENKO, 1960.

Geological range: Oligocene to Miocene.

Geographical distribution: Western and eastern Europe.

Features: Small fishes of oval outline, laterally flattened. Head deep. Eyes large. Snout pointed. Dorsal fin begins shortly behind the head, hard-rayed anteriorly, soft-rayed posteriorly, extending as a fringe almost the whole length of the back. Pectoral fins small. Pelvic fins close to the pectorals. Tail fin not forked.

Remarks: Predators.

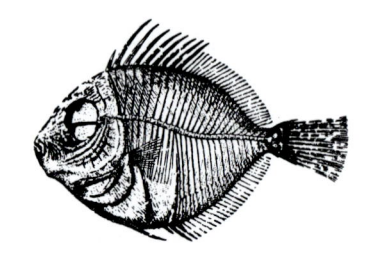

Recent relatives: None. Died out in Oligocene.

Caprovesposus, reconstruction after Akademia Nauk, Moscow.

894

EUTELEOSTEI
Order: Perciformes
Family: Kushlukiidae

Higher Bony Fishes
Suborder: Acanthuroidei

Kushlukia permira DANILTCHENKO (length c. 17 cm) from the Lower Eocene of Turkmenistan, C.I.S. Original: Paleontologicheskii Muzei Russkoi Akademii Nauk, Moscow, Russia.

Genus: *Kushlukia* DANILTCHENKO, 1968.

Geological range: Lower Eocene.

Geographical distribution: Western Asia.

Features: Middle-sized fishes of oval outline, deep anteriorly and strongly decreasing in height posteriorly. Head deep. Eyes large. Snout pointed. Gape rather long. Anterior dorsal fin tall, hard-rayed. Posterior dorsal fin soft-rayed, fringe-like. Caudal fin not forked.

Remarks: Predators.

Recent relatives: Genus extinct. Nevertheless perhaps related to recent rabbitfishes.

Siganus guttatus, a recent rabbitfish.

895

EUTELEOSTEI
Order: Perciformes
Family: Gempylidae

Higher Bony Fishes
Suborder: Scombroidei
Snake Mackerels

Epinnula cancellata ARAMBOURG (length c. 5 cm) from the Lower Oligocene of Iran. Original: Muséum National d'Histoire Naturelle, Paris, France. Photograph: Serette, Paris.

Genus: *Epinnula* POEY, 1854.

Geological range: Oligocene to recent.

Geographical distribution: Middle East.

Features: Small fishes with very slender elongate bodies. Head relatively large. Eyes small. Snout strongly pointed. Gape long. Anterior dorsal fin elongate, hard-rayed. Posterior dorsal fin soft-rayed. Pectoral fins pointed. Pelvic fins vertically beneath pectorals and very small. Anal fin triangular. Caudal fin forked.

Remarks: Gregarious.

Recent relatives: Closely related to recent fishes of the genus *Epinnula*.

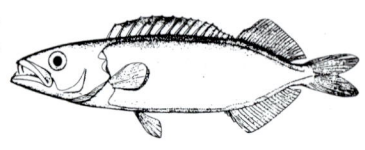

Epinnula orientalis, a recent fish of the family Gempylidae.

896

EUTELEOSTEI
Order: Perciformes
Family: Gempylidae

Higher Bony Fishes
Suborder: Scombroidei
Snake Mackerels

Hemithyrsites maicopicus DANILTCHENKO (length c. 6 cm) from the Lower Miocene of Azerbaijan, C.I.S. Original: Paleontologicheskii Muzei Russkoi Akademii Nauk, Moscow, Russia.

Genus: *Hemithyrsites* SAUVAGE, 1873.

Geological range: Miocene.

Geographical distribution: Western and eastern Europe, northern Africa.

Features: Small fishes with very slender elongate bodies. Head shallow. Eyes large. Snout pointed. Dorsal fin fringe-like, hard-rayed. Anal fin small, like the pectoral and pelvic fins. Caudal fin forked.

Remarks: Probably gregarious predators.

Recent relatives: Genus extinct. Nevertheless distantly related to recent snake mackerels of the genus *Thyrsites*.

Thyrsites atun, a recent snake mackerel. Lithograph from CUVIER.

EUTELEOSTEI
Order: Perciformes
Family: Trichiuridae

Higher Bony Fishes
Suborder: Scombroidei
Cutlassfishes

Eutrichiurides delheidi LERICHE (length c. 8 cm) from the Oligocene of Wiesloch, Baden, Germany. Original: Staatliches Museum für Naturkunde, Karlsruhe, Germany.

Genus: *Eutrichiurides* CASIER, 1944.

Geological range: Paleocene to Oligocene.

Geographical distribution: Europe, Africa.

Features: Small fishes with slender, laterally flattened bodies. Head shallow. Eyes large. Snout pointed. Gape rather long. Dorsal fin low and fringe-like. Caudal fin very small, forked.

Remarks: Predators.

Recent relatives: Perhaps related to recent cutlassfishes of the genus *Trichiurs* which live in the oceans.

Trichiurus lepturus, a recent cutlassfish. Lithograph from BLOCH.

EUTELEOSTEI
Order: Perciformes
Family: Trichiuridae

Higher Bony Fishes
Suborder: Scombroidei
Cutlassfishes

Lepidopus sp. (length c. 24 cm) from the Pliocene of Licata, Sicily, Italy. Original: Siber & Siber Collection, Aathal, Switzerland.

Genus: *Lepidopus* GOUAN.

Synonyms: *Acanthonotus, Anenchelum, Lepidopides.*

Geological range: Eocene to recent.

Geographical distribution: Europe, South America, western and northern Africa.

Features: Middle-sized fishes with very slender elongate, laterally flattened bodies. Head shallow. Eyes large. Snout pointed. Gape long. Dorsal fin low, extending along the whole body. Anal fin likewise low and fringe-like, but nevertheless considerably shorter. Pelvic fins completely lost. Caudal fin very small, forked.

Remarks: Predators.

Recent relatives: Closely related to recent scabbardfishes of the genus *Lepidopus* which live in the oceans.

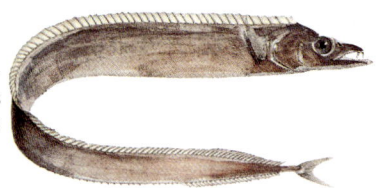

Lepidopus sp., a recent scabbardfish. Lithograph from CUVIER.

899

EUTELEOSTEI
Order: Perciformes
Family: Scombridae

Higher Bony Fishes
Suborder: Scombroidei
Mackerels and Tunas

Auxis propterygius (AGASSIZ) (length c. 7 cm) from the Middle Eocene of Bolca, Italy. Original: National Museum of Natural History, Smithsonian Institution, Washington, D.C., U.S.A.

Genus: *Auxis* CUVIER, 1829.

Geological range: Eocene to recent.

Geographical distribution: Europe.

Features: Small fishes of slender shape. Head shallow. Eyes large. Snout somewhat produced, pointed. Two small dorsal fins. Caudal fin deeply forked.

Remarks: Predators.

Recent relatives: Closely related to recent bullet mackerels of the genus *Auxis* which are placed among the smaller tunas.

Auxis sp., a bullet mackerel. Lithograph from CUVIER.

EUTELEOSTEI
Order: Perciformes
Family: Scombridae

Higher Bony Fishes
Suborder: Scombroidei
Mackerels and Tunas

Grammatorcynus scomberoides ARAMBOURG (length c. 15 cm) from the Lower Oligocene of Iran. Original: Muséum National d'Histoire Naturelle, Paris, France. Photograph: Serette, Paris.

Genus: *Grammatorcynus* GILL, 1862.

Geological range: Oligocene to recent.

Geographical distribution: Middle East.

Features: Small to middle-sized fishes, outline becoming deeper anteriorly. Head elongate. Eyes small. Snout pointed. Gape rather long. Anterior dorsal fin hard-rayed, posterior dorsal fin soft-rayed. Anal fin opposite the posterior dorsal fin. Pelvic fins vertically beneath the pectoral fins.
Caudal fin forked.

Remarks: Gregarious.

Recent relatives: Closely related to recent mackerels of the genus *Grammatocynus*.

Grammatorcynus bicarinatus, the recent double-lined mackerel, after WEBER.

901

EUTELEOSTEI
Order: Perciformes
Family: Scombridae

Higher Bony Fishes
Suborder: Scombroidei
Mackerels and Tunas

Isurichthys orientalis WOODWARD (length c. 9 cm) from the Oligocene of Shuster, Iran. Original: The Natural History Museum, London, U.K. (P7130).

Genus: *Isurichthys* WOODWARD, 1901.

Geological range: Oligocene.

Geographical distribution: Europe, western Asia.

Features: Small fishes of slender shape. Head shallow. Eyes large. Snout pointed. Dorsal fin fringe-like. Anal fin likewise fringe-like and very low. Caudal fin deeply forked, with narrow lobes.

Remarks: Predators.

Recent relatives: None. Died out in Oligocene.

EUTELEOSTEI
Order: Perciformes
Family: Scombridae

Higher Bony Fishes
Suborder: Scombroidei
Mackerels and Tunas

Palimphyes longirostratus DANILTCHENKO (length c. 11 cm) from the Lower Oligocene of the Caucasus, C.I.S. Original: Paleontologicheskii Muzei Russkoi Akademii Nauk, Moscow, Russia (Bannikov Collection).

Genus: *Palimphyes* AGASSIZ, 1844.

Synonym: *Krambergeria*.

Geological range: Oligocene.

Geographical distribution: Europe.

Features: Small to middle-sized fishes of slender shape. Head shallow. Eyes relatively large. Snout pointed. Two dorsal fins, respectively opposite the pelvic fins and the anal fin. Pectoral fins narrow. Caudal fin deeply forked.

Remarks: Gregarious.

Recent relatives: None. Died out in Oligocene.

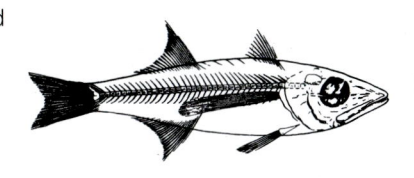

Palimphyes, reconstruction after Akademia Nauk, Moscow.

EUTELEOSTEI
Order: Perciformes
Family: Scombridae

Higher Bony Fishes
Suborder: Scombroidei
Mackerels and Tunas

Sarda rara BANNIKOV (length c. 7.5 cm) from the Lower Oligocene of the northern Caucasus, C.I.S. Original: Paleontologicheskii Muzei Russkoi Akademii Nauk, Moscow, Russia (Bannikov Collection).

Genus: *Sarda* CUVIER, 1829.

Synonym: *Pelamys*.

Geological range: Paleocene to recent.

Geographical distribution: Europe, North America, northern Africa.

Features: Small fishes of slender shape. Head narrow. Eyes large. Snout pointed. Gape deep. Dorsal fin on a broad base, beginning about body center. Anal, pectoral and ventral fins small. Caudal fin deeply forked.

Remarks: Schooling fishes.

Recent relatives: Closely related to recent fishes of the genus *Sarda*.

Sarda australis, a recent bonito

EUTELEOSTEI
Order: Perciformes
Family: Scombridae

Higher Bony Fishes
Suborder: Scombroidei
Mackerels and Tunas

Scomber sujedanus STEINDACHNER (length c. 33 cm) from the Oligocene of Raduboj, Yugoslavia. Original: Naturhistorisches Museum, Vienna, Austria.

Genus: *Scomber* LINNAEUS, 1758.

Synonym: *Pneumatophorus*.

Geological range: Eocene to recent.

Geographical distribution: Europe, Africa, North America, eastern Asia.

Features: Middle-sized fishes of slender elongate shape. Head shallow. Snout pointed. Two dorsal fins, respectively opposite the pelvic fins and the anal fin. Pectoral fins narrow. Caudal fin deeply forked.

Remarks: Gregarious.

Recent relatives: Closely related to recent mackerels of the genus *Scomber* which live in great schools in tropical and subtropical seas.

Scomber scomber, a recent mackerel. Lithograph from BLOCH.

905

EUTELEOSTEI
Order: Perciformes
Family: Scombridae

Higher Bony Fishes
Suborder: Scombroidei
Mackerels and Tunas

Scomberomorus speciosus Agassiz (length c. 40 cm) from the Middle Eocene of Bolca, Italy. Original: Rijksmuseum van Geologie en Mineralogie, Leiden, Netherlands.

Genus: *Scomberomorus* de Lacépède, 1802.

Synonym: *Cybium*.

Geological range: Paleocene to recent.

Geographical distribution: Europe, Africa, Middle East.

Features: Small fishes of slender outline, but somewhat deeper in the middle of the body. Head shallow. Eyes small. Snout pointed. Gape long. Two dorsal fins, respectively opposite the pelvic fins and the anal fin. Caudal deeply forked.

Remarks: Gregarious.

Recent relatives: Closely related to recent Spanish mackerels of the genus *Scomberomorus* which belong among the tunas and occur in huge schools in the Atlantic and Pacific.

Scomberomorus queenslandicus, a mackerel.

EUTELEOSTEI
Order: Perciformes
Family: Scombridae

Higher Bony Fishes
Suborder: Scombroidei
Mackerels and Tunas

Scombrosarda cernerurae (Ciobanu) (length c. 21 cm) from the Lower Oligocene of the northern Caucasus, C.I.S. Original: Paleontologicheskii Muzei russkoi Akademii Nauk, Moscow, Russia.

Genus: *Scombrosarda* Daniltchenko, 1962.

Geological range: Eocene to Oligocene.

Geographical distribution: Western and eastern Europe.

Features: Middle-sized fishes of slender shape. Head shallow. Eyes large. Snout pointed. Gape long. Two small dorsal fins. Anal fin triangular. Pelvic and pectoral fins small. Caudal fin rather deeply forked.

Remarks: Gregarious.

Recent relatives: Genus extinct. Possibly related to recent mackerels.

Scombrosarda, reconstruction after Akademia Nauk, Moscow.

907

EUTELEOSTEI
Order: Perciformes
Family: Scombridae

Higher Bony Fishes
Suborder: Scombroidei
Mackerels and Tunas

Thunnus lanceolatus (AGASSIZ) (length c. 33 cm) from the Middle Eocene of Bolca, Italy. Original: Museo Civico di Storia Naturale, Verona, Italy.

Genus: *Thunnus* SOUTH, 1845.

Synonyms: *Orcinus*, *Thynnus*.

Geological range: Eocene to recent.

Geographical distribution: Europe, North America, Africa.

Features: Small fishes of slender outline, but deepest in the middle of the body and tapering towards the caudal fin. Head shallow. Eyes small. Snout pointed. Two dorsal fins, respectively opposite the pelvic fins and the anal fin. Pectoral fins narrow and relatively long. Caudal fin deeply forked and sickle-shaped.

Remarks: Gregarious.

Recent relatives: Closely related to recent tunas of the genus *Thunnus* which live in huge swarms in warm and temperate seas.

Thunnus thynnus, the recent tuna. Lithograph from BLOCH.

EUTELEOSTEI
Order: Perciformes
Family: Scombridae

Higher Bony Fishes
Suborder: Scombroidei
Mackerels and Tunas

Turio wilburi (GILBERT & JORDAN) (length c. 30 cm) from the Miocene of California, U.S.A. Original: National Museum of Natural History, Smithsonian Institution, Washington, D.C., U.S.A.

Genus: *Turio* GILBERT & JORDAN, 1920.

Geological range: Miocene.

Geographical distribution: North America.

Features: Middle-sized fishes of slender elongate outline. Head shallow. Eyes large. Snout pointed. Pelvic fins small. Caudal fin deeply forked.

Remarks: Predators. *Turio* is occasionally considered a synonym of *Scomber*.

Recent relatives: None. Died out in Miocene.

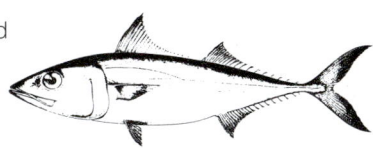

Turio, reconstruction after JORDAN.

EUTELEOSTEI
Order: Perciformes
Family: Scombridae

Higher Bony Fishes
Suborder: Scombroidei
Mackerels and Tunas

Xiphopterus falcatus (VOLTA) (length c. 55 cm) from the Middle Eocene of Bolca, Italy. Original: Museo Civico di Storia Naturale, Verona, Italy.

Genus: *Xiphopterus* AGASSIZ, 1835.

Geological range: Middle Eocene.

Geographical distribution: Europe.

Features: Middle-sized fishes of very slender elongate outline. Head shallow. Eyes small. Upper and lower jaws produced to a point, the upper being shorter. Two small dorsal fins, the posterior being opposite the anal fin and the anterior opposite the pelvic fins. Caudal fin deeply forked.

Remarks: Rapidly swimming predators.

Recent relatives: None. Died out in Eocene.

EUTELEOSTEI
Order: Perciformes
Family: Xiphiidae

Higher Bony Fishes
Suborder: Scombroidei
Swordfishes

Blochius longirostris VOLTA (length c. 60 cm) from the Middle Eocene of Bolca, Italy. Original: Interfoss, Munich, Germany.

Genus: *Blochius* VOLTA, 1800.

Geological range: Middle Eocene.

Geographical distribution: Europe.

Features: Middle-sized fishes of very slender elongate outline. Head shallow. Eyes large. Upper and lower jaws set with pointed teeth and extended to form an unusually long rostrum. Dorsal fin fringe-like and extending over the whole length of the body. Anal fin likewise fringe-like, but beginning only in the middle of the body. Pelvic and pectoral fins small, fan-shaped. Caudal fin deeply forked.

Remarks: Predators. The rostrum probably served to deflect the prey and strike it from the side.

Recent relatives: None. Died out in Eocene.

Blochius, reconstruction after ZITTEL.

EUTELEOSTEI
Order: Perciformes
Family: Xiphiidae

Higher Bony Fishes
Suborder: Scombroidei
Swordfishes

Xiphias gladius Linnaeus (length c. 134 cm) from the Pliocene of Fiume Marecchia, Italy. Original: Museo Civico di Storia Naturale, Verona, Italy.

Genus: *Xiphias* Linnaeus, 1758.

Geological range: Eocene to recent.

Geographical distribution: Europe, western and northern Africa.

Features: Large to very large fishes of streamlined shape. Head shallow. Eyes large. Upper and lower jaws produced to form a sword-like rostrum, with the lower jaw considerably shorter than the upper. Anterior dorsal fin tall, immediately behind the head. Posterior dorsal fin small, shortly in front of the end of the body. Anal fin large. Pelvic fins very anterior in position. Pectoral fins long and pointed, placed rather ventrally. Caudal fin large, sickle-shaped.

Remarks: Pelagic predators.

Recent relatives: The fossil species is identical to the recent one. The swordfish *Xiphias gladius* lives in all the world's oceans.

Xiphias gladius, the recent swordfish. Lithograph from Bloch.

EUTELEOSTEI
Order: Perciformes
Family: Palaeorhynchidae

Higher Bony Fishes
Suborder: Scombroidei

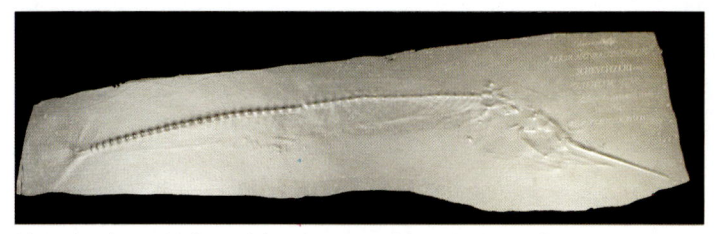

Homorhynchus colei (AGASSIZ) (length c. 81 cm) from the Lower Oligocene of Glarus, Switzerland. Original: Teylers Museum, Haarlem, Netherlands.

Genus: *Homorhynchus* van BENEDEN, 1873.

Synonym: *Hemirhynchus*.

Geological range: Eocene to Miocene.

Geographical distribution: Europe.

Features: Middle-sized fishes of very slender elongate outline. Head shallow. Eyes large. Upper and lower jaws produced to form a rostrum, with the lower jaw considerably shorter than the upper. Dorsal and anal fins fringe-like. Caudal fin deeply forked.

Remarks: Predators.

Recent relatives: None. Died out in Miocene.

EUTELEOSTEI
Order: Perciformes
Family: Palaeorhynchidae

Higher Bony Fishes
Suborder: Scombroidei

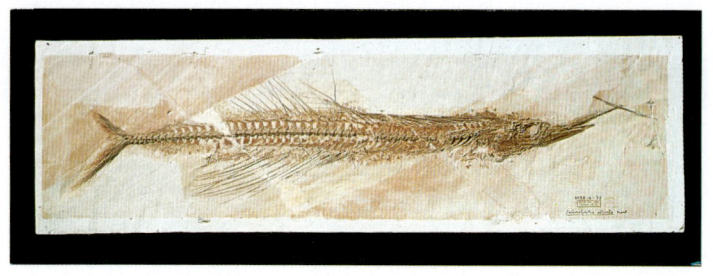

Palaeorhynchus altivelis ARAMBOURG (length c. 60 cm) from the Lower Oligocene of Iran. Original: Muséum National d'Histoire Naturelle, Paris, France. Photograph: Serette, Paris.

Genus: *Palaeorhynchus* de BLAINVILLE, 1818.

Geological range: Eocene to Miocene.

Geographical distribution: Europe, Middle East.

Features: Middle-sized fishes of slender elongate outline. Head shallow, elongate. Eyes large. Upper and lower jaw produced to form a rostrum. Dorsal fin extending over the whole body, arcuate upwards. Anal fin similar, but only half as long. Pectoral fins very small. Pelvic fins elongate. Caudal fin relatively small, deeply forked.

Remarks: Predators.

Recent relatives: None. Died out in Miocene.

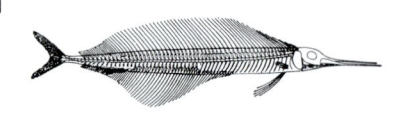

Palaeorhynchus, reconstruction after ORLOV.

EUTELEOSTEI
Order: Perciformes
Family: Nomeidae

Higher Bony Fishes
Suborder: Stromateoidei
Driftfishes

Carangodes cephalus HECKEL (length c. 16 cm) from the Middle Eocene of Bolca, Italy. Original: Museo Civico di Storia Naturale, Verona, Italy.

Genus: *Carangodes* HECKEL, 1856.

Geological range: Middle Eocene.

Geographical distribution: Europe.

Features: Small fishes of slender outline. Head deep. Eyes large. Gape long. Anterior dorsal fin small, consisting of a few hard rays. Posterior dorsal fin long, arcuate behind. Anal fin large, triangular. Pectoral fins large, rounded. Pelvic fins likewise large, elongate. Caudal fin deeply forked.

Remarks: Perhaps even at that time there was a sort of symbiosis between these fishes and large jellyfishes.

Recent relatives: Perhaps related to recent driftfishes of the family Nomeidae which is represented in tropical and subtropical seas by three genera and about 15 species.

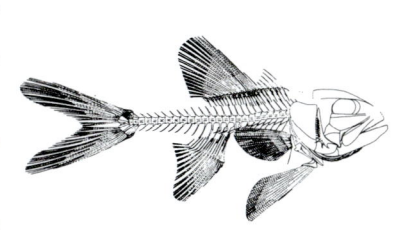

Carangodes, reconstruction after BLOT.

915

EUTELEOSTEI
Order: Perciformes
Family: Nomeidae

Higher Bony Fishes
Suborder: Stromateoidei
Driftfishes

Psenicubiceps alatus DANILTCHENKO (length c. 12 cm) from the Lower Oligocene of northern Caucasus, C.I.S. Original: Paleontologicheskii Muzei Russkoi Akademii Nauk, Moscow, Russia (Bannikov Collection).

Genus: *Psenicubiceps* DANILTCHENKO, 1980.

Geological range: Lower Oligocene.

Geographical distribution: Eastern Europe.

Features: Small fishes of elongate oval outline. Head relatively deep. Eyes large. Gape short. Anterior dorsal fin tall, hard-rayed. Posterior dorsal fin soft-rayed. Pectoral fins broad. Pelvic fins narrow. Caudal fin deeply forked.

Remarks: Perhaps even at that time these fishes live in symbiosis with large jellyfishes.

Recent relatives: Genus extinct. Probably related to recent driftfishes of the family Nomeidae and to their close relatives the Ariommidae.

Ariomma indica, a recent ariommid.

EUTELEOSTEI
Order: Perciformes
Family: Tetragonuridae

Higher Bony Fishes
Suborder: Stromateoidei
Squaretails

Tetragonurus sp. (length c. 18 cm) from the Pliocene of Fiume Marecchia, Italy. Original: Museo Civico di Storia Naturale, Verona, Italy.

Genus: *Tetragonurus* Risso, 1810.

Geological range: Pliocene to recent.

Geographical distribution: Europe.

Features: Middle-sized fishes with elongate, torpedo-shaped bodies. Head shallow. Eyes large. Snout rounded. Gape short. Dorsal fin anteriorly hard-rayed and very low, passing posteriorly into a rounded soft-rayed portion which lies opposite the anal fin. Pelvic fins very small, vertically beneath the pectoral fins which are considerably larger. Caudal fin arcuate above and below, emarginate posteriorly, heart-shaped in outline. Keeled rhombic scales arranged in transverse rows.

Remarks: Probably fed on jellyfishes.

Recent relatives: Closely related to recent squaretails of the genus *Tetragonurus*.

Tetragonurus cuvieri, a recent squaretail. Lithograph from Cuvier.

917

EUTELEOSTEI
Order: Perciformes
Family: Stromateidae

Higher Bony Fishes
Suborder: Stromateoidei
Butterfishes

Pinichthys pulcher BANNIKOV (length c. 11 cm) from the Lower Oligocene of northern Caucasus, C.I.S. Original: Paleontologicheskii Muzei Russkoi Akademii Nauk, Moscow, Russia (Bannikov Collection).

Genus: *Pinnichthys* BANNIKOV, 1985.

Geological range: Lower Oligocene.

Geographical distribution: Eastern Europe.

Features: Small fishes of rhombic outline, laterally flattened. Head small in relation to the total body size. Eyes small. Gape short. Dorsal fin begins at the highest part of the body, tall anteriorly but continuing posteriorly as a low fringe. Anal fin similar. Pelvic fins probably absent. Pectoral fins rounded. Caudal fin deeply forked, with rather broad lobes.

Remarks: Probably fed on small animals.

Recent relatives: Genus extinct. Distantly related to recent butterfishes of the family Stromateidae.

Stromateus flatola, a recent butterfish. Lithograph from BLOCH.

EUTELEOSTEI
Order: Perciformes
Family: Stromateidae?

Higher Bony Fishes
Suborder: Stromateoidei
Butterfishes

Unnamed butterfish (length c. 13 cm) from the Eocene of Mors, Denmark. Original: Paleontologiska Muséet, Uppsala, Sweden.

Genus: Not named.

Geological range: Eocene.

Geographical distribution: Europe.

Features: Fishes with oval outline, laterally flattened. Head deep. Eyes large. Gape short. Dorsal fin narrow, beginning in the anterior third of the body and running rearwards to a raised arcuate end near the caudal fin. Anal fin large, triangular. Pelvic fins narrow. Pectoral fins small, fan-shaped. Caudal fin large, slightly emarginate.

Remarks: Probably lived in open water near the coast.

Recent relatives: Genus probably extinct. Perhaps related to recent butterfishes of the family Stromateidae.

EUTELEOSTEI
Order: Pleuronectiformes
Family: Bothidae

Higher Bony Fishes
Suborder: Pleuronectoidei
Lefteye Flounders

Arnoglossus distinctus SVITCHENSKA (length c. 4.5 cm) from the Lower Miocene of northern Caucasus, C.I.S. Original: Paleontologicheskii Muzei Russkoi Akademii Nauk, Moscow, Russia.

Genus: *Arnoglossus* BLEEKER, 1862.

Geological range: Miocene to recent.

Geographical distribution: Western and eastern Europe.

Features: Very small fishes of oval outline with strongly flattened, asymmetrical bodies. Eyes small, both on the right side of the body. Dorsal and anal fins fringe-like. Pectoral fins small. Caudal fin not forked.

Remarks: Predators lying on the bottom.

Recent relatives: Closely related to recent scaldfishes of the genus *Arnoglossus*.

Arnoglossus sp., a recent scaldfish. Lithograph from COUGH.

920

EUTELEOSTEI
Order: Pleuronectiformes
Family: Bothidae

Higher Bony Fishes
Suborder: Pleuronectoidei
Lefteye Flounders

Bothus sp. (length c. 7 cm) from the Pliocene of Fiume Marecchia, Italy. Original: Museo Civico di Storia Naturale, Verona, Italy.

Genus: *Bothus* Bonaparte, 1841.

Geological range: Oligocene to recent.

Geographical distribution: Europe.

Features: Small fishes of rounded oval outline with strongly flattened asymmetrical bodies. Eyes small. Both on the right side. Snout slightly pointed. Dorsal and anal fins fringe-like. Pectoral fins small. Caudal fin not forked.

Remarks: Predators lying on the bottom.

Recent relatives: Closely related to recent lefteye flounders of the genus *Bothus*.

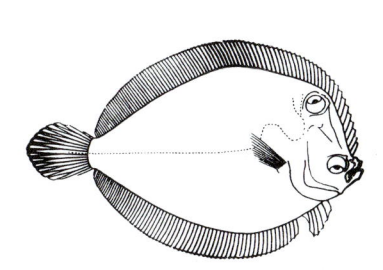

Bothus podas, a recent flounder, after Whitehead.

EUTELEOSTEI
Order: Pleuronectiformes
Family: Bothidae

Higher Bony Fishes
Suborder: Pleuronectoidei
Lefteye Flounders

Eobothus minimus (AGASSIZ) (length c. 6 cm) from the Middle Eocene of Bolca, Italy. Original: Museo Civico di Storia Naturale, Verona, Italy.

Genus: *Eobothus* EASTMAN, 1914.

Synonym: *Rhombus*

Geological range: Middle Eocene.

Geographical distribution: Europe, Asia.

Features: Small fishes of rounded oval outline with very flattened asymmetrical bodies. Eyes small, both on the right side. Dorsal and anal fins fringe-like. Pectoral fins small, fan-shaped. Caudal fin not forked, rounded.

Remarks: Bottom-dwelling predators.

Recent relatives: Related to recent flounders of the genus *Bothus*.

Eobothus, reconstruction after MAC-MILLAN.

EUTELEOSTEI
Order: Pleuronectiformes
Family: Bothidae

Higher Bony Fishes
Suborder: Pleuronectoidei
Lefteye Flounders

Scophthalmus heckeli (KNER) (length c. 6 cm) from the Middle Miocene of St. Margarethen, Austria. Original: Weiss Collection, Vienna, Austria.

Genus: *Scophthalmus* RAFINESQUE, 1810.

Geological range: Miocene to recent.

Geographical distribution: Europe.

Features: Small fishes of rounded oval outline, with strongly flattened asymmetrical bodies. Eyes small, both on the left side. Snout pointed. Dorsal fin and anal fin fringe-like. Pectoral fins small and narrow. Caudal fin not forked.

Remarks: Bottom-dwelling predators.

Recent relatives: Closely related to the recent brill (*Scophthalmus rhombus*) and other turbots.

Scophthalmus maximus, the recent turbot. Lithograph from BLOCH.

EUTELEOSTEI
Order: Pleuronectiformes
Family: Pleuronectidae

Higher Bony Fishes
Suborder: Pleuronectoidei
Righteye Flounders

Liopsetta sp. (length c. 11 cm) from the Pliocene of Sakhalin, Siberia, C.I.S. Original: Paleontologicheskii Muzei Russkoi Akademii Nauk, Moscow, Russia.

Genus: *Liopsetta* GILL, 1864.

Geological range: Pliocene to recent.

Geographical distribution: Eastern Asia.

Features: Small fishes with greatly flattened asymmetrical bodies. Eyes small, both on the right side. Dorsal and anal fins fringe-like. Pectoral fins small and fan-shaped. Caudal fin rounded, not forked.

Remarks: Bottom-dwelling predators.

Recent relatives: Closely related to recent arctic flounders of the genus *Liopsetta* which live off arctic coasts.

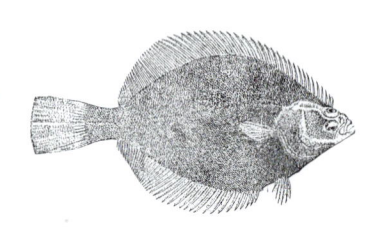

Liopsetta glacialis, the recent arctic flounder. From JORDAN.

EUTELEOSTEI
Order: Pleuronectiformes
Family: Soleidae

Higher Bony Fishes
Suborder: Pleuronectoidei
Soles

Solea kirchbergeana MEYER (length c. 7 cm) from the Miocene of Unterkirchberg, Württemberg, Germany. Original: Bayerische Staatssammlung für Paläontologie, Munich, Germany.

Genus: *Solea* GOUAN, 1770.

Geological range: Paleocene to recent.

Geographical distribution: Europe, northern Africa, western Asia.

Features: Small fishes of oval outline with greatly flattened, asymmetrical bodies. Eyes small. Both on the right side of the body. Snout rather rounded. Dorsal fin and anal fins fringe-like. Pectoral fins pointed. Caudal fin not forked, rounded.

Remarks: Bottom-dwelling predators.

Recent relatives: Closely related to recent soles of the genus *Solea*.

Solea solea, the recent sole. Lithograph from BLOCH.

925

EUTELEOSTEI
Higher Bony Fishes
Order: Tetraodontiformes
Family: Aracanidae
Suborder: Balistoidei
Ancient Trunkfishes

Eolactoria sorbinii TYLER (length c. 5 cm) from the Middle Eocene of Bolca, Italy. Original: Museo Civico di Storia Naturale, Verona, Italy.

Genus: *Eolactoria* TYLER, 1975.

Geological range: Middle Eocene.

Geographical distribution: Europe.

Features: Small fishes with rounded bodies, almost entirely armoured with bony plates - only the snout and the stalk of the tail are free. Eyes large. Snout rounded. Mouth small. Upper and lower jaws with teeth. All fins small. The forehead region and the posterior ventral part of the body each carry a pair of spines with small thorn-like outgrowths. Two small broad spines at the horizontal level of the eyes.

Remarks: Lived on small organisms.

Recent relatives: Genus extinct. Distantly related to recent cowfishes of the genus *Lactoria*.

Lactoria fornasini, the thornback cowfish.

EUTELEOSTEI
Order: Tetraodontiformes
Family: Aracanidae

Higher Bony Fishes
Suborder: Balistoidei
Ancient Trunkfishes

Plectocretacicus clarae Sorbini (length c. 2 cm) from the Upper Cretaceous of Lebanon. Original: Museo Civico di Storia Naturale, Verona, Italy.

Genus: *Plectocretacicus* Sorbini, 1979.

Geological range: Upper Cretaceous.

Geographical distribution: Middle East.

Features: Very small fishes of almost circular outline. Head small. Eyes large. Gape rather long. Head and body enclosed in an armour of bony plates with only the stalk of the caudal fin and the bases of the other fins free of it.

Remarks: Counts as the oldest known boxfish. Probably fed on small organisms taken from the bottom.

Recent relatives: Genus extinct. Distantly related to recent boxfishes.

EUTELEOSTEI
Order: Tetraodontiformes
Family: Aracanidae

Higher Bony Fishes
Suborder: Balistoidei
Ancient Trunkfishes

Proaracana dubia (de BLAINVILLE) (length c. 4 cm) from the Middle Eocene of Bolca, Italy. Original: Museo Civico di Storia Naturale, Verona, Italy.

Genus: *Proaracana* TYLER, 1975.

Synonym: *Ostracion*.

Geological range: Middle Eocene.

Geographical distribution: Europe.

Features: Very small fishes with rounded outline and laterally rather flattened bodies. Head deep. Eyes large. Gape short. Head and body enclosed in an armour of hexagonal bony plates, except for the stalk of the tail and the bases of the fins. First dorsal fin pointed, at the highest part of the body. Second dorsal fin soft-rayed, opposite the anal fin. Caudal fin elongate, not forked, rounded.

Remarks: Probably preferred hard-shelled food.

Recent relatives: Related to recent cowfishes of the genus *Aracana*.

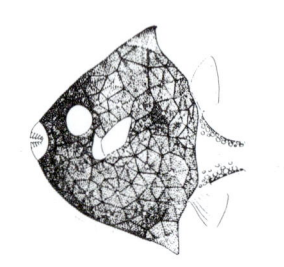

Proaracana, reconstruction after TYLER.

928

EUTELEOSTEI
Order: Tetraodontiformes
Family: Triacanthodidae

Higher Bony Fishes
Suborder: Balistoidei
Spikefishes

Eoplectus bloti TYLER (length c. 10 cm) from the Middle Eocene of Bolca, Italy. Original: Museo Civico di Storia Naturale, Verona, Italy.

Genus: *Eoplectus* TYLER, 1973.

Geological range: Middle Eocene.

Geographical distribution: Europe.

Features: Small fishes of circular outline, rather laterally flattened. Head short and deep. Eyes large. Gape short, rather produced. First dorsal fin hard-rayed. Second dorsal fin soft-rayed, opposite the anal fin. Pelvic fins small. Caudal fin on a thick peduncle, elongate, rounded, not forked.

Remarks: Probably preferred hard-shelled food.

Recent relatives: None. Died out in Eocene.

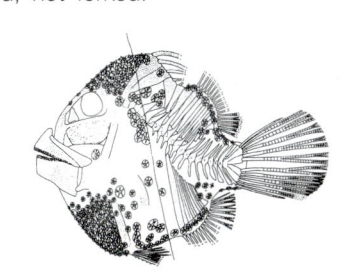

Eoplectus, reconstruction after TYLER.

EUTELEOSTEI — Higher Bony Fishes

Order: Tetraodontiformes
Family: Triacanthodidae
Suborder: Balistoidei
Spikefishes

Spinacanthus imperialis (MASSALONGO) (length c. 66 cm) from the Middle Eocene of Bolca, Italy. Original: Museo Civico di Storia Naturale, Verona, Italy. Photograph: G. Bonato, Verona.

Genus: *Spinacanthus* AGASSIZ, 1835.

Synonym: *Protobalistum*.

Geological range: Middle Eocene.

Geographical distribution: Europe.

Features: Middle-sized to large fishes of oval outline, laterally flattened. Head deep. Eyes large. Gape somewhat anterior. First dorsal fin carried by five strong hard rays which decrease in length posteriorly. Second dorsal fin small, soft-rayed. Anal fin opposite the second dorsal fin, rather larger. Caudal fin peduncolated, not forked, rounded.

Remarks: Free-swimming predators which certainly also took hard-shelled prey.

Recent relatives: None. Died out in Eocene.

EUTELEOSTEI
Order: **Tetraodontiformes**
Family: **Triacanthodidae**

Higher Bony Fishes
Suborder: **Balistoidei**
Spikefishes

Zignoichthys oblongus (de Zigno) (length c. 18 cm) from the Middle Eocene of Bolca, Italy. Original: Università di Padova, Padua, Italy. Photograph: Università di Padova.

Genus: *Zignoichthys* Tyler, 1975.

Geological range: Middle Eocene.

Geographical distribution: Europe.

Features: Middle-sized fishes of oval outline, laterally compressed. Head deep. Eyes small. Snout somewhat produced. First dorsal fin borne by three hard rays. Second dorsal fin soft-rayed, short and fringe-like, like the anal fin opposite. Caudal fin not forked.

Remarks: Probably fed on bivalves, gastropods, crabs and also corals.

Recent relatives: Genus extinct. Nevertheless related to recent triggerfishes.

Balistoides conspicillum, the clown triggerfish.

EUTELEOSTEI
Higher Bony Fishes
Order: Tetraodontiformes
Family: Triacanthodidae
Suborder: Balistoidei
Spikefishes

Protacanthodes ombonii de Zigno (length c. 16 cm) from the Middle Eocene of Bolca, Italy. Original: Università di Padova, Padua, Italy.

Genus: *Protacanthodes* Gill, 1888.

Geological range: Middle Eocene.

Geographical distribution: Europe.

Features: Middle-sized fishes in outline deep in the middle of the body and tapering rearwards. Head deep. Eyes large. Snout pointed. Gape short. Jaws set with powerful teeth. First dorsal fin with a long powerful ray and three smaller rays. Second dorsal fin soft-rayed, broad-based. Anal fin considerably smaller. Pectoral fins likewise small. Pelvic fins each with one long hard ray. Caudal fin elongate and rounded.

Remarks: Probably fed mostly on hard-shelled prey.

Recent relatives: Genus extinct. Nevertheless related to recent spikefishes of the family Triacanthodidae.

Triacanthus biaculeatus, the common tripodfish.

EUTELEOSTEI
Order: Tetraodontiformes
Family: Balistidae

Higher Bony Fishes
Suborder: Balistoidei
Triggerfishes and Filefishes

Alutera sp. (length c. 3 cm) from the Pliocene of Fiume Marecchia, Italy. Original: Museo Civico di Storia Naturale, Verona, Italy.

Genus: *Alutera* OKEN, 1817.

Geological range: Pliocene to recent.

Geographical distribution: Europe.

Features: Small to middle-sized fishes of elongate, laterally flattened shape. Head deep but with a long produced snout. Mouth small. First ray of the first dorsal fin elongated as a spine and with thorn-like outgrowths. Second dorsal fin short, fringe-like and soft-rayed. Pelvic fins absent. An obvious ventral keel begins at the throat. Tail fin not forked.

Remarks: Fed on plants.

Recent relatives: Related to recent filefishes of the genus *Alutera*.

Alutera scripta, the scribbled filefish.

EUTELEOSTEI
Order: Tetraodontiformes
Family: Balistidae

Higher Bony Fishes
Suborder: Balistoidei
Triggerfishes and Filefishes

Monacanthus sp. (length c. 14.5 cm) from the Pliocene of Fiume Marecchia, Italy. Original: Staatliches Museum für Naturkunde, Karlsruhe, Germany.

Genus: *Monacanthus* OKEN, 1817.

Geological range: Pliocene to recent.

Geographical distribution: Europe.

Features: Small fishes of elongate oval outline. Head deep. Eyes relatively small. Mouth produced somewhat forward, very small. First ray of the first dorsal fin very long and powerful. Second dorsal fin very posterior, short and fringe-like, opposite the anal fin. Belly with an obvious keel. Pelvic fins absent. Caudal fin not forked, rounded.

Remarks: Fed on small organisms and probably also on plants.

Recent relatives: Closely related to recent filefishes of the subfamily Monacanthinae.

Monacanthus hispidus, the recent planehead filefish.

EUTELEOSTEI
Order: **Tetraodontiformes**
Family: **Balistidae**

Higher Bony Fishes
Suborder: **Balistoidei**
Triggerfishes and Filefishes

Oligobalistes robustus DANILTCHENKO (length c. 9 cm) from the Lower Oligocene of the northern Caucasus, C.I.S. Original: Paleontologicheskii Muzei Russkoi Akademii Nauk, Moscow, Russia.

Genus: *Oligobalistes* DANILTCHENKO, 1960.

Geological range: Lower Oligocene.

Geographical distribution: Eastern Europe.

Features: Small fishes of oval outline, laterally flattened. Head deep. Eyes small. Snout somewhat produced. First dorsal fin with three hard rays, the first being considerably stronger and longer than the two others. Second dorsal fin fringe-like like the anal fin. Caudal fin not forked, rounded.

Remarks: Fed on bivalves and snails, crabs and possibly also corals.

Recent relatives: Closely related to recent triggerfishes of the family Balistidae.

Pseudobalistes fuscus, the recent blue-and-gold triggerfish.

935

EUTELEOSTEI
Order: Tetraodontiformes
Family: Balistoidei

Higher Bony Fishes
Suborder: Balistoidei
Triggerfishes and Filefishes

Unnamed fish (length c. 38 cm) from Fiume Marecchia, Italy. Original: Staatliches Museum für Naturkunde, Karlsruhe, Germany.

Genus: Not named.

Geological range: Pliocene to recent?

Geographical distribution: Europe.

Features: Middle-sized fishes of elongate oval outline, laterally flattened. Eyes large. Gape very small. First ray of the first dorsal fin elongate, powerful and anteriorly serrated. Second dorsal fin very posterior, short and fringe-like, opposite the similar anal fin. Caudal fin elongate, not forked, rounded. Belly keeled.

Remarks: Fed on small organisms and perhaps also on plants.

Recent relatives: Closely related to recent filefishes of the subfamily Monacanthinae.

Monacanthus melanocephalus, the recent redtail filefish.

936

EUTELEOSTEI
Order: Tetraodontiformes
Family: Tetraodontidae

Higher Bony Fishes
Suborder: Tetraodontoidei
Puffers

Eotetraodon pygmaeus TYLER (length c. 2 cm) from the Middle Eocene of Bolca, Italy. Original: Museo Civico di Storia Naturale, Verona, Italy.

Genus: *Eotetraodon* TYLER, 1980.

Geological range: Eocene.

Geographical distribution: Europe.

Features: Small to very small fishes with rounded plump bodies. Head large. Eyes large. Mouth small, somewhat produced. Teeth fused to form beak-like plates. First dorsal fin absent, as also are the pelvic fins. Second dorsal fin opposite the anal fin. Caudal fin stalked, not forked.

Remarks: Fed preferably on hard-shelled prey. Perhaps even then were able to inflate themselves.

Recent relatives: Closely related to recent puffers which live in tropical and subtropical seas but also occur in brackish and fresh water.

Arothron hispidus, the recent stars and stripes puffer.

937

EUTELEOSTEI
Order: Tetraodontiformes
Family: Diodontidae

Higher Bony Fishes
Suborder: Tetraodontoidei
Porcupinefishes

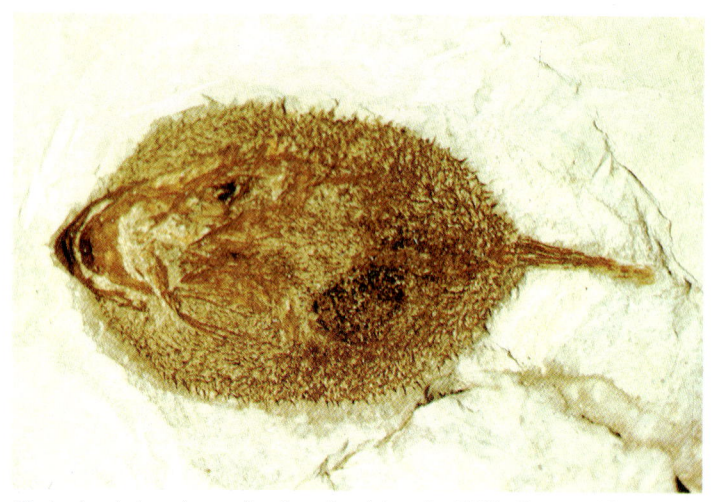

Diodon tenuispinus AGASSIZ (length c. 7 cm) from the Middle Eocene of Bolca, Italy. Original: Museo Civico di Storia Naturale, Verona, Italy.

Genus: *Diodon* LINNAEUS, 1758.

Synonyms: *Heptadiodon*, *Megalurites*.

Geological range: Eocene to recent.

Geographical distribution: Europe, Asia, Africa, North America, Indonesian Archipelago, Caribbean, Australia.

Features: Small fishes with plump oval bodies. Skin set with short powerful spines. Head small. Mouth relatively large. Mouth beak-like. Fused dental ridges. Dorsal and anal fins small, opposite each other, near the root of the tail. Caudal fin on a stalk, not forked, rounded.

Remarks: Fed mainly on hard-shelled prey. Could probably already inflate themselves.

Recent relatives: Closely related to recent porcupine fishes of the genus *Diodon* which live in warm seas.

Diodon hystrix, a recent porcupinefish.

CROSSOPTERYGII — Crossopterygians or Lobe-Finned Fishes

The lobe-finned fishes are assigned to the Osteichthyes. They differ from other bony fishes, however, in possessing true nostrils and choanae (ducts leading from the nostrils into the mouth). The skull is extensively ossified in the older forms, but incompletely so in the Coelacanthiformes. The eyes are protected by bony sclerotic rings consisting of more than four elements. The jaws are set with more or less longitudinally ribbed teeth. The vertebrae are only partly ossified. Pelvic and pectoral fins arise from a quadripartite base. The caudal fin is heterocercal in the older representatives, with a small upper lobe. In the course of evolution, however, this lobe became gradually bigger and finally reached the size of the lower lobe. Later forms have a third lobe at the end of the vertebral column. There are usually two dorsal fins and an anal fin separate from the caudal fin.

In the primitive members of the group the body is covered by thick rhombic scales with a cosmine layer and a thin shiny ganoine layer. In later forms these cosmine scales tend to transform into cycloid scales by gradual loss of the cosmine and ganoine layers. The length of these fishes varies from 20 cm to 2.5 metres or even more.

Lobe-finned fishes originally lived in fresh water. Later they moved into the sea, especially the members of the order Coelacanthiformes. The oldest ones appear in the Lower Devonian and the group reached its first maximum in the Middle Devonian. There was a second maximum, though only of short duration, in the Lower Triassic. After some oscillations they came to be uniformly distributed in the Upper Cretaceous. After that time, in the Tertiary, no fossil lobe-fins have ever been found, and they were believed to have died out.

In 1938, however, the famous *Latimeria* was discovered living in the depths of the ocean around the Comores Islands so the lobe-fins had survived after all. About 90 fossil genera have so far been described. Many of these are based on fragments though others are very well preserved. The particular importance of lobe-fins lies in the fact that they are seen as the immediate ancestors of all terrestrial vertebrates.

CROSSOPTERYGII — Lobe-Finned Fishes

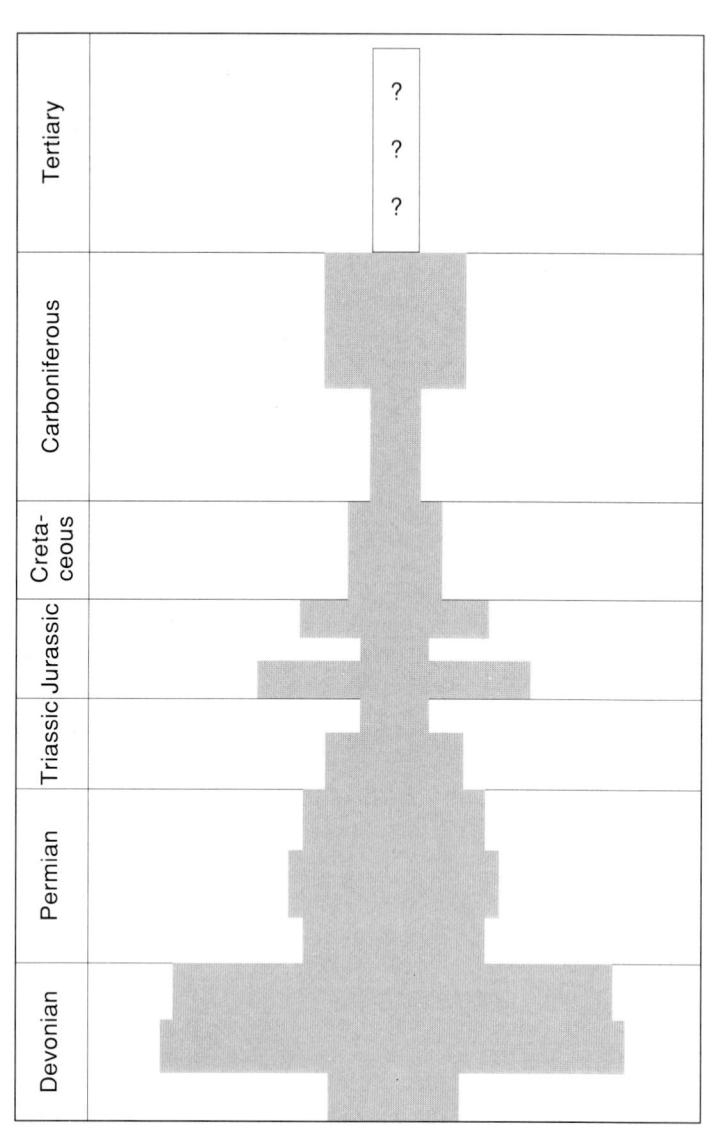

The approximate stratigraphical distribution of the crossopterygians, changed after MÜLLER.

CROSSOPTERYGII
Lobe-Finned Fishes
Order: Coelacanthiformes
Family: Diplocercidae

Chagrinia sp. (length c. 10 cm) from the Upper Devonian of the U.S.A. Original: American Museum of Natural History, New York, N.Y., U.S.A.

Genus: *Chagrinia* Schaeffer, 1962.

Geological range: Upper Devonian.

Geographical distribution: North America.

Features: Small fishes of slender shape. Head shallow. Eyes large. Snout pointed. Gape rather long. First dorsal fin anterior to the middle of the body. Second dorsal fin in the posterior third of the body. Anal fin small. Pectoral fins relatively large. An obvious ventral keel begins at the throat. Caudal fin three-lobed with the middle lobe brush-like.

Remarks: Predators.

Recent relatives: None. Died out in Upper Devonian.

CROSSOPTERYGII
Lobe-Finned Fishes
Order: Coelacanthiformes
Family: Diplocercidae

Lochmocercus aciculiodontus Lund & Lund (length c. 11 cm) from the Lower Carboniferous (Mississippian) of Bear Gulch, Montana, U.S.A. Original: Adelphi University, Garden City, N.Y., U.S.A.

Genus: *Lochmocercus* Lund & Lund, 1984.

Geological range: Lower Carboniferous (Mississippian).

Geographical distribution: North America.

Features: Small fishes with laterally compressed bodies. Head deep. Eyes large. Gape rather long. Two small dorsal fins, the first being approximately in the middle of the body and the second in the posterior third of the body. The pelvic and anal fins are likewise small and lie obliquely opposite the first and second dorsal fins respectively. Caudal fin rounded, three-lobed, with a prominent brush-like middle lobe.

Remarks: Predators.

Recent relatives: None. Died out in Lower Carboniferous.

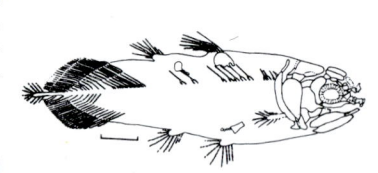

Lochmocercus, reconstruction after Lund.

CROSSOPTERYGII
Order: Coelacanthiformes
Family: Hadronectoridae

Lobe-Finned Fishes

Allenypterus montanus MELTON (length c. 14 cm) from the Lower Carboniferous (Mississippian) of Bear Gulch, Montana, U.S.A. Original: Field Museum of Natural History, Chicago, Illinois, U.S.A.

Genus: *Allenypterus* MELTON, 1969.

Geological range: Lower Carboniferous (Mississippian).

Geographical distribution: North America.

Features: Small fishes, approximately half-pear-shaped in outline. Head deep. Eyes large. Gape rather long. First dorsal fin at the highest part of the body. Second dorsal fin begins shortly behind the first and extends rearwards as a fringe. Anal fin and pelvic fins small. Pectoral fins considerably larger. Caudal fin consists only of a small extension of the vertebral axis.

Remarks: Predators.

Recent relatives: None. Died out in Lower Carboniferous.

Allenypterus, reconstruction after Lund.

CROSSOPTERYGII
Lobe-Finned Fishes
Order: Coelacanthiformes
Family: Hadronectoridae

Hadronector donbairdi LUND & LUND (length c. 9 cm) from the Lower Carboniferous (Mississippian) of Bear Gulch, Montana, U.S.A. Original: Carnegie Museum of Natural History, Pittsburgh, Penna., U.S.A.

Genus: *Hadronector* LUND & LUND, 1984.

Geological range: Lower Carboniferous (Mississippian).

Geographical distribution: North America.

Features: Small fishes with laterally compressed bodies, deepest in the middle. Head deep. Eyes large. Gape rather long. First dorsal fin approximately in the middle of the body, the second dorsal fin in the posterior third. Pelvic and anal fins opposite the two dorsal fins, small. Pectoral fins somewhat larger. Caudal fin broad, three-lobed, the middle lobe prominent and brush-like.

Remarks: Predators.

Recent relatives: None. Died out in Lower Carboniferous.

Hadronector, reconstruction after LUND.

CROSSOPTERYGII
Lobe-Finned Fishes
Order: Coelacanthiformes
Family: Hadronectoridae

Polyosteorhynchus simplex Lund & Lund (length c. 12 cm) from the Lower Carboniferous (Mississippian) of Bear Gulch, Montana, U.S.A. Original: Adelphi University, Garden City, N.Y., U.S.A.

Genus: *Polyosteorhynchus* Lund & Lund, 1984.

Geological range: Lower Carboniferous (Mississippian).

Geographical distribution: North America.

Features: Small fishes with laterally compressed bodies. Head deep. Eyes large. Gape rather long. Two small dorsal fins, the first being at the highest part of the body, the second in the posterior third. Pelvic, pectoral and anal fins small. Caudal fin three-lobed, the middle lobe prominent and brush-like.

Remarks: Predators.

Recent relatives: None. Died out in Lower Carboniferous.

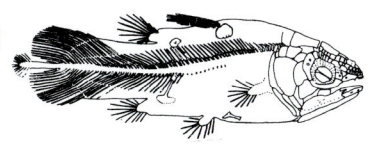

Polyosteorhynchus, reconstruction after Lund.

CROSSOPTERYGII
Lobe-Finned Fishes
Order: Coelacanthiformes
Family: Rhabdodermatidae

Caridosuctor populosum LUND & LUND (length c. 19 cm) from the Lower Carboniferous (Mississippian) of Bear Gulch, Montana, U.S.A. Original: Bayerische Staatssammlung für Paläontologie, Munich, Germany.

Genus: *Caridosuctor* LUND & LUND, 1984.

Geological range: Lower Carboniferous (Mississippian).

Geographical distribution: North America.

Features: Small to middle-sized fishes of slender shape. Head shallow. Eyes large. Snout slightly rounded. Gape rather long. First dorsal fin approximately in the middle of the body. Second dorsal fin in the posterior third of the body. Pelvic and anal fins small, opposite the dorsal fins. Pectoral fins rounded. Caudal fin elongate, three-lobed, the middle lobe greatly extended and brush-like.

Remarks: Predators.

Recent relatives: None. Died out in Lower Carboniferous.

Caridosuctor, reconstruction after LUND.

CROSSOPTERYGII
Order: Coelacanthiformes
Family: Rhabdodermatidae

Lobe-Finned Fishes

Coelacanthopsis curta TRAQUAIR (length c. 9 cm) from the Lower Carboniferous of Eskdale, U.K. Original: National Museum of Scotland, Edinburgh, U.K.

Genus: *Coelacanthopsis* TRAQUAIR, 1901.

Synonym: *Dumfregia*.

Geological range: Lower Carboniferous (Mississippian).

Geographical distribution: Europe.

Features: Small fishes with slender bodies. Head shallow. Eyes large. Snout rounded. Gape rather long. First dorsal fin shortly behind the middle of the body. Second dorsal fin just in front of the root of the tail. Pelvic and anal fins opposite the dorsal fins. Caudal fin three-lobed, the middle lobe brush-like.

Remarks: Predators. Now reclassified into the genus *Rhabdoderma*.

Recent relatives: None. Died out in Lower Carboniferous.

CROSSOPTERYGII
Lobe-Finned Fishes
Order: Coelacanthiformes
Family: Rhabdodermatidae

Rhabdoderma elegans (Newberry) (length c. 14 cm) from the Lower Carboniferous of Scotland, U.K. Original: The Natural History Museum, London. (P 5379)

Genus: *Rhabdoderma* Reis, 1888.

Synonyms: *Conchiopsis*, *Holopygus*.

Geological range: Lower to Upper Carboniferous.

Geographical distribution: Western and eastern Europe, North America, northern Africa.

Features: Small to middle-sized fishes of slender shape. Head shallow. Eyes large. Snout rounded. Gape rather long. Both dorsal fins small, the first approximately in the middle of the body, the second in the posterior third. Caudal fin three-lobed, the middle lobe brush-like.

Remarks: Predators.

Recent relatives: None. Died out in Upper Carboniferous.

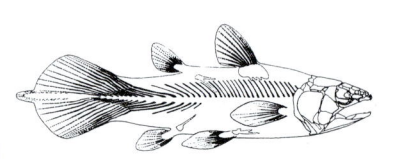

Rhabdoderma, reconstruction after Forey.

CROSSOPTERYGII
Order: Coelacanthiformes
Family: Coelacanthidae

Lobe-Finned Fishes

Axelrodichthys araripensis MAISEY (length c. 42 cm) from the Lower Cretaceous of Ceará, Brazil. Original: Staatliches Museum für Naturkunde, Karlsruhe, Germany.

Genus: *Axelrodichthys* MAISEY, 1986.

Geological range: Lower Cretaceous.

Geographical distribution: South America.

Features: Middle-sized fishes with laterally compressed bodies. Head shallow. Eyes small. Gape long. First dorsal fin in the anterior third of the body. Second dorsal fin probably smaller, in the posterior part of the body. Pelvic and anal fins elongate. Pectoral fins broad, fan-shaped. Caudal fin very large, probably three-lobed.

Remarks: Predators.

Recent relatives: None. Died out in Lower Cretaceous.

Axelrodichthys araripensis, reconstruction after MAISEY.

CROSSOPTERYGII
Lobe-Finned Fishes
Order: Coelacanthiformes
Family: Coelacanthidae

Coccoderma nudum REIS (length c. 17 cm) from the Upper Jurassic of Solnhofen (Kelheim), Bavaria, Germany. Original: Bayerische Staatssammlung für Paläontologie, Munich, Germany.

Genus: *Coccoderma* ZITTEL, 1887.

Synonym: *Dokkoderma*.

Geological range: Upper Jurassic.

Geographical distribution: Europe.

Features: Small to middle-sized fishes of slender shape. Head shallow. Eyes large. Snout somewhat pointed. Gape rather long. First dorsal fin anterior to the middle of the body. Second dorsal fin in the posterior half of the body. Pelvic and anal fins opposite the respective dorsal fins. Pectoral fins rounded. Caudal fin approximately lozenge-shaped, three-lobed, the middle lobe prominent and brush-like. Scales with granular surface.

Remarks: Predators.

Recent relatives: None. Died out in Upper Jurassic.

CROSSOPTERYGII
Lobe-Finned Fishes
Order: Coelacanthiformes
Family: Coelacanthidae

Coelacanthus granulatus Agassiz (length c. 32 cm) from the Permian of Bad Sachsa, Hesse, Germany. Original: Interfoss, Munich, Germany.

Genus: *Coelacanthus* Agassiz, 1836.

Geological range: Upper Carboniferous to Lower Triassic.

Geographical distribution: Europe, Madagascar, North America.

Features: Small to middle-sized fishes of slender shape. Head shallow. Eyes large. Snout rounded. Gape rather long. First dorsal fin in anterior third of body. Second dorsal fin in posterior third of body. Pelvic fins small. Anal and pectoral fins rounded. Caudal fin three-lobed, the middle lobe brush-like.

Remarks: Predators.

Recent relatives: None. Died out in Lower Triassic.

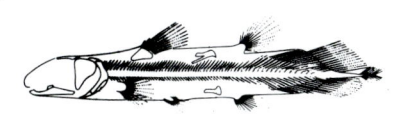

Coelacanthus, reconstruction after Moy-Thomas.

CROSSOPTERYGII
Lobe-Finned Fishes
Order: Coelacanthiformes
Family: Coelacanthidae

Diplurus newarki BRYANT (length c. 10 cm) from the Upper Triassic of Newark, N.J., U.S.A. Original: Interfoss, Munich, Germany.

Genus: *Diplurus* NEWBERRY, 1878.

Synonyms: *Osteoplurus, Holophagoides, Pariostegus, Rhabdiolepis*.

Geological range: Upper Triassic.

Geographical distribution: North America.

Features: Small fishes of slender outline. Head shallow. Eyes large. Snout pointed. First dorsal fin anterior to the middle of the body. Second dorsal fin somewhat larger, in the posterior half of the body. Pelvic and anal fins obliquely opposite the respective dorsal fins. Caudal fin three-lobed, the middle lobe prominent and brush-like.

Remarks: Predators.

Recent relatives: None. Died out in Upper Triassic.

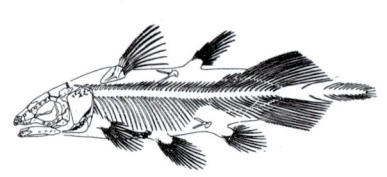

Diplurus, after SCHÄFFER.

CROSSOPTERYGII
Lobe-Finned Fishes
Order: Coelacanthiformes
Family: Coelacanthidae

Libys superbus Zittel & Reis (length c. 42 cm) from the Upper Jurassic of Solnhofen (Eichstätt), Bavaria, Germany. Original: Bayrische Staatssammlung für Paläontologie, Munich, Germany.

Genus: *Libys* Münster, 1842.

Geological range: Upper Jurassic.

Geographical distribution: Europe.

Features: Middle-sized fishes of laterally compressed shape. Head deep. Eyes large. Snout somewhat produced. Gape rather long. Both dorsal fins relatively large, the first anterior to the middle of the body, the second in the posterior third. Pelvic and anal fins rounded and slightly pointed. Caudal fin very large, three-lobed, the middle lobe prominent and brush-like.

Remarks: Predators.

Recent relatives: None. Died out in Lower Carboniferous.

CROSSOPTERYGII
Lobe-Finned Fishes
Order: Coelacanthiformes
Family: Coelacanthidae

Macropomoides orientalis Woodward (length c. 8 cm) from the Upper Cretaceous of Lebanon. Original: Henne Collection, Stuttgart, Germany.

Genus: *Macropomoides* Woodward, 1942.

Geological range: Upper Cretaceous.

Geographical distribution: Middle East.

Features: Small fishes with rather laterally compressed bodies. Head deep. Eyes large. Snout produced. Gape rather long. First dorsal fin shortly behind the middle of the body. Second dorsal fin much more posterior. Pelvic and anal fins rounded. Caudal fin three-lobed, the middle lobe prominently brush-like.

Remarks: One of the last lobe-fins before the discovery of *Latimeria*.

Recent relatives: Possibly related to the recent genus *Latimeria*.

Latimeria chalumnae. The only recent lobe-fin.

CROSSOPTERYGII
Lobe-Finned Fishes
Order: Coelacanthiformes
Family: Coelacanthidae

Miguashaia bureaui SCHULTZE (length c. 7.5 cm) from the Upper Devonian of Miguasha, Gaspé Peninsula, Quebec, Canada. Original: Musée de Géology, University Laval, Quebec, Canada.

Genus: *Miguashaia* SCHULTZE, 1973.

Geological range: Upper Devonian.

Geographical distribution: North America.

Features: Small fishes of slender shape. Head deep. Eyes rather large. Snout somewhat produced. First dorsal fin approximately in the middle of the body. Second dorsal fin very posterior. Caudal fin three-lobed, the middle lobe brush-like.

Remarks: Predators.

Recent relatives: None. Died out in Upper Devonian.

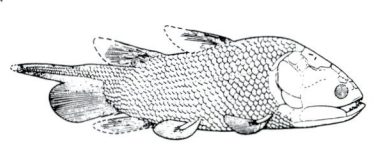

Miguashaia, reconstruction after SCHULTZE.

955

CROSSOPTERYGII
Order: Coelacanthiformes
Family: Coelacanthidae

Lobe-Finned Fishes

Piveteauia madagascariensis LEHMAN (length c. 12 cm) from the Lower Triassic of Madagascar. Original: Muséum National d'Histoire Naturelle, Paris, France. Photograph: Serette, Paris.

Genus: *Piveteauia* LEHMAN, 1952.

Geological range: Lower Triassic.

Geographical distribution: Madagascar.

Features: Small fishes of slender shape. Head deep. Snout pointed. Gape rather long. First dorsal fin narrow, in the anterior third of the body. Second dorsal fin with a rather broader base. Pectoral and pelvic fins narrow, obliquely opposite each other. Caudal fin three-lobed, the middle lobe prominently brush-like.

Remarks: Probably predators.

Recent relatives: None. Died out in Triassic.

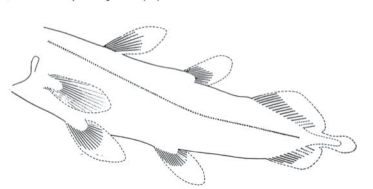

Piveteauia, reconstruction after LEHMAN

CROSSOPTERYGII
Lobe-Finned Fishes
Order: Coelacanthiformes
Family: Coelacanthidae

Whiteia woodwardi Moy-Thomas (length c. 26 cm) from the Lower Triassic of Madagascar. Original: Staatliches Museum für Naturkunde, Karlsruhe, Germany.

Genus: *Whiteia* Moy-Thomas, 1935.

Geological range: Lower to Upper Triassic.

Geographical distribution: Madagascar, Greenland, North America.

Features: Middle-sized fishes of rather laterally compressed shape. Head shallow. Eyes large. Snout elongate and pointed. Gape rather long. First dorsal fin long and narrow. Second dorsal fin in the posterior third of the body, rounded. Anal, pelvic and pectoral fins likewise rounded. Caudal fin three-lobed, the middle lobe prominently brush-like.

Remarks: Predators.

Recent relatives: None. Died out in Upper Triassic.

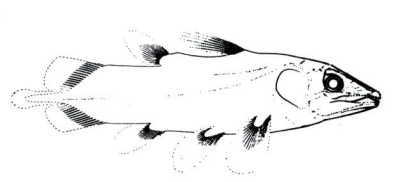

Whiteia, reconstruction after Lehman.

CROSSOPTERYGII — Lobe-Finned Fishes
Order: Coelacanthiformes
Family: Coelacanthidae?

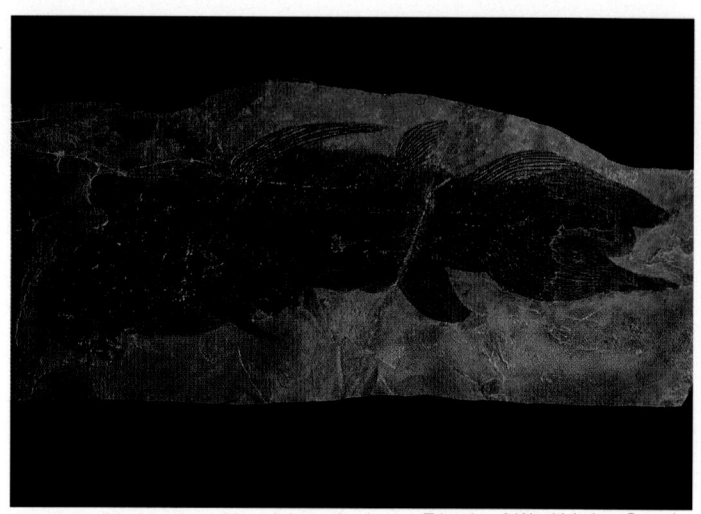

Unnamed fish (length c. 67 cm) from the Lower Triassic of Wapiti Lake, Canada. Original: Staatliches Museum für Naturkunde, Karlsruhe, Germany.

Genus: Not named.

Geological range: Lower Triassic.

Geographical distribution: North America.

Features: Middle-sized fishes with rather laterally compressed bodies. Head elongate. Eyes small. Snout slightly produced. Gape rather long. First dorsal fin in the anterior third of the body. Second dorsal fin in the posterior third of the body, opposite the larger anal fin. Pectoral fins long, narrow and pointed. Caudal fin very large, the upper and lower lobes arcuate anteriorly, produced into a point posteriorly, the middle lobe brush-like.

Remarks: Predators.

Recent relatives: None. Probably died out in the Triassic.

CROSSOPTERYGII
Lobe-Finned Fishes
Order: Coelacanthiformes
Family: Laugiidae

Holophagus sp. (length c. 25 cm) from the Upper Triassic of Zogno, Bergamo, Italy. Original: Museo Civico dei Scienze Naturali Caffi, Bergamo, Italy.

Genus: *Holophagus* EGERTON, 1861.

Synonym: *Trachymetopon*.

Geological range: Upper Triassic.

Geographical distribution: Europe, Australia.

Features: Middle-sized fishes of rather laterally compressed shape. Head shallow. Eyes large. Snout pointed. Gape rather long. Dorsal fins rounded, the first in the middle of the body, the second very posterior. Anal and pelvic fins likewise rounded. Pectoral fins long and rounded. Caudal fin three-lobed, the middle lobe prominently brush-like.

Remarks: Predators.

Recent relatives: None. Died out in Upper Triassic.

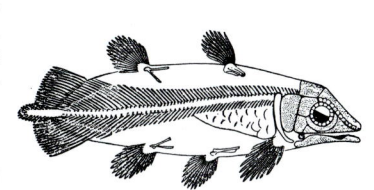

Holophagus, reconstruction after WOODWARD.

CROSSOPTERYGII
Lobe-Finned Fishes
Order: Coelacanthiformes
Family: Laugiidae

Laugia groenlandica STENSIÖ (length c. 17 cm) from the Lower Triassic of Greenland. Original: The Natural History Museum, London, U.K. (P2641-2).

Genus: *Laugia* STENSIÖ, 1932.

Geological range: Lower Triassic.

Geographical distribution: Greenland.

Features: Middle-sized fishes of slender shape. Head shallow. Eyes large. Gape rather long. First dorsal fin slightly anterior to the middle of the body. Second dorsal fin in the posterior third, opposite the relatively long anal fin. Caudal fin long and narrow, three-lobed, the middle lobe prominently brush-like.

Remarks: Predators.

Recent relatives: None. Died out in Lower Triassic.

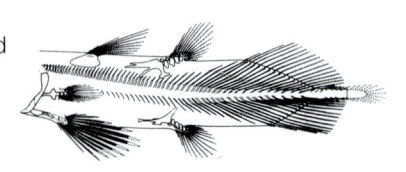

Laugia, reconstruction after STENSIÖ.

CROSSOPTERYGII
Lobe-Finned Fishes
Order: Coelacanthiformes
Family: Laugiidae

Undina penicillata MÜNSTER (length c. 32 cm) from the Upper Jurassic of Solnhofen (Eichstätt), Bavaria, Germany. Original: Interfoss, Munich, Germany.

Genus: *Undina* MÜNSTER, 1834.

Geological range: Upper Jurassic.

Geographical distribution: Europe.

Features: Middle-sized fishes of rather laterally compressed shape. Head deep. Eyes large. Gape rather long. First dorsal fin approximately in the middle of the body, the second very posterior. Pelvic and anal fins rounded. Pectoral fins elongate. Caudal fin broad, three-lobed, the middle lobe prominently brush-like.

Remarks: Predators. *Undina* is occasionally considered a synonym of *Holophagus*.

Recent relatives: None. Died out in Upper Jurassic.

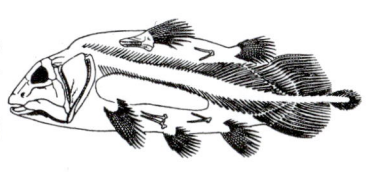

Undina, reconstruction after NORMAN.

961

CROSSOPTERYGII
Order: Onychodontiformes
Family: Onychodontidae

Lobe-Finned Fishes

Callistiopterus clappi ROMER (length c. 7 cm) from the Upper Devonian of Miguasha, Gaspé Peninsula, Quebec, Canada. Original: Museum for Comparative Zoology, Harvard University, Cambridge, Mass., U.S.A.

Genus: *Callistiopterus* THOMSON & HAHN, 1968.

Geological range: Upper Devonian.

Geographical distribution: North America.

Features: Small fishes with very slender elongate bodies. Head shallow. Eyes small. Gape long. The two dorsal fins very posterior in position, respectively opposite the anal and pelvic fins. Caudal fin heterocercal with large lower lobe. Rounded scales. The taxonomic classification of this specimen is disputed.

Remarks: Predators. The taxonomic classification of this specimen is disputed.

Recent relatives: None. Died out in Upper Devonian.

Callistiopterus, reconstruction after SCHULTZE.

CROSSOPTERYGII
Order: Onychodontiformes
Family: Onychodontidae

Lobe-Finned Fishes

Quebecius quebecensis (WHITEAVES) (length c. 6 cm) from the Upper Devonian of Miguasha, Gaspé Peninsula, Quebec, Canada. Original: Museum of Natural History, Lawrence, Kansas, U.S.A.

Genus: *Quebecius* SCHULTZE, 1973.

Geological range: Upper Devonian.

Geographical distribution: North America.

Features: Small fishes with rather laterally compressed bodies. Head deep. Eyes small. Gape very long. Two dorsal fins, the first smaller, both very posterior in position. Anal fin elongate, rounded. Pelvic fins broad-based. Pectoral fins long and very narrow. Caudal fin directed downwards, heterocercal, with the lower lobe bigger than the upper. Rounded, strongly overlapping scales.

Remarks: Predators. Now reclassified into the genus *Holoptychiidae*.

Recent relatives: None. Died out in Upper Devonian.

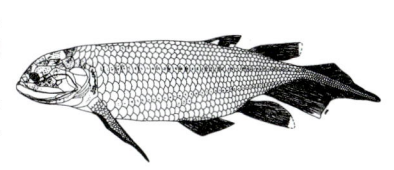

Quebecius, reconstruction after SCHULTZE.

CROSSOPTERYGII   Lobe-Finned Fishes
Order: Rhipidistiiformes
Family: Porolepididae

Porolepis brevis JARVIK (length c. 20 cm) from the Middle Devonian of Spitzbergen. Original: Muséum National d'Histoire Naturelle, Paris, France. Photograph: Serette, Paris.

Genus: *Porolepis* WOODWARD, 1891.

Synonym: *Gyrolepis*.

Geological range: Lower to Middle Devonian.

Geographical distribution: Europe, Spitzbergen, northern Asia.

Features: Small to middle-sized fishes of rather laterally compressed shape. Head deep. Eyes relatively large. Snout rounded. Two pairs of nostrils. Body covered with thick rhombic scales. Paired fins probably long and pointed, with fleshy lobes.

Remarks: Probably predators.

Recent relatives: None. Died out in Devonian.

CROSSOPTERYGII
Order: Rhipidistiiformes
Family: Holoptychiidae

Lobe-Finned Fishes

Glyptolepis paucidens AGASSIZ (length c. 62 cm) from the Middle Devonian of Caithness, Scotland. Original: National Museum of Scotland, Edinburgh, U.K.

Genus: *Glyptolepis* AGASSIZ, 1841.

Synonyms: *Hamodus*, *Phlyphlepis*, *Sclerolepis*.

Geological range: Middle to Upper Devonian.

Geographical distribution: Western and eastern Europe, Spitzbergen, Greenland.

Features: Middle-sized to large fishes with rather laterally compressed bodies tapering strongly rearwards. Head rather deep. Eyes small. Gape long. Two dorsal fins, both of them narrow and gently pointed and situated very posteriorly. Pelvic and anal fins obliquely opposite the respective dorsal fins. Pectoral fins very long and narrow. Caudal fin heterocercal, with the lower lobe considerably larger and almost fringe-like. Rounded, overlapping scales.

Remarks: Predators.

Recent relatives: None. Died out in Upper Devonian.

Glyptolepis, reconstruction after ZITTEL.

CROSSOPTERYGII
Lobe-Finned Fishes
Order: Rhipidistiiformes
Family: Holoptychiidae

Holoptychius quebecensis (WHITEAVES) (length c. 45 cm) from the Middle Devonian of Scaumenac Bay, Canada. Original: American Museum of Natural History, New York, N.Y., U.S.A.

Genus: *Holoptychius* EGERTON, 1837.

Synonyms: *Apedodus*, *Apendulus*, *Dendrodus*, *Lamnodus*.

Geological range: Middle Devonian to Lower Carboniferous.

Geographical distribution: Europe, North America, Greenland, Australia, Antarctic, northern Asia.

Features: Middle-sized fishes with rather laterally compressed bodies. Head shallow. Eyes small. Gape long. First dorsal fin very small, second considerably larger, both very posterior. Pelvic fins small, rather pointed, opposite the first dorsal fin. Anal fin somewhat larger. Pectoral fins unusually long and narrow. Caudal fin heterocercal with the lower lobe larger. Rounded overlapping scales.

Remarks: Predators.

Recent relatives: None. Died out in Lower Carboniferous.

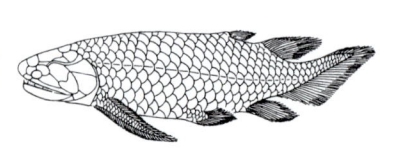

Holoptychius, reconstruction after TRAQUAIR.

CROSSOPTERYGII   Lobe-Finned Fishes
Order: Rhipidistiiformes
Family: Osteolepididae

Ectosteorhachis sp. (length c. 40 cm) from the Lower Permian of Texas, U.S.A. Original: American Museum of Natural History, New York, N.Y., U.S.A.

Genus: *Ectosteorhachis* Cope, 1880.

Geological range: Lower Permian.

Geographical distribution: North America.

Features: Middle-sized fishes with long narrow bodies. Head broad. Eyes small. Gape long. Dorsal fins very posterior. Pectoral fins rounded. The whole body covered with thick rhombic scales.

Remarks: Predators.

Recent relatives: None. Died out in Lower Permian.

CROSSOPTERYGII
Order: Rhipidistiiformes
Family: Osteolepididae

Lobe-Finned Fishes

Gyroptychius agassizi TRAILL (length c. 30 cm) from the Middle Devonian of the Orkney Islands, U.K. Original: Bayerische Staatssammlung für Paläontologie, Munich, Germany.

Genus: *Gyroptychius* McCoy, 1848.

Synonyms: *Diplopterax, Diplopterus, Diptopterus.*

Geological range: Middle to Upper Devonian.

Geographical distribution: Europe, Greenland.

Features: Middle-sized fishes with elongate slender bodies. Head shallow. Eyes small. The two dorsal fins very posterior, with the first smaller than the second. Anal and pelvic fins opposite the respective dorsal fins. Caudal fin rhombic in shape, pointed posteriorly. Body covered with rectangular, diagonally arranged scales.

Remarks: Predators.

Recent relatives: None. Died out in Upper Devonian.

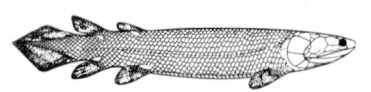

Gyroptychius, reconstruction after JARVIK.

CROSSOPTERYGII
Order: Rhipidistiiformes
Family: Osteolepididae

Lobe-Finned Fishes

Osteolepis macrolepidotus AGASSIZ (length c. 18 cm) from the Middle Devonian of the Orkney Islands, U.K. Original: Frickhinger Collection, Munich, Germany.

Genus: *Osteolepis* VALENCIENNES, 1829.

Synonyms: *Pleiopterus, Pliopterus, Triplopterus, Tripterus.*

Geological range: Middle to Upper Devonian.

Geographical distribution: Europe, northern Asia, Antarctica.

Features: Small to middle-sized fishes with slender elongate bodies. Head shallow. Eyes small. Gape long. The two dorsal fins small, rounded, very posterior in position. Anal and pelvic fins obliquely opposite the respective dorsal fins. Pectoral fins likewise rounded. Caudal fin heterocercal with the lower lobe larger. Scales rectangular, arranged in diagonal rows.

Remarks: Predators.

Recent relatives: None. Died out in Upper Devonian.

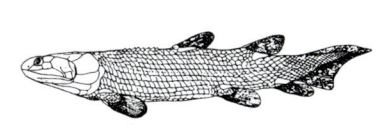

Osteolepis, reconstruction after JARVIK.

969

CROSSOPTERYGII
Order: Rhipidistiiformes
Family: Osteolepididae

Lobe-Finned Fishes

Thursius pholidotus TRAQUAIR (length c. 19 cm) from the Middle Devonian of Caithness, Scotland, U.K. Original: Bayerische Staatssammlung für Paläontologie, Munich, Germany.

Genus: *Thursius* TRAQUAIR, 1888.

Geological range: Middle Devonian.

Geographical distribution: Europe.

Features: Small to middle-sized fishes with slender elongate bodies. Head shallow. Eyes small. Gape long. Both dorsal fins rounded, very posterior. Pelvic and anal fins opposite the respective dorsal fins. Pectoral fins elongate and narrow. Caudal fin heterocercal with lower lobe considerably larger. Body covered with rectangular, diagonally arranged scales.

Remarks: Predators.

Recent relatives: None. Died out in Middle Devonian.

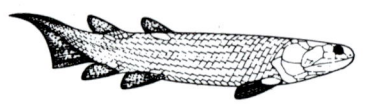

Thursius, reconstruction after JARVIK.

CROSSOPTERYGII
Order: Rhipidistiiformes
Family: Eusthenopteridae

Lobe-Finned Fishes

Eustenopteron foordi Whiteaves (length c. 31 cm) from the Upper Devonian of Miguasha, Gaspé Peninsula, Quebec, Canada. Original: Musée d'Histoire Naturelle, Miguasha, Quebec, Canada.

Genus: *Eusthenopteron* Whiteaves, 1881.

Geological range: Upper Devonian.

Geographical distribution: Europe, North America.

Features: Middle-sized fishes with long, anteriorly dorso-ventrally flattened bodies. Head shallow. Eyes small. Gape long. Two elongate and pointed dorsal fins, both of them very posterior. Pelvic and anal fins opposite the respective dorsal fins and somewhat broader. Pectoral fins elongate, rounded. Caudal fin with three lobes, the middle one extending beyond the two others. Scales round and thin, overlapping.

Remarks: Commonly seen as the most typical example of the lobe-fins which first moved onto land.

Recent relatives: None. Died out in Upper Devonian.

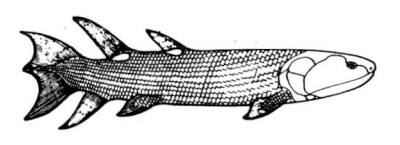

Eusthenopteron, reconstruction after Whiteaves.

CROSSOPTERYGII
Order: Rhipidistiiformes
Family: Eusthenopteridae

Lobe-Finned Fishes

Tristichopterus alatus EGERTON (length c. 28 cm) from the Middle Devonian of the Orkney Islands, U.K. Original: National Museum of Scotland, Edinburgh, U.K.

Genus: *Tristichopterus*   Egerton, 1861.

Geological range: Middle Devonian.

Geographical distribution: Europe.

Features: Middle-sized fishes with slender elongate bodies. Head shallow. Eyes small. Gape long. Two narrow dorsal fins, both very posterior. Anal and pelvic fins opposite the respective dorsal fins, somewhat longer and pointed. Pectoral fins long and narrow, somewhat fan-shaped. Caudal fin tripartite, with all three lobes of about the same length. Rounded, overlapping scales.

Remarks: Predators.

Recent relatives: None. Died out in Middle Devonian.

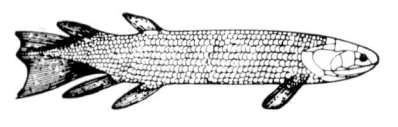

Tristichopterus, reconstruction after WATSON.

CROSSOPTERYGII
Order: Rhipidistiiformes
Family: Panderichthyidae

Lobe-Finned Fishes

Elpistostege watsoni Westoll (length c. 17 cm) from the Upper Devonian of Miguasha, Gaspé Peninsula, Quebec, Canada. Original: Musée d'Histoire Naturelle, Miguasha, Quebec, Canada.

Genus: *Elpistostege* Westoll, 1938.
Geological range: Upper Devonian.
Geographical distribution: North America.
Features: Middle-sized to large fishes with head deep behind and tapering forwards. Snout rounded. Eyes small and close together. Gape long.
Remarks: Already has a very amphibian-like head and therefore may have played an important role in evolution.
Recent relatives: None. Died out in Upper Devonian.

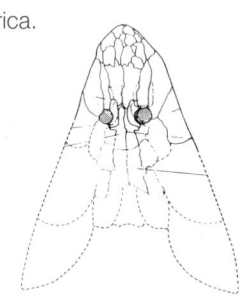

Elpistostege, reconstruction after Schultze.

973

CROSSOPTERYGII
Order: Rhipidistiiformes
Family: Rhizodontidae

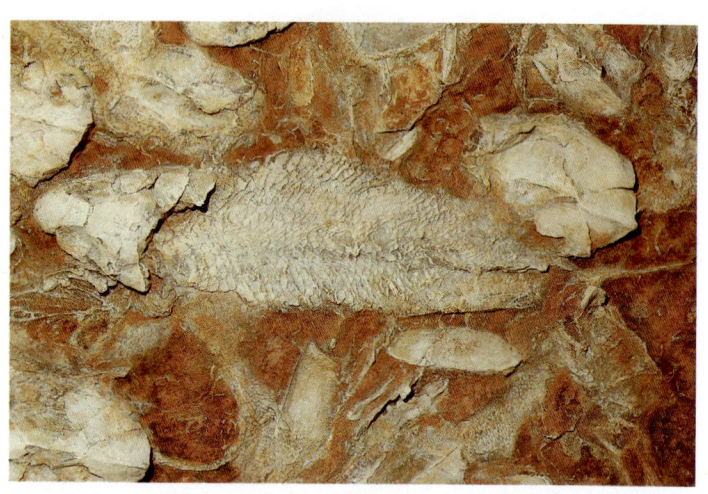

Lobe-Finned Fishes

Canowindra grossi THOMSON (length c. 52 cm) from the Devonian of Canowindra, New South Wales, Australia. Cast: Tyrell Museum of Natural History, Drumheller, Alberta, Canada.

Genus: *Canowindra* THOMSON, 1973.

Geological range: Upper Devonian.

Geographical distribution: Australia.

Features: Middle-sized fishes with slender elongate bodies. Head shallow. Eyes small. Gape long. First dorsal fin smaller than the second, both very posterior. Pelvic and anal fins similar. Pectoral fins small and pointed. Caudal fin heterocercal with the lower lobe larger. Body covered with round overlapping scales.

Remarks: Predators.

Recent relatives: None. Died out in Upper Devonian.

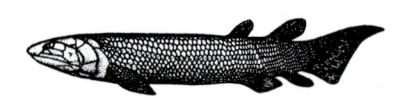

Canowindra, reconstruction after West Australian Museum.

DIPNOI — Lungfishes

Lungfishes are bony fishes with a lung branching ventrally from the esophagus. The lung is a primitive organ comparable to that of other primitive teleosts and amphibians. External gills form in the larval stages but are later lost. In the earliest stages there is bone in the skull, but cartilage predominates later. Most lungfishes have massive tooth plates which have arisen by the fusion of primitive tooth rows. There are usually two tooth plates on the palate and one on the lower jaw. Some Devonian genera have remarkable flange-like bones on the upper and lower jaws which have been interpreted as gripping tools helping in the capture of food. The internal skeleton is partly bony and partly cartilaginous. The paired fins are narrow-based and consist of a jointed main ray and numerous side rays. The caudal fin is primitively heterocercal but tends to become diphycercal. The first dorsal fin tends to be lost, while in the course of evolution the second dorsal fin fuses with the caudal and anal fin. Primitively there are thick cosmoid scales, but in younger genera these become thinner cycloid scales with the loss of the cosmine and ganoine layers. At the same time the scales increase in size. Lungfishes feed predominantly on molluscs but also on plants. All lungfishes live, and always have lived, in fresh water.

Formerly the lungfishes were seen as the forerunners of the amphibians. It turns out, however, that, from the phylogenetic point of view, they must be regarded as a side branch of the crossopterygians.

They first appeared towards the end of the Lower Devonian and in the Upper Devonian reached their all-time maximum. They were never so common again, although they have persisted, with a few genera, to the present day. These recent forms are distributed over a wide area, occurring in Africa, Australia and South America. Not more than 45 fossil genera have so far been described which indicates that lungfishes were always relatively rare. The smaller specimens are often extremely well preserved as fossils.

DIPNOI — Lungfishes

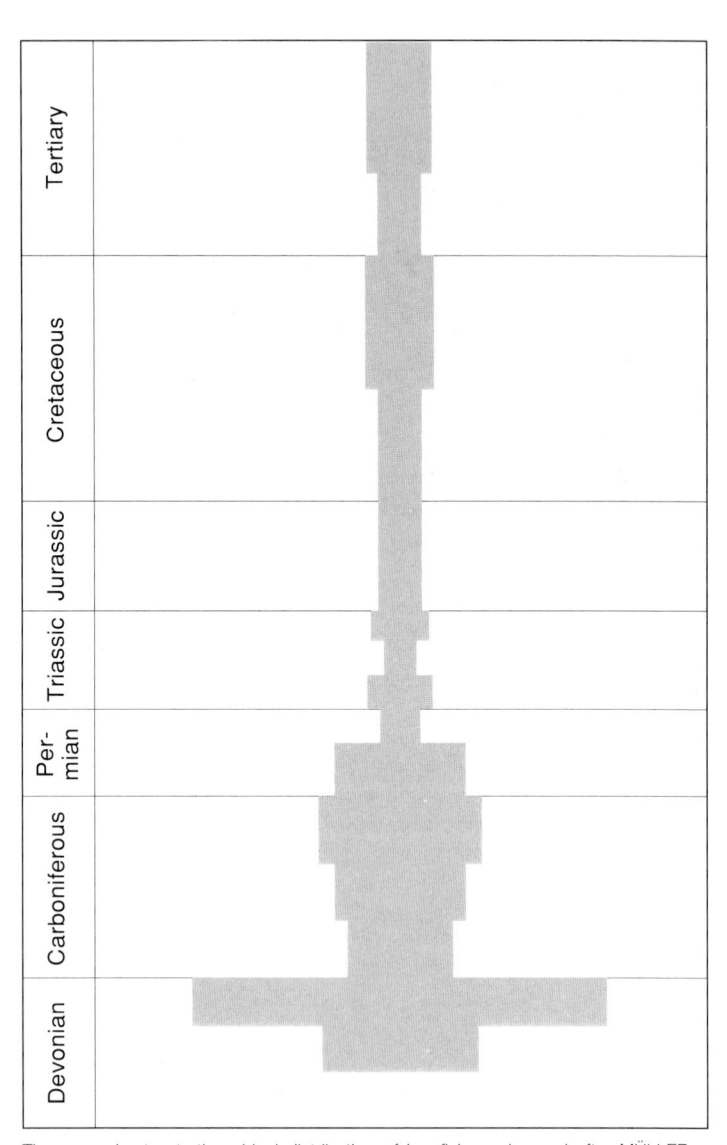

The approximate stratigraphical distribution of lungfishes, changed after MÜLLER.

DIPNOI
Family: Uranolophidae

Lungfishes

Uranolophus wyomingensis DENISON (length c. 30 cm) from the Lower Devonian of Wyoming, U.S.A. Original: Field Museum of Natural History, Chicago, Illinois, U.S.A.

Genus: *Uranolophus* DENISON, 1967.

Geological range: Lower Devonian.

Geographical distribution: North America.

Features: Middle-sized fishes with laterally bodies but rather broader in the middle. Head deep. Body covered with very thick rhombic scales. Both dorsal fins low. Caudal fin broad and short.

Remarks: Fresh-water predators.

Recent relatives: None. Died out in Lower Devonian.

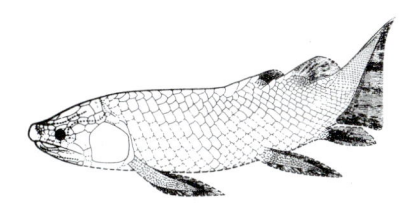

Uranolophus, reconstruction after SCHULTZE.

DIPNOI
Family: Dipnorhynchidae

Lungfishes

Dipnorhynchus suessmilchi (ETHERIDGE) (length c. 12 cm) from the Lower Devonian of Taemas, New South Wales, Australia. Original: Australian National University, Canberra, Australia.

Genus: *Dipnorhynchus* JAEKEL, 1927.

Geological range: Lower Devonian.

Geographical distribution: Europe, Australia.

Features: Middle-sized fishes of slender shape. Head shallow and flat. Eyes small. Snout rounded. Gape rather long. Two dorsal fins. Anal fin small. Pelvic and pectoral fins long and pointed. Caudal fin with a lower lobe. Body covered with rounded overlapping scales.

Remarks: Fresh-water predators.

Recent relatives: None. Died out in Lower Devonian.

Dipnorhynchus, reconstruction after MACMILLAN.

DIPNOI
Family: Dipnorhynchidae

Lungfishes

Griphognathus sculpta SCHULTZE (length c. 25 cm) from the Upper Devonian of Bergisch Gladbach, Rhineland, Germany. Original: Naturhistoriska Riksmuseet, Stockholm, Sweden.

Genus: *Griphognathus* GROSS, 1956.

Geological range: Upper Devonian.

Geographical distribution: Europe, Australia.

Features: Middle-sized fishes with rather laterally compressed bodies. Head shallow. Eyes small. Snout produced to form a sort of beak. Gape long. Two dorsal fins in the posterior third of the body, the first being small and pointed and the second considerably larger. First dorsal fin. Second dorsal fin. Anal, pectoral and pelvic fins elongate, narrow and pointed. Caudal fin with a lower lobe. Body covered with rounded, overlapping scales.

Remarks: Fresh-water predators.

Recent relatives: None. Died out in Upper Devonian.

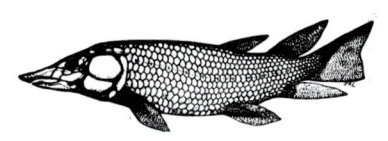

Griphognathus, reconstruction after SCHULTZE.

979

DIPNOI
Family: Dipnorhynchidae

Lungfishes

Holodipterus gogoensis MILES (length c. 8 cm) from the Upper Devonian of Paddy's Springs, Western Australia, Australia. Original: Australian National University, Canberra, Australia.

Genus: *Holodipterus* WHITE & MOY-THOMAS, 1940.

Synonyms: *Archaeotylus*, *Holodus*.

Geological range: Upper Devonian.

Geographical distribution: Europe, Australia.

Features: Middle-sized fishes. Head shallow. Snout produced into a sort of beak. Lower jaw extends further than upper jaw. Strong intermeshing tooth plates.

Remarks: Fresh-water predators.

Recent relatives: None. Died out in Upper Devonian.

DIPNOI
Family: Dipteridae
Lungfishes

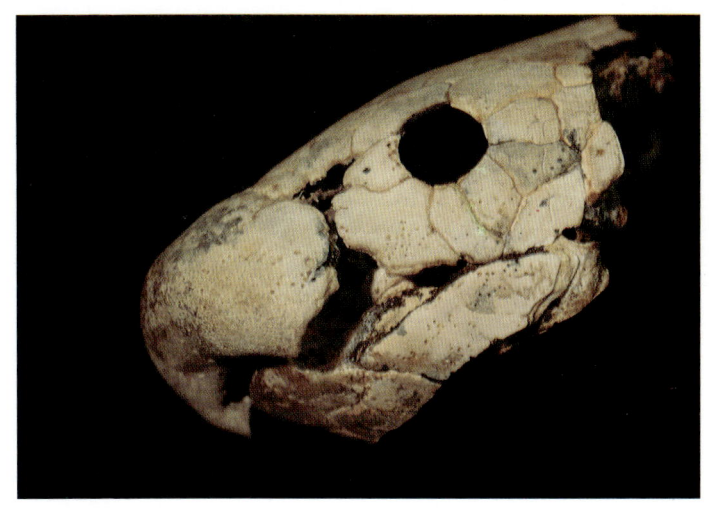

Chirodipterus australis MILES (length c. 12 cm) from the Upper Devonian of Paddy's Springs, Western Australia, Australia. Original: Australian National University, Canberra, Australia.

Genus: *Chirodipterus* GROSS, 1933.

Geological range: Upper Devonian.

Geographical distribution: Europe, Australia.

Features: Middle-sized fishes. Head shallow. Eyes large. Snout slightly produced, rounded. Lower jaw placed rather posteriorly, acting against the upper jaw as in a parrot's beak. Body covered with rounded scales.

Remarks: Fresh-water predators.

Recent relatives: None. Died out in Upper Devonian.

DIPNOI
Family: Dipteridae

Lungfishes

Dipterus valenciennesi SEDGWICK & MURCHISON (length c. 12 cm) from the Middle Devonian of Caithness, Scotland, U.K. Original: Naturmuseum Senckenberg, Frankfurt-am-Main, Germany.

Genus: *Dipterus* SEDGWICK & MURCHISON, 1829.
Synonyms: *Catopterus, Eoctenodus, Paradipterus, Polyphractus*.
Geological range: Lower to Upper Devonian.
Geographical distribution: Europe, North America, northern Asia, Australia.
Features: Small fishes of slender shape. Head shallow. Eyes relatively large. Snout produced, pointed. Gape long. Two dorsal fins, the first very small, the second elongate and broad. Caudal fin with lower lobe. Pelvic and pectoral fins elongate, narrow and pointed. Body covered with round overlapping scales.
Remarks: Fresh-water predators.
Recent relatives: None. Died out in Upper Devonian.

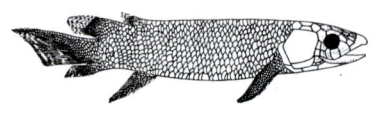

Dipterus, reconstruction after FORSTER-COOPER.

DIPNOI
Family: Dipteridae

Lungfishes

Pentlandia macroptera (Traquair) (length c. 12 cm) from the Middle Devonian of the Orkney Islands, U.K. Original: National Museum of Scotland, Edinburgh, U.K.

Genus: *Pentlandia* Watson & Day, 1916.

Geological range: Middle Devonian.

Geographical distribution: Europe.

Features: Small fishes with slender bodies. Head rather deep. Eyes large. Snout rounded. Two dorsal fins near the posterior end of the body. First dorsal fin very small. Second dorsal fin considerably larger and rounded at the end. Caudal fin with lower lobe only. Anal fin just separate from the caudal fin, elongate and narrow. Pelvic and pectoral fins elongate and pointed. Caudal fin heterocercal. Round overlapping scales.

Remarks: Fresh-water predators.

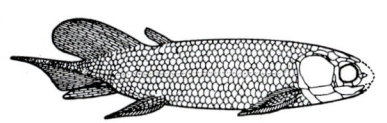

Recent relatives: None. Died out in Middle Devonian.

Pentlandia, reconstruction after Watson.

DIPNOI
Family: Dipteridae

Lungfishes

Rhinodipterus sp. (length c. 11 cm) from the Upper Devonian of Bergisch-Gladbach, Rhineland, Germany. Original: Naturhistoriska Riksmuseet, Stockholm, Sweden.

Genus: *Rhinodipterus* GROSS, 1956.

Geological range: Middle to Upper Devonian.

Geographical distribution: Europe.

Features: Small fishes of slender shape. Head shallow. Eyes relatively large. Snout produced. Gape long. Two dorsal fins, close together at the posterior end of the body. First dorsal fin considerably smaller than the second. Caudal fin with lower lobe only. Anal, pelvic and pectoral fins elongate and pointed. Body covered with round overlapping scales.

Remarks: Fresh-water predators.

Recent relatives: None. Died out in Upper Devonian.

DIPNOI
Family: Phaneropleuridae
Lungfishes

Fleurantia denticulata Graham-Smith & Westoll (length c. 21 cm) from the Upper Devonian of Bonaventura County, Canada. Original: The Natural History Museum, London, U.K. (P24745-6).

Genus: *Fleurantia* Graham-Smith & Westoll, 1937.

Geological range: Upper Devonian.

Geographical distribution: North America.

Features: Middle-sized fishes with rather laterally compressed bodies, deepest out in the middle. Head shallow. Eyes relatively large. Snout produced to form a sort of beak. Gape long. Teeth pointed. First dorsal fin very small. Second dorsal fin broad. Caudal fin with lower lobe only. Anal, pelvic and pectoral fins elongate and pointed. Body covered with thin round scales.

Remarks: Fresh-water predators.

Recent relatives: None. Died out in Upper Devonian.

Fleurantia, reconstruction after Graham-Smith & Westoll.

DIPNOI
Family: Phaneropleuridae

Lungfishes

Phaneropleuron andersoni HUXLEY (length c. 33 cm) from the Upper Devonian of Fife, Scotland, U.K. Original: National Museum of Scotland, Edinburgh, U.K.

Genus: *Phaneropleuron* HUXLEY, 1859.

Geological range: Upper Devonian.

Geographical distribution: Europe.

Features: Middle-sized fishes of slender shape. Head shallow. Eyes small. Snout somewhat produced, pointed. Gape rather long. Dorsal fin fused with the caudal fin to form a fringe which begins in the anterior third of the body and becomes rather taller posteriorly. Anal fin separate from the caudal fin. Pelvic and pectoral fins elongate and pointed. Thin overlapping scales.

Remarks: Fresh-water predators.

Recent relatives: None. Died out in Upper Devonian.

Phaneropleuron, reconstruction after DOLLO.

986

DIPNOI
Family: Phaneropleuridae

Lungfishes

Scaumenacia curta (WHITEAVES) (length c. 25 cm) from the Upper Devonian of Miguasha, Gaspé Peninsula, Quebec, Canada. Original: American Museum of Natural History, New York, N.Y., U.S.A.

Genus: *Scaumenacia* TRAQUAIR, 1893.

Synonym: *Canadipterus*.

Geological range: Upper Devonian.

Geographical distribution: North America.

Features: Middle-sized fishes of laterally compressed, high-backed shape. Head shallow. Eyes small. Snout somewhat produced, pointed. First dorsal fin beginning at the highest part of the body and forming a very blow fringe. Second dorsal broad, rounded posteriorly. Caudal fin with the lower lobe considerably larger than upper. Anal, pelvic fins and pectoral fins elongate and pointed. Body covered with round scales.

Remarks: Fresh-water predators.

Recent relatives: None. Died out in Upper Devonian.

Scaumenacia, reconstruction after PIVETEAU.

DIPNOI
Lungfishes
Family: Ctenodontidae

Ctenodus tardus FRITSCH (length c. 45 cm) from the Permian of Kostalov, Czechoslovakia. Original: American Museum of Natural History, New York, N.Y., U.S.A.

Genus: *Ctenodus* AGASSIZ, 1838.

Synonyms: *Campylopleuron*, *Proctenodus*, *Rhadamista*.

Geological range: Lower Carboniferous to Permian.

Geographical distribution: Europe, Australia, North America.

Features: Middle-sized fishes with slender, laterally flattened bodies. Head shallow. Eyes small. Snout somewhat produced, pointed. Gape rather long. Dorsal and anal fins fused with caudal fin to form a narrow fringe. Body covered with thin round scales.

Remarks: Fresh-water predators.

Recent relatives: None. Died out in Permian.

DIPNOI
Family: Sagenodontidae
Lungfishes

Sagenodus copeanus WILLISTON (length c. 34 cm) from the Upper Carboniferous of Kansas, U.S.A. Original: Museum of Natural History, Lawrence, Kansas, U.S.A.

Genus: *Sagenodus* OWEN, 1867.

Synonyms: *Petalodopsis, Yonodus.*

Geological range: Lower Carboniferous to Lower Permian.

Geographical distribution: Europe, North America.

Features: Middle-sized fishes with slender, laterally flattened bodies. Head shallow. Eyes small. Snout rounded. Dorsal and anal fins fused with the caudal fin to form a low fringe. Body covered with round scales.

Remarks: Fresh-water predators.

Recent relatives: None. Died out in Upper Permian.

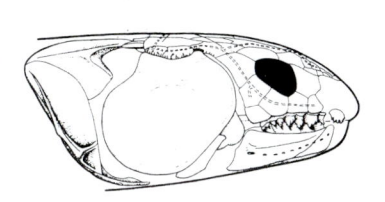

Sagenodus, reconstruction after WATSON & GILL.

DIPNOI
Family: Uronemidae

Lungfishes

Uronemus lobatus Traquair (length c. 13 cm) from the Lower Carboniferous of Edinburgh, Scotland, U.K. Original: National Museum of Scotland, Edinburgh, U.K.

Genus: *Uronemus* Agassiz, 1844.

Synonym: *Ganopristodus*.

Geological range: Lower Carboniferous.

Geographical distribution: Europe.

Features: Small fishes of slender shape. Head shallow. Eyes small. Snout somewhat produced and pointed. Gape rather long. Dorsal fin and anal fins fused with the caudal fin to produce a narrow fringe which begins dorsally in the anterior third of the body and reaches ventrally almost to the pelvic fins. Pelvic and pectoral fins elongate, pointed. Body covered with round scales.

Remarks: Fresh-water predators.

Recent relatives: None. Died out in Lower Carboniferous.

Uronemus, reconstruction after Forster-Cooper.

DIPNOI
Family: Conchopomidae
Lungfishes

Conchopoma edesi DENISON (length c. 10 cm) from the Upper Devonian of Francis Creek, Illinois, U.S.A. Original: Field Museum of Natural History, Chicago, Illinois, U.S.A.

Genus: *Conchopoma* KNER, 1868.

Synonyms: *Conchiopsis*, *Peplorhina*.

Geological range: Upper Carboniferous to Lower Permian.

Geographical distribution: Europe, North America.

Features: Small to middle-sized fishes of slender shape. Head shallow. Eyes small. Snout rounded. Gape rather long. Lower jaw somewhat posterior in position. Dorsal and anal fins fused with the caudal fin to form a low fringe tapering rearwards. Anal fins small, pointed oval in outline. Pectoral fins considerably bigger, elongate and pointed. Body covered with round scales.

Remarks: Fresh-water predators.

Recent relatives: None. Died out in Lower Permian.

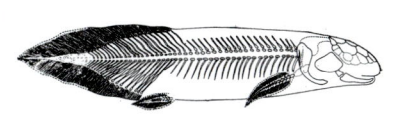

Conchopoma, reconstruction after WEITZEL.

DIPNOI
Family: Ceratodontidae

Lungfishes
Australian Lungfishes

Gosfordia truncata Woodward (length c. 27 cm) from the Lower Triassic of Gosford, Australia. Original: Australian Museum, Sydney, Australia.

Genus: *Gosfordia* Woodward, 1890.

Geological range: Lower Triassic.

Geographical distribution: Australia.

Features: Middle-sized fishes with laterally compressed bodies. Head deep. Eyes small. Snout produced and pointed. Gape rather long. Dorsal fins fused with caudal fin and anal fin to form a broad fringe. Pelvic fins very narrow and elongate. Pectoral fins likewise very narrow but considerably longer.

Remarks: Fresh-water predators.

Recent relatives: Related to recent Australian lungfishes of the genus *Neoceratodus*.

Gosfordia, reconstruction after Ritchie.

DIPNOI
Family: Ceratodontidae

Lungfishes
Australian Lungfishes

Paraceratodus germaini LEHMAN (length c. 110 cm) from the Lower Triassic of Madagascar. Original: Muséum National d'Histoire Naturelle, Paris, France. Photograph: Serette, Paris.

Genus: *Paraceratodus* LEHMAN, 1959.

Geological range: Lower Triassic.

Geographical distribution: Madagascar.

Features: Middle-sized to large fishes with slender bodies tapering rearwards. Head shallow and elongate. Eyes small. Snout pointed. Dorsal fin beginning approximately in the middle of the body, probably joined to form a fringe with the caudal and anal fins. Pelvic and pectoral fins probably elongate.

Remarks: Had a durophagous diet.

Recent relatives: Genus extinct. Perhaps related to the Australian lungfish *Neoceratodus*.

Neoceratodus forsteri, the Australian lungfish.

993

DIPNOI
Family: Not named

Lungfishes

Esconichthys apopyris BARDACK (length c. 5 cm) from the Upper Carboniferous (Pennsylvanian) of Mazon Creek, Illinois, U.S.A. Original: Field Museum of Natural History, Chicago, Illinois, U.S.A.

Genus: *Esconichthys* BARDACK, 1974.

Geological range: Upper Carboniferous (Pennsylvanian).

Geographical distribution: North America.

Features: Small fishes with slender bodies. Head shallow. Eyes small. Snout rounded. Pectoral fins very narrow and strikingly long. This fish represents a larval stage.

Remarks: Adult specimens not known.

Recent relatives: None. Presumably died out in Carboniferous.

The Bolca fishes came from this cliff. It seems clear, unfortunately, that the locality will be exhausted in the foreseeable future.

Literature

For reasons of space, this bibliography is essentially confined to works on morphology, systematics or phylogeny. Further references can be found in the bibliographies of all major paleontological works.

GENERAL LITERATURE

Agassiz, L. (1833–44). Recherches sur les poissons fossils.–5 Vol., 1420 pp, 369 tables.

Baensch, H. A. and Riehl, R. (1982, 1985, 1990). Mergus Aquarien-Atlas, Band 1, 2 and 3, Mergus Verlag, Melle, total of 3312 pages and as many color photos. Recent fisches.

Berg, L. S. (1958). System der rezenten und fossilen Fischartigen und Fische.– Deutsch. Verl. d. Wissensch., Berlin, 310 pp., 263 ills.

Berril, N. J. (1955). The Origin of Vertebrates.–Oxford University Press, Oxford.

Carroll, R. L. (1987). Vertebrate Paleontology and Evolution.–Freeman and Co., New York.

Gregory, W. K. (1951). Evolution emerging.–2 Vol., Macmillan, New York.

Grzimek, B. (1970). Tierleben, volume 4 and 5, Kindler Verlag, Zürich, in total 918 pp., many color ills. and diagrams. Recent fishes.

Klausewitz, W. (1965). Fischartige und Fische. In F. Gessner (ed.) Handbuch der Biologie, Vol. VI, 2, pp. 32–628, 215 ills., Athenaion, Konstanz, recent fishes.

Nelson, J. S. (1984). Fishes of the World.–John Wiley & Sons, New York. 523 pp., numerous drawings. Recent fishes.

Moy-Thomas, J. A. and Miles, R. S. (1971). Paleozoic fishes.–Chapman and Hall, London. 259 pp., numerous ills.

Müller, A. H. (1985). Lehrbuch der Paläozoologie, vol III, part I, Gustav Fischer, Jena. pp. 1–458, 526 ills.

Norman, J. R. (1966). Die Fische, eine Naturgeschichte.–Parey, Hamburg and Berlin. Recent fishes.

Piveteau, J. (Publisher), Traité de Paléontologie, Band IV, Teil 1, 387 pp., 201 ills. Teil 2, 790 pp., 339 ills. Part 3, 442 pp., 357 ills., Paris, Masson, (1964–1966).

Romer, A. S. (1966). Vertebrate Paleontology.–University of Chicago Press.

Schultze, H.-P. (ed.). Handbook of Paleoichthyologie.–Volume 2, Denison, R. (1978). Placodermi, 128 pp., 94 ills. Volume 3A, Zangerl, R. (1981). Chondrichthyes I, 115 pp., 116 ills. Volume 3B, Cappetta, H. (1987). Chondrichthyes II, 191 pp., 148 ills. Volume 5, Denison, R. (1979). Acanthodii, 62 pp., 35 ills. Gustav Fischer Verlag, Stuttgart. Additional volumes in preparation.

Woodward, A. S. (1899–1901). Catalogue of the Fossil Fishes in the British Museum. 4 Vol., 2493 pp., 70 tables.

Zittel, K. A. (1887–1890). Palaeozoologie. 5 Vol., Band III, Fische, Oldenbourg, München, Seite 5–336, numerous illustrations.

Literature

FOSSIL FISH FAUNAS

Aldinger, H. (1937). Permische Ganoidfische aus Ostgrönland.–Meddel om Gronland, 102 (3), 1–392.

Arambourg, C. (1925). Revision des poissons de Licata (Sicilie).–Ann. Paléont. 14, 1–96.

Arambourg, C. (1927). Les poissons fossiles d'Oran.–Matér. Carte Géol. Algérie. ser. 1. No. 6 p. 218.

Arambourg, C. (1954). Les poissons Crétacés du Jebel Tselfat (Maroc).–Notes Mém. Serv. Géol. Maroc. No. 118, 185 pp.

Arambourg, C. and Signeux, J. (1952). Les vertébrés fossiles des gisements de phosphates (Maroc-Algérie-Tunisie).–Notes Mém. Serv. Géol. No. 92, 374 pp.

Barthel, K. W. (1978). Solnhofen.–Ott Verlag, Thun, CH. Seite 164–172, zahlr. ills., 4 Farbt.

Blot, J. (1980). La faune ichthyologique des gisement du Monte Bolca (Province de Vérona, Italie). Catalogue systématique présentant l'actuel des recherches concernant cette faune.–Bull. Mus. ntl. Hist. nat., Paris. 4. serie2, section C, no 4, 339–396.

Brough, (1939). The Triassic fishes of Besano, Lombardy.–Brit. Mus. (Nat. Hist.), London, 117 pp.

Capetta, H. (1980). Les selachiens du Crétacé supérieur du Liban. I: Requins.–Palaeon tographica A168, 69–148.

Capetta, H. (1980). Les selachiens du Crétacé supérieur du Liban. II:Batoides.–Palaeon tographica A168, 149–229.

Casier, E. (1946). La faune ichthyologique de l'Yprèsien de la Belgique.–Mém. Mus. Hist. Nat. Belg. 104, 3–267.

Frickhinger, K. A. (1984). Fische aus Brasilien.–Fossilien1, Heft 4. Goldschneck-Verlag, Korb.

Frickhinger, K. A. (1989–1990). Die Fische von Solnhofen.–Fossilien 6, booklets 5 and 7, Booklets 1, 2 and 3. Goldschneck Verl., Korb

Frickhinger, K. A. (1994) The Fossils of Solnhofen, Goldschneck Verlag, Korb, Germany

Dartevelle, E. and Casier, E. (1943, 1949, 1959). Les poissons fossiles du Bas-Congo et des régions voisines.–Ann. Mus. Roy. Congo Belge, ser. A, 2, 1–586.

David, L. R. (1943). Miocene fishes of southern California.–Geol. Soc. Amer., Spec. Papers. No. 43, 193.

Davis, J. W. (1883). On the fossil fishes of the Carboniferous limestone series of Great Britain.–Trans. Roy. Dublin Soc., ser. 2, 1, 327–548.

Grande, L. (1984). Paleontology of the Green River Formation, with a review of the fish fauna.–Part II, pp. 16–185, 103 ills., Bull. 63, Geol. Surv., Wyoming.

Gross, W. (1933–37). Die Wirbeltiere des rheinischen Devons.–Abhandl. preuss. geol. Landesanst., new. ser. No. 154, 1–83, No. 176, 1–83.

Haubold, H. (1982). Die Lebewelt des Rotliegenden.–Neue Brehm-Bücherei, 164–176, 13 ills.

Literature

Haubold, H. and Schaumberg, G. (1985). Die Fossilien des Kupferschiefers. Neue Brehm Bücherei, 112–176, 57 ills.

Hauff, B. and R. B. (1981). Das Holzmadenbuch.–Eigenverlag, Seite 58–85, 42 ills.

Jörg, E. (1969). Eine Fischfauna aus dem oberen Buntsandstein (Unter- Trias) von Karlsruhe-Durlach.–Beitr. naturkundlich. Forschung SW-Deutschland 28, 87–102. 997

Jubb, R. A. and Gardiner, B. G. (1975). A preliminary catalogue of identifiable fossil fish material from Southern Africa.–Ann. of the South. Afric. Mus. 67, 381–440.

Kuhn, O. (1977). Die Tierwelt des Solnhofer Schiefers.–Neue Brehm-Bücherei, Seite 26–30, 44 ills.

Lambers, P. (1992) On the Ichthyofauna of the Lithographie Limestone (Upper Jurassic, Germany) Rijksuniversität Groningen, Netherlands.

Lehman, J. P. (1952). Étude complémentaire des poissons de l'Éotrias de Madagascar.–Handl. K. Svenska Vetenskapsakad. 2, 1–201.

Lehman, J. P., Chateau, C., Laurain, M. and Nauche, M. (1959). Paléontologie de Madagascar. 28. Les poissons de la Sakamena Moyenne.–Ann. Paléont. 45, 3–45.

Leriche, M. (1951). Les poissons Tertiaires de la Belgique (suppl.).–Mém. Inst. Roy. Sci. Nat. Belg. 118, 474–600.

Maisey, J.G. (1992) Santana Fossils, T.F.H. Publications, Inc., Neptune City, NJ. / USA

Malz, H. (1976). Solnhofer Plattenkalk : Eine Welt im Stein.–Museum beim Solenhofer Aktien-Verein, Maxberg, Seite 64–93, 29 ills.

Meyer, H. v. (1852). Fossile Fische aus dem Tertiärthon von Unter-Kirchberg an der Iller.–Palaeontogr. 2, 85–113.

Nielsen, E. (1942, 1949). Studies on Triassic fishes from East Greenland. Palaeozool. Groenl. 1, 1–403, Meddel om Gronland 146, 1–309.

Nitecki, M. H. (publ., 1979). Mazon Creek Fossils. Acad. Press, New York.

Orvig, T. (1957). Remarks on the vertebrate fauna of the lower Upper Devonian of Escuminac Bay, P. Q., Canada, with special reference to the porolepiform crossoptery gians. Arkiv Zool. ser. 2, 10, 367–426.

Piveteau, J. (1934). Paléontologie de Madagascar. No. 21. Les poissons du Trias infé rieur.–Ann. Paléont. 23, 81–180.

Saint-Seine, P. (1949). Les poissons des calcaires lithographique de Cerin (Ain).–Nouv. Arch. Mus. Hist. Nat. Lyon. Fasc. 2, 1–357.

Saint-Seine, P. (1955, 1962). Poissons fossiles de l'étage de Stanleyville (Congo Belge).–Ann. Mus. Roy. Congo Belge, Sér. in 8, Sci. Géol. 14 1–125 (1955).–Ann. Mus. Roy. Afrique Centrale, 8, 44, 1–52 (1962) (with Casier, E.).

Schmidt, M. (1928). Die Lebewelt unserer Trias.–Oehringen, Seite 330–369, num. ills.

Siber, H. J. (1982). Green River Fossilien.–Eigenverlag, pp. 6–29, 23 ills.

Silva Santos, Rubens da (1968). A Formacao Santana e sua Paleoichtiofauna.–Divisao de Geologia e Mineralogia, D. N. P. M., Rio de Janeiro.

Sorbini, L. (1983). La collezione Baja di Pesci e Piante fossili di Bolca.–75 Farbtafeln. Mus. Civ. di Stor. Naturale, Verona.

Literature

Sorbini, L. (1987). Biogeography and Climatology of Pliocene and Messinian fossil fish of Eastern-Central Italy.–Boll. Mus. Civ. St. Nat. Verona 14, 1–85.

Wade, R. T. (1935). The triassic fishes of Brookvale, New South Wales.–Brit. Mus. Nat. Hist. 1935, 1–89.

Wade, R. T. (1940). The triassic fishes of Gosford, New South Wales.–J. and Proc. Roy. Soc., South Wales 73, 206–217.

Woodward, A. S. (1902–1912). The fishes of the Englisch chalk.–Monogr. Palaeontogr. Soc. London, 264 pp.

Woodward, A. S. (1916–1919). The fossil fishes of the English Wealden and Purbeck formations.–Monogr. Palaeontogr. Soc., London, 148 pp.

AGNATHA (Agnathans)

Afanassieva, O. B. (1985). The pecularities of the exoskeleton of Thyestinae (Agnatha).–Palaeontolog. Acad. of Sci. USSR, 4, 70–75.

Afanassieva, O. B. (1989). New cephalaspids (Agnatha) from the Lower Devonian of Podolia.–Palaeontolog. Acad. of Sci. USSR, 8, 51–59.

Afanassieva, O. B. and Janvier, P. (1985) Tanuaspis, Tuvaspis, Ilemoraspis endemic osteostracan genera from the Silurian and Devonian of Tuva and Khakassia (USSR).–Geobios 18, 493–506.

Bardack, D. and Richardson, E. S. (1977). New agnathous fishes from the Pennsylvanian of Illinois.–Fieldiana, Geol., 33, 489–510.

Bardack, D. and Zangerl, R. (1968). First fossil lamprey: A record from the Pennsylvanian of Illinois.–Science, 162, 1265–1267.

Bardack, D. and Zangerl, R. (1971). Lampreys in the fossil record.–In M. W. Hardisty and I. C. Potter (Herausgeber), The Biology of Lampreys, 67–84. Academic Press, New York.

Bendix-Almgreen, S. E. (1986). Silurian ostracoderms from Washington Land (North Greenland), with comments on cyathaspid structure, systematics and phyletic posi tion.–Rapp. Gronlands geol. Unders. 132, 89–123.

Blieck, A. (1984). Les Hetérostracés Pteraspidiformes, Agnathes du Silurien-Dévonien du Continent Nord-Atlantique et des Blocs Avoisiments: Révision systematique, phylogénie, biostratigraphie, biogéographie.–Editions du Centre National de la Recherche Scientifique, Paris.

Bockelie, T. and Fortey, R. A. (1976). An early Ordovician vertebrate.–Nature, 260, 36–38.

Denison, R. H. (1951). Evolution and classification of the Osteostraci.–Fieldiana, Geol., 11, 157–196.

Denison, R. H. (1952). Early Devonian fishes from Utah. Part 1. Osteostraci. Fieldiana, Geol. 11, 263–87.

Denison, R. H. (1953). Early Devonian fishes from Utah. Part 2. Heterostraci. Fieldiana, Geol. 11 (7), 299–355

Literature

Denison, R. H. (1964). The Cyathaspididae: A family of Silurian and Devonian jawless vertebrates.–Fieldiana, Geol., 13, 309–473.

Denison, R. H. (1967). Ordovician vertebrates from western United States.–Fieldiana, Geol., 16, 131–192.

Denison, R. H. (1970), Revised classification of Pteraspididae with description of new forms from Wyoming.–Fieldiana, Geol., 20, 1–41.

Dineley, D. L. and Loeffler, E. J. (1976). Ostracoderm faunas of the Delorme and associated Siluro-Devonian Formations, North West Territories, Canada.–Spec. Papers Palaeont., 18, 1–214.

Elliot, D. K. (1987). A Reassessment of Astraspis desiderata, the Oldest North American Vertebrate.–Am. Ass. Advanc. Sci. 237, 190–192.

Gross, W. (1947). Die Agnathen und Acanthodier des obersilurischen Beyrichiakalkes.–Paläontographica 96A, 91–112.

Gross, W. (1963). Drepanaspis gemuendensis SCHLÜTER, Neuuntersuchung. Palaeonto graphica 121A, 133–155.

Halstead, L. B. (1973). The heterostracan fishes.–Biol. Rev., 48, 279–332.

Halstead, L. B., Liu, Y.–H. and P'an, K. (1979). Agnathans from the Devonian of China.–Nature, 282, 831–833.

Heintz, A. (1939). Cephalaspida from Downtonian of Norway.–Skr. norsk. vidensk. Akad. i Oslo, mat.–nat. Kl. No. 5, 119.

Hoppe, K. (1931). Die Coelolepiden und Acanthodier des Obersilurs der Insel Oesel.–Palaeontographica 76A, 35–94.

Janvier, P. (1984). The relationships of the Osteostraci and Galeaspida. J. Vert. Paleont., 4 , 344–358.

Janvier, P. (1985). Les Céphalaspides du Spitsberg.–Cahiers de Pal., Section Vertébrés, Ed. CNRS, Paris.

Janvier, P. (1985). Preliminary description of Lower Devonian Osteostraci from Podolia (Ukrainian S. S. R.).–Bull. Br. Mus. 38, 309–334.

Janvier, P. and Lund, R. (1983). Hardistiella montanensis n. gen. et sp. (Petromyzontidae) from the Lower Carboniferous of Montana, with remarks on the affinities of lampreys.–J. Vert. Paleont., 2, 407–413.

Karatajute-Talimaa, V. (1978). Silurian and Devonian Thelodonts of the USSR and Spitsbergen.–Mokslas Publishers, Vilnius.

Kiaer, J. (1924). The Downtonian fauna of Norway. 1. Anaspida.–Skr. vidensk. selsk. Kristiania, mat.–nat. Kl. Volume 1. No. 6, 139 S.

Kiaer, J. (1932). The Downtonian and Devonian Vertebrates of Spitzbergen. 4. Suborder Cyathaspida.–Skr. om Svalbard og Ishavet 52, 1–26.

Kiaer, J. (1932). New coelolepids from the Upper Silurian of Oesel (Esthonia).–Arch. Naturk. Estlands ser. 1, 10, 169–174.

Lehman, J.–P. (1937). Les Poissons du Downtonien de la Scanie (Suède).–Faculté Sci. Univ. Paris. Mém. pour Dipl. d'études supérieures, 62–64, Rennes.

Lund, R. and Janvier, P. (1986). A second lamprey from the Lower Carboniferous (Namurian) of Bear Gulch, Montana (USA).–Geobios 19, 647–652.

Literature

Moy-Thomas, J. A. and Miles, R. S. (1971). Palaeozoic Fishes–(2nd ed.) Chapman and Hall, Ltd., London.

Novitskaya, L. I. (1971). Les amphiaspides (Heterostraci) du Dévonien de la Sibérie.–Cahiers de Paléontologie, Paris, 1–130.

Novitskaya, L. (1972). Liliaspis–ein Poraspide aus dem Unterdevon des Urals und einige Bemerkungen über die Phylogenie der Poraspiden.–Palaeontographica, Vol. 143A, 25–34.

Novitskaya, L. (1983). Morphology of ancient agnathans (Russian).–Trans. of Palaeontol. Inst. Akad. Sci. USSR, 196, 1–182 Moscow.

Pander, C. H. (1856). Monographie der fossilen Fische des silurischen Systems der russisch-baltischen Gouvernements.–43–91, Petersburg.

Repetzki, J. E. (1978). A fish from the Upper Cambrian of North America.–Science, 200, 529–531.

Ritchie, A. (1964). New light on the morphology of the Norwegian Anaspida Skr. norsk. vidensk.–Akad. i Oslo. Mat.-nat. Kl. new ser. 14, 1–35.

Ritchie, A. (1968). New evidence of Jaymoythius kerwoodi WHITE, an important ostraco derm from the Silurian of Lanarkshire. Scotland Palaeontology, 11, 21–39.

Ritchie, A. (1968) Phlebolepis elegans PANDER, an Upper Silurian thelodont from Oesel, with remarks on the morphology of thelodonts.–In T. Orvig (publisher), Current Problems of Lower Vertebrate Phylogeny.–Proc. 4th Nobel Symp., 81–88. Almquist and Wiksell, Stockholm.

Ritchie, A. and Gilbert-Tomlinson, J. (1977). First Ordovician vertebrates from the Southern Hemisphere.–Alcheringa, 1, 351–368.

Stensiö, E. A. (1927). The Downtonian and Devonian Vertebrates of Spitzbergen. I. Family Cephalaspidae.–Skr. om Svalbard og Nordishavet 12, XXII+391 pp.

Stensiö, E. A. (1932). The Cephalaspids of Great Britain.–London 220+66

Stensiö, E. A. (1939). A new anaspid from the Upper Devonian of Scaumenac Bay in Canada, with remarks on the other anaspids.–Handl. K. Svenska Vetenskapsakad. ser. 318, 1–25.

Stetson, H. C. (1928). A new American Thelodus.–Am. J. Sci., 16, 221–231.

Wängsjö, G. (1952). The Downtonian and Devonian vertebrates of Spitsbergen. 9. Morphologic and systematic studies of the Spitsbergen cephalaspids.–Norsk Polarinst. Skrift. No. 97, 615.

Westoll, T. S. (1945). A new Cephalaspid fish from Downtonian of Scotland, with notes on the structure and classification of Ostracoderms.–Trans. R. Soc. Edinburgh 61, part II, 341–357.

PLACODERMI (Placoderms)

Denison, R. H. (1975). Evolution and classification of Placoderm fishes.–Breviora, 432, 1–24.

Literature

Denison, R. H. (1978). Placodermi. In H.-P. Schultze (publ.) Handbook of Paleoichthyologie. 2., Gustav Fischer Verlag, Stuttgart.

Denison, R. H. (1958). Early Devonian fishes from Utah. Teil 3. Arthrodira. Fieldiana: Geol. 11, 459–551.

Dunkle, D. H. (1947). A new genus and species of arthrodirian fish from the Upper Devonian Cleveland Shale.–Sci. Publ. Clevel. Mus. Nat. Hist. 8, 103–117.

Forey P. L. and Gardiner. B. G. (1986). Observations on Ctenurella (Ptyctodontida) and the classification of Placoderm fishes.–Zool. J. Linn. Soc., 86, 43–74.

Gardiner, B. G. (1984). The relationship of Placoderms.–J. Vert. Paleont. 4, 379–395.

Goujet, D. (1975). Dicksonosteus, un nouvel arthrodire du Dévonien du Spitzberg.–Coll. Intl. C. N. R. S., Problèmes actuels de paléontol. 218, 81–99.

Goujet, D. (1984). Les Poissons placodermes du Spitzberg.–Cahiers de Paléontologie. Section vértebrés. Editions du Centre National de la Recherche Scientifique, Paris.

Goujet, D. (1984). Placoderm interrelationships: A new interpretation with a short review of placoderm classification.–Proc. Linn. Soc. N. S. W. 107, 211–243.

Gross, W. (1961). Lunaspis broilii und Lunaspis heroldi aus dem Hunrückschiefer (Unterdevon, Rheinland).–Notizbl. Hess. Landesamt. Bodenforschung 89, 17–84.

Gross, W. (1962). Neuuntersuchung der Stensiöllida (Arthrodira, Unterdevon). Notizbl. Hess. Landesamt. Bodenforsch. 90, 48–96.

Gross, W. (1963). Gemuendina stuertzi TRAQUAIR, Neubearbeitung. Hessisches Landes amt für Bodenforschung, Wiesbaden, Notizblatt 91, 36–73.

Heintz, A. (1929). Die downtonischen und devonischen Vertebraten von Spitzbergen. 2. Acanthaspida.–Skr. om Svalbart og Ishaved 22, 81 pp.

Lehman, J. P. (1956). Les Arthrodires du Dévonien supérieur du Tafilalet.–Not. et Mém. Serv. géol. Maroc. 129, 70 pp.

Long, J. A. (1984). New phyllolepids from Victoria and the relationships of the group.–Proc. Linn. Soc. N. S. W., 107, 263–308.

Miles, R. S. (1967). Observations on the ptyctodont fish Rhamphodopsis WATSON. Linn. Soc. 47, Nr. 311, 99–120.

Miles, R. S. and Westoll, T. S. (1968). The Placoderm fish Coccosteus cuspidatum MILLER from the Middle Old Red Sandstone of Scotland.–Trans. Roy. Soc. Edinburgh 67, 373–476.

Miles, R. S. and Young, G. C. (1977). Placoderm interrelationships reconsidered in the light of new ptyctodontids from Gogo, Western Australia. In S. M. Andrews, Miles and Walker (eds.), Problems in Vertebrate Evolution.–Linn. Soc. Sympos. 4, 123–198, Acad. Press, London.

Moy-Thomas, J. A. (1940). The Devonian fish Palaeospondylus gunni TRAQUAIR.–Phil. Trans. Roy. Soc., London 230, 391–413.

Moy-Thomas, J. A. and Miles, R. S. (1971). Palaeozooic fishes. Chapman and Hall, Ltd., London.

Literature

Ritchie, A. (1973). Wuttagoonaspis, an unusual arthrodire from the Devonian of Western New South Wales, Australia.–Palaeontographica 143, 58–72.

Ritchie, A. (1975). Groenlandaspis in Antarctica and Europe.–Nature 254, 569–573.

Schaeffer, B. and Thomson, K. S. (1980). Reflections on agnathan- gnathostome relation ships. In L. L. Jacobs (ed.), Aspects of Vertebrate History.–Essays in Honor of Edwin Harris Colbert, 19–33. Museum of Northern Arizona Press, Flagstaff.

Schultze, H. P. (1973). Large Upper Devonian arthrodires from Iran.–Fieldiana, Geol. 23, 53–78.

Stensiö, E. (1948). On the Placodermi of the Upper Devonian of East Greenland. 2. Antiarchi, Subfamily Bothriolepinae.–Palaeozool. Groenland. 2, 1–622.

Traquair, R. H. (1894–1914). A Monograph of the fishes of the Old Red Sandstone of Britain. II: Nr. 1: The Asterolepidae.–Monogr. Palaeont. Soc. 48, 63–134.

Watson, D. M. S. (1938). On Rhamphodopsis, a ptyctodont from the Middle Old Red Sandstone of Scotland.–Trans. Roy. Soc., Edinburgh 59, 397–410.

Wells, J. W. (1964). The Antiarch Asterolepis in the Upper Devonian of New York.–J. Paleont. 43, 492–495.

White, E. I. (1952). Australian arthrodires.–Bull. Brit. Mus. (Nat. Hist.) Geol. 1, 249–304.

Young, G. C. (1980). A new early Devonian placoderm from New South Wales, Australia, with a discussion of placoderm phylogeny.–Palaeontographica 167, 10–76.

Young, G. C. (1986). The relationships of placoderm fishes.–Zool. J. Linn. Soc. 88, 1–57.

CHONDRICHTHYES (Cartilaginous Fishes)

Baird, D. (1978). Studies on Carboniferous freshwater fishes.–Am. Mus. Novitates 2641, 1–22.

Bendix-Almgreen, S. E. (1966). New investigations on Helicoprion from the Phosphoria Formation of south-east Idaho, USA.–Biol. Skr. Dan. Vid. Selskab 14, 1–54.

Cappetta, H. (1980). Les selachiens du Crétacé supérieur du Liban. I: Requins.–Palaeon tographica A 168, 69–148, Stuttgart.

Cappetta, H. (1980). Les selachiens du Crétacé supérieur du Liban. II: Batoides.–Palaeontographica A 168, 149–229, Stuttgart.

Cappetta, H. (1987). Chondrichthyes II. Mesozoic and Cenozoic Elasmobranchii. In H. P. Schultze (ed.), Handbook of Paleoichtyologie, Band 3B. Gustav Fischer, Stuttgart.

Compagno, L. J. V. (1977). Phyletic relationships of living sharks and rays.–Amer. Zool. 17, 303–322.

Dick, J. R. F. (1978). On the Carboniferous sharkTristychius arcuatus AGASSIZ from Scot land.–Trans. Roy. Soc., Edinburgh 70, 63–109.

Literature

Dick, J. R. F. (1980). A new euselachian shark from the Upper Triassic of Germany.–Neues Jb. Geol. Paläont. 1, 1–16.

Dick, J. R. F. (1981). Diplodoselache woodi, an early Carboniferous shark from the Midland Valley of Scotland.–Trans. Roy. Soc. Earth Sci., Edinburgh, 72, 99–113.

Dick, J. R. F. and Maisey, J. G. (1980). The Scotish Lower Carboniferous shark Onychoselache traquairi.–Paleontology 23, 363–374.

Frickhinger, K. A. (1989). Die Fische von Solnhofen, Teil 1: Knorpelfische-Fossilien 6, 211–214.

Jaekel, O. (1894). Die eozänen Selachier von Monte Bolca.–Springer, Berlin.

Johnson, G. D. (1980). Xenacanthoidi (Chondrichthyes) from the Tecovas Formation (Late Triassic) of West Texas.–J. Paleont. 54, 923–932.

Klausewitz, W. (1986). Redescription of Orthacanthus senckenbergianus FRITSCH.–Indo- Pacific Fish Biology, 125–132, Ichtholog. Soc. of Japan, Tokyo.

Lund, R. (1974). Stethacanthus altonensis (Elasmobranchii) from the Bear Gulch Lime stone of Montana.–Ann. Carnegie Mus. 45, 161–178.

Lund, R. (1977). New information on the evolution on the bradyodont. Fieldiana, Geol. 33, 521–539.

Lund, R. (1977). A new petalodont from the Upper Mississipian of Montana. Ann. Carnegie Mus. 46, 129–155.

Lund, R. (1977). Echinochimaera meltoni, a new genus and species from the Mississipian of Montana.–Ann. Carnegie Mus. 46, 195–221.

Lund, R. (1980). Viviparity and Intrauterine Feeding in a New Holocephalan fish from the Lower Carboniferous of Montana.–Science 209, 697–699.

Lund, R. (1982) Harpagofututor volsellorhinus new genus and species from the Namurian Bear Gulch Limestone.–J. Paleontol. 56 , 938–958.

Lund, R. (1985). Stethacanthid Elasmobranch remains from the Bear Gulch Limestone of Montana.–Amer. Mus. Novitates 2828, 1–24.

Lund, R. (1985). The morphology of Falcatus falcatus (ST. JOHN & WORTHEN) a Missis sipian stethacanthid chondrychthian from the Bear Gulch Limestone of Montana.–J. Vertebr. Paleont. 5, 1–19.

Lund, R. (1985). Ces étranges bètes du Montana.–La Recherche 162 , 98–101.

Lund, R. (1986). On Damocles serratus. nov. gen. et sp. from the Upper Mississipian Bear Gulch Limestone of Montana.–J. of Vertebr. Paleont. 6, 12–19.

Lund, R. (1986). New Mississipian Holocephali and the evolution of the Holocephali.–Mém. Mus. natl. Hist. nat., 53, 195–205, Paris.

Lund, R. (1986). The Diversity and Relationships of the Holocephali.–Indo-Pacific Fish Biology, 97–106, Ichthyolog. Soc. of Japan, Tokyo.

Lund, R. (1989). New. Petalodonts (Chondrichthyes) from the Upper Mississipian Bear Gulch Limestone (Namurian) of Montana.–J. Vertebr. Paleont. 9, 350–368.

Lund, R. (1990). Chondrichthyan life history styles as revealed by the 320 million years old Mississipian of Montana.–Env. Biol. Fish. 27, 1–19. Kluver Academic Publishers.

Literature

Lund, R. and Zangerl, R. (1974). Squatinactis caudispinatus, a new elasmobranch from the Upper Mississipian of Montana.–Ann. Carnegie Mus. 45, 43–55.

Maisey. J. G. (1975). The interrelationships of phalacanthous selachiens.–Neues Jahr buch Geol. Paläontol. Mh., 9, 553–567.

Maisey, J. G. (1976). The Jurassic selachian fish Protospinax WOODWARD. Palaeontology, 19, 733–747.

Maisey, J. G. (1977). The fossil selachian fishes Palaeospinax EGERTON 1872 and Nema canthus AGASSIZ 1837.–Zool. J. Linn. Soc., 60, 259–273.

Maisey, J. G. (1982). The Anatomy and Interrelationships of Mesozoic Hybodont Sharks.–Am. Mus. Novitates 2724, 1–48.

Maisey, J. G. (1982). Studies on the Paleozoic selachien genus Ctenacanthus AGASSIZ, Bythiacanthus ST:JOHN & WORTHEN, Amelacanthus, new genus, Eumenacanthus ST. JOHN & WORTHEN, Sphenacanthus AGASSIZ and Wodnika MÜNSTER. Amer. Mus. Novitates 2706, 1–24

Maisey, J. G. (1984). Chondrichthyan phylogeny: A look at the evidence.–J. Vert. Paleont. 4359–371.

Maisey, J. G. (1986). Anatomical Revision of the Fossil Shark Hybodus fraasi.– Americ. Museum Novitates 2857, 1–16.

Maisey, J. G. (1989). Hamiltonichthys mapesi, gen. and sp. nov. from the Upper Pennsylvanian of Kansas.–Amer. Mus. Novitatates 2931, 1–42.

Malzahn, E. (1968). Über neue Funde von Janassa bituminosa (SCHLOTHEIM) im nieder rheinischen Zechstein.–Geol. Jb. 85 , 67–96.

Moy-Thomas, J. A. (1939). The early evolution and relationships of the elasmobranchs. Biol. Rev. 14, 1–26.

Moy-Thomas, J. A. and Miles, R. S. (1971). Palaeozoic fishes.–Chapman and Hall, London.

Norman, J. R. (1926). A synopsis of the rays of the family Rhinobatidae.–Proc. Zool. Soc., London, 941–982.

Patterson, C. (1965). The phylogeny of the chimaeroids.–Phil. Trans. Roy. Soc., London 249, 101–219.

Patterson, C. (1968). Menaspis and the Bradyodonts. In T. Orvig (ed.), Current problems of Lower vertebrate Phylogeny.–Nobel Symp. 4, 171–205. Almquist and Wiksell, Stockholm.

Regan, C. T. (1908). A synopsis of the sharks of the Family Scyliorhinidae. Ann. Mag. Nat. Hist. 1, 453–465.

Regan, C. T. (1908). A synopsis of the sharks of the family Squalidae. Ann. Mag. Nat. Hist. 2, 39–56.

Rieppel, O. (1981). The hybodontiform sharks from the Middle Triassic of Monte San Giorgio.–Neues Jb. Geol. Paläont. 161, 324–353.

Saint-Seine, P. de(1949). Les poissons des calcaires lithographiques de Cerin (Ain).– Nouv. Arch. du Musée d'Hist. Nat. de Lyon, 2 , 1–357.

Schaeffer, B. and Williams, M. (1977). Relationships of fossil and living elasmobranchs.–Amer. Zool. 17, 293–302.

Literature

Schaumberg, G. (1977). Der Richelsdorfer Kupferschiefer und seine Fossilien.–Auf schluss 28, 297–352.

Schweitzer, R. (1964). Die Elasmobranchier und Holocephalen aus den Nusplinger Plattenkalken.–Palaeontographica 123 A, 58–110.

Stahl, B. J. (1980). Non-autostylic Pennsylvanian iniopterygian fishes.–Palaeontology 23, 315–324.

Thies, D. (1981). Vier neue Neoselachier-Haiarten aus der NW-deutschen Unterkreide.–Neues Jb. Geol. Paläont., 475–486.

Tintori, A. (1980). Teeth of the selachian genus Pseudolatias (SYKES) from the Norian (Upper Triassic) of Lombardy.–Riv. ital. paleont. stratigr. 86, 19–26.

Young, G. C. (1982). Devonian sharks from south-eastern Australia and Antarctica.–Palaeontology 25, 817–843.

Zangerl, R. (1969). Bandringa rayi, a new ctenacanthoid from the Pennsylvanian Essex Fauna of Illinois.–Fieldiana, Geol. 12 , 157–169.

Zangerl, R. (1979). New Chondrichthyes from the Mazon Creek fauna (Pennsylvanian) of Illinois. In M. H. Nitecki (ed.), Mazon Creek Fossils, 449–500. Academic Press, New York.

Zangerl, R. (1981). Chondrichthyes I. Paleozoic elasmobranchs. In H.-P. Schultze (ed.), Handbook of Paleoichthyologie, Band 3a. Gustav Fischer, Stuttgart.

Zangerl, R. and Case, G. R. (1973). Iniopterygia, a new order of chondrichthyan fishes from the Pennsylvanian of North America.–Fieldiana, Geol. Mem. 6, 1–67.

Zangerl, R. and Case, G. R. (1976). Cobelodus aculeatus (COPE), an anacanthous shark from Pennsylvanian black shales of North America. Palaeontographica 154 A, 105– 157.

ACANTHODII   (Acanthodians)

Bendix-Almgreen, S. P. (1974). Early devonian vertebrates from Hall Land, North Greenland.–Rapp. Gronl. Geol. Unders., Copenhagen 65, 13–16.

Bernacsek, G. M. and Dineley, D. L. (1977). New acanthodians from the Delorme formation (Lower Devonian) of N. W. T., Canada.–Palaeontographica, 158 A, 1–25.

Denison, R. (1979). Acanthodii.–In: H.-P. Schultze (ed.) Handbook of Paleoichthyology 5, 62 pp., 35 ills., Stuttgart-New York.

Dunkle, D. H. and Mamay, S. H. (1956). An Acanthodian fish from the lower Permian of Texas.–J. Washington Acad. Sci. 46, 308–310.

Egerton, P. (1861). British fossils. (Descriptions of Tristichopterus, Acanthodes, Climatius, Diplacanthus, Cheiracanthus).–Mem. Geol. Surv. United Kingdom (British Organic Remains), X, 51–75.

Gross, W. (1940). Acanthodier und Placodermen aus den Heterostius-Schichten Estlands und Lettlands.–Ann. Soc. Reb. Natur. Invest. Univ. Tartuensis Const. 46, 1–89.

Literature

Jarvik, E. (1977). The systematic position of acanthodian fishes. In:Andrews, S. M., Miles, R. S. & Walker, A. D., (ed.), Problems in Vertebrate Evolution,–Linn. Soc. Symp. Ser., 4, 199–225.

Jensen, S. R. (1975). Acanthodians from the Permo-Carboniferous boundary of central East Greenland.–Coll. Internat. C. N. R. S., 218, 125–131.

Liu Shi-Fan (1973). Some new acanthodian fossil materials from the Devonian of South China. (in Chinese)–Vertebrata Palasiatica 11, 144–148.

Miles, R. S. (1966). The acanthodian fishes of the Devonian Plattenkalk of the Paffrath trough in the Rhineland.–Ark. Zoolog. 18, 147–194.

Miles, R. S. (1973). Articulated acanthodian fishes from the Old Red Sandstone of England, with a review of the structure and evolution of the acanthodian shoulder-girdle.–Bull. Brit. Mus. (Nat. Hist.), Geol. 24, 113–213.

Miles, R. S. (1973). Relationships of acanthodians.–Zool. J. Linn. Soc. 53, Suppl. 1, 63–103.

Moy-Thomas, J. A. and Miles. R. S. (1971). Paleozoic fishes.–61–78, Chapman und Hall, London.

Orvig, T. (1967). Some new acanthodian material from the Lower Devonian of Europe.–J. Linn. Soc. (Zool.) 47, 131–153.

Reis, O. M. (1895). Illustrationen zur Kenntnis des Skeletts von Acanthodes bronni AGASSIZ.–Abh. Senckenberg. Naturforsch. Ges. 19, 49–64.

Reis, O. M. (1896). Über Acanthodes bronni AGASSIZ.–In: G. Schwalbe (ed.), Morphol. Arb. 6, 143–220.

Russel, L. S. (1951). Acanthodians of the Upper Devonian Escuminac Formation, Miguasha, Quebec.–Ann. Mag. nat. Hist. (12) 3, 401–407.

Schultze, H.–P. and Zidek, J. (1982). Ein primitiver Acanthodier (Pisces) aus dem Unterdevon Lettlands.–Paläont. Z. 56, 95–105.

Schultze, H.–P. (1990). A new Acanthodian from the Pennsylvanian of Utah, USA., and the distribution of otoliths in Gnathostomes.–Vertebr. Paleont. 10 (1), 49–58.

Simpson, L. C. (1974). Acanthodes and Hybodus in the Permian of Texas and Oklahoma.–J. Paleont. 48, 1291–1293.

Traquair, R. H. (1884). Notes on the genus Gyracanthus AGASSIZ.–Ann. Mag. Nat. Hist 13, 37–48.

Traquair, R. H. (1894). On a new species of Diplacanthus, with remarks on the acantho dian shoulder-girdle.–Geol. Mag. 4, 254–257.

Traquair, R. H. (1898). Notes on paleozoic fishes., Nr. II.–Ann. Mag. Nat. Hist. 7, 67–70.

Watson, D. M. S. (1937). The Acanthodian fishes.–Phil. Trans. Roy. Soc. London, Biol. Sci. 228B, 49–146, London.

Zidek, J. (1973). Remarkes on acanthodian specimen from Texas.–Oklahoma Geol. Notes 33, 201–202.

Zidek, J. (1980). Acanthodes lundi, new species and associated Coprolites from upper most Mississipian Heath Formation of Central Montana.–Ann. Carnegie Mus. 49, 49–78.

Literature

CHONDROSTEI (Chondrosteans)

Abel, O. (1906). Fossile Flugfische.–Jb. K. K. Reichsanstalt 56, 1–88.

Aldinger, H. (1937). Permische Ganoidfische aus Ostgrönland.–Medd. om Gronland 102, Nr. 3, 392 pp.

Andersson, E. (1916). Über einige Trias-Fische aus der Cava Trefontane (Tessin).–Bull. Geol. Inst., Uppsala 15, 13–34.

Baird, D. (1962). A haplolepid fish fauna in the early Pennsylvanian of Nova Scotia.–Palaeontology 5, 22–29.

Blot, J. (1966). Etude des Palaeoniscifornes du bassin de Commentry.–Cah. Paléont. C. N. R. S., Paris, 99 pp.

Brough, J. (1931). On fossil fishes from the Karroo system and some general considerations on the bony fishes of the Triassic Period.–Proc. Zool. Soc., London, 1931, 235–296.

Brough, J. (1936). On the evolution of bony fishes during the Triassic period.–Biol. Rev. 11, 385–405.

Brough, J. (1939). The Triassic fishes of Besano, Lombardy.–Brit. Mus. (Nat. Hist.), London, 117 pp.

Dunkle, D. H. (1939). A new Palaeoniscid fish from the Texas Permian.–Amer. J. Sci. 237, 262–274.

Dunkle, D. H. (1946). A new palaeoniscoid fish from the Lower Permian of Texas.–J. Washington Acad. Sci. 36, 402–409.

Dunkle. D. H. and Schäffer, B. (1956). Preliminary description of a palaeoniscoid fish from the late Paleozoic of Brasil.–Univ. Sao Paulo, Bol. Geol. 193, Br. 13, 5–22.

Egerton, P. (1858). On Chondrosteus, an extinct genus of Sturionidae, found in the Lias Formation at Lyme Regis.–Trans. Roy. Soc. Phil. 148, 871–886.

Gardiner, B. G. (1967). Further notes on palaeoniscoid fishes with a classification of the Chondrostei.–Bull. Brit. Mus. (Natural History) Geol., 14 143–206.

Gardiner, B. G. (1969). New palaeoniscoid fish from the Witteberg Series of South Africa.–J. Linn. Soc. (Zool.) 48 423–452.

Gardiner, B. G. (1984). The relationsships of the palaeoniscid fishes, a review based on new specimen of Mimia and Moythomasia from the Upper Devonian of Western Australia.–Bull. Brit. Mus. (Nat. Hist.) Geol. 37, 173–428.

Gardiner, B. G. and Jubb, R. A. (1975). A ne genus Acentrophorus.–Proc. Zool. Soc., London 1923, 19–40.

Gill, E. L. (1925). The Permian fish Dorypterus.–Trans. Roy. Soc., Edinburgh 53, 643–661.

Goodrich, E. S. (1927). Polypterus, a palaeoniscid ?–Palaeobiologica 1, 87–92.

Gottfried, M. D. (1987). A Pennsylvanian aeduelliform from North America with comments on aeduelliform interrelation ships.–Paläont. Z. 61 141–148.

Gottfried, M. D. (1987). A New Long-snouted Actinopterygian Fish from the Pennsylvanian of North-central New Mexico.–New Mexico J. Sci. 27, 7–19.

Gürich, G. (1923). Acrolepis lotzi und andere Ganoiden aus den Dwyka-Schichten von Ganikobis, Südwestafrika.–Beitr. geol. Erforschung deutsch. Schutzgebiete 19-26–73.

Literature

Hauff, B. (1938). Über Acidorhynchus aus den Posidonienschiefern von Holzmaden.–Paläontol. Z. 20, 214–248.

Heller, F. (1953). Ein Ganoidfisch (Aphetolepis delpi n. g. n. sp.) aus dem Grenzdolomit Mittelfrankens.–Geol. Bl. NO-Bayern 3, 81–87.

Henning, E. (1926). Chondrosteus hindenburgi. ein Stör des württembergischen Ölschie fers.–Palaeontographica 65, 115–134.

Heyler, D. (1969). Vertébrés de l'Autunien de France.–Cahiers Paléont. 1969, 1–255. ßn:Heyler, D. (1976). Sur le genre Amblypterus AGASSIZ (actinopterygien du Permien inférieur).–Cahiers Paléont. 78 , 17–37.

Heyler, D. (1977). Aeduelliformes de l'Autunien francais.–Cahiers Paléont. 83, 9–19.

Hussakof, L. (1911). The Permian fishes of North America.–Publ. Carnegie Inst. Washington, 146, 155–175.

Hutchinson, P. (1973). A revision of the redfieldiiform and perleidiform fishes from the Triassic of Bekker's Kraal (South Africa) and Brookvale (New South Wales).–Bull. Brit. Mus. (Nat. Hist.) Geol. 22, 135–354.

Jessen, H. (1968). Moythomasia nitida GROSS and Moythomasia cf. striata GROSS, devonische Palaeonisciden aus dem oberen Plattenkalk der Bergisch-Gladbach-Paff rather Mulde (Rheinisches Schiefergebirge.)–Palaeontographica 128A, 87–114 Stuttgart.

Jubb, R. A. (1965). A new palaeoniscid fish from the Witteberg Series of South Africa.–Ann. South Afric. Mus. 48, 267–272.

Jubb, R. A. and Gardiner, B. G. (1975). A preliminary catalogue of identifiable fossil fish material from Southern Africa.–Ann. South. Afric. Mus. 67, 381–440.

Lambe, L. M. (1914). Description of a new species of Platysomus from the neighbourhood of Banff, Alberta.–Trans. Roy. Soc., Canada 4, 17–23.

Lehman, J.-P. (1947). Description des quelques exemplaires de Cheirolepis canadensis (WHITEAVES). Handl. K. Svenska Vetenskap. 24, 1–40.

Lehman, J.-P. (1952). Etude complémentaire des poissons de L'Eotrias de Madagaskar.–Kungl. Svenska Vetenskapsakad. Handlingar. 2, 1–201.

Lehman, J.-P. (1956). Compléments l'étude des genres Ecrinesomus et Bobasatrania de l'eotrias de Madagascar.–Ann. Paléont. 42, 1–30.

Lehman, J. P. (1980). Le genre Scanilepis ALDINGER du Rhétien de la Scanie (Suède). Bull. Geolog. Inst. Univ. Uppsala 8, 113–125.

Long, J. A. (1988). Devonian and Carboniferous fish studies.–Assoc. Australasian Palaeontologists, Sydney, 144 pp.

Lowney, K. A. (1980). A revision of the family Haplolepidae from Linton, Ohio (Westphalian D, Pennsylvanian).–J. Paleont. 54, 942–953.

Moy-Thomas, J. A. (1934). The structure and affinities of Tarrasius problematicus TRA QUAIR. -Proc. Zool. Soc., London 1934, 367–376.

Moy-Thomas, J. A. (1937). The palaeoniscids from the Cement stones of Tarras Waterfoot Eskdale, Dumfrieshire.–Ann. Mag. Nat. Hist. 20, 345–356.

Moy-Thomas, J. A. (1938). Carboniferous Palaeoniscids from Northhumberland and Berwickshire.–Geol. Mag. 75, 308–318.

Literature

Moy-Thomas, J. A. (1938). A revision of the fishes referred to the genus Canobius from Lower Carboniferous localities other than Glencartholm.–Ann. Mag. Nat. Hist. 2, 291–299.

Moy-Thomas, J. A. and Dyne, B. M. (1938). Actinopterygian fishes from the Lower Carboniferous of Glencartholm, Eskdale, Dumfrieshire.–Trans. Roy. Soc. Edinburgh 59, 437–480.

Moy-Thomas, J. A. (1939). Notes on some Carboniferous Palaeoniscids.–Ann. Mag. Nat. Hist. 3 622–625.

Moy Thomas, J. A. (1942). Carboniferous palaeoniscids from East Greenland. Ann. and Mag. Nat. Hist. 9, 937–959.

Moy-Thomas, J. A. and Miles, R. S. (1971). Palaeozoic fishes.–Chapman and Hall, London.

Müller, A. H. (1962). Körperlich erhaltene Fische (Palaeoniscoidea) aus dem Zechstein (Kupferschiefer) von Ilmenau, Thüringen.–Geologie 11, 845–856.

Müller, A. H. (1969). Ein Flugfisch (Dollopterus volitans) aus dem oberen Muschelkalk von Apolda (Thüringen).–Freiberger Forschungshefte 256 C, 37–45.

Müller, A. H. (1970). Ein neuer Colobodus-Fund aus dem oberen Muschelkalk des germanischen Triasbeckens.–Mbr. dt. Akad. Wiss., Berlin 12, 511–520.

Nielsen, E. (1952): A preliminary note on Bobasatrania groenlandica.–Medd. Dansk. Geol. Fören 12, 197–204.

Nielsen, E. (1955). Notes on Triassic fishes from Madagascar.–Medd. Dansk. Geol. Fören 12, 563–578.

Patterson, C. (1982). Morphology and interrelationships of primitive actinopterygian fishes.–Amer. Zool. 22, 241–259.

Pearson, D. M. (1982). Primitive bony fishes, with especial reference to Cheirolepis and palaeonisciform actinopterygians.–Zool. J. Linn. Soc. 74, 35–67.

Pearson, D. M. and Westoll, T. S. (1979). The Devonian actinopterygian Cheirolepis AGASSIZ. -Trans. Roy. Soc. Edinburgh 70, 337–399.

Rieppel, O. (1980). Additional specimens of Saurichthys madagascariensis PIVETEAU from the Eotrias from Madagascar.–Neues Jb. Geol. Paläont. Mh. 1980, 43–51.

Rieppel O. (1935). Die Triasfauna der Tessiner Kalkalpen XXV. Die Gattung Saurichthys aus der mittleren Trias des Monte San Giorgio, Kanton Tessin.–Schweiz. Paläontolog. Abhandl. 108 , 1–103.

Romer, A. S. (1942). Notes on certain American Paleozoic fishes.–Amer. J. Sci. 240, 216–227.

Saxon, J. (1975). The fossil fishes of the North of Scotland.–John Humphries, Turso, Caithness, Scotland.

Schaeffer, B. (1973). Interrelationships of chondrosteans. In P. H. Greenwood, R. S. Miles and C. Patterson (eds.), Interrelationships of Fishes, Seite 207–226. Suppl. Nr. 1, Zool. J. Linn. Soc. 53, Academic Press, London.

Schaeffer, B. (1978). Redfieldiid fishes from the Triassic-Liassic Newark Supergroup of Eastern North America.–Bull. Am. Mus. Nat. Hist. 159, 133–173.

Literature

Schaeffer, B. (1984). On the ralationships of the Triassic-Liassic Redfieldiform fishes.– Am. Mus. Noviates 2795, 1–18.

Schaumberg, G. (1977). Erster Nachweis von Elonichthys punctatus ALDINGER in Mittel europa, im Kupferschiefer von Richelsdorf. Geol. Jb. Hessen 105, 65–68.

Schaumberg, G. (1989). Muensterichthys buergeri n. gen. n. sp., ein neuer Palaeoniscoide (Actinopterygii, Pisces) aus dem permischen Kupferschiefer von Richelsdorf (Hessen, Westdeutschland).–Paläont. Z. 63, 119–131.

Schultze, H. P. (1970). Indaginilepis rhombifera n. gen et n. sp., ein altertümlicher Palaeoniscide aus dem Wealden von Norddeutschland.–Paläont. Z. 44, 10–24, Stuttgart.

Schwarz, W. (1970) Birgeria stensiöi ALDINGER. - Schweiz. Paläontol. Abhandl. 89, 1–93.

Stensiö, E. (1921). Triassic fishes from Spitzbergen I., 307 pp, Wien

Stensiö, E. (1925). Triassic fishes from Spitzbergen II.–Kgl. Svensk. Vetensk. Handl. 2, 261 pp, Stockholm.

Stolley, E. (1920). Beiträge zur Kenntnis der Ganoiden des deutschen Muschelkalkes.– Palaeontographica 63, 25–86.

Wade, R. T. (1935). The triassic fishes of Brookvale, New South Wales.–Bull. Brit. Mus. Nat. Hist. 1935, 1–89.

Wade, R. T. (1940). The triassic fishes of Gosford, New South Wales.–J. and Proc. Roy. Soc., South Wales 73, 206–217.

Watson, D. M. S. (1925). The structure of certain palaeoniscids and the relationships of the group with other bony fish.–Proc. Zool. Soc., London, 815–870.

Westoll, T. S. (1941). The Permian fishes Dorypterus and Lektanichthys.–Proc. Zool. Soc., Series B, 111, 39–58.

Westoll, T. S. (1944). The Haplolepidae, a new Family of late Carboniferous bony fishes.–Bull. Amer. Mus. Nat. Hist. 83, 1–121.

White, E. I. (1939). A new type of palaeoniscoid fish, with remarks on the evolution of the actinopterygian pectoral fins.–Proc. Zool. Soc., London 109 B, 41–61.

"HOLOSTEI" (Holosteans)

Accordi, B. (1955). Archaeolepidotus leonhardii n. gen. n. sp. e altri pesci Permo-Werfe niani delle Dolomiti.–Mem. Ist. Geol. Min. Univ. Padova 19, 1–25.

Accordi, B. (1956). A new genus of lower Triassic holostean fishes from the Dolomite Alps.–J. Paleont. 30, 345–351.

Agassiz, L. (1878). The development of Lepidosteus.–Proc. Amer. Acad. Arts Sci. 13, 65–76.

Aldinger, H. (1937). Permische Ganoidfische aus Ostgrönland.–Medd. om Gronland 102, 392 pp., Kopenhagen.

Andersson, E. (1916). Über einige Trias-Fische aus der Cava Trefontane, Tessin.– Bull. Geol. Inst. Uppsala 15, 13–34.

Literature

Arambourg, C. (1925). Contribution l'étude des poissons du Lias Supérieur.–Ann. paléontol. 24, 3–32.

Arambourg, C. (1935). Observations sur quelques poissons fossiles de l'ordre des Halécostomes et sur l'origine des Clupeidae.–C. R. A. S. 200, 2100–2111.

Arambourg, C. (1954). Les poissons crétacés du Djebel Tselfat (Maroc).–Notes Mém. Serv. Geol. Maroc 118, 1–188.

Bartram, A. W. H. (1977). The Macrosemiidae, a Mesozoic family of holostean fishes.– Bull. Brit. Mus. Nat. Hist. (Geol.) 29, 137–234.

Berger, H. A. (1832). Die Versteinerungen der Fische und Pflanzen im Sandsteine der Coburger Gegend.–Coburg.

Blot, J. (1987). L'ordre de Pycnodontiformes.–Studi e richerche sui giacimenti Terziari di Bolca, 211 pp, Mus. Civ. St. Nat., Verona.

Boreska, J. R. (1974). A review of the North American fossil amiid fishes.–Bull. Mus. Comp. Zool. 146, 1–87.

Browne, M. (1890). Revision of a genus of fossil fishes. Dapedius.–Transact. Leicester Lit. Phil. Soc. 1890, 196–203.

Dechaseaux, C. (1937). Le genre Amia, son histoire paléontologique.–Ann. Paléont. 26, 1–16.

Dechaseaux, C. (1943). Contribution à l'étude du genre Lepidotus–Ann. Paléont. 30, 1–13.

Frickhinger, K. A. (1990). Die Fische von Solnhofen. Teil II, Schmelzschupper I.– Fossilien 7, 1, 19–22.

Frickhinger, K. A. (1990). Die Fische von Solnhofen. Teil III, Schmelzschupper II.– Fossilien 7, 2, 75–78.

Hennig, E. (1906). Gyrodus und die Organisation der Pycnodonten.–Palaeontographica 53, 137–208.

Jaekel, O. (1929). Lepidotus und Leptolepis aus dem oberen Lias von Dobbertin, Mecklenburg.–Mitt. meckl. geol. L.-A. 38, 1–14.

Jörg, E. (1969). Eine Fischfauna aus dem oberen Buntsandstein (Unter-Trias) von Karls ruhe-Durlach.–Beitr. naturk. Forsch. SW-Deutschland 28, 87–102.

Lange, S. (1968). Zur Morphologie und Taxonomie der Fischgattung Urocles aus Jura und Kreide Europas.–Palaeontographica 131A, 1–78.

Lehman: J. P. (1949). Etude d'un Pachycormus du Lias de Normandie. Kgl. Svensk. Vetensk. Handl. 1, 1–44.

Loomis, F. B. (1900). Die Anatomie und Verwandtschaft der Ganoid-und Knochenfische aus der Kreideformation von Kansas, USA.–Palaeographica 45 213–284.

Malzahn, E. (1963). Lepidotus elvensis BLAINVILLE aus der Dobbertiner Liasscholle mit speziellen Untersuchungen zur Histologie des Operculums.–Geol. Jb. 80 539–560.

Nielsen, E. (1955). Notes on Triassic Fishes from Madagascar.–Medd. dansk. Geol. Fören 12 563–578.

Literature

Patterson, C. (1965). A review of Mesozoic acanthopterygian fishes with special reference to those of the English chalk.–Phil. Trans. Roy. Soc., London, 247 B, 213–482.

Patterson, C. (1973). Interrelationships of holosteans. In P. H. Greenwood, R. S. Miles und C. Patterson (eds.), Interrelationships of fishes, Seite 223–305. Suppl Nr. 1, Zool. J. Linn. Soc. 53, Academic Press, London.

Patterson, C. (1982). Morphology and interrelationships of primitive actinopterygian fishes.–Amer. Zool. 22, 242–259.

Rayner, D. M. (1941). The structure and evolution of the holostean fishes.–Biol. Rev. 60, 218–237.

Saint-Seine, P. de (1949). Les Poissons de calcaires lithographiques de Cerin (Ain).– Nouv. Arch. Mus. Hist. Nat. Lyon. 2, 1–357.

Saint-Seine, P. de (1955). Poissons fossiles de l'étage de Stanleyville (Congo belge). Ann. illustr. Roy. Congo belg. 14, 126 pp.

Schaeffer, B. (1947). Cretaceous and tertiary actinopterygian fishes from Brazil.– Bull. Amer. Mus. Nat. Hist. 89, Seite 39 ff.

Schaeffer, B. (1960). The Cretaceous Holostean fish Macrepistius.–American Museum Novitates 2011, 1–18.

Stensiö, E. (1935). Sinamia zdanskyi, a new Amiid from the Lower Cretaceous of Shan tung, China.–Palaeont. Sinica 3c, 1–48.

Tintori, A. (1980). Two new Pycnodonts from the Upper Triassic of Lombardy (N. Italy).–Riv. ital. paleont., 86, 795–823.

Tintori, A. (1982). Hypsisomatic Semionotidae from the Upper Triassic of Lombardy (N. Italy).–Riv. Ital. Paleont., 88, 417–442.

Tintori, A. and Renesto, S. (1983). The Macrosemiidae from the Upper Triassic of Lombardy (N. Italy).–Riv. Ital. Paleont., 89, 209–222.

Viohl, G. (1987). Raubfische der Solnhofer Plattenkalke mit erhaltenen Beutefischen.– Archaeopteryx 5, 33–64.

Wade, R. T. (1935). The Triassic fishes of Brookvale, New South Wales.–Brit. Mus. Nat. Hist. 1935, 1–89.

Wade, R. T. (1940). The Triassic fishes of Gosford, New South Wales.–Roy. Soc. New South Wales 76, 206–217.

Wagner, A. (1859). Monographie der fossilen Fische des fränkisch- oberpfälzischen lithografischen Schiefers.–Gel. Anz. Akad. Wiss. 49, 13–19.

Wiley, E. O. (1976). Phylogeny and biogeography of fossil and recent gars.–Univ. Kansas Mus. Nat. Hist. Misc. Publ. 64, 1–111.

Woodward, A. S. (1895). The fossil fishes of the Talbragar beds (Jurassic) Mem. Geol. Surv. New South Wales.–Palaeontographica 9, 1–27.

Woodward, A. S. (1908). On some remains of Pachycormus and Hypsocormus from the Jurassic of Normandy.–Mem. Soc. Linn. Normandie 23, 29–34.

Woodward, A. S. (1929). The Upper Jurassic Ganoid fish Heterostrophus.–Proc. Zool. Soc. 1929 Part 3, 561–574.

Literature

TELEOSTEI (True Bony Fishes)
EUTELEOSTEI (Higher Teleosts)

Arambourg, C. (1925). Les poissons fossiles de Licata (Sicile).–Ann. Paléont. 14, 39–132.

Arambourg, C. (1927). Les poissons fossiles d'Oran.–Matériaux carte géol. d'Algerie, ser. 1, 6, 1–218.

Arambourg, C. (1935). Contribution l'étude des poissons du Lias supérieur.–Ann. Paléont. 24, 1–32, Paris.

Arambourg, C. (1952). Les Vertébrés fossiles des gisement de phosphates (Maroc-Algerie- Tunesie).–Notes et Mém. Serv. Géol. Maroc 92, 1–372.

Arambourg, C. (1954). Les poissons crétacés du Jebel Tselfat.–Notes et Mém. Serv. Géol. Maroc 118, 1–188.

Arratia, G. (1981). Varasichthys ariasi n. gen. et spec. from the Upper Jurassic of Chile.–Palaeontographica, A. 175, 105–107.

Arratia, G. and Schultze, H.-P. (1985). Late Jurassic teleosts from nothern Chile and Cuba.–Palaeontogr., Abt. A 189, 29–61.

Arratia, G. (1987). Anaethalion and similiar teleosts from the late Jurassic (Tithonian) of Southern Germany and their relationships.–Palaeontographica, A 200, 1–44.

Arratia, G. (1987). Orthogonikleithrus leichi n. gen. n. spec., from the Late Jurassic of Germany.–Paläont. Z. 61 309–320.

Bachmayer, F. (1980). Eine fossile Schlangennadel (Syngnathidae) aus dem Leithakalk (Badenien) von St. Margarethen, Burgenland (Österreich).–Ann. Naturhist. Mus. Wien 83, 29–33.

Bachmayer, F. and Symeonidis, N. (1978). Eine fossile Seenadel (Syngnathidae) aus dem Obermiozän Ierapetra.–Ann. Naturhist. Mus. Wien 81, 121–127.

Bannikov, A. F., Parin and Pinna, G. (1985). Rhamphexocoetus volans gen. et spec. nov.–Mus. Civ. St. Nat. Milano, 343–346.

Bannikov, A. F. (1985). Fossil scombrids of the USSR.–Moskau, Nauka, 111 pp.

Bannikov, A. F. (1986). The first finding of fossil wrassers (Teleostei) in the Sarmatian of Moldavia.–Paleontol. J., N 1, 78–83.

Bannikov, A. F. (1988). The new species of stromateid fishes (Perciformes) from the Lower Oligocene of the Caucasus.–Paleontol. J., N 4, 108–113.

Bannikov, A. F. (1989). The first finding of clinids (Teleostei) in the Sarmatian of Mol davia.–Palaeontol. J., N 2, 64–70.

Bardack, D. (1965). Anatomy and evolution of chirocentrid fishes.–Paleont. Contr. Univ. Kansas, Vertebrata 10, 1–88.

Bertin, L. (1951). Les Anguilles.–2. ed., 193 pp., Paris (Payot).

Bjerring, H. C. (1985). Facts and thougts on piscine phylogeny. In Forman, Gorbman, Dodd, Olsen (eds.), Evolutionary Biologie of primitive fishes. Plenum Press, New York.

Blot, J. (1969). Les poissons fossiles du Monte Bolca classés jusqu'ici dans les familles des Carangidae-Menidae-Ephippidae-Scatophagidae. Studi e Ricerche sui Giacimenti Ter ziari di Bolca. I. Mem. Mus. Civ. Storia Nat. Verona. Mem. out

Literature

of normal ser. no. 2, vol. I (Text), 526 pp. Band II(Bilder), Museo Civico di Storia Naturale di Verona.

Blot, J. (1978). Les apodes fossiles du Monte Bolca.–Studi e Ricerche sui Giacimenti Terziari di Bolca. Vol. III/1, 260 pp., Museo Civico di Storia Naturale di Verona, Verona.

Blot, J. (1980) La faune ichthyologique des gisements du Monte Bolca (Province de Vérone, Italie). Catalogue systématique présentant l' actuel des recherches concernant cette faune.–Bull. Mus. ntl. Hist. nat., Paris. 4. serie 2 section C, no 4, 339–396.

Blot, J. (1984). Actinopterygii. Ordre des Scorpaeniformes? Famille des Pterygocephali dae. In Studi e Ricerche sui Giacimenti Terziari di Bolca. Band IV, Miscellanea Paleon tologica. II. Seite 265–299. Museo Civico di Storia Naturale di Verona.

Blot, J. and Voruz, C. (1975). La famille de Zanclidae. In Studi e Ricerche sui Giacimenti Terziari di Bolca. Band II. Miscellanea Paleontologica, Seite 223–278. Museo Civico di Storia Naturale di Verona.

Crane, J. M. jr. (1966). Late Tertiary radiation of viperfishes (Chauliodontidae) based on a comparision of Recent and Miocene Species.–Contrib. Sci., Los Ang. Country Mus. 115, 1–29.

Daniltshenko, P. G. (1960). Teleost fishes of Maikopian deposits of Caucasus.–Moskau, Nauka, 208 pp.

Daniltshenko, P. G. (1968). Fishes of Upper Paleocene of Turkmenia.–In: Ocherki po filogenii i systematike iskopayemykh ryb i beschelynstnykh. Moskau, Nauka, 113–156.

Daniltshenko, P. G. (1980). Order Lampridiformes. In: Fossil teleost fishes of the USSR.–Moskau, Nauka, 91–95.

Daniltshenko, P. G. (1980). Order Perciformes. In: Fossil teleost fishes of the USSR.–Moskau, Nauka, 115–169.

David, L. R. (1943). Miocene fishes of Southern California.–Geol. Soc. Amer. Spec. Papers 43, 181 pp.

Dunker, G. (1912). Die Gattungen der Syngnathidae.–Mitt. Naturhist. Mus. Hamburg 29, 219–240.

Dunker, G. (1915). Revision der Syngnathidae.–Mitt. Naturhist. Mus. Hamburg 32, 9–120.

Dunkle, D. H. (1958). Three North American Cretaceous fishes.–Proc. U. S. Nat. Mus. 108, 269–277.

Estes, R. (1964). Fossil vertebrates from the late Cretaceous Lance formation Eastern Wyoming.–Univ. California Publ. Geol. Sci. 49, 1–180.

Fedotov, V. F. (1985). Fossil mugiliforms of the USSR.–Moskau, Nauka, 63 pp.

Fink, S. V. and Fink, W. L. (1981). Interrelationships of the ostariophysan teleost fishes.–Zool. J. Linn. Soc. 72, 297–352.

Fink, W. L. and Weitzman, S. H. (1982). Relationships of the stomiiform fishes (Teleostei), with a description of Diplophos.–Bull. Mus. Comp. Zool. 150, 31–93.

Forey, P. L. (1973). Relationships of elopomorphs.–Zool. J. Linnean Soc. 53, Suppl. 1, 351–368.

Literature

Forey, P. L. (1973). A revision of the elopiform fishes, fossil and recent Bull. Brit. Mus. Nat. Hist. Geol. Suppl. 10, 1–222.

Forey, P. L. (1973). A primitive clupeomorph fish from the Middle Cenomanian of Hakel, Lebanon.–Can. J. Earth Sci. 10, 1302–1318.

Frickhinger, K. A. (1990). Die Fische von Solnhofen. Teil IV, Knochenfische Fossilien 7, 3. 122–124.

Gardiner, B. G. (1973). Interrelationships of teleostomes.–Zool. J. Linn. Soc. 53, Suppl. 1, 105–135.

Gaudant, J. (1980). Mise au point sur l'ichthyofaune miocène d'Öhningen (Baden, Allemagne).–C. R. Acad. Sc. Paris 291 Serie D, 1033–1036.

Gasman, S. (1895). The Cyprinodonts.–Mem. Mus. Comp. Zool. 19, 1–179.

Gaudant, J. (1978). Découverte du plus ancien représentant connu du genre Esox L. (Poisson Téléostéen, Esocoidei) dans le Stampien moyen du bassin d'Apt (Vaucluse).–Géol. Méditer. 5 , 257–268.

Gayet, M. (1980). Découverte dans le Crétacé de Hadjula (Liban) du plus ancien Caproi dae connu.–Etude anat. et phylog. Bull. Mus. Nat. Hist. Sci. terre 2 (3), 259–269.

Goody, P. C. (1969). The relationships of certain Upper Cretaceous teleosts with special reference to the myctophoids.–Bull. Brit. Mus. (Nat. Hist.) Geol. Suppl., 7, 1–255.

Grande, L. (1979). Eohiodon falcatus, a new species of Hiodontid from the Late Early Eocene Green River formation of Wyoming.–J. Palaeont. 5, 103–111.

Grande, L. (1982). A revision of the fossil genus Diplomystus with comments on the interrelationships of the clupeomorph fishes.–Am. Mus. Novitates, 2728, 1–34.

Grande, L. (1982). A revision of the fossil genus Knightia, with a description of a new genus from the Green River formation (Teleostei, Clupeidae).–Am. Mus. Novitates 2731, 1–22.

Grande, L., Eastman E. T. and Cavender, T. M. (1982). Amyzon gosiutensis, a New Catostomid Fish from the Green River Formation.–Copeia 1982 (3), 523–532.

Grande, L. (1984). Paleontology of the Green River Formation with a review of the fish fauna.–Geolog. Surv. Wyoming, 63, 1–333.

Grande, L. (1985). Recent and fossil Clupeomorph fishes with materials for revision of the subgroups of Clupeoids.–Bull. Am. Mus. Nat. Hist. 181 Art. 2, 235–372.

Grande, L. (1985). Interrelationships of Fossil and Recent Anchovies and Description of a New species from the Miocene of Cyprus.–Am. Mus. Novitates 2826, 1–16.

Grande, L. (1986). The first articulated freshwater Teleost fish from the Cretaceous of North America.–Palaeont. 29, Part 2, 365–371.

Grande, L. (1987). Redescription of Hypsidoris farsonensis with a reassessment of its phylogenetic relationships.–J. Vertebr. Paleont. 7, 1, 24–54.

Grande, L. (1988). A well preserved Paracanthopterygian fish from Freshwater Lower Paleocene Deposits of Montana.–J. Vertebr. Paleont. 8, 117–129.

Grande, L. and Lundberg, J. G. (1988). Revision and redescription of the genus Astephus with a discussion of its phylogenetic relationships.–J. of Vertebr. Paleont. 8 No. 2, 139–171.

Literature

Greenwood, P. H. (1973). Interrelationships of osteoglossomorphs.–Zool. J. Linn. Soc. 53, Suppl. 1, 307–332.

Greenwood, P. H. (1977). Notes on the anatomy and classification of elopomorph fishes.–Bull. Brit. Mus. (Nat. Hist.) Zool. 32, 65–102.

Greenwood, P. H., Rosen, D. E., Weitzman, S. H. and Myers, G. S. (1966). Phyletic studies of Teleostean fishes, with a provisional classification of living forms.– Bull. Amer. Mus. Nat. Hist. 131, 341–455, New York.

Griffith, J. and Patterson, C. (1963). The structure and relationships of the Jurassic fish Ichthyokentema purbeckensis.–Bull. Brit. Mus. Nat. Hist., Geol. 8, 1–43

Hay, O. P. (1903). On a collection of Upper Cretaceous fishes from Mount Lebanon, Syria, with description of four new genera and nineteen new species.–Bull. Amer. Mus. Nat. Hist. 19, 395–452.

Iljin, B. S. and Branner, J. C. (1908) The Cretaceous fishes of Ceára, Brazil.–Smithon. Misc. Coll. 52, 1–19.

Iljin, B. S. and Branner, J. C. (1919). New genera of fossil fishes from Brazil.–Proc. Akad. Nat. Sci. Philadelphia 71, 208–210.

Jerzmanska, A. (1958). Scorpaena ensiger (JORDAN & GILBERT) Miocenu Pinczowa.– Acta Palaeontol. Polonica 3, 151–159.

Jerzmanska, A. (1960). Ichthyofauna from the Jaslo shales at Sobniow (Poland).– Acta Palaeontol. Polonica 5, 367–419.

Jerzmanska, A. (1962). Fossil Bony fishes from the Miocene of Upper Silesia, Poland.–Acta Palaeontol. Polonica 7, 235–247.

Jerzmanska, A. (1967). Argentinidés (Poissons) fossiles de la série ménilitique des Kar pates.–Acta Palaeontol. Polonica 22 , 195–211.

Jerzmanska, A. (1977a). The freshwater fishes from the Middle Eocene of Geiseltal.– Wiss. Beitr. Martin Luther-Univ. Halle-Wittenberg 1977/2 (P5), 41–65.

Jerzmanska, A. (1977b). Süsswasserfische des älteren Tertiärs von Europa. Wiss. Beitr. Martin Luther Univ. Halle 1977/2 (P5), 67–76.

Jerzmanska, A. (1979). Oligocene alepocephaloid fishes from the Polish Carpathians.– Acta Palaeontol. Polonica 24 , 65–76.

Jungersen, H. (1908). The structure of the genera Amphisile and Centriscus.–Kgl. Dansk. Vidensk. Selsk. Sk. 6, 1–71.

Jungersen, H. (1910). The structure of the Aulostomidae, Syngnathidae and Solenostomi dae.–Kgl. Dansk. Vidensk. Selsk. Sk. 8, 1–98.

Kalabis, V. and Schultz, O. (1974). Die Fischfauna der paläogenen Menelitschichten von Speitsch in Mähren, CSSR.–Ann. Naturhist. Mus. Wien 78, 183–192.

Klausewitz, M. (1965). Fischartige und Fische. In F. Gessner (ed.) Handbuch der Biologie, Band VI, 2, Seite 32–628, Athenaion, Konstanz

Kyle, H. M. (1923). The asymmetry, metamorphosis and origin of Flat fishes.–Phil. Trans. R. Soc. 211, 75–129.

Lauder, G. V. and Liem, K. F. (1983). The evolution and interrelationships of the actinop terygian fishes.–Bull. Mus. Comp. Zool., 150, 95–197.

Lees, T. and Bartholomai, A. (1987). Study of a Lower Cretaceous actinopterygian Cooyoo australis from Queensland, Australia.–Mem. Queensl. Mus. 25 , 177–192.

Literature

Leidenfrost, J. (1925). Die fossilen Siluriden Ungarns.–Mittl. Jb. K. ungar. Geol. Anst. 24, 117–123.

Leriche, M. (1910). Les poissons oligocènes de la Belgique.–Mém. Mus. Roy. Hist. Nat. Belg. 5.

Leriche, M. (1926). Les poissons néogène de la Belgique.–Mém. Mus. Roy. Hist. Nat. Belg. 32.

Leriche, M. (1927). Les poissons de la molasse suisse.–Mém. Soc. Paléont. Suisse 46/47.

Leriche, M. (1951). Les poissons tertiaires de la Belgique (supplément).–Mém. Inst. Roy. Sci. Nat. Belg., 118, 475–600.

Lundberg, J. G. (1975). The fossil catfishes of North America.–Mus. Paleont., Univ. Michigan, Papers on Paleont., 11, (Claude W. Hibbard Memorial Volume 2), 1–51.

Meyer, H. v. (1852) Fossile Fische aus dem Tertiärthon von Unter-Kirchberg an der Iller.–Palaeontographica 2, 85–113.

Micklich, N. (1978). Palaeoperca proxima, ein neuer Knochenfisch aus dem Mittel-Eozän von Messel bei Darmstadt.–Senckenbergiana lethaea 59, 483–501.

Nelson, G. J. (1973). Notes on the structure and relationships of certain Cretaceous and Eocene Teleostean fishes.–Am. Mus. Novitates 2524, 1–31.

Nelson, G. J. (1973). Relationships of clupeomorphs, with remarks on the structure of the lower jaw in fishes.–Zool. J. Linn. Soc. 53, Suppl. 1, 333–349.

Nybelin, O. (1964). Versuch einer taxonomischen Revision der jurassischen Fischgattung Thrissops AGASSIZ.–Göteborgs K. Vet. Vitterh. Samh. Hand. F. 9B, 1–44.

Nybelin, O. (1966). On certain Triassic and Liassic representatives of the family Pholido phoridae.–Bull. Brit. Mus. (Nat. Hist.) Geol., 11, 351–432.

Nybelin, O. (1967). Versuch einer taxonomischen Revision der Anaethalion- Arten des Weissjura Deutschlands.–Acta Reg. Soc. Sci. Litt. Gothoburg., Zoologica 2, 1–53.

Nybelin, O. (1973). Comments on the caudal skeleton of actinopterygians.–Zool. J. Linn. Soc. 53, Suppl. 1, 369–372.

Nybelin, O. (1974). A revision of the leptolepid fishes.–Acta Regiae Societatis scientia rum et litterarum gothoburgensis. Zoologica, 9, 1–202.

Obrhelova, N. (1967). Cyprinoidei (Pisces) aus dem Hangenden des miozänen Braunkoh lenflözes Nordböhmens.–Palaeontographica 126A, 141–179.

Obrhelova, N. (1969). Die Karpfenfische im tschechoslowakischen Süsswassertertiär.–Casopsis pro mineral. a. geol. 14, 39–52.

Obrhelova, N. (1978). Die Gattung Umbra WALBAUM im nordböhmischen Tertiär. Ent wicklungsgeschichte der Esocoidei BERG im Lichte der funktionalen Analyse.–Acta Mus. Nat. Pragae 36b, 119–171, Prag.

Parenti, L. R. (1981). A phylogenetic and biogeographic analysis of cyprinodontiform fishes (Teleostei, Atherinomorpha).–Bull. Am. Mus. Nat. Hist., 168, 335–557.

Patterson, C. (1963). A review of Mesozoic Acanthopterygian fishes with special reference to those of the English Chalk. .–Phil. Trans. R. Soc., London 739B, 213–482.

Literature

Patterson, C. (1970). Two Upper Cretaceous salmoniform fishes from the Lebanon.–Bull. Brit. Mus. (Nat. Hist.) Geol., 19, 205–296.

Patterson, C. (1984). Chanoides, a marine Eocene otophysan fish (Teleostei: Ostario physi).–J. Vert. Paleont., 4, 430–456.

Patterson, C. and Rosen, D. E. (1977). Review of ichthyodectiform and other Mesozoic teleost fishes and the theory and practice of classifying fossils.–Bull. Am. Mus. Nat. Hist., 158, 81–172.

Pauca, M. (1931). Die fossile Fauna und Flora aus dem Oligozän von Suslanesti-Muscel in Rumänien.–Ann. Inst. Gel. Romanien, 16 , 9–99.

Pictet, F.-J. and Humbert, A. (1866). Nouvelles recherches sur les poissons fossiles du Mont Liban.–J.-B. Baillière et fils, Paris.

Rayner, D. H. (1937). On Leptolepis bronni AGASSIZ. - Ann. Mag. Nat. Hist. 19, 46–74.

Roberts, T. R. (1973). Interrelationships of ostariophysans.–Zool. J. Linn. Soc. 53, Suppl. , 373–395.

Rosen, D. E. (1973). Interrelationships of higher euteleostean fishes.–Zool. J. Linnean Soc. 53, Suppl. 1, 397–513.

Rosen, D. E. (1982). Teleostean interrelationships, morphological function and evolution ary inference.–Amer. Zool., 22, 261–273.

Rosen, D. E. and Parenti, L. R. (1981). Relationships of Oryzias, and the groups of atherinomorph fishes.–Amer. Mus. Novitates, 2719, 1–25.

Rosen, D. E. and Patterson, C. (1969). The structure and relationships of the paracanthop terygian fishes.–Bull. Am. Mus. Nat. Hist. 141, 357–474.

Saint-Seine, P. de (1949). Les Poissons de calcaires lithographiques de Cerin (Ain).–Nouv. Arch. Mus. Hist. Nat. Lyon 2, 1–357.

Saint-Seine, P. de (1955). L'évolution des Actinoptérygiens.–Probl. actuels Paléont. (1955), 27–34.

Schaeffer, B. (1947). Cretaceous and Tertiary Actinopterygian fishes from Brazil.–Bull. Amer. Mus. Nat. Hist. 89, 40 pp.

Siegfried, P. (1954). Die Fischfauna des westfälischen Ober-Senons.–Palaeontographica 106 A, 1–36.

Silva Santos, Rubens da, (1968). A Formacao Santana e sua Paleoictiofauna.–Divisao de Geologia e Mineralogia, D. N. P. M., Rio de Janeiro.

Sorbini, L. (1975). Evoluzione e distribuzione del genere fossile Eolates e suoi rapporti con il genere attuale Lates (Pisces, Centropomidae).–In Studi e Ricerche sui Giace menti Terziari di Bolca. II. Miscellanea Paleontologica, 1–54, Museo Civico di Storia Naturale di Verona, Verona.

Sorbini, L. (1975). Studio paleontologico di Acropoma lepidotus (AGASSIZ). Pisces, Acropomidae.–In Studi e Ricerche sui Giacementi Terziari di Bolca. II. Miscellanea Paleontologica, 205–232. Museo Civico di Storia Naturali di Verona, Verona.

Sorbini, L. (1979). Segnalazione di un plettognato cretacico Plectocretacicus nov. gen.–Boll. Mus. Civ. St. Nat. Verona IV 1–4.

Sorbini, L. (1983). L'ittiofauna fossile di Bolca e le sue relazioni biogeografiche con i pesci attuali: Vicarianza o Dispersione?–Boll. della Soc. Paleont. Ital. 22, n. 1–2, 108–118.

Literature

Sorbini, L. and Bottura, C. (1987). Bajaichthys elegans, an Eocene Lampridiform from Bolca (Italy).–Boll. Mus. Civ. St. Nat. Verona 14, 369–380.

Sorbini, L. and Bottura, C. (1987). Antigonia veronensis, an Eocene caproid from Bolca (Italy).–Boll. Mus. Civ. St. Nat. Verona 14, 255–260.

Sorbini, L. (1987). Biogeography and Climatology of Pliocene and Messinian fossil fish of Eastern-Central Italy.–Boll. Mus. Civ. St. Nat. Verona 14, 1–85.

Switchenskaya, A. A. (1973). Fossil mugiliforms of the USSR.–Moskau, Nauka, 63 pp.

Sytchevskaya, E. K. (1987). Palaeogene freshwater fish fauna of the USSR and Mon golia.–Transactions 29, 157 pp.

Taverne, L. (1975). Considérations sur la position systématique des genres Leptolepis et Allothrissops au sein des Téléostéens primitifs et sur l'origine et le polyphylétisme des poissons Téléostéens.–Act. Roy. Belg. Bull. Cl. Sci. 61, 336–371.

Taverne, N. (1977). Ostéologie et position systématique du genre Thrissops AGASSIZ (Jurassique supérieur de l'Europe occid. au sein des Téléostéens primitifs).–Geobios 10, 5–33.

Tintori, A. (1990) The actinoperygian fish *Prohalecites* from the Triassic of Northern Italy. Palaeontologie, 33, 1 , 155 - 174

Tyler, J. C. (1975). A new species of Boxfish from the Eocene of Monte Bolca, Italy, the first unquestionable fossil record of the Ostraciontidae. In Studie e Ricerche sui Giaci menti Terziari di Bolca. II. Miscellanea Paleontologica, 103–126. Museo Civico di Storia Naturale di Verona, Verona.

Tyler, J. C. (1975). A new species of triacanthid fish (Plectognathi) from the Eocene of Monte Bolca, Italy, representing a new subfamily ancestral to the Triodontidae and the other gymnodonts.–In Studi e Ricerche sui Giacimenti Terziari di Bolca. II. Miscellanea Paleontologica, 103–126. Museo Civico di Storia Naturale di Verona.

Voigt, E. (1934). Die Fische aus der mitteleozänen Braunkohle des Geiseltales.–Nova Acta Leopoldina 2, 42–62.

Wagner, A. (1859). Monographie der fossilen Fische des fränkisch- oberpfälzischen litographischen Schiefers.–Geol. Anz. Akad. Wiss. München 49, 13–19.

Weiler, W. (1922–1928). Beiträge zur Kenntnis der tertiären Fische des Mainzer Beckens. I and II.–Abh. Hess. Geol. L.-A. 6 and 8.

Weiler, W. (1928). Fische aus dem rumänischen Tertiär.–Senckenbergiana 10.

Weiler, W. (1932). Die Fischfauna der oberen und unteren Meeresmolasse Oberbayerns.–N. Jb. Min. Geol. etc. 68 B 305–352.

Weiler, W. (1956). Über eine neue Gattung der Welse (Siluridae) aus dem Pliozän von Willershausen.–Paläont. Z. 30, 180–189.

Weitzmann, S. H. (1974). Osteology and evolutionary relationships of the Sternoptychi dae, with a new classification of stomiatoid families.–Bull. Am. Mus. Nat. Hist. 153, 329–478.

White, E. J. (1956). Eocene fishes in Alabama.–Bull. Amer. Palaeont. 36, Nr. 156, 1–34.

Wilson, M. V. H. (1977). Middle Eocene Freshwater Fishes from British Columbia.–Life Sci. Contrib. Roy. Ont. Mus. 113, 1–61.

Literature

Wilson, M. V. H. (1978). Eohiodon woodruffi n. spec. from the Middle Eocene Klondike Mountain Formation near Republic, Washington.–Can. J. Earth Sci. 15, 679–678.

Wilson, M. V. H. (1979). A second species of Libotonius from the Eocene of Washington State.–Copeia 1979, 399–405.

Wilson, M. V. H. (1980). Oldest known Esox (Pisces: Esocidae), part of a new Palaeocene teleost fauna from western Canada.–Can. J. Earth Sci. 17, 307–312.

Wilson, M. V. H. (1984). Osteology of the Palaeocene teleost Esox tiemani.–Palaeontology, 27, 597–608.

Wilson, M. V. H. (1984). Year classes and sexuell dimorphism in the Eocene Catostomid fish Amyzon aggregatum.–J. Vertebr. Paleont. 3, 137–142.

Woodward, A. S. (1891–1901). Catalogue of the fossil fishes in the British Museum.– Band I–IV., London.

Woodward, A. S. (1895). The fishes of the Talbragar Beds (Jurassic).–Mem. Geol. Surv. New South Wales–Palaeontographica 9, 1–27.

Woodward A. S. (1916). The fossil fishes of the English Wealden and Purbeck Formations.–Part II. Publ. Palaeont. Soc., London, 70 , 49–104.

Woodward, A. S. (1942). Some new and little known Upper Cretaceous fishes from Mount Lebanon.–Ann. Mag. Nat. Hist. 9, 537–568.

Woodward, A. S. (1942). The beginning of the Teleostean fishes.–Ann. Mag. Nat. Hist. 9, 902–912.

Zambelli, R. (1975). Note sui Pholidophoriformes. I. Parapholidophorus nybelini gen. n. sp. n.–Istituto Lombardo. Accademia di Scienze e Lettere. (B) 109, 3–49.

Zambelli, R. (1977–1978). Note sui Pholidophoriformes. II. Pholidoctenus serianus gen. n. sp. n.–Accademia Nazionale dei XL, Serie V, III, 1–125.

Zambelli, R., (1980). Note sui Pholidophoriformes. III Contributo Pholidophorus gerva suttii sp. n.–Riv. del Mus. Civ. Sc. Nat. "E. Caffi" 1 5–37.

Zambelli, R. (1980). Note sui Pholidophoriformes. IV Contributo Pholidorhynchodon malzannii gen. n. sp. n.–Riv. Mus. Sc. Nat. BG. 2, 129–159.

Zambelli, R. (1980). Note sui Pholidophoriformess. V Contributo: I Pholidophoridae dell'alta Valvestino (Brescia, Italia)–"Natura Bresciana" Ann. Mus. Civ. St. Nat. Brescia 17, 77–88.

SARCOPTERYGII (Lobe-finned Fishes)

Andrews, S. M. (1973). Interrelationships of crossopterygians.–Zool. J. Linn. Soc. 53, Suppl. 1, 137–177.

Andrews, S. M. (1985). Rhizodont crossopterygian fish from the Dinantian of Foulden, Berwickshire, Scotland, with a re-evaluation of this group.–Trans. Roy. Soc. Edinburgh, Earth Sci. 76, 67–95.

Bardack, D. (1974). A larval from the Pennsylvanian of Illinois.–J. Paleont. 53, 988–993.

Bjerring, H. C. (1973). Relationships of coelacanthiforms.–Zool. J. Linnean. Soc. 53, Suppl. 1, 179–205, London.

Literature

Broom, R. (1905). On a species of Coelacanthus from the Upper Beaufort Beds of Aliwal North.–Rec. Albany Mus. 1, p. 5.

Compagno, L. J. V. (1979). Coelacanths: Shark relatives or bony fishes ? In McCoster and Lagios (eds.), The Biology and Physiology of the living coelacanth.–Calif. Acad. Sci. Occ. Papers 134, 45–55.

Cooper, C. F. (1937). The middle Devonian fish fauna of Achanarras.–Trans. Roy. Soc. Edinburgh 59, 223–240.

Dehm, R. (1956). Ein Coelacanthide aus dem mittleren Keuper Frankens.–N. Jb. Geol. Paläont., Mh., 148–153.

Denison, R. H. (1968). Early Devonian lungfishes from Wyoming, Utah and Idaho.–Fieldiana, Geol. 17, 353–413.

Denison, R. H. (1968). The evolutionary significants of the earliest known lungfish Urano lophus.–Nobel. Symp. No. 4, 247–257.

Denison, R. H. (1974). New Pennsylvanian lungfishes from Illinois.–Fieldiana, Geol. 12, 193–211.

Dollo, L. (1895). Sur la phylogénie des Dipneustes.–Bull. Soc. Belge Géol. 9, 79–128.

Fraas, E. (1904). Ceratodus priscus FRAAS aus dem Hauptbuntsandstein.–Mitt. Ber. oberrhein. geol. Ver. 37, 30–32.

Gardiner, B. G. (1960). A revision of certain Actinopterygian and Coelacanth fishes, chiefly from Lower Lias.–Bull. Brit. Mus. (Nat. Hist.) Geol. 4 239–384.

Graham-Smith, W. and Westoll. T. S. (1937). On a new long-headed Dipnoan fish from the Upper Devonian of Scaumenac Bay, P. Q., Canada.–Trans. Roy. Soc. Edinburgh 59, 241–266.

Gregory, W. K. (1951). Evolution emerging. Macmillan, New York.

Gross, W. (1956). Über Crossopterygier und Dipnoer aus dem baltischen Oberdevon im Zusammenhang einer vergleichenden Untersuchung des Porenkanalsystems paläozoi scher Agnathen und Fische.–Kgl. Svensk. Vetensk. Handl. (4) 5, 1–140.

Gross, W. (1964). Polyphyletische Stämme im System der Wirbeltiere ?–Zool. Anz. 173, H 1, 1–22.

Hills, E. S. (1933). On a primitive Dipnoan from the Middle Devonian rocks of New South Wales.–Ann. Mag. Nat. Hist. (10) 11, 634–643.

Hills, E. S. (1943). The ancestra of Choanichthyes.–Australian J. Sci. 6, Nr. 1, 21–23, Sydney.

Holmes, E. B. (1985). Are lungfish a sister group of tetrapods.–Biol. J. Linn. Soc. 25, 379–397.

Jaekel, O. (1890). Über Phaneropleuron und Hemictenodus.–S.üB. Ges. Naturforsch. Freunde Berlin, 21. January, 1–8.

Jarvik, E. (1937). On the species of Eusthenopteron found in Russia and the Baltic states.–Bull. Geol. Inst. Uppsala 27, 62–127.

Jarvik, E. (1949). On the Middle Devonian Crossopterygians from the Hornelan Field in Western Norway.–Univ. Bergen Arb. 1948, 1–48.

Jarvik, E. (1950). Middle Devonian Vertebrates from Canning Land and Wegeners Halvö (East Greenland). Part II. Crossopterygii.–Medd. om Gronland 96, Nr. 4, 1–132.

Literature

Jarvik, E. (1950). Note on Middle Devonian Crossopterygians from the eastern part of Gauss Halvö, East Greenland. Appendix: An attempt at a correlation of the Upper Old Red Sandstone of East Greenland with the marine sequence.–Medd. om Gronland 149, Nr. 6, 1–20.

Jarvik, E. (1950). On some osteolepiform Crossopterygians from the Upper Old Red Sandstone of Scotland.–Kgl. Svensk. Vetensk. Handl. (3) 2, 1–35.

Jarvik, E. (1962). Les Porolepiformes et l'origine des urodèles.–Colloques internat. Cent. nat. Rech. scient. 104, 87–101.

Jarvik, E. (1968). The systematic position of the Dipnoi.–Nobel. Symp. 4, 223–245.

Jarvik, E. (1972). Middle and Upper Devonian Porolepiformes from East Greenland with special reference to Glyptolepis groenlandica n. sp. and a discussion on the structure of the head in the porolepiformes.–Medd. Gronland 187 , 1–307.

Jarvik, E. (1980). Basic Structure and Evolution of Vertebrates.–Academic Press, London.

Jessen, H. (1966). Die Crossopterygier des Oberen Plattenkalkes (Devon) der Bergisch- Gladbach-Paffrather Mulde (Rheinisches Schiefergebirge) unter Berücksichtigung von amerikanischem und europäischem Onychodus-Material.–Ark. Zool. 18, 305–389.

Jessen, (1980). Lower Devonian Porolepiformes from the Canadian Arctic with special reference to Powichthys thorsteinssoni JESSEN.–Palaeontographica, 167 A, 180–214.

Kulczycki, J. (1960). Porolepis (Crossopterygii) from the Lower Devonian of the Holy Cross Mountains.–Acta Palaeont. Polonica 5, 66–106.

Lagios, M. D. (1979). The Coelacanths and the Chondrichthyes as sister groups: A review of shared apomorph characters and a cladistic analysis and reinterpretation. In McCosker und Lagios(Herausgeber), The biology and physiology of the living coela canth.–Calif. Acad. Sci. Occ. Papers 134, 25–44.

Lehman, J.-P. (1952). Etude complémentaire des Poissons de l'Eotrias de Madagascar.–Kgl. Svensk. Vetensk. Handl. (4) 2, 1–201.

Lehman, J.-P. (1955b). Les Dipneustes du Dévonien supérieur du Groenland.–C. R. Acad. Sci. 240, 995–997.

Lehman, J. P. (1959). Les Dipneustes du Dévonien Supérieur du Groenland.–Meddel. om Gronland 160 (4), 358.

Lehmann, W. M. and Westoll, T. S. (1952). A primitive dipnoan fish from the Lower Devonian of Germany.–Proc. Roy. Soc. 140 B.

Lehmann, W. M. and Westoll, T. S. (1956). Dipnorhynchus lehmanni WESTOLL, ein primitiver Lungenfisch aus dem rheinischen Unterdevon.–Paläont. Z. 30, 21–25.

Linck, O. (1962). Neuer Beitrag zur Kenntnis der Ceratodontiden der germanischen Trias (mit Ceratodus planasper n. sp. aus dem Oberen Muschelkalk, Ceratodus bovisrivi n. sp. und anderen Arten aus dem Mittleren Keuper.)–Jh. ver. vaterl. Naturkde. Würt temberg 117, 195–209.

Lund, R. and Lund, W. (1984). New genera and species of coelacanths from the Bear Gulch Limestone (Lower Carboniferous) of Montana, U. S. A.–Geobios 17 237–244.

Literature

Maisey, J. G. (1986). Coelacanths from the Lower Cretaceous of Brazil.–Am. Mus. Novitates 2866, 1–30.

Martin, M. (1979). Arganodus atlantis et Ceratodus arganensis, deux nouveaux Dipneu stes du Trias supérieur continental marocain.–C. R. Acad. Sci. Paris 289D, 89–92.

Martin, M. (1980). Revision of Ceratodus concinnus PLIENINGER–Stuttgarter Beitr. Naturk. 56B, 1–15.

Martin, M. (1981). Les Dipneustes et Actinistiens du Trias supérieur continental maro cain.–Stuttgarter Beitr. Naturk. 69B, 1–30.

Miles, R. S. (1977). Dipnoan (lungfish) skulls and the relationships of the group. : A study based on new species from the Devonian of Australia.–Zool. J. Linn. Soc. 61, 1–328.

Moy-Thomas, J. A. (1937). The Carboniferous Coelacanth fishes of Great Britain and Ireland.–Proc. Zool. Soc. London 107 B, 383–415.

Moy-Thomas, J. A. and Miles, R. S. (1971). Palaeozooic fishes (2d ed.). Chapman and Hall, London.

Nybelin, O. (1961). Über die Frage der Abstammung der rezenten primitiven Teleostier.–Paläont. Z. 35, 114–117.

Panchen, A. L. (1967). The nostrils of choanate fishes and early tetrapods.–Biol. Rev. 42, 374–420.

Reis, O. M. (1888). Die Coelacanthinen, mit besonderer Berücksichtigung der im Weissen Jura Bayerns vorkommenden Gattungen.–Palaeontographica 35, 1–96.

Ritchie, A. (1981). First complete specimen of the dipnoan Gosfordia truncata WOOD WARD from the Triassic of New South Wales.–Rec. Austral. Mus. 33, 606–615.

Romer, A. S. and Smith, H. J. (1934). American Carboniferous Dipnoans.–J. Geol. 42, 700–719.

Rosen, D. E., Forey, P. L., Gardiner, B. G. and Patterson, C. (1981). Lungfishes, tetra pods, paleontology and plesiomorphy.–Bull. Am. Mus. Nat. Hist. 167, 163–275.

Säve-Söderbergh, G. (1934). Some points of view concerning the evolution of the vertebrates and the classification of this group.–Ark. Zool. 26 A, 1–20.

Säve-Söderbergh, G. (1937). On Rhynchodipterus elginensis n. g. n. sp., representing a new group of Dipnoan-like Choanata from the Upper Devonian of East Greenland and Scotland.–Ark. Zool. 29 B , 1–18.

Säve-Söderbergh, G. (1952). On the skull of Chirodipterus wildungensis GROSS, an Upper Devonian dipnoan from Wildungen.–Handl. K. Svenska Vetenskapsakad. 3, 1–28.

Saint-Seine, P. de. (1949). Les poissons des calcaires lithographiques de Cerin.–Arch. Mus. Hist. Nat. Lyon 2, 1–357.

Schaeffer, B. (1941). A revision of Coelacanthus newarki and notes on the evolution of the girdles.–Am. Mus. Novitates 1110, 1–17.

Schaeffer, B. (1952). The triassic Coelacanth fish Diplurus, with observations on the evolution of the Coelacanthini.–Bull. Amer. Mus. Nat. Hist. 99, 25–78.

Schaeffer, B. (1954). Pariostegus, a Triassic Coelacanthid.–Notulae Nature Acad. nat. Sci. Philadelphia 251, 1–5.

Literature

Schaumberg, G. (1978). Neubeschreibung von Coelacanthus granulatus AGASSIZ (Actini stia, Pisces) aus dem Kupferschiefer von Richelsdorf (Perm, W.-Deutschland)–Paläont. Z. 52, 169–197.

Schultze, H.-P. (1973). Crossopterygier mit heterozerker Schwanzflosse aus dem Oberdevon Kanadas, nebst einer Beschreibung von Onychodontida-Resten aus dem Mitteldevon Spaniens und aus dem Karbon der USA.–Palaeontographica, 143 A, 188–208.

Schultze, H.-P. (1975). Die Lungenfisch-Gattung Conchopoma (Pisces, Dipnoi).–Senckenbergiana lethae 56, 191–231.

Schultze, H.-P. and Arsenault, M. (1985). The Panderichthyid fish Elpistostegea close relative of Tetrapods ?.–Palaeontology 28, 293–309.

Schultze, H.-P. and Arsenault, M. (1986). Quebecius quebecensis (WHITEAVES), a porolepiform crossopterygian from the late Devonian of Quebec, Canada.

Schweizer, R. (1966). Ein Coelacanthide aus dem Oberen Muschelkalk Göttingens.–Neues Jb. Geol. Paläont. Abh. 125, 216–225.

Stensiö, E. (1921). Triassic Fishes from Spitzbergen.–Part 1, Vienna, 307 pp.

Stensiö, E. (1932). Triassic fishes from East Greenland.–Medd. om Gronland 83, 1–345.

Thomson, K. A. and Hahn, K. V. (1968). Growth and form in fossil rhipidistian fishes (Crossopterygii).–J. Zool. 156, 199–223.

Thomson, K. S. (1962) Rhipidistian classification in relation to the origin of the tetra pods.–Breviora, Mus. Comp. Zool. 166, 1–12.

Thomson, K. S. (1968). A critical review on certain aspects of the diphyletic theory of tetrapod relationships.–Nob. Symp. 4, 285–305.

Thomson, K. S. and Campbell, K. S. W. (1971). The structure and relationships of the primitive Devonian lungfish Dipnorhynchus suesmilchi (ETHERIDGE).–Peabody Mus. Nat. Hist. Bull. 38, VI + 109 S.

Vorobjeva, E. I. (1959). A new genus of a crossopterygian fish, Platycephalichthys, from the Upper Devonian of Lovat River.–Paleont. J. Akad. Nauka UdSSR 1959, 95–106, (russ.).

Vorobjeva, E. I. (1967). Triassic Ceratods from South Fergana and remarks on the systematics and phylogeny of Ceratodontids.–Paleont. J. Transl. 1, 80–87.

Vorobjeva, E. I. (1975). Formenvielfalt und Verwandtschaftsbeziehungen der Osteolepi dida (Crossopterygii, Pisces).–Paläont. Z. 49, 44–45.

Vorobjewa, E. I. (1977). Morphology and the features of the evolution of crossopterygian fish.–Trudy Paleont. Inst. 163, 1–240. (russ.)

Watson, D. M. S. (1921). On the Coelacanth fish.–Ann. Mag. Nat. Hist. London (9) 8, 320–337.

Weitzel, K. (1926). Conchopoma gadiforme KNER, ein Lungenfisch aus dem Rotliegenden. Abh. Senckenberg. naturforsch. Ges. 40, 159–178.

Westoll, T. S. (1937). The Old Red Sandstone fishes of the north of Scotland.–Proc. Geol. Assoc. London 48, 13–45.

Westoll, T. S. (1948). On the evolution of Dipnoi.–In: G. L. Jepsen et al. (publ.), Genetics, Paleontology and Evolution, 121–184, Princeton.

White, E. (1954). The Coelacanthid fishes.–Ann. Rep. Smithsonian Inst. 1933, 351–360.

This is a quarry in the famous Posidonia Shales of the Lias of southern Germany at Holzmaden in Württemberg. As well as interesting fishes, many ichthyosaurs have been found here. Photo: Staatliches Museum für Naturkunde

Index of Genera and Synonyms

Current scientific names are normal.
Synonyms are in *italics*.

A

Acanthaspis = Macropetalichthys	126
Acanthodes	245
Acanthonemus	888
Acanthoniscus	299
Acanthonotus = Lepidopus	899
Acanthophoria = Acrogaster	716
Acanthopsis = Cobitis	591
Acanthorhina	231
Acanthurus	889
Acanus	792
Acentrophorus	375
Aceraspis	97
Acidorhynchus = Saurichthys	366
Acrodus = Acronemus	166
Acrodus = Janassa	164
Acrogaster	716
Acrolepis	277
Acronemus	166
Acropholis	278
Acropoma	816
Adiapneustes = Acronemus	166
Aechmodus = Dapedium	377
Aeduella	285
Aellopos	195
Aeoliscoides	766
Aeoliscus	763
Aeothrissa = Ctenothrissa	669
Aethalion = Anaethalion	500
Aethalionopsis	578
Aetheodontus	363
Aetheretmon	261
Aganodus = Orthacanthus	151
Agassizia = Asthenocormus	438
Agassizichthys = Macropetalichthys	126
Aipichthys	736
Alaspis	100
Alausa = Alosa	551
Albertonia	415
Allenypterus	943
Allothrissops	479
Alonsina = Clupea	552
Alosa	551
Alutera	933
Amblypterops = Paramblypterus	288
Amblypterus	283
Amblysemius	426
Amblyurus = Dapedium	377
Ameiurus	599
Amia	431
Amiatus = Amia	431
Amiopsis	432
Ammodytes	886
Amphicentrum = Chirodus	315
Amphiperca	793
Amphiplaga	674
Amphisile = Centriscus	764
Amphistium	850
Amyzon	593
Anacorax = Squalicorax	180
Anaethalion	500
Analectis	713
Ananogmius = Bananogmius	491
Anapterus = Paralepis	640
Anatiftopsis = Vernonaspis	77
Anelia = Pachylebias	708
Anenchelum = Lepidopus	899
Anglaspis	71
Anguilla	523
Anguillavus	524
Anguilloides	531
Anogmius = Bananogmius	491
Anomiophthalmus = Coelodus	393
Antigonia	750
Aoria	601
Apateolepis	258
Apateopholis	643
Apedodus = Holoptychius	966
Apendulus = Holoptychius	966
Aphanepygus	405
Aphanius	702
Aphnelepis	462
Apholidotos	327
Apogon	814
Apsopelix	501
Arambourgella	868
Araripichthys	744
Archaeogadus = Halec	634
Archaeoides = Archaeus	819
Archaeomaene	463
Archaeosemionotus = Semionotus	387
Archaeoteuthis = Pteraspis	84

1027

Index of Genera and Synonyms

Archaeotylus = Holodipterus	980
Archaephippus	851
Archaeus	819
Arduafrons	391
Argyropelecus	626
Arnoglossus	920
Ascalabos	469
Asiatolepis = Lycoptera	498
Asima = Menaspis	230
Asineops	675
Aspidopleurus = Prionolepis	653
Aspidorhynchus	446
Aspidorhynchus = Vinctifer	448
Aspius	579
Astephas	600
Asterodermus	196, 197
Asterodon = Colobodus	351
Asterolepis	141
Asthenocormus	438
Atherina	710
Atherstonia	300
Atopocephala	338
Atracauda	301
Atractosteus	373
Auchenaspis = Thyestes	104
Aulorhamphus	761
Aulostoma = Eoaulostomus	755
Aulostomoides	754
Auluxacanthus = Ischyodus	233
Aurata = Sparus	843
Australosomus	330
Auxis	900
Axelrodichthys	949

B

Bajaichthys	712
Baleiichthys	451
Bananogmius	491
Bathylagus	611
Batrachoides	693
Beaconia	339
Belantsea	165
Belemnobatis	198
Belgicaspis = Rhinopteraspis	85
Belichthys	302
Belone	701
Belonorhynchus = Saurichthys	366
Belonostmus = Belonostomus	447
Belonostomus	447
Belonostomus = Vinctifer	448
Benedenichthys = Benedenius	269
Benedenius	269
Benthesikyme = Dercetis	649
Berybolcensis	724
Berycomorus	723
Berycopsis = Platycormus	742
Besania	336
Birgeria	296
Birkenia	106
Blabe	794
Blenniomogeus = Notagogus	410
Blochius	911
Blotichthys	787
Bobasatrania	316
Bolcanguilla	541
Bolcyrus	535
Boltyshia	606
Boops	835
Boreaspis	101
Boreocentrarchus	803
Boreosomus	279
Bothriolepis	139, 140
Bothryolepis = Bothriolepis	140
Bothus	921
Bourbonella	286
Box = Boops	835
Brachipteraspis = Pteraspis	84
Brachyichthys = Heterolepidotus	428
Brachylebias	703
Brachyosteus	138
Brachyrhamphus	698
Brama	832
Brannerion	503
Bregmacerina	680
Bregmaceros	679
Brembodus	389
Broiliina = Gemuendina	120
Brookvalia	340
Brychaetus	496
Brycon	595
Byzenos = Janassa	164

C

Calamopleurus	433

Index of Genera and Synonyms

Calamostoma	768
Callignathus = Notagogus	410
Callipterys	882
Callistiopterus	962
Callopterus	465
Camptaspis = Cephalaspis	103
Camylopleuron = Ctenodus	988
Canadapteraspis	79
Canadipterus = Scaumenacia	987
Canobius	265
Canowindra	974
Capros	751
Caprovesposus	894
Carangodes	915
Carangopsis	820
Carangopsis = Seriola	826
Caranx	821
Carcharocles	178
Carcharodon = Carcharocles	178
Cardipeltis	86
Caridosuctor	946
Carrionellus	704
Caspiolus = Alosa	551
Cassandra = Leptosomus	661
Catervariolus	459
Catopterus = Dipterus	982
Catopterus = Redfieldius	348
Caturus	424
Centriscus	764
Centrophoroides	190
Cephalaspis	102, 103
Cephenoplosus = Pachycormus	442
Ceratoichthys	822, 823
Ceratoscopelus	655
Cestracion = Heterodontus	171
Chaenobryttus	804
Chaetodon	857
Chagrinia	941
Chanoides	575
Chanos	573
Charitosomus	576
Cheiracanthus	246
Cheirodopsis	314
Cheirodus = Chirodus	315
Cheirolepis	254
Cheirothrix	645
Chimaeracanthus = Ischyodus	233
Chirocentrites	480
Chirodipterus	981
Chirodus	315
Chirothrix = Cheirothrix	645
Chondrenchelys	217
Chondrosteus	368
Chrysophrys = Sparus	843
Cimolichthys	652
Cionichthys	341
Citula = Caranx	821
Cladocyclus	481
Cladodus = Cladoselache	154
Cladodus = Stethacanthus	159
Cladodus = Symmorium	156
Cladoselache	154
Cleithrolepidina	360
Cleithrolepis	361
Climatius	238
Climaxodus = Janassa	164
Clinitrachus	884
Clinus	885
Clupavus	470
Clupea	552
Clupeops = Clupea	552
Clupionella = Alosa	551
Cobitis	591
Cobitopsis	697
Coccoderma	950
Coccodus	392
Coccolepis	298
Coccosteus	131, 132
Coelacanthopsis	947
Coelacanthus	951
Coelodus	393
Coeloperca = Perca	810
Colobodus	351
Colpopholis = Notogoneus	577
Commentrya	287
Compsacanthus = Orthacanthus	151
Conchiopsis = Conchopoma	991
Conchiopsis = Rhabdoderma	948
Conchopoma	991
Conger	536
Conodus = Caturus	424
Cooyoo	482
Copeichthys = Diplomystus	545
Corax = Squalicorax	180
Coregonus	616
Cornuboniscus	268
Corydoras	604
Corysodon	173

1029

Index of Genera and Synonyms

Cosmodus = Coelodus	393
Cosmopoma = Paramblypterus	288
Cottopsis	780
Cottus	781
Crossognathus	502
Crossopholis	370
Crossorhinops = Phorcynis	176
Crossorhinus = Phorcynis	176
Cryptoberyx	733
Ctenocephalichthys	725
Ctenodentex	836
Ctenodus	988
Ctenothrissa	669
Ctenurella	122
Cybium = Scomberomorus	906
Cyclobatis	206
Cyclopoma	785
Cyclospondylus = Euthynotus	439
Cyclothone	621
Cymatodus = Janassa	164
Cyprinus	580, 581

D

Dactylopogon	656
Dactylopterus	775
Daitingichthys	510
Dalpiaziella	525
Damocles	157
Dandya	376
Dapalis	795
Dapedium	377
Dapedius = Dapedium	377
Dapedoglossus = Phareodus	497
Daptinus = Saurodon	490
Dartmuthia	95
Dastilbe	504
Dasyatis = Heliobatis	213
Dasybatus = Heliobatis	213
Davichthys	505
Delphyodontos	234
Deltoptychius	228
Dendrodus = Holoptychius	966
Dentex	837
Dercetis	649
Dermatoptychus = Osmeroides	513
Diademodus	155
Diaphorognathus = Boreosomus	279
Dicellopyge	295
Dichelospondylus = Belonostomus	447
Dictaspis = Irregulareaspis	72
Dictea = Janassa	164
Dictyopyge	342
Digoria	739
Dinichthys = Dunkleosteus	136
Dinopteryx	735
Diodon	938
Diplacanthus	242
Diplodus	838
Diplodus = Orthacanthus	151
Diplognathus	146
Diplolepis = Sauropsis	444
Diplomystus	545
Diplopterax = Gyroptychius	968
Diplopterus = Gyroptychius	968
Diplurus	952
Dipnorhynchus	978
Dipterichthys	867
Dipteroma = Paramblypterus	288
Dipteronotus	362
Dipterus	982
Diptoterus = Gyroptychius	968
Discoserra	320
Dissodus = Orthacanthus	151
Disticholepis	406
Ditaxiodus = Caturus	424
Dokkoderma = Coccoderma	950
Domeykos	553
Doryaspis	81
Dorypterus	326
Drepanaspis	87, 88
Drepanephorus = Heterodontus	171
Drydenius	273
Ductor	824
Dules	807
Dumfregia = Coelacanthopsis	947
Dunkleosteus	136
Dyctiaspidella = Irregulareaspis	72

E

Eastmanosteus	137
Ebenaqua	317
Echeneis	818
Echidnocephalus	521
Echinochimaera	232

Index of Genera and Synonyms

Ecrinesomus	318
Ectosteorhachis	967
Edestes = Edestus	161
Edestodus = Edestus	161
Edestus	161
Elaveria = Commentrya	287
Ellimma	546
Ellimma = Knightia	559
Ellimmichthys	547
Ellipos = Knightia	559
Elonichthys	274
Elpistostege	973
Emmachaere = Epinephelus	796
Empedaspis	78
Empo = Cimolichthys	652
Enchelion	537
Enchodus	630
Endactis = Caturus	424
Engraulis	571
Enigmaichthys	378
Enneles = Calamopleurus	433
Enoplosus	859
Enzichthys	309
Eoarchegonaspis = Vernonaspis	77
Eoaulostomus	755
Eobothus	922
Eoclupea = Gaudryella	612
Eocottus	782
Eoctenodus = Dipterus	982
Eoeugnathus	425
Eogaleus	185
Eohiodon	499
Eoholocentrum	726
Eolabroides	876
Eolactoria	926
Eolamprogrammus	690
Eolates	786
Eomesodon	394
Eomyctophum	657
Eomyrophis	527
Eomyrus = Eomyrophis	527
Eoperca = Perca	810
Eoplatax	854, 855
Eoplectus	929
Eoproscinetes	399
Eosalmo	617, 618
Eosemionotus	379
Eosphaeramia	815
Eotetraodon	937
Eozanclus	890
Ephippus	852
Ephippus = Archaephippus	851
Epinephelus	796
Epinnula	896
Equula = Leiognathus	831
Eretima = Apogon	814
Erichalcis	554
Erisichthe = Protosphyraena	443
Erismatopterus	676
Esconichthys	994
Escuminaspis = Cephalaspis	103
Esox	607, 608
Etrumeus	555
Eubiodectes	483
Eucephalaspis = Cephalaspis	103
Eucompsacanthus = Orthacanthus	151
Eulepidotus = Heterolepidotus	428
Eupalaeoniscus = Palaeoniscum	292
Euplorodus = Colobodus	351
Eurecana = Turseodus	294
Euryarthra = Aellopos	195
Eurycormus	452
Eurygnathus = Enchodus	630
Eurylepis = Haplolepis	323
Eurynothus	312
Eurynotus = Eurynothus	312
Eurypholis	633
Eurysomus	313
Eusthenopteron	971
Euthacanthus	239
Euthynotus	439
Eutrichiurides	898
Exellia	853
Exocoetoides	646
Expleuracanthus	150
Expleuracanthus = Triodus	152

F

Falcatus	158
Fistularia = Parasynarcualis	760
Fistularioides	759
Fleurantia	985
Fraenkelaspis = Anglaspis	71
Fubarichthys	303
Fundulus	705
Furo	427

Index of Genera and Synonyms

G

Gadella	678
Gadus	681
Galeorhinus	186
Ganocrodus = Elonichthys	274
Ganolepis	275
Ganopristis = Sclerorhynchus	209
Ganopristodus = Uronemus	990
Gardineria	304
Gasteracanthus = Mene	830
Gasterorhamphosus	762
Gasterosteus	752
Gaudryella	612
Gemuendina	119, 120
Geomichthys = Palaeoniscum	292
Geophagus	861
Gephyroberyx	717
Gephyrura = Fundulus	705
Gharbouria	620
Gibbodon	390
Gillicus	484
Gilpichthys	115
Glaucolepis = Pteronisculus	293
Globulodus = Eurysomus	313
Glossodus = Coelodus	393
Glyphisoma = Capros	751
Glyptolepis	965
Glyptosteus = Bothriolepis	140
Gobio	582
Gobius	887
Gonatodus	276
Goniolepis = Hoplopteryx	718
Gonostoma	622
Gosfordia	992
Gosiutichthys	556
Goslinophis	534
Grammatorcynus	901
Griphognathus	979
Guildayichthys	319
Gwynnedichthys = Turseodus	294
Gymnoniscus = Phanerosteon	264
Gymnosaurichthys = Saurichthys	366
Gyrodus	395
Gyrolepis	289
Gyrolepis = Porolepis	964
Gyronchus	396
Gyropleurodus = Heterodontus	171
Gyroptychius	968

H

Habroichthys	333
Hadronector	944
Hajulia	514
Hakelia	658
Halec	634
Halecula = Etrumeus	555
Hamiltonichthys	167
Hamodus = Glyptolepis	965
Haplolepis	323
Hardistiella	113
Harpagofututor	218
Haywardia	321
Heintzaspis = Macropetalichthys	126
Helichthys	343
Helicoprion	160
Heliobatis	212, 213
Helmintholepis = Apsopelix	501
Hemicalypterus	380
Hemicladodus = Chirodus	315
Hemicyclaspis	98
Hemicyclolepis = Hoplopteryx	718
Hemigonolepis = Hoplopteryx	718
Hemirhamphus	699
Hemirhynchus = Belonostomus	447
Hemirhynhus = Homorhynchus	913
Hemisaurida	635
Hemiteleaspis = Aceraspis	97
Hemithyrsites	897
Heptadiodon = Diodon	938
Heterodontus	171
Heterolepidotus	428
Heteropetalus	170
Heterostrophus	381
Heterothrissa	670
Heterothrissops = Euthynotus	439
Hexanchus	188
Hilsa	557
Hippocampus	770, 771
Hirella	99
Histiocephalus = Histionotophorus	695
Histionotophorus	695
Histionotus	407
Histiothrissa	558
Histiurus = Diplomystus	545

Index of Genera and Synonyms

Holaspis = Poraspis	74
Holcodon = Enchodus	630
Holocentrus	727
Holodipterus	980
Holodus = Holodipterus	980
Holophagoides = Diplurus	952
Holophagus	959
Holoptychius	966
Holopygus = Rhabdoderma	948
Holurus	270
Homalacanthus	247
Homoeolepis = Tetragonolepis	388
Homorhynchus	913
Homosteus	129
Homostius = Homosteus	129
Homothorax = Bothriolepis	140
Hoplopteryx	718
Howqualepis	290
Hulettia	468
Humbertia	613
Humilichthys	666
Hybodus	168
Hygophum	659
Hyperlophus = Diplomystus	545
Hyporhamphus	700
Hypospondylus = Xenacanthus	153
Hypsidoris	598
Hypsocormus	440
Hypterus = Atherstonia	300

I

Ianassa = Janassa	164
Ichthyoceros	397
Ichthyodectes	485
Ichthyokentema	460
Ichthyorhynchus = Saurichthys	366
Ichthyotringa	644
Ictalurus = Ameiurus	599
Idrissia	623
Iniopera	220
Iniopteryx	219
Ionoscopus	466
Irregulareaspis	72
Ischnacanthus	244
Ischnolepis	344
Ischyodus	233
Ischypetrus = Semionotus	387
Ischyrecephalus = Enchodus	630
Ismene = Prolebias	709
Isodon = Enchodus	630
Isopholis = Furo	427
Istieus	515
Isurichthys	902

J

Jacobulus	416
Jagorina	121
Jamoythius	105
Janassa	164

K

Kentuckia	255
Knightia	559
Krambergeria = Palimphyes	903
Kushlukia	895

L

Labrax = Acropoma	816
Labrus	877
Lambdodus = Stethacanthus	159
Lamnodus = Holoptychius	966
Lampanyctus	660
Lanarkia	89
Larnovaspis	82
Lasalichthys	345
Lasanius	112
Laugia	960
Lawnia	284
Lebias	706
Lebonichthys	517
Lednevia	817
Legendrelepis	111
Legnonotus	408
Leiacanthus = Hybodus	168
Leiognathus	831
Lepidaspis	94
Lepidocottus	783
Lepidopides = Lepidopus	899
Lepidopus	899
Lepidotes	382

1033

Index of Genera and Synonyms

Lepidotus = Lepidotes	382
Lepisosteus	374
Leptecodon	631
Leptichthys = Apsopelix	501
Leptolepides	471
Leptolepis	472
Leptolepis = Leptolepides	471
Leptosomus	661
Leptotrachelus = Dercetis	649
Lerichaspis = Pteraspis	84
Lestidiops	639
Leuciscus	583
Liassolepis = Leptolepis	472
Libanoberyx	719
Libotonius	673
Libys	953
Lichia = Seriola	826
Lignobrycon = Triportheus	597
Liodesmus	434
Liopsetta	924
Lissoberyx	720
Lissolepis = Furo	427
Lissoprion = Helicoprion	160
Listracanthus = Deltoptychius	228
Lithofundulus	707
Lochmocercus	942
Logania	91
Lompoquia	844
Lophiurus = Liodesmus	434
Lophius	694
Lophosteus = Dartmuthia	95
Lota	682
Lotimorpha = Palaeogadus	686
Luganoia	337
Lunaspis	124, 125
Lusitanichthys	594
Lycoptera	498
Lyctaspis = Doryaspis	81

M

Macracara = Geophagus	861
Macraulostomus	756
Macrepistius	429
Macroaethes	331
Macrobrachius = Bothriolepis	140
Macromesodon = Gyronchus	396
Macropetalichthys	126
Macropomoides	954
Macrosemius	409
Macrostoma = Amphistium	850
Macrourogaleus	181
Mallotus	614
Manlietta	352
Maurolicus	627
Mayomyzon	114
Mcconichthys	671
Mecolepis = Haplolepis	323
Megalolepis = Palaeogadus	686
Megalurites = Diodon	938
Megalurus = Urocles	436
Megapteriscus	259
Megapus = Cheirothrix	645
Megaselachus = Carcharocles	178
Megastoma = Leptolepis	472
Megistopuspholis = Cheirothrix	645
Meidiichthys	353
Mekolepis = Haplolepis	323
Meletta = Sprattus	569
Menaspis	229, 230
Mendocinia = Mendocinichthys	354
Mendocinichthys	354
Mene	829, 830
Mentzichthys	262
Meriamella = Gasterosteus	752
Meridensia	355
Meristodon = Hybodus	168
Merluccius	689
Mesacanthus	248
Mesembroniscus	280
Mesiteia	177
Mesodon = Gyronchus	396
Mesogaster = Ramphognathus	711
Mesolepis	310
Mesopoma	266
Mesturus	398
Metapomichthys = Capros	751
Micraspis = Hirella	99
Microbrachium = Microbrachius	142
Microbrachius	142
Microcoelia = Sendenhorstia	512
Microdon = Eoproscinetes	399
Microdon = Proscinetes	402
Microhaplolepis	324
Micromesistius	683
Micropristis	207
Micropteryx = Seriola	826

Index of Genera and Synonyms

Miguashaia	955
Milananguilla	533
Millerosteus	133
Minestaspis = Cephalaspis	103
Mioplosus	808, 809
Molybdichthys	346
Monacanthus	934
Morhus = Gadus	681
Morone	788
Moythomasia	256
Muensterichthys	305
Mugil	873
Mullus	846
Mylomyrus	528
Myriolepis	291
Myripristis	728

N

Nannolepis	334
Narcine	211
Narcobatus = Torpedo	210
Naseus	891
Naseus = Tylerichthys	893
Naso = Naseus	891
Nematonotus	662
Nematoptychius	271
Nemopteryx	684
Neopercis	883
Noemacheilus	592
Notagogus	410
Notelops	520
Notidanus = Hexanchus	188
Notogoneus	577
Nursallia	400
Nyctophus	663

O

Ochlodus = Orthacanthus	151
Odonteus	865
Ohiodurolites = Macropetalichthys	126
Oligobalistes	935
Oligoplarchus	805
Omalopleurus = Dapedium	377
Omosoma	740
Omosomopsis	741
Onobrosmius	685
Ophichthys = Goslinophis	534
Ophidion	691
Ophidium = Ophidion	691
Ophiopsis	414
Ophirachis = Belonostomus	447
Ophisurus = Goslinophis	534
Opistopteryx	664
Opsigonus = Ionoscopus	466
Orcynus = Thunnus	908
Orectolobus	174
Ornategulum	560
Orthacanthus	151
Orthocormus	441
Orthogonikleithrus	473
Orthybodus = Hybodus	168
Oshunia	467
Osmeroides	513
Osmerus	615
Osteolepis	969
Osteoplurus = Diplurus	952
Ostracion = Proaracana	928
Ottaviania	869
Oxyosteus	130

P

Pachycormus	442
Pachycormus = Saurostomus	445
Pachylebias	708
Pachyrhizodus	518
Pachystetus = Prolebias	709
Pachythrissops	511
Pagellus	839
Pagrus	840
Palaeobalistes = Palaeobalistum	401
Palaeobalistum	401
Palaeobrosmius = Palaeogadus	686
Palaeocarcharias	175
Palaeoclupea = Apsopelix	501
Palaeocrossorhinus = Phorcynis	176
Palaeodenticeps	550
Palaeodasybatis = Heliobatis	213
Palaeogadus	686
Palaeolycus	632
Palaeomolva	687
Palaeoniscionotus = Coccolepis	298
Palaeoniscum	292

Index of Genera and Synonyms

Palaeoniscus = Palaeoniscum	292
Palaeoperca	797
Palaeorhynchus	914
Palaeoscyllium	182
Palaeospondylus	149
Palaeoteuthis = Pteraspis	84
Palaeothrissum = Palaeoniscum	292
Palimphyes	903
Pangasius	602
Paracentrophorus	383
Paraceratodus	993
Paracestracion	172
Parachanos	574
Paradipterus = Dipterus	982
Paraelops	506
Paraeoliscus	767
Parafundulus = Fundulus	705
Parahalecula = Etrumeus	555
Parahaplolepis = Haplolepis	323
Paralepidotus	384
Paralepis	640
Paramblypterus	288
Paramiatus = Amia	431
Paramphisile	765
Paranguilla	526
Parapercis = Neopercis	883
Parapholidophorus	453
Parapristipoma	833
Parapteraspis = Pteraspis	84
Parapygaeus	892
Pararaja	205
Parascopelus	641
Parasemionotus	417
Parasphyraena	874
Paraspinus	729
Parasyllaemus	507
Parasynarcualis	760
Paratarrasius	328
Parathrissops = Euthynotus	439
Paratrachinotus	825
Paratriakis	187
Parexus	240
Parhybodus = Hybodus	168
Pariestegus = Diplurus	952
Parmphractus = Bothriolepis	140
Pasaichthys	847
Patavichthys	542
Pateroperca	561
Pattenaspis = Cephalaspis	103
Pattersonichthys	667
Pavelichthys	538
Pegasus	753
Pelamys = Sarda	904
Pelargorhynchus	650
Pelecopterus = Protosphyraena	443
Pelecorapis = Apsopelix	501
Peltodus = Janassa	164
Peltopleurus	364
Pentaceros	860
Pentagonolepis = Phyllolepis	127
Pentlandia	983
Peplorhina = Conchopoma	991
Perca	810, 811
Percalates	789
Percichthys	790
Percostoma = Perca	810
Perequula = Caranx	821
Pericentrophorus	385
Periodus = Pycnodus	403
Perleidus	356
Petalodopsis = Sagenodus	989
Petalopteryx	411
Phaidrosoma	418
Phalacropholis = Notogoneus	577
Phaneropleuron	986
Phanerosteon	264
Phareodus	497
Pharmacichthys	605
Pharyngolepis	107
Phelidophorus = Pholidophorus	456
Phigeacanthus = Deltoptychius	228
Phlebolepis	90
Phlyctaenichthys	347
Phoebammon = Bothriolepis	140
Phoenicolepis	668
Pholidoctenus	454
Pholidolepis	455
Pholidophorus	456
Pholidopleurus	332
Pholidorhynchodon	457
Pholidosteus	135
Pholidotus = Dapedium	377
Pholis	881
Phorcynis	176
Photichthys	628
Phylactocephalus	636
Phyllolepis	127
Physichthys = Macropetalichthys	126

Index of Genera and Synonyms

Physocephalus = Pachylebias	708	Prionolepis	653
Physonemus = Falcatus	158	Priscacara	866
Physonemus = Stethacanthus	159	Pristigenys	813
Pimelodus	603	*Pristipoma* = Pomadasys	834
Pinichthys	918	Pristisomus	357
Pionaspis	73	*Pristiurus* = Macrourogaleus	181
Piveteauia	956	*Proantigonia* = Capros	751
Placopleurus	365	Proaracana	928
Placothorax = Bothriolepis	140	*Procarcharodon* = Carcharocles	178
Platacanthus = Deltoptychius	228	Procheirichthys	358
Platax = Eoplatax	855	*Proctenodus* = Ctenodus	988
Platinx	572	Prohalecites	458
Platops = Brychaetus	496	Prolates	799
Platyacrodus = Heterodontus	171	Prolebias	709
Platycanthus = Deltoptychius	228	*Prolepidotus* = Lepidotes	382
Platycormus	742	Proleptolepis	474
Platyosteus = Oxyosteus	130	Promecosomina	420
Platyrhina	204	Promyliobatis	215
Platysomus	311	Pronotacanthus	522
Plectocretacicus	927	*Propalaeoniscus* = Elonichthys	274
Plectrolepis = Eurynothus	312	Properca	800
Pleiopterus = Osteolepis	969	Proportheus	486
Plesioberyx	734	Propteridium	692
Plesiodus = Lepidotes	382	Propterus	412
Plesiopteraspis = Pteraspis	84	*Prosauropsis* = Saurostomus	445
Pleurolepis = Tetragonolepis	388	Proscinetes	402
Pleuropholis	461	Proserrivomer	540
Plioplarchus	812	Prosolenostomus	769
Pliopterus = Osteolepis	969	Protacanthodes	932
Plyphlepis = Glyptolepis	965	*Protamia* = Amia	431
Pneumathophorus = Scomber	905	Protaspis	83
Pnigeacanthus = Deltoptychius	228	Proteomyrus	530
Pododus = Mesolepis	310	*Protobalistum* = Spinacanthus	930
Podopteryx = Bregmaceros	679	Protobrama	494
Polyosteorhynchus	945	*Protocarostomus* = Notogoneus	577
Polyphractus = Dipterus	982	Protoclupea	563
Polysephis = Proscinetes	402	Protolophotus	715
Polysephus = Eoproscinetes	399	*Protosauropsis* = Saurostomus	445
Pomadasys	834	Protosphyraena	443
Pomognathus = Halec	634	Protospinax	191, 192
Pomolobus	562	*Protospirata* = Edestus	161
Pomoxis	806	Protostomias	624
Pomphractus = Brychaetus	496	Prymnites	487
Poraspis	74	Psenicubiceps	916
Porolepis	964	Psettopsis	848
Portheus = Xiphactinus	489	*Pseudacrodus* = Heterodontus	171
Praesemionotus	419	Pseudoberyx	564
Priacanthopsis	798	*Pseudolates* = Prolates	799
Priconolepis = Hoplopteryx	718	*Pseudolota* = Palaeogadus	686

1037

Index of Genera and Synonyms

Pseudopriacanthus = Pristigenys	813
Pseudopteraspis = Pteraspis	84
Pseudoraniceps	688
Pseudorasbora	584
Pseudorhina	193, 194
Pseudosyngnathus	772
Pseudothrissops = Euthynotus	439
Pseudovomer	878
Psilacanthus = Acronemus	166
Pteraspis	84
Pterichthyodes	143, 144
Pterichthys = Pterichthyodes	144
Pternodus = Orthacanthus	151
Pterolepidops = Pterygolepis	108
Pterolepis = Pterygolepis	108
Pteronisculus	293
Pteroniscus	306
Pterygocephalus	777
Pterygolepis	108
Pterygopterus = Thoracopterus	335
Ptycholepis	392
Pychnodus = Pycnodus	403
Pycnodus	403
Pycnosterinx	743
Pycnosteroides	737
Pygaeus	858
Pygopterus	272
Pyritocephalus	325

Q

Quebecius	963

R

Radamas = Wodnika	169
Radamus = Menaspis	230
Redfieldius	348
Regenius = Cyclothone	621
Remigolepis	145
Reticulepis	281
Rhabdiolepis = Diplurus	952
Rhabdoderma	948
Rhabdolepis	260
Rhacolepis	519
Rhadamista = Ctenodus	988
Rhadinacanthus	243
Rhadinacanthus = Diplacanthus	242
Rhadinichthys	263
Rhamphexocoetus	696
Rhamphodopsis	123
Rhamphognathus	711
Rhamphosus	778
Rhina = Pseudorhina	194
Rhineastes = Astephas	600
Rhinellus = Ichthyotringa	644
Rhinobatos	199, 200
Rhinobatus = Rhinobatos	200
Rhinodipterus	984
Rhinopteraspis	85
Rhodeus	585
Rhombopterygia	201
Rhombus = Eobothus	922
Rhombus = Scophthalmus	923
Rhynchodercetis	651
Rhyncholepis	109
Rhytmias	841
Richardsonius	586
Ruffoichthys	870
Ruppelianus = Palaeogadus	686
Rutilus	587

S

Sacabambaspis	70
Sagenodus	989
Sahelinia = Clupea	552
Santosius	791
Sarda	904
Sardina	565
Sardinella	566
Sardinioides	654
Sardinius	637
Sarginites = Leptolepis	472
Sargocentron = Sargocentrum	730
Sargocentrum	730
Sargodon	386
Sargus = Diplodus	838
Saurichthys	366
Saurodon	490
Sauropsis	444
Saurorhynchus	367
Saurostomus	445
Scanilepis	297
Scapanorhynchus	179

Index of Genera and Synonyms

Scaphaspis = Doryaspis	81
Scaphodus = Gyronchus	396
Scatophagus	856
Scaumenacia	987
Sceletophorus = Phanerosteon	264
Schizurichthys	349
Sciaena	845
Sciaenops = Sciaena	845
Sclerolepis = Glyptolepis	965
Sclerorhynchus	208, 209
Scolenaspis = Cephalaspis	103
Scomber	905
Scomberomorus	906
Scombroclupea	567
Scombrosarda	907
Scopeloides	625
Scophthalmus	923
Scorpaena	776
Scrobodus = Lepidotes	382
Scyliorhinus	183
Scyllium = Scyliorhinus	183
Selachidea = Hybodus	168
Semionotus	387
Semiophorus = Exellia	853
Sendenhorstia	512
Seriola	826
Serranus	801
Shurcobroma = Bothriolepis	140
Sibyrhynchus	221
Simopteraspis = Pteraspis	84
Sinamia	435
Siphonostoma = Syngnathus	773
Smerdis = Dapalis	795
Solea	925
Solenodon = Enchodus	630
Solenognathus = Charitosomus	576
Spaniodon	508
Sparnodus	842
Sparus	843
Spathobatis = Aellopos	195
Sphaerodus = Lepidotes	382
Sphenocephalus	672
Sphenolepis = Notogoneus	577
Sphenonchus = Acronemus	166
Sphyraena	875
Spinacanthus	930
Spinogadus = Merluccius	689
Spratelloides	568
Sprattus	569
Squalicorax	180
Squatina = Pseudorhina	194
Stanacanthus = Bothriolepis	140
Stegotrachelus	257
Stemmatodus	404
Stensioella	118
Stethacanthus	159
Stichoberyx	731
Stichocentrus	738
Stichopterus	369
Stichopteryx	721
Stolephorus = Spratelloides	568
Streblodus = Deltoptychius	228
Strematodus = Gyrodus	395
Strigilina = Janassa	164
Strobilodus	430
Sudis	642
Sundayichthys	267
Syllaemus = Apsopelix	501
Symmorium	156
Symphodus	879
Synergus = Urocles	436
Syngnathus	773
Synodus	638
Synorichthys	350

T

Tachynectes	665
Tarsichthys = Tinca	590
Teleopterina = Pyritocephalus	325
Telepholis	647
Tenuicentrum	732
Tetheodus = Enchodus	630
Tetragonolepis	388
Tetragonopterus	596
Tetragonurus	917
Tharrhias	476
Tharsis	475
Thaumas = Pseudorhina	194
Thaumaturus	619
Thectodus = Acronemus	166
Thelodus	92
Thelolepis = Thelodus	92
Thelolepoides = Thelodus	92
Thelyodus = Thelodus	92
Thlattodus = Caturus	424
Tholonotus	282

1039

Index of Genera and Synonyms

Thoracodus = Janassa	164
Thoracopterus	335
Thrissopater = Pachyrhizodus	518
Thrissops	488
Thrissopteroides	516
Thunnus	908
Thursius	970
Thyellina = Scyliorhinus	183
Thyestes	104
Thynnichthys	588
Thynnus = Thunnus	908
Tiarodontus = Diademodus	155
Tilapia	862
Tinca	589, 590
Todiltia	477
Torpedaspis	75
Torpedo	210
Tortonesia	880
Toxotes	849
Trachurus	827
Trachymetopon = Holophagus	959
Traquairichthys	249
Trematina = Esox	607
Triazeugacanthus	250
Trichophanes	677
Trigenodus = Pseudorhina	194
Trigla	779
Trigonorhina	202
Trilobites = Janassa	164
Triodus	152
Tripelta	359
Triplopterus = Osteolepis	969
Triportheus	597
Tripterus = Osteolepis	969
Tristichopterus	972
Tropidotus = Heterodontus	171
Trygon	214
Trygonaspis	80
Tselfatia	495
Tubantia	722
Turinia	93
Turio	909
Turkmene	714
Turseodus	294
Tydeus = Paralepis	640
Tylerichthys	893
Typodus = Gyronchus	396
Tyriaspis	96

U

Uarbryichthys	413
Umbra	609
unnamed (Amiiformes?)	437
unnamed (Anguilliformes)	544
unnamed (Argentinidae)	610
unnamed (Balistidae)	936
unnamed (Beryciformes)	775–777
unnamed (Birkeniidae?)	110
unnamed (Cheirothricidae?)	648
unnamed (Cichlidae)	863, 864
unnamed (Cochliodontoidei)	224–227
unnamed (Coelacanthidae?)	958
unnamed (Cyathaspididae)	76
unnamed (Edestidae)	162
unnamed (Ellimmichthyiform.)	548, 549
unnamed (Elopidae?)	509
unnamed (Galeiformes?)	189
unnamed (Holocephali)	235
unnamed (Ichthyodectiformes)	493
unnamed (Iniopterygiformes)	222, 225
unnamed (Orodontiformes)	163
unnamed (Parasemionotidae?)	422, 423
unnamed (Percoidei)	871, 872
unnamed (Scorpaeniformes)	784
unnamed (Scyliorhinidae?)	184
unnamed (Serranidae)	802
unnamed (Stromateidae)	919
unnamed (Syngnathiformes)	774
Undina	961
Uraeus = Caturus	424
Uranolophus	977
Urenchelys	543
Urocles	436
Urolophus	216
Uronemus	990
Uropteryx = Platysomus	311
Urosphen	757
Urosphenopsis	758
Urosthenes	322
Utahacanthus	251

Index of Genera and Synonyms

V

Varasichthys	478
Vernicomacanthus	241
Vernonaspis	77
Veronanguilla	532
Vinciguerria	629
Vinctifer	448
Voltaconger	539
Vomeropsis	828

W

Wadeichthys	464
Watsonosteus	134
Watsonulus	421
Whitapodus	529
Whiteia	957
Willomorichthys	307
Wodnika	169
Woodwardichthys = Amphistium	850
Wuttagoonaspis	128

X

Xenacanthus	153
Xenestes = Birgeria	296
Xenolamia = Squalicorax	180
Xiphactinus	489
Xiphias	912
Xiphopterus	910
Xiphotrygus = Heliobatis	213
Xyne	570
Xystodus = Synodus	638

Y

Yogoniscus	308
Yonodus = Sagenodus	989

Z

Zalarges = Vinciguerria	629
Zanclites	492
Zapteryx	203
Zenaspis = Cephalaspis	103
Zenopsis	748
Zeus	749

This is a quarry in the famous Lithographic Limestone of the upper Jurassic of southern Germany, at Daiting, near Solenhofen, Bavaria. Unfortunately not all beds are rich in fossils. Good luck is required to find anything.

Index of Orders, Suborders, and Families

Families are in SMALL CAPS.
Terms preceeding an equal sign (=) are common names.

A

ACANTHODIDAE	45, 245–251
Acanthodiformes	45, 245–251
ACANTHORHINIDAE	44, 231
ACANTHURIDAE	65, 888–893
Acanthuroidei	65, 888–895
Acipenseriformes	47, 368–370
ACROLEPIDIDAE	46, 277–282
ACROPOMATIDAE	62, 816
Actinistia = Coelacanthiformes	67, 941–961
ADRIANICHTHYIDAE	58
Adrianichthyids = ADRIANICHTHYIDAE	58
AEDUELLIDAE	46, 285–286
AETHEODONTIDAE	47, 363
African hillstream catfs. = AMPHILIIDAE	53
African lungfishes = PROTOPTERIDAE	67
AGASSIZODONTIDAE	41, 160
AGENEIOSIDAE	53
AGONIDAE	61
Aholeholes = KUHLIIDAE	62
AIPICHTHYIDAE	59, 736
Airbreathing catfishes = CLARIIDAE	53
Airsac catfishes = HETEROPNEUSTIDAE	53
AKYSIDAE	53
ALBULIDAE	50, 517
Albuloidei	50, 513–517
ALEPISAURIDAE	55
Alepisauroidei	55, 637–642
ALEPOCEPHALIDAE	54
Alfonsinos = BERYCIDAE	59, 723
Algae eaters = GYRINOCHEILIDAE	52
ALLOTHRISSOPIDAE	49, 479
ALOPIIDAE	42
AMBLYCIPITIDAE	53
AMBLYOPSIDAE	56
AMBLYPTERIDAE	46, 283–284
AMIIDAE	48, 431–436
Amiiformes	48, 415–437
Amiommids = ARIOMMATIDAE	65
AMMODYTIDAE	64, 886
Ammodytoidei	64, 886
AMPHIASPIDIDAE	37, 78
AMPHILIIDAE	53
AMPHISTIIDAE	63, 850
ANABANTIDAE	66
ANACORACIDAE	42, 180
ANAETHALIONIDAE	50, 500
ANABLEPIDAE	58
ANARHICHADIDAE	64
Anaspidiformes	38, 105–112
ANASTOMIDAE	52
Anchovies = ENGRAULIDIDAE	52, 571
Angelfishes = POMACANTHIDAE	63
Angel sharks = Squaloidei	43, 190–192
Angel sharks = SQUATINIDAE	43, 193–194
Anglerfishes = Lophiiformes	57, 694–695
ANGUILLAVIDAE	50, 524
ANGUILLIDAE	50, 523
Anguilliformes	50, 523–544
ANGUILLOIDIDAE	51, 531–532
ANOMALOPIDAE	59
ANOPLOGASTRIDAE	59
ANOPLOPOMATIDAE	61
ANOTOPTERIDAE	55
Antenna catfishes = PIMELODIDAE	53, 603
ANTENNARIIDAE	57, 695
Antennarioidei	57, 695
Antiarchiformes	40, 139–145
APHREDODERIDAE	56, 674–677
Aphredoderoidei	56, 674–677
APLOACTINIDAE	61
APLOCHEILIDAE	58
APOGONIDAE	62, 814–815
APTERONOTIDAE	54
ARACANIDAE	66, 926–928
ARAMBOURGELLIDAE	63, 868
ARANDASPIDIDAE	37, 70
Araripichthoidei	59, 744
ARARIPICHTHYIDAE	59, 744
ARCHAEOMAENIDAE	49, 462–464
Archerfishes = TOXOTIDAE	62, 849

1043

Index of Orders, Suborders, and Families

ARGENTINIDAE	54, 610
Argentinoidei	54, 610–613
ARIIDAE	53
ARIOMMATIDAE	65
Armoured catfishes = LORICARIIDAE	53
Armourhead catfishes = CRANOGLANIDIDAE	53
Armourheads = PENTACEROTIDAE	63, 860
ARRIPIDAE	62
Arthrodiriformes	39, 128–146
Asiatic torrent catfishes = AMBLYCIPITIDAE	53
ASPIDORHYNCHIDAE	49, 446–448
Aspidorhynchiformes	49, 446–448
ASPREDINIDAE	53
ASTEROLEPIDIDAE	40, 141–145
ASTEROSTEIDAE	39, 119–121
Astraspidiformes	37, 70
ASTROBLEPIDAE	53
ASTRONESTHIDAE	55
ATELEASPIDIDAE	38, 97–99
ATHERINIDAE	58, 710–711
Atheriniformes	58, 710–711
AUCHENIPTERIDAE	53
Aulopiformes	55, 630–653
AULOPODIDAE	55
Aulopus = AULOPODIDAE	55
AULORHYNCHIDAE	60
AULOSTOMIDAE	60, 754–756
Aulostomoidei	60, 754–767
Australian lungfishes = CERATODONTIDAE	67, 992–993
Australian salmon = ARRIPIDAE	62

B

BAGRIDAE	53, 601
Bagrid catfishes = BAGRIDAE	53, 601
Baikal oilfishes = COMEPHORIDAE	61
BALISTIDAE	66, 933–936
Balistoidei	66, 926–936
Bandfishes = CEPOLIDAE	63
Bannertail catfishes = OLYRIDAE	53
Banjo catfishes = ASPREDINIDAE	53
Barbel-less catfishes = AGENEIOSIDAE	53
Barracudas = SPHYRAENIDAE	63, 874–875
Barracudinas = PARALEPIDIDAE	55, 639–642
Barreleyes = OPISTHOPROCTIDAE	54
Basking sharks = CETORHINIDAE	42
Basslets = GRAMMIDAE	61
Batfishes = OGCOCEPHALIDAE	57
BATHYLAGIDAE	54, 611
BATHYMASTERIDAE	63
BATRACHOIDIDAE	57, 693
Batrachoidiformes	57, 693
Beachsalmon = LEPTOBRAMIDAE	62
Beardfishes = POLYMIXIIDAE	59, 740–743
BELANTSEIDAE	41, 165
BELONIDAE	58, 701
BELONTIIDAE	66
BERYCIDAE	59, 723
Beryciformes	59, 716–747
Berycoidei	59, 716–734
Bichirs = POLYPTERIDAE	45
Bigeyes = PRIACANTHIDAE	62, 813
Bigscale fishes = MELAMPHAIDAE	59
Billfishes = ISTIOPHORIDAE	65
Birgeriidae	46, 296
Birkeniidae	38, 106–110
Black dragonfishes = IDIACANTHIDAE	55
Blackfish = GADOPSIDAE	63
BLENNIIDAE	64
Blennioidei	64, 884–885
Bluefishes = Pomatomidae	62, 817
Boarfishes = Caproidae	60, 750–751
Bobasatraniidae	46, 316–318
Bonefishes = Albulidae	50, 517
Bonnetmouths = EMMELICHTHYIDAE	62
Bonytongues = Osteoglossidae	49, 496–497
Bonytongues = Osteoglossiformes	49, 496–497
BOTHIDAE	66, 920–923
BOTHRIOLEPIDIDAE	40, 139–140
Bowfins = AMIIDAE	48, 431–436
Bowfins = Amiiformes	48, 415–437
Boxfishes = OSTRACIIDAE	66

Index of Orders, Suborders, and Families

BRACHIONICHTHYIDAE	57
BRACHYDEIRIDAE	40, 130
Bramble sharks = ECHINORHINIDAE	43
BRAMIDAE	62, 832
BREGMACEROTIDAE	57, 679–680
BREMBODONTIDAE	48, 389–390
Bristlemouths = GONOSTOMATIDAE	55, 621–625
Brotulas = OPHIDIIDAE	57, 690–692
Burrowing gobies = TRIPAUCHENIDAE	65
Butterfishes = STROMATEIDAE	65, 918–919
Butterfly rays = GYMNURIDAE	43
Butterflyfishes = CHAETODONTIDAE	63, 857–858
Butterflyfishes = PANTODONTIDAE	49

C

Callichthyid armoured catfishes = CALLICHTHYIDAE	53, 604
CALLICHTHYIDAE	53, 604
CALLORHYNCHIDAE	45
CANOBIIDAE	46, 265–267
CAPROIDAE	60, 750–751
CAPROVESPOSIDAE	65, 894
CARACANTHIDAE	60
Caracins = Characiformes	52, 594–597
CARANGIDAE	62, 819–828
CARAPIDAE	57
Carapids = CARAPIDAE	57
CARBOVELIDAE	46, 264
CARCHARHINIDAE	42, 185
Carcharhinoidei	42, 181–187
CARCHARIIDAE	42
Cardinalfishes = APOGONIDAE	62, 814–815
CARDIPELTIDAE	37, 86
CARISTIIDAE	62
Carps = CYPRINIDAE	52, 579–590
Carps = Cypriniformes	52, 579–593
CATOSTOMIDAE	52, 593
Cat sharks = SCYLIORHINIDAE	42, 181–184
Catfish eels = PLOTOSIDAE	53
Cavefishes = AMBLYOPSIDAE	56
CATURIDAE	48, 424–430
CENTRARCHIDAE	62, 803–806
CENTRISCIDAE	60, 763–765
CENTROLOPHIDAE	65
CENTROPHRYNIDAE	57
CENTROPOMIDAE	61, 785–786
CEPHALASPIDIDAE	38, 100–104
Cephalaspidiformes	38, 95–104
CEPOLIDAE	63
CERATIIDAE	57
CERATODONTIDAE	67, 992–993
CETOPSIDAE	53
CETORHINIDAE	42
CENTROPHRYNIDAE	57
CHACIDAE	53
CHAETODONTIDAE	63, 857–858
CHANNICHTHYIDAE	64
CHANIDAE	52, 573–574
CHANNIDAE	66
Chanoidei	52, 573–575
CHARACIDAE	53, 595–597
Characiformes	52, 594–597
CHAULIODONTIDAE	55
CHAUNACIDAE	57
CHEILODACTYLIDAE	63
CHEIROLEPIDIDAE	45, 254
CHEIROTHRICIDAE	55, 645–648
Chimaeras = CHIMAERIDAE	45, 233
CHIMAERIDAE	45, 233
Chimaeriformes	45, 232–234
CHIROCENTRIDAE	52, 572
CHIRODONTIDAE	46, 312–315
CHIRONEMIDAE	63
CHLOROPHTALMIDAE	55
CHONDRENCHELYIDAE	44, 217–218
Chondrenchelyiformes	44, 217–218
CHONDROSTEIDAE	47, 368–369
Chondrosteoidei	47, 368–369
CICHLIDAE	63, 861–864
Cichlids = CICHLIDAE	63, 861–864
CIMOLICHTHYIDAE	56, 652
CIRRHITIDAE	63
CITHARIDAE	66
Citharids = CITHARIDAE	66

1045

Index of Orders, Suborders, and Families

Citharinidae	52
Citharins = Citharinidae	52
Cladoselachian sharks = Cladoselachiformes	41, 154
Cladoselachidae	41, 154
Cladoselachiformes	41, 154
Clamydoselachidae	42
Clariidae	53
Cleithrolepididae	47, 360–362
Climatiidae	45, 238–241
Climatiiformes	45, 238–243
Climbing gourami = Anabantidae	66
Clingfishes = Gobiesosocidae	65
Clinidae	64, 884–885
Clinids = Clinidae	64, 884–885
Clupavidae	52, 594
Clupeidae	52, 551–570
Clupeiformes	51, 550–572
Clupeoidei	52, 551–570
Cobia = Rachycentridae	62
Cobitididae	52, 591–592
Coccolepididae	46, 298
Coccosteidae	40, 131–134
Coccosteoidei	39, 129–145
Cochlidontoidei	44, 224–227
Cod icefishes = Nototheniidae	64
Codlets = Bregmacerotidae	57, 679–680
Cods = Gadidae	57, 681–688
Coelacanthidae	67, 949–958
Coelacanthiformes	67, 941–961
Coelacanths = Coelacanthiformes	67, 941–961
Combfishes = Zaniolepididae	61
Combtooth blennies = Blenniidae	64
Comephoridae	61
Commentryidae	46, 287–288
Conchopomidae	67, 991
Congers = Congridae	51, 535–539
Congiopodidae	61
Congridae	51, 535–539
Congrogadidae	64
Coracinidae	62
Cornetfishes = Fistulariidae	60, 759
Cornuboniscidae	46, 268
Coronodontiformes	41, 155
Coryphaenidae	62
Cottidae	61, 780–783
Cottoidei	61, 780–783
Cow sharks = Hexanchidae	42, 188
Cow-nosed rays = Rhinopteridae	43
Cranoglanididae	53
Crestfishes = Lophotidae	58, 715
Crocodile icefishes = Channichthyidae	64
Crossognathidae	50, 501–502
Crossopterygii	67
Cryptacanthodidae	64
Ctenacanthiformes	41, 166–170
Ctenodontidae	67, 988
Ctenoluciidae	53
Ctenothrissidae	56, 669–670
Ctenothrissiformes	56, 669–670
Cub sharks = Carchariidae	42
Curimatas = Curimatidae	52
Curimatidae	52
Cusk eels = Ophidiidae	57, 690–692
Cutlassfishes = Trichiuridae	65, 898–899
Cuthroat eels = Synaphobranchidae	51
Cyathaspididae	37, 71–77
Cyclobatidae	43, 206
Cyclopteridae	61
Cynoglossidae	66
Cyprinidae	52, 579–590
Cypriniformes	52, 579–593
Cyprinodontidae	58, 702–709
Cyprinodontiformes	58, 696–709
Cyprinodontoidei	58, 702–709

D

Dactylopteridae	60, 775
Dactylopteriformes	60, 775
Dactyloscopidae	64
Daggertooths = Anotopteridae	55
Dalatiidae	43
Damselfishes = Pomacentridae	63, 865
Dartmuthiidae	38, 95–96
Dasyatidae	43, 212–214
Deep-sea anglerfishes = Centrophrynidae	57

Index of Orders, Suborders, and Families

Deep-sea smelts = BATHYLAGIDAE 54, 611
DENTICIPITIDAE 51, 550
Denticipitoidei 51, 550
Denticle herrings = DENTICIPITIDAE 52, 550
DERCETIDAE 56, 649–651
DERICHTHYIDAE 51
Devonian cladoselachian sharks = Cladoselachiformes 41, 154
Devil rays = MOBULIDAE 43
DICELLOPYGIDAE 46, 295
DIGORIIDAE 59, 739
DINICHTHYIDAE 40, 136–137
DINOPTERYGIDAE 59, 735
Dinopterygoidei 59, 735–739
DIODONTIDAE 66, 938
DIPLACANTHIDAE 45, 242–243
DIPLOCERCIDAE 67, 941–942
DIPLOMYSTIDAE 53
Diplomystid catfishes = DIPLOMYSTIDAE 53
DIPNORHYNCHIDAE 67, 978–980
DIPTERICHTHYIDAE 63, 867
DIPTERIDAE 67, 981–984
DIRETMIDAE 59
DISSOMIDAE 51
Dogfish shark = Squaloidei 43, 190–192
Dolphins = CORYPHAENIDAE 62
DORADIDAE 53
Dories = ZEIDAE 60, 748–749
Dorypteriformes 46, 326
Dottybacks = PSEUDOCHROMIDAE 61
Dragonets = CALLIONYMIDAE 65
DRACONETTIDAE 65
DREPANASPIDIDAE 37, 87–88
Driftfishes = NOMEIDAE 65, 915–916
Driftwood catfishes = AUCHENIPTERIDAE 53
Drums = SCIAENIDAE 62, 844–845
Duckbilled eels = NETTASTOMATIDAE 51

E

Eagle rays = MYLIOBATIDAE 43, 215
ECHENEIDIDAE 62, 818
ECHINOCHIMAERIDAE 45, 232
ECHINORHINIDAE 43
EDESTIDAE 41, 161–162
Eelblennies = CONGROGADIDAE 64
Eel cods = MURAENOLEPIDIDAE 56
Eellike gobies = GOBIOIDIDAE 65
Eelpouts = ZOARCIDAE 63
Eels = Anguilliformes 50, 523–544
Electric catfishes = MALAPTERURIDAE 53
Electric eels = ELECTROPHORIDAE 54
Electric rays = TORPEDINIDAE 43, 210
ELECTROPHORIDAE 54
ELEOTRIDIDAE 65
Elephantfishes = MORMYRIDAE 50
ELLIMMICHTHYIDAE 51, 545–547
ELLIMMICHTHYIFORMES 51, 545–549
ELONICHTHYIDAE 46, 273–276
ELOPIDAE 50, 503–509
Elopiformes 50, 500–520
Elopoidei 50, 503–512
EMBIOTOCIDAE 63
EMMELICHTHYIDAE 62
Emperors = LETHRINIDAE 62
ENCHODONTIDAE 55, 630–632
Enchodontoidei 55, 630–633
ENDEIOLEPIDIDAE 38, 111
ENGRAULIDIDAE 52, 571
ENOPLOSIDAE 63, 859
EPHIPPIDAE 63, 851–853
ERYTHRINIDAE 52
ESOCIDAE 54, 607–608
Esocoidei 54, 606–609
Eugeneodontiformes 41, 160–162
EUPHARYNGIDAE 51
Eurasian catfishes = SILURIDAE 53
EURYPHOLIDAE 55, 633
EUSTHENOPTERIDAE 67, 971–972
EUTAENIOPHORIDAE 59
EVERMANNELLIDAE 55
EXOCOETIDAE 58, 696
Exocoetoidei 58, 696–701

F

False morays = XENOCONGRIDAE 51, 527–

1047

Index of Orders, Suborders, and Families

	529
False trevallies = LACTARIIDAE	62
Fangtooth = ANOPLOGASTRIDAE	59
Featherbacks = Notopteroidei	50, 498–499
Filefishes = BALISTIDAE	66, 933–936
Fingerfishes = MONODACTYLIDAE	62, 847–848
FISTULARIIDAE	60, 759
Flatheads = PLATYCEPHALIDAE	61
Flying fishes = EXOCOETIDAE	58, 696
Flying gurnards = DACTYLOPTERIDAE	60, 775
Footballfishes = HIMANTOLOPHIDAE	57
Four-eyed fishes = ANABLEPIDAE	58
Freshwater hatchetfishes = GASTEROPELECIDAE	53
Frill sharks = CHLAMYDOSELACHIDAE	42
Frogfishes = ANTENNARIIDAE	57, 695

G

GADIDAE	57, 681–688
Gadiformes	56, 678–689
Gadoidei	56, 678–689
GADOPSIDAE	63
GALAXIIDAE	54
Galaxiids = GALAXIIDAE	54
Galeiformes	42, 171–189
Galjoen fishes = CORACINIDAE	62
Garpikes = LEPISOSTEIDAE	48, 373–374
GASTEROPELECIDAE	53
GASTEROSTEIDAE	60, 752
Gasterosteiformes	60, 752
GEMPYLIDAE	65, 896–897
GERREIDAE	62
Ghost flatheads = HOPLICHTHYIDAE	61
Ghost pipefishes = SOLENOSTOMIDAE	60, 768–769
Giant gourami = OSPHRONEMIDAE	66
GIBBERICHTHYIDAE	59
Gibberfish = GIBBERICHTHYIDAE	59
GIGANTURIDAE	55
Goatfishes = MULLIDAE	62, 846
Gobies = GOBIIDAE	65, 887
GOBIESOSOCIDAE	65
GOBIIDAE	65, 887
Gobioidei	65, 887
GOBIOIDIDAE	65
Gombessa = LATIMERIIDAE	67
GONORHYNCHIDAE	52, 576–577
Gonorhynchiformes	52, 573–578
Gonorhynchoidei	52, 576–578
GONOSTOMATIDAE	55, 621–625
Gonostomatoidei	55, 621–627
GOODEIDAE	58
Goodeids = GOODEIDAE	58
Goosefishes = LOPHIIDAE	57, 694
Gouramis = BELONTIIDAE	66
GRAMMICOLEPIDIDAE	60
Grammicolepids = GRAMMICOLEPIDIDAE	60
GRAMMIDAE	61
GRAMMISTIDAE	61
Graveldiver = SCYTALINIDAE	64
Greeneyes = CHLOROPHTALMIDAE	55
Greenlings = HEXAGRAMMIDAE	61
Grenadier fishes = MACROURIDAE	57
Grunts = HAEMULIDAE	62, 833–834
Guitar fishes= RHINOBATIDAE	43, 195–203
Gulper eels = Saccopharyngoidei	51
Gulpers = EUPHARYNGIDAE	51
Gunnels = PHOLIDIDAE	64, 881
GYMNOTIDAE	54
GYMNURIDAE	43
GYRINOCHEILIDAE	52

H

HABROICHTHYIDAE	47, 333–334
HADRONECTORIDAE	67, 943–945
HAEMULIDAE	62, 833–834
Hagfishes = MYXINIDAE	37
Hairyfish = MIRAPINNIDAE	59
Halfbeaks= HEMIRHAMPHIDAE	58, 697–700
HALECIDAE	55, 634–636
Halecoidei	55, 634–636
Halosaurid eels = Notacanthiformes	

1048

Index of Orders, Suborders, and Families

	50, 521–522
HALOSAURIDAE	50, 521
Halosaurs = HALOSAURIDAE	50, 521
Hammerhead sharks = SPHYRNIDAE	42
HAPLOLEPIDIDAE	46, 323–325
Haplolepiformes	46, 323–325
HARPAGIFERIDAE	64
Hawkfishes = CIRRHITIDAE	63
Headstanders = ANASTOMIDAE	52
HELOGENIDAE	53
HELOSTOMATIDAE	66
Herniodids = HEMIODONTIDAE	52
HEMIODONTIDAE	52
HEMIRHAMPHIDAE	58, 697–700
HEMISCILLIIDAE	42, 177
HEPSETIDAE	53
Herring smelts = ARGENTINIDAE	54, 610
Herrings = CLUPEIDAE	52, 551–570
HETERODONTIDAE	42, 171–172
Heterodontoidei	42, 171–172
HETEROPNEUSTIDAE	53
HEXAGRAMMIDAE	61
Hexanchoidei	42, 188
HIMANTOLOPHIDAE	57
HIODONTIDAE	50, 499
HOLOCENTRIDAE	59, 724–732
HOLOPTYCHIIDAE	67, 965–966
HOLURIIDAE	46, 270
HOMALOPTERIDAE	52
HOMOSTEIDAE	40, 129
HOPLICHTHYIDAE	61
Horn sharks = HETERODONTIDAE	42, 171–172
Hound sharks = TRIAKIDAE	42, 186–187
HYBODONTIDAE	42, 166–169
HYPOPHTHALMIDAE	53
HYPOPTYCHIDAE	60
HYPSIDORIDAE	53, 598

I

Icefishes = SALANGUIDAE	54
ICHTHYODECTIDAE	49, 480–489
Ichthyodectiformes	49, 479–493
ICHTHYOKENTEMIDAE	49, 459–460
ICHTHYOTRINGIDAE	55, 643–644
Ichthyotringoidei	55, 643–653
ICTALURIDAE	53, 599–600
IDIACANTHIDAE	55
Iniopterygiiformes	44, 219–223
INIOPTERYGIIDAE	44, 219
ISCHNACANTHIDAE	45, 244
Ischnacanthiformes	45, 244
ISONIDAE	58
ISTIOPHORIDAE	65

J

Jacks = CARANGIDAE	62, 819–828
JAMOYTHIIDAE	38, 105
Jawfishes = OPISTHOGNATHIDAE	64

K

Kafue pike = HEPSETIDAE	53
KATOPORIDAE	38, 89–90
Kelpfishes = CHIRONEMIDAE	63
Killifishes = CYPRINODONTIDAE	58, 702–709
Kissing gourami = HELOSTOMATIDAE	66
Knife eels = GYMNOTIDAE	54
Knifefishes = Notopteroidei	50, 498–499
Knifefishes = RHAMPHICHTHYIDAE	54
Knifejaws = OPLEGNATHIDAE	63
KRAEMERIIDAE	65
KUHLIIDAE	62
KURTIDAE	65
KUSHLUKIIDAE	65, 885
KYPHOSIDAE	63

L

LABRIDAE	63, 876–880

Index of Orders, Suborders, and Families

Labroidei	63, 876–880
LACTARIIDAE	62
Lamnoidei	42, 178–180
LAMNIDAE	42
Lampreys= Petromyzontiformes	38, 113–114
Lampreys = PETROMYZONTIDAE	38
LAMPRIDAE	58, 712
Lampridiformes	58, 712–715
Lampridoidei	58, 712–714
Lancetfishes = ALEPISAURIDAE	55
Lanterneye fishes = ANOMALOPIDAE	59
Lanternfishes = MYCTOPHIDAE	56, 655–665
Largenose fishes = MEGALOMYCTERIDAE	59
LASANIIDAE	38, 112
LATIMERIIDAE	67
LATRIDIDAE	63
LAUGIIDAE	67, 959–961
Leaffishes = NANDIDAE	63
LEBIASINIDAE	52
Lefteye flounders = BOTHIDAE	66, 920–923
LEIOGNATHIDAE	62, 831
LEPIDOSIRENIDAE	67
LEPISOSTEIDAE	48, 373–374
Lepisosteiformes	48, 373–374
LEPTOBRAMIDAE	62
LEPTOLEPIDIDAE	49, 469–477
Leptolepiformes	49, 469–478
LETHRINIDAE	62
Livebearers = POECILIIDAE	58
Lizardfishes = SYNODONTIDAE	55, 637–638
Loaches = Cobitididae	52, 591–592
Loach gobies = RHYACICHTHYIDAE	65
Lobe-finned fishes = Crossopterygii	67
LOBOTIDAE	62
Longneck eels = DERICHTHYIDAE	51
Longnose chimaeras = RHINOCHIMAERIDAE	45
LOGANIIDAE	38, 91–92
Loosejaws = MALACOSTEIDAE	55
LOPHIIDAE	57, 694
Lophiiformes	57, 694–695
Lophioidei	57, 694
LOPHOTIDAE	58, 715
LORICARIIDAE	53
Louvar = LUVARIIDAE	65
Low-eyed catfishes. = HYPOPHTHALMIDAE	53
LUCIOCEPHALIDAE	66
LUGANOIIDAE	47, 336–337
Luganoiiformes	47, 333–337
Lumpfishes = CYCLOPTERIDAE	61
LUTJANIDAE	62
LUVARIIDAE	65
LYCOPTERIDAE	50, 498

M

MACROPETALICHTHYIDAE	39, 124–126
MACRORHAMPHOSIDAE	60, 761–762
MACROSEMIIDAE	48, 405–412
Macrosemiiformes	48, 405–414
MACROURIDAE	57
Mackerels = SCOMBRIDAE	65, 900–910
Mackerel sharks = LAMNIDAE	42
MALACOSTEIDAE	55
MALAPTERURIDAE	53
Manefishes = CARISTIIDAE	62
Marbled catfishes = HELOGENIDAE	53
Marine hatchetfishes = STERNOPTYCHIDAE	55, 626–627
MASTACEMBELIDAE	66
MAYOMYZONTIDAE	38, 113–114
MCCONICHTHYIDAE	56, 671
Medusafishes = CENTROLOPHIDAE	65
MEGALOMYCTERIDAE	59
MEGALOPIDAE	50, 511–512
MELAMPHAIDAE	59
MELANONIDAE	56
MELANOSTOMIIDAE	55
MELANOTAENIIDAE	58
MENASPIDAE	44, 228–230
Menaspoidei	44, 228–230

Index of Orders, Suborders, and Families

MENIDAE	62, 829–830
Merluccid hakes = MERLUCCIIDAE	57, 689
MERLUCCIIDAE	57, 689
MICRODESMIDAE	65
MILANANGUILLIDAE	51, 533
Milkfishes = CHANIDAE	52, 573–574
Minnows = CYPRINIDAE	52, 579–590
MIRAPINNIDAE	59
MITSUKURINIDAE	42, 179
MOCHOKIDAE	53
Mojarras = GERREIDAE	62
Molas = MOLIDAE	66
MOLIDAE	66
MONOCENTRIDIDAE	59
MONODACTYLIDAE	62, 847–848
Mooneyes = HIODONTIDAE	50, 499
Moonfishes = MENIDAE	62, 829–830
Moray eels = MURAENIDAE	51
Morid cods = MORIDAE	57, 678
MORIDAE	57, 678
MORINGUIDAE	51
MORMYRIDAE	50
Morwongs = CHEILODACTYLIDAE	63
Mudminnows = UMBRIDAE	54, 609
MUGILIDAE	63, 873
Mugiloidei	63, 873
MUGILOIDIDAE	64, 883
Mullets = MUGILIDAE	63, 873
MULLIDAE	62, 846
MURAENESOCIDAE	51
MURAENIDAE	51
MURAENOLEPIDIDAE	56
Mustard eels = DISSOMIDAE	51
MYCTOPHIDAE	56, 655–665
Myctophiformes	56, 654–665
MYLIOBATIDAE	43, 215
Myliobatoidei	43, 212–216
Myriacanthoidei	44, 231
MYXINIDAE	37

N

NANDIDAE	63
NARCINIDAE	43, 211
Needlefishes = BELONIDAE	58, 701
NEMIPTERIDAE	62
NETTASTOMATIDAE	51
New Zealand smelts = RETROPINNIDAE	54
NIMICHTHYIDAE	51
NOMEIDAE	65, 915–916
North American catfishes = ICTALURIDAE	53, 599–600
NOTACANTHIDAE	50, 522
Notacanthiformes	50, 521–522
NOTELOPIDAE	50, 520
Notopteroidei	50, 498–499
NOTOTHENIIDAE	64
Nurseryfishes = KURTIDAE	65
Nurse sharks = ORECTOLOBIDAE	42, 173–176

O

Oarfishes = REGALECIDAE	58
OGCOCEPHALIDAE	57
OLIGOPLEURIDAE	49, 465–467
OLYRIDAE	53
ONYCHODONTIDAE	67, 962–963
Onychodontiformes	67, 962–963
Opah = LAMPRIDAE	58, 712
OPHICHTHIDAE	51, 534
OPHIDIIDAE	57, 690–692
Ophidiiformes	57, 690–692
OPISTHOGNATHIDAE	64
OPISTHOPROCTIDAE	54
OPLEGNATHIDAE	63
Orbicular velvetfishes = CARACANTHIDAE	61
ORECTOLOBIDAE	42, 173–176
Orectoloboidei	42, 173–177
Oreos = OREOSOMATIDAE	60
OREOSOMATIDAE	60
ORODONTIDAE	41, 163
Orodontiformes	41, 163
OSMERIDAE	54, 614–615
Osmeroidei	54, 614–615

Index of Orders, Suborders, and Families

OSMEROIDIDAE	50, 513
OSPHRONEMIDAE	66
OSTEOGLOSSIDAE	49, 496–497
Osteoglossiformes	49, 496–499
Osteoglossoidei	49, 496–497
Osteolepidiformes	67, 964–974
OSTRACIIDAE	66
OTODONTIDAE	42, 178

P

PACHYCORMIDAE	48, 438–445
PACHYRHIZODONTIDAE	50, 518–519
Pachyrhizodontoidei	50, 518–520
Paddlefishes = Polyodontoidei	48, 370
PALAEOESOCIDAE	54, 606
PALAEONISCIDAE	46, 289–294
Palaeonisciformes	45, 254–322
Palaeoniscoidei	45, 254–308
Palaeoniscoids = Palaeoniscoidei	45, 254–308
PALAEORHYNCHIDAE	65, 913–914
PALAEOSPONDYLIDAE	149
Palaeospondyliformes	149
PANDERICHTHYIDAE	67, 973
PANGASIIDAE	53, 602
PANTODONTIDAE	49
PARAEOLISCIDAE	60, 766–767
PARALEPIDIDAE	55, 639–642
PARANGUILLIDAE	51, 525–526
PARASEMIONOTIDAE	48, 415–423
Parasitic catfishes = TRICHOMYCTERIDAE	53
PARASYNARCUALIDAE	60, 760
Parazen = PARAZENIDAE	59
PARAZENIDAE	59
Parrotfishes = SCARIDAE	63
PATAVICHTHYIDAE	51, 541–542
PATTERSONICHTHYIDAE	56, 666–668
Pattersonichthyiformes	56, 666–668
Pearleyes = SCOPELARCHIDAE	55
PEGASIDAE	60, 753
Pegasiformes	60, 753
PELTOPLEURIDAE	47, 364–365
Peltopleuriformes	47, 363–365
PEMPHERIDIDAE	62
Pencil fishes = LEBIASINIDAE	52
PENTACEROTIDAE	63, 860
Perches = PERCIDAE	62, 807–812
PERCICHTHYIDAE	61, 787–791
PERCIDAE	62, 807–812
Perciformes	61–66, 785–919
Percoidei	61–63, 785–872
PERCOPSIDAE	56, 673
Percopsiformes	56, 672–677
Percopsoidei	56, 673
PERLEIDIDAE	47, 351–359
Perleidiformes	47, 351–363
Petalichthyiformes	39, 124–126
PETALODONTIDAE	41, 164
Petalodontiformes	41, 164–165
Petromyzontiformes	38, 113–114
PETROMYZONTIDAE	38
PHANEROPLEURIDAE	67, 985–987
PHOLIDIDAE	64, 881
PHOLIDOPHORIDAE	49, 451–458
Pholidophoriformes	49, 451–468
Pholidopleuridae	47, 330–332
Pholidopleuriformes	47, 330–332
Pholidosteidae	40, 135
PHOTICHTHYIDAE	55, 628–629
Photichthyoidei	55, 628–629
PHYLLOLEPIDIDAE	39, 127
Phyllolepidiformes	39, 127
Pike-characins = CTENOLUCIIDAE	53
Pike eels = MURAENESOCIDAE	51
Pikehead = LUCIOCEPHALIDAE	66
Pikes = ESOCIDAE	54, 607–608
PIMELODIDAE	53, 603
Pinecone fishes = MONOCENTRIDIDAE	59
Pipefishes = SYNGNATHIDAE	60, 770–774
Pirate perch = APHREDODERIDAE	56, 674–677
PLATACIDAE	63, 854–855
PLATYCEPHALIDAE	61
PLATYRHINIDAE	43, 204
PLATYSOMIDAE	46, 309–311
Platysomoidei	46, 309–318
PLESIOPIDAE	61

Index of Orders, Suborders, and Families

PLEURONECTIDAE	66, 924
Pleuronectiformes	66, 920–925
Pleuronectoidei	66, 920–924
PLEUROPHOLIDAE	49, 461
PLOTOSIDAE	53
Ploughnose chimaeras = CALLORHYNCHIDAE	45
Plunderfish = HARPAGIFERIDAE	64
Poachers = AGONIDAE	61
POECILIIDAE	58
POLYMIXIIDAE	59, 740–743
Polymixoidei	59, 740–743
POLYNEMIDAE	63
POLYODONTIDAE	48, 370
Polyodontoidei	48, 370
POLYPTERIDAE	45
POMACANTHIDAE	63
POMACENTRIDAE	63, 865
POMATOMIDAE	62, 817
Pomfrets = BRAMIDAE	62, 832
Pompanos = CARANGIDAE	62, 819–828
Ponyfishes = SCYLIORHINIDAE	42, 181–184
Porcupinefishes = DIODONTIDAE	66, 938
Porgies = SPARIDAE	62, 835–843
POROLEPIDIDAE	67, 964
POTAMOTRYGONIDAE	43
PSEUDOCHROMIDAE	61
PRIACANTHIDAE	62, 813
Pricklebacks = STICHAEIDAE	63
Pricklefishes = STEPHANOBERYCIDAE	59
PRIONOLEPIDIDAE	56, 653
PRISCACARIDAE	63, 866
PRISTIOPHORIDAE	43
PROTEOMYRIDAE	51, 530
PROTOPTERASPIDIDAE	37, 79–80
PROTOPTERIDAE	67
Prowfish = ZAPORIDAE	64
PSETTODIDAE	66
Psettotids = PSETTODIDAE	66
PTERASPIDIDAE	37, 81–85
Pteraspidiformes	37, 71–88
PTEROTHRISSIDAE	50, 514–516
PTERYGOCEPHALIDAE	61, 777
PTILICHTHYIDAE	64
PTYCHOLEPIDIDAE	47, 329
Ptycholepiformes	47, 329
PTYCTODONTIDAE	39, 122–123
Ptyctodontiformes	39, 122–123
Puffers = TETRAODONTIDAE	66, 937
PYCNODONTIDAE	48, 391–404
PYCNOSTEROIDIDAE	59, 737
Pycodontiformes	48, 389–404
PYGOPTERIDAE	46, 271–272
Pyrrhulinins = LEBIASINIDAE	52

Q

Quillfish = PTILICHTHYIDAE	64

R

Rabbitfishes = SIGANIDAE	65
Racehorses = CONGIOPODIDAE	61
RACHYCENTRIDAE	62
Rainbowfishes = MELANOTAENIIDAE	58
RAJIDAE	43, 205
Rajiformes	43, 195–216
Rajoidei	43, 205–206
Rays = Rajiformes	43, 195–216
REDFIELDIIDAE	47, 338–350
Redfieldiiformes	47, 338–350
REGALECIDAE	58
Remoras = ECHENEIDIDAE	62, 818
Requin sharks = CARCHARHINIDAE	42, 185
RETROPINNIDAE	54
RHABDODERMATIDAE	67, 946–948
RHABDOLEPIDIDAE	46, 260
RHADINICHTHYIDAE	46, 261–263
RHAMPHICHTHYIDAE	54
RHAMPHOSIDAE	61, 778
Rhenaniformes	39, 119–121
RHINCODONTIDAE	42
RHINOBATIDAE	43, 195–203
Rhinobatoidei	43, 195–204
RHINOCHIMAERIDAE	45

1053

Index of Orders, Suborders, and Families

RHINOPRENIDAE 63
RHINOPTERIDAE 43
Rhipidiiformes 67, 964–974
RHIZODONTIDAE 67, 974
RHYACICHTHYIDAE 65
Ribbonfishes = TRACHIPTERIDAE 58
Righteye flounders = PLEURONECTIDAE 66, 924
River stingrays = POTAMOTRYGONIDAE 43
Rivulines = APLOCHEILIDAE 58
Ronquils = BATHYMASTERIDAE 63
Roundheads = PLESIOPIDAE 61
Round rays = UROLOPHIDAE 43, 216

S

Sablefishes = ANOPLOPOMATIDAE 61
Sabretooth fishes = EVERMANNELLIDAE 55
SACCOPHARYNGIDAE 51
Saccopharyngoidei 51
SAGENODONTIDAE 67, 989
SALANGUIDAE 54
SALMONIDAE 54, 616–619
Salmonids = SALMONIDAE 54, 616–619
Salmoniformes 54, 606–620
Salmonoidei 54, 616–619
Sand eels = HYPOPTYCHIDAE 60
Sandfishes = TRICHODONTIDAE 64
Sandfishes = TRICHONOTIDAE 64
Sand gobies = KRAEMERIIDAE 65
Sand lances = AMMODYTIDAE 64, 886
Sandperches = MUGILOIDIDAE 64, 883
Sand stargazers = DACTYLOSCOPIDAE 64
Sarcopterygii 67
Sarcopterygians = Sarcopterygii 67
SARDINOIDIDAE 56, 654
SAURICHTHYIDAE 47, 366–367
Saurichthyiformes 47, 366–367
Sauries = SCOMBEROSOCIDAE 58
SAURODONTIDAE 49, 490
Sawfishes = Pristoidei 43
Saw sharks = PRISTIOPHORIDAE 43
Scaleless black dragonfishes = MELANOSTOMIIDAE 55

SCANILEPIDIDAE 46, 297
SCARIDAE 63
SCATOPHAGIDAE 63, 856
Scats = SCATOPHAGIDAE 63, 856
Scavengers = LETHRINIDAE 62
Schilbeid catfishes = SCHILBEIDAE 53
SCHILBEIDAE 53
SCIAENIDAE 62, 844–845
SCLERORHYNCHIDAE 43, 207–209
Sclerorhynchoidei 43, 207–209
SCOMBEROSOCIDAE 58
SCOMBRIDAE 65, 900–910
Scombroidei 65, 896–914
SCOPELARCHIDAE 55
SCORPAENIDAE 60, 776
Scorpaeniformes 60, 776–784
Scorpaenoidei 60, 776–779
Scorpionfishes = SCORPAENIDAE 61, 776
Sculpins = COTTIDAE 61, 780–783
SCYTALINIDAE 64
Sea basses = SERRANIDAE 61, 792–802
Sea catfishes = ARIIDAE 53
Sea chubs = KYPHOSIDAE 63
Sea devils = CERATIIDAE 57
Seahorses = SYNGNATHIDAE 60, 770–774
Seamoths = PEGASIDAE 60, 753
Searobins = TRIGLIDAE 61, 779
Sea toads = CHAUNACIDAE 57
SEMIONOTIDAE 48, 375–388
Semionotiformes 48, 375–388
SERRANIDAE 61, 792–802
SERRIVOMERIDAE 51, 540
Shark catfishes = PANGASIIDAE 53, 602
Shrimpfishes = CENTRISCIDAE 60, 763–765
SIBYRHYNCHIDAE 44, 220–221
SIGANIDAE 65
SILLAGINIDAE 62
Siluriformes 53, 598–604
Sisorid catfishes = SISORIDAE 53
SISORIDAE 53
SILURIDAE 53
Silversides = ATHERINIDAE 58, 710–711
SIMENCHELYIDAE 51

1054

Index of Orders, Suborders, and Families

Skates = Rajidae	43, 205
Skates = Rajiformes	43, 195–216
Sleepers = Eleotrididae	65
Sleeper sharks = Dalatiidae	43
Slickheads = Alepocephalidae	54
Slimeheads = Trachichthyidae	59, 716–722
Slimys = Scyliorhinidae	42, 181–184
Slipmouths = Scyliorhinidae	42, 181–184
Smelts = Osmeridae	54, 614–615
Smelt-whitings = Sillaginidae	62
Snaggletooths = Astronesthidae	55
Snailfishes = Cyclopteridae	61
Snake eels = Ophichthidae	51, 534
Snakeheads = Channidae	66
Snake mackerels = Gempylidae	65, 896–897
Snappers = Lutjanidae	62
Snipe eels = Nemichthyidae	51
Snipefishes = Macrorhamphosidae	60, 761–762
Snooks = Centropomidae	61, 785–786
Snubnose parasitic eels = Simenchelyidae	51
Soapfishes = Grammistidae	61
Soleidae	66, 925
Solenostomidae	60, 768–769
Soleoidei	66, 925
Soles = Soleidae	66, 925
South American hillstream catf. = Astroblepidae	53
South American lungfishes = Lepidosirenidae	67
Spadefishes = Ephippidae	63, 851–853
Sparidae	62, 835–843
Speckeled knifefishes = Apteronotidae	54
Sphenocephalidae	56, 672
Sphenocephaloidei	56, 672
Sphyraenidae	63, 874–875
Sphyraenoidei	63, 874–875
Sphyrnidae	42
Spikefishes = Triacanthodidae	66, 929–932
Spiny eels = Mastacembelidae	66
Spiny eels= Notacanthidae	50, 522
Spiny eels = Notacanthiformes	50, 521–522
Spinyfins = Diretmidae	59
Squaliformes	43, 190–194
Squalidae	43, 190–192
Squaloidei	43, 190–192
Squarehead catfishes = Chacidae	53
Squaretails = Tetragonuridae	65, 917
Squatinidae	43, 193–194
Squatinoidei	43, 193–194
Squirrelfishes = Holocentridae	59, 724–732
Stargazers = Uranoscopidae	64
Stegotrachelidae	46, 255–257
Stensioellidae	39, 118
Stensioelliformes	39, 118
Stephanoberycidae	59
Sternoptychidae	55, 626–627
Stethacanthidae	41, 157–159
Stichaeidae	63
Stichocentridae	59, 738
Sticklebacks = Gasterosteidae	60, 752
Stingrays = Dasyatidae	43, 212–214
Stomiiformes	54, 621–629
Stream catfishes = Akysidae	53
Stromateidae	65, 918–919
Stromateoidei	65, 915–919
Sturgeons = Acipenseriformes	47, 368–370
Stylephoridae	59
Styracopteridae	46, 269
Suckers = Catostomidae	52, 593
Sunfishes = Centrarchidae	62, 803–806
Surfperches = Embiotocidae	63
Surf sardines = Isonidae	58
Surgeonfishes = Acanthuridae	65, 888–893
Swallowers = Saccopharyngidae	51
Swamp-eels = Synbranchidae	60
Sweepers = Pempherididae	62
Swordfish = Xiphiidae	65, 911–912
Symmoriidae	41, 156
Symmoriiformes	41, 156–159
Synanceiidae	60

Index of Orders, Suborders, and Families

Synancejidae = SYNANCEIIDAE	60
SYNAPHOBRANCHIDAE	51
SYNBRANCHIDAE	60
SYNGNATHIDAE	60, 770–774
Syngnathiformes	60, 754–774
Syngnathoidei	60, 768–774
SYNODONTIDAE	55, 637–638

T

Tapetails = EURAENIOPHORIDAE	59
Tarpons = Megalopidae	50, 511–512
Tarpons = Elopiformes	50, 500–520
Tarrasiiformes	46, 327–328
Tegeolepididae	46, 258–259
Temperate basses = Percichthyidae	61, 787–791
Tenches = CYPRINIDAE	52, 579–590
Tenpounders = Elopidae	50, 503–509
TERAPONIDAE	61
Tetragonuridae	65, 917
Tetraodontidae	66, 937
Tetraodontiformes	66, 926–938
Tetraodontoidei	66, 937–938
Thelodontiformes	38, 89–94
Thoracopteridae	47, 335
Thorny catfishes = DORADIDAE	53
Threadfin breams = NEMIPTERIDAE	62
Threadfin scat = RHINOPRENIDAE	63
Threefin blennies = TRIPTERYGIIDAE	64
Threadfins = POLYNEMIDAE	63
Three-toothed puffer = TRIODONTIDAE	66
Thresher sharks = Alopiidae	42
THRYPTODONTIDAE	49, 491–492
Tigerperches = TERAPONIDAE	61
Toadfishes = Batrachoididae	57, 693
Tonguefishes = CYNOGLOSSIDAE	66
TORPEDINIDAE	43, 210
Torpedinoidei	43, 210–211
Torrentfishes = HOMALOPTERIDAE	52
TOXOTIDAE	62, 849
TRACHICHTHYIDAE	59, 716–722
TRACHINIDAE	64, 882
Trachinoidei	64, 882–883
TRACHIPTERIDAE	58
Trachipteroidei	58, 715
Trahiras = ERYTHRINIDAE	52
TREMATOSTEIDAE	40, 138
TRIACANTHIDAE	66
TRIACANTHODIDAE	66, 929–932
TRIAKIDAE	42, 186–187
TRICHIURIDAE	65, 898–899
TRICHODONTIDAE	64
TRICHOMYCTERIDAE	53
TRICHONOTIDAE	64
Triggerfishes = BALISTIDAE	66, 933–936
TRIGLIDAE	61, 779
TRIODONTIDAE	66
TRIPAUCHENIDAE	65
Triplespines = TRIACANTHIDAE	66
Tripletails = LOBOTIDAE	62
TRIPTERYGIIDAE	64
True American characins = CHARACIDAE	53, 595–597
True eels = ANGUILLIDAE	50, 523
True rays = RAJIDAE	43, 205
Trumpeters = LATRIDIDAE	63
Trumpetfishes = AULOSTOMIDAE	60, 754–756
TSELFATIIDAE	49, 494–495
Tube-eye = STYLEPHORIDAE	59
Tubesnouts = AULORHYNCHIDAE	60
Tunas = SCOMBRIDAE	65, 900–910
TURINIIDAE	38, 93
TURKMENIDAE	58, 713–714

U

UARBRYICHTHYIDAE	48, 413
UMBRIDAE	54, 609
Upside-down catfishes = MOCHOKIDAE	53
URANOLOPHIDAE	67, 977
URANOSCOPIDAE	64
URENCHELYIDAE	51, 543
UROLOPHIDAE	44, 216

Index of Orders, Suborders, and Families

Uronemidae	67, 990	Zoarcidae	63
Urosphenidae	60, 757–758	Zoarcoidei	63, 881

V

Varasichthyidae	49, 478
Velvetfishes = Aploactinidae	61
Viperfishes = Chauliodontidae	55

W

Warty anglers = Brachionichthyidae	57
Weeverfishes = Trachinidae	64, 882
Whale-like catfishes = Cetopsidae	53
Whale sharks = Rhincodontidae	42
Wolffishes = Anarhichadidae	64
Wolf herrings = Chirocentridae	52, 572
Worm eels = Moringuidae	51
Wormfishes = Microdesmidae	65
Wrasses = Labridae	63, 879–880
Wrymouths = Cryptacanthodidae	64
Wuttagoonaspididae	39, 128
Wuttagoonaspidoidei	39, 128

X

Xenacanthidae	40, 150–153
Xenacanthiformes	40, 150–153
Xenocongridae	51, 527–529
Xiphiidae	65, 911–912

Z

Zaniolepididae	61
Zaporidae	64
Zeidae	59, 748–749
Zeiformes	59, 748–751

A slab being split. Looking for fossils can seem like hard labour, but determination will be rewarded by success.

Index of Genera Arranged by Formation

ORDOVICIAN

Sacabambaspis	70

SILURIAN

Birkenia	106
Dartmuthia	95
Hemicyclaspis	98
Hirella	99
Jamoythius	105
Lanarkia	89
Lasanius	112
Logania	91
Pharyngolepis	107
Phlebolepis	90
Pterygolepis	108
Thelodus	92
Thyestes	104
Tyriaspis	96
unnamed (Birkeniidae)	110
unnamed (Cyathaspididae)	76
Vernonaspis	77

DEVONIAN

Aceraspis	97
Alaspis	100
Anglaspis	71
Asterolepis	141
Boreaspis	101
Bothriolepis	140
Brachyosteus	138
Callistiopterus	962
Canadapteraspis	79
Canowindra	974
Cardipeltis	86
Cephalaspis	103
Chagrinia	941
Cheiracanthus	246
Cheirolepis	254
Chirodipterus	981
Cladoselache	154
Climatius	238
Coccosteus	132
Ctenurella	122
Diademodus	155
Diplacanthus	242
Diplognathus	146
Dipnorhynchus	978
Dipterus	982
Doryaspis	81
Drepanaspis	88
Dunkleosteus	136
Eastmanosteus	137
Elpistostege	973
Empedaspis	78
Eusthenopteron	971
Euthacanthus	239
Fleurantia	985
Gemuendina	120
Glyptolepis	965
Griphognathus	979
Gyroptychius	968
Holodipterus	980
Holoptychius	966
Homalacanthus	247
Homosteus	129
Irregulareaspis	72
Ischnacanthus	244
Jagorina	121
Kentuckia	255
Larnovaspis	82
Legendrelepis	111
Lepidaspis	94
Lunaspis	125
Macropetalichthys	126
Mentzichthys	262
Mesacanthus	248
Microbrachius	142
Miguashaia	955
Millerosteus	133
Moythomasia	256
Osteolepis	969
Oxyosteus	130
Palaeospondylus	149
Parexus	240
Pentlandia	983
Phaneropleuron	986
Pholidosteus	135
Phyllolepis	127
Pionaspis	73
Poraspis	74
Porolepis	964
Protaspis	83
Pteraspis	84

Index of Genera Arranged by Formation

Pterichthyodes	144	Drydenius	273
Quebecius	963	Echinochimaera	232
Remigolepis	145	Edestus	161
Rhadinacanthus	243	Enzichthys	309
Rhamphodopsis	123	Esconichthys	994
Rhinodipterus	984	Eurynothus	312
Rhinopteraspis	85	Expleuracanthus	150
Rhyncholepis	109	Falcatus	158
Scaumenacia	987	Fubarichthys	303
Stegotrachelus	257	Gilpichthys	115
Stensioella	118	Gonatodus	276
Sundayichthys	267	Guildayichthys	319
Thursius	970	Hadronector	944
Torpedaspis	75	Hamiltonichthys	167
Triazeugacanthus	250	Haplolepis	323
Tristichopterus	972	Hardistiella	113
Trygonaspis	80	Harpagofututor	218
Turinia	93	Heteropetalus	170
Uranolophus	977	Holurus	270
Vernicomacanthus	241	Howqualepis	290
Watsonosteus	134	Iniopera	220
Willomorichthys	307	Iniopteryx	219
Wuttagoonaspis	128	Lochmocercus	942
		Mayomyzon	114
		Mesolepis	310
CARBONIFEROUS		Mesopoma	266
		Microhaplolepis	324
Acanthoniscus	299	Nematoptychius	271
Acrolepis	277	Paratarrasius	328
Aetheretmon	261	Polyosteorhynchus	945
Allenypterus	943	Rhabdoderma	948
Apholidotos	327	Rhadinichthys	263
Atracauda	301	Sagenodus	989
Belantsea	165	Sibyrhynchus	221
Benedenius	269	Stethacanthus	159
Canobius	265	Symmorium	156
Caridosuctor	946	unnamed (Cochliodontoidei)	224
Cheirodopsis	314	unnamed (Cochliodontoidei)	225
Chirodus	315	unnamed (Cochliodontoidei)	225
Chondrenchelys	217	unnamed (Cochliodontoidei)	226
Coelacanthopsis	947	unnamed (Cochliodontoidei)	227
Commentrya	287	unnamed (Holocephali)	235
Conchopoma	991	unnamed (Iniopterygiformes)	222
Cornuboniscus	268	unnamed (Orodontiformes)	163
Damocles	157	Uronemus	990
Delphyodontos	234	Utahacanthus	251
Deltoptychius	228	Yogoniscus	308
Discoserra	320		

Index of Genera Arranged by Formation

PERMIAN

Acanthodes	245
Acentrophorus	375
Acropholis	278
Aeduella	285
Amblypterus	283
Atherstonia	300
Bourbonella	286
Coelacanthus	951
Ctenodus	988
Dorypterus	326
Ebenaqua	317
Ectosteorhachis	967
Elonichthys	274
Eurysomus	313
Ganolepis	275
Gardineria	304
Helicoprion	160
Janassa bituminosa	164
Lawnia	284
Menaspis	230
Muensterichthys	305
Orthacanthus	151
Palaeoniscum	292
Paramblypterus	288
Phanerosteon	264
Platysomus	311
Pygopterus	272
Pyritocephalus	325
Reticulepis	281
Rhabdolepis	260
Tholonotus	282
Traquairichthys	249
triodus	152
Urosthenes	322
Wodnika	169
Xenacanthus	153

TRIASSIC

Acronemus	166
Aetheodontus	363
Albertonia	415
Apateolepis	258
Atopocephala	338
Australosomus	330
Beaconia	339
Belichthys	302
Besania	336
Birgeria	296
Bobasatrania	316
Boreosomus	279
Brembodus	389
Brookvalia	340
Cionichthys	341
Cleithrolepidina	360
Cleithrolepis	361
Colobodus	351
Dandya	376
Dicellopyge	295
Dictyopyge	342
Diplurus	952
Dipteronotus	362
Ecrinesomus	318
Enigmaichthys	378
Eoeugnathus	425
Eosemionotus	379
Gibbodon	390
Gosfordia	992
Gyrolepis	289
Habroichthys	333
Haywardia	321
Helichthys	343
Hemicalypterus	380
Heterolepidotus	428
Holophagus	959
Ischnolepis	344
Jacobulus	416
Lasalichthys	345
Laugia	960
Legnonotus	408
Luganoia	337
Macroaethes	331
Manlietta	352
Megapteriscus	259
Meidiichthys	353
Mendocinichthys	354
Meridensia	355
Mesembroniscus	280
Molybdichthys	346
Myriolepis	291
Nannolepis	334
Paracentrophorus	383
Paraceratodus	993

Index of Genera Arranged by Formation

Paralepidotus	384	Pachycormus	442
Parapholidophorus	453	Pholidolepis	455
Parasemionotus	417	Proleptolepis	474
Peltopleurus	364	Ptycholepis	392
Pericentrophorus	385	Saurorhynchus	367
Perleidus	356	Saurostomus	445
Phaidrosoma	418	Tetragonolepis	388
Phlyctaenichthys	347	Todiltia	477
Pholidoctenus	454	Uarbryichthys	413
Pholidopleurus	332	unnamed (Amiiformes?)	437
Pholidorhynchodon	457	unnamed (Galeiformes?)	189
Piveteauia	956	unnamed (Parasemionotidae)	423
Placopleurus	365		
Praesemionotus	419		
Pristisomus	357	**UPPER JURASSIC**	
Procheirichthys	358		
Prohalecites	458	Aellopos	195
Promecosomina	420	Allothrissops	479
Pteronisculus	293	Amblysemius	426
Redfieldius	348	Anaethalion	500
Sargodon	386	Arduafrons	391
Saurichthys	366	Ascalabos	469
Scanilepis	297	Aspidorhynchus	446
Schizurichthys	349	Asterodermus	197
Semionotus	387	Asthenocormus	438
Synorichthys	350	Belemnobatis	198
Thoracopterus	335	Belonostomus	447
Tripelta	359	Callopterus	465
Turseodus	294	Catervariolus	459
unnamed (Coelacanthidae?)	958	Caturus	424
unnamed (Edestidae)	162	Coccoderma	950
unnamed (Parasemionotidae?)	422	Coccolepis	298
Watsonulus	421	Corysodon	173
Whiteia	957	Daitingichthys	510
		Disticholepis	406
		Domeykos	553
LOWER JURASSIC		Eomesodon	394
		Eurycormus	452
Acanthorhina	231	Furo	705
Aphnelepis	462	Gyrodus	395
Archaeomaene	463	Gyronchus	396
Chondrosteus	368	Heterodontus	171
Dapedium	377	Heterostrophus	381
Euthynotus	439	Histionotus	407
Hulettia	468	Hypsocormus	440
Hybodus	168	Ichthyokentema	460
Lepidotes	382	Ionoscopus	466
Leptolepis	472	Ischyodus	233

Index of Genera Arranged by Formation

Leptolepides	471
Libys	953
Liodesmus	434
Lycoptera	498
Macrosemius	409
Macrourogaleus	181
Mesturus	398
Notagogus	410
Ophiopsis	414
Orectolobus	174
Orthocormus	441
Orthogonikleithrus	473
Pachythrissops	511
Palaeocarcharias	175
Palaeoscyllium	182
Paracestracion	172
Pholidophorus	456
Phorcynis	176
Pleuropholis	461
Propterus	412
Proscinetes	402
Protoclupea	563
Protospinax	192
Pseudorhina	194
Pteroniscus	306
Sauropsis	444
Strobilodus	430
Tharsis	475
Thrissops	488
Undina	961
unnamed (Ichthyodectiformes)	493
Urocles	436
Varasichthys	478

LOWER CRETACEOUS

Amiopsis	432
Araripichthys	744
Axelrodichthys	949
Brannerion	503
Calamopleurus	433
Chirocentrites	480
Cladocyclus	481
Clupavus	470
Coelodus	393
Cooyoo	482
Crossognathus	502
Dastilbe	504
Ellimmichthys	547
Eoproscinetes	399
Idrissia	623
Macrepistius	429
Notelops	520
Omosomopsis	741
Oshunia	467
Pachyrhizodus	518
Paraelops	506
Proportheus	486
Protostomias	624
Rhacolepis	519
Sinamia	435
Stemmatodus	404
Stichoberyx	731
Stichopterus	369
Tharrhias	476
Tselfatia	495
unnamed (Cheirothricidae?)	648
Vinctifer	448
Wadeichthys	464

UPPER CRETACEOUS

Acrogaster	716
Aipichthys	736
Anguillavus	524
Apateopholis	643
Aphanepygus	405
Apsopelix	501
Bananogmius	491
Centrophoroides	190
Charitosomus	576
Cheirothrix	645
Cimolichthys	652
Coccodus	392
Cryptoberyx	733
Ctenocephalichthys	725
Ctenothrissa	669
Cyclobatis	206
Dactylopogon	656
Davichthys	505
Dercetis	649
Dinopteryx	735
Echidnocephalus	521
Enchelion	537

1063

Index of Genera Arranged by Formation

Enchodus	630	Platycormus	742
Eubiodectes	483	Plectocretacicus	927
Eurypholis	633	Plesiobery x	734
Exocoetoides	646	Prionolepis	653
Gasterorhamphosus	762	Prolates	799
Gaudryella	612	Pronotacanthus	522
Gharbouria	620	Protobrama	494
Gillicus	484	Protosphyraena	443
Hajulia	514	Pseudoberyx	564
Hakelia	658	Pycnosterinx	743
Halec	634	Pycnosteroides	737
Hemisaurida	635	Rhinobatos	200
Heterothrissa	670	Rhombopterygia	201
Hexanchus	188	Rhynchodercetis	651
Histiothrissa	558	Sardinioides	654
Hoplopteryx	718	Sardinius	637
Humilichthys	666	Saurodon	490
Ichthyoceros	397	Scapanorhynchus	179
Ichthyodectes	902	Sclerorhynchus	209
Ichthyotringa	644	Scombroclupea	567
Istieus	515	Scyliorhinus	183
Lebonichthys	517	Sendenhorstia	512
Leptecodon	631	Spaniodon	508
Leptosomus	661	Sphenocephalus	672
Libanoberyx	719	Squalicorax	180
Lissoberyx	720	Stichocentrus	738
Macropomoides	954	Stichopteryx	721
Mesiteia	177	Tachynectes	665
Micropristis	207	Telepholis	647
Nematonotus	662	Thrissopteroides	516
Omosoma	740	Tubantia	722
Opistopteryx	664	unnamed (Beryciformes)	775
Ornategulum	560	unnamed (Beryciformes)	776
Osmeroides	513	unnamed (Beryciformes)	777
Palaeobalistum	401	unnamed (Ellimmichthyiformes)	548
Palaeolycus	632	unnamed (Ellimmichthyiformes)	549
Parachanos	574	unnamed (Scyliorhinidae?)	184
Pararaja	205	Urenchelys	543
Paraspinus	729	Xiphactinus	489
Parasyllaemus	507	Zanclites	492
Paratriakis	187		
Pateroperca	561		
Pattersonichthys	667	**PALEOCENE**	
Pelargorhynchus	650		
Petalopteryx	411	Boltyshia	606
Pharmacichthys	605	Mcconichthys	671
Phoenicolepis	668		
Phylactocephalus	636		

Index of Genera Arranged by Formation

EOCENE

Acanthonemus	888
Acanthurus	889
Acropoma	816
Aeoliscoides	766
Amia	431
Amphiperca	793
Amphiplaga	674
Amphistium	850
Amyzon	593
Anguilloides	531
Antigonia	750
Apogon	814
Arambourgella	868
Archaephippus	851
Asineops	675
Astephas	600
Atractosteus	373
Aulorhamphus	761
Aulostomoides	754
Auxis	900
Bajaichthys	712
Berybolcensis	724
Blochius	911
Blotichthys	787
Bolcanguilla	541
Bolcyrus	535
Bolthyshia	606
"Brachyrhamphus"	698
Brychaetus	496
Calamostoma	768
Callipterys	882
Carangodes	915
Carangopsis	820
Ceratoichthys	823
Chanoides	575
Crossopholis	370
Ctenodentex	836
Cyclopoma	785
Dalpiaziella	525
Dentex	837
Diodon	983
Diplomystus	545
Ductor	824
Dules	807
Ellimma	546
Enoplosus	859
Eoaulostomus	755
Eobothus	922
Eocottus	782
Eogaleus	185
Eohiodon	499
Eoholocentrum	726
Eolabroides	876
Eolactoria	926
Eolamprogrammus	690
Eolates	786
Eomyrophis	527
Eoplatax	855
Eoplectus	929
Eosalmo	618
Eosphaeramia	815
Eotetraodon	937
Eozanclus	890
Ephippus	852
Erismatopterus	676
Exellia	853
Fistularioides	759
Galeorhinus	186
Gobius	887
Gosiutichthys	556
Goslinophis	534
Heliobatis	213
Hemirhamphus	699
Histionotophorus	695
Holocentrus	727
Humbertia	613
Hypsidoris	598
Knightia	559
Kushlukia	895
Lepisosteus	374
Libotonius	673
Lophius	694
Macraulostomus	756
Mcconichthys	671
Mene	830
Milananguilla	533
Mioplosus	809
Mylomyrus	528
Myripristis	728
Narcine	211
Naseus	891
Notogoneus	577
Nursallia	400
Odonteus	865

1065

Index of Genera Arranged by Formation

Ophidion	691
Ottaviania	869
Pagellus	839
Palaeoperca	797
Paraeoliscus	767
Paramphisile	765
Paranguilla	526
Parapygaeus	892
Parasynarcualis	760
Paratrachinotus	825
Pasaichthys	847
Patavichthys	542
Pegasus	753
Percalates	789
Phareodus	497
Platinx	572
Platyrhina	204
Pomadasys	834
Priscacara	866
Pristigenys	813
Proaracana	928
Promyliobatis	215
Prosolenostomus	769
Protacanthodes	932
Proteomyrus	530
Psettopsis	848
Pseudosyngnathus	772
Pterygocephalus	777
Pycnodus	403
Pygaeus	858
Rhamphexocoetus	696
Rhamphognathus	711
Rhamphosus	778
Ruffoichthys	870
Scatophagus	856
Scomberomorus	906
Scopeloides	625
Seriola	826
Serranus	801
Sparnodus	842
Sphyraena	875
Spinacanthus	930
Syngnathus	773
Tenuicentrum	732
Thaumaturus	619
Thunnus	908
Torpedo	210
Tortonesia	880
Toxotes	849
Trachurus	827
Trigonorhina	202
Trygon	214
Turkmene	714
Tylerichthys	893
unnamed (Argentinidae)	610
unnamed (Cichlidae)	864
unnamed (Percoidei)	872
unnamed (Scorpaeniformes)	784
unnamed (Serranidae)	802
unnamed (Stromateidae)	919
Urolophus	216
Urosphen	757
Urosphenopsis	758
Veronanguilla	532
Voltaconger	539
Vomeropsis	828
Xiphopterus	910
Zapteryx	203
Zignoichthys	931

OLIGOCENE

Acanus	792
Aeoliscus	763
Ammodytes	886
Analectis	713
Aoria	601
Archaeus	819
Atherina	710
Berycomorus	723
Capros	751
Caprovesposus	894
Caranx	821
Chanos	573
Cobitopsis	697
Cottopsis	780
Dapalis	795
Digoria	739
Dipterichthys	867
Echeneis	818
Eomyctophum	657
Epinnula	896
Eutrichiurides	898
Gephyroberyx	717
Grammatorcynus	901

Index of Genera Arranged by Formation

Homorhynchus	913	Brachylebias	703
Isurichthys	902	Bregmacerina	680
Leiognathus	831	Brycon	595
Lepidocottus	783	Carcharocles	178
Merluccius	689	Carrionellus	704
Morone	788	Chaenobryttus	804
Mugil	873	Chaetodon	857
Nemopteryx	684	Clinitrachus	884
Noemacheilus	592	Clinus	885
Oligobalistes	935	Clupea	552
Oligoplarchus	805	Cobitis	591
Palaeogadus	686	Corydoras	604
Palaeorhynchus	914	Cottus	781
Palimphyes	903	Cyclothone	621
Pangasius	602	Cyprinus	581
Paralepis	640	Diplodus	838
Pavelichthys	538	Engraulis	571
Pinichthys	918	Epinephelus	796
Plioplarchus	812	Esox	608
Pomolobus	562	Gasterosteus	752
Priacanthopsis	798	Geophagus	861
Prolebias	709	Gobio	582
Propteridium	692	Gonostoma	622
Proserrivomer	540	Hemithyrsites	897
Protolophotus	715	Labrus	877
Psenicubiceps	916	Lampanyctus	660
Pseudoraniceps	688	Lebias	706
Sarda	904	Lednevia	817
Sardinella	566	Lepidopus	899
Scomber	905	Leuciscus	583
Scombrosarda	907	Lithofundulus	707
Sprattus	569	Lompoquia	844
Trichophanes	677	Mullus	846
Zenopsis	748	Neopercis	883
		Nyctophus	663
		Onobrosmius	685
MIOCENE		Pachylebias	708
		Pagrus	840
Alosa	551	Palaeodenticeps	550
Ameiurus	599	Palaeomolva	1046
Anguilla	523	Palaeodenticeps → Palaeomolva	687
Argyropelecus	626	Parapristipoma	833
Arnoglossus	920	Parascopelus	641
Aspius	579	Parasphyraena	874
Bathylagus	611	Pentaceros	860
Batrachoides	693	Percichthys	790
Blabe	794	Photichthys	628
Boreocentrarchus	803	Pimelodus	603
		Pomoxis	806

1067

Index of Genera Arranged by Formation

Properca	800
Pseudorasbora	584
Pseudovomer	878
Rhodeus	585
Rhytmias	841
Santosius	791
Sciaena	845
Scophthalmus	923
Scorpaena	776
Solea	925
Sparus	843
Sudis	642
Symphodus	879
Tetragonopterus	596
Tinca	590
Trigla	779
Triportheus	597
Turio	909
Umbra	609
unnamed (Anguilliformes)	544
Xyne	570

PLIOCENE

Alutera	933
Aphanius	702
Belone	701
Boops	835
Bothus	921
Brama	832
Bregmaceros	679
Centriscus	764
Ceratoscopelus	655
Conger	536
Dactylopterus	775
Etrumeus	555
Fundulus	705
Gadella	678
Gadus	681
Hilsa	557
Hippocampus	771
Hygophum	659
Hyporhamphus	700
Lestidiops	639
Liopsetta	924
Maurolicus	627
Micromesistius	683
Monacanthus	934
Perca	811
Richardsonius	586
Sardina	565
Sargocentrum	730
Spratelloides	568
Synodus	638
Tetragonurus	917
unnamed (Balistidae)	936
unnamed (Cichlidae)	863
unnamed (Syngnathiformes)	774
Vinciguerria	629
Xiphias	912
Zeus	749

PLEISTOCENE

Coregonus	616
Lota	682
Mallotus	614
Osmerus	615
Pholis	881
Rutilus	587
Tilapia	862

The oblique rays of the evening sun make the contures of fossils visible in a stone in Wyoming. A marker is placed on the plate...

...to be worked on the following day.

Index of Genera Arranged by Locality

BAD WILDUNGEN, GERMANY

Brachyosteus	138
Jagorina	121
Oxyosteus	130
Pholidosteus	135

BEAR GULCH, MONTANA, USA

Acanthoniscus	299
Allenypterus	943
Apholidotos	327
Atracauda	301
Belantsea	165
Caridosuctor	946
Damocles	157
Delphyodontos	234
Discoserra	320
Echinochimaera	232
Falcatus	158
Fubarichthys	303
Guildayichthys	319
Hadronector	944
Harpagofututor	218
Heteropetalus	170
Lochmocercus	942
Mcconichthys	671
Paratarrasius	328
Polyosteorhynchus	945
unnamed (Cochliodontoidei)	224
unnamed (Cochliodontoidei)	225
unnamed (Cochliodontoidei)	225
unnamed (Cochliodontoidei)	226
unnamed (Cochliodontoidei)	227
unnamed (Holocephali)	235
unnamed (Iniopterygiformes)	222
unnamed (Orodontiformes)	163
Yogoniscus	308

BERGAMO, ITALY

Birgeria	296
Brembodus	389
Dandya	376
Gibbodon	390
Holophagus	959
Legnonotus	408
Paralepidotus	384
Pholidoctenus	454
Pholidorhynchodon	457
Sargodon	386
Thoracopterus	335

BERGISCH GLADBACH, GERMANY

Griphognathus	979
Moythomasia	256
Rhinodipterus	984

BOLCA, ITALY

Acanthonemus	888
Acanthurus	889
Acropoma	816
Aeoliscoides	766
Amphistium	850
Anguilloides	531
Antigonia	750
Apogon	814
Arambourgella	868
Archaephippus	851
Aulorhamphus	761
Aulostomoides	754
Auxis	900
Bajaichthys	712
Berybolcensis	724
Blochius	911
Blotichthys	787
Bolcanguilla	541
Bolcyrus	535
"Brachyrhamphus"	698
Calamostoma	768
Callipterys	882
Carangodes	915
Carangopsis	820
Ceratoichthys	823
Chanoides	575
Cyclopoma	785
Dalpaziella	525
Dentex	837
Diodon	983
Ductor	824

Index of Genera Arranged by Locality

Dules	807	Pristigenys	813
Enoplosus	859	Proaracana	928
Eoaulostomus	755	Promyliobatis	215
Eobothus	922	Prosolenostomus	769
Eocottus	782	Protacanthodes	932
Eogaleus	185	Proteomyrus	530
Eoholocentrum	726	Psettopsis	848
Eolabroides	876	Pseudosyngnathus	772
Eolactoria	926	Pterygocephalus	777
Eolates	786	Pycnodus	403
Eomyrophis	527	Pygaeus	858
Eoplatax	855	Rhamphexocoetus	696
Eoplectus	929	Rhamphognathus	711
Eosphaeramia	815	Rhamphosus	778
Eotetraodon	937	Ruffoichthys	870
Eozanclus	890	Scatophagus	856
Ephippus	852	Scomberomorus	906
Exellia	853	Seriola	826
Fistularioides	759	Serranus	801
Galeorhinus	186	Sparnodus	842
Gobius	887	Sphyraena	875
Goslinophis	534	Spinacanthus	930
Hemirhamphus	699	Syngnathus	773
Histionotophorus	695	Tenuicentrum	732
Holocentrus	727	Thunnus	908
Humbertia	613	Torpedo	210
Lophius	694	Tortonesia	880
Macraulostomus	756	Toxotes	849
Mene	830	Trachurus	827
Milananguilla	533	Trigonorhina	202
Myripristis	728	Trygon	214
Narcine	211	Tylerichthys	893
Naseus	891	unnamed (Percoidei)	872
Nursallia	400	Urolophus	216
Odonteus	865	Urosphen	757
Ophidion	691	Veronanguilla	532
Ottaviania	869	Voltaconger	539
Pagellus	839	Vomeropsis	828
Paraeoliscus	767	Whitapodus	529
Paramphisile	765	Xiphopterus	910
Paranguilla	526	Zignoichthys	931
Parapygaeus	892		
Parasynarcualis	760		
Paratrachinotus	825		
Pasaichthys	847	**BRAZIL**	
Patavichthys	542		
Pegasus	753	Araripichthys	744
Platinx	572	Axelrodichthys	949
Platyrhina	204	Brannerion	503
Pomadasys	834	Brycon	595

Index of Genera Arranged by Locality

Calamopleurus	433
Cladocyclus	481
Dastilbe	504
Ellimma	546
Ellimmichthys	547
Eoproscinetes	399
Geophagus	861
Notelops	520
Oshunia	467
Paraelops	506
Pimelodus	603
Rhacolepis	519
Santosius	791
Tetragonopterus	596
Tharrhias	476
Tholonotus	282
Triportheus	597
Vinctifer	448

BROOKVALE, AUSTRALIA

Beaconia	339
Belichthys	302
Brookvalia	340
Manlietta	352
Megapteriscus	259
Mesembroniscus	280
Molybdichthys	346
Phlyctaenichthys	347
Procheirichthys	358
Schizurichthys	349

BUNDENBACH, GERMANY

Drepanaspis	88
Gemuendina	120
Lunaspis	125
Stensioella	118

CERIN, FRANCE

Belemnobatis	198
Corysodon	173
Disticholepis	406
Phorcynis	176

CLEVELAND, OHIO, USA

Cladoselache	154
Diademodus	155
Diplognathus	146
Dunkleosteus	136
Kentuckia	255

FIUME MARECCHIA, ITALY

Alutera	933
Belone	701
Boops	835
Bothus	921
Brama	832
Bregmaceros	679
Centriscus	764
Ceratoscopelus	655
Conger	536
Dactylopterus	775
Etrumeus	555
Gadella	678
Gadus	681
Hippocampus	771
Hygophum	659
Hyporhamphus	700
Lestidiops	639
Maurolicus	627
Micromesistius	683
Monacanthus	934
Sardina	565
Sargocentrum	730
Spratelloides	568
Synodus	638
Tetragonurus	917
unnamed (Balistidae)	936
unnamed (Syngnathiformes)	774
Vinciguerria	629
Xiphias	912
Zeus	749

GLARUS, SWITZERLAND

Acanus	792
Echeneis	818
Homorhynchus	913
Nemopteryx	684

Index of Genera Arranged by Locality

GOSFORD, AUSTRALIA

Apateolepis	258
Cleithrolepis	361
Dictyopyge	342
Gosfordia	992
Myriolepis	291
Pristisomus	357
Promecosomina	420
Tripelta	359

GREENLAND

Acropholis	278
Laugia	960
Pholis	881
Phyllolepis	127

HOLZMADEN, GERMANY

Acanthorhina	231
Chondrosteus	368
Dapedium	377
Hybodus	168
Lepidotes	382
Pachycormus	442
Ptycholepis	392
Saurorhynchus	367
Saurostomus	445
Tetragonolepis	388
unnamed (Amiiformes?)	437
unnamed (Galeiformes?)	189
unnamed (Parasemionotidae?)	423

ILLINOIS, USA

Conchopoma	991
Edestus	161
Gilpichthys	115
Haplolepis	323
Mayomyzon	114

IRAN

Berycomorus	723
Brachylebias	703
Cottopsis	780
Dipterichthys	867
Epinnula	896
Grammatorcynus	901
Isurichthys	902
Palaeorhynchus	914
Priacanthopsis	798
Propteridium	692
Proserrivomer	540
Protolophotus	715
Scopeloides	625

CALIFORNIA, USA

Argyropelecus	626
Bathylagus	611
Cyclothone	621
Gasterosteus	752
Lampanyctus	660
Lompoquia	844
Rhytmias	841
Turio	909
Xyne	570

KANSAS, USA

Apsopelix	501
Bananogmius	491
Chaenobryttus	804
Cimolichthys	652
Fundulus	705
Gillicus	484
Hamiltonichthys	167
Ichthyodectes	902
Leptecodon	631
Pomoxis	806
Protosphyraena	443
Sagenodus	989
Saurodon	490
Squalicorax	180
Xiphactinus	489
Zanclites	492

Index of Genera Arranged by Locality

CAUCASUS, former USSR

Aeoliscus	763
Analectis	713
Arnoglossus	920
Bregmacerina	680
Caprovesposus	894
Digoria	739
Gephyroberyx	717
Lednevia	817
Leiognathus	831
Merluccius	689
Oligobalistes	935
Onobrosmius	685
Palaeogadus	686
Palaeomolva	687
Palimphyes	903
Pavelichthys	538
Pinichthys	918
Pomolobus	562
Psenicubiceps	916
Pseudoraniceps	688
Sarda	904
Sardinella	566
Sciaena	845
Scombrosarda	907
Zenopsis	748

LEBANON

Acrogaster	716
Aipichthys	736
Anguillavus	524
Apateopholis	643
Aphanepygus	405
Centrophoroides	190
Charitosomus	576
Cheirothrix	645
Coccodus	392
Cryptoberyx	733
Ctenocephalichthys	725
Ctenothrissa	669
Cyclobatis	206
Davichthys	505
Dercetis	649
Dinopteryx	735
Enchelion	537
Eubiodectes	483
Eurypholis	633
Exocoetoides	646
Gaudryella	612
Gharbouria	620
Hajula	514
Hakelia	658
Halec	634
Hemisaurida	635
Heterothrissa	670
Hexanchus	188
Humilichthys	666
Ichthyoceros	397
Lebonichthys	517
Libanoberyx	719
Lissoberyx	720
Macropomoides	954
Mesiteia	177
Micropristis	207
Nematonotus	662
unnamed (Scyliorhinidae?)	184
unnamed (Ellimmichthyiformes)	548
unnamed (Beryciformes)	775
unnamed (Beryciformes)	776
unnamed (Beryciformes)	777
Omosoma	740
Opistopteryx	664
Ornategulum	560
Osmeroides	513
Palaeobalistum	401
Pararaja	205
Paraspinus	729
Paratriakis	187
Pateroperca	561
Pattersonichthys	667
Petalopteryx	411
Pharmacichthys	605
Phoenicolepis	668
Phylactocephalus	636
Plectrocretacicus	927
Plesioberyx	734
Prionolepis	653
Pronotacanthus	522
Protobrama	494
Pseudoberyx	564
Pycnosterinx	743
Pycnosteroides	737
Rhinobatos	200
Rhombopterygia	201

Index of Genera Arranged by Locality

Rhynchodercetis	651
Scapanorhynchus	179
Sclerorhynchus	209
Scombroclupea	567
Scyliorhinus	183
Spaniodon	508
Stichocentrus	738
Stichopteryx	721
Telepholis	647
Urenchelys	543

LICATA, ITALY

Gonostoma	622
Lepidopus	899
Parascopelus	641
Photichthys	628
Pseudovomer	878
Sudis	642
Trigla	779

MADAGASCAR

Australosomus	330
Bobasatrania	316
Ecrinesomus	318
Jacobulus	416
Paracentrophorus	383
Paraceratodus	993
Parasemionotus	417
Perleidus	356
Piveteauia	956
Pteronisculus	293
Watsonulus	421
Whiteia	957

MESSEL, GERMANY

Amia	431
Amphiperca	793
Atractosteus	373
Palaeoperca	797
Thaumaturus	619

MIGUASHA, CANADA

Alaspis	100
Bothriolepis	140
Callistiopterus	962
Elpistostege	973
Eusthenopteron	971
Homalacanthus	247
Legendrelepis	111
Miguashaia	955
Quebecius	963
Scaumenacia	987
Triazeugacanthus	250

MONTE S. GIORGIO, SWITZERLAND

Acronemus	166
Aetheodontus	363
Besania	336
Eoeugnathus	425
Eosemionotus	379
Luganoia	337
Meridensia	355
Placopleurus	365
Saurichthys	366

NARDO, ITALY

Gasterorhamphosus	762
Lusitanichthys	594
unnamed (Elopidae?)	509

ÖHNINGEN, GERMANY

Anguilla	523
Aspius	579
Cobitis	591
Esox	608
Gobio	582
Lebias	706
Leuciscus	583
Rhodeus	585
Umbra	609

Index of Genera Arranged by Locality

ORAN, ALGIERS

Alosa	551
Batrachoides	693
Chaetodon	857
Diplodus	838
Epinephelus	796
Neopercis	883
Pagrus	840
Parapristipoma	833

PADDY'S SPRINGS, AUSTRALIA

Chirodipterus	981
Eastmanosteus	137
Holodipterus	980

PALATINATE, GERMANY

Acanthodes	245
Aeduella	285
Elonichthys	274
Orthacanthus	151
Paramblypterus	288
Rhabdolepis	260
Triodus	152
Xenacanthus	153

QUEENSLAND, AUSTRALIA

Cooyoo	482
Ebenaqua	317
Pachyrhizodus	518
Percalates	789
unnamed (Cheirothricidae?)	648

RICHELSDORF, GERMANY

Coelacanthus	951
Dorypterus	326
Eurysomus	313
Muensterichthys	305
Palaeoniscum	292
Platysomus	311
Pygopterus	272
Reticulepis	281
Wodnika	169

RINGERIKE, NORWAY

Aceraspis	97
Hirella	99
Pharyngolepis	107
Pterygolepis	108
Rhyncholepis	109
Tyriaspis	96

SCOTLAND, GREAT BRITAIN

Acrolepis	277
Aetheretmon	261
Asterolepis	141
Birkenia	106
Canobius	265
Cephalaspis	103
Cheiracanthus	246
Cheirodopsis	314
Cheirolepis	254
Chondrenchelys	217
Climatius	238
Coccosteus	132
Deltoptychius	228
Diplacanthus	242
Dipterus	982
Drydenius	273
Eurynothus	312
Euthacanthus	239
Glyptolepis	965
Gonatodus	276
Gyroptychius	968
Holoptychius	966
Holurus	270
Homosteus	129
Ischnacanthus	244
Jamoythius	105
Lanarkia	89

Index of Genera Arranged by Locality

Lasanius	112	Eurycormus	452
Logania	91	Furo	705
Mesacanthus	248	Gyrodus	395
Mesolepis	310	Gyronchus	396
Mesopoma	266	Heterodontus	171
Microbrachius	142	Heterostrophus	381
Millerosteus	133	Histionotus	407
Nematoptychius	271	Hypsocormus	440
Osteolepis	969	Ionoscopus	466
Palaeospondylus	149	Ischyodus	233
Parexus	240	Leptolepides	471
Pentlandia	983	Libys	953
Phaneropleuron	986	Liodesmus	434
Pteraspis	84	Macrosemius	409
Pterichthyodes	144	Macrourogaleus	181
Rhabdoderma	948	Mesturus	398
Rhadinacanthus	243	Notagogus	410
Rhadinichthys	263	Ophiopsis	414
Rhamphodopsis	123	Orectolobus	174
Stegotrachelus	257	Orthocormus	441
Stethacanthus	159	Orthogonikleithrus	473
Thelodus	92	Pachythrissops	511
Thursius	970	Palaeocarcharias	175
Tristichopterus	972	Palaeoscyllium	182
Turinia	93	Paracestracion	172
Uronemus	990	Pholidophorus	456
Vernicomacanthus	241	Pleuropholis	461
Watsonosteus	134	Propterus	412
		Proscinetes	402
		Protospinax	192
		Pseudorhina	194
SOLNHOFEN, GERMANY		Sauropsis	444
		Strobilodus	430
Aellopos	195	Tharsis	475
Allothrissops	479	Thrissops	488
Amblysemius	426	Undina	961
Anaethalion	500	unnamed (Ichthyodectiformes)	493
Arduafrons	391	Urocles	436
Ascalabos	469		
Aspidorhynchus	446		
Asterodermus	197	**SPITZBERGEN, NORWAY**	
Asthenocormus	438		
Belonostomus	447	Anglaspis	71
Callopterus	465	Boreaspis	101
Caturus	424	Doryaspis	81
Coccoderma	950	Irregulareaspis	72
Coccolepis	298	Larnovaspis	82
Daitingichthys	510	Poraspis	74
Eomesodon	394	Porolepis	964

Index of Genera Arranged by Locality

ST. MARGARETHEN, AUSTRIA

Labrus	877
unnamed (Anguilliformes)	544
Scophthalmus	923
Scorpaena	776

SOUTH AFRICA

Atherstonia	300
Atopocephala	338
Cleithrolepidina	360
Dicellopyge	295
Helichthys	343
Meidiichthys	353
Mentzichthys	262
Sundayichthys	267
Willomorichthys	307

TALBRAGAR, AUSTRALIA

Aphnelepis	462
Archaeomaene	463
Leptolepis	472
Uarbryichthys	413

TURKMENIA, former USSR

Eolamprogrammus	690
Kushlukia	895
Turkmene	714
Urosphenopsis	758

TSELFAT, MOROCCO

Clupavus	470
Idrissia	623
Omosomopsis	741
Protostomias	624
Stichoberyx	731
Tselfatia	495

UNTERKIRCHBERG, GERMANY

Clupea	552
Cottus	781
Cyprinus	581
Solea	925

WAPITI LAKE, CANADA

Albertonia	415
Boreosomus	279
unnamed (Coelacanthidae)	958
unnamed (Edestidae)	162
unnamed (Parasemionotidae?)	422

WESTFALIA, GERMANY

Crossognathus	502
Dactylopogon	656
Echidnocephalus	521
Enchodus	630
Euthynotus	439
Histiothrissa	558
Hoplopteryx	718
Istieus	515
Leptosomus	661
Palaeolycus	632

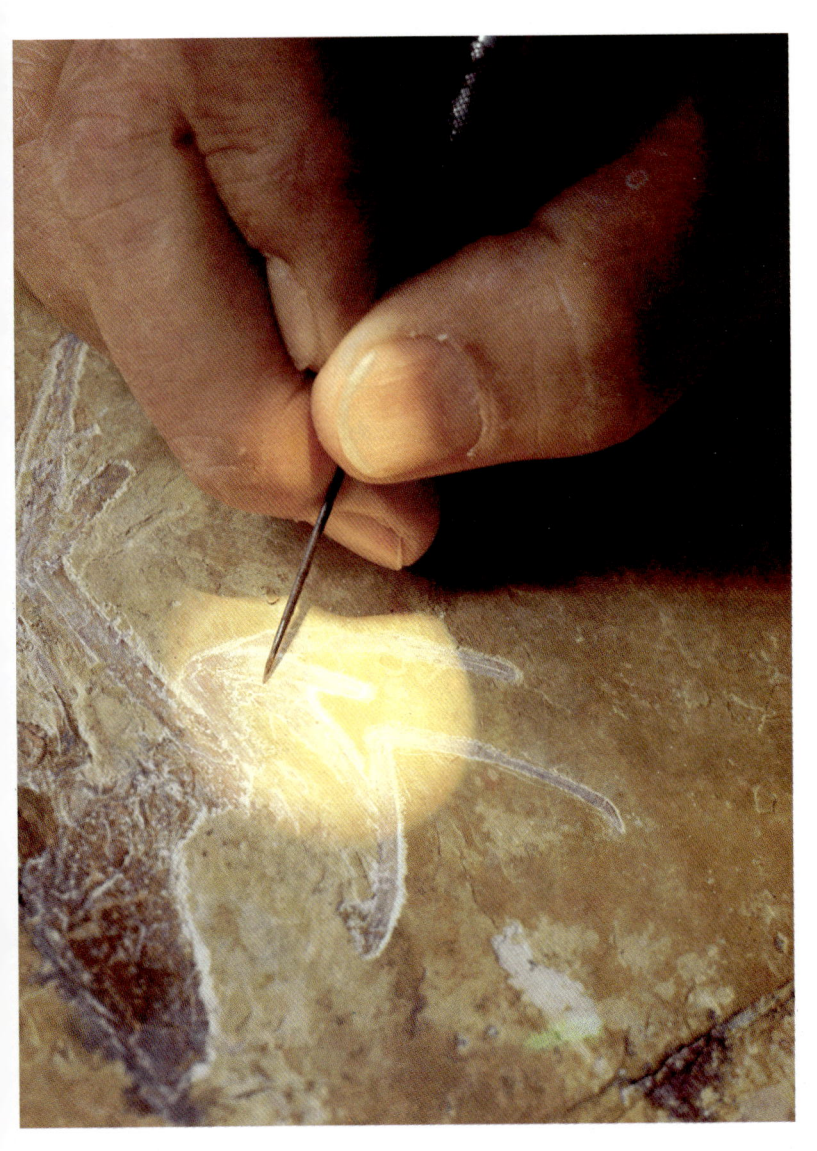

Reclaiming a fossil demands utmost care. The smallest tools are used under a dissecting scope to clean a fossil—here a crustacean. Photo: K. Götz.

Index of Recent Families and Genera

Common names normal.
Genera in *italics*.
Families in SMALL CAPS.

A

Acanthurus	889
Acipenser	369
ACIPENSERIDAE	47, 368
Acropoma	816
Aeoliscus	763, 766, 767
Aetobatus	215
Albula	517
ALBULIDAE	50, 513, 517
Alosa	551
Alutera	933
Amberjack = *Seriola*	826
Ameiurus	599
Amia	431–433, 435, 436
Ammodytes	886
Anchovy = *Engraulis*	571
Angel shark = *Squatina*	194
Angler fishes = ANTENNARIIDAE	57, 695
Anguilla	523
Anglerfish = *Antennarius*	695
Anglerfish = *Lophius*	694
Antenna catfish = *Pimelodus*	603
Antenna codlet = *Bregmaceros*	679, 680
ANTENNARIIDAE	57, 695
Antigonia	750
Aphanius	702
Aphredoderus	675
Apogon	814, 815
Aptychotrema	197
Aracana	928
Archerfish = *Toxotes*	849
ARGENTINIDAE	54, 610
Argyropelecus	626
Ariomma	916
Ariommid = *Ariomma*	916
Armourhead = *Pentaceros*	860
Arnoglossus	920
Asp = *Aspius*	579
Aspius	579
Atherina	710
ATHERINIDAE	58, 710, 711
Atractosteus	373
Aulostomus	755, 756
Australian lungfish = *Neoceratodus*	992, 993
Auxis	900

B

Bagrid catfishes = BAGRIDAE	53, 601
BAGRIDAE	53, 601
Balistoides	931
Barb = *Pseudorasbora*	584
Barracudas = *Sphyraena*	874, 875
Barracudina = *Lestidium*	639
Barracudina = *Paralepis*	640
Barracudina = *Sudis*	642
Barramundi = *Lates*	786
Bass = *Morone*	788
Bathylagus	611
Batrachoides	693
Beardfish = *Polymixia*	743
Belone	701
Beryx	717
Bigeye = *Pristigenys*	813
Bitterling = *Rhodeus*	585
Bitterlings = *Leuciscus*	583
Blueback = *Alosa*	551
Bluefish = *Pomatomus*	817
Bluefishes = POMATOMIDAE	62, 817
Boarfish = *Antigonia*	750
Boarfish = *Capros*	751
Bodianus	880
Bonefish = *Albula*	517
Bonefishes = ALBULIDAE	50, 513, 517
Boneytongues = OSTEOGLOSSIDAE	50, 497
Boops	835
Bothus	921, 922
Bowfin = *Amia*	431–433, 435–436
Bregmaceros	679, 680
Bristlemouth = *Cyclothone*	621
Bristlemouth = *Gonostoma*	622
Bristlemouths = GONOSTOMATIDAE	55, 625
Brotulas and cusk-eels = OPHIDIIDAE	57, 690, 691
Brycon	595
Bullet mackerel = *Auxis*	900
Bullhead catfishes = *Ameiurus*	599
Bullhead shark = *Heterodontus*	171

Index of Recent Families and Genera

Burbot = *Lota* — 682
Butterfish = *Stromateus* — 918
Butterfishes = STROMATEIDAE — 65, 918, 919
Butterflyfish = *Chaetodon* — 857

C

Capelin = *Mallotus* — 614
Capros — 751
Caranx — 821
Cardinalfish = *Apogon* — 814, 815
Carp = *Cyprinus* — 580, 581
Catfish = *Ictalurus* — 598
Catostomus — 593
Cat shark = *Galeus* — 185
Cat shark = *Scyliorhinus* — 183
Cat sharks = SCYLIORHINIDAE — 42, 181, 182, 184
CENTRARCHIDAE — 62, 803
Centriscus — 764, 765
Centroberyx — 718
Ceratoscopelus — 655
Chaenobryttus — 804
Chaetodon — 857
CHANIDAE — 52, 574
Chanos — 573
Characin = *Brycon* — 595
Chimaera — 233
CHIROCENTRIDAE — 52, 480, 481, 483, 487, 488
Chirocentrus — 572
CICHLIDAE — 63, 863, 866
Cichlids = CICHLIDAE — 63, 863, 866
Clinid = *Clinus* — 885
Clinids = *Clinitrachus* — 884
Clinitrachus — 884
Clinus — 885
Clupea — 552
Cobitis — 591
Cod = *Gadus* — 681, 684, 686
Cod = *Micromesistius* — 683
Codlets = *Gadella* — 678
Conger — 536
Conger eel = *Conger* — 536
Conger eels = CONGRIDAE — 51, 535, 536, 539
CONGRIDAE — 51, 535, 536, 539
Coregonus — 616

Cornetfish = *Fistularia* — 759
Cornetfishes = *Fistulariidae* — 60, 760
Corycats = *Corydoras* — 604
Corydoras — 604
Cottidae — 61, 780, 783
Cottus — 781, 782
Cow-fish = *Lactoria* — 926
Cow shark = *Hexanchus* — 188
"Crappie" = *Pomoxis* — 806
Crestfish = *Lophotus* — 715
Croaker = *Sciaena* — 845
Cutlassfish = *Trichiurus* — 898
Cyclothone — 621
Cynolebias — 703
Cyprinodon — 704
CYPRINODONTIDAE — 58, 703, 704, 706–709
Cyprinus — 580, 581

D

Dactylopterus — 775
Damselfish = *Dascyllus* — 865
Damselfishes = POMACENTRIDAE — 63, 865
Dascyllus — 865
Deep sea smelt = *Bathylagus* — 611
Dentex — 837
Denticeps — 550
Denticle herring = *Denticeps* — 550
Diodon — 938
Diplodus — 838
Dories = *Zenopsis* — 748
Dories = *Zeus* — 749
Driftfishes = NOMEIDAE — 65, 915, 916
Drums = SCIAENIDAE — 62, 844

E

Eagle ray = *Aetobatus* — 215
Eagle ray = *Myliobatis* — 215
"Earth eater" = *Geophagus* — 861
Echeneis — 818
Eel = *Anguilla* — 523
Electric ray = *Narcine* — 211
Electric ray = *Torpedo* — 210
ELOPIDAE — 50, 505, 507, 508
Elops — 509

Index of Recent Families and Genera

Engraulis	571
Enoplosus	859
EPHIPPIDAE	62, 851
Ephippus	852
Epinephelus	796
Epinnula	896
Esox	607, 608
Etrumeus	555
Exocoetus	646

F

False morays = XENOCONGRIDAE	51, 527–529
Filefish = *Alutera*	933
Filefish = *Monacanthus*	934
Fistularia	759
FISTULARIIDAE	60, 760
Flounder = *Bothus*	921, 922
Flounder = *Liopsetta*	924
Flying fish = *Exocoetus*	646
Flying gurnard = *Dactylopterus*	775
Fundulus	705

G

Gadella	678
Gadus	681, 686
Galeorhinus	186
Galeus	185
Gar = *Atractosteus*	373, 374
Gasterosteus	752
Geophagus	861
Gephyroberyx	717
Ghost pipefish = *Solenostomus*	768
Ghost pipefishes = SOLENOSTOMIDAE	60, 769
Goatfish = *Mullus*	846
Gobio	582
Gobius	887
Goblin shark = *Scapanorhynchus*	179
Goby = *Gobius*	887
Gonorhynchid = *Gonorhynchus*	577
GONORHYNCHIDAE	52, 576, 577
Gonorhynchus	577

Gonostoma	622
GONOSTOMATIDAE	55, 625
Grammatorcynus	901
Grouper = *Epinephelus*	796
Grunt = *Parapristipoma*	833
Gudgeon = *Gobio*	582
Guitarfish = *Aptychotrema*	197
Guitarfish = *Rhinobatos*	200
Guitarfishes = RHINOBATIDAE	43, 195, 197, 201, 202
Gunnel = *Pholis*	881

H

Hake = *Molva*	687
Hake = *Raniceps*	688
Halfbeak = HEMIRHAMPHIDAE	58, 697
HALOSAURIDAE	51, 521
Halosaurs = HALOSAURIDAE	50, 521
Hatchetfish = *Argyropelecus*	626
Hatchetfish = *Triportheus*	597
HEMIRHAMPHIDAE	58, 697
Hemirhamphus	699
Herring = *Clupea*	552
Herring smelts = ARGENTINIDAE	54, 610
HETERODONTIDAE	42, 172
Heterodontus	171
Hexanchus	188
Hilsa	557
Hiodon	499
Hippocampus	770, 771
HOLOCENTRIDAE	59, 725, 732
Holocentrus	726, 727
Horn sharks = HETERODONTIDAE	42, 172
Hundshai = *Galeorhinus*	186
Hygophum	659
Hyporhamphus	700

I

ICTALURIDAE	53, 598, 600
Ictalurus	598

Index of Recent Families and Genera

J

Jack mackerel = *Trachurus*	827

K

Kaupichthys	527
Killifishes = CYPRINODONTIDAE	58, 702–709

L

LABRIDAE	63, 879, 880
Labrus	877
Lactoria	926
Lampanyctus	660
Lampetra	114
Lampris	713, 714
Lamprey = *Lampetra*	114
Lampreys = PETROMYZONTIDAE	38, 114
Lanternfish = *Myctophum*	657
Lanternfishes = MYCTOPHIDAE	56, 658, 661, 663, 664
Lates	786
Latimeria	25, 954
Leiognathus	831
Lepidopus	899
Lepisosteus	374
Lestidium	639
Leuciscus	583
Lightfish = *Maurolicus*	627
Lightfish = *Photichthys*	628
Lightfishes = *Viniciguerria*	629
Liopsetta	924
Lizardfish = *Synodus*	638
Lizardfishes = SYNODONTIDAE	55, 637
Loach = *Cobitis*	591
Loach = *Noemacheilus*	592
Lobe-fin = *Latimeria*	954
Longnose = *Lepisosteus*	374
Lophius	694
Lophotus	715
Lota	682

M

Mackerel = *Scomber*	905
Mackerels = *Grammatorcynus*	901
MACRORHAMPHOSIDAE	60, 761
Macrorhamphosus	762
Mallotus	614
Marine halfbeak = *Hyporhamphus*	700
Maurolicus	627
MEGALOPIDAE	50, 511, 512
Megalops	512
Mene	830
Merluccid hake = *Merluccius*	689
Merluccius	689
Micromesistius	683
Milkfish = *Chanos*	573
Milkfishes = CHANIDAE	52, 574
Molva	687
Monacanthus	934, 936
MONODACTYLIDAE	62, 847, 848
Monodactylus	847
Monos = MONODACTYLIDAE	62, 847, 848
Mooneye = *Hiodon*	499
Moonfish = *Mene*	830
Moorish idol = *Zanclus*	890
Moray eel = *Muraena*	526
Morone	788
Mud minnow = *Umbra*	609
Mugil	873
Mullet = *Mugil*	873
Mullus	846
MYCTOPHIDAE	56, 658, 661, 663, 664
Myctophum	657
Myliobatis	215
Myrichthys	534
Myripristis	728

N

Narcine	211
Naso	891
Needlefish = *Belone*	701
Neoceratodus	992, 993
Neopercis	883
Noemacheilus	592
NOMEIDAE	65, 915, 916

Index of Recent Families and Genera

North American catfishes = ICTALURIDAE 53, 600
Notacanthus 522
Nurse sharks = ORECTOLOBIDAE 42, 173, 175, 176

O

Opah = *Lampris* 713, 714
OPHICHTHIDAE 51, 534
OPHIDIIDAE 57, 690
Ophidion 691
Orbiculate batfish = *Platax* 855
Orectolobus 174
Osmerus 615
OSTEOGLOSSIDAE 50, 497

P

Paddlefish = *Polyodon* 370
Pagellus 839
Pagrus 840
Pangasius 602
Paralepis 640
Parapristipoma 833
Pegasus 753
Pentaceros 860
Perca 810, 811
Percalates 789
Perch = *Perca* 810, 811
Percichthys 790, 791
PETROMYZONTIDAE 38, 114
Pholis 881
Photichthys 628
Pike = *Esox* 607, 608
Pike perch = *Stizostedion* 808, 809
Pimelodus 603
Pipefish = *Syngnathus* 773, 774
Pirate perch = *Aphredoderus* 675
Platax 855
Platyrhina 204
Platyrhinid guitarfish = *Platyrhina* 204
Plioplarchus 812
Polymixia 743

Polyodon 370
POMACENTRIDAE 63, 865
Pomadasys 834
POMATOMIDAE 62, 817
Pomfret = *Brama* 832
Pomolobus 562
Pomoxis 806
Pompano = *Trachinotus* 825
Porcupinefish = *Diodon* 938
Porgies = SPARIDAE 62, 842
Porgy = *Boops* 835
Porgy = *Dentex* 837
Porgy = *Diplodus* 838
Porgy = *Pagellus* 839
Porgy = *Pagrus* 840
Porgy = *Sparus* 843
Pristigenys 813
Pseudobalistes 935
Pseudorasbora 584
Puffer = *Tetraodon* 937

R

Rabbitfishes = *Siganus* 895
RAJIDAE 43, 205, 206
Raniceps 688
Remora = *Echeneis* 818
RHINOBATIDAE 43, 195, 197, 201, 202
Rhinobatos 200
Rhodeus 585
Richardsonius 586
River herrings = *Pomolobus* 562
Roach = *Rutilus* 587
Round herring = *Etrumeus* 555
Round herring = *Spratelloides* 568
Round ray = *Urolophus* 216
Rutilus 587

S

Salmo 617, 618
Salmon = *Salmo* 617, 618, 619
Sandfishes = GONORHYNCHIDAE 52, 576, 577

Index of Recent Families and Genera

Sandlance = *Ammodytes*	886
Sandperch = *Neopercis*	883
Sarda	904
Sardina	565
Sardine = *Sardina*	565
Sardine = *Sardinella*	566
Sardinella	566
Sargocentrum	730
Scabbardfish = *Lepidopus*	899
Scaldfish = *Arnoglossus*	920
Scapanorhynchus	179
Scatophagus	856
Scats = *Scatophagus*	856
Sciaena	845
SCIAENIDAE	62, 844
Scomber	905
Scomberomorus	906
Scophthalmus	923
Scorpaena	776
Scorpionfish = *Scorpaena*	776
Sculpin = *Cottus*	781, 782
Sculpins = COTTIDAE	61, 780, 783
SCYLIORHINIDAE	42, 181, 182, 184
Scyliorhinus	183
Sea bass = *Serranus*	801
Sea basses = SERRANIDAE	61, 802
Seahorse = *Hippocampus*	770, 771
Seamoth = *Pegasus*	753
Searobin = *Trigla*	779
Seriola	826
SERRANIDAE	802
Serranus	801
Serrivomer	540
Serrivomerid eels = SERRIVOMERIDAE	51, 540
Shad = *Hilsa*	557
Shark catfish = *Pangasius*	602
Shrimpfish = *Centriscus*	764, 765
Shrimpfishes = *Aeoliscus*	763, 766, 767
Siganus	895
Silverside = *Atherina*	710
Silversides = ATHERINIDAE	58, 710, 711
Silver tetra = *Tetragonopterus*	596
Slimehead = *Gephyroberyx*	717
Slipmouth = *Leiognathus*	831
Smipefishes = *Macrorhamphosus*	762
Smooth dogfish = *Triakis*	187
Snake eels = OPHICHTHIDAE	51, 534
Snake mackerel = *Epinnula*	896
Snipefishes = MACRORHAMPHOSIDAE	60, 761
Solea	925
SOLENOSTOMIDAE	769
Solenostomus	768
Soles = *Solea*	925
Spadefish = *Ephippus*	852
Spadefishes = EPHIPPIDAE	63, 851
SPARIDAE	62, 842
Sparus	843
Sphyraena	874, 875
Spiny dogfish = *Squalus*	190
Spiny dogfishes = SQUALIDAE	43, 190, 192
Spiny eel = *Notacanthus*	522
Spratelloides	568
Sprats = *Sprattus*	569
Sprattus	569
SQUALIDAE	43, 190, 192
Squalus	190
Squaretail = *Tetragonurus*	917
Squatina	194
Squirrelfish = *Holocentrus*	726, 727
Squirrelfish = *Myripristis*	728
Squirrelfishes = HOLOCENTRIDAE	59, 725, 732
Stickleback = *Gasterosteus*	752
Stingrays = DASYATIDAE	43, 213, 214
Stints = *Osmerus*	615
Stizostedion	808, 809
STROMATEIDAE	65, 918.919
Stromateus	918
Sturgeon = *Acipenser*	369
Sucker = *Catostomus*	593
Sudis	642
Sunfish = *Chaenobryttus*	804
Sunfishes = CENTRARCHIDAE	62, 803
Surgeonfishes = *Acanthurus*	889
Sweetlip = *Pomadasys*	834
Swordfish = *Xiphias*	912
Symphodus	879
Syngnathus	773
SYNODONTIDAE	55, 637
Synodus	638

1085

Index of Recent Families and Genera

T

Tarpons = CROSSOGNATHIDAE	50, 500–502
Tarpons = MEGALOPIDAE	50, 511, 512
Tench = Tinca	589, 590
Tenpounders = ELOPIDAE	50, 505, 507–509
Tetragonopterus	596
Tetragonurus	917
Tetraodon	937
Thunnus	908
Thyrsites	897
Tilapia = *Tilapia*	862
Tinca	589, 590
Toadfish = *Batrachoides*	693
Torpedo	210
Toxotes	849
Trachinotus	825
Trachinus	882
Trachurus	827
TRIACANTHIDAE	66, 932
Triacanthus	932
Triakis	187
Trichiurus	898
Triggerfish = *Balistoides*	931
Triggerfish = *Pseudobalistes*	935
Trigla	779
Trigonorhina	202
Triplespines = TRIACANTHIDAE	66, 932
Tripodfish = *Triacanthus*	932
Triportheus	597
True rays = RAJIDAE	43, 205, 206
True sturgeons = ACIPENSERIDAE	47, 368
Trumpetfish = *Aulostomus*	755, 756
Tuna = *Thunnus*	908
Turbot = *Scophthalmus*	923

U

Umbra	609
Unicornfish = *Naso*	891
Urolophus	216

V

Vinciguerria	629

W

Weeverfishes = *Trachinus*	882
Whitefish = *Corregonus*	616
Wolf herring = *Chirocentrus*	572
Wolf herrings = CHIROCENTRIDAE	52, 480, 481, 483, 487, 488
Wrasses = LABRIDAE	63, 876, 879, 880

X

Xiphias	912

Y

Yellow jack = *Caranx*	821

Z

Zanclus	890
Zapteryx	203
Zenopsis	748
Zeus	740

The Author

Karl Albert Frickhinger was born in 1924. Science always interested him so that, even as a boy, he was an enthusiastic fossil collector. This, however, was only an episode. Coming from an old family of pharmacists, he was predestined to study pharmacy. At the same time he took an interest in botany and finally opened his own pharmaceutical shop in Munich. Here, for the first time, he had an opportunity to spend some of this time on scientific research and turned his attention to fish parasitology. He invented several preparations for the prevention of fish diseases in the aquarium and, after a few years, founded the firm Zoomedica to market his products worldwide. He sold the firm in 1977 and so, at last, had time to pursue his old hobby of paleontology. By methodical acquisition, guided by evolutionary considerations, he built up an impressive collection. Since, however, he had always been under the Sign of the Fish, it is no surprise that finally he specialized entirely on fishes. This gave him the determination needed to produce this book.

Picture Credits

All photos by the author unless otherwise indicated.

Dr. Allen: 174b, 509b, 534b, 573b, 730b, 843b, 875b, 906b
Bayer. Landesanstalt für Wasserforschung: 114b
Debelius: 171b, 183b, 194, 215b, 197b
Dr. Foersch: 856b
Dr. Frank: 584b
Hansen: 374b, 512b, 849b
Kahl: 598b, 781b
Dr. Krupp: 702b
Kuiper: 886b, 895b
Linke: 862b
Norman: 187b, 211b, 431b, 593b, 595b, 596b, 597b, 675b, 695b, 755b, 775b, 788b, 801b, 804b, 806b, 813b, 814b, 815b, 821b, 825b, 826b, 831b, 847b, 859b, 865b, 890b, 931b, 934b, 935b, 936b
Nieuwenhuizen: 752b
Paysan: 591b
Dr. Randall: 200, 527b, 577b, 700b, 743b, 723b, 750b, 768b, 816b, 904b, 916b, 932b
Reinhard: 523b, 582b, 583b, 585b, 587b, 592b, 602b, 603b, 609b, 979b
Richter: 370b
Scharger: all reproductions
Schmida: 710b, 786b, 993b
Schraml: 767b, 638b, 695b, 727b, 728b, 751b, 761b, 773b, 801b, 835b, 852b, 838b, 864b, 865b, 879b, 933b, 934b, 937b
Seegers: 704b, 705b
Senckenberg Museum: 954b
Stawikowski: 861b
Dr. Stehmann: 188b, 204b, 216b, 599b, 626b, 628b, 642b, 683b, 748b